BTEC National

Early Years

2nd Edition

Edited by Penny Tassoni

...Thames
KT1 2AQ

www.heinemann.co.uk
✓ Free online support
✓ Useful weblinks
✓ 24 hour online ordering

01865 888058

Heinemann Educational Publishers
Halley Court, Jordan Hill, Oxford OX2 8EJ
Part of Harcourt Education

Heinemann is the registered trademark of
Harcourt Education Limited

© Penny Tassoni, Maureen Smith, Andy Boak, Joan Butcher, Maureen
Daly, Harriet Eldridge, Sarah Horne, Carol Runciman, 2006

First published 2006

11 10 09 08 07 06
10 9 8 7 6 5 4 3 2 1

British Library Cataloguing in Publication Data is available
from the British Library on request.

10-digit ISBN: 0 435 46372 1
13-digit ISBN: 978 0435 46372 4

Edited by Christopher Clark and Natasha Goddard
Typeset and illustrated by 🅣 Tek-Art, Croydon, Surrey

Original illustrations © Harcourt Education Limited, 2005
Cover design by Wooden Ark
Printed in the UK by Scotprint
Cover photo: © Getty Images

Acknowledgements
Every effort has been made to contact copyright holders of material reproduced in this book.
Any omissions will be rectified in subsequent printings if notice is given to the publishers.

Contents

Author Acknowledgements

Penny Tassoni would like to thank her co-authors for their support on this project. She would also like to thank all those who have been involved at Heinemann in the production of this book, especially Beth Howard and Lucy Hyde. Penny would also like to thank all those students and tutors who have provided helpful feedback that has helped to shape this book. Special thanks are due to Wendy and Sophie Bristow for permission to use the home-school communication sheet in unit 16. Finally, she would like to thank the Tassoni Team once again.

Picture Acknowledgements

The authors and publisher would like to thank the following for permission to reproduce photographs.

Alamy Images, page 211

John Birdsall, page 30

Corbis, page 389

Digital Vision, page 452

Rex Features, page 6

Getty Images, pages 222, 260, 344, 402

Getty Images/PhotoDisc, pages 240, 273, 294

Harcourt Education Ltd/Gareth Boden, pages 84, 159, 374

Harcourt Education Ltd/Gerald Sunderland, page 446

Harcourt Education Ltd/Haddon Davies, pages 183, 428

Harcourt Education Ltd/Jules Selmes, pages 13, 49, 102, 109, 113, 136, 216, 257, 286, 306, 393

Harcourt Education Ltd/Tudor Photography, pages 51, 96, 269, 413

Sarah Horne, page 164

Photolibrary.com, page 65

photos.com, pages 300, 424

Science Photo Library, pages 352, 360

Introduction

Working with children and their families is a rewarding and special career. Time spent with children is usually hard work, but exhilarating and varied. Not many careers offer people the opportunity to genuinely influence and shape young lives. The BTEC National in Early Years is a qualification that gives students many entry routes into the early years sector. It will provide you with a firm foundation for your future work.

About this book

This book contains the information that you will need in order to complete your BTEC National Early Years course. The units have been carefully written to match the specifications of the syllabus. The book contains all of the core units and some of the popular optional units. The units have been written with the needs of students in mind and so should provide you with the depth of knowledge that you need, but also be easy to follow.

The eight core units for the certificate and diploma are:

* Equality, Diversity and Rights in Early Years Work
* Communication and Interpersonal Skills in Early Years Work
* Protection of Children
* Learning in the Early Years
* Child Care Practice
* Professional Practice
* Human Growth and Development
* Observation of Children

Further core units for the diploma (optional for the certificate) are:

* Research Methodology for Early Years (including support for specialist unit 20: Early Years Project)
* Child Health

Optional units for the certificate and the diploma are:

* Play and Learning Activities
* Developmental Psychology
* Children with Special Needs

Course structure

In order to complete the BTEC National, you will need to complete core units as well as optional units. The diploma has ten core units whilst the certificate has eight core units. The optional units are designed to give you some specialist knowledge. This book contains three of the most popular specialist units.

Assessment

All units are assessed and graded and an overall grade for the qualification is awarded. Core units 1 and 2 are externally graded. Other units will be marked by your tutors. You will need to complete all of the assessments in order to gain the qualification.

Features of this book

It is always useful to check your understanding and also to reflect on some of the issues in the text. We have therefore included a range of features that should help you to do this.

What you will need to learn	a list of the knowledge points that you will have learnt by the end of the unit
Think it over	thought-provoking questions and dilemmas that can be used for individual reflection or group discussion
Theory into practice	practical activities that require you to apply your theoretical knowledge to the workplace

Key issues	contemporary issues in childcare that you should be aware of
Assessment activities	activities that address the assessment requirements of the course
Case studies	examples of 'real' situations to help you link theory to practice
End-of-unit test	several numbered questions covering the entire content of the unit
References and further reading	publications, videos and websites to consolidate and extend your learning

A wide range of experienced professionals have contributed their expertise to this book: their purpose in doing so is to support you in your chosen studies and to provide you with a firm knowledge foundation from which you can extend and develop your particular interests.

We all wish you success in the completion of your BTEC National in Early Years and hope that you enjoy your career working with children.

Penny Tassoni
General Editor

UNIT 1

Equality, diversity and rights in early years work

What you need to learn

1 The meaning of diversity in today's society

2 The importance of equality, diversity and rights in early years services

3 How early years services can recognise and promote equality, diversity and rights

4 Promoting equality, diversity and rights in your own early years practice

Introduction

This unit introduces the concepts of equality, diversity and rights. These concepts form the foundation of your work with young children and their families. Some of the language used may be new to you, so each time you see a new word look it up so that you understand precisely what it means. As your understanding of equality, diversity and rights grows, you will see that these important concepts are integral to the way in which early years settings and early years practitioners provide their services.

How you will be assessed

This unit is assessed internally.

1 The meaning of diversity in today's society

Diversity is about the differences between people – you need to understand this in order to practise in early years and childcare settings. Contemporary British society today is diverse, with many different languages, ethnic groups and cultures. There are many aspects of diversity, or difference, but those most commonly recognised are described in the following table.

DIFFERENCE	COMMENT
Gender	In the past men had more rights than women and were seen as more important. Women still earn less than men for similar work and find difficulty in breaking through the 'glass ceiling' to the most senior positions at work. There are far more derogatory terms, such as 'slag', used to describe women than men.
Race and ethnicity	People categorise themselves and others based on race and ethnicity, such as being black or white, European or Asian. Many people in our society still place a preference on white skin and Western European background, and derogatory terms for black people are still used. Ethnic origin is different from race and usually covers a shared history, social customs and common ancestry.
Culture	All of us have a cultural background – activities, beliefs, values, knowledge and ideas shared by a group of people. White, middle-class culture still dominates the media and is often seen as more valuable. People feel more comfortable with others of a similar cultural background and groups who hold power and influence in society tend to value others like themselves.
Place of origin	Immigration into the UK has been taking place throughout our history. Waves of immigrants have come here from many countries of the world and have chosen to settle here. Today is no exception and many are here fleeing from persecution, war and disruption in their home countries, or simply to make a better life for themselves. Some groups have formed significant communities in different parts of the UK, whereas others are more integrated into our society. We are now part of an enlarged European Union and many immigrants to the UK are now coming from countries right across Europe. These people have a right to be here and to work in the UK.

Terminology used in this unit

Equality – In our society, equality is about fairness and ensuring people have the same rights regardless of their background or who they are. Any society that ensures its people have equal chances and equal treatment is building for its future by encouraging equality of opportunity for all.

Diversity is about differences, such as differences in gender, disability, race, age, culture, religion, social class, child-rearing practices, appearance, employment status or sexuality. Differences enrich our society and make it an exciting and challenging place to be.

Rights are what we are entitled to as members of society. Our society recognises that rights often come with responsibilities. For example, we have a right to live in peace, but a corresponding responsibility to be peaceful ourselves. These rights are sometimes called 'moral rights' and are based on ideas about what is right or wrong, fair or unfair and just or unjust.

DIFFERENCE	COMMENT
Beliefs	People are brought up with varying religious backgrounds. Religion is closely linked with culture. In the UK there is religious freedom and people are allowed to practise their religion without fear of prejudice. But criticism of a religion is often used as a cover for prejudice. As early years practitioners we have a duty to respect the beliefs that children and families hold.
Values	Values are held by all of us – they are the beliefs and moral principles by which we live. We are likely to share many of the values of our society, such as respect for human life and opposition to murder, but there is less agreement on other issues, such as capital punishment for people who commit murder. We need to make sure our values do not lead us to make negative judgments about other people.
Age	Youth is generally valued above old age, although the very young are also often not valued. There are problems for older people in employment and in relation to issues such as health care.
Health status	People with illnesses are often made to feel different and outside mainstream society. This is especially true for mental health problems. People can also be treated differently if they are seen as somehow being responsible for their situation, such as with diseases like AIDS or lung cancer.
Physical ability	People have different levels of physical ability, ranging from those who are super fit and physically able to those who may have severe physical disabilities which hinder them in taking a full part in our society. People make assumptions about disability and make negative judgements about those who are seen as disabled. The 'social model' of disability is one which sees the problems as lying in society's lack of provision for disabled people, who could achieve substantially more given the right support. Another view is the 'medical model' which concentrates on the person's disability and sees them as a 'condition' rather than as a whole person with the ability to achieve. In early years settings the 'social model' is the one that is used, as it encourages us to look at the whole child, regardless of their physical ability, and help them to achieve as best they can.
Learning needs	People learn differently and have different abilities. Children with special educational needs learn differently from most children of the same age. These children may need extra or different help from that given to other children.
Economic status	This refers to a person's income or wealth, and so can also refer to differences in social background, education, income or lifestyle. Assumptions are made about people who are poor or have a limited lifestyle. People who are employed are often valued above those who are unemployed, regardless of the reasons. One of the first questions people ask each other is 'What do you do?'.
Family structure	This refers to differences in family or social relationships, such as lone parents or same sex relationships. These are often not valued as much as heterosexual relationships and two-parent families. Even today divorced, separated or single people are often made to feel different.
Language	English is seen as the UK's mainstream language, but Welsh is also a mainstream language with a statutory basis. Children in Wales are routinely taught Welsh in state schools and many are essentially bilingual. Some children are multilingual, speaking a variety of home languages,

DIFFERENCE	COMMENT
Language (contd.)	as well as English and Welsh. Languages other than English or Welsh are often seen as less important, but in early years settings all children's languages should be valued and respected.
Accents	Within the UK there are a number of regional accents. Sometimes these are mocked and judged as 'inferior', although this is less likely to happen than 20 years ago. People who have English as an additional language may also have accents based on their first language.
Sexuality	Being a gay man or lesbian woman is a difference. Homosexual relationships are often not valued as much as heterosexual relationships, and can suffer prejudice.
Codes of behaviour	People have different codes of behaviour according to their beliefs, values and backgrounds. People may have different codes of behaviour for different aspects of their lives. For example, people who live quiet and law-abiding lives may behave differently at football matches or when with certain friends. As early years practitioners, it is important to make sure our behaviour at work is highly professional at all times and adheres to the policies and procedures of the setting. Its also important to remember that our work is in a regulated setting and requires the confidence of parents and families. Therefore our behaviour outside of work may also affect our work status.
Families with a history of offending	This refers to families who may have been in trouble with the law. Many children are punished for their families' offending behaviour by being separated from their parents or looked after by the state. It is important to remember that children who come from families with a history of offending should not be labelled or viewed as potential offenders themselves. Some families may require high degrees of support from early years services.

The table can only include broad categories. For example, the category 'gender' is a broad term but we all know there are huge differences between men and other men, and women and other women. The main lesson is that the similarities between us are usually greater than the differences and we should always see people as individuals rather than as part of a particular group. We are all different. Also, it is important not to judge by appearances, as people with hidden disabilities, such as autism, deafness or mental health problems, may look just like anyone else. This can lead to reverse discrimination, where people with real needs are overlooked because they look like everyone else.

It is important that we do not judge people who are 'different' from us as either inferior or lacking in some way. Our society, in common with most others, values particular characteristics. These messages are often not deliberate but are picked up

The UK is multicultural and early years practitioners are responsible for helping all children to recognise and appreciate diversity.

by young children from their families and the world around them and reinforced throughout life by experiences, influential people and the media.

For many of us, learning about diversity and relating to those who are different can be stressful, as we may feel that our own culture and values are under threat. We need to be aware of this and be willing to see the benefits of diversity in our society and in the workplace.

2 The importance of equality, diversity and rights in early years services

Equity

Equity is about fairness, natural justice, and being impartial and reasonable. Many people will use the term equity in the same way as they would talk about equality. The principle of equity is very important and should be the hallmark of a civilised, mature society. British society, through its laws and practices, supports the view that fairness, tolerance and equity are important moral principles. A society that is not based on principles of equity will be an unequal and divided society. But even where society, at least in its laws and constitution, supports equity, there are still many gaps between rich and poor. Equity is not just about poverty but, if you are poor, you suffer most from a range of different problems and deprivations.

The Child Poverty Action Group published, in 2005, a summary leaflet called *Poverty: the Facts*. This leaflet states that:

* children face a higher risk of income poverty. In 2003/04 28 per cent of children (3.5 million) were poor

* of all those income poor in 2003/04, 19 per cent were pensioner households, 52 per cent were in households containing a child and

30 per cent were in households of working age not containing children

* income poverty increased in the 1980s and 1990s, from 13 per cent in 1979, to 25 per cent in 1996/97 and to 21 per cent by 2003/04.

Children in poverty have lower educational attainments. In 2004 in England, 56.1 per cent of children not receiving free school meals got five or more GCSEs at grades A to C. This was double the rate (26.1 per cent) of children in receipt of free school meals. Children's health is also affected: children of manual workers are five times more likely to die in accidents.

The leaflet states that the causes of equality are as follows.

* **High income inequality**. In 2003/04, the poorest fifth of the population had a median income (the mid-point of incomes in this group) of £128 a week; for the richest fifth this was £616, nearly five times as much.

* **Worklessness**. In 2003/04, 1.5 million people lived in households where either the head or spouse were unemployed. A total of 6.0 million individuals lived in households where adults

of working age were not working (for reasons including ill health and caring responsibilities).

* **Inadequate safety net**. In 2005/06, 'safety net' benefits and tax credits were worth around £192 a week for a couple with children aged 5 and 11 – £80 less than the poverty line (£272, uprated from 2003/04). For a lone parent with children aged 5 and 11 the safety net was worth £160, some £29 less than the poverty line of £189.

Groups of people at greater than average risk of experiencing poverty are identified as follows.

* Where the head of the family or their spouse were unemployed – in these cases 78 per cent of people in such families were income poor.

* 19 per cent of white people were income poor, while 58 per cent of Pakistani and Bangladeshi people and 40 per cent of black or black British people were income poor.

* 47 per cent of those in lone parent households were income poor, compared to 23 per cent of single people without children. For those households containing children, 20 per cent were income poor compared to 11 per cent where there were no children. For pensioner couples, 20 per cent were income poor.

The Child Poverty Action group is a campaigning group to help our poorest children and families and is a rich source of information.

Many children grow up in poverty in the UK.

It is clear that, despite efforts to bring about a more equitable society, there is still a long way to go. It remains to be seen whether the government's agenda for social inclusion, and a more equal society with better public services for all, will be achieved.

KEY ISSUES

Recently the government has introduced a major strategy for reform of services for children, young people and their families called 'Every Child Matters: Change for Children'. This includes an extensive overhaul of the way services are provided. The programme identifies five key outcomes for children. These are:

* being healthy
* staying safe
* enjoying and achieving
* making a positive contribution
* economic well-being.

Tolerance

British society is widely regarded as a society that tolerates the beliefs and opinions of others.

Although there are people who hold intolerant views, our laws and way of life mean that most of society is open minded and tolerant of differences. Being tolerant of others and of differences between people is an important principle in early years services.

Think it over...

Imagine you are a young Asian woman in a bus queue and everyone keeps ignoring you and pushing past to get on the bus. When you eventually get to the front of the queue the bus driver does not let you on and is hostile and unhelpful. You might feel angry and argue the point or decide to go by train next time. Discuss how you would feel if this was your experience every day, in all sorts of different situations.

Tackling social exclusion and the cycle of disadvantage

Generally, groups that experience discrimination do not have power or influence in our society and are often marginalised to a greater or lesser extent. These people are sometimes called the socially excluded.

Currently, government policy is to promote social inclusion with such initiatives as Sure Start and to empower communities and give people the skills for employment. Sure Start's aim is:

'To work with parents, parents-to-be and children to promote the physical, intellectual and social development of babies and young children – particularly those that are disadvantaged – so that they can flourish at home and when they get to school, and thereby break the cycle of disadvantage for the current generation of young children.'

(DfES, 2001.)

The cycle of disadvantage is where generations of the same families are trapped in a vicious circle and face multiple problems such as poverty, unemployment, poor environments and low aspirations. Often these are fragile families located in troubled communities. Sure Start and other initiatives are usually focused on the family and local community. These often have many strengths and successful programmes will build on them.

Think it over...

Research information on Sure Start on both a local and national level. In a group, discuss how you would answer the following questions, using your research to help.

• Is the UK an equitable society?
• How can the cycle of disadvantage be broken?
• How can the Sure Start programme help with this?

Equal access to services

Tied up with social exclusion is the issue of access to services. To gain access to services people need to know they exist and that they can use them. This means information must be open and available in all community languages. The services also need to be accessible and affordable. Finally, services must welcome children and families and involve them at all levels, including management and service development.

KEY ISSUES

In December 2004 the government published a ten-year strategy for childcare ('Choice for Parents: The best start for children'). This policy document sets out many ideas but, its main purposes, outlined in paragraph 1.8, are:

• many families still have difficulty finding childcare services that fit their circumstances and that adapt as their children grow
• many parents still find childcare services hard to afford
• the quality of childcare services can vary, which can undermine parents' confidence and, at its worst, have harmful impacts on children's development
• services can be poorly joined up, making them more difficult to access
• parents would like flexible working arrangements to enable them to spend more time with their children
• too many parents, especially mothers, who would like to stay in work and develop their careers after their children are born, are not able to do so, which can result in considerable costs to the family and to the wider economy
• many parents would like more time with their children when they are very young
• childcare and family support could be used more effectively in helping families break out of the cycle of poverty and worklessness.

Obtain a copy of the strategy and write a short leaflet on how it might help families in poverty.

Early years values and principles

Most occupations have some kind of value base or professional code of ethics that underpins how they work. These value statements generally recognise the importance of good standards of provision and public safety, according to the type of occupation, and many recognise principles of equality and rights.

CASE STUDY

A rural initiative has been set up to work with children under five and their families in several small villages. There are real difficulties for these families, as many have been affected by lower prices for their produce and have lost their jobs or their farms. The initiative has been very successful due to its motivated and talented organiser and has attracted funding for several projects to help children and families. The success has been in taking the services to the communities and meeting the real needs of young families in isolated settings.

- Research the needs of rural communities for early years services. Identify ways in which the needs have been met or could be met.

The code of ethics or value base covers an occupation's approach to its service users and to the work it actually undertakes. These values will be evident in the work of the setting and demonstrated through the kind of service offered and the attitudes and behaviour of the staff.

Early years services have a set of values and principles stated clearly within the national occupational standards for the sector. The values and principles are listed later in this unit. The occupational standards for early years services are called standards for 'Children's Care, Learning and Development' (CCLD). Occupational standards are based on the functions people undertake when working and are published by standard-setting bodies for different types of employment, such as early years, catering or engineering. They are grouped into units that lay out the standard of service expected by employers and government and include the values of the occupation. These units form NVQs. It is important for you to become familiar with the values of the early years sector, as you will need to make sure you can work to these values when you are in placement and in employment.

The values and principles are so important that they are integrated into every unit within the occupational standards for Children's Care, Learning and Development. You can find out more about occupational standards by contacting the relevant standard-setting body, in this case the sector skills council Skills for Care and Development.

Attitudes and values

To be able to work using the values of any sector it is important to understand your own attitudes and values. Attitudes are about the way you view something and usually include how you judge or evaluate. For example, your attitude to war is likely to include views about whether you agree or disagree with the idea. Together, your attitudes and values are of major importance for how you view the world and the people in it.

KEY ISSUES

You are aware that there are several families using the nursery who are asylum seekers and that part of a local estate seems to have many houses and flats where families claiming asylum live. The press reports that local children cannot get school places near to home due to the influx of children from abroad.

- Do we think of asylum seekers as one group or many groups, each with different reasons for being here?
- Are we prejudiced – if so, why?
- Do we mind if someone accuses us of prejudice?
- Do we think we are superior?
- Do we think asylum seekers are getting something they don't deserve?

How we learn our attitudes and values

Attitudes, values and prejudices are usually learned in our early years. Children as young as two years old are able to make judgements based on race or gender as they learn to put a higher value on certain types of physical appearance.

Young children develop their attitudes and values as a result of early learning from their families, friends, nursery, school and from television and other media. The family is a very powerful influence on children's values and attitudes and it is often in the home that they first learn to stereotype other people or groups. Children pick up the attitudes of their parents or carers through observing their behaviour and then copying it. Boys who are always given 'boys' toys', such as construction equipment for making cars, and girls who are always given 'girls' toys', such as dolls, and who are also encouraged to behave in stereotyped ways, are likely to hold back from trying new ideas and ways of relating that cross those stereotypes.

Most people make friends with and have family members who share their values and attitudes. This often means that communities and individuals are less likely to be able to explore similarities and differences with others who are different. When children have the chance to mix with and make friends with other children who may have different social and cultural backgrounds of their own this will help them to become more tolerant and to understand the feelings of others about what it is to be different.

Often individual prejudices have come about through history and experience as well as misinformation. Prejudices are often shared with a larger social group and have become part of what we all believe and what we express to our children, regardless of whether there is any factual basis for them. For example, a common prejudice is against obese people who are often judged as lazy or out of control.

Remember: children have a right not to learn negative attitudes and prejudices from people around them.

Think it over...

Ask yourself the following questions:
- Can I remember examples of times when I felt I was receiving unfair treatment?
- How did that experience make me feel?
- Do I hold stereotyped views about race, gender, disability or other people who are different from me?

How people using early years services may be subject to inequality in our society

Most people in our society are subject to some forms of inequality, but some groups experience it much more than others. As we have already discussed, being different in some way often brings discrimination. The following are examples of vulnerable groups who may feel the effects of inequality:

* disabled people, who may experience high levels of inequality, such as not being able to travel freely or go to a theatre and being prevented from doing certain jobs

* older people, who may be considered not able to work or to care for children

* economically disadvantaged people, who may not be able to afford things they would wish to buy for their family, such as healthy food

* Educationally disadvantaged people, who for various reasons have not achieved at school either for social reasons or through learning disabilities.

Why don't you go and play with the dolls? I'm sure you'd enjoy that more.

Gender stereotypes can hold children back from exploring new ideas.

Effects of inequality

Inequality affects everyone and is closely linked to discrimination. People, including children, who experience inequality and discrimination, are damaged in many ways. Discrimination affects children from birth. During their early years, children are developing their sense of identity, self-worth and self-esteem. They are learning how others see them and react to them, especially outside the home. For example, overweight children may be bullied or called names. Alongside this, they may encounter advertising where slim and active children are portrayed positively as successful and beautiful. It is important to ensure a balance between encouraging healthy lifestyles, including healthy eating and exercise, without portraying those who are overweight in negative and demoralising ways.

If children grow up with a view of themselves as inferior (or superior), this will affect their whole future. Children with poor self-esteem may achieve less at school and may have serious emotional and behavioural problems.

Marginalised and disempowered

As well as personal feelings which hold people back from realising their true potential, the effects of inequality spread out to the wider community. This can lead to increased marginalisation (being pushed to the fringe or edge of society) and the social exclusion of whole groups, such as young males. Some communities find increased levels of violence and aggression and social problems like crime or drug taking. Inequality is both a moral issue and a social issue with wide consequences. As well as being marginalised, people can also feel disempowered. This means they feel that they have no control over their lives. In this situation people wonder what they have to lose and may find it difficult to invest in or support the society they live in. Being marginalised and disempowered leads to low self-esteem and low self-confidence with people lacking faith in themselves or their ability to succeed and improve their chances in life.

KEY ISSUES

The effects of inequality and discrimination on self-esteem include:

- lack of confidence
- low self-esteem
- being unwilling to take risks
- fear of rejection
- feeling unsafe and vulnerable
- withdrawal
- feeling excluded
- loss of motivation to achieve
- stress and illness
- depression and hopelessness.

Social exclusion and marginalisation can cause problems for the wider community as well as for the individuals experiencing it.

The Race Relations (Amendment) Act 2000

This act identifies four types of discrimination.

* **Direct discrimination**. Treating a person less favourably on racial grounds, such as refusing children places at nursery because they are black, Asian or white.

* **Indirect discrimination**. Applying a requirement to everyone that certain racial groups either cannot fulfil or only a small proportion can fulfil. For example, insistence that girls wear skirts as part of school uniform can be unlawful as it indirectly discriminates against certain religions.

* **Victimisation**. Being treated less favourably because someone is using race relations legislation or alleging discrimination.

* **Segregation**. Segregating on racial grounds may constitute discriminatory treatment, such as grouping children by colour at mealtimes or when in line.

These definitions of discrimination are equally applicable to other groups that might suffer discrimination such as in disability discrimination, gender discrimination, or religious discrimination.

Anti-discrimination

Anti-discrimination means actively opposing discrimination by implementing policies and practices designed to rid society of barriers and discrimination, such as when women are paid less for the same work as men and legal action is taken against the employer under the Equal Pay Act.

Anti-discrimination puts equal opportunities into action and means that positive steps are taken to combat the various types of discrimination, such as racism.

Within early years settings, anti-discriminatory practice is considered to be best practice and this is dealt with in more detail later in the unit.

Stereotyping and labelling

A stereotype is defined as 'a standardised image or conception of a type of person'. Most stereotypes are based on prejudices (prejudice usually means an unfavourable view of someone or something based on inadequate facts). They involve labelling and all are untrue as they do not look at all the aspects of the entire individual. You will need to be sure that you are aware of holding any prejudiced and stereotyped attitudes as these may lead you to behave unfairly towards people. Most of us hold stereotypes without necessarily realising it and apply those stereotypes to people we meet. There are people, for example, who are long-term unemployed because they are disabled, ill or not able to move to another part of the country because of family commitments. People in this position are sometimes labelled lazy or scroungers because the very good reasons why they cannot get a job are not considered. When people are labelled, often this can act as a self-fulfilling prophecy. Children who are labelled as lazy may act in a lazy way, not because of themselves but because of the adults around them having low expectations or treating them differently.

Stereotyping affects the ways we treat individual children. For example, we may feel that girls, in general, enjoy quiet activities and are less competitive than boys. We may feel that boys are usually noisier and enjoy competitive games and vigorous outdoor play. Equally we may think that black children are stronger and more athletic than others or that Asian girls are quiet and submissive. Our expectations of children are known to be a key factor in their achievement. If we hold stereotypes we may expect less of some children in some areas of their learning and development and they may not reach their true potential.

Early years best practice looks at individual children with their individual needs, personalities, likes and dislikes rather than whether they are boys or girls, or black or white.

Discriminatory practices are sometimes present because no one in an organisation realises they are discriminating and there is lack of thought or understanding or, on rare occasions, where staff simply can't be bothered. Examples include:

* where a setting uses books and learning materials that only feature white children

* where a setting only allows the English language to be used when it has many bi-lingual children and/or children with English as an additional language

Welcoming children and families from all cultures and linguistic backgrounds is very important.

* asking boys to play outside and girls to stay in and help staff clear away
* when disabled children are steered away from certain activities that, with appropriate support, they could undertake very successfully.

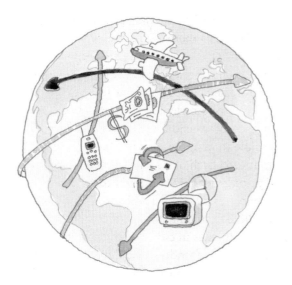

We live in a globalised society.

Holding stereotypical views about children based on their gender, race, ability or any other feature is not acceptable within early years settings and should never be tolerated.

Advantages of diversity

The UK has a rich cultural and ethnic mix that has many positive effects. Today we live in a globalised society. Countries have links with other countries across the world, communication is instant and understanding other cultures has positive benefits to business and commerce. Immigration has brought skills and knowledge into the UK and has enriched our national life. Highly skilled people come here to work in arts and science and many top experts, such as specialists in reproductive medicine, come to work here because of the UK's more open attitude.

CASE STUDY

Egyptian-born Dr Mohammed Taranissi, the director of the Assisted Reproduction and Gynaecology Centre in London, has been a strong voice within the UK for more progress in human embryology research. For a number of years he has supported parents with children who have serious illnesses that can be helped by donations of stem cells from brothers and sisters who are a genetic match. This can only be achieved by genetic screening of embryos – those that are a suitable match are implanted and become what has sometimes been called 'designer babies'. Dr Taranissi is anxious to help parents whose existing children have real health issues and believes that all the babies that are born as a result of this technique will be loved and cared for. He has said, 'It's not a commodity, as the baby will be loved and cherished on its own merit. It's not just being produced as a spare part.'

Cultural enrichment takes many forms. On a day-to-day basis there are new foods to try, different clothes to wear and new forms of relating. For example, Asian communities are well known for their hospitality and for their respect for and care of the elderly. Cultural enrichment is also present in music and the arts. It is almost impossible to imagine UK society without reggae or rap music, both of which have their origins in immigrant groups. Different cultures are represented in the media and sports and help the UK to succeed in all these areas. People who accept differences in culture can be more flexible and creative, and understand the needs of others.

In the past, specific economic activities have been strongly associated with specific groups of people. However, different communities are increasingly moving into mainstream business activities. It would be wrong, for example, to assume that Asians are only involved in the food industry. Equally, black people of African or Caribbean backgrounds are moving forward in the arts, science and politics.

Early years and diversity

There are particular advantages in recognising diversity within early years settings. In schools and nurseries there are children from many different races and cultures speaking many different languages. Being positive about diversity can enrich our lives and those of the children in our care. It is important to make sure that different people and groups are equally respected.

Early years settings can develop and use the differences in culture, ethnic group, gender, language and religion to help make attending a nursery a learning experience for all children and their families. Looking positively at other cultures and ways of life helps children to understand the wider world, to grow up to be tolerant and to accept, without fear and as equals, people who are different.

Children who, as part of their overall social development, learn to respect the views and needs of others and to value difference, are more likely to become tolerant adults who are able to contribute to a fairer society.

Appreciation of diversity promotes tolerance and acceptance without fear.

CASE STUDY

Baroness Amos was born in Guyana and studied at the Universities of Warwick, Birmingham and East Anglia. She was awarded an Honorary Professorship at Thames Valley University in 1995 in recognition of her work on equality and social justice. Valerie Amos was appointed a government Whip in the House of Lords in July 1998. In addition to her role as a Spokesperson on International Development, she also spoke on Social Security and Women's Issues. She was created a life peer in August 1997. She joined the Cabinet as International Development Secretary in May 2003 before becoming Leader of the House of Lords and President of the Council in October 2003.

• Find out about black MPs or MEPs. Are their numbers growing? What posts of responsibility do they hold?

Human rights

Moral rights

Moral rights are based on views about what is just and moral and consist of universal values that are generally agreed to apply to all human beings, regardless of gender, race, culture or difference. Some are truly global – theft, murder or perjury are recognised as immoral activities throughout the world and protecting people's rights would involve protecting them from these activities.

Some moral rights may not be recognised globally. Freedom of speech or capital punishment may not be regarded in the same way in different countries or areas of the world. In the European Union there are shared human rights laws and conventions. The Human Rights Act is discussed in more detail later in this unit.

Rights of children

Children are increasingly seen to have rights and their voice heard in decisions affecting their lives. This is reflected in our legislation and social policy. The UN Convention on the Rights of the Child, described later in the unit and which the UK government has ratified (agreed to), sets out rights for our children.

Assessment activity 1.2

You have read an article in a newspaper saying that 'children should not be the subject of all this nonsense about being equal'. Write a letter back to the paper stating why in your view it is important to understand equality issues in the service we provide for children.

3 How early years services can recognise and promote equality, diversity and rights

Early years and care services are operated within a framework of laws and regulations designed, among other things, to support equality, diversity and rights. They have policies, procedures and codes of practice in place as a matter of best practice and to make sure that the law is upheld. The main thrust of these policies is to ensure that people are allowed equal treatment and that an individual's rights are protected. Work practices, administration and organisation should all reflect this.

Formal policies

Policies are overall statements, aims and intentions and include the general goals and values of the organisation. Policies are powerful tools to make sure that the organisation's values and beliefs are implemented in everyday practice.

Policies that cover equality, diversity and rights have a role in ensuring high-quality services relating closely to the values of the sector. Quality services are difficult to achieve if systems and anti-discriminatory policies and practices are not in place to protect staff and service users.

Each policy will have a code of practice and/or statements of procedures that set out in general terms how the policy will operate and what actions are to be taken in particular situations, such as what staff do if a parent makes a racist comment.

Many policies are primarily designed to promote an individual's rights and freedoms when in employment, whereas other policies are designed to protect service users. For example, a harassment policy protects employees from different forms of harassment or bullying,

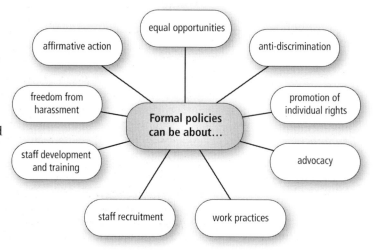

affirmative action · equal opportunities · anti-discrimination · freedom from harassment · **Formal policies can be about...** · promotion of individual rights · staff development and training · advocacy · staff recruitment · work practices whereas a policy on behaviour is designed both to give staff clear guidance and to protect children.

Policies covering equality are required in early years settings' legislation, and they should include an appeals and complaints procedure that is implemented fairly and without prejudice.

Every organisation and setting should have an equal opportunities policy that includes all areas of potential discrimination, even areas where they do not feel it is relevant. For example, an early years setting in a rural area where all the children attending are white should still ensure that equipment, activities, books and so on clearly reflect positive images of black and Asian children. Children need to understand that they live in a diverse society and learn to value and respect other people.

COMMON POLICIES IN EARLY YEARS SETTINGS	EXAMPLES OF POLICY GOALS
Recruitment and selection of staff	Open and transparent recruitment and selection that does not put up barriers to any section of the community. Designed to encourage a multi-racial workforce that reflects the proportion of different races in the community, and also including male staff and those with disabilities.
Equal opportunities	For staff as well as children and families. Equal opportunities should form a part of all other policies to bring about equal treatment and equal chances. A 'no blame' culture to cope with change and service development.
Inclusion	This is defined in the CCLD occupational standards as 'a process of identifying, understanding and breaking down barriers to participation and belonging'. Making sure, in everyday practice, that barriers are broken down for individual and groups of children is a goal for a number of policies and is sometimes used to refer specifically to disabled children or children with special educational needs.
Anti-discrimination	Actively opposing and challenging discrimination in every area of work, including discriminatory language, bullying, and hidden or unintentional discrimination.
Harassment	Giving clear guidance on all forms of harassment experienced by staff, children and families, such as racial or sexual harassment.
Admissions	Open, fair and transparent admissions systems, ensuring access to service by all parts of the community. Providing materials translated into community languages and extending knowledge of the services into 'hard to reach' groups, such as travellers.
Curriculum	The curriculum, resources, equipment and activities should be fully accessible to all children, including disabled children, those with special needs or with English as an additional language. Positive images of groups that experience discrimination should be used throughout. Links with the community should be strong and diversity celebrated.
Relations with parents	This policy will state the setting's attitudes and values regarding parents as partners.
Staff development and training	On-going training to raise awareness of discrimination and to ensure staff both understand the issues and support the solutions. Staff development is vital to ensure the best possible service for children and families.

▶

COMMON POLICIES IN EARLY YEARS SETTINGS	EXAMPLES OF POLICY GOALS
Quality assurance	This may incorporate elements of other policies but is designed to ensure that levels of service meet high quality standards across all the work of the setting. Settings may have written quality standards that they aim to achieve and a quality-assurance policy will include these, together with mechanisms for obtaining and using feedback from service users and other agencies involved. Inspections, regulations, codes of practice and the underlying principles will all contribute to the quality standards.
Complaints	For use by families who may have a complaint or grievance and who should also know about how to make complaints to a regulatory authority, such as Ofsted. Human resources policies also allow for staff to make complaints in various circumstances if they feel they have received discrimination.

Work practices

It is very easy to have a policy, but it is more difficult to make sure that the policy is put into practice and that everybody knows about it and sticks to it. Organisations and settings should regularly evaluate the success of their policy in achieving its objectives. This also means that organisations will have to use management strategies, such as appraisal and performance management, to make sure policies and procedures are followed by individuals and monitored regularly. Many organisations now have whistle-blowing procedures whereby staff can report problems of all types, including bullying, harassment and poor work practice. A whistle-blowing policy should protect, not penalise, the whistle-blower. Adequate staff training and development follows on from appraisal. Regular in-house and off-the-job training sessions on equality of opportunity, anti-discriminatory practice and so forth will help the organisation to meet its goals. Staff should work together on developing policies for their work with children and policies that affect them as an employee. They should be clear on what policies protect them and how they do so.

As well as working closely with families, work practices should ensure that the voices of children are heard in decisions affecting their lives and experiences.

Positive promotion of individual rights

It is important that individual rights are promoted in a positive way and this applies to both adults and children in early years settings. Staff who respect themselves and are respected by others find it easier to respect the children they care for and to set a positive example. Lack of respect easily communicates itself to children and families and damages self-esteem. Policies and procedures concerning equality and anti-discrimination are designed to protect individual rights and should form a normal part of the culture of the setting.

Advocacy

Disability legislation and practice stresses the need to encourage children to make their own decisions and gain some control over their lives. This is known as empowerment and is a right for every child. Children with special needs may find it difficult to communicate their needs and desires and require an independent adult (an advocate) to speak for them. Sometimes parents can be their child's advocate, while at other times a child's health visitor or social worker can perform the task. Some local authorities employ children's rights officers. Legal advocates are appointed by courts for children taken into care. Adults who may have severe learning or communication difficulties may also require advocates.

Affirmative action

Affirmative action occurs when employers and others can take positive action to overcome discrimination or to put right previous discrimination. For example, where there are few people from a particular ethnic group in the workforce the aim of positive action would be to enable these people to compete on equal terms with others. Positive action in this case could take the form of printing leaflets in relevant languages or arranging extra training for the minority ethnic group. However, selection itself must be based on merit and all applicants must be treated equally. There are cases when being of a particular ethnic group might be a genuine occupational requirement and the law allows this to happen, for example, when working in a particular ethnic restaurant.

Harassment

Harassment is illegal under both the Race Relations Act and the Sex Discrimination Act. Harassment in these contexts can mean subjecting people to unwanted sexual attention or racial abuse. This covers a whole range of behaviours, such as verbal or physical bullying, jokes and taunts or excluding people because of their race or gender. No one should have to put up with this sort of behaviour and people can expect the law to be on their side if harassment is proven.

Success of legislation in opposing discrimination

It would be wrong to assume that all legislation designed to oppose discrimination is entirely successful. Despite laws being in place, certain groups still experience discrimination. For example, black people are still under-represented in professions such as law or medicine and women are under-represented in parliament.

Under the Race Relations Act, it is still difficult to prove discrimination and obtain evidence that makes comparisons with other racial groups. Cases take a long time and are often stressful. There are possibilities under the Act for positive action in certain cases, such as where an employer wishes to advertise for a black member of staff and can justify why they are allowed to do so, perhaps to work with people from a specific ethnic group.

The Sex Discrimination Act has still not succeeded in bringing equality for women, who earn on average 82 per cent of men's hourly earnings for broadly the same work. The pay gap isn't just bad news for women. It means that women's abilities and skills are not being fully used in businesses and in the economy.

Women are still kept from rising to top positions at work because of the 'glass ceiling'. This is a term used to describe the barriers in place to prevent women getting beyond middle management.

There are other structural barriers to women succeeding, such as poor childcare facilities, lack of family-friendly policies at work, inflexible working hours and low status given to part-time work. Many UK employers expect staff to work long hours if they are to rise in the company and women still take the major burden of caring for the home and family, making the pressures on them enormous.

The 'glass ceiling' at work.

The Children Act 1989 and National Standards for Under Eights Day Care and Childminding

The Children Act is a very important piece of legislation that affects many aspects of the way in which children are cared for. The Act covers children who are disabled and states that health, education and social services for children should be co-ordinated so that a seamless service may be offered.

In England the regulations under the Children Act (DFES, 2001) require early years providers to meet a set of fourteen standards and supporting criteria. Ofsted inspect early years settings, taking account of these standards. The standards most closely linked to equality, diversity and rights are as follows.

* **Standard 9, Equal opportunities:** This standard will ensure that settings actively promote equality of opportunity and anti-discriminatory practice for all children.

* **Standard 10, Special needs (including special educational needs and disabilities):** This standard will ensure that settings are aware that some children will have special needs and that they are proactive in taking action when

such children are identified or admitted to the provision. This means settings will have to take steps to promote the welfare and development of the child in partnership with parents/carers.

Human Rights Act 1998

The Human Rights Act incorporates the European Convention on Human Rights into UK law across England, Wales, Scotland and Northern Ireland. The Act allows residents to seek justice through the courts if they feel a public authority has infringed their human rights. The term 'public authority' covers:

* local authorities (including social services)

* government departments

* police

* NHS (including GPs, dentists, etc.) when doing NHS work

* other public bodies (covers a wide range of organisations that have a public function).

The Act is designed to modernise relationships between people and the state based on the values of fairness, respect for human dignity, and inclusiveness in public services. The law is divided into sections, all of which affect broad human rights. The main exceptions to the goal of promoting individual human rights are to do with ensuring the safety of the individual or the wider common good.

The main areas that have been incorporated into UK law are listed in the table below with a brief commentary of those sections most relevant to early years work.

RIGHTS AND FREEDOMS (PART 1)	COMMENTARY
Article 2 Right to life	Public authorities must not cause death. There are some exceptions, such as when necessary force has been used to protect someone from unlawful violence and this has resulted in death. This article could affect decisions on abortion, life-saving operations or end-of-life decisions. It will also affect decisions about access to treatment, withdrawal of treatment, and investigations of suspicious deaths while in health or care settings.
Article 3 Prohibition of torture	No one should be subjected to inhumane and degrading treatment. This article could affect decisions about taking children into care where they are experiencing inhumane or degrading conditions.
Article 4 Prohibition of slavery and forced labour	People must not be 'owned' by anyone as if they were slaves or forced to work and unable to leave. There are some exceptions, such as during emergencies affecting the community or for people in prison.
Article 5 Right to liberty and security	Everyone has rights to liberty except when detained by law, such as convicted criminals, those with mental illness or people entering the country illegally. This article could affect people detained under Mental Health Acts when there is a delay in dealing with their case.
Article 6 Right to a fair trial	People have a right to a fair trial within a reasonable time and are innocent until proved guilty. This part of the Act gives everyone the right to a public trial or hearing by an independent tribunal. It covers criminal and many civil cases, tribunals and hearings.
Article 7 No punishment without law	No one can be held guilty of a criminal offence for something they did in the past when, under the law at the time, what they did was not criminal.
Article 8 Right to respect for private and family life	Public authorities are not allowed to interfere in people's private affairs unless they have legal authority to do so, such as in cases of national security, public safety or protecting others. Health and social care services can affect family life, for example, when taking children into care.
Article 9 Freedom of thought, conscience and religion	Freedom to change religions, and to practise religion. Covers issues such as taking time off for religious festivals, refusing life-saving treatment such as blood transfusions on religious grounds, children practising religion when in care, and adoption practices based on religion.
Article 10 Freedom of expression	Freedom to hold opinions, and to receive and impart information. This covers the media, the Internet, books – any type of communication.
Article 11 Freedom of assembly	Right to demonstrate and to join (or not to join) trade unions and associations.
Article 12 Right to marry	Right to marry and found a family. The article will affect adoption and fostering. Local authorities' policies on who can adopt may need reviewing to ensure they do not discriminate on grounds of race or age or other criteria, such as obesity.
Article 13 Prohibition of discrimination	The rights and freedoms under the Act do not discriminate between people on grounds of race, colour, sex, language, religion, political opinion, national or social origin, being part of a minority, property, birth or other status.

▶

RIGHTS AND FREEDOMS (PART 1)	COMMENTARY
Article 14 Freedom from discrimination in respect of protected rights (not a separate article)	Prohibits discrimination. It could cover a whole range of different scenarios, such as organ donation or denying treatment because of age. This article recognises not all differences in treatment are discriminatory, only those with no reasonable justification.
RIGHTS AND FREEDOMS (PART 2 THE FIRST PROTOCOL OF THE ACT)	
Article 1 Protection of property	Gives people entitlement to peaceful enjoyment of their property and possessions so long as the public interest is not affected or removing property is allowed under the law.
Article 2 Right to education	No one is to be denied education and the state will respect the right of parents to ensure education for their children conforms with their principles, for example in terms of religion. The rights have to be measured against the available resources. This article could affect the rights of children with special educational needs or children who are excluded from schools.
Article 3 Right to free elections	Covers rights to a free election with secret ballot.
RIGHTS AND FREEDOMS (PART 2 THE SIXTH PROTOCOL OF THE ACT)	
Article 1 The death penalty shall be abolished	No one shall be executed. Exceptions to this Article cover times of war.

UN Convention on the Rights of the Child

The UN Convention on the Rights of the Child has influenced law and public policy with respect to children in the UK. The UN Convention is a formal statement designed to protect children's rights agreed by almost all nations. The Convention on the Rights of the Child outlines in 41 Articles the human rights to be respected and protected for every child under the age of 18 years and requires that these rights are implemented in the light of the Convention's guiding principles. The following highlights some of the rights that are included.

* All rights apply to all children, whatever their background, and the state has an obligation to protect children against discrimination. (Article 2)

* Children's best interests must come first. (Article 3)

* Children have a right to be heard. (Article 12)

* Children must be protected from violence, abuse and neglect. (Article 19)

* Children with disabilities and learning difficulties must have their rights protected. (Article 23)

* Children have a right to education. (Article 28)

* Children have a right to play and recreation activities according to their age. (Article 31)

* Children have a right to freedom from economic exploitation. (Article 32)

* Children have a right to be protected from sexual exploitation. (Article 33)

Think it over...

Read about the UN Convention on the Rights of the Child. In groups, discuss what rights covered are used in your everyday work with children.

CASE STUDY

Article 12 of the UN Convention talks about children having a right to be heard. In 2000, Coram Family (a London based charity) began its 'Listening to young children' project. This work aimed to understand how to really listen to young children under the age of eight. It aimed to identify the kinds of relationships and opportunities that help children to articulate their feelings, experiences and concerns.

This project is helping practitioners to move from a model of practice which centres on adults promoting young children's welfare to one that acknowledges children's rights by recognising that even at a young age they are competent to make or contribute to informed decisions.

The UN Convention on the Rights of the Child has radically changed early years practice as well as attitudes to children. Here are some examples of how early years practice has changed over the years in line with the Convention and subsequent UK legislation.

1 The rights of disabled children to be included within mainstream education where this is appropriate for them.

2 Avoiding humiliating practices in work with children such as the 'naughty chair'.

3 Consulting with and listening to children.

4 Involving children in decision-making.

5 Maintaining contact with families for 'looked-after' children.

6 A child's right to privacy in cases of child protection.

7 Making voluntary payments for school trips rather than compulsory payments.

Overriding individuals' rights

Practitioners working in early years settings have to be very careful not to override individual rights and freedoms. This is particularly the case when dealing with vulnerable children and families. The principle of parents as the most important people in the child's life is very important. What parents want for their children or children want for themselves should be respected. Practitioners do not always agree with parents' or children's choices and this can cause some difficulties. However, in most cases practitioners should not

Think it over...

Young girls in some parts of the world are subjected to what is known as female genital mutilation (female circumcision). Parts of their external genital organs are altered or removed in order to minimise sexual pleasure and encourage chastity. This is illegal in the UK but sometimes young girls who live here are taken to other countries to be circumcised as it is considered to be a part of their culture.

Discuss in a group how the UK views this practice and how prevalent it is in the rest of the world. Can any culture justify female genital mutilation?

How does the practice accord with the UN Convention on the Rights of the Child?

force the child or family to undertake a certain course of action even when it is perceived as being for their 'own good' but should allow them to make an informed decision.

There are cases when individual rights have to be put aside, sometimes by the exercise of authority and the use of force. Sectioning people under Mental Health Acts usually means the person is taken away from their home without their consent. The law allows this to happen to ensure public safety or the safety of the individual concerned by giving statutory powers to the health authorities or to the police to take this action. If mental health professionals decide that the patient has a mental illness and treatment is 'in their best interests' a doctor has a duty of care under common law to provide treatment in the patient's best interests where the patient lacks a capacity to consent to or refuse treatment and there is no valid advance statement. Common law is based on the principle of deciding cases by reference to previous decisions (precedents), rather than to written statutes drafted by legislative bodies such as parliament. Common law focuses more intently on the facts of the particular case to arrive at a fair and equitable result. The patient's best interests are not simply confined to what is in his or her best medical interests, as there are other factors that may be taken into account, which include the patient's values and preferences when able, their psychological health, well-being, quality of life, relationships with family or other carers, spiritual and religious welfare and their own financial interests.

In cases of child protection the Children Acts 1989 and 2004 and other relevant legislation clearly outline principles for safeguarding children and this can mean children are forcibly removed from their home. These laws give statutory powers to local authorities or other agencies involved, such as the NSPCC, when the safety of a child is at stake. These statutory powers can be seen to override parents' rights, making the welfare of the child paramount.

In many situations dealing with young children, practitioners have 'power' over the children or their families and must use this ethically. For example, where a child discloses abuse, or where you suspect that a child is being abused, a particularly difficult situation arises. The child may well say that 'This is a secret'. In this case you will have to say immediately to the child that it cannot remain a secret and make clear that you are obliged to tell other people. Equally, if a parent states they suspect a third party of abuse you cannot collude with secrecy and have to override their rights for confidentiality.

Promoting equality and individual rights

As an early years practitioner you will be required to treat both children and adults fairly and equally, ensuring their individual rights. Treating everyone fairly is not the same as treating everyone in the same way. Fair treatment in any organisation or in an early years setting means meeting the needs of individuals. Individual needs are always different and need to be met in different ways as long as these are fair in terms of the law and the policies of the setting. This is not favouritism – giving all children the same activity and materials does not allow for the fact that some children will not be able to do the activity without additional assistance. For example, a disabled child will be treated differently but only to ensure he or she has an equal chance with everyone else of completing a task.

Allowing choice

There have been occasions when children who are fussy about food have been 'force fed' in early years settings, sometimes with the best of motives. This kind of behaviour is totally unacceptable. No matter how young children are their views and opinions should be sought and should generally direct what happens to them.

CASE STUDY

An early years setting in an inner city had an established equal opportunities policy which ensured that discrimination, when identified, was dealt with immediately. The officer in charge insisted that all staff had training in anti-discriminatory practice as soon as they started at the nursery.

A new family had a place for their two-year-old at the nursery and were assigned a black key worker. They met with the officer in charge and stated that they did not wish their child's key worker to be black or Asian. The officer in charge was able to show the family the equal opportunities policy and to talk to them about the benefits to their child of meeting people from other backgrounds. The family understood that the policy meant that their request could not be granted although they were free to take their child elsewhere.

- What positive actions had the officer in charge taken? Why were the actions appropriate?
- How might the family be feeling? How could their attitudes affect their own child?

Children should be allowed choice and autonomy within the bounds of safe practice. This is not the same as a free for all where children are not given boundaries and frameworks for positive behaviour. Practitioners do need to prevent children hurting one another or to prevent and manage self-destructive behaviour.

KEY ISSUES

The same principles of fairness and equality should underpin your work with colleagues and with the families using the service. This can lead to tensions and contradictions. For example you may find that families have different values and do not support equal treatment for all. Some families do not like it if boys engage in domestic play or girls are noisy and enjoy football. In some cases, families are overtly prejudiced against other groups, such as travellers, who may be using the service.

Recruitment practices

Recruitment practices are very important indicators of fair employment. Recruitment to your setting should be open and transparent and all staff should have access to training and development opportunities. By ensuring that your recruitment practices meet the needs of your community, such as accessible information in community languages, you are much more likely to recruit from groups, such as ethnic minorities, who may not have worked there before. Training all staff in equality and diversity, inclusion and anti-discriminatory practice means better outcomes for children and families. You should take every opportunity open to you for further training as, in early years work, things move quickly and your initial training soon becomes out of date.

Implications of confidentiality

Confidentiality is an important principle in work with children and families. If confidences are broken and sensitive information leaks out through accident or careless practice, this has major implications for all concerned and leads to loss of confidence in the setting. Parents or other service users are at liberty to take legal action against the setting in some cases.

Communication

Positive and effective communication is essential in early years settings and practitioners have to be able to communicate with:

* colleagues
* visiting professionals
* children
* parents and families
* emergency services.

Sharing information, both in a single organisation and with other agencies, may save children's lives and will certainly contribute to their well-being. Most cases when children known to social services are murdered by their carers involve a breakdown in communication between the people and agencies involved. The government is taking steps to redress this by ensuring anyone working with children, young people and their families learns about information sharing and multi-agency work as part of the DfES Common Core of Skills and Knowledge. You can find the Common Core on the DfES website.

Information about services and policies should be provided in all community languages and the information should be available to those who need it through signing, large print or Braille. As described elsewhere in this unit, advocates can be useful if parents or children require them. Where necessary, interpreters and translators should be provided. Positive relationships with local communities often bring with them useful contacts that can help to provide these services.

Partnership with parents

Partnership with parents is a key value within early years services. Parents and carers know more about their young children than anyone else and are the most important influence in their lives. The role of the parent is not easy and practitioners should not be judgemental when different family patterns are encountered. In today's society there is a wide range of different family patterns, such as lone parents, blended families (two existing families merging) or same-sex relationships. Families may need support from the setting to undertake their parenting role. Positive relationships with families help children to develop and thrive in the early years setting, as most children are acutely aware of tensions and may respond negatively. When problems arise, discussion should take place as soon as possible, before the situations become difficult.

Early years settings should welcome and value parents, regardless of their backgrounds or differences. Two-way sharing of information with parents is essential for the well-being of the child. When children start at the setting, a whole range of information is obtained and recorded to ensure that appropriate action can be taken in emergencies and the child's and families' preferences about care are known. Some of these may be vital to a child's life – for example, some allergies may be life threatening. There are many ways to share information, including daily diaries left out for busy parents to see when collecting their child after work or formal and informal conversations. Children's records are normally available for parents to see.

Parents can be involved in many ways in the setting if they wish to be and feel welcomed.

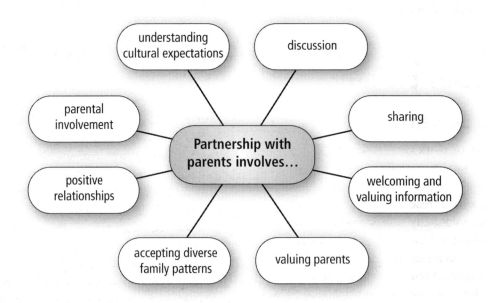

The relationship between the early years practitioner and parent should be based on trust.

They can:

* participate as volunteers, supporting everyday activities

* help with the management of the setting, as in many voluntary pre-schools

* provide help with specific activities within their expertise, such as dentists giving advice or equipment

* help with visits and outings.

Parents from other cultures may need to be approached in different ways and encouraged to become involved. Some parents may find leaving the home setting and participating culturally acceptable while other activities are not. Parents may enjoy language classes based in the setting or find their self-esteem raised through helping with children who have additional needs or who need language support.

Cultural expectations of care and education in the early years sector may vary with different parents or groups of parents. Some parents may not be accustomed to allowing the kinds of freedom that are given to children in the setting – for example, children may be taking part in messy activities, such as painting or digging in the garden. Other parents may have strict gender roles at home and find it difficult to understand why children are encouraged to explore different roles. A play-based curriculum is also controversial for some families who would prefer to see a more formal learning programme.

It is important for you to know why you do what you do with respect to equality, diversity and rights and be able to explain this sensitively to parents. You also need to know when to refer to other members of staff.

> **Assessment activity 1.3**
>
> • Find examples of policies covering equality, diversity and rights in your placement or get them from a college tutor.
>
> • Compare them and see if they cover the same areas. Ask yourself if there are missing areas.
>
> • Discuss in groups or pairs how such a policy helps early years services to promote rights and monitor good practice.

4 Promoting equality, diversity and rights in your own early years practice

Personal awareness

As you study or work with children in early years settings, you need to be aware of your own prejudices and beliefs. This means taking time to note your personal reactions when faced with difficult and potentially discriminatory situations, such as working with a family where the mother has recently been released from prison. How would your contact with her make you feel? Would you be concerned about her ability to look after her children? Beliefs are opinions, assumptions, prejudices, judgments, ideas and attitudes through which everything we experience in life is filtered. They are the lenses through which we see the world. Some of your beliefs were probably influenced by your parents, grandparents, teachers or come from books, the media, magazines and films.

Beliefs and prejudices dictate our experience, whether we recognise it or not. We automatically notice things we're expecting to see, because we're looking for them. In this way, the world largely conforms to our beliefs about it. The outer world is a reflection of our inner world. If you believe, for instance, that boys are always noisy, then you may not notice all the boys being quiet.

Our beliefs and prejudices

Maintaining your beliefs and prejudices feels safe because they are familiar to you, but in reality they can be dangerous. On the pretence of helping you, they may be severely limiting. Though beliefs are supposed to define your world, they can narrowly shape what you think and how you experience life. Sticking to your beliefs and prejudices may harm both you and the children and families you work with, so you need to think hard about change or ask for help in sorting out prejudices that are not in line with the early years value base and the policies of your setting. Remember that you are responsible for your beliefs and prejudices and how we behave to each other and to those around is the outward face of our inner beliefs.

None of us is likely to be completely free of prejudice, but we must make sure that the way we behave at work is always true to the values and principles of the sector. In other words, we must never behave in ways that discriminate, either intentionally or unintentionally. This means constantly checking the ways in which we relate to service users and the kind of service we provide. Settings do this in many different ways, including feedback from parents and children and through inspections and self-assessment. All the work of the setting will be covered and the feedback will inform future planning. Individual staff can use this feedback to inform their own practice.

Theory into practice

Write a list of things you believe about people – be honest with yourself as no-one needs to see it. What does your list tell you about your beliefs? Start each item with the words 'I believe'. Here is an example of a common prejudice to help you start:

'I believe that most fat people are lazy.'

Challenging discrimination

It is important to challenge oppressive and discriminatory behaviour. Anti-discrimination is defined in the Children's Care, Learning and Development occupational standards as 'Taking positive action to counter discrimination: this will involve identifying and challenging discrimination and being positive in your practice about differences and similarities between people.' So it's not enough to just not be discriminatory yourself – this is too passive. You must challenge discrimination when you see or experience it. Remember that you act as a role model to children and families as well as colleagues and others in the setting. Children will copy the behaviour of people they respect or care for.

Anti-discrimination in the early years setting

All forms of discrimination should be removed immediately as soon as they are evident in the setting. This means tackling discrimination and discriminatory remarks as soon as possible. Staff need to be clear about the policies they are working to and be sure of the support of management.

As well as dealing with discrimination from people and organisations, early years practitioners have a duty to provide a curriculum that, in addition to promoting children's development

You must challenge discrimination whenever you come across it.

and learning, is also in itself anti-discriminatory. Louise Derman Sparks (1989) uses the term 'anti-bias' to describe a curriculum that should permeate every aspect of the early years provision and goes beyond celebrating the occasional non-mainstream festival. All nursery activities and equipment should reflect anti-bias and ensure that all children feel valued and at home in the setting, regardless of their background.

Children and parents discriminate too

Occasionally you will have to deal with children who behave inappropriately or make discriminatory remarks. Children may not know the views they are expressing are inappropriate and need to be told clearly and calmly, with appropriate explanation. For example, in a home corner a group of girls say to a boy wishing to join them 'We don't want boys in here – they're dirty,' or comments are made in the school playground to an Asian child, 'Go home, we don't like pakis'. In these circumstances you should explain clearly to the child that you do not like what they have said and explain why their remarks were hurtful. According to Iram Siraj-Blatchford (1994), you should support and physically comfort the abused child, making sure they know you support their identity.

If parents are openly racist and ask that their child does not sit with a child from a different

ethnic group or if children use abusive and discriminatory language or behaviour, there is usually an established procedure for these situations. This behaviour needs to be addressed – doing nothing is not an option.

Appropriate use of language

It is important to be careful not to use discriminatory language and to check that you are accurately using descriptive terms. Terminology changes and develops over time. For example, many disability groups prefer the term 'disabled people' to 'people with disabilities', or today the term 'black' is often preferred to 'coloured'.

It is important not to define people by their differences but by their similarities, so that you do not limit what they can achieve. Ask for 'strong children' not 'strong boys'. Don't group children by gender, such as saying 'boys this side, girls the other'. Why would you do this?

Check your language

Some languages are considered more important than others. Bullying or teasing children because of their home language or their name seriously affects how they feel about themselves.

Many people find it difficult to know what language is acceptable when talking about discrimination. They are afraid of offending someone by being unintentionally insulting. For example, many older people describe black people as 'coloured' as they feel using the term 'black' could be offensive, whereas many black people find the word 'coloured' reminds them of the days of slavery and apartheid. Similarly, words to describe disability are not always clear.

Most people know what constitutes discriminatory language. There are many derogatory terms used against women, black people or disabled people – there are far fewer against white men, although any group may be addressed in inappropriate language.

It is also important to learn the names of the children and their families and to know which is their first name and which is their family name – this can change depending on cultural or ethnic background. Correct pronunciation is also important, as this shows concern and respect for the individual.

Theory into practice

Learn the names of the children in your group and how to pronounce names correctly. Find out some of the rules for naming children in different ethnic groups. Learn a few words in some of the community languages in your setting – such as 'please' or 'thank you'.

Role modelling

Early years practitioners model good practice to children by the way they behave and what they say. 'Actions speak louder than words' is never truer than for young children who are watching you very carefully and soon see if you say one thing and do another. The key issue is to demonstrate respectful attitudes and fairness and to positively welcome and build on the diversity in our society.

Disability discrimination

The effects of discrimination are discussed earlier in this unit and apply equally to disabled people.

Each child is different and has areas where they are especially talented or skilled, and areas where they may lag behind others of their age. Yet when we think about children who have a disability, it is easy to think about the disability first, putting the child into a category with other 'disabled children', and rarely stopping to think further about the individual behind the label.

KEY ISSUES

Some disability groups prefer to be called 'disabled people' which they feel is a straightforward description of the situation; others prefer the term 'people with disabilities' which they say concentrates on the person not the disability. The term 'handicapped' is not often used today.

- Research the terms commonly used to describe different aspects of disability and identify which groups use particular terms and why.

Children who are disabled or who have other special needs have the same rights and should receive the same opportunities as other children. They should be treated as unique individuals and should not be labelled or stereotyped, as this is discrimination.

Think it over...

Do you demonstrate respectful attitudes to children and their families, visiting adults and other staff? How can you be sure your approach is effective?

The early years value base

Early years practitioners have to ensure that they promote equality, diversity and rights in their own practice and work to the values and principles of the sector. The basis of the principles and values is respect for individual differences and the identity and dignity of children and families.

Study the rest of this section and copy and complete the table, working in a group or on your own.

PRINCIPLES	PRACTICE IMPLICATIONS – HOW DO WE DO IT?
The welfare of the child is paramount.	
Practitioners contribute to children's care, learning and development and this is reflected in every aspect of practice and service provision.	
Practitioners work with parents and families who are partners in the care, learning and development of their children and are the child's first and most enduring educators.	
The needs, rights and views of the child are at the centre of all practice and provision.	
VALUES	**PRACTICE IMPLICATIONS – HOW DO WE DO IT?**
Individuality, difference and diversity are valued and celebrated.	
Equality of opportunity and anti-discriminatory practice are actively promoted.	
Children's health and well-being are actively promoted.	
Children's personal and physical safety is safeguarded, while allowing for risk and challenge as appropriate to the capabilities of the child.	
Self-esteem, resilience and a positive self-image are recognised as essential to every child's development.	
Confidentiality and agreements about confidential information are respected as appropriate, unless a child's protection and well-being are at stake.	
Professional knowledge, skills and values are shared appropriately in order to enrich the experience of children more widely.	
Best practice requires reflection and a continuous search for improvement.	

Inclusive practice

Inclusion is about removing barriers to access and participation for individual children and their families. It is often used in relation to children who have additional needs, perhaps because of disability or learning difficulties. However, inclusion is a much broader concept and means making sure that all children feel that they 'belong' in the setting and have equal access to resources, activities and services. Observing and assessing individual children and identifying their needs in partnership with parents and families will give you a clear idea of those who may feel excluded or need extra help to get the most out of their experiences.

Empowering children

Children need to be encouraged from a very early age to deal with bullying and discriminatory attitudes – although adults must also always be there to support and protect them when they are needed. Children can be taught techniques which empower them or, in other words, give them strategies to use to defend themselves. Children's self-esteem and confidence grow if they feel they have some control over their lives and if they feel that they and their families are valued. Derman Sparks (1989) suggests that for children to feel good and confident about themselves they need to be able to say 'That's not fair' or 'I don't like that' if they are the targets of discrimination. If they see a child abusing another child they should have the confidence to say 'I don't like what you are doing'. We should help children as much as we can to have the confidence to stand up for themselves and others in these situations.

Children with English as an additional language are vulnerable to discrimination if they cannot communicate well in English, as are other children with different communication difficulties. Communication support is very important and may involve using interpreters and bringing in those who speak the child's language. Children who cannot understand or communicate in English will need to be clear that their home language is valuable and examples of bi-lingual books, story tapes and posters need to be available. Multi-lingual children often cope very well if they have more than one language and can derive real benefits but may also need support. Children with other communication difficulties must have appropriate specialist support. Practitioners will find that drawing attention to dialect, accents, sign language and so forth is a good way of complementing discussions on community languages.

Environment

It is important to make sure the environment is accessible to all children who use the setting and supports their development. The environment is both the physical environment and the emotional environment. Removing physical barriers, using appropriate support for children who have additional needs and differentiating the curriculum so that children of all abilities can participate are all important. The emotional

The environment needs to be physically and emotionally safe.

environment is more difficult to precisely describe but should be positive and affirming for everyone, building on and encouraging achievement, not denigrating or criticising or focusing on the negative. A safe emotional environment allows children to take risks and encourages their self esteem.

Care routines

Your everyday routines should ensure that every child is treated as an individual and all individual needs are met. Allow children who require it more time to complete activities or care routines, give appropriate praise and reward. Make sure your expectations for children are high but realistic, building in lots of opportunities for praise and encouragement

Play and curricular activities

Play is the most important aspect of provision in early years settings, as children learn best through their play and their social relationships. They learn all about themselves and who they are in the world. Well-thought-out play provision will provide many opportunities for development of positive self-esteem and resilience and this is vital if children are to achieve the best they can. Play-based activities should allow children to succeed and to take risks in their relationships, as well as physical challenges.

* Promote equality, diversity and rights through play.

* Encourage boys to talk and express their feelings appropriately.

* Encourage girls to use construction equipment and outdoor equipment such as bikes or climbing frames.

* Encourage boys to use the home corner.

* Don't expect girls to tidy up after boys.

* Don't condone overly boisterous behaviour from boys or allow it to disrupt other children's experiences.

* Encourage all parents to participate in the life of the nursery.

Think it over...

It is very easy to stereotype boys or to believe that natural physical differences are solely responsible for their behaviour. This could lead to aggressive and sometimes difficult behaviour being tolerated from boys where the same behaviour in girls would not be allowed. It is important that we see both boys and girls as individuals with their own personalities, strengths and weaknesses and avoid stereotyping.

Circle time with children

Circle time is when children gather together in small groups and sit in a circle with an adult they know, such as a key worker, and where they can see and hear each other. Circle time varies between settings but is often used to:

* provide an opportunity for children to share views, ideas and feelings

* develop skills in language and communication

* support personal, social and emotional development.

Usually circle time is kept to around ten minutes or so, but this may vary depending on the children involved. It should never be used with children who are too young or who are not developmentally ready to 'sit still'. Properly conducted circle time works well with primary age children and can be used with older nursery children. Children should not be forced to take part and speaking in the group should be voluntary.

Skilled adults should support circle time. Many use the time for questions and discussion appropriate to the age of the children in ways that stress similarities between people and races, rather than emphasising differences. This is a much more effective way of ensuring co-operation and respect. It is also important to encourage children to look at other points of view. For example, if a child is upset at something that has been said to them, encourage empathy by asking the other children to consider how they would feel if someone said something similar to them?

You can also:

* use the time to suggest ways of sharing and resolving conflicts

* discuss differences, such as in colour or shape of face or features, personality or ability, always in a positive and sensitive way without labelling

* set rules for circle time such as no interruptions and accepting that others have comments and feelings to share.

Activities, equipment, books and pictures

* Learn to use these thoughtfully and with understanding.

* Use equipment with which children can identify and that reflects diversity, such as black-skinned dolls, dressing up clothes from different cultures, multi-ethnic kitchen utensils.

* Ensure that there are positive images of girls, disability and ethnic minority groups in the nursery.

* Value languages that are not English and support bi-lingual children.

* Encourage children to use their home language during role play.

* Use dual-language books, labels and posters.

* Ensure that all nursery activities are adaptable for use by children with special needs.

Theory into practice

* Undertake an audit of two or three types of resources in your setting, such as books, domestic play equipment, posters and pictures, dolls, puzzles and games.

* Check the resources for an anti-bias approach and whether they promote equality, diversity and rights.

* Select the resource that best encourages equality of opportunity. Say why you have chosen this resource instead of one of the others.

Persona dolls

Persona dolls are special dolls that represent different people and are not usually kept with the other toys and equipment.

These dolls can be very helpful in explaining diversity and exploring concepts of discrimination with children. For example, the doll could represent a child from an ethnic minority and can be used to discuss feelings and difficult issues one step removed from the children.

Events and opportunities

* Settings should explore with their communities whether celebrating religious and cultural events is appropriate.

* Use festivals to celebrate diversity not just to pay lip service to different cultures or religions. Be authentic and don't just dwell on the exotic aspects.

* Invite parents and members of the community in to talk to children and work with them.

Assessment activity 1.5

Devise a leaflet for an early years setting explaining to parents the policy on equality, diversity and rights and how early years practitioners will promote these. Talk to other candidates and think of frequently asked questions (FAQs) about these topics to include in your leaflet, with a model answer for each.

Practice implications of confidentiality

How confidential information comes into the setting, how it is recorded and stored and how it is retrieved from storage are all points where the wrong people can find out things. For example, if information is received by fax or email it can sometimes be seen by those for whom it is not intended. Therefore, a setting will need to have systems for receiving, recording and storing confidential information.

Clearly children's records should be stored securely as well as medical or court reports, case conference material and so forth. Staff must be clear about who has access to what and in what circumstances. Use of IT can be controlled and made secure by the use of passwords and other means of limiting access. Storage of data is controlled by the Data Protection Act 1998 and involves limitations on what basis data can be stored and who is entitled to see it. This Act repealed the Access to Personal Files Act 1987 – together with its subsidiary regulations – and the Access to Health Records Act 1990. Except on rare occasions, people are entitled to see records kept about them, including medical, social work, housing and school records and children's records kept by early years settings.

Where face-to-face interviews and discussions take place, participants should be clear at the start that what is said must be confidential, including any notes or minutes taken and where recording devices or video have been used.

In most circumstances the relationship between children, their parents and the early years practitioner is one of trust, based on a professional relationship where confidentiality is the rule. Parents must feel able to share with staff any issues that affect children and many of these will be deeply personal, such as changes to the household when a parent moves out or another adult moves in. Students in placements must never discuss or write about the children and families in their care outside the setting, except with prior written permission.

Day-to-day work with children and families will necessitate some recording of information; this should be done sensitively and accurately. You should record what you see and hear objectively and without bias. You should not express opinion unless it is firmly based on evidence.

There are, however, some circumstances where confidentiality cannot be guaranteed and these are mainly to do with child protection. If a child discloses abuse of any type or where the practitioner suspects abuse, they must report this immediately to a responsible, senior member of staff. In turn, senior staff will act according to the setting's policies and procedures for child protection. If a child or anyone close to the child reports abuse they must be told that this information cannot remain confidential (see Unit 5 for more information).

(see Unit 5 for more information)

Assessment activity 1.6

- Identify scenarios when you may wish to discuss children and/or families outside the setting.
- How might families feel if you break their confidence?
- Identify legislation that both protects the rights of the individual and sometimes may override the rights of individuals and think of examples affecting children and families.
- Write a report evaluating your examples and how legislation works to provide for the rights of individuals.

There are other issues that may interfere with the confidential relationship between families and the setting, for example drug dealing on the setting's premises, or where theft is a problem. These issues always have to be dealt with on their own merits, but are likely to involve the police and may result in the necessary sharing of confidential information.

All individuals in the UK have some protection through the Data Protection Act 1998. This Act gives legal rights to individuals in respect of personal data held about them by others. However, there is no other requirement or absolute right to confidentiality. In practice it would be difficult to keep confidentiality in settings where information has to be exchanged between staff and between agencies. If information is sensitive, permission should be sought before passing to others.

END-OF-UNIT TEST

1 Explain the term 'diversity'.

2 Evaluate the statement 'the UK is an equal society'.

3 Identify the meaning of the terms 'values' and 'beliefs'.

4 Describe three key points from the UN Convention on the Rights of the Child and explain how these affect early years practice.

5 Describe what is meant by the term 'human rights'.

6 Identify and explain three reasons why an understanding of equality, diversity and rights is important to early years services.

7 Describe three ways in which diversity in our society can be celebrated within the early years setting.

8 Explain how holding prejudiced views can affect our work with children and families. Give two examples.

9 Explain how children learn attitudes and values.

10 Identify an example of when a family's right to confidentiality may be overridden.

11 In the nursery you overhear a member of staff telling a parent, 'We treat all the children exactly the same in this nursery'. Analyse whether this attitude encourages equality of opportunity.

12 Evaluate how Persona dolls could assist children's understanding of equality and diversity.

13 Describe why partnership with parents is important for early years practitioners.

14 Explain how circle time with children can be used to promote anti-discrimination.

15 Evaluate the reasons why confidentiality is important in early years practice.

References and further reading

Commission for Racial Equality, (1989), *From Cradle to School*, London: CRE

Council for the Disabled, (1995), *Help Starts Here*, London: NCB

Brown, B (1998), *Unlearning Discrimination in the Early Years*, Trentham Books

Dare, A and O'Donovan, M (1997), *Good Practice in Caring for Young Children with Special Needs*, Cheltenham: Stanley Thornes

Denziloe, J and Dickins, M (revised 2002), *All Together: How to create inclusive services for disabled children and their families*, National Early Years Network

Department of Health (1989), *Children Act*, London: HMSO

Derman-Sparks, L (1989), *Anti-Bias Curriculum*, Washington, DC: National Association for the Education of Young Children

DfES (2003), *Every Child Matters*, London: DfES

DfES (2001), *SEN Code of Practice*, London: DfES

DfES (2001), *SEN Toolkit*. London: DfES

Early Years Trainers Anti Racist Network – EYTARN (revised 1999), *All Our Children: A guide for those who care*

Early Childhood Education Forum (1998), *Quality and Diversity in Early Learning*, London: National Children's Bureau

Equal Opportunities Commission, *An Equal Start*, Manchester: EOC

Equal Opportunities Commission (Scotland), *An Equal Opportunities Guide for Parents*, Glasgow: EOC

Hyder, T and Kenway, P (1995), *An Equal Future: A guide to anti-sexist practice in the early years*, National Early Years Network

Hyder, T and Rutter, J (1998), *Refugee Children in the Early Years: Issues for policymakers and providers*, Save the Children/Refugee Council

Lane, J (1999), *Action for Racial Equality in the Early Years: Understanding the past, thinking about the present, planning for the future*, National Early Years Network

Maxime, J (1991), *Towards a Transcultural Approach to Working with Under Sevens*, Conference report for the Early Years Trainers Anti-racist network and the National Children's Bureau, Wallasey: EYTARN

Lancaster, P and Broadbent, V (2003), *Listening to Young Children*, Open University Press

Milner, D (1983), *Children and Race: 10 years on*, Ward Lock Educational

Pre-school Learning Alliance (2001), *Equal Chances: Eliminating discrimination and ensuring equality in pre-school settings*

Siraj-Blatchford, I and Clarke, P (2000), *Supporting Identity, Diversity and Language in the Early Years*, Oxford: OUP

Siraj-Blatchford, I (1994), *The Early Years: Laying the foundation for racial equality*, Staffordshire: Trentham Books

Woolfson, R (1991), *Children with Special Needs*, London: Faber and Faber

Working Group against Racism in Children's Resources (1990), *Guidelines for the Evaluation and Selection of Toys and Other Resources for Children*, London: WGARCR

Working Group against Racism in Children's Resources, *Early Years Student Information Pack*, a series of articles regularly updated costing £7 at time of writing

Useful websites

Commission for Racial Equality – www.cre.org.uk

Equal Opportunities Commission – www.eoc.org.uk

Every Child Matters – www.everychildmatters.gov.uk

Home Office (for information on Human Rights Unit) – www.homeoffice.gov.uk

National Disability Council – www.disability-council.gov.uk

Refugee Council – www.refugeecouncil.org.uk

Sure Start – www.surestart.gov.uk

Articles

Bandura, A, 'Perceived self-efficacy in the exercise of personal agency', *The Psychologist*, 1989, Volume 2, Issue 10

Dickins, M, 'All about Anti-discriminatory Practice', *Nursery World*, 3 January 2002, Volume 102, No. 3796

Lane, J, 'Dealing with prejudice and discrimination: the issues and in practice', *Practical Pre-School*, January 2001, Issue 2

Lane, J, 'Working together within a "no-blame culture"', *Network News* (the newsletter of the Early Years Trainers Anti Racist Network), July 2002, Volume 4, Issue 2

Videos

Persona Doll Training (2001), *Persona Dolls in Action* with support book. Available from 51 Granville Road, London N12 OJH. Also available from EYTARN

Save the Children/The Refugee Council (2001), *In Safe Hands*, a resource and training pack to support work with young refugee children. Also available from EYTARN

Organisations that provide publications on equality issues

Alliance for Inclusive Education, Unit 2, Ground Floor, 70 South Lambeth Road, London SW8 1RL
Tel: 0207 735 5277

Early Years Equality, PO Box 3428, Chester, CH1 9BX, Tel/Fax: 01244 310569
Email: eyequality@tiscali.co.uk

Persona Doll Training United Kingdom, 51 Granville Road, London, N12 0JH
Fax: 0208 446 7591
Email: personadoll@ukgateway.net

Working Group against Racism in Children's Resources, Unit 63A, Eurolink Business Centre, 49 Effra Road, London SW2 1BZ
Tel: 0207 501 9992

UNIT 2

Communication and interpersonal skills in early years work

What you need to learn

1 Features of interpersonal communication and the factors that affect communication

2 How to develop and maintain relationships with children, families and others

3 How interpersonal skills contribute to the care of distressed individuals

4 How to reflect on the effectiveness of your own interpersonal and communication skills

Introduction

In order to work in the care and education sector, adults must have high levels of communication and interpersonal skills. This unit describes the skills that are required in order to develop strong relationships, not only with children and their families, but also with other professionals. Practitioners working with babies and very young children will also need to be good communicators in order to stimulate their language development.

Communication is an essential part of most people's everyday lives. Without good communication, we would not gain information, form relationships or maintain friendships. Babies and children rely on adults around them to be good interpreters of their body language and first words, so early years practitioners have to be skilled communicators.

How you will be assessed

This unit is assessed internally.

1 Features of interpersonal communication and the factors that affect communication

Types of communication

Adults who work within the childcare and education sector need to have strong communication skills and to be able to apply them to colleagues, parents and children.

While language often springs to mind when considering communication, it is important to remember that there are several ways in which communications can be sent. There are four key types of communication:

* verbal communication

* non-verbal communication

* written communication

* visual communication.

Within each of the four key types of communication, there are further sub-classifications. Developments in technology and people's work and social patterns have had an effect on everyday communication. There has also been a greater understanding of the need to find ways to communicate with groups of people who previously may have found communication difficult. This has resulted in the development of systems such as Makaton, BLISS boards and the use of interpreters and advocates.

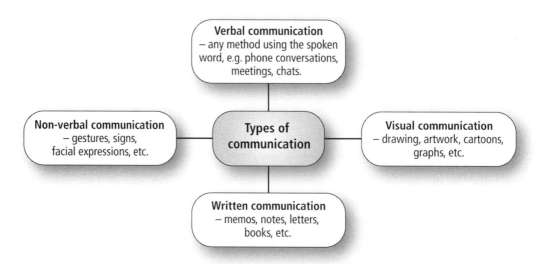

TYPES OF COMMUNICATION	EXAMPLES
Language – spoken	Face-to-face, by telephone, through video and webcams, story telling, radio, story tapes, taped information
Signing	British Sign Language, Makaton, social signs such as thumbs up, pointing
Music and drama	Rap, country and western, opera, classical music, pop music, ballads, plays, dialogues
Arts and crafts	Painting, drawing, collage, ceramics, embroidery, tapestry
Body language	Frowns, smiles, shrugging of shoulders, hand gestures
Written language, including Braille	Letters, text messages, notice boards, emails, websites, newspapers, memos

In pairs, think about the communications that you have 'sent' and 'received' today. Copy and complete the following table.

TYPE OF COMMUNICATION	SENT OR RECEIVED	MESSAGE
Written		
Verbal		
Visual		
Non-verbal		

Describe the purpose of two of the communications that you have either received or sent.

Personal space

The type of interactions that take place are often governed by physical distance and the environment. Some environments and layouts are better than others for communication. Noisy, bustling environments will make it harder for people to share sensitive information, while calmer and more relaxed environments can help communication. The importance of the environment in helping communication is increasingly being recognised and many early years settings now pay attention to creating welcoming reception areas. The seating arrangements and the way in which people are placed can also affect communication. In early years settings communication is encouraged between children, so chairs may be grouped around tables to stimulate discussion. In other educational situations, tables and chairs may be in straight lines to encourage children to focus on and observe the teacher, such as in science lessons.

As well as considering the environment, it is also important to think about the physical space between those who are communicating and even the way in which they are positioned. These are referred to respectively as proximity and orientation (see also page 51).

Written skills

As well as interacting with people using spoken language, early years practitioners need to be able to use written language effectively. Writing is a useful form of communication, but a reader can misunderstand the tone of the writing, something that can be communicated more easily in spoken language, through voice or body language. This means that being able to write using an appropriate style, as well as relaying information, is an important skill.

TYPE	PURPOSE	AUDIENCE	COMMENTS
Letter	To give information To make a request	Parents Other professionals Organisations	Letters are formal ways of recording information and requests. They might be used in settings to inform parents of trips, to confirm a place or to invite parents to open days and evenings.
Memo	To give information To make a request	Colleagues	Memos are informal ways of passing information or making requests.

TYPE	PURPOSE	AUDIENCE	COMMENTS
Noticeboards	To give information To advertise To make requests	Parents Visitors	Noticeboards are public ways of passing on information. It is essential that writing on display is accurate and appropriate.
Emails	To give information	Colleagues Other professionals	Emails are a popular way of passing information quickly. They tend to be informal in tone.
Records	To store information for future reference	Parents Colleagues Other professionals Oneself	Records may include observations of children or assessment records. They must be accurate, legible and conform to data protection laws and policies.
Reports	To record summarised information	Parents Colleagues Other professionals	Reports might be given to parents to summarise their child's progress. Reports might also be sent to other professionals when a child starts at another setting.

Many people find writing difficult and even daunting. Common fears include worries about spelling and punctuation or not being sure about the layout and style. There are many points to consider before starting any writing project – see the diagram below.

Spelling

Spelling is an area that many people identify as one of their weaknesses. There are, however, some strategies that can be used to overcome this difficulty.

Using a spell checker

This is a useful tool if you are working on a computer, but check carefully that the computer has not altered the meaning or ignored words that are spelled correctly but are the wrong words. For example, 'quite' and 'quiet' are two words that have different meanings but are spelled very similarly – and if you intended to write quiet, a spell checker would not note if you typed quite instead. Also note that some computers show American spellings by default.

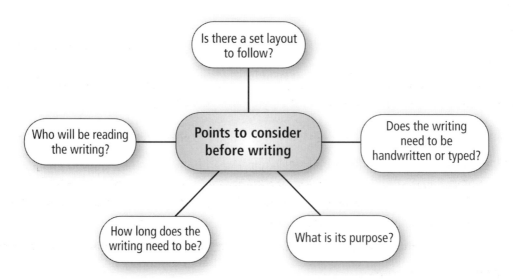

Ask others to read through the document

This is one of the best ways of getting help. Choose someone who is a good speller, but is also sympathetic. Asking for help shows a mature attitude rather than being seen as a weakness.

Use a dictionary

This is helpful when the first few letters of a word are already known. Check carefully that the word found has the same meaning as the one intended.

Report writing

Most early years practitioners will need to be able to write reports. Reports are ways of passing on summarised information, such as an accident report form or a report on a child's progress. The easiest types of reports to write are those which need completing on a form. Organisations use report forms to ensure that all the information that needs to be noted is recorded. Headings or boxes provide guidance as to the content.

Where reports are not to be recorded on forms, it is important to find out if there is a set organisational style in terms of order, headings and whether it needs to be typed or handwritten. It is essential to consider who will be reading the report and to ensure that it is as accurate and factual as possible. Most reports require:

* clear headings and structure
* formal style of writing
* accurate and concise language.

References

The word 'plagiarism' is used to describe copying or using written material or ideas without the author's permission or without acknowledging them as the source. In report or essay writing this is considered to be unacceptable as it is seen as taking credit for someone else's work. To avoid plagiarism, references should be used to source the material that is being used.

Record keeping

A range of records is kept in most early years settings. These include registers or records about children's progress as well as records which ensure the smooth running of a setting, such as stock ordering. It is essential that records comply with data protection rules.

Data Protection Act 1998

The Data Protection Act 1998 (DPA) came into force in March 2000, replacing the Data Protection Act 1984 which covered only information that was stored on computer systems. It also replaced the Access to Personal Files Act 1987 and the Access to Health Records Act 1990.

The current Act requires anyone who is processing personal information to register with the Data Protection Commission. This includes paper-based information as well as anything held on computers.

There are eight enforceable principles of good practice as listed below. Information must be:

* fairly and lawfully processed
* not kept for longer than necessary
* processed for limited purposes
* processed in accordance with data subjects' rights
* secure
* adequate, relevant and not excessive
* accurate
* not transferable to other countries without adequate protection.

In this observation, I saw that Alice was looking for the hidden object. This shows an understanding of object permanence as described by Jean Piaget. According to Tassoni (2004) this 'may explain why most babies begin to protest when their carer leaves the room'. Meggit (2000) states that this is usually seen at nine months.

Referencing avoids plagiarism.

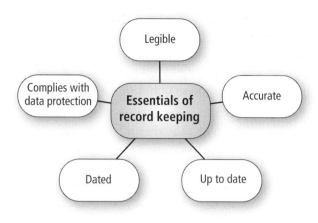

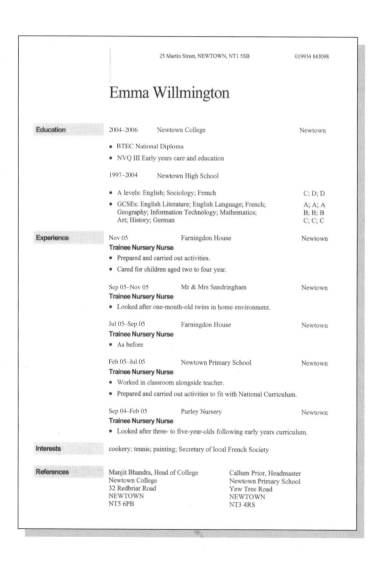

emergency contact details and health information, as well as notes and observations to help staff and parents evaluate children's progress (see Unit 8).

Curriculum vitae

A curriculum vitae or CV gives an employer a summary of your working life, including your qualifications, experience and education. The best CVs are concise and are usually no longer than two pages of A4. They need to be typed, and several computer word-processing packages are available to help people lay out this information. It is usual for CVs to end with the names and addresses of two referees who will be able to provide more information about you. It is courteous to inform people that you would like to use them as referees before adding their names.

Children's records

Keeping children's records up to date is an essential task in early years settings. Most settings have a folder for each child. This may contain

Letter of application

Letters of application are sometimes asked for by employers instead of or as well as a curriculum vitae. A letter of application should provide the employer with information about your skills, qualifications and experience, as well as details about why you feel that you would be suitable for the post. It is now usual to present employers with a typed letter of application, although some employers state that they require a handwritten letter.

Visual forms of presenting information

There is a range of visual forms of presenting information. These include photographs, posters, videos and cartoons. Information that is visual is often more easily remembered, as the brain can store images more easily than words. Visual forms of presenting information can be particularly helpful for communicating when people have difficulties with either the spoken language or with handling written information.

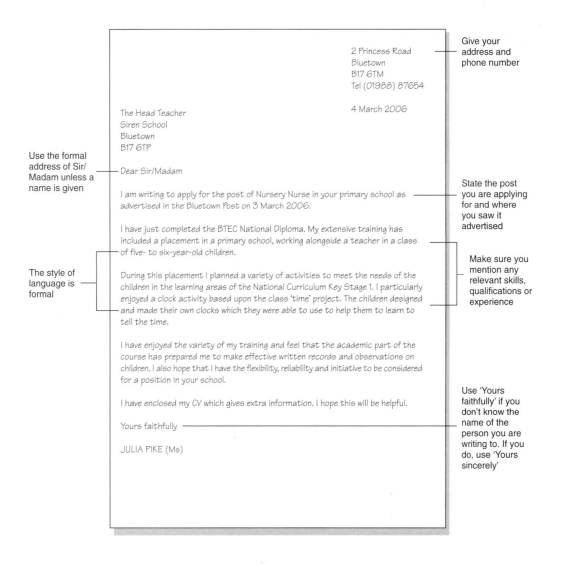

Give your address and phone number

2 Princess Road
Bluetown
B17 6TM
Tel (01988) 87654

4 March 2006

The Head Teacher
Siren School
Bluetown
B17 6TP

Use the formal address of Sir/Madam unless a name is given

Dear Sir/Madam

I am writing to apply for the post of Nursery Nurse in your primary school as advertised in the Bluetown Post on 3 March 2006.

State the post you are applying for and where you saw it advertised

I have just completed the BTEC National Diploma. My extensive training has included a placement in a primary school, working alongside a teacher in a class of five- to six-year-old children.

The style of language is formal

During this placement I planned a variety of activities to meet the needs of the children in the learning areas of the National Curriculum Key Stage 1. I particularly enjoyed a clock activity based upon the class 'time' project. The children designed and made their own clocks which they were able to use to help them to learn to tell the time.

Make sure you mention any relevant skills, qualifications or experience

I have enjoyed the variety of my training and feel that the academic part of the course has prepared me to make effective written records and observations on children. I also hope that I have the flexibility, reliability and initiative to be considered for a position in your school.

I have enclosed my CV which gives extra information. I hope this will be helpful.

Yours faithfully

Use 'Yours faithfully' if you don't know the name of the person you are writing to. If you do, use 'Yours sincerely'

JULIA PIKE (Ms)

A refugee family has been settled into accommodation in the local town. The youngest child is attending the nursery class attached to the primary school and the teacher is keen to communicate with the parents. She decides to take a series of pictures of the child during the day doing a variety of different activities. She hopes that this will help communication between her and the parents when they next meet.

In pairs consider the following questions:

- Why might the photographs help the parents to feel welcomed?
- Come up with two other situations where photographs might act as a tool for communication.

Non-visual forms of presenting information

The majority of methods of communicating have some visual element – but for groups of people who have a visual impairment these can be handicapping. Non-visual forms of presenting information can therefore be useful, such as tape recordings, telephone and touch.

Tape recordings

Tape recordings are often used as a way of presenting information to people who have a visual impairment. Newsletters, reports and messages can be put onto tape as a way of helping to stay in contact. Remember the following to help produce better recordings.

* Keep background noises to a minimum.

* If possible use a hand-held microphone, rather than the built-in microphone.

* Speak naturally, but as clearly as possible.

* Try to visualise the listener as you speak, to inject warmth into your voice.

* Prepare a script or list of points to avoid lengthy hesitations.

Telephone

The telephone is one of the most used forms of communication when people are not face to face. It is immediate and allows people to respond to each other. The tone of voice used on a telephone is critical and so it is essential to visualise the other speaker and also to avoid distractions during a call. Remember the following.

If you smile when talking on the phone, you will sound (and feel) more welcoming and friendly.

* Use your normal voice – do not put on a 'phone' voice.

* Speak clearly and slightly slower than usual if necessary.

* Show the speaker that you are listening and understanding by using phrases such as 'Yes, I see' – a telephone version of nodding and smiling.

* Always repeat or spell out unusual names.

* Repeat and take care over numbers – for example, 14 and 40 sound similar.

Making a call

- Consider whether using the phone is the best form of communication – the telephone is not usually a suitable form of communication to discuss sensitive issues such as a child's behaviour.
- Mentally run through the purpose of the call beforehand.
- Consider the timing of the call – is this an appropriate time?
- Establish identity at the start of a call.
- Be courteous – do not attempt to do any other tasks during the call.
- Have a pen and paper to hand to keep notes of a conversation or to record information.

Answering a call

- Establish your identity and if necessary your position in the setting.
- Listen carefully to the needs of the caller, such as who they wish to speak to.
- Respond to the caller appropriately, for example, answering their questions where you are able to and ensuring they know you are listening and taking in what they are saying.
- If a message is to be left, note down the name of the person calling, the message and repeat it back to the caller to ensure that the details are correct.
- If a call needs to be returned, ask for the contact number.
- Immediately following the call, write up the message along with the time and date of the call.
- Make sure that the message is passed on swiftly.

Barriers to interpersonal interaction

Good communicators also have to be aware of potential difficulties that some people may have in communicating.

Language

Spoken language relies on both speakers finding a common language in which to communicate. An inequality in levels of language can create frustration as one person may not feel that they are adequately able to express what they wish to say or may misinterpret what is being said. Young children who have a different home language from the one used in their setting will need particular support in order to convey their needs. To overcome this potential barrier to interaction, interpreters may be used in early years settings (see page 53).

Language disorders

Some interaction may be hindered by specific language and speech disorders such as aphasia and dysphasia as well as communication impairments caused by conditions such as autism. Aphasia and dysphasia result from brain damage, such as from an accident or disease, and they cause difficulties in articulating ideas and understanding language. Autism can cause difficulties in communication and social interaction.

Disability

It is a mistake to imagine that anyone with a disability will necessarily have difficulties in making their wishes and needs understood. Difficulties in interpersonal interaction are sometimes the result of others feeling uncomfortable with a person with a disability. Overcompensation, withdrawal and embarrassment sometimes create situations where interaction becomes tense.

Personality

People have different personalities and behaviour types. Some personality types find it easier than others to communicate with others. A person who is very shy may find it hard to engage in conversation or respond if they are approached.

In some cases, people's differences in personality can create difficulties. This is sometimes called a 'personality clash', although the root cause is often the inability of one party to respect and value the other or to listen carefully. Practitioners working with children cannot use 'personality differences' as an excuse for not forming an effective relationship with a child, as children tend only to reflect back (see page 52 for more information on reflecting back).

Time

Time can be a strong barrier to communication. Most relationships take some time to develop, for people to become familiar with others and for confidence in a relationship to grow. In situations where time is not easily available, it is harder to communicate and the level of relationship is therefore limited. For example, in the morning, a child may be dropped off at nursery or school and there may be little time for parents and early years practitioners to communicate. In situations where time is limited, misunderstandings can take place.

Self-esteem

Self-esteem plays a major part in the way in which people communicate. The feelings that we have towards ourselves affect the way in which we talk to and relate to others. Someone who feels that they are inferior in some way or is made to feel this way may not talk as much or may, through nervousness, find it hard to listen. We look again at this issue later in the unit on pages 57–8.

Whatever way we choose to communicate with children, parents, colleagues or other professionals, it is essential that respect and courtesy is shown. Flippant remarks, lack of interest or even tone of voice can make people feel insecure and can create a barrier to future communication. A poorly presented letter or hastily scribbled note can equally give the recipient the impression that they are not valued. Remember the following.

* Always acknowledge another speaker by making eye contact, nodding or smiling.

* Find out how parents and children wish to be addressed.

* Make sure that remarks and speech are respectful and appropriate.

Response to different types of behaviour

It is useful as a communicator to be able to recognise different types of behaviour that people may show, as this allows us to consider ways

of best working with them. Responses to each type of behaviour can be found later in this unit on pages 60–61.

Assertive behaviour

People showing assertive behaviour have accepted themselves and have self-confidence. They do not need to be competitive with others, they accept and can cope with responsibility and are accepting of others. They are likely to be able to accept change, constructive criticism and feel in control of their work and lives.

Key characteristics

* Self confidence and high self-esteem

* Interested in others' thoughts and feelings

* Listens to others and not afraid of conflicting viewpoints

* Takes on responsibility

* Asks others for feedback

Submissive behaviour

This type of behaviour is sometimes referred to as 'passive' behaviour. People showing submissive behaviour may have reached the conclusion that others around them are 'better' than them and so merely go along with others' demands and views. In situations such as team meetings they may never volunteer an alternative viewpoint and are likely to listen rather than be active.

Key characteristics

* Lack of confidence and self-esteem

* Puts down self in front of others and inwardly

* Feelings of insecurity

* Assumes others' viewpoints are superior

* Prefers others to take responsibility and to be in control

* Feels guilty

Aggressive behaviour

People showing aggressive behaviour are often lacking in self-confidence and have adopted a defensive and aggressive attitude as a coping mechanism. They tend to appear as though they are confident.

Key characteristics

* Lack of self-confidence and low self-esteem
* Lack of respect towards others
* Feelings of superiority
* Like to be in control of situations
* Not interested in others' points of view
* See others' viewpoints as a personal challenge or slight to them
* May make fun at others' expense

Manipulative behaviour

A person showing manipulative behaviour may well blame others around them rather than take on any responsibility for what has happened. People showing this type of behaviour are ill at ease with themselves and therefore find fault with everything and everyone. They feel 'hard done by' and are usually lacking in self-esteem and confidence.

Key characteristics

* Lack of confidence and self-esteem
* May spread rumours or dissatisfaction
* Mistrustful of others' intentions
* Depressed and demotivated

Management of behaviour

The way we respond when we communicate can, as we have seen, affect others' responses towards us. With children, it is important that our communication skills are good when dealing with negative aspects of their behaviour. Children may, for example, need to hear clear messages about what is and is not expected. We can also reinforce wanted behaviour through non-verbal and verbal communication. We might, for example, smile at a child or verbally acknowledge, using praise, what a group of children has done. In the same way, it is important to think about what type of messages we are sending out at other times. Children who are showing negative behaviours might carry on repeating them, if they notice that adults will spend time and attention on them.

2 How to develop and maintain relationships with children, families and others

It is useful to understand the skills that are needed in order to work effectively with children, families and other people. This section looks at ways in which we can help this to take place.

What is communication?

The process of communication is often shown as a model called the **communication cycle**. There are seven stages in this model (see the diagram on page 48).

Stage 1 – Information: the sender has to decide what they want to convey.

Stage 2 – Encoding: the sender chooses a medium in which to send their message. This can be using spoken language, written, non-verbal or visual.

Stage 3 – Transfer of information: at this point the information is sent out.

Stage 4 – Reception of information: the receiver now hears or takes in the information.

Stage 5 – Decoding of information: the information is now interpreted.

Stage 6 – Feedback: the receiver of the information may show some reaction. Sometimes the sender of the information may not see the feedback, for example if the medium used is a letter.

Stage 7 – Response: they may then wish to send information themselves, in which case the cycle continues.

Difficulties during the communication cycle

There are many factors that can interrupt and disrupt the communication cycle. These include factors that are known as 'noise' and 'disruption'. Other barriers to communication were covered earlier in the unit (see page 45).

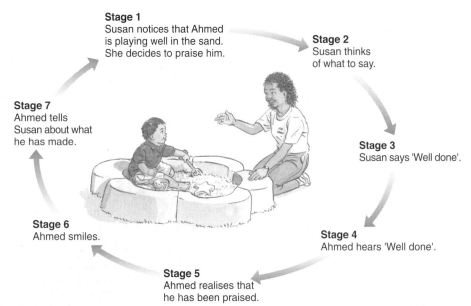

Stage 1
Susan notices that Ahmed is playing well in the sand. She decides to praise him.

Stage 2
Susan thinks of what to say.

Stage 3
Susan says 'Well done'.

Stage 4
Ahmed hears 'Well done'.

Stage 5
Ahmed realises that he has been praised.

Stage 6
Ahmed smiles.

Stage 7
Ahmed tells Susan about what he has made.

Noise

Factors that are not caused by the sender or receiver are sometimes referred to as 'noise'. Sometimes these factors can be technical, such as email failing to send a message or noise on the telephone line. Other examples of 'noise' include:

* lack of lighting – this can affect non-verbal and written communication
* background noise – noisy environment, loud music
* poor handwriting
* poor telephone line.

Distortion

The communication cycle can also be disrupted if the way the message is sent is unclear or if the sender does not pick up the message properly. This means that the message becomes distorted. This is a common cause of misunderstandings – for example, a cartoon may have been drawn in order to make someone laugh, but the receiver may not have the same sense of humour. This will mean that the message will have been distorted.

Verbal and non-verbal behaviour

In order to maintain the communication cycle, good communicators need a variety of skills and have to be able to interpret correctly others' verbal and non-verbal behaviour.

Form and tone of expression

The tone of voice that is used during spoken language, either in face-to-face situations or when using the telephone, is extremely important. Tone of voice can actually be stronger than the words that are said and can also reflect what the speaker is truly thinking. Good communicators use warm voice tones and this means that conversations are comfortable with them. Warmth in the voice has to be 'thought' which means warm thoughts are also needed. Trainers teaching people to use the telephone effectively encourage them to smile as they speak so that their voices develop warm tones.

Questioning skills

In some situations, questions might be used to help the person we are communicating with express themselves in order to give us more information. For example, if a child comes in crying, we may need to help them tell us what has happened. If we ask some questions while we are listening to someone, it can help them feel that we are listening to them. Questions can be used as a positive tool although, if not used carefully and with the wrong tone of voice, they can make others feel defensive and threatened.

There are two types of question – open and closed. Closed questions allow the other person to reply using very few words. For example, 'Did you tell Mrs Smith about this?' will probably elicit either a 'yes' or 'no' response. Closed questions do not therefore yield much information, but can make the other person feel safe, as they do not have to reveal much. Open questions encourage the other person to reveal more information and can be used to help people explain their thoughts or their reactions. For example, 'Why did you not tell Mrs Smith that you had fallen over?' would require a longer answer.

Combining open and closed questions

Many skilled communicators use a combination of open and closed questions to help others express themselves. This can be a useful technique, especially with children who may need some guidance and encouragement to talk.

For example:

Early years practitioner:	Did you have a nice birthday tea yesterday?
Child:	Yes.
Early years practitioner:	Tell me about your cake. What was it like?
Child:	It was really big and had lots and lots of candles that I blew out by myself.

Silence

There are times when communicators need to be quiet! Generally, people who do not know each other tend to fill in natural silences within conversations, as these can sometimes feel uncomfortable. Silence can, however, be necessary when people need time to collect their thoughts or consider questions, especially if they have had to absorb information as in the example below:

Early years practitioner:	I am afraid that Matt fell over and bumped his head today. He seems much better now. I have filled in an accident report, but you may need to keep an eye on him.
	(Short silence)
Parent:	Yes, I will – is he all right now?

Eye contact

Eyes are powerful tools when interacting with someone face to face. In many European cultures, eye contact is considered an important

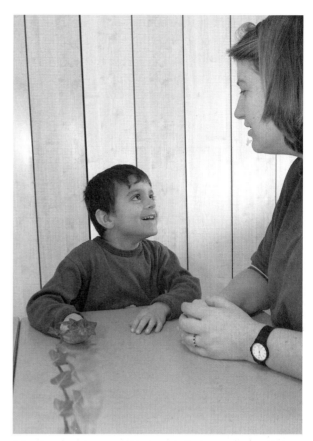

Making eye contact is especially important when talking to young children.

part of interacting with someone else and withholding eye contact can signal a range of feelings, including displeasure, anger and embarrassment. Speakers usually notice whether or not the listener's eyes are focused on them – looking behind the speaker or down sends signals of not being interested. However, in some cultures **not** making eye contact is a sign of respect. Whenever you are dealing with people from cultures with which you are unfamiliar, you need to be aware that both your body language and theirs may send mixed signals.

Gazing

Eye contact which is comfortable for both parties usually consists of gazing and glancing at someone's whole face, rather than just at their eyes. Looking at someone when they are speaking provides reassurance that they are being listened to.

Intense eye contact/staring

Intense eye contact can be threatening and unnerving. It sends out a range of messages including intimidation and aggressiveness, as well as intimacy and confusion.

Body direction

Non-verbal communication refers to the signals that our bodies send out. The way we stand, move or even touch someone can send out signals. Good communicators notice and react to the signals that other people are sending out. They also monitor their own body language, with the aim of making it as positive and non-threatening as possible.

Body movement and gesture

Body movements and gestures can reflect our moods. Children who suck their thumb may be indicating that they are tired, bored or distressed, while adults who point and jab their finger towards another person are likely to be showing anger. Accurately reading someone's body language requires experience, but some signs are easy to read, such as a child fiddling nervously with a sleeve. Good communicators monitor their own movements and gestures to ensure that they are not distracting a speaker by, for example, rubbing their eyes or tapping their feet!

Head movements

Nodding and shaking are the most common head movements. Nodding suggests agreement and understanding while shaking usually conveys disagreement. The more vigorous the movements, the stronger the signals given out. Good communicators usually tend to moderate their head movements to avoid distracting the speaker. Early years practitioners need to look at babies' and toddlers' head movements and acknowledge them. For example, a practitioner might say to a baby, 'You don't want any more?' when he turns his head away from a spoon. Remember to:

* avoid gestures that might distract
* be aware that some gestures may be misinterpreted
* acknowledge babies' and children's gestures and head movements by paraphrasing what you think they mean.

Posture

The way someone stands, leans forward or sits back in a chair sends out signals about their state of confidence and their interest in the conversation. Sitting forward slightly is a good position to adopt when listening and speaking to another person, especially children, because it makes them feel listened to.

It is important to monitor your body posture, as leaning forward too close may appear intimidating. It is also interesting to note changes in body posture. People who are feeling increasingly relaxed may gradually 'unfold' by uncrossing their legs or arms. This is a positive signal as it shows that they are feeling more confident in your company.

Muscle tension

Good communicators tend to notice the 'whole' person when they are communicating with them. As part of this process, it is useful to look for tension in the body. Stress causes muscular tension in people's bodies and common signs include raised shoulders, tight hands or nervous twitches and ticks. Once signs of stress have been noted, it will be important to look for ways to help the other person feel more at ease.

The way we hold ourselves can send signals about our confidence – or lack of confidence.

Touch

Physical contact with another person is extremely powerful. In the right circumstances it can show understanding, give comfort and show warmth and friendship. It can also be seen as invasive and threatening if misunderstood. Touch is often an important element in communicating with babies and young children whose receptive language is limited and who need physical reassurance. Touch is not usually an immediate response to adults or even children, as most people need to have established some type of interaction first. It is also important to recognise that some adults and children dislike being touched and that trying to touch them may make them withdraw, as they feel uncomfortable.

The way in which the touch is delivered affects its interpretation. A pat on the arm is less threatening than being held by the hand, which is usually perceived as being a more intimate gesture. Wherever possible, a touch should be offered rather than forced upon the other person – an early years practitioner may offer an outstretched hand for a child to take rather than automatically take the child's hand. Avoid touching or patting children on the head – this suggests that you are in control. With babies and toddlers, it is essential to use touch, as it is linked with emotional development. Cuddling babies and toddlers can help them to feel reassured.

Physical contact is one way in which babies and toddlers can gain reassurance.

Proximity

Proximity refers to the distance between the speakers. Being very close can suggest intimacy, while a large distance can make people feel that they are being treated impersonally. Early years practitioners often find they need to be quite near to a child so that the child feels listened to. Young children also get a feeling of comfort and reassurance from a familiar adult's close presence. Being very close to an adult, however, may not be appropriate, as most people need 'personal space' and getting too close will make them feel uncomfortable.

Orientation

The term orientation is used to refer to the way in which the body is facing. Turning away while another person is talking will give the impression of being uninterested, while facing another person signifies more involvement. People who are finding it hard to communicate particular details may look away while they are speaking – for example, a child who is embarrassed may talk to the floor rather than directly to you.

As a communicator, it is a good idea to sit slightly to the side of people, as this is not an intense position, but allows people to make or break eye contact with you easily. Make sure that you are facing babies and young children when you are talking to them – children rely on facial expression. Face adults or children with a hearing impairment so that they can see you more clearly, especially if they are lip reading.

Cultural differences in verbal and non-verbal communication

Verbal and non-verbal communication is not universal. Every culture has different ways of using non-verbal and verbal communication with, for instance, a large variance between the way touch and proximity is used. It is not uncommon for some cultures to use handshaking at the start and end of routine interactions, such as shaking hands with the hairdresser before having a haircut. People may also sit closer to each other in some cultures, while in others this would feel intimidating. The differences in verbal and non-verbal communication can therefore lead to misunderstandings when a person from one culture interacts with someone from another culture. Early years practitioners need to be aware of the cultural background of the people they are working with, including children, to avoid potential misunderstandings. If you are unsure about whether eye contact or physical contact is appropriate, it is worth finding out from an interpreter or from the person themselves.

Listening skills

Being able to communicate using verbal communication and signing is partly linked to being able to listen/respond to others effectively. The term 'listening' in this section will be used to cover situations where people may also be signing. By listening carefully to others, we can gain trust and find out more about others' points of view.

Active listening

Active listening can be used as a way of understanding another person's perspective, as well as checking that we have understood what someone really means. Active listening is a skill that takes time to learn, as it means thinking carefully about what other people are saying and formulating thoughts after they have finished talking. We are more used to thinking about what we are going to say next while the other person is still talking. Listening to others is also about making sure that they have enough time and opportunity to fully explain themselves, make their points and feel valued.

It is also important to remember things that people have said, especially when you meet them again, as this shows that you have really thought and listened to what they have said. An early years practitioner might, for example, ask a child

'Did you have a nice time yesterday at Jo's house?'. This would show the child that the practitioner had listened, as well as giving the child an opportunity to use language.

Good communicators, including counsellors, use a range of strategies that help them to listen actively. While learning and using these techniques will help you to communicate more effectively, remember that they do not confer 'counsellor' status!

Reflecting and paraphrasing

This strategy makes people feel that they are being listened to and understood. Essentially, the strategy is quite simple as the listener takes what the speaker has said and either directly repeats the words (direct reflection) or summarises what has been said (paraphrasing) using an interested tone of voice. This strategy allows the focus of the conversation to stay with the speaker while acknowledging what the speaker is saying. Paraphrasing also helps us to check with the speaker that we are correctly interpreting the meaning of what is being said. This clarification is important, as we can sometimes make assumptions about what we think is meant.

It is important that reflection is not taken to extremes, otherwise the conversation will be stilted. Generally, paraphrasing is considered to be the better method of reflection, providing that the summary is accurate. Reflective listening is a technique that is used to help counsel people because, in some ways, it acts like a mirror on people's thoughts and so can help them to clarify them.

Communication differences

There are many potential communication differences that can cause a barrier to understanding – see the table below.

Interpretation of expression	Tone of voice or facial expressions can be misunderstood. A puzzled tone of voice may appear to the receiver as being 'difficult' or 'bored'.
Language differences	Regional expressions as well as changes in tone resulting from translating a language may cause distortion of the message. People using signed language also find that there can be differences in the way that signs are produced. British Sign Language is different to American Sign Language. There are also variations with some of the visual signs that Makaton users produce.

Emotional distress	Misunderstandings can easily occur when people are in distressed states. This is usually because they are not able to take in information as efficiently because they are distracted. People in distress may easily misread or mishear what is being said to them and may also not be in control of their own body language.
Environment: noise, room layout, lighting	Communication can be hindered by the environment. Noises can distract the listener, interrupt the speaker or even prevent the listener hearing the message. Room layout can be a distraction and can cause difficulties, such as if people are walking by or if a sensitive conversation needs privacy. Lighting can cause difficulties, as hearing impaired people using lip reading need to be able to see the speaker's face clearly.
Assumptions, belief systems and attitudes	People can interpret situations and language differently depending on their lifestyles and cultural background. This is why communicators need to be aware of their own values and attitudes (see pages 8–9), as well as those of others. A common cause of misunderstanding is making assumptions about what is being said, rather than listening actively.

Early years practitioners have to be proactive in finding solutions to communication differences as it is essential that they are able to communicate effectively with parents, children and others in the setting.

Using interpreters and translators

Interpreters and translators can be invaluable in enabling early years practitioners to bridge the language gap. There are, however, many potential difficulties when using interpreters and translators.

Impartiality and objectivity of interpreters and translators

Professional translators and interpreters are often used because they have been trained to deliver, but not alter, the message. This is essential in translation because otherwise there is a danger of interpreters putting forward their own viewpoints or advice to the other speaker.

Inherent difficulties in accurate translation

Every language has its own expressions and levels of vocabulary. This means that it can be hard to directly translate concepts or expressions from one language into another without losing some of the underlying values or feelings.

Think it over...

A good example of an English expression that is difficult to translate into other languages is 'looking forward'. It is used in everyday situations, for example, 'I am looking forward to meeting you'.

- In pairs, work out exactly what this expression means. What is the underlying concept and feeling that it is expressing?
- Can you find another way of saying the same thing without losing any of the sense of this expression?

Using non-professional interpreters and translators

There may be occasions when settings ask for a family member or even an older child to translate documents or act as an interpreter. While this may be a good arrangement for everyday issues, there is always a danger that the quality of interpretation may not be sufficient when tackling sensitive issues. Older children might also find the information they receive an emotional burden. Using older children to interpret should therefore be avoided. Non-professional interpreters may not be aware of potential pitfalls in translating or may not have sufficient skill in each of the languages to accurately translate. There is also the danger that they may find it hard to stay in the role of 'translator' and begin acting as an advisor. It can also be hard for non-professional interpreters to remember to keep sensitive information confidential.

Communication aids

There is a range of communication aids that facilitate interaction between people when one or more person has difficulties in communicating. While aids are extremely valuable in allowing people with difficulties to break through the potential communication barrier, many still rely on the other person to actively try to understand the other person's needs through questioning and observing reactions.

* **Talking aids**: these allow the user to press a picture or a symbol which then produces a word or phrase.

* **Picture cards/communication boards**: a bank of pictures or words gives users the opportunity to communicate by selecting the picture or word that they need. Communication boards allow users to see at a glance the visual sign that they wish to select.

* **Non-verbal aids**: these allow people with limited physical movement and severe visual impairment or limited limb movements to show others what they want.

Using picture cards can aid communication.

* **Adaptive aids**: some equipment that is used for communication is adapted to allow people to use it. Telephones can be made with large keypads and have boosted sound to help a user, while keypads attached to a computer can produce voice messages.

Clear speech and accuracy

To avoid potential misunderstandings, it is essential for communicators to speak clearly and at a suitable pace to meet the listener's needs. People with English as an additional language may need to be spoken to more slowly and time will need to be spent checking that they have understood. Babies and young children need a more repetitive style of speech, with emphasis being placed on key words. Most early years practitioners do this naturally and linguists call this style of speech 'motherese'. Language also needs to be accurate to avoid misunderstandings. For example, vague statements such as 'I still need some things' may create confusion if the listener is not sure what is meant by 'things'.

Think it over...

Look at the conversation below:

Parent:	Sometimes he doesn't want to play with other children when they come around and he just goes up to his room.
Early years practitioner:	So he just goes up into his room.
Parent:	Yes, he just goes into his room and then I get really cross with him because I'm the one who has to sort out his friends and that really makes me angry.
Early years practitioner:	So there you are left with his friends and feeling angry.
Parent:	And I don't really know what I should do – does he act like this when he's here?

* Find examples of direct reflection and paraphrasing in this conversation.
* As a group or individually, examine the importance of correctly paraphrasing what a speaker has said.

Communication skills for calming a situation

When people are distressed it is harder for them to give and receive information. This means that communicators need to find ways of calming situations to allow communication to take place. Children, for instance, may need to be physically soothed if they have fallen down or are upset, while adults may need to sit down and be allowed a moment to collect their thoughts (see page 60).

Remember to:

✴ encourage adults to sit down

✴ get down to children's level

✴ make sure that your tone of voice is gentle and lower it if necessary

✴ avoid bombarding children or adults with information.

Getting down to children's level can help with soothing them when they are upset.

Interpreting non-verbal behaviour

Looking at another person's non-verbal behaviour will provide important clues as to how they are feeling. Good communicators use this to consider their approach to the situation. For example, if you see that a child has clenched fists and is physically restless, it will be important to begin any interaction by calming the child down and making the child feel more relaxed.

Advocacy

Vulnerable groups, such as 'looked-after' children or adults with severe learning difficulties, may find it hard to be listened to or to express their needs and feelings powerfully. To empower such groups so that they can be active rather than passive in decisions being taken about them, an advocate might be appointed for them. An advocate speaks and argues for someone else so that their viewpoints can be put forward, and should be completely independent, although family members and friends can be advocates provided they do not have a conflict of interest. For advocacy to work well, it is important that a trusting relationship is established. This means that arrangements have to made in plenty of time so that children can feel comfortable with their advocates.

The importance of empowering people who may have communication differences is being increasingly recognised and many support groups are able to give information about paid or volunteer advocates. Legal advocates are appointed by the court when children are taken into the care of the local authority.

CASE STUDY

Katie is in a residential children's home. She is four years old and, under the Children Act 1989, has been appointed an advocate. The advocate represents her when her case is being discussed by social services and lawyers for her parents. Her advocate is independent and, although she is a trained solicitor, she does not have any involvement with social services or the solicitors representing her parents. She visits Katie before her case is reviewed to find out clearly what Katie is feeling.

• How would the advocate communicate with Katie to make her feel comfortable?

• Why is it so important that Katie is able to communicate clearly with her advocate?

Adapting the environment

Creating a good environment can prevent communication differences. In some situations it will be important to find an area that will give some privacy, especially if a conversation is personal or sensitive. This may mean taking someone into an office or altering an environment by adjusting the layout of furniture. Comfort is also important – standing outside or against a wall might make a conversation feel rushed, while taking time to sit somewhere will give the communication more importance.

Try to find somewhere private to talk if a parent wants to discuss a personal or sensitive issue.

Checking understanding

One of the key ways in which communication differences can be overcome or avoided is by carefully checking that each person understands what is being said and has the same perceptions about how it is meant. The skills of active listening are important here, as well as using questions to check and clarify. Many good communicators rephrase important points that they are making to ensure that the other person can take in the information. Good communicators also make sure that the other person has time to think and reflect. Allowing enough time is particularly important with young children.

Using other skilled communicators

In some situations, early years practitioners will need to recognise that they are not the best people to communicate with somebody. A child who is having behavioural difficulties because of a bereavement may need to be helped by a counsellor or play therapist. Recognising that people may need the assistance and support of others is therefore an important part of interacting.

Understanding tensions

A good starting point is to understand that people have a right to be as they are. This requires practitioners to adopt an accepting attitude towards others if communication is to be open and honest. This is not always easy to do because sometimes our value bases can prevent us from being tolerant and accepting. Value bases are the set of values and attitudes that are developed during people's lives, especially during the formative years of childhood. They envelope us like a hidden cloak that remains invisible to us but can be perceived by others. People's sets of values determine who they are likely to feel at ease with, as most people subconsciously relate better to others who have similar values. Having different value bases can affect the way we communicate with people. Most people simply feel ill at ease without necessarily understanding why – their body language in turn often reflects their unease, causing potential alienation from the person with whom they wish to communicate. Different attitudes stemming from value bases can also be the cause of prejudice and discrimination against others. A practitioner who feels ill at ease with a parent may not spend as much time with that parent as with another with whom they do feel comfortable. This is discrimination and is therefore unprofessional.

Self-esteem

The way we think of ourselves can influence the quality of our interactions. People with high self-esteem are likely to be more confident and able to put forward their views, while people who are unsure about themselves may find it harder. The level of self-esteem can affect people's behaviour types (see pages 46–47).

The development of self-esteem

People are not born with high or low self-esteem. It develops as babies, and then children, learn about themselves mainly from looking at the reactions of others to them. Children or adults who have repeated bad experiences in their interactions with others are therefore likely to develop low self-esteem. This has several implications for early years practitioners, as they will be in part responsible for building the self-esteem of the children they work with. Children will need to feel listened to and have their comments respected. They will also need to see positive facial expressions from adults and feel that they are being supported and encouraged as they speak.

How self-esteem may be developed and maintained as a result of positive interactions

It is not unusual for early years practitioners to work with children, adults and others who may have low self-esteem. While there is no magic cure for low self-esteem, it is possible to raise people's self-esteem by making them feel that they are valued and that the relationship with them is important.

※ Positively acknowledge them, for example, by greeting them in a friendly manner.

※ Use active listening skills (see page 52).

※ Avoid rushed 'interactions' – if you cannot talk to someone, explain why and if possible arrange a better time to talk.

※ Look for ways of acknowledging their achievements and contributions. For example, 'I saw that Sam had a new haircut. He said that you did it. It looks really good.'

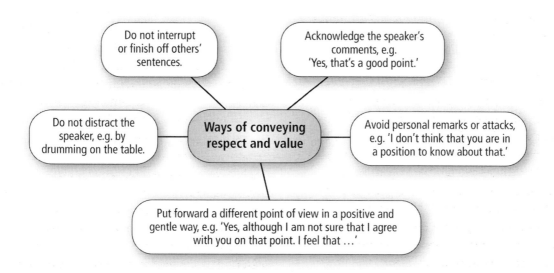

Do not interrupt or finish off others' sentences.

Acknowledge the speaker's comments, e.g. 'Yes, that's a good point.'

Do not distract the speaker, e.g. by drumming on the table.

Ways of conveying respect and value

Avoid personal remarks or attacks, e.g. 'I don't think that you are in a position to know about that.'

Put forward a different point of view in a positive and gentle way, e.g. 'Yes, although I am not sure that I agree with you on that point. I feel that …'

The importance of conveying respect and value

All of our interactions should be positive and convey respect to others. Failure to show respect creates tension and prevents people from sharing information. This in turn can cause misunderstandings which sometimes develop into feelings of alienation and mistrust.

3 How interpersonal skills contribute to the care of distressed individuals

There are times when children or adults may show distressed behaviour. Early years practitioners may find that children will become upset when their parent leaves or parents may come into a setting feeling angry about the care of their child. Finding ways to communicate and be supportive in these situations is therefore important.

Distressed behaviour

The reactions of people to being stressed can vary enormously and depends on the coping skills and mechanisms that they have acquired. Children's reactions are often more straightforward, as they are less able to control their feelings and therefore show strong reactions.

Reasons for distressed behaviour

There are many reasons why people may show distressed behaviour. These include family bereavements, misunderstandings and pressure at work or at home. Early years practitioners find that one of the most common causes of babies' and young children's distressed behaviour is separation anxiety. From around eight months, babies begin to become distressed if their primary carer leaves them. The table opposite outlines the causes and signs of distressed behaviour in children.

Withdrawal
- Little or no interest in what is happening
- Little or no speech
- Eye contact withheld
- Closed body language

Types of distressed behaviour

Anger and aggression
- Non-verbal – slamming, banging, large gestures, pointing
- Verbal anger – swearing, shouting, sarcasm, exaggeration
- Controlled anger may also be noticed, e.g. tension in face, colour of face, quick responses, curt tones

Distress
- Uncontrollable crying, intermittent crying
- Restless, difficult to be distracted
- Difficulty in speaking and responding

CAUSE	SIGNS	EXAMPLES IN CHILDREN
Pain	Children in pain often cry or show their distress by using comfort behaviour, such as rocking or sucking their thumb. Adults' reaction to pain can vary according to their coping skills but includes irritation, withdrawal and tearfulness.	Falling down Feeling poorly Minor/major accidents
Grief	The loss of someone or something creates powerful emotions. Children who feel upset when they leave their parents are actually grieving. As grief is a process, the behaviour shown by people may change – shock and disbelief may change into anger.	Absence of parent Death of pet Lost toys or comfort objects
Communication differences	Misunderstandings can cause distressed behaviour. Feelings of hurt and betrayal can create aggressive or withdrawn behaviour.	Stammering Children misunderstanding what has been said to them
Frustration	Frustration occurs when people feel that they are not in control of what is happening. Toddlers may become frustrated because they cannot convey to an adult what they need, while adults may become frustrated because they are late for work. Feelings of frustration are often translated into aggressive behaviour as a way of protesting; if someone is constantly frustrated they may use withdrawal as a way of coping.	Tantrums
Perceived loss of rights or unfairness	Protecting family members and property creates powerful feelings. Early years practitioners often find that angry parents are 'protecting' their children in some way. For example, parents may complain if they feel that their child has not received proper care or has been disadvantaged in some way. Squabbles and aggression in young children are often caused by problems over toys or objects, as children find it difficult to share but quickly learn to defend possessions.	Squabbles over turns, toys and possessions
Threats to self-esteem	Negative actions or words from others that are taken personally create distressed behaviour. An aggressive stance taken by an adult can be the result of a defence mechanism to avoid being 'hurt'. Children often show withdrawal or aggression if their confidence is being undermined.	Distress because of bullying (school-aged children)

Skills for working with individuals

Ability to remain calm

When working with an adult or child who is distressed, it is important to remain calm. Strong reactions can often fuel the distressed behaviour rather than defuse it. Shouting back at someone who is shouting tends to increase the anger and likelihood of more aggressive behaviour. It is also important to judge the seriousness of a situation quickly and seek help if necessary.

Communication techniques that encourage calm responses

Most early years practitioners will find that they quite often have to work with children who are distressed, such as a child who has fallen down or is upset because of a lost toy.

The following techniques are often helpful in calming down children, but can also be adapted in some situations with adults.

* Use gentle, soft tones.

* Get down to the child's level.

* Tell the child that you are listening.

* Use paraphrasing and reflection to help the child feel listened to.

* Use questioning skills to help children express themselves logically.

* Physically soothe the child (if appropriate).

* Look for practical ways of addressing the source of the distress. For example, ask children if they would like to help you to look for their lost teddy bear.

* Do not dismiss the child's feeling as being petty.

Responding to submissive, aggressive and manipulative behaviour

Submissive, aggressive and manipulative behaviours are ways that people have developed to cope with their feelings of low self-esteem. At times of distress, people may clearly show these types of behaviour. Responding can be difficult, but good communicators need to develop their own assertiveness and aim to nurture others' self-confidence.

The difference between aggressiveness and assertiveness

Many people confuse assertiveness with aggressiveness. The two are very different, as assertiveness is about having enough confidence in yourself to be able to put forward your viewpoint in a positive way, while aggressiveness is about trying to take control away from others.

Strategies for assertiveness

There is a range of strategies that can help us to be assertive, while also responding to others' behaviour.

Positive recognition

Positive recognition means thinking positively about ourselves and others. It shows in our interactions with others and is therefore likely to

---

Assessment activity 2.2

Write a reflective account of how you calmed a distressed child. Your account should evaluate the effectiveness of the communication skills that you used.

* Describe the communication skills that you used to support the child.
* Explain how effective you felt that your communication style was.

Discuss strategies that could have been used in a situation where the child had limited understanding of language, such as not understanding English or other communication difficulties.

Smiling and making eye contact can help defuse tensions.

attract positive responses from others. Positive recognition can be non-verbal as well as verbal. Examples of non-verbal positive recognition can include making eye contact with others, nodding in agreement with them and smiling. These non-verbal behaviours can defuse tensions and aggressiveness while encouraging a person showing submissive behaviour to interact.

As well as showing non-verbal recognition, it is also important to verbalise positive recognition and acknowledge others' contributions. Making comments such as, 'Thank you for taking the time to come in and talk to me,' is an example of positive recognition and may be helpful at the start of a potentially hostile exchange.

Being able to receive positive comments is also an important part of positive recognition. Refusing to take a compliment or praise can make the other person feel less positive about themselves and you.

Positive visualisation

Positive visualisation is a technique designed to help people imagine their way through a potentially difficult encounter. The idea behind this technique is that if you are able to visualise yourself behaving positively, you will be able to

CASE STUDY

Sam is working in a family centre and is uncomfortable working with one of the parents. The parent had been in to see him to say that his son had come home with paint on his clothes and was angry. Sam in response had shown manipulative behaviour saying that it was not his fault and that the parents would be better off making sure that their child was wearing more sensible clothes in the future. The interaction ended with both parties feeling irritated with each other and since then Sam has avoided meeting this particular parent.

Sam is now learning some techniques of assertiveness and is considering how, at the next parents' meeting, he will interact with this parent.

Using positive visualisation he imagines he will:

- acknowledge the parent warmly
- make eye contact and smile
- make a positive comment about the child
- make a positive comment about the parents' involvement with the child
- use active listening skills to show the parent that he wants to understand any concerns.

In his mind he can imagine that the meeting will be positive so, on the day of the meeting, feels more positive. The parent is at first defensive, but gradually responds to the more positive attitude and the meeting is mutually beneficial.

go on into the situation and create a positive outcome. This is particularly useful for situations where poor communication has previously taken place.

Using language for assertiveness

In order to be assertive, it is important that the language we use is positive and reflects our thoughts and needs. People who are not confident often find difficulty in expressing clearly what they need to say.

'I statements'

One of the ways in which to make communication simple is to use 'I statements'. For example, instead of saying 'We need to tidy up the cloakroom', the statement may be 'I think that we need to sort out the cloakroom'. 'I statements' show that we are taking responsibility for our thoughts, words and actions. They help others understand what we are trying to do or say.

Using language accurately

Using language accurately is important, as it prevents misunderstandings and also allows others to put forward their own points of view. As part of using language accurately, good communicators

distinguish between facts, feelings and ideas in their speech – it is common for most people to mix these up. Phrases such as 'I know' should be used for facts rather than for thoughts and feelings, especially in cases where we might be trying to empathise with others. 'I know how you are feeling' is a classic example of using unhelpful language and potentially alienating the other speaker.

Sources of support for carers

People working in emotionally charged situations should seek support from others. This provides a 'safety mechanism' for all concerned.

Supervision

Supervision is usually used by counsellors as a way of preventing them from becoming too emotionally involved with the people they are working with. It helps them spread the emotional load and assists them in evaluating and reflecting upon their work. Early years practitioners who are not counsellors may seek support from senior members of the setting. This can help as they may be experienced and able to give advice about how best to manage future situations.

Counselling

There are times when early years practitioners may feel that they need counselling in order to 'offload' and cope with their strong feelings. For example, an early years practitioner may find it hard to cope if a child they work with dies suddenly or a child has made a disclosure about abuse. Receiving counselling is no longer seen as being 'weak', as it is recognised that denying feelings can lead to psychological damage.

Training

Working with children and adults is a skill and learning to communicate effectively in difficult circumstances does not come naturally to everyone. Communication and assertiveness training is therefore very popular among people who care for others.

Peer support

Support from colleagues can be invaluable when coping with stressful situations. Colleagues are

---

Assessment activity 2.3

It is first thing in the morning and the setting is bustling with parents dropping off their children and hanging up coats. A parent has come into the setting to complain that her baby had been sent home with a nappy that obviously needed changing. She is on her way to work and is very angry. She is standing in the doorway of the setting demanding to speak to her baby's key worker. You are the key worker!

In pairs, role play how you would deal with this situation. (This role play could be videotaped or recorded as evidence.)

Write a report about how this type of situation could be managed successfully. Your report should:

- analyse the reasons behind the parent's distress
- consider potential barriers to effective communication and ways of managing these
- evaluate the strategies that might be used in this situation.

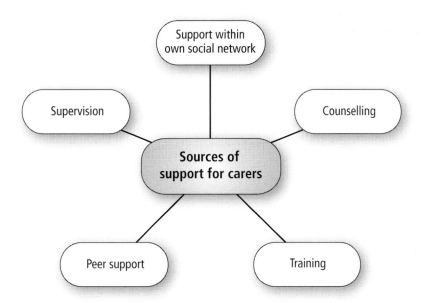

likely to be sympathetic, although may lack the necessary objectivity to guide you if you have mishandled a situation.

Support within own social network

Many early years practitioners find support from within their family and friends. While they can provide a sympathetic ear, it is essential that talk about work should be kept in the broadest terms to avoid possible breaches of confidentiality. Most people use their social network as a way of 'switching off' from work, which allows them to relax.

4 How to reflect on the effectiveness of your own interpersonal and communication skills

This section looks at the skills that you need to develop in order to be an effective communicator.

Personal skills

Verbal skills

You will need to consider how easy you find it to articulate your own thoughts and ideas. Verbal skills are important in many situations, but if you work with babies and young children, you will need to remember that they will partly be learning how to use language from you.

Non-verbal skills

Children and adults are quickly able to identify those people who appear to be good listeners and

> **Theory into practice**
>
> **Working with parents**
> - Be courteous.
> - Provide regular feedback about their child's progress and development.
> - Take time to tell parents about their child's day and achievements.
> - Ask parents about how their child is when at home.
> - Find out about any preferences that they may have regarding diet, skin care or behaviour management.
> - Listen carefully to parents' concerns and acknowledge them.

Reporting and feedback

Parents need us to report and provide feedback to them. They may want to know about their child's progress as well as on a day-to-day basis what they have been doing. Parents of babies and toddlers also need information about day-to-day care of their children such as nappy changing or feeds.

Running commentary

Talking to babies and toddlers is essential. The style that is often used with babies and toddlers is known as 'running commentary'. Adults talk to children about what is happening and what they are doing. Children learn from this new vocabulary, but also hear the sounds and expressions that they will later use.

Recasting and expanding

When young children talk they often make grammatical mistakes or pronunciation errors. Babies or toddlers may also only provide one or two words. Recasting is a technique that is used to help babies and toddlers hear a grammatically correct sentence. It also shows we have been listening.

Verbal skills when working with children and parents

Questioning

One way in which children can learn more in situations is by adults using questions. An adult might ask a child to consider why things are happening. Questions help children to learn to articulate their thoughts.

Giving instructions

There are times when children will need clear instructions such as what to do when the fire alarm goes off or how to act at home time. Adults must be able to speak clearly and also concisely in a way that children can understand.

Acknowledging

One of the ways in which we can encourage wanted behaviour is by praising or remarking on wanted behaviour. It is important to be precise about what a child is doing that is so good. Expressions such as 'well done' or 'good boy' do not tell children exactly what they are doing that is gaining approval.

---

skilful communicators. This comes through body language.

Acceptance, gentleness and empathy

Carl Rogers, whose work has greatly influenced counselling methods, suggests that there are three important elements that are needed to create situations where people could talk openly: acceptance, gentleness and empathy.

Acceptance is about trying not to judge others as we listen to them. To do this we have to understand our own values and attitudes.

Gentleness, sometimes referred to as sincerity, is about responding in an open and positive way – not just saying things because they are the 'right' things to say.

Empathy is about trying to understand how the other person is feeling and seeing things from their perspective.

Positive body language

Body language is a powerful tool in interpersonal interaction and communication. Good communicators use positive body language to help others feel at ease. The three elements of acceptance, gentleness and empathy can be conveyed through positive body language. Children are very quick to pick up on adults' body language and respond well to caring, open gestures. It is also important for you to notice babies' and children's body language, especially where children have limited language.

Stance – the way people sit and stand sends out silent messages. You need to be able to monitor your stance as you communicate with others.

Crossed arms and legs – these can indicate that people are not comfortable in a situation. It is as if they are trying to hold themselves back or defend themselves.

Learning forward or back – in some situations, a listener who sits back from a speaker can send out a message of not being interested, while a listener who leans slightly forward can give the impression of attention.

Facial expression

Facial expression is a strong element in non-verbal communication, although in some cultures facial expressions are more restricted and may not, therefore send out as many messages. People can show a lot of their feelings through their faces, as facial muscles tense when people are anxious or under stress. As a practitioner, it is helpful to note people's expressions because, if they are particularly stressed or tense, this might mean that we will need to alter our approach. As a communicator, you should try to show warmth and interest in your face. Smiling and inclining the head are ways of conveying interest and warmth non-verbally. It is also interesting to note whether or not hands are being used to cover up the mouth or face. This can mean that someone is not comfortable or trying to conceal their feelings.

Identification of areas of development

It is important to think about ways in which we might be able to improve or further develop our own communication practice. Practitioners who are able to think about how well they communicate will find that they can work more effectively and also gain in confidence.

Gaining feedback

It can be useful for others to provide us with feedback about our communication skills. This only works well if we are ready to really listen to what is being said and to avoid the trap of being defensive. Colleagues and tutors can be helpful,

but the key is to see any criticism in a positive rather than negative way. Gaining feedback is particularly helpful when it comes to our written skills. Spelling, punctuation or even the format of the way a document is written might need to be improved.

Reflection

During the communication cycle, it is important to monitor how well it is going and consider what is, as well as what is not, being said. It also means monitoring one's own communication skills and considering if the approach taken is working. Evidence that we are communicating well will often be communicated through other people's body language (non-verbal communication) as well as their contributions. In some situations it is very easy to take over a conversation rather than listen to what is being said – monitoring whether this is happening is therefore an important skill.

Observing others

Learning by watching others can be a very powerful tool. Look out for those people that you consider to be skilled communicators. Think about what they do that helps other people to respond positively towards them. You can also learn communication skills, such as sign language, from watching others.

You may like to use sign language.

Action planning

The term 'reflective practice' is currently popular. It means thinking carefully about areas of our work with children and their families and considering ways in which we might build on our strengths and further develop areas of weakness. The starting point for this is to be objective about ourselves. This is not always easy and is one reason why we might seek help form others (see Gaining feedback above).

Below is a list of questions that might be useful when reflecting on your communication skills. It is not an exhaustive list and you will need to add to it.

Parents

* How easy do I find it to talk to parents?
* Do I always acknowledge parents?
* Do I make good eye contact with parents as I talk to them?
* Do parents approach me and chat to me?
* Do I show that I have time for parents?
* Do parents choose to come to me when they have difficulties?
* How aware of cultural and lifestyle differences am I?

Children

* Do I use active listening skills with children?
* With babies and toddlers, do I use a running commentary style?
* Are children able to follow my instructions?
* Do children often come freely to see and talk to me?
* How well do I know the children and their interests?
* Do I use language to help children's thinking skills?

Colleagues and professionals

* Do I acknowledge colleagues and professionals when I meet them, such as at the start of the day?
* Am I able to put forward my own viewpoints in a positive way?
* Do I respect viewpoints that are different to my own?
* Do colleagues and professionals offer advice and also ask my advice from time to time?
* Am I able to listen to criticism in a constructive way?

Written skills

* How easy do I find it to write?
* Do I ever make spelling or punctuation errors?
* Do I encourage others to comment and check my written work?
* Do other people understand what I have written?

Signing skills

* Am I able to use some Makaton signs?
* Am I able to use some British sign language?

Assessment activity 2.4

* Write a report on your own communication skills in the workplace. Your report should:
  - describe your strengths and weaknesses with examples
  - evaluate the impact of these strengths and weaknesses on your working practice.
* Devise an action plan based on your report. The plan should:
  - reflect your strengths and weaknesses
  - set realistic targets as to how to improve your skills
  - demonstrate how these targets are to be met.

END-OF-UNIT TEST

1 Give one example of a non-verbal method of communication.

2 How can the layout of the environment affect interaction?

3 Give three factors that might act as a barrier to effective communication.

4 Explain how the communication cycle works.

5 List three factors that might disrupt the communication cycle.

6 Give one advantage and one disadvantage of using a translator.

7 What is meant by the term 'active listening'?

8 Explain three ways in which a person can show active listening.

9 What is the difference between an open and a closed question?

10 Explain what is meant by 'advocacy' and give an example of when it might be used.

11 What is the difference between assertive and aggressive behaviour?

12 How might early years practitioners convey 'respect' in their interactions with parents and children?

13 Suggest two ways in which we might help a young child to calm down.

14 List three strategies that you might use to communicate effectively with young children.

15 Why is it important for adults to reflect on their communication skills?

References and further reading

Burton, G and Dimbleby, R (1996), *Between Ourselves: A guide to interpersonal communication*, Hodder Arnold

Gill, D and Adams, B (1998), *ABC of Communication Studies*, Nelson Thornes

Hartley, P (1999), *Interpersonal Communication*, Routledge

Protection of children

What you need to learn

1 How to recognise and understand the signs and symptoms of child abuse

2 What to do if there are concerns about a child, using the current legal framework for child protection

3 The range of strategies to support children and their families

4 Multi-agency working to protect all children

Introduction

The majority of families care for their children appropriately and will not need intervention from professional services. However, there are adults who intentionally harm children or put them at risk from harm through neglect. Early years practitioners are in a prime position to alert others to possible abuse, support the child through any investigation that might take place and provide help for children who are known to have been abused. Because of this, it is important that early years practitioners equip themselves with knowledge about child abuse, why it may occur, how it may be recognised, its effects on young children and their families and what to do if they are concerned. It is also important for practitioners to understand the importance of co-operating with other professionals, using community support networks to assist in the protection of children.

How you will be assessed

This unit is assessed internally.

1 How to recognise and understand the signs and symptoms of child abuse

The work addressed in this unit is of a sensitive nature. Child abuse may be a hidden aspect of some people's lives. It is important that when discussing issues in class you are aware of this. The need for confidentiality will be a vital aspect of your practice. Much of your practice will require that you have a sound knowledge of:

* indicators of abuse
* predisposing factors – factors which make an abusive situation more likely
* theories of abuse
* variations in family functioning.

Indicators of abuse

This section sets out to look at the possible indicators of abuse. When considering these indicators, practitioners must exercise caution, as it could be tempting to see these as absolutes which always indicate abuse, when there may be a perfectly reasonable explanation. These indicators are to be used as a guide. It is important that the practitioner always follows the guidelines and policies of the setting, without jumping to conclusions or making assumptions.

Physical abuse and injury

'Physical abuse may involve hitting, shaking, throwing, poisoning, burning or scalding, drowning, suffocating, or otherwise causing physical harm to a child. Physical harm may also be caused when a parent or carer feigns the symptoms of, or deliberately causes ill health to a child whom they are looking after. This situation is commonly described as Munchausen syndrome by proxy.'

(*Working Together to Safeguard Children*, 1999)

The table below shows characteristics that may be observed in a physically abused child.

PHYSICAL INDICATORS	BEHAVIOURAL INDICATORS
Unexplained multiple bruises in unusual places (thighs, behind the knee, upper arm, back, neck, back of legs, etc. – see page 70)	Unlikely or inconsistent explanations for injuries
Frequent bruises at different stages of healing	Withdrawn and overly compliant
Bruises in the shape of objects, e.g. belts, rope, etc.	Aggressive
Fingertip bruises	Poor social skills
Unexplained/untreated burns and scalds	Low self-esteem
Unexplained/untreated fractures	Unusually fearful
Any bruising on a young baby who is not yet mobile	Hyper-alert to the environment (frozen watchfulness)
Cigarette burns	Reluctant to change clothing for swimming or PE
Bite marks	Playing inappropriately with or without toys
Internal injuries which can cause pain, fever, vomiting, etc.	Inappropriately clinging to, or cowering from, parent or carer

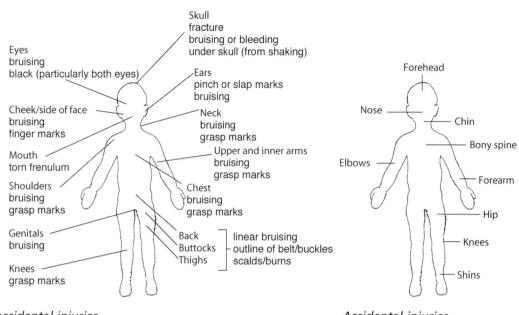

Non-accidental injuries.   *Accidental injuries.*

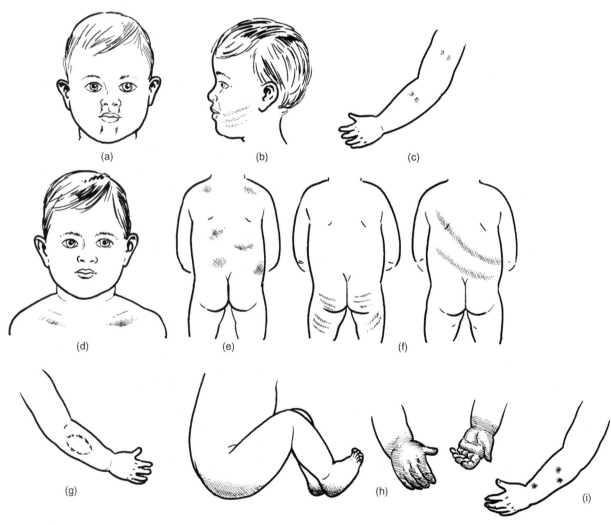

Signs of physical abuse: (a) facial squeezing, (b) diffuse facial bruising, (c) pinch marks, (d) grip marks, (e) body bruising, (f) identifiable lesions, (g) bite marks, (h) burns or scalds, (i) cigarette burns.

It is important to remember that young children regularly develop bumps and bruises through falls or squabbles with siblings. You should also consider the age and stage of development of the child. For example, regular bumps on the head of a toddler who may fall or bang his head on furniture may be viewed differently from that of a six-year-old who regularly appears with bumps or bruises on the head. When making a decision about a specific injury you should also consider any explanation that has been given to you regarding the injury.

However, the physical signs of abuse are often different from those acquired through normal causes, as shown in the figures opposite.

Parental attitude is important in assessing accidental and non-accidental injuries – when a child is suffering a severe and painful injury most parents would seek medical help. It is also important to remember that children of mixed race, of African or Asian heritage, may have dark pigmented areas at the tip of the spine, which at times extends into the buttocks. These spots are known as 'Mongolian Blue Spot'. They are always of the same colour and do not go through changes of colour like bruises do.

Think it over...

- A child has fallen over in the playground grazing both knees and his elbow.
- A child has bumped his head on the sharp corner of a cupboard.
- A child has pinch marks to her forearm.
- A child has bruising on his upper chest.

With a partner, discuss which of these injuries would be recorded on a body map.

Emotional abuse

'Emotional abuse is the persistent emotional ill-treatment of a child such as to cause severe and adverse effects on the child's emotional development. It may involve conveying to children that they are worthless or unloved, inadequate, or valued only insofar as they meet the needs of another person… Some level of emotional abuse is involved in all types of ill-treatment of a child, though it may occur alone.'

(*Working Together to Safeguard Children*, 1999)

Emotional abuse is perhaps the most difficult and under-estimated form of abuse to detect because there are no physical indicators. There are also many other reasons why a child may be displaying these signs. Children may be unsettled by a change in the family function. There may be a new baby, a loss in the family or parents may have recently separated. There may be domestic violence in the home or an adult with mental health problems putting the child under enormous stress. Emotional abuse can include:

- parents or carers not giving love and attention
- constant shouting and screaming and insulting remarks
- continual criticism and threats
- humiliating punishments
- lack of approval – the child is never good enough, undermining their sense of self-worth.

Often parents are unaware that the way in which they are treating their children is abusive. Some emotional abuse can take place when families are under particular stress, such as bereavement, depression or separation. If this continues and becomes part of the normal day-to-day treatment of the child, this would constitute abuse.

It is important to have a good knowledge of child development and use regular observation as part of good practice to alert you to the subtle changes in a child's behaviour.

The table on the next page shows characteristics that may be observed in an emotionally abused child.

BEHAVIOURAL INDICATORS	
Attention seeking	Developmental delay
Withdrawn and isolated	Indiscriminately affectionate
Stealing or telling lies	Fearful of parents/carers – reluctant to go home
Inability to have fun	
Low self-esteem	Self-mutilation, e.g. head banging, hair pulling, picking at skin
Tantrums at an inappropriate age – over-reacting	Comfort-seeking behaviour, thumb sucking or rocking
Speech disorders	Over-anxious to please
Inability to play	Poor concentration
	Frequent toileting accidents in older children

In the Birth to Three Matters framework (DfES 2002) emotional well-being is recognised as an essential part of a child's right to be 'a healthy child'. It is important to be aware that parents are only human and may have moments of stress when they feel they cannot cope and consequently treat their children inappropriately. This may only be a temporary period of stress, but children need healthy dependent relationships in order to develop and express their feelings and this kind of treatment, even in the short term may have long-term effects.

Sexual abuse

'Sexual abuse involves forcing or **coercing** a child or young person to take part in sexual activities, whether or not the child is aware of what is happening. The activities may involve physical contact, including penetrative (e.g. rape or buggery) or non-penetrative acts. They may include non-contact activities, such as involving children in looking at, or in the production of, pornographic material or watching sexual activities, or encouraging children to behave in sexually inappropriate ways.'
(*Working Together to Safeguard Children*, 1999)

The table opposite shows characteristics that may be observed in a sexually abused child.

Neglect

'Neglect is the persistent failure to meet a child's basic physical and/or psychological needs, likely to result in the serious impairment of the child's health or development. It may involve a parent or carer failing to provide adequate food, shelter and clothing.'
(*Working Together to Safeguard Children*, 1999)

The table opposite shows characteristics that may be observed in a child who is neglected.

Bullying

Although not in a category of its own, bullying is a form of emotional abuse and can cause long-term damage to a child. Abuse by older children can also be physical and sexual. In 1993 Jamie Bulger died at the hands of two ten-year-old boys Jon Venables and Robert Thompson in Liverpool. This highlighted that children can also be the aggressors and abusers. Children who are bullied at school or at home by older siblings often have low self-esteem and self-worth, they may begin to believe their attackers and feel worthless. Bullies may pick on the seemingly more vulnerable children; those less likely to fight back. They have often learnt this behaviour from their parents or older siblings, having been victims of violence themselves. Children who are the victims of bullying may go on to miss school in later years.

PHYSICAL INDICATORS OF SEXUAL ABUSE	BEHAVIOURAL INDICATORS
Pain, itching or discomfort in the genital area	Nightmares, night terrors and sleep disturbances
Difficulty when having a bowel movement, urinating or swallowing	Dramatic behavioural changes, causing disruption of child care activities
Recurring complaints, such as frequent stomach aches and headaches	Clinging or compulsively seeking attention, from both boys and girls
Eating disorders such as refusing to eat or eating constantly	Overly co-operative or aggressive
Torn, stained or bloody underwear	Destructive or anti-social behaviour
Bruising/bites to breasts, buttocks, lower abdomen, thighs, genital or anal areas	Apparent sadness almost all the time
Sexually transmitted diseases, promiscuity or pregnancy	Poor relationships with other children and lack of self-confidence
Semen on skin, clothes or in the vagina or anus	Frequent lying without apparent reason
	Self-destructive behaviour, e.g. biting oneself, pulling out hair, wrist-cutting, head banging
	Unusual distrust or fear of adults or specific adults
	May fear going home or being left alone
	Unusually secretive, 'special' relationship with an older person
	Unusual sexual knowledge and persistent, inappropriate sexual play for the child's age and stage of development

PHYSICAL INDICATORS OF NEGLECT	BEHAVIOURAL INDICATORS
Poor hygiene	Lack of interest, difficult to stimulate
Clothing is inadequate, dirty, torn or inappropriate for weather conditions	Indiscriminately affectionate
Untreated medical problems	Persistently late to school or frequently missing school
Persistent nappy rash	Withdrawn
Poor nourishment	Low self-esteem
Emaciation	

Pre-disposing factors

In this section we will examine some of the factors that may lead to a child being abused. However, it is important for the practitioner to understand that children are never responsible for being abused. It is the adult or 'abuser' who is always responsible for the abuse taking place; the child is always the victim.

Abuse within families

Contrary to popular belief, most child abuse and neglect takes place within the child's own home and family, by somebody (usually a parent) who the child knows. Child abuse and neglect crosses all boundaries of culture, ethnic origin, religion and social status.

While no single factor can be seen to be responsible for causing an abusive situation, there are some factors which may make an abusive situation more likely.

Parents

Research into child abuse has shown that certain characteristics and experiences may predispose particular individuals to be more likely to abuse a child in their care than another individual. These include:

* parents who themselves have been abused
* parents who have experienced poor parenting themselves
* very young parents, who may be unaware of the child's needs or are in fact still growing up themselves
* parents who have unrealistic expectations of their child's behaviour
* parents who experience poverty, poor housing and social isolation
* parents who have a low self-esteem
* parents with a history of alcohol or drug abuse
* parents with mental health issues
* where the child was an unwanted pregnancy and/or difficult birth.

None of these categories is applicable to all adults who may abuse or neglect their children, but they do need to be considered when addressing individual issues of child protection.

Children

Some children are more vulnerable to abuse than others, such as the following.

* **A child with a disability** – a parent who has responsibility for significant physical care could become frustrated and resentful of the responsibility, taking it out on the child.
* **An eldest child** – often the eldest child will be given more responsibility in a family under stress and this can lead to them being held accountable for problems, and abused emotionally or physically as a result.
* **Looked-after children** – unfortunately, children who are being looked after by the state may be cared for by an abusive person who is betraying their position of trust.
* **A loner** – a child who does not have friends or social support may be preyed upon by paedophiles who exploit their vulnerability.
* **A child who cries a lot or is difficult to feed** – parents who are tired or stressed can find it harder to keep calm and control their emotions.

These factors are obviously not applicable for all children, but may be pre-disposing factors. Can you think of any more?

Children with disabilities

All the indicators listed above apply to children with disabilities; however, the question still remains why children with disabilities are more vulnerable. Some reasons are listed below.

* They receive less information on abuse and their rights, and may be less likely to understand it.
* They are often more dependent on physical care from different people.
* They may be less likely to tell what has happened, due to communication barriers.
* They may be more likely to have low self-esteem and feel less in control.
* They may find it difficult to distinguish between good and bad touches.

Working Together to Safeguard Children (DoH 1999) also suggests that children with disabilities are at increased risk from abuse.

All families have differing values and standards. These will have developed as a result of the personal experiences of the parents, who will bring their values and family practices from their own childhood and past experiences. You will see that they have different ways in which they discipline their children as a result of these differences. What is acceptable behaviour in one family may be unacceptable in another. You need to take this into account as part of good practice. You may also need to support and advise a parent when their child's development is suffering as a result of their concept of discipline. You can do this primarily by being a good role model in the way you handle and work with their children.

Consequences and effects of child abuse and neglect

Studies have shown that child abuse has been a consistent factor in the backgrounds of criminals, substance abusers, prostitutes and runaways. Children who have experienced child abuse are likely to continue or create the cycle of abuse when they become adults. They assume that pain naturally accompanies intimacy. They are more likely to turn to physical abuse, as well as substance abuse, in order to forget what has happened or is happening to them. Child abuse and neglect lower self-esteem and have a long-term damaging effect on the person's confidence, faith, relationships and future. Long-term effects of child abuse include fear, anxiety, depression, anger, hostility, inappropriate sexual behaviour, poor self-esteem, tendency towards substance abuse and difficulty with close relationships (Browne and Finkelhor, 1986).

While these effects are not always obvious, they are very important. Knowing this, there can be little doubt that children who are abused, as well as adults who were abused as children, need assistance to resolve the questions that the abuse experience has raised, even if that assistance does not come until years after the abuse.

In 2003, National Children's Homes (NCH) published *Working with Children*. This book provided a statistical analysis of the latest government statistics on children and their families, looking at children's services; health; population; education; children at risk; poverty and social exclusion. It stated that in 2003 the following numbers were recorded on the child protection register:

* 4,200 children under 1 year

* 7,600 children between 1–4 years

* 7,600 children between 5–9 years

* 7,000 children between 10–15 years

At 31 March 2002 there were 25,700 children on child protection registers in England, a 4 per cent increase on the previous year. These were not all cases of abuse in the home. In 2002 a new 'mixed' category was introduced in recording these registrations because of the concerns about multiple risks. At 31 March 2002 the most commonly recorded risk category was neglect (39 per cent), followed by physical abuse (19 per cent), and then emotional abuse (17 per cent).

(12th Annual Report of the Chief Inspector of Social Services 2002–2003, DoH, 2003)

CASE STUDY

'When we were children we were expected to adhere to certain rules – we were not allowed to eat, except at the table, and were expected to sit together every evening for our meal. Table manners were very important in our house – if you did not follow certain etiquette my father would ask you to leave the table and you went without your dinner.'

This is an example of differing expectations of family life. You may find this strange, even unacceptable. With your group, come up with some similar examples of family life as you remember them and discuss whether or not you share the same experiences. Do you find some of these experiences unacceptable?

There are also other areas of high risk and concern, where children are being abused:

* child prostitution – this takes place in Britain today
* runaways
* drug-use-related incidents
* trafficked children
* domestic violence
* looked-after children.

Think it over...

In small groups, research the following reports, and other secondary sources, to present a poster to inform your fellow learners about the areas of concern mentioned above.
- Trafficked children – *Stop the Traffic*, Unicef UK, 2003
- Domestic violence – *The Hidden Victims – children and domestic violence*, NCH, 1994/Routes to Safety, Women's Aid Federation of England, 2002, www.avenueswomen.co.uk

Theories of abuse

In spite of the large number of theories put forward as to why child abuse occurs, there is no one theory which can be applied to all cases of abuse and neglect. Each situation is different and occurs for different reasons and therefore needs to be viewed individually. The five main models of why child abuse and neglect occur are defined in the following diagram.

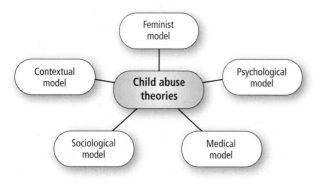

Medical model

This theory addresses issues around the idea that the causes of child abuse are best viewed as a disease. This came from the phrase coined by Kempe and Kempe (1962): the 'battered child syndrome'. This was later changed in 1976 to 'child abuse and neglect'. Kempe and Kempe applied Bowlby's thinking around 'attachment theory' directly to child abuse and neglect. They concluded that many mothers (the main caregiver who the bond is made with) who had abused their children had themselves suffered from poor attachment experiences in early childhood. Their response to this was to ensure that children in abusive situations were removed to places of safety and the parents were given 'treatment' to help with the bonding process.

Sociological model

This theory looks at changing patterns within society and believes that unemployment, poverty, poor housing and health deprivation are reasons for people abusing their children. Children need to live in healthy environments if they are to grow up healthy and well adjusted. Research has shown that there are links between rates of reported abuse and characteristics of social deprivation. Research also shows that many people who abuse children have very often been victims of abuse during their own childhood. Sadly, these adults may go on to treat their children in the same way, as this is an integral part of their socialisation. This is referred to as the cycle of abuse. It is necessary, however, that practitioners do not make judgements about a family based on something the parent has told them about their background. Parents who have had poor parenting experiences may need extra support to enjoy being parents themselves and to get the very best from their relationships with their children.

Psychological model

Family dysfunction theorists look at the dynamics within a family relationship. If this becomes poor or distorted, the family ceases to function as a unit. Dysfunction usually begins with the adult partners who may then 'scapegoat', which means that all the family's problems become identified with one family member. Theorists argue that the 'scapegoat' has become necessary for the survival of the family unit.

Feminist model

This perspective addresses the imbalance of power between men and women within society and with particular reference to child sexual abuse and the abuse of adult male power.

Contextual model

Abuse can occur anywhere or at any time, but there is no particular type of family where abuse always occurs. Research has shown that there are four groups of factors which may lead to an increased chance of abuse.

* **Exceptional context** – this is when parents who would usually meet the needs of their children have particular stresses or problems which prevent them from being able to cope in their normal way.

* **Rigid context** – parents are very strict and controlling and children appear to be fearful of making their parents angry. Parents are intolerant and focus on the negative, with high expectations of the child.

* **Deviant context** – one or two of the parents abuse their power and are often mentally unwell themselves. For example, Munchausen by proxy syndrome would come under this category.

* **Chaotic context** – discipline within the family is inconsistent and there is a lack of appropriate boundaries. Care of the children is often erratic and older children may be given adult responsibility.

Think it over...

Victoria Climbie was eight years old when she died in February 2000. She had been tortured and died at the hands of an aunt, Marie Theresa Kouao, and her partner Carl Manning. Research this case and, in a presentation to your group, do the following.

* Discuss some of the background information on the case.
* Link the case to one or more of these theoretical models.
* Give reasons for your choice.

There are references at the end of this unit that may be useful (see page 106).

Variation in family functioning

Family types

The family, in whatever form, is the unit that provides a home and care for dependent children. There is a variety of family types within our society.

* **Nuclear family** – Parents and children live in an independent unit, separate from other relatives. This may mean that the family is better off economically, but may also mean that if anything goes wrong between the parents, the family will experience considerable disruption.

* **Reconstituted family** – Partners with children from previous relationship live together. This may provide a good level of support, but may also bring tensions for some individuals.

* **Extended family** – Parents, children, grandparents, uncles and aunts live together in a supportive unit which has many advantages, but may limit the personal independence of some members.

* **Lone parent** – A single parent, father or mother, living alone with a child. This may lead to financial hardship, or may induce feelings of isolation and lack of support.

Changing face of the family

While these definitions are fairly specific, it is important to be aware that there are many different combinations. The structure of the family has altered as a result of changes within the wider society. The increased incidence of divorce and remarriage, the development of a multi-cultural society and increased life expectancy have resulted in changes in family lifestyles and practices. Children may live in two households, moving from one to another at weekends or holidays, live with parents who are in a homosexual relationship or grow up living with foster carers. While family structures may vary in different cultures, it is very important not to generalise about any family situation.

More specifically, a change within any individual family structure, such as moving away from relatives, a grandparent dying or moving to a different country, can be quite disruptive for the

FACTOR	EFFECT
Poor housing which may be overcrowded, damp and unheated, with limited outside play space	Chest infections from living in damp conditions Lack of privacy or personal space Noise No safe outdoor play, which may leave young children playing on the streets
Poor diet, cheap food with limited nutrients, high intake of fast foods, too much sugar and starch and too little fruit and vegetables	Illness and infections May affect growth Sets a pattern of poor eating habits which will last for life
Inadequate clothing	Discomfort in bad weather and may produce illness
Lack of stimulation and quality play resources, no holidays and limited travel	May effect intellectual development Makes times like Christmas additionally stressful
Low self-esteem	Feeling of worthlessness May cause depression May develop alcohol or drug dependency Leads to a feeling of being 'trapped'

family and the child. All families are different, have different practices and different values – there is no one particular ideal model. What is important is that the children are fed, clothed and sheltered, are loved and have the opportunity to learn within a protective and caring environment.

Social disadvantage

There are many pressures on families, not least those caused by social or financial hardship. The cycle of poverty is difficult to escape and places added pressures on the family. The table above identifies some of the factors which affect families.

Different concepts of discipline

Parents have different ideas about what is appropriate discipline – for example, some parents may feel that smacking their children is appropriate. There are many types of discipline that are considered to be good parenting; these may have been learnt from the parent's own upbringing or they could also be a culturally accepted view. Early years practitioners need to acknowledge these views and offer support and advice, ensuring that they are always a good role model for parents. Settings will also have policies on discipline, which can be discussed with the parents.

2 What to do if there are concerns about a child, using the current legal framework for child protection

In this section we will be looking at:

* historical perspectives
* the legal framework for protection of children
* supporting children who disclose
* reporting concerns
* the role of the key worker.

Historical perspectives

Before we look at the present framework, we need to understand something about how we came to this point. Prior to the implementation of the Children Acts of 1989 and, more recently, 2004, there were many pieces of child care legislation which were thought to be far too complex and incomplete for the needs of children, their families and the professionals working with them. As society's ideas and attitudes were changing towards child abuse, for example, more people were becoming aware of its existence and were no longer prepared to 'bury their heads in the sand'. It was evident that the existing legislation had to be updated. Another reason for this was the reports into the deaths of Jasmine Beckford (1985), Kimberley Carlile (1985), Tyra Henry (1985) and an inquiry into the handling of alleged child sexual abuse in Cleveland (1987).

Human Rights Act 1998

This Act came into force on 2 October 2000 and details the basic rights of humans in our society. The Human Rights Act outlines rules to order and protect every person. Rules of the Human Rights Act include the right to life, protection from slavery, the right to education and the right to marriage. These seem as though they go without saying, but without these concepts of human rights we could live in a very different society. There are places around the world where freedom is restricted, people are made to work as slaves or are not allowed an education. The Human Rights Act is vital in keeping our society as fair and equal as possible and fortunately most of us have no idea what it would be like without such laws.

The United Nations Convention on the Rights of the Child

Children have rights and there is legislation to protect their rights. The League of Nations drafted the first Declaration of the Rights of the Child in 1924. In 1989 the United Nations Convention on the Rights of the Child, (CRC) containing 54 Articles addressing the rights of children, was ratified by the UK in 1991. Only the United States and Somalia have not ratified this declaration. The 54 Articles within the CRC address children's right to:

* survival
* development
* protection
* participation.

The following articles, among others, are key in the protection of children.

* Article 19 – To protect children from all form of physical or mental violence while in the care of parents or others.
* Article 37a – No child shall be subjected to torture or other cruel inhuman or degrading treatment or punishment.

The principles stated in the CRC underpin much of the current legislation of this country designed to ensure that the views and the rights of the child are sought and upheld

Think it over...

Research a child abuse or neglect case that occurred before the Children Act 1989, such as the case of Maria Colwell or Tyra Henry.
* How did the system fail to protect the children?
* Could the case have been handled differently?
* Think about how the case would be handled now, in light of the Children Act 1989, the Human Rights Act 1998 and the United Nations Convention on the Rights of the Child.

The Special Educational Needs and Disability Act (SENDA) 2001

This Act is in two parts. Part one of the Act makes reforms to former legislation and gives rights to children with special educational needs to access mainstream education, where they were formerly educated primarily in specialist schools for moderate and severe learning difficulties and specialist units. The Disability Discrimination Act of 1995 is extended in part two of the Act, which increases the civil rights of disabled children and adults in schools and further and higher education – giving them rights to equal access and the right to inclusion.

The SEN Code of Practice 2001 was developed from this Act and this gives guidance to parents, schools and any establishments receiving government funding. The guidance works on fundamental principles based on the social model of disability, so that their individual needs can be met.

For more information on the Act or the Code of Practice see Unit 16, pages 439–442.

The legal framework for the protection of children

The Children Act 1989

The Children Act 1989 came into force on 14 October 1991. It is one of the most important reforms of the law concerning children over the last century. It made the law simpler and easier to use. It brought together the legislation concerning the care and upbringing of children in both private law, which applied to children affected by a private dispute such as divorce proceedings, and public law, which covered children who are in need of help from a local authority.

The five principles underpinning the Act were as follows.

* At all times, the *welfare of the child* must be the paramount consideration.

* A new concept of *parental responsibility* was introduced.

* The '*no order*' principle was introduced, whereby courts are instructed not to make statutory orders unless they are satisfied that the only way to safeguard the first principle (welfare of the child) is to make such an order.

* The '*no delay*' principle was introduced – where children are involved in cases before the court, the court must set a timetable and ensure that the case is heard as quickly as possible.

* The principles of '*corporate responsibility*' and '*partnership*' were introduced.

These principles have remained valid in the 2004 Act.

The Children Act 2004

Built on the principals of the 1989 Act, and following the Children Bill, the 2004 Act is part of a wider reform programme of change set out in the Green Paper 'Every Child Matters' – discussed further on page 81 and in section four of this unit.

The Children Bill finished its passage through Parliament and received Royal Assent on 15 November 2004, from when it became known as the Children Act 2004.

The Act amends sections 17, 20 and 47 of the former Children Act and includes a new framework of duties and accountabilities to develop high-quality services, including:

* closer joint working between various agencies involved with children

* wishes of the children to be taken into account

* greater sharing of information between professionals through databases

* limits on the use of reasonable chastisement

* a Children's Commissioner for England

* better information sharing between practitioners

* Local Safeguarding Children Boards (LSCBs), of which there are 150

* groups to review unexpected child deaths in their area

* improved local accountability (through a local Director of Children's Services and a lead council member for children's services)

* a duty on local authorities to promote the educational achievement of looked-after children.

> **Think it over...**
>
> With a partner, research the new 2004 Children Act and make a list of at least **four** ways in which it helps to meet the needs of children more effectively than the 1989 Act.
>
> You might want to use the current Children Act Report to aid your research. This can be found at www.dfes.gov.uk.

Who has parental responsibility?

All mothers automatically have parental responsibility for their children. The 2004 Act made changes to the 1989 Act which had said that all *married* fathers had parental responsibility, by giving parental responsibility to all fathers who had been named on the child's birth certificate – this was a significant change. In cases of divorced or separated married parents, both parents, regardless of who the child lives with, retain parental responsibility.

Parental responsibility is very rarely lost, except on adoption. Even where a care order is made, parental responsibility is retained, although the local authority may limit the extent to which that responsibility is exercised.

Parental responsibility covers both rights and duties. It includes the following rights:

* to give consent to medical treatment
* to determine the child's religion
* to choose the child's surname
* to apply discipline
* to give consent to marriage from the age of 16 to 18
* to give consent before their child can be adopted
* to appoint a guardian in the event of the death of the other parent.

It also includes the following duties:

* to look after children in a way which is not cruel or deliberately neglectful, and does not expose children to the risk of significant harm
* to provide maintenance
* to ensure that children of five and over receive full-time education.

Every Child Matters

On 8 September 2003, the government launched the long-awaited Green Paper 'Every Child Matters' (Department for Education and Skills, 2003). Improved information sharing across agencies had been called for as result of the 2003 inquiry into the death of Victoria Climbie in 2000. Victoria's tragic death highlighted the need for more effective communication and information sharing.

The Green Paper listed five key outcomes for children:

1 **being healthy** – enjoying a healthy lifestyle – good physical and mental health

2 **staying safe** – to be protected from neglect and harm

3 **enjoying and achieving** – to get the most out of life – to gain the skills needed for a productive adulthood

4 **making a positive contribution** – to not become engaged in anti-social behaviour but to make a positive contribution to the community and society

5 **economic well-being** – to not be held back by socio-economic difficulties.

Chapter 2 of the Green Paper confirmed the government's commitment to:

* ensure children are safe from bullying and homelessness
* the Sure Start project
* tackling child poverty
* raising school standards
* improving children's access to health services
* more investment in the youth service.

There will be further reference to the Green Paper later in this unit, in section four.

Framework for Assessment of Need 2000

The *Framework for the Assessment of Children in Need and their Families* (DoH, The Stationery Office 2000) is a common framework to be used by all professionals when an initial assessment establishes there are child protection issues. In the majority of cases, Social Services will take the lead in carrying out the assessments. The framework lays out the roles and responsibilities of all the agencies involved, providing a common approach to assessment that everyone can understand when collecting information about the family. It also provides guidance on how education and day care services might contribute to an assessment.

CASE STUDY

Alicia is four years old and attends nursery. She has lived in England with her mother for three years and they are refugees. Alicia and her mother have moved around the country a great deal and have never stayed anywhere longer than six months. Alicia's mother is being supported by a social worker from the local health authority and takes Alicia to the hospital for regular appointments because she has severe eczema. Recently practitioners at the nursery have become concerned because Alicia asks them if they can change her bandages and put her cream on – her bandages are often dirty and smelly and she is continually scratching. When staff approach her mother, she does not appear to appreciate the importance of the situation. She says that the hospital social worker is dealing with that.

- After having looked at the various legislation working for the protection of children, consider which, if any, of the pieces of legislation could be put into effect here.

The process for carrying out an assessment is as follows.

❋ Look at the referral to clarify if there is concern.

❋ Gather information.

❋ Look at all the facts and the feelings of the child and family involved – ask their opinions.

❋ Gain an understanding of what is happening within the family.

❋ Come to a conclusion about the needs of the family and the parenting capacity.

The framework is based on three domains and is called the *assessment triangle*:

❋ **Child's development needs** – their relationships, identity, emotional and behavioural development, health and education, social presentation

❋ **Family and environmental needs** – income, employment, family history and functioning, wider family, community, housing

❋ **Parenting capacity** – basic care, emotional warmth, stability, ensuring safety, guidance and boundaries, stimulation.

The assessment will look at all these three domains in detail in order to make the assessment and gain a greater understanding of what is happening within the family (see also page 101).

Think it over...

With a partner, discuss possible ways in which an early years practitioner might be able to contribute to the assessment process. Using the three domains, make separate lists of ideas for each.

Supporting children who disclose

In this section we will be considering how to deal with and support a child who may disclose they have been abused. When a child tells you that they are being abused or have been abused, this is known as disclosure. There are two ways in which a child may disclose – directly and indirectly.

It is important that all practitioners are aware of the policy of their setting should this arise. Some of the guidance may change in line with the most recent legislation, so you should ensure it is kept up to date. How a child is dealt with should this happen is crucial as the practitioner will have no advance warning and may be caught off guard. On the rare occasion a child does directly disclose the practitioner may be alone with the child. In these circumstances the practitioner is also vulnerable and must follow correct procedures.

The practitioner must also be aware of the boundaries of confidentiality. Although all practitioners and student workers are bound by confidentiality in all aspects of their work, disclosure or concern for a child is the only occasion when there may be a need to divulge information. This is, of course, to protect the child and ensure that their needs are paramount. If there are concerns or a disclosure, direct or indirect, the practitioner is bound to report whatever information is needed, in line with the policies of the setting.

Direct disclosure

We need to be aware that direct disclosure rarely happens in the majority of early years settings. In a direct disclosure situation you must ensure that you give the child your full attention. The child obviously feels they can trust you and you must not betray this trust. You may feel shocked by what the child tells you, but you must remain calm and not allow your own feelings to show, as this may affect what information the child then shares. Above all, you must ensure that you show the child that you believe him or her and demonstrate unconditional acceptance of everything disclosed. It is vital that the child feels believed and can trust you not to question or suggest it is in any way the fault of the child. Below is a list of do's and don'ts when dealing with disclosure and responding to the child.

Once the child has divulged this information it is your responsibility to record what has been said as soon as you can after the event, and report it to your supervisor or line manager. When recording the event it is important to give a factual account stating what the child said as clearly as you can remember. Do not make assumptions about the child's feelings or about the truth of what the child has told you. The good practice guidelines for observations and reporting should be followed. It is also important that you tell the child that he or she can come back and discuss it further if he or she wishes.

Indirect disclosure

Indirect disclosure is when a child identifies abuse through play and is more often the way a child demonstrates pain about being abused. For example, children might demonstrate knowledge of abuse while playing in the home corner, using sexually explicit language or acting out an abusive situation. Children might make comments during a painting activity, or present paintings that reflect images or ideas that cause you concern. When and if this happens, you must record the conversation or observation and present it to your line manager or designated child protection person, in line with your setting's policy.

DO	DON'T
Listen to the child calmly.	Make promises that you cannot keep, such as keeping 'secrets'.
Tell the child he or she was right to tell you.	Ask the child lots of questions – investigation of the alleged abuse will be undertaken by a trained social worker.
Believe the child.	
Tell the child that what has happened is not his or her fault or responsibility.	Cast doubt on what the child tells you – it has taken a great deal of courage to tell you.
Acknowledge that the child has been brave to tell you.	Say anything which may make the child feel responsible for the abuse, such as 'Why haven't you told anyone before?'
Reassure the child, telling him or her that the situation is not unique.	Communicate feelings of anger.
Be honest about your own position, who you will have to tell and why.	Ask leading questions, such as 'Was it your mummy that hurt you?'
Keep the child fully informed about what you are doing and what is happening at every stage.	Panic. When confronted with the reality of abuse there is often a feeling of needing to 'act immediately'. Action taken too hastily can be counter-productive.
Give the child information about other confidential sources of help, like Childline.	

One of the children in your nursery has been causing you concern. You have noticed that whenever she is playing alone in the role play area she appears to be 'playing out' acts of violence using the dolls. She also uses an aggressive tone and swears quite a lot. You are also concerned that during a cooking activity she becomes very frustrated with another child and shouts at the child, 'I will burn you in the oven.'

In a small group, discuss this scenario and decide:

- whether you should tell anyone your concerns and if so, who
- how you would record these incidents in line with your setting's procedures and policy
- whether you should discuss it with the child's parents

(You may want to look at the next section, 'Reporting concerns', and use copies of your setting's policies.)

Why children do not disclose

You can understand children's reluctance to talk about their abuse if you consider the following.

* Very young children may not have the language skills to tell you.
* The abusing adult may threaten the child physically or emotionally to keep the secret.

Children may often feel it is their fault.

* Some children may think it is normal, if they have never experienced anything else.
* Children may be afraid that adults will not believe them.
* Children may feel that it is their fault.
* Some children may emotionally separate home from the outside world, expecting that both are different – some children will isolate the traumatic feelings so that they can enjoy their time in the setting. This is of course far more difficult to identify.

CASE STUDY

One case of child abuse was that of a health visitor who was neglecting and emotionally abusing her children. A friend had reported concerns about her ability to cope since having her second child. The social worker visited her home on two occasions – the downstairs of her house was extremely clean and tidy, with no visible signs of her two children (aged two and three) living there, such as their toys. The children came downstairs to talk to the adults and were told to go upstairs and play after a few minutes. She became anxious when asked if the social worker could use the bathroom and directed her to a downstairs bathroom.

Some months later Social Services were called in – they found the children living in appalling conditions on the top floor of the house. It was unsanitary and the children were sleeping on urine-drenched mattresses. The children showed visible signs of neglect on examination.

- Discuss this case study in your group.
- What would be your first reaction to this case study – would you be less likely to question the possibility of neglect of these children? If so, why? Examine your reasons – you may want to debate these in a larger group.

Potential impact of disclosure on the child and the family

Disclosure may result in:

* the provision of services to support the family and enable the child to remain at home

* the abusing parent being asked to leave the family home

* the child being removed to a place of safety

* break-up of the family structure.

If the abuser comes from outside the direct family circle, such as an uncle or babysitter, additional pressures relating to the wider community will be apparent.

Any of these situations will make the family feel very threatened. Parents may be angry because the setting has raised concerns. The initial shock may be hard to take in and promote a feeling of disbelief. The shock is quickly followed by anger. This anger may be directed at the setting, the child or the partner.

There may often be feelings of guilt, as the non-abusing parent worries about his or her inability to protect the child and the abusing parent may feel guilty about what he or she has done. The abusing parent, however, may feel that the complaint is unjustified: 'I was only disciplining the child'. There will also be a feeling of shame and embarrassment that the situation may become public. The child will also experience feelings of guilt and feel responsible for the family situation. This is particularly relevant if the abusing parent has issued threats about secrecy during the abuse.

Reporting concerns

As a practitioner you are required firstly to follow the policies of the setting. Therefore it is vital that you know and understand your setting's policy. (There is an example of a child protection policy on page 92.) You will also need to refer to the child protection procedures produced by the Area Child Protection Committee (ACPC). This is a multi-agency body in every local authority which has responsibility for producing a child protection procedure in line with the *Working Together to Safeguard Children* document. There should be a copy of the ACPC procedure in every setting for staff to refer to.

Reporting within the setting

As a practitioner or student, your first priority in relation to any suspicions of abuse is to talk to your line manager or supervisor. The procedures for reporting abuse will be described in the setting's child protection policy and will usually include the following details.

* Staff should be aware of the signs of abuse.

* All incidents and concerns should be recorded in the incident book.

* If appropriate, additional observations may be carried out to gather supporting evidence.

* Confidential discussions may be held with some other staff.

* Concerns may be discussed with the parents.

The decision to refer a cause for concern to the appropriate body (this could be social services or the local child protection team) needs to be objective and with the best interests of the child in mind.

Record keeping

Early years settings all have their own procedures for recording issues relating to child protection. Any suspicions of abuse or instances of disclosure will be recorded in the accident report book (see page 195).

Staff who are working directly with a family in relation to issues of concern maintain a contact sheet which provides details of all contact with the family.

While record keeping is an important aspect of the care and education of all children, recording issues relating to child protection has particular importance. Any decisions that are made for a family may rely on the evidence gathered within the child's individual record. For this reason it is important that all recording is:

* completed as soon after the incident as possible

* factual

* relevant

* detailed

* clearly written

* free from opinion.

Gathering information

When reporting information relating to individual children, it is important to distinguish between directly observed evidence and evidence that someone else has told you. Second-hand stories may not actually be true, or they may have someone else's interpretation, which could be misleading. For example, the statement from a concerned neighbour that, 'It's a terrible house, the children are screaming all night,' may simply mean that there is a new baby in the house who cries all evening, or it may mean that children are being abused. As an early years practitioner you need to be able to identify relevant information that is directly observed, factual and relevant.

Confidentiality and security of records

In early years settings, children's records are always shared with the parents. However, when a family is receiving specific support in relation to issues of child protection, there will be an additional section within a child's file for the storage of confidential records, which will be clearly marked as confidential.

While records relating to child protection may be available to the parents, only the manager or key worker would access these records – they would not automatically be available for all members of staff. The diagram below provides guidelines for the storage of records.

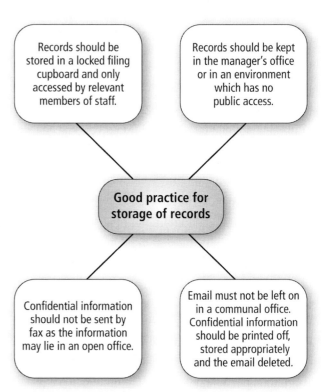

Records should be stored in a locked filing cupboard and only accessed by relevant members of staff.

Records should be kept in the manager's office or in an environment which has no public access.

Good practice for storage of records

Confidential information should not be sent by fax as the information may lie in an open office.

Email must not be left on in a communal office. Confidential information should be printed off, stored appropriately and the email deleted.

After the referral

Once a referral has been made, the child protection team will consider the level of risk and then decide whether any further action is needed. They will then carry out an investigation. If necessary, a child protection enquiry, under section 47 of the Children Act, will be instigated. Details of these procedures can be found in *What to do if You're Worried a Child is Being Abused* (DoH, 2003).

Part V of the Children Act 2004 contains all the relevant orders for protecting children. It is these

CASE STUDY

Saheera is four years old and has been at the nursery for a year now. When she began nursery, staff found her shy and a little withdrawn but, in the last few months, she had begun to take part in activities more and communicate more confidently with her key worker, Mita. Her mother was managing her and her baby brother alone until about three months ago, when a new partner moved in with them. Saheera's mother told staff about him and seemed very happy. Almost right away her new partner, Michael, began picking the children up from nursery and discussing their progress with staff. Michael was very likeable and friendly and always made the staff laugh – sometimes joking about his new role as a father. After about six weeks, Saheera became more withdrawn and participated less in activities. She didn't want to talk about home at all, even to her key worker. When her mother dropped her off in the morning Saheera begged her to come back and collect her. She had been overheard saying to her mother that she didn't want 'nasty Michael' to come and collect her. Saheera became more easily upset and, when asked why she didn't want to join in activities, she would say, 'I can't do it... I'm stupid... I will make a mess.'

In a group, discuss what action you would take as a team.

- Would you talk to the mother?
- Would you ask Saheera questions?
- Would you have cause for concern?
- Which procedures would you consider?
- What would you do to monitor the situation?

that local authorities or the NSPCC will apply to the courts for in order to safeguard children who are deemed to be at risk.

* **Child Assessment Order** – a child is removed for an assessment of their physical or mental condition. Lasts for seven days.

* **Emergency Protection Order** – gives the power to remove a child to a place of safety. Lasts for eight days and can be extended for a further seven days.

* **Care Order** – the child is placed in the care of the local authority. Lasts until the child is eighteen. Parental responsibility is shared between the parent and the local authority.

* **Police Protection Order** – gives the police the power to remove children to a place of safety. Lasts for 72 hours.

* **Supervision Order** – the child is placed under the supervision of the local authority, which does not have parental responsibility.

If further action is taken, the assessment process will begin. The *Framework for Assessment of Children in Need and their Families* (DoH, 2000) underpins this process of assessing the needs of the child.

A case conference will be held and information about the child will be shared at this point, so that decisions can be made to ensure the child's safety and well-being. Families are asked to attend the conference and occasionally the designated child protection coordinator from the setting, if it is felt necessary. It is at this point that records from the setting may be used to help create a holistic picture of the child's development and behaviour.

Think it over...

Using the document *What to do if You're Worried a Child is Being Abused* (DoH, 2003), investigate what happens after an initial referral of concern. Find out what is meant by:
- significant harm
- a core assessment
- the child protection plan.

Present your findings to your group.

You may also want to refer to the *Framework for Assessment of Children in Need and their Families* (DoH, 2000).

Both of these documents can be found at The Stationery Office.

The role of the key worker

Following the introduction of the Early Years Curriculum, the concept of key workers is now firmly established within early years care and education settings. However, settings that provide for children's care have been operating key worker systems for many years. Advantages of a key worker system are as follows.

* The key worker becomes a familiar figure for the child.
* The parent has one specific individual to communicate with.
* The key worker can build up a meaningful relationship with the family.
* The key worker can monitor and record progress and details of the child's care.
* Greater knowledge of the family situation will make the key worker more responsive to individual needs.
* When representing the family at meetings with other professionals the close relationship and knowledge of the individual family is an asset.
* It provides consistency of care which is of particular advantage for a child who is experiencing a traumatic period in their life.

Dealing with inconsistent care

As a key worker, you will work with many different families, and you need to be aware of different cultures and social status within our society and ensure you are not judgemental in any way. It is essential that key workers are not critical of parenting styles, just because they do not view them as the 'norm'. For example, if a child is allowed to stay up in the evenings until the parents go to bed it may be a concern in terms of how much sleep the child is getting, but it may be necessary to consider the additional adult attention the child may gain during this period. Families under stress may be able to take some advice about new strategies of coping with their children. However, when they are distracted by other problems or start to feel that the strategies are not having an immediate effect, they might give up and would then need encouragement to persevere.

3 The range of strategies to support children and their families

In this section we will be considering:

* how to teach children self-protection and empower them
* good practice in early years settings
* support for children who disclose
* alleviating the effects of abuse
* alternative forms of care
* encouraging the development of parenting skills.

How to teach children self-protection and empower them

Teaching children self-protection

The most important aspect of self-protection is the promotion of children's confidence and self-esteem. However, there are many other ways in which early years practitioners can empower children to protect themselves. Giving them information, promoting awareness and encouraging coping skills can all help achieve this.

You can teach children:

* the difference between good and bad touches
* to say 'No!' to adults they know, as well as to strangers
* the difference between good and bad 'secrets'
* that their body belongs to them
* that they have a right to privacy
* ways of coping with bullying
* how to get help.

The following table identifies specific strategies that can be introduced to enable children to protect themselves. It is important to remember that children should not be made to feel totally responsible for their own protection as, in reality, the adults who care for them are ultimately responsible.

CONCEPT	STRATEGIES
Good and bad touches Children should be able to identify good and bad touches – touches that hurt, are rude or make them feel uncomfortable are not acceptable.	Promote through appropriate daily physical care routines. Support children who say 'No' to tickling games, hugs or kisses. For older children, discussions such as 'I like hugs from... I would not like a hug from...'
To say 'No!' to adults they know as well as to strangers While it is important to promote the concept of 'stranger danger', more children are at risk from adults that they know well.	Role play. Books and videos, e.g. NSPCC 'Emily and the Stranger' or Rolf Harris 'Say No' video. Visits from a police officer. Discussion about people you trust.
Good and bad secrets You can provide opportunities for children to discuss good and bad secrets.	Discussion about good and bad secrets. No-one should ever ask children to keep a hug, touch or smack secret. 'Don't tell Mummy what we have bought for her birthday.' = good secret 'Don't tell Mummy that I hit you.' = bad secret
That their body belongs to them Children should be encouraged to know that their body belongs to them and that they have control over what happens to it.	Young children can be helped by learning body vocabulary. Songs such as 'Head, shoulders, knees and toes...' Books such as *My First Body Book* (Early Learning Centre). Appropriate physical care routines. Draw a picture of a body and discuss which parts of the body are the 'private' parts. Body 'beetle game'.
That they have the right to privacy Children have the right to their own privacy.	Physical care routines.
Getting help There are some situations where children can help themselves by getting help.	Children should be taught their address and phone number, in case they get lost. Learning about which adults they can go to for help, e.g. the police, the person at the shop till, a lollipop lady, a mother with a pram or school teacher. Visits from a police officer. Shouting 'No!'

Make a game and plan an activity for children to develop body awareness. Include the following.

- Provide a rationale for the activity.
- Identify some of the language or conversation you may promote.
- What will the children gain from taking part in the game?

Remember to ensure that your communication with children is age appropriate. Your experience of working with children will be your guide.

- Use age-appropriate language.

- Check vocabulary and ensure that the child understands.
- Use pictures or drawings with younger children.
- Communicate at the child's pace; do not force the subject.
- Play therapists may use anatomically correct dolls to promote conversation.
- Do not lead the child.
- Employ effective listening.
- Work at the child's level; ensure good eye contact.

Empowering children to protect their rights

In protecting children, we need to ensure that we *advocate* for them, if they cannot do so for themselves. To advocate is to work on someone's behalf – to speak for or to support someone. In supporting the child, we need to be aware of the rights of the parents so that we do not challenge their parental responsibilities. Parents' 'rights' was changed to 'responsibilities' under the Children Act 1989 and the new concept of 'parental responsibility' was added (see page 81 for definition). This

means that, since children are no longer seen as possessions of their parents, parents no longer have 'absolute rights' for their children. The parents never lose parental responsibility, unless the child is adopted or when the child is taken into care on a care order (when parental responsibility is 'shared').

Children's rights have become increasingly important and grown from the Children Act 1989, the United Nations Convention on the Rights of the Child and, more recently, the Children Act of 2004. The table below shows some of the European and national rights of children.

CHILDREN ACT 2004	UNITED NATIONS CONVENTION ON THE RIGHTS OF THE CHILD
Wishes and feelings of child must be taken into consideration	Right to non-discrimination
	Right to have best interests as a primary consideration
Right to be brought up within own families wherever possible	Right to an identity
	Rights when separated from parents
Right to decline medical treatment (Gillick v West Norfolk Health Authority)	Right to express views and opinions
	Right to freedom of thought, conscience and religion
Right to adequate/appropriate services	Right to protection from abuse and neglect
	Rights of disabled children
	Rights to an adequate standard of living
	Right to an education
	Rights of children from minority ethnic communities

Good practice in early years settings

Good practice within any early years setting involves working as part of a team, both within the setting and in respect of other professionals. This section enables you to explore specific issues of good practice related to protecting children. We will consider:

* what a child protection policy is

* guidelines and support for staff

* visiting and access rights.

What is a child protection policy?

All early years settings must have a number of policies which outline procedures that workers must follow in particular situations, such as health and safety or anti-bullying. They must also have a child protection policy which contains information about what to do if staff suspect that a child in their care is being abused or neglected. These procedures should be written in a format that is easy to read for early years workers, volunteers and parents. It is important that they are reviewed regularly, keeping abreast of any local and national changes in policy and law.

Standard 13 of the *National Standards for Under Eights Day Care and Childminding – Full Day Care* states:

'The registered person has a written statement based on the ACPC procedures clearly stating staff responsibilities with regard to reporting of suspected child abuse or neglect, including contact names and telephone numbers. It also includes procedures to be followed in the event of an allegation being made against a member of staff or volunteer.'

The standards also state that there must be a designated member of staff who is responsible for liaison with child protection agencies in any child protection situation. The guidance to the *National Standards – Full Day Care* provides the following advice to help settings prepare their child protection policy:

* their commitment to the protection of children

* the responsibilities of all staff in child protection matters

* the steps to be taken when a concern is raised

* the name of the designated member of staff for child protection liaison and this person's role and responsibilities

* how and under what circumstances parents will be informed about concerns and any actions taken, and how confidentiality will be managed.

The guidance in relation to allegations made against a member of staff could include:

* the action to be taken with regard to the member of staff

* who should be informed

* how any investigation will be conducted and by whom

* how confidentiality will be managed.

Settings will also include statements about training opportunities, and the need to share the policy with all parents. An example of a child protection policy is shown on page 92. It is also necessary to have separate policies for:

* behaviour

* reporting concerns

* accidents

* observation of children.

Child Protection Policy

Happy Days Nursery aims to provide an environment where children are safe from abuse and where any suspicion of abuse is promptly and appropriately responded to. In order to achieve this we will do the following:

- We will ensure that all staff have police clearance prior to the onset of employment.
- We will require at least one reference, which will always be followed up. Doubts regarding previous employment or gaps in employment will need to be clearly explained.
- We will require all appointments to be subject to a probationary period.
- We will ensure that all staff are trained in the identification of signs and symptoms of possible abuse.
- We will be vigilant when undertaking everyday routines, to allow for observation of the children.
- We will refer any suspicions to the manager, who will then take the decision as to whether further investigation is needed.
- We will ensure that all matters in relation to any child protection issue are treated according to the Confidentiality Policy of the setting.
- We will ensure that all parents are made aware of the Child Protection Policy when their children first enter the nursery.
- We will ensure that parents are informed of any changes noticed in the behaviour or appearance of their child.
- We will contact Social Services or the NSPCC, at the discretion of the manager.
- We will recognise the expertise of professional statutory and voluntary organisations and will endeavour to work closely with them, should the need arise.
- We will comply with the local ACPC procedures. The file is kept in the manager's office and can be examined at any time.
- Allegations of abuse against staff members/volunteers will be investigated immediately and relevant staff members will be suspended from their posts until investigations are complete. The manager will inform the Area Child Protection Team, who will undertake the necessary investigations. Persons found to be guilty of abuse of any nature will be referred to the appropriate agency. Support will be given to staff who may be the subject of wrongful allegations.

Child Protection Officer – The Manager

Guidelines for staff

As an essential part of good practice, all settings will have policies and procedures that are set down in line with local authority guidelines – we have already mentioned some of these in considering what to do if a child should disclose abuse or if staff at the setting should have concerns about a child. All staff employed to work with children will have a 'police check' (CRB – Criminal Records Bureau) in line with the legal requirements for working with children. They will have also had an induction and regular staff training to ensure that they are up-to-date with current legal requirements and ways of working.

Support for staff

As a member of staff, it can be very distressing dealing with disclosure of abuse from a child or listening to details of an abusive situation, especially as you will know the child and family involved. You might find it particularly difficult if you have been abused in the past. In this situation it is vital that you discuss your concerns with your line manager and ask for support. This distress may not occur initially, as you will be concerned with the needs of the child and it often becomes a reality some time later. It may be possible to consider one of the following solutions.

* Discuss with your GP and ask advice about local counselling services – some sessions should be available on the NHS.

* Talk to the Social Services contact, as they have opportunities for supervision within their job role and may be able to offer advice and guidance.

It is important not to neglect these concerns, as you will need to remain professional when dealing with the child and family and cannot do so if you are upset and unable to remain objective.

Protecting staff from allegations of abuse

You need to be aware that you are also accountable for your actions and therefore vulnerable. You will need to protect yourself from possible accusations of abuse by:

* following the procedures of the setting

* seeking advice before speaking to parents or implementing a strategy with a child

* remaining professional at all times – it is all too easy to become involved with a child and family, particularly if they are experiencing difficulties, but you need to remain objective

PROMOTING GOOD PRACTICE	EXAMPLES OF PRACTICAL EXPERIENCES
Appropriate physical care enables children to have respect for their body and to learn about the personal control they should have over their own body and what their personal boundaries are.	Providing privacy during toileting. Respecting privacy when dressing. Encouraging independence in physical care routines, such as bathing, feeding, toileting. Promoting discrete behaviour, such as not pulling your trousers down in public. Drawing activities where children can discuss: • who has the right to touch their body, e.g. doctors • what parts of the body should not be touched by others, e.g. areas covered by swimwear.
Appropriate physical care enables children to learn about their body.	Younger children learn body-part vocabulary. Age-appropriate discussion about bodily functions.
Appropriate physical care gives young children the opportunity for individual attention and appropriate affectionate touch, which will enable them to recognise inappropriate touches.	The cuddles a baby receives during nappy changing. The physical touch during dressing activities. The appropriate bed-time routine with bathing, story and cuddle.
Appropriate physical care enables children to develop good self-image and self-esteem.	Demonstrating respect during physical care activities, explaining to the child what you are doing – 'We are going to take your socks off now,' rather than just pulling the socks off. Positive comments during dressing activities can promote self-image.
Appropriate physical care demonstrates how adults should behave towards children.	Appropriate support for toileting and bathing.

and keep colleagues informed in line with the policies of the setting

* never making inappropriate promises to a child or a parent – never agree to keep a secret or not divulge particular information

* being aware of confidentiality.

Affection

All children need physical demonstrations of affection. They need to experience appropriate touches during respectful contact. If they do not have experience of appropriate affection, they will not be able to judge what is inappropriate. Similarly, children with limited experience of physical affection may be so desperate for affection that they accept inappropriate advances from adults. For this reason, it is important to role model appropriate expressions of affection.

All children are different and all families have different ways of demonstrating affection. It is wrong to demand expressions of affection, such as sitting on your knee or being kissed, if the child does not offer them spontaneously. Some children who crave affection may approach any new adult in the setting with overt physical attention. They may want to hold your hand, sit on your knee and always be physically close. For many new students in placement this message can be misunderstood and it is important that, in this situation, you do not promote unnecessary physical contact and that you maintain a professional approach to all children.

Visiting and access rights

In every setting practitioners are responsible for the children in their care. This includes access to the children during the session times and what happens at the end of the session – 'going home time'. As part of the records kept on each child, there will be written clarification from the parent as to who is allowed to collect the child from the setting. A record of who is allowed to collect the child will be kept in the register. Should there be any changes to this, the setting will need to ensure that parents are aware of how to inform the staff of these changes. If a different adult should come to collect the child, members of staff would not be allowed to let the child go with the adult unless a prior arrangement was made with the parent. This is when good communication is essential.

During the sessions, the building needs to be secure. In some settings this can be in the form of an intercom or a reception area where visitors are met by a member of staff and not allowed to wander in to rooms occupied by the children. It is also necessary to ask all visitors to sign the visitors book, not only to protect the children but also for their own safety. Outside areas must also be secure, with locked gates permitting no access from outside, but easy exit should there be a fire or emergency.

Think it over...

Read the following descriptions of children being welcomed into a nursery.

* Zareena arrives at nursery with her grandmother. Zareena's grandmother does not speak English. Kate (her key worker) bends down to talk to Zareena and asks her if she has enjoyed the weekend. She takes her hand and walks in to the nursery. As she does so, she turns and quickly says, 'Say goodbye to Grandma Zareena.'

* Mark is a newly qualified practitioner. While the children are arriving, he keeps busy trying not to make eye contact with anyone. Kelly walks up behind him and says, 'My Mummy wants you Mark.' Mark replies, 'Can you ask her to talk to Marcia [the head of room] please, Kelly. I am a little bit busy now.'

* Brandon is not cooperating with his mother as she tries to change his shoes in the crowded hallway. His mother is looking a little anxious, as some of the other mothers are staring. Louise (the practitioner) walks over to them and smiles at Brandon's mother. She says, 'Hello Brandon, how are you today? Have you told your mummy about the model you made yesterday? If you want we can show it to mummy. Do you want to change your shoes and we can go through together?'

Look at each of these examples and identify areas of good and bad practice in communicating with the families. Give reasons for your choices.

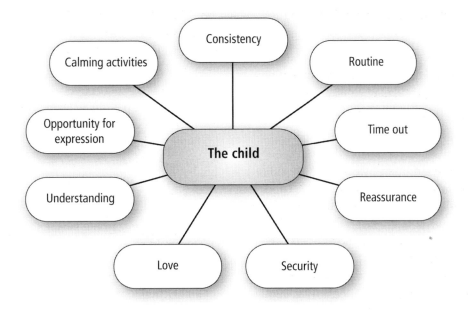

The child needs to be surrounded with security in order to feel safe and accepted.

Support for children who disclose

It is essential that a child who has disclosed abuse is *unconditionally accepted* and never made to feel as if they are to blame. It is at this time that the child is most vulnerable and they will need the following:

Impact on the family

An allegation of abuse within a family will have a devastating effect. Many parents will feel intimidated and embarrassed. Alternatively they may be hostile and angry. They will need support in the following ways.

* Focus precisely on the desired outcomes – this involves creating a specific action plan with specific outcomes, and may be implemented with the support of other professionals.

* Support them to do what is best for the child and ensure the child is the focus.

* It is easier to be responsive to parents' needs if you show some empathy for their difficulties.

* Provide opportunities for parents to talk.

* Keep parents informed.

All human interactions involve communication, and many difficulties or conflicts may arise from failure to communicate effectively. Situations relating to abuse and the challenging of a parent's basic care of a child are very sensitive and, as such, require particularly sophisticated communication skills. For this reason, much of the direct work with children and families who are in abusive situations may be undertaken by other professionals. However, it is important that you develop an understanding of essential communication skills. Much of this communication may be non-verbal, requiring careful observation to accurately interpret the messages being sent, especially emotions or feelings for example, through facial expression, gestures, body posture, lack of eye contact or tone of voice.

Good communication firstly involves establishing and maintaining a good working relationship with the child and parent.

Recognising diversity

Here are some issues to consider with regard to child protection.

* Don't assume that parents from a particular background are more or less likely to abuse their children.

* Ensure that children and parents for whom

English is an additional language use their preferred interpreter and access all the information they may need.

* Promote anti-discriminatory practice with the children. Challenge inappropriate behaviour.

It is important when responding to disclosure of abuse that the practitioner does not make assumptions about the family's situation based on culture, racial background or gender. Very often we make assumptions based on what we think we know about a certain group in society or race of people. For example, we may assume that parents using physical punishment such as smacking are abusive, whereas many families consider this to be a fair discipline. We may assume that it is more natural for a man to be strict and less affectionate towards their children, or we may decide he is a particularly 'good dad' if he spends time playing with his child.

In the case of Victoria Climbie, assumptions were made about Caribbean methods of discipline, suggesting that they were more authoritarian, and some of these assumptions led to Victoria being ignored by the authorities. While it is important to respect all parents and their styles of parenting, it is necessary to look deeper and think first before making an assumption. There may be times when a form of punishment considered reasonable by a certain culture is considered unreasonable in Britain, and those parents may need support in recognising this. In such a case, it is important that the practitioner seeks advice from other professionals involved and actively challenges other team members who may make judgmental comments about the family.

Alleviating the effects of abuse

Once a child has disclosed abuse, or you have observed indicators of abuse and referred to social services, your work with that child is just beginning. Below is a list of suggestions which may help with the after-effects of abuse.

* Consult other professionals for advice.
* Help the child to build trusting relationships – this could be achieved through a one-to-one relationship with a key worker.

* Remain consistent and allow times for rest and quiet periods.
* Always be willing to listen to the child should he or she wish to talk further about the abuse, but do not question the child.
* Meet the child's individual needs. Remember that many children who have been abused display challenging behaviour and may need specialist help with this.
* Children may need support with language skills to express themselves.
* Provide appropriate play experiences to allow the child to explore feelings and promote self-image and self-esteem.

Play experiences

Children may be referred to a play therapist whose role is to help children express trauma or emotions through play. You should **not** undertake play therapy experiences yourself, unless you are working directly with a play therapist. You will, however, be able to offer a range of different play experiences to support all children's emotional and social development. The table opposite identifies some of these.

Creative play can give vent to powerful feelings.

CHILDREN'S NEEDS	PLAY ACTIVITIES
Expressing their feelings	Appropriate books dealing with issues such as bullying, or moving into foster care Dough, clay and malleable materials where children can give vent to powerful feelings Sand, water and messy play activities Happy/sad face drawing activities to allow the children to give words to their feelings Self-portrait activities with sensitive, non-questioning discussion Expressing feeling through music and dance Opportunities to explore feelings through role play activities Controlled noise-making activities, such as banging a drum, shouting out loud, etc. Puppet and doll play, where children can describe feelings
Improving self-image	Body image activities, such as self-portraits, use of mirrors, etc. Dressing up with mirrors and supportive discussion Books and stories, such as 'Little duck and the bad eye glasses' Circle time and discussion about objects from home Create 'A book about me' Inviting parents from different cultural groups to the setting to share cooking or clothing experiences
Building self-esteem	Positive feedback during all interactions Dressing up activities to develop independence skills Providing tasks and responsibilities, such as handing out biscuits, feeding the animals, looking after younger children

Theory into practice

- How do you think a child who has been abused might feel? Make a list of these possible feelings.
- Plan a list of one-to-one activities you might provide for the child and give reasons for your choice.

Alternative forms of care

If, due to child abuse and neglect, a child has to be removed from the family home, he or she will be placed in foster care or in a children's home. Fostering, however, is seen as a good alternative to residential care in that:

* it can provide a family environment
* it can be used for short- or long-term placements
* it avoids children becoming institutionalised
* it enables children who have been abused and, as a result, are possibly experiencing

behavioural problems, the opportunity to experience family life.

If a child is fostered, temporarily, it may also be possible for him or her to remain at the normal setting and have continuity of care.

Residential establishments for children are mainly provided by local authorities. However, voluntary organisations such as Barnardos and the NCH also provide this service. There has also been an increase in privately run children's homes. These establishments consist of small family group homes, community homes and resource and reception centres.

Adoption is seen as another alternative to a child growing up in an abusive situation. This is governed by the Adoption Act 1976 and the Children Act 2004 and is a legal undertaking with all the responsibilities of caring for a natural child. As mentioned previously, with adoption, the birth parents lose parental responsibility, which is automatically given to the adoptive parents once the adoption certificate is processed.

Respite care can also be advantageous for children who have been abused or neglected. Residential care is given to a child for a short period only, giving the parent and child the opportunity for some 'time out'.

Encouraging the development of parenting skills

The majority of parents, even those who abuse their children, do love them very much and want to do the best for them. It is important that you do not judge any parent and, despite any personal feelings you may have about their management of the child, you must treat them with professional respect. We are taught that to promote self-esteem we respond to a child who is behaving inappropriately by saying, 'I do not like what you are doing, but I still love you.' In the same way, we can encourage a parent's self-esteem by acknowledging that, as people and parents, they are valued even though they may not be meeting all their child's needs. If you can initiate good relationships with the parents and work to promote their self-esteem, they will develop confidence in your ability to help and advise them.

Many people learn parenting skills within their own family but some parents, particularly young people and parents who have not experienced parenting themselves, may need help to develop these skills.

There are many ways of helping families to develop parenting skills. Working with parents is important because:

* parenting programmes can work in changing parents' behaviour and increasing their range of skills

* programmes can reduce the proportion of negative parenting

* parenting must be seen in the context of the relationship between the couple and other external stresses.

The following table addresses some of the difficulties experienced by parents and identifies strategies to support them. Many of these activities will be introduced in all early years settings, but some will be used within settings

SKILLS	DIFFICULTIES FACED BY SOME PARENTS	STRATEGIES TO SUPPORT PARENTS
Relating to children	Parents may not have experienced good parenting themselves and do not know how to relate to children. In a stressful family situation, responding to children is a low priority, e.g. mental health, drug-related situations.	Provide positive feedback whenever possible. Encourage parents to work beside you positively (role modelling). Help parents to develop listening skills. Provide opportunities for parents to talk to and share experiences with children. Address any additional difficulties parents may be experiencing, such as accessing financial support.
Informing parents about child care and development	Parents may not see it as a priority to know about their child's development. Parents may feel that the nursery is the expert and will deal with all such matters. Parents may have literacy difficulties themselves and be reluctant that this should be 'found out', or have difficulty accessing information.	Positively reinforce the value of shared care. Exchange information on a daily basis. Have regular parent meetings to discuss children's learning. Have visits from the health visitor or dental hygienist. Display signs and pictures around the setting describing development milestones related to individual activities. Write reports about development in a jargon-free format that is accessible to parents.

SKILLS	DIFFICULTIES FACED BY SOME PARENTS	STRATEGIES TO SUPPORT PARENTS
Developing practical caring skills	Parents may not have experienced the basic caring skills. Parents may be isolated and have no support network and therefore no role models.	Do not challenge the parents' method of working with their child. Suggest that there may also be some other ways of managing the situation. For example, rather than saying a diet of spaghetti hoops is not nourishing, suggest additional things that the child could eat. Demonstrate practical skills, such as nappy changing and bottle and hygiene routines. Involve the parents in cooking activities or meal times. Identify or instigate support networks within the family and the community.
Participating in play and learning	Parents may not have experienced play themselves. Play may not be seen as a priority. Learning may be viewed as the role of the nursery or school. Financial difficulties may limit the provision of play materials or stimulating experiences	Provide opportunities for parents to share play experiences with children in the early years setting. Provide workshop activities where parents can enjoy the play experience and make games or puppets to share with their child at home. Use toy libraries. Provide in-house 'stress-free' courses.
Adapting as children develop	For first children, parents may not know what to expect at different ages and stages, e.g. some parents will continue baby food long after the time the child should be on solid food. Some parents have a need to be needed and are reluctant to allow their children to develop.	Discuss future developments, e.g. preparing for temper tantrums. Talk on a daily basis, preparing the way for additional development. Link the parents into family and community support networks. Run family workshop activities to enable parents to meet other parents and observe the development of different children.
Facilitating change	Accepting the need to change requires an individual to confront the fact that they may not have been doing well enough. This is very threatening.	Parents need all the support they can to accept the need for change and to move forward positively. This relies on them receiving positive feedback and encouragement and the belief that they are valued as parents.

where parents are required to bring their child under a child protection order.

Support for behaviour management

In the latest government guidance we are asked to work together with both parents and other professionals to support families who are in need. This can be facilitated in all settings, not only family centres.

A family may get stuck in a cycle where the child's inappropriate behaviour causes the parent to behave in an inappropriate manner. To ensure change, both children and parents may need help to modify their behaviour. There are many strategies for promoting positive behaviour. These can be reinforced through a variety of shared experiences, as shown in the table on page 100.

ACTIVITY	STRATEGIES TO ENCOURAGE BEHAVIOUR MODIFICATION
Women's group	The process is started by promoting the parents' self-esteem by providing the parents with some quality time where they can experience activities such as aromatherapy, make-up sessions, relaxation or stress management. It is an opportunity to have time for themselves and pamper themselves.
Family workshop	This is an opportunity for staff to work with the whole family, promoting positive behaviour, such as encouraging parents to praise good behaviour, give children lots of attention and encourage the child's self-control. There are opportunities for one-to-one support to help parents reduce the need to smack.
Outings such as shopping	This is a situation where children and parents often behave inappropriately. Staff can demonstrate effective behaviour management, such as giving the child responsibility or using distraction techniques and reinforcing appropriate behaviour.
Residential	This is an opportunity for children and parents to experience new and stimulating activities while staff introduce effective management techniques during normal family activities such as meal times and bed-time routines. Staff reinforce the importance of a consistent approach, of not nagging the child and of firmly reinforcing appropriate behaviour.
Home visit	Staff can visit at meal times to support what may be difficult situations, encouraging the family to sit at the table and to participate in conversation. Parents will be encouraged to set a good example and reward desirable behaviour. They can then encourage play experiences with new and exciting resources from the toy library.

Providing feedback to parents about their parenting

Factors to consider when providing feedback to parents are outlined in the diagram below.

Cultural and social variations

While helping parents with their child's behaviour, it is important to take into account cultural and social factors. What might be viewed as unacceptable in one society may be viewed as the norm in another. We have already seen that standards of acceptable behaviour vary in different families (see

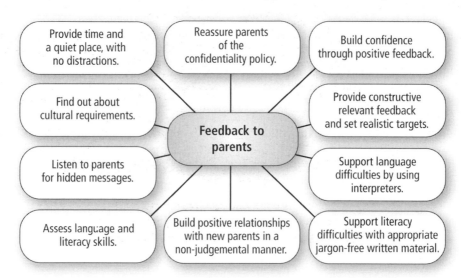

Provide time and a quiet place, with no distractions.

Reassure parents of the confidentiality policy.

Build confidence through positive feedback.

Find out about cultural requirements.

Provide constructive relevant feedback and set realistic targets.

Feedback to parents

Listen to parents for hidden messages.

Support language difficulties by using interpreters.

Assess language and literacy skills.

Build positive relationships with new parents in a non-judgemental manner.

Support literacy difficulties with appropriate jargon-free written material.

pages 95–6) and it may be difficult for children to conform to another expected standard within the early years setting. It is therefore very important to work with parents to achieve a consistent approach to managing behaviour. Communication barriers may also pose a problem when working with parents for whom English is an additional language – therefore a translator should be called upon. The same is said for parents with a hearing impairment, when a signer should be requested.

4 Multi-agency working to protect all children

In this section we will look at:

* how to cooperate with other professionals
* community support networks
* the range of professionals involved.

How to cooperate with other professionals

The *Framework for Assessment of Children in Need and their Families* (DoH, 2000) is used to assess the needs of a child. Early years settings, therefore, can provide key information to aid the process and cooperate with other professionals. They can share information about:

* the child's development
* their relationships with family members
* the child's health
* how the child interacts with others.

Everyday observation and monitoring of a child's progress will enable the setting to have a holistic view of the child. Other professionals may only see the child for short periods of time in a particular set of circumstances.

The triangle model of the framework looks at three aspects:

1 the child's developmental needs
2 parenting capacity
3 family and environmental factors.

Early years settings can share information with other professionals to support the family and in

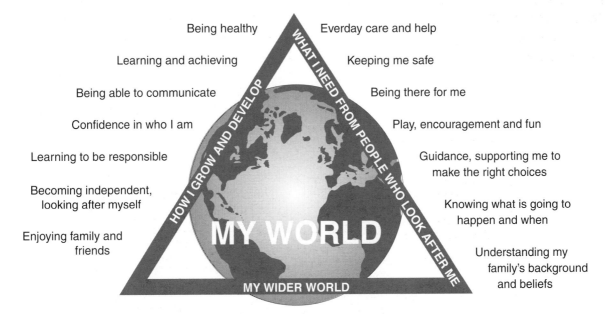

Being healthy

Learning and achieving

Being able to communicate

Confidence in who I am

Learning to be responsible

Becoming independent, looking after myself

Enjoying family and friends

HOW I GROW AND DEVELOP

Everday care and help

Keeping me safe

Being there for me

Play, encouragement and fun

Guidance, supporting me to make the right choices

Knowing what is going to happen and when

Understanding my family's background and beliefs

WHAT I NEED FROM PEOPLE WHO LOOK AFTER ME

MY WORLD

MY WIDER WORLD

Support from family, friends and other people, School, Enough money, Work opportunities for my family, Local resources, Comfortable and safe housing, Belonging

The assessment triangle.

It is essential that professionals work together to support children and their families.

some cases prevent an abusive situation occurring. This is what the Green Paper *Every Child Matters* called for by stating the need for:

✳ a common assessment framework (see above)

✳ improved sharing of information between agencies

✳ a lead professional to be identified when children are involved with several agencies, such as health, social services and voluntary agencies.

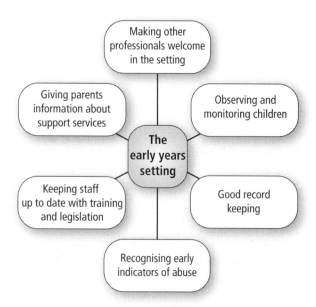

It may not be necessary to allocate specialist services for the child if part of the protection plan can be supported in the early years setting where the child and their parents will have already formed good trusting relationships.

The early years setting can perform a role that supports a multi-disciplinary approach.

In all early years settings it is important to promote a collaborative approach to meeting the needs of a child.

Community support networks

The challenges faced by families who are involved in abusive situations are considerable and cannot always be addressed by one agency. A range of professionals with different skills and expertise will be able to work together to support the family.

Under the Children Act social services have a duty to provide services for children and families in need. The law defines 'in need' in a very broad way. It covers:

✳ children who are not achieving a reasonable standard of health or development

✳ children whose health or development is likely to be damaged

✳ children with disabilities.

The services provided by social services may include:

* advice, guidance and counselling
* access to a family or children's centre
* occupational, social, cultural and leisure activities
* home help
* holiday provision
* day care provision for under-fives and specified activities after school and in the holidays for under-eights
* accommodation for children where the person caring for them has been prevented for any reason from providing accommodation or care, such as hospitalisation.

Voluntary and private organisations also offer services to families who are in need. The NSPCC is a voluntary organisation which has the statutory power to remove children who are deemed to be at risk of significant harm from their homes. The NSPCC has been providing support to families in many communities for many years. Services vary widely based on the needs of the local community.

KEY ISSUES

Visit the NSPCC website and identify the role of the following organisations. Then visit the appropriate websites to identify additional facts about these organisations.
* The Children's Legal Centre
* Deafchild International
* National Association of Child Contact Centres
* Parentline Plus
* The Samaritans
* Women's Aid

Sure Start

Sure Start is a vital part of the government's anti-poverty strategy, aiming to break the cycle of deprivation and give children under the age of four a 'Sure Start' in life. Sure Start is also an example of good inter-agency collaboration. One of the national targets in relation to improving social and emotional development is a 20 per cent

reduction of children re-registered within the space of one year on the Child Protection Register. Sure Start works in certain wards or areas of the country where there are more disadvantaged families. Sure Start has recognised a need for:

* the involvement of parents as well as children
* not labelling families as 'problem families'
* consultation with communities
* culturally appropriate services.

Sure Start has endeavoured to put 'joined-up thinking' into place and target the very youngest children and their families. In these areas it provides:

* free education for three- and four-year-olds
* affordable high-quality childcare
* after-school care and activities
* children's centres.

Children's centres and neighbourhood nurseries

Responsibility for neighbourhood nurseries lies with the Early Years Development and Childcare Partnerships. They work with other services to provide a service for families in their area. Many of these services will be provided under one roof alongside:

* parent groups
* crèche facilities
* language groups
* baby massage
* mother-and-baby support groups
* fathers' groups.

Many of the families will have been referred by a social worker or health visitor.

Children's centres are very often centres of vocational excellence and provide care and education for children from six months to school age. Many offer 'wraparound care' to enable parents to work longer hours. Children attending such a centre will have access to a range of facilities, as the centres work closely with other professionals, usually on the same premises.

Working in a small group, research one of the following voluntary organisations.

- NSPCC
- Barnardos
- Kidscape
- National Children's Homes

Prepare a presentation for the rest of your group. Address the following points, and present your findings.

- The history of the organisation
- The aims and objectives
- The main areas of work
- Funding issues
- Local contacts
- The role of the organisation in offering joint services with local authorities

Now discuss how you would disseminate this information to parents.

The range of professionals involved

The following list demonstrates the roles of some of the professionals who may support families to enable them to stay together and work to prevent problems.

* **Social workers** – many families will have regular contact with a social worker to support them. They are able to request services for the family.

* **Health visitors** – parents will have visits from their health visitor when the children are young. The health visitor may also pay regular visits to the early years setting on an informal basis to see if there are any concerns.

* **Drug and alcohol counsellors** – these may be involved with parents or older siblings.

* **Educational psychologists** – support from an educational psychologist may be short term if there are behaviour or development problems or if a child has been abused.

* **Psychiatrists** – these may be working with family members if there is a mental health issue or if a child has been abused.

* **Family workers** – these are very often attached to a family or children's centre. They may also do some outreach work.

* **Play therapists** – play therapy has been found to be beneficial to children traumatised by abuse.

* **Child protection teams** – these may only have contact in the initial stages of an investigation and assessment of a child. They may ask the setting for information to aid the assessment process.

* **Teachers** – schools can contact and refer for all sorts of concerns, including child protection concerns or individual needs.

* **General Practitioners** – these are often the first port of call for many families and will refer a child or family to the relevant services and also be able to reassure and offer ongoing support to the family, having often secured their trust.

* **Hospital staff** – there are many ways in which families may become involved with hospital staff. This could initially be through the accident and emergency department. Vigilant staff will recognise a concern and offer support. The hospital will also have their own social workers who can be called in to help with things such as long-term illnesses, eczema, and related problems.

* **Religious ministers** – many people will find talking to the minister of their own faith or religion an enormous comfort. Very often a religious minister can be involved with many of the family problems and challenges and will refer them to other services and professionals for support and help. A religious community can often be a source of strength for a family or child in need of support, because they will feel they belong and are able to trust the advice given to them. Also, religious communities offer a good role model for family life and stability in parenting.

END-OF-UNIT TEST

1 Name the four main types of child abuse. Provide a definition of the most common form of abuse. List four indicators of emotional abuse.

2 List four types of family structure.

3 In considering pre-disposing factors related to child abuse, list five factors that may make a parent more likely to abuse a child in his or her care and three factors that may make a child more vulnerable to abuse.

4 List five ways in which your setting can promote good practice with children.

5 Name the five key outcomes listed in the Green Paper 'Every Child Matters'.

6 State the five main principles of the Children Act 1989.

7 List three factors of social disadvantage.

8 Define parental responsibility.

9 Name four things that the United Nations Convention on the Rights of the Child addresses.

10 Which piece of legislation followed the Green Paper?

11 List the techniques you should use when responding to a child's disclosure.

12 Describe the effects on the family following a child's disclosure that the father has been abusing her.

13 Describe two ways in which you could work with a two-year-old to promote self-protection.

14 Which piece of legislation states that an early years setting needs to have a child protection policy? What other guidance on child protection should a setting have?

15 State two ways in which a setting can provide security of records and security of access to the premises.

References and further reading

Brown, A and Finkelhor, D (1986), 'Impact of Child Sexual Abuse: A review of research', *Psychological Bulletin*, vol 99, pp. 66–77

Bruce, T and Meggitt, C (1999), *Childcare and Education* (2nd Edition), London: Hodder and Stoughton

DoH (2003), *What to do if You're Worried a Child is Being Abused*, London: The Stationery Office

Finkelhor, D (1984), *Child Sexual Abuse: New theory and research*, New Jersey: Prentice Hall

Framework for the Assessment of Children in Need and their Families (2000), London: The Stationery Office

Flynn, H & Starns, B (2004), *Protecting Children*, Heinemann

Full Day Care Guidance to the National Standards (2001), DfES

Herbert, M (1996), *Working with Children and the Children Act*, Leicester: BPS Books

Hobbart and Frankel (1998), *Good Practice in Child Protection*, Cheltenham: Nelson Thornes

Horton, C (ed) (2004), *Working with Children 2000–05 Facts, Figures, Information*, Guardian Books, London in association with NCH

Kemp, C et al (1962), 'The Battered Child Syndrome', *Journal of American Medical Association*, vol 181, pp. 17–24

Kempe, R and Kempe, C (1978), *Child Abuse*, London: Fontana

Lindon, J (1998), *Child Protection and Early Years Work*, London: Hodder and Stoughton

National Standards for Under Eights Day Care and Childminding – Full Day Care (2001), DfES

Reder, P et al (1999), *Beyond Blame: Child abuse tragedies revisited*, London: Routledge

Tassoni, P (2003), *Supporting Special Needs*, Heinemann

Tassoni, P and Bulman, K (1999), *Early Years Care and Education NVQ 3*, Oxford: Heinemann

Victoria Climbie Inquiry – Report of an Inquiry by Lord Lamming (January 2003)

Working Together to Safeguard Children (1999), London: The Stationery Office

Resources for children

Emily and the Stranger, NSPCC

Elliott, M (1998), *Feeling Happy, Feeling Safe*, London: Hodder and Stoughton (colour picture book for ages 3–7)

Jody and the Biscuit Bully, NSPCC

Videos

Cosmo and Dibs Keep Safe, Kidscape and BBC (for children aged 3–6, teaching notes included)

Useful websites

Barnado's – www.barnardos.org.uk

Bullying Online – www.bullying.co.uk

Childline – www.childline.org.uk

Children 1st – www.children1st.org.uk

Children's Legal Centre – www.childrenslegalcentre.com

Children's Society – www.the-childrens-society.org.uk

Gingerbread – www.gingerbread.org.uk

Daycare Trust – www.daycaretrust.org.uk

Deafchild International – www.deafchild.org

Department of Health publications – www.dh.gov.uk

Every Child Matters – www.dfes.gov.uk/everychildmatters

Kidscape – www.kidscape.org.uk

National Association of Child Contact Centres – www.nacc.org.uk

National Children's Bureau – www.ncb.org.uk

NCH – www.nch.org.uk

NSPCC – www.nspcc.org.uk

Ofsted – www.ofsted.gov.uk

Parentline Plus – www.parentlineplus.org.uk

Planet One Parent – www.planetoneparent.com

Save the Children – www.savethechildren.org.uk

The Stationery Office – www.opsi.gov.uk

UNICEF www.unicef.org.uk

Victoria Climbie – www.victoria-climbie-inquiry.org

Women's Aid – www.womensaid.org.uk

UNIT 4

Learning in the early years

What you need to learn

1 Theories of how children develop and learn

2 The work of the early years educators

3 Curriculum frameworks for children from 0–8 years of age

4 Learning opportunities for young children

Introduction

Children's learning is a major focus within most early years settings and one that is rewarding and exciting for early years practitioners. Understanding how children learn and how to promote learning requires extensive and in-depth knowledge from those people who care for and educate young children. The term 'early years' covers children from birth to eight years of age and is applied to all mainstream settings where children under eight receive care and education.

To meet the requirements of this unit you will need a thorough understanding of how children learn and develop. You will need to know about the curriculum frameworks that are used in early years settings and the historical perspectives from the early years educators that have influenced practice. You will use this knowledge to identify and promote learning opportunities for young children.

How you will be assessed

This unit is assessed internally.

1 Theories of how children develop and learn

Theories of how children develop and learn have been central to debates between philosophers, psychologists, scientists and educators over many years. A lot of these debates are still taking place and they have a direct influence on the type of education and care given to young children. It is therefore very important for early years practitioners to understand these theories and to draw conclusions regarding their own practice and that of the setting in which they work.

This section will help you to understand how theories affect our views of children as learners and influence provision for young children.

Development and learning

Development is how a child grows, matures and functions. It is often divided into different strands, for example:

* physical
* intellectual/cognitive
* language
* emotional
* social
* cultural
* spiritual/moral.

These strands come together to form a complete view of the child. Child development is a relatively new discipline based on psychology, sociology, anthropology, genetics, physiology and health disciplines, such as paediatrics.

Children's development generally follows the same pattern. The pattern of development covers the sequence or order in which development takes place, what development you would expect to see and the rate of development. For example, the sequence is that children normally sit unaided before they walk unaided. However, the rate will vary, for example, some will walk at twelve months and others at eighteen months. When children can walk unaided they are at the 'walking stage'.

Learning is what takes place as a response to something the child experiences. This may be through solving problems, through trial and error, in everyday interactions or through being taught. The mechanisms of how learning actually takes place are still not fully understood and the theories considered below all have different viewpoints.

Development occurs rapidly in the early years and it is the child's stage of development and readiness to learn that should control the learning they are offered. This means that each child needs to be considered as an individual. It would be bad practice to treat a group of young children as if they were exactly the same and could all learn the same things at the same time.

By carefully observing children, most early years practitioners will assess the individual child's stage of development and will make sure the time is right for each child to move on in their learning. They will do this by creating an environment where children can grow and develop freely, with adult support offered sensitively and in a way that will not dominate the child's learning.

> **Think it over...**
>
> Some people believe that a group of children aged four can sit together in a classroom, pick up their pencils at the same time and learn to write simple words. They are surprised when an early years practitioner says that some of the children are not ready to hold and control a pencil, others need a good deal of practice, while others can already write their names clearly.
>
> * Discuss the difference between these points of view. How does this link to ideas about development and learning?

Neuroscience and brain development

Research into babies' brain development has shown them to be alert and responsive to everything around them. The brain responds to information babies receive through their senses and starts to make connections between brain cells, based on the range of experiences the babies have encountered. Babies and young children have

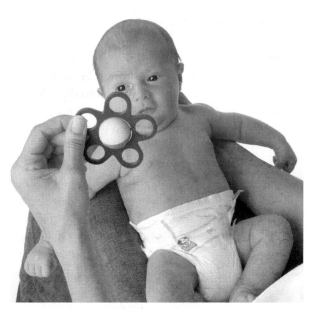

Research shows that early stimulation is essential for healthy brain development.

far more brain activity than adults and this makes it vital to ensure they have a wide and rich range of experiences to help their future learning. As babies and children develop, the experiences they encounter need to build on each other to strengthen early learning. The more children learn, the more their brains will have the capacity to learn. Early years practitioners need to remember that children's brains thrive on stimulation and new experiences, especially play. Young children soon get bored with toys that only do one thing or with dull and monotonous surroundings.

Gopnik et al (1999) compare babies' early brain development to that of a computer, with inbuilt programs for learning about people, objects and language, and special learning mechanisms to help them revise their learning. They note that babies have excellent technical support from their parents, siblings and other adults and all of their learning is supported by language and love.

Factors affecting development and learning

Meeting basic needs first

A range of issues affect the pattern of development and of learning. Maslow's hierarchy of needs (see diagram below) suggests that basic needs, at the bottom of the hierarchy, must be met before effective learning takes place.

Timing

Learning and development take place when the time is right and the opportunities are there. For example, it is pointless trying to force children to write their names before they are developmentally ready. To write their name, children have to be able to hold a pencil securely, confidently and with control. This ability comes when children's nerves and muscles are able to cope with handling small objects with control, when they understand something about making marks on paper and when opportunities to practise and develop these skills are available. It is important that children are regularly observed and assessed to make sure that opportunities are not missed by underestimating what children can actually do.

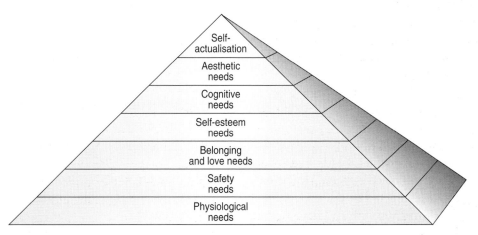

Maslow's hierarchy of needs.

Settings

The type of setting in which a child receives care is also important in terms of learning and development. From birth there are many different settings where babies and children receive care and education. These services are provided by different parts of the early years sector and can be home based, such as childminders and nannies, or group settings, such as nurseries and schools.

Early years care and education takes place wherever there are young children, and usually starts in the home. By its very nature, caring for a young child is also educating the child and encouraging learning and development. Early education integrates care and education and extends children's learning and experience.

Services for families and young children increasingly offer an integrated service, as both care and education need to be included in order to look after the needs of the whole child. Children will learn well in whatever settings they are in, given the correct conditions.

Genetics

Children's genetic blueprints affect their development and learning, although it is not clear how much these effects determine children's ability to reach their potential.

Unless there is a genetic abnormality, such as in Down's syndrome, each person has 46 chromosomes – 23 from each parent. The chromosomes are subdivided into genes and each gene is responsible for some parts of development, such as eye colour or temperament. The genes from each of the parents may be similar or very different. For each corresponding gene, one of them (the one from the mother or the one from the father) is likely to be the dominant one that affects a particular aspect of the child. This is why you sometimes find children in the same family who are very different – because they have different dominant genes.

Heredity also affects how people grow and mature, for example, how tall they will grow or how quickly they will reach puberty. However, this potential is also affected by the environment. For example, children's growth and development will be affected if they do not get enough food.

Other factors that can affect the potential of genetic inheritance include drug use and diseases, such as the mother having rubella during pregnancy.

Today scientists can investigate an unborn baby's genetic code and this can lead to serious ethical decisions about whether to abort a foetus who may have an inherited illness or disability.

Environment

Children need an environment which encourages them to learn and develop. The environment is not just physical surroundings, but also covers the emotional and social environment. Children need to explore freely and safely from an early age and to mix with other children. They also need encouragement and praise for their efforts, as well as for their achievements.

Health factors

Most children in the UK today are born healthy and have a healthy childhood. However, this has not always been the case and in some parts of the world there are still high levels of child mortality and ill-health. In cases where children themselves are healthy, they may be affected by the ill health of their parents or siblings.

The effect of health factors on children's development and learning itself depends on many factors, including access to health care and family support. Most children and families who are given adequate support and good health care cope very well with short periods of acute illness, as do children with chronic illness such as cystic fibrosis.

It is important to remember that children with health needs are children first and therefore still need opportunities to play and enjoy life. Focus should be on meeting their individual needs and enabling them to live happy and fulfilled lives, achieving the best they can. Practitioners should have high expectations of children with health problems but need to remain sensitive to the child's needs. For example, being aware that the child may tire easily or find it more difficult to concentrate will help the practitioner to react appropriately.

Support

All children need appropriate support to encourage their development and learning. This includes rich interactions with caring adults and a responsive physical environment. The physical environment should contain stimulating activities alongside opportunities to rest and relax without constant noise. Practitioners need to tailor support to the needs of each individual child and recognise that, where children have disabilities or special educational needs, they may require additional support.

Children need to be given the opportunity to develop. For example, in some orphanages in Eastern Europe it was found that toddlers were being kept in cots all the time. As a result, they had not learnt to walk, because their muscles, co-ordination and balance had not been given the opportunity to develop.

Children also need motivation and positive encouragement. For example, if toddlers, who are usually intrepid explorers, are constantly told 'no', they become discouraged and frustrated. When trying new skills, most children need encouragement and support in order to move on. Children with low self-esteem, such as those who have been abused or neglected, also need special encouragement to take risks and do new things.

Major theories

Early years settings base their provision on what they believe about children and learning. The setting's beliefs will be linked to the theories they accept as valid and important for children's learning in their early years. This section looks at some of the most important theoretical models of children's learning, each of which has influenced current early years provision in the UK. The models themselves have their origins in the work of philosophers and thinkers and have more recently been developed by psychologists. You will see evidence of theories and theorists in your work placements, although you may not always recognise them.

Nature/nurture debate

This is a very important debate that influences how we view children's learning and how we provide for it. The debate is about how much either nature (genetic inheritance – inborn abilities) or nurture (the environment – the people, places and influences on a child) contribute to children's development, learning and potential achievement.

If theorists consider that nurture is a strong influence, this means that there is a greater emphasis on the environment. This is because it is believed that a child's early experiences will be the most important factor affecting their ability to achieve. If theorists consider that nature is a strong influence, this will mean less emphasis on the environment, as the potential to achieve is thought to be inborn. Theorists supporting 'nature' believe children cannot perform at a higher level than their genetic inheritance may allow.

For example, if a child had learning difficulties, the 'nature' approach could offer love and care, but might not expect the child to achieve very much. It might not offer a very stimulating environment, as this would not make much difference in the end. The 'nurture' approach would say that the child should have an enriched learning environment to make sure they achieve their full potential and who knows what that might be!

Transmission model

The transmission model of learning builds on the thinking of the philosopher John Locke (1632–1704), who thought of the child as an empty clay tablet (*tabula rasa*) or an 'empty vessel' capable of being moulded and shaped by adults. People working in this tradition are often called behaviourists. This theory sees human beings as basically passive, learning through their experiences and reacting predictably to outside stimulation. It also recognises that human behaviour can be modified by reinforcement. For example, if you put your hand in the fire, it will be burned and you are unlikely to repeat the act.

Transmission theories are less concerned with what goes on inside the mind and more concerned with the external inputs and influences on learning, such as learning programmes, activities and experiences. Transmission models are concerned with the person's environment and experiences, not their genetic inheritance – nurture not nature. There are two main components of transmission theory: **learning theory** and **social learning theory**.

Learning theory (learning from experience)

Classical conditioning

Pavlov's (1849–1936) work on the behaviour of dogs is a well-known example of how learning theory developed during the twentieth century. Pavlov fed his dog when the church bells rang or a light was flashed before feeding; at the sight of the food the dog salivated. After some time the dog would salivate at the sound of the bell or when the light was flashed, even when no food was in sight as it associated the bell ringing or light flashing with the arrival of food. Salivation at the sound of the bell or flash of light indicated a conditioned response.

Operant conditioning

Operant conditioning was a further development of Pavlov's work by the psychologist B. F. Skinner (1904–90). It is concerned mainly with shaping and modifying behaviour. Skinner also worked with animals but only rewarded them with food if they did as he required. The food reward acted as a positive reinforcement. When animals did not do as Skinner required he subjected them to unpleasant stimuli such as electric shocks; the unpleasant stimuli acted as negative reinforcers and these gradually eliminated the behaviour. Learning theory has greatly influenced how adults shape or modify children's behaviour. By selectively reinforcing behaviour that is wanted, adults can change the way children behave. This is called **behaviour modification**.

Social learning theory (learning through example)

Social learning theory accepts the basics of learning theory but also emphasises that children learn behaviours by observing and imitating adults, especially those adults who are important to them. As well as adults, it has also been shown that children imitate each other too. Albert Bandura (1925–) is a well-known social learning theorist and he found that many behaviours were learned by observation, including aggression, sharing, sex roles, and altruism (willingness to do things that benefit other people, even if it results in disadvantage for yourself). Social learning theory emphasises the need to model socially acceptable behaviour to children. For example, if staff within the nursery regularly become angry and shout, children will learn that this is an acceptable way to behave and will copy the behaviour.

Food arrives when the bell has rung.

After some time the dog associates food with the bell ringing and salivates ready to eat. This is a conditioned response.

Classical conditioning (Pavlov).

How has this child learned about cooking?

Laissez-faire model (learning just happens)

This model is based on the work of the French philosopher Rousseau (1712–78). Rousseau thought that children learned naturally like the opening of a flower bud, and were programmed to learn certain things at certain times. Rousseau's thinking was that children's development would proceed anyway, whether or not there was a significant influence from adults or the environment. Developmental scales were first developed as a result of the laissez-faire approach.

Expanding Rousseau's thinking, some psychologists (e.g. Fodor, 1983) believe that the development of mental concepts such as number, space, music and time, are 'wired in' to inborn internal structures and that the role of the adult in the child's development is limited. Noam Chomsky's (1968) work on language development is similar. Chomsky believed that children learned the complex grammatical structures of language just by hearing it spoken. He taught that children have innate structures within their brain that allow them to develop language and that children develop new sentences and apply rules of grammar to their speech rather than just copy sentences they have heard. This is often borne out by children making errors by applying speech rules to new situations. For example, 'sheeps' instead of 'sheep' applies a common rule (adding an 's' to form a plural).

Freud

Freudian theory is based on the work of Sigmund Freud (1856–1939) who is known as the father of psychoanalysis. Psychoanalysis is based on the theory of personality development, introduced by Freud, that focuses on the unconscious mind. Freud's theory sees the child as passing through a series of pre-determined psychological stages in the development of personality based on the child's level of physical maturation. Freud's stages are called psycho-sexual stages, as they are all part of the human being's drive to feed, grow and reproduce. Freud's view was that people were born with unconscious biological instincts, much like animals, and that we have to learn to control these instincts to live in society. Passing through these stages helps to ensure that children learn control and become mature.

FREUD'S PSYCHO-SEXUAL STAGES	
Oral stage	This is where the baby has a drive to feed and engage in activities involving the mouth and lips, e.g. sucking, biting, exploring with the mouth. How children are weaned from the breast or bottle was thought by Freud to affect their future personality.
Anal stage	This is about young children learning to control their muscles, especially anal muscles, e.g. during toilet training. How children are toilet trained was thought to affect their future personality. For example, over-strict toilet training was thought to lead to a more obsessive personality.

FREUD'S PSYCHO-SEXUAL STAGES	
Phallic stage	This stage relates to children having sexual feelings towards their parents. Freud believed that boys had sexual feelings towards their mothers and wished their fathers did not exist. He called this the Oedipus complex. Freud also believed that girls had sexual feelings towards their fathers and called this the Electra complex. By about the age of five or six years, children had to learn to give up these feelings and to identify with the parent of the same sex. How children managed this transition was thought by Freud to have an important impact on future relationships, especially with the opposite sex.
Latency stage	This period covers middle childhood from about six years until puberty. It is a latent period, as children are not yet ready to express their sexuality.
Genital stage	This refers to the onset of puberty, when adolescents become ready for full sexual activity.

Freud's view is that the environment is important, as children are involved in ongoing conflict situations with their parents and it is therefore not strictly a laissez-faire model, though it does have many similarities.

Psychoanalysis and psycho-analytic therapy look at how these experiences are stored in the unconscious mind and how they affect people's personality, feelings and behaviour.

Social constructivist model

This model is based on the work of Piaget (1896–1980), Bruner (1915–) and Vygotsky (1896–1934) and is influential in current early years provision. The social constructivist model originated in the work of Kant (1724–1804) and views children as partly 'empty vessels' (transmission model) and partly pre-programmed (laissez-faire model), with an interaction between the two. The social constructivist model emphasises environmental, biological and cultural factors and sees children as active participants in their own learning and development.

Piaget

Piaget was a constructivist whose work has been a major influence both on developmental psychology and on learning and education. Piaget's influence cannot be underestimated, as he changed the way in which young children's learning was viewed and opened the door to further research and development.

Piaget's view was that, from birth, a child actively selects and interprets information from the environment and has the ability to adapt and learn. He believed that children construct higher levels of knowledge by drawing on their own innate capacities to interpret the information coming through the environment. Piaget stated that children pass through a series of stages of cognitive or mental development, always in the same order but at different rates. He emphasised that the child was an active participant in his or her own learning and development. Although recognising the social world of the child as having a role in development and learning, Piaget did not emphasise this and his work focuses on the role of the individual child in his or her own development.

Piaget believed that children learn through processes of adaptation known as assimilation, accommodation and equilibration.

Key definitions from the work of Piaget
Schemas These are early ideas or concepts based on linked patterns of behaviour and are part of children's powerful drive to understand their experiences. Adults take for granted that they know how objects relate together or about shapes and where things are positioned. Children have to learn about this. Schemas include the idea or concept in the mind of the child and the actions

PIAGET'S STAGES	
Sensori-motor (birth to about two years)	The child moves from basic reflexes and learns through senses, gradually moving toward organising more complex physical action schemes such as hitting and grasping.
Pre-operational (two to about seven years)	The child begins to think and represents actions with symbols. Early language is the best example of representation, as words begin to represent objects and people in the child's thinking. At this stage, thought is very different from the ways adults think and has different logic.
Concrete– operational (seven to about twelve years)	Children become capable of more systematic logical thought and begin to grasp abstract notions. They still need to relate their thinking to concrete objects and activities.
Formal- operational (twelve years and onwards)	Children become capable of abstract thought and are able to make hypotheses and test them. Children are able to grasp abstract concepts, such as truth or justice. Critics state that not all adults fully reach this stage.

PIAGET'S PROCESSES OF ADAPTATION		
PROCESS	**DESCRIPTION**	**EXAMPLE**
Assimilation	Taking in new information from the environment through the child's existing patterns of action (sometimes called schemas)	Toddler established concept of cats as black
Accommodation	Modifying existing patterns of actions to accommodate new information and knowledge	Toddler has 'accommodated' new information that cats can be different colours
Equilibration	Balancing what they already know with new experience to make sense of the world	Toddler needs to have this reinforced by further experiences before accommodating this into his understanding

Assimilation   Accommodation   Equilibration

Many young children explore the transporting schema.

the child takes as a result of the idea. Often schemas occur in clusters. For example, children can be fascinated by positioning objects in certain ways, such as on top of something, around the edge or behind. They spend a lot of time positioning objects or people in this manner and will show this in their paintings as well. They are learning about position. Children will develop their schemas for hours on end and in many ways.

Athey (1990) has developed the concept of schema. She believes that particular schemas can dominate a child's play at any one time. Early years practitioners can identify which schema a child is working with and use this information to provide additional learning experiences for the child.

There are many types of schema identified by early years practitioners, teachers and psychologists. Examples of common types of schema clusters include the following.

* Transporting – moving objects or collections from one place to another. Look out for children doing this using bags, trucks or containers.

* Orientation – looking at things from different angles. Children turn things upside down or hang upside down themselves.

* Horizontal and vertical schemas – often shown in actions taken by the child, such as climbing or stepping up and down or lying flat. They will also construct in this way using blocks or show the schema in drawings and collage. When both horizontal and vertical schema have been explored separately, children merge them by exploring grids and crosses.

Conservation of mass Young children judge situations on what they can see. Piaget's classic test for conservation of mass is when a child who is pre-operational is shown two equal-sized pieces of clay. The child agrees they are the same size but when one is rolled into a sausage shape the child will say that it is larger. This means the child cannot 'conserve' mass (cannot understand the concept of reversibility of materials).

Conservation is not just about mass, as children have to learn to 'conserve' in other areas,

Conservation of mass.

such as volume, number and weight (which is a more difficult concept and comes about a year later than the conservation of mass).

Egocentricity Piaget described young children as egocentric, because they could not make a distinction between objects in the world and their own actions towards the objects – they cannot see from another's point of view.

Discovery learning Piaget felt that young children learned best by discovery – working out for themselves how to think and solve problems. In other words, the child is a solitary learner and the role of the adult was not emphasised.

Other social constructivists

Margaret Donaldson

Donaldson repeated some of Piaget's classic tasks which related to abstract reasoning and concluded that children show their expertise best in situations which are socially meaningful to them. She argued that Piaget's tasks were too disconnected from everyday life for children to fully show their understanding. Donaldson and others, such as Vygotsky, recognised the importance of the child's social world and became known as 'social constructivists'.

Bruner and Vygotsky

Bruner and Vygotsky build on Piaget's work but stress the role of play, talking with adults and interacting with the social world. Piaget's view of the child as a solitary learner is replaced by that of the child as a social being. Children use the tools of learning and their knowledge of their own culture, received from adults, to develop ideas and learning that they could not do alone.

Like Piaget, Vygotsky saw children as active organisers of their own lives but, unlike Piaget, he believed that social relationships and interaction with another person were needed for human beings to develop intellectually. Vygotsky emphasised the role of adults in helping children learn. He identified the 'zone of proximal development', which is when children begin to show signs that they are ready to move on in their development and learning. Adults need to intervene and help children to move into

the zone of actual development and the cycle goes on.

Bruner believed that children learn through doing – imagining what they have been doing and then turning what they know into symbols, such as speech, drawing, and writing. Bruner viewed the adult as important in supporting children's learning, especially when informal, everyday interactions are used to help children make sense of the world. Social constructivism is widely acknowledged as underpinning and influencing much early years provision. It emphasises that children have distinct and different ways of thinking, behaving and feeling at different stages of development and that children's thinking is different from that of adults.

How children learn

Active learning

Children are active learners, not passive recipients of learning. They engage with adults, materials, events and ideas in ways that are immediate, direct and meaningful to them. Children learn best when they engage with familiar objects or situations that mean something to them and adults can extend this experience more effectively. Social constructivists emphasise the role of the adult in supporting learning and this is backed up by the Effective Pre-School Practice Research study (EPPE) – a long-term research project by a team from the Institute of Education and Birkbeck, University of London and the University of Oxford on the impact of pre-school education.

> **Theory into practice**
>
> Children need first-hand experiences, rather than seeing things on television or in pictures in books. They need to handle items and materials and explore them with their senses:
>
> * seeing
> * hearing
> * touching
> * feeling
> * smelling.
>
> Think of some of the everyday activities you do with children and identify which senses are used.

EPPE set out to investigate the following questions.

* What is the impact of pre-school on young children's intellectual and social/behavioural development? Can the pre-school experience reduce social inequalities?

* Are some pre-schools more effective than others in promoting children's development?

* What are the characteristics of an effective pre-school setting?

* What is the impact of the home and childcare history (before age 3) on children's intellectual and behavioural development?

* Do the effects of pre-school continue through Key Stage 1 (ages 6 and 7 years)?

EPPE found that pre-school children do best when they are engaged in activities that make them think. Sustained shared thinking (defined by EPPE as 'an episode in which two or more individuals "work together" in an intellectual way to solve a problem, clarify a concept, evaluate activities, extend a narrative etc. Both parties must contribute to the thinking and it must develop and extend') between adults and children enables children to make better learning and developmental progress. EPPE has found that it is not enough to create a stimulating environment and simply let children play. Children learn best when staff actively teach the children, which means modelling appropriate language and behaviour, sharing intelligent conversations, asking open-ended questions (questions which have more than one answer) and using play to motivate and encourage them.

EPPE found that the best balance for children was a more equal emphasis on free play, where children could select their activity from a range of choices, and direct learning opportunities, often led by adults who actively 'taught' the children. Adults should sensitively intervene in children's play to extend and 'teach'. This means carefully observing children and intervening appropriately. For example, if children are deeply absorbed in a meaningful learning activity or dialogue with other children, then this may not be the best time to intervene, but the opportunity for intervention

is likely to occur some time during the play sequence.

The EPPE findings encourage:

* asking open-ended questions to extend children's thinking

* children initiating activities as often as staff

* seeing learning and social development as complementary, rather than separate

* helping children to talk through conflicts and become assertive, rather than using distraction or telling them to stop

* parental involvement in educational aims for their children and supporting learning at home.

The EPPE findings are closely linked to the DfES curriculum guidance for the foundation stage.

Language

As the EPPE study has shown, using language is a key element of supporting children's learning. Use every opportunity to extend language. Encourage children to talk about what they do or are experiencing, through general everyday activities and routines, as well as language activities such as books and stories, poems, rhymes and songs, writing and mark making. Use new language and repeat existing language – where children make errors don't correct them, but repeat the correct usage back to them. Encourage children to be interested in environmental print, such as road signs or advertisements, and to learn that written words and symbols have meaning.

Theory into practice

Note how experienced early years practitioners or teachers take opportunities to develop children's language. Note how children respond to both open-ended and closed questions.

Think it over...

Choose an area of the setting and plan how you can use that area to encourage children to extend their language.

Working with others

Most children learn best when they work with others co-operatively and there is significant teaching input from adults. Children do best in settings where staff are consistent and pro-active in supporting the children to develop their social skills, for example, using story books and group discussions to work through common conflicts.

Feeling secure

As well as a safe and stimulating environment for learning, children need to feel emotionally and physically secure. The best atmosphere for learning is one of encouragement and support, not one of criticism. Children need lots of praise and encouragement to take risks and need to feel that someone is there to support them should they fail. Key workers who have special responsibility for individual children are an important source of emotional security for children.

Physical security is often best displayed by the presence of caring adults who know how to let children take risks without over-protecting, but who will intervene if situations get out of hand.

How theories influence early years provision

The table below summarises good practice in supporting children's learning.

THEORIES OF HOW CHILDREN LEARN			
	TRANSMISSION MODEL	LAISSEZ-FAIRE MODEL	SOCIAL CONSTRUCTIVIST MODEL
Advantages	• Behaviour modification • Learning through experience • Insights into learning through observing and imitating	• Stages identified when children are sensitive to particular learning • Children encouraged to take lead in learning • Developmental scales are useful	• Rewarding for children and adults involved • Many centres of excellence today use this model • Includes communities and families and recognises cultural diversity
Disadvantages	• Does not explain complexity of children's learning and behaviour • Children do not direct learning • Children less likely to explore or try new things • Does not consider how children's developmental stage affects how learning occurs	• Children pre-programmed to develop, regardless of adult or environment • May be labelled backward if they do not conform with developmental scales • Cultural differences in milestones not recognised	• Costly to operate, demanding high staffing ratios and resourcing levels
Role of adult and interaction with child	• Children seen as passive, with adults making good what is lacking (as in compensatory education movement of 1960s)	• 'Leave it to nature' model, with limited role for adult • Adults may not intervene at appropriate time or offer sufficient stimulation • Children seen as mostly passive	• Children seen as active agent in own learning • Requires highly-skilled multi-disciplinary teams to work together • Adults observe and assess children, work closely with children, support their learning and extend play opportunities • Parents involved as partners

▶

THEORIES OF HOW CHILDREN LEARN		
	TRANSMISSION MODEL	LAISSEZ-FAIRE MODEL	SOCIAL CONSTRUCTIVIST MODEL
Organisation of the learning environment	• Adults control environment • Formal programmed approach to learning, using small steps, each building on the other • Children sit quietly, getting on with activities, with little exploration, movement or need for much equipment	• Well-resourced, with plenty of equipment and activities • Children allowed to explore freely • Low adult intervention, so may miss learning opportunities	• Carefully structured and well-resourced • Encourages exploration and discovery • Emphasis on crucial role of play in learning • Balance of adult-structured activities and play and learning opportunities freely chosen by child • Outdoors important
Nature/ nurture debate	• Supports nurture, as little notice taken of genetic or innate abilities	• Supports nature, as environment does not really affect development	• Both nature and nurture important • Development and learning interdependent
Links to current research	• Dowling (1995) argues behaviour modification is not long term • Little support for model in current UK practice	• Current research, especially concerning brain development, supports view that child has sensitive periods	• Approach supported by current research, e.g. Athey (1990) and Pascal (1993)

2 The work of the early years educators

As well as basing early years provision on key theories of how children learn, current early years practice has also grown out of the work of early years educators. This section explores the work of Froebel, Steiner, Montessori, McMillan and Isaacs and notes where their ideas are incorporated into mainstream practice today.

Friedrich Froebel (1782–1852)

Key beliefs and emphasis

Froebel emphasised the importance of physical activity and exploration involving real experiences, especially creative play, finger plays, songs and rhymes. His work stressed the importance of making one thing stand for another (symbolism). He stated how symbolic behaviour is best developed through play, especially imaginative and pretend play. Froebel developed play activities and materials to promote symbolic play. He called the play materials, such as wooden blocks, 'the gifts'. Activities such as songs, movements and dancing were called 'the occupations'. Froebel also felt that children were helped to think through being introduced to opposites, such as hard and soft, and this was a theme followed through in the play materials he used.

Froebel believed that everything in the world was linked and that children perceived the world best through integrated activities. He stressed the importance of encouraging art, literature, natural sciences, mathematical understanding and the appreciation of beauty. Froebel recognised that parents are the child's first educator and stated that teachers should be like 'mothers' to young children. He welcomed parents into schools and into the 'communities' where the children were cared for.

Influence on current practice and provision

Most mainstream early years provision in the UK is based on Froebelian principles and most of his ideas are now taken for granted, although in his lifetime they were ground breaking.

Current mainstream settings encourage learning through first-hand experiences, and play remains central to provision for children's learning, including language development through rhymes and finger plays. Most early years settings encourage imagination to flow freely in play, and symbolic play is seen as very important for children's development.

Early years settings integrate care and education and today this is emphasised more than ever. Children's development is still encouraged through provision of a wide range of materials and activities tailored to the needs of the individual child. Current best practice still emphasises creativity, science and the humanities and learning opportunities are integrated across curriculum areas.

Current mainstream provision places emphasis on positive relationships and social development and values parent/educator partnerships.

Susan Isaacs (1885–1948)

Key beliefs and emphasis

Susan Isaacs worked in the Froebelian tradition but was influenced by Melanie Klein, a psychoanalyst, who believed in encouraging children to express their feelings. Isaacs valued play as giving children opportunity to think and learn and to express feelings. Isaacs saw parents as the main educators of young children and felt that nurseries were an extension of home. She felt that children should remain in nursery until the age of seven before starting formal school and kept careful records of children's time at nursery. Through these records she demonstrated how children regressed after starting formal school.

Influence on current practice and provision

Mainstream early years settings today give opportunities for children to 'let off steam' in a controlled way through vigorous physical play. They also encourage controlled expression of feelings through language and imaginative play. Play is still seen as central to learning and parents/carers are seen as partners. Careful observation of children and accurate record keeping is emphasised in early years settings.

In many countries throughout the world children do not start school until they are six or seven years and many early years educators in the UK argue that this should be the case here.

Margaret McMillan (1860–1931)

Key beliefs and emphasis

Margaret McMillan worked in the Froebel tradition. She believed in active learning through first-hand experiences and emphasised feelings and relationships, as well as physical aspects of movement and learning. McMillan believed that play helped a child to become a 'whole person' and was an integrating force in learning and development. McMillan was a pioneer in nursery education. She believed in the introduction of nursery schools as an extension of home and as communities in themselves. She emphasised the value of the open air and introduced gardens for families to play in and explore. She believed in partnership with parents who developed with their children in the nursery environment. McMillan was the first to introduce school meals and medical services and stressed the importance of trained adults to work with children.

Influence on current practice and provision

McMillan has had a powerful influence on the provision of nursery education in the UK and many of her principles are widespread. Today children are given access, wherever possible, to outdoor areas and encouraged to make gardens and use natural materials. Early years settings provide opportunities for children's physical, social, imaginative and creative play, and encourage expression of feelings. Active learning is encouraged through provision of a wide range of materials and equipment, together with a skilled and qualified workforce.

McMillan's views on the nursery school as a community are followed through today as parents are invited into schools and seen as partners in the care and education of their children. As well as being communities in themselves, early years settings extend provision into the community and become part of the community.

School meals and medical services are now an accepted part of provision.

Maria Montessori (1870–1952)

Key beliefs and emphasis

Maria Montessori was a doctor who practised in a poor part of Italy and who spent a good deal of time observing children, especially those with special needs. There are Montessori schools in the UK within the private sector. Children are seen as active learners who go through sensitive periods in their development when they are more open to learning particular skills and concepts.

The Montessori method involves a series of graded activities through which every child progresses, working through specially designed Montessori materials, such as solid geometric forms, knobbed puzzle maps, coloured beads, and various specialised rods and blocks. Each material isolates one quality for the child to discover, such as size, colour or shape. The materials are self-correcting – when a piece does not fit or is left over, the child can easily see what went wrong.

Montessori did not emphasise play or the free flow of ideas and did not allow children to draw or undertake creative activities until they had worked through all the graded learning activities. The child is thought to solve problems

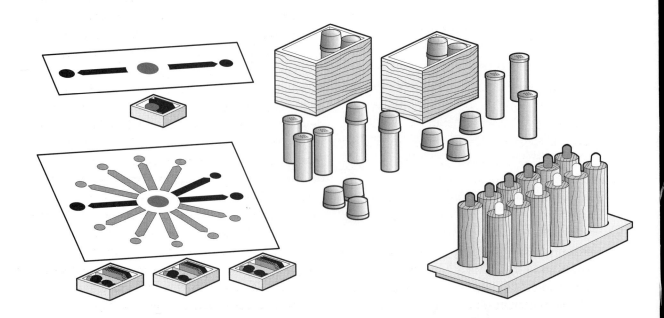

Montessori equipment is graded so that children can develop skills sequentially.

independently, building self-confidence, analytical thinking, and the satisfaction that comes from accomplishment. Montessori did not think there was a need for adult 'correction'. The role of the adult was limited to facilitating the child's own activity; the teacher is known as 'directress'. Children are not seen as part of a community, but work largely on their own in a quiet and peaceful environment of total concentration. Little parental involvement is encouraged.

Influence on current practice and provision

Mainstream provision also sees the child as an active learner and some Montessori ideas and materials are used, for example, graded sizes of particular shapes, such as small, medium and large blocks.

Many of the other aspects of Montessori provision are different from mainstream early years practice. For example, mainstream settings emphasise the role of adults in intervening and supporting the child's learning. Current mainstream practice would not usually leave children to work through activities alone, but encourages group work and sensitive intervention by adults to support learning. Sometimes quiet concentration is encouraged, but according to individual children's needs rather than a basic approach to all learning activities.

Rudolph Steiner (1861–1925)

Key beliefs and emphasis

Steiner believed in childhood as a special phase of life and that the young child needs a protected environment where all-round development can take place. He believed that a child's temperament was important in overall development and learning, as well as academic progress. Steiner also emphasised the spiritual, moral, social, artistic and creative and the need to care for each other. He did not emphasise what is taught, but how and when.

Steiner believed that young children need to be protected from formal learning and learn through imaginative and creative play using simple tasks and activities with natural materials. In Steiner schools, the learning opportunities are often repeated as many times as necessary so that all children are confident, including those with special needs.

Influence on current practice and provision

Mainstream settings believe in early childhood as a unique phase of life that is more than just preparation for adulthood and that the individual child's needs and personality are important. As in Steiner schools, establishing relationships is valued and reaching out and serving the community is considered part of the nursery's role.

Mainstream settings consider the how and when (the process of learning), but also the content. Mainstream settings do not emphasise the spiritual dimension as much as Steiner.

Approaches to practice

Practice in early years work is based on the work of the early educators as well as newer research and thinking. The following represent newer approaches.

Reggio Emilia

Loris Magaluzzi began his work in 1945 in the Reggio Emilia area of Italy. Since that time, his work has greatly influenced early childhood education in many countries throughout the world. Loris Magaluzzi emphasised an image of children as rich, strong and powerful, with rights rather than needs. He refers to the 'hundred languages' through which children can express themselves, such as through drama, play and language, as well as the importance of adults listening to the child's expressions. Magaluzzi emphasises the role of society, which is to nurture children who can think and act for themselves.

Reggio Emilia has no written curriculum or learning goals and the child is seen as a starting point for learning. The nature of the adult–child relationship is key to this approach, which focuses on the views and ideas of the child and that children and adults co-construct knowledge together. Some people have criticised the Reggio approach for its lack of a formal curriculum, leading to lack of accountability to parents.

Settings that use the Reggio approach often have a central area where children can meet, play and talk together. The settings concentrate on the use of light, mirrors and reflective surfaces and usually have large windows, white walls and mirrored surfaces where children can view themselves from different angles. Children's work is displayed and their achievements documented using photographs, slides and film.

High/Scope

High/Scope is a structured programme developed in the 1960s in the US, and now extended for use with pre-school children and babies. Some mainstream settings in the UK use the High/Scope approach. The method was well resourced in the US and involved parents and children in more deprived areas. It was designed to meet the gaps in the child's learning and everyday experiences. The results seem to promise good long-term benefits for children. In the UK, evidence for the success of High/Scope is less clear, but new work is taking place in different parts of the country, involving parents who themselves have basic skills needs, and this seems to be opening new possibilities for High/Scope. High/Scope is based on well-accepted educational principles.

* *Active learning*: the child is encouraged to become an active learner, involved directly in his or her own learning.

* *Personal initiative*: the child is encouraged to use personal initiative to plan/do/review his or her own learning. For example, children are encouraged to plan their own learning at the start of the session, to undertake the learning experiences and to review how it went at the end of the session.

* *Consistency*: High/Scope believes children need consistent, stable daily routines and an

organised learning environment to help them become confident and independent learners.

* *Genuine relationships*: High/Scope practitioners aim to bring genuine warmth and trust to their relationships with children and respect and value cultural diversity.

* *Appropriate curriculum*: High/Scope has been developed through extensive observations of children and is designed to provide key learning experiences. The settings have a range of resources similar to most mainstream early years settings.

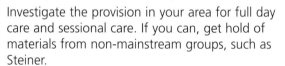

Think it over...

• Investigate further the High/Scope or Reggio approaches to children's learning.

• Imagine you are a young child and describe three things you like best about your nursery based on either the High/Scope or Reggio approaches.

Assessment activity 4.2

Investigate the provision in your area for full day care and sessional care. If you can, get hold of materials from non-mainstream groups, such as Steiner.

Collect examples of marketing leaflets, information for parents, inspection reports, or planning documents – anything that will tell you about the provision.

Develop a checklist to see which theoretical model(s) are used in the settings you investigate. You could use headings such as learning environment, parents as partners, role of play, organisation.

3 Curriculum frameworks for children from 0–8 years of age

This section looks at the curriculum and learning opportunities offered to babies and young children. It focuses on the provision in England and, although there are similarities between the four Home Countries of the UK, there are separate

curriculum frameworks and different underpinning legislation. You should be aware that documents supporting the early years curriculum are frequently updated and you will need to make sure you work with up-to-date versions which may be slightly different from the content below. In this section we consider the Birth to Three Matters Framework, the Curriculum Guidance for the Foundation Stage and the National Curriculum Key Stage 1. You will need to check which framework is used within your own setting, but many of the broad principles in this unit apply to provision across the UK.

Current curriculum frameworks

In England, the government is planning to introduce the Early Years Foundation Stage to support the delivery of quality integrated care and education for children from birth to five years. This is likely to merge Birth to Three Matters with the existing Foundation Stage.

Birth to Three Matters: a framework to support children in the earliest years (Sure Start Unit 2002)

Birth to Three Matters is a framework of effective practice for those who work with children from birth to three years of age in day care settings. It has been widely welcomed as a big step forward in caring for our youngest children. It is not to be seen as a curriculum, which is often more structured and prescribed, for example teaching literacy or maths, but provides a firm basis and clear links with the Foundation Stage.

The purpose of the framework is to support and inform practitioners who work with this age range and the following is a statement of the principles which underpin the framework.

❋ Parents and families are central to the well-being of the child.

❋ Relationships with other people (both adults and children) are of crucial importance in a child's life.

❋ A relationship with a key person at home and in the setting is essential to young children's well-being.

❋ Babies and young children are social beings; they are competent learners from birth.

❋ Learning is a shared process and children learn most effectively when, with the support of a knowledgeable and trusted adult, they are actively involved and interested.

❋ Caring adults count more than resources and equipment.

❋ Schedules and routines must flow with the child's needs.

❋ Children learn when they are given appropriate responsibility, allowed to make errors, decisions and choices, and respected as autonomous and competent learners.

❋ Children learn by doing rather than being told.

❋ Young children are vulnerable; they learn to be independent by having someone they can depend upon.

There are four aspects around which the framework is organised. These are:

❋ a strong child

❋ a skilful communicator

❋ a competent learner

❋ a healthy child.

The framework itself develops and explains each of these aspects and how to promote development. You should familiarise yourself with the framework and understand how it can be used with our youngest children. Birth to Three

> **Think it over...**
>
> The text of Birth to Three Matters can be downloaded from the DfES website at www.standards.dfes.gov.uk or a pack obtained free from DfES Publications by phoning 0845 602 2260. The pack comprises an introductory booklet, poster, video, CD-ROM and 16 'component cards' relating to the four aspects identified above.
>
> - Many early years settings or partnerships are providing training in the best use of the Birth to Three Matters framework, including how to use the cards and reinforcing knowledge on development. Find out what is being offered in your area.
> - Pick one of the 'component cards' relating to one of the aspects and observe a child in your setting. (See unit 8 for more on observation techniques.) In the light of the information provided and what you have observed, how might you support this child?

Matters provides a firm basis for and clear links with the Foundation Stage.

The Curriculum Guidance for the Foundation Stage

The Foundation Stage applies to children in England aged three until the end of the school year in which they become five years of age, who are being cared for and educated in settings that receive public funding. These can be group- or home-based care and education settings.

The Foundation Stage is organised into six areas of learning:

* personal, social and emotional development (PSED)
* communication, language and literacy (CLL)
* mathematical development (MD)
* knowledge and understanding of the world (KUW)
* physical development (PD)
* creative development (CD).

Each area of learning has early learning goals which most children are expected to achieve by the end of the Foundation Stage. Some children will have exceeded these goals. Others will still be working towards some or all of them. The Curriculum Guidance for the Foundation Stage is intended to help practitioners plan to meet the diverse needs of all children.

To help practitioners in planning, the guidance identifies 'stepping stones' that show the knowledge, skills, understanding and attitudes that children need to develop in the Foundation Stage in order to achieve the Early Learning Goals. The stepping stones are not related to children's ages but they are colour coded. The Early Learning Goals form the final stepping stones. Earlier stepping stones are shown as yellow, moving through blue to green (normally describing children at the end of the Foundation Stage). Although, for many children, these can be related to their age, not all children conform so neatly to this sequence of learning. The government recognises that some children will exceed the goals, whereas others may still be working towards them, especially if they have not had high-quality learning experiences, have special educational needs or are learning English as an additional language.

The Early Learning Goals are expectations for most children to reach by the end of the Foundation Stage but are not a curriculum in themselves and children's learning in the

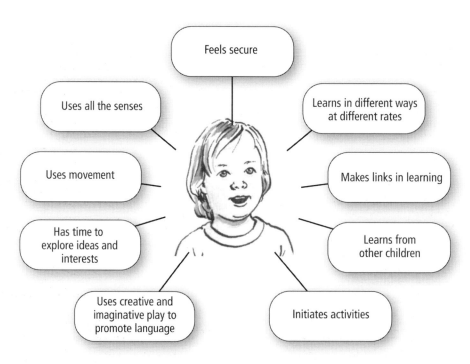

Strategies for effective learning.

Foundations Stage is holistic – they do not see the world in areas of learning. The main strategies for learning in young children are through playing and talking. In early years settings, the six areas of learning will usually be presented to children through integrated activities, experiences, themes and projects and skilled practitioners will support, assess and record learning. Children will approach the learning in different ways according to their age, level of experience, interest and confidence.

Effective teaching

The QCA Guidance (QCA, 2000) defines early years teaching as 'systematically helping children to learn so that they are helped to make connections in their learning and are actively led forward, as well as helped to reflect on what they have already learnt'. Teaching has many aspects, including planning and creating a learning environment, organising time and material resources, interacting, questioning and responding to questions, working with and observing children, assessing and recording children's progress and sharing knowledge gained with other practitioners. The strategies shown in the following diagram draw on that definition.

The National Curriculum

Early years practitioners will work with children from birth to eight years and will need to have some understanding of the National Curriculum Key Stage 1, both if they work with children aged five to seven years in schools, and if they work with younger children to prepare them for moving into Key Stage 1.

The National Curriculum follows on from the Foundation Stage and should form a seamless progression for children moving into Key Stage 1, as it covers some of the same broad areas. Children entering Key Stage 1 who have achieved the ELGs will be well prepared to enter formal schooling.

The National Curriculum was established by the Education Reform Act 1988. It defines the minimum educational entitlement for pupils of compulsory school age, and builds on the ELGs. The National Curriculum applies to all pupils aged five to sixteen in maintained (state) schools. It does not apply in independent schools, although those schools may choose to follow it.

There is no single curriculum within the four countries of the UK. For example, Curriculum Cymreig applies to schools in Wales and stresses the need to provide a curriculum which includes

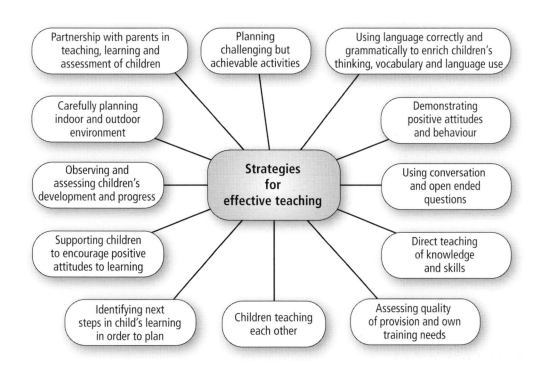

NATIONAL CURRICULUM CONTENT AT KEY STAGE 1 (NORMALLY CHILDREN AGED 5–7 YEARS)	
English	Speaking and listening
	Reading
	Writing
Mathematics	Using and applying mathematics
	Number
	Shape, space and measures
Science	Scientific enquiry
	Life processes and living things
	Materials and their properties
	Physical processes
Design and technology	Designing
	Making
Information technology	Using, exploring and discussing experiences of IT
	Communicating and handling information
	Controlling and modelling
History	Chronology
	Range and depth of historical knowledge and understanding
	Interpretations of history
	Historical enquiry
	Organisation and communication
Geography	Geographical skills and vocabulary
	Places
	Thematic study
Art	Investigating and making
	Knowledge and understanding
Music	Performing and composing
	Listening and appraising
Physical education	Games
	Gymnastic activities
	Dance
Religious education	While this is a statutory area, the content is organised by individual schools according to their needs.
Personal, health, social education (PHSE) and citizenship	This is not a statutory area, but some primary schools include it within their planning.

the teaching of Welsh as a first or second language and the culture and heritage of Wales.

The National Curriculum does not constitute the whole curriculum for schools. Schools have discretion to develop the curriculum to reflect their particular needs and circumstances.

The content of each National Curriculum subject is defined in a **Statutory Order**. Statutory Orders are legal requirements stating what has to be taught to children. Each Order consists of:

* **common requirements** which relate to access to the curriculum for all pupils, pupils' use of language, pupils' access to information technology and the Curriculum Cymreig (in Wales)

* the **programme of study** which sets out the minimum knowledge, understanding and skills for each subject at each Key Stage

* **attainment targets** which define the expected standards of pupil performance in terms of level descriptions or end of Key Stage descriptions.

The National Curriculum and the early years practitioner

The early years practitioner has to understand the National Curriculum Key Stage 1 in order to:

* support children through the Foundation Stage

* work with children at National Curriculum Key Stage 1.

It is important that you familiarise yourself with these aspects of children's learning to be able to understand learning from birth to eight years of age (the early years). Early years practitioners are unique in that they consider the whole child from birth to eight years of age and are able to see children's learning progress from babyhood until they are well established at formal school.

Characteristics of the early years curriculum

The early years curriculum starts at birth, as babies are exposed to learning and development activities right from the start. There are some characteristics which make the early years curriculum distinctive and should be borne in

mind while planning for babies and young children.

* Babies and children are seen as active learners.

* Learning is play based and child centred.

* Observation is used to plan activities.

* The adult role is to facilitate learning rather than formally 'teach'.

* Babies and children are seen as individuals.

* Activities are differentiated to meet children's needs.

* The curriculum is designed to build skills and positive attitudes rather than knowledge.

* The curriculum is broad and balanced.

* Learning builds on the child's existing knowledge.

* Parents are viewed as equal partners in children's education.

Routine of the day

This will vary between settings, depending on the age of the children and the length of their stay in the setting. A baby attending full daycare will, for example, need a routine which includes plenty of one-to-one interaction with an adult. It is also good practice for the routine to be based upon following the baby's individual routine, rather than expecting the baby to slot into to a pre-determined routine. With older children, the situation changes, although most settings aim to develop a routine that is flexible. An example of a routine for children in a pre-school setting attending a three-hour session could include:

* a greeting and settling-down period

* open play and supported workshop activities

* free use of indoor and outdoor spaces

* circle games and singing

* opportunity for drinks throughout the session or perhaps with a snack at a set time

* clearing-away time

* opportunities for stories and language

* going home.

Staff will be deployed according to an agreed plan. For example, one may greet the children, comfort those who are distressed and help everyone to settle. Others may facilitate the workshops and be 'anchored' to that area during most of the session, giving opportunities for long conversations and support to the children.

Children should be given time to engage in periods of uninterrupted play when they are totally involved. During the session, an adult will need to be free to cope with visits to the washrooms, comforting, clearing up accidents, pointing children towards the activities and ensuring safe supervision, both indoors and outside. Adults will need to carefully observe and assess the children during the session and record their progress.

The role of play

Wherever you see young children you are likely to see play taking place. Play is a term used to describe both adult and children's activity – for example, an adult playing golf or cards or a child playing with their friend or with blocks in the garden. Although human beings play throughout their lives, adult play tends to be seen as something extra to do when work is over, whereas for young children the term 'play' is used to describe much of how they spend their time and energy.

> ### Think it over...
>
> What can you remember about your early play experiences? Discuss this question in a group and see if you remember similar things. Take it a step further and remember what it was like when an adult stopped your play, even for good reasons – how did you feel?

Valuing play

Different cultures place different value on play. For some it is a fundamental right of the child (see UN Convention on Rights of the Child on page 20), while for other cultures childhood is seen as a preparation for adulthood, rather than a time unique and important in itself. Here, the role of play is given less prominence and children are expected to engage in adult work from a very early age. In some cultures play is highly valued and encouraged throughout early childhood and formal schooling is postponed until the age of six or seven years.

> ### KEY ISSUES
>
> Get a copy of the Department of Health booklet 'The Rights of the Child – A Guide to the UN Convention (CAG9)' or read Article 31 of the Convention. What does this say about the child's right to play?

Children's play contributes both to their all-round development and has generally agreed characteristics and benefits such as:

* freely chosen and initiated by the child – no one can make a child play
* spontaneous
* content and intent of the play owned and directed by the child
* child is actively involved
* involves first-hand experiences
* usually pleasurable even where children are concentrating deeply
* usually a process not a product
* pretending is an important feature.

Through play children can:

* take risks and make mistakes in a safe environment
* practise and build up ideas, concepts and skills
* explore, develop and represent their learning experiences
* learn how to control impulses and behaviour
* explore the identities and feelings of others
* express fears or feelings in a controlled way
* be creative and imaginative
* communicate and be sociable.

Common terms used to describe play

You will often notice that practitioners and researchers use a variety of terms to describe categories of play. These categories relate to the way the child is playing and are not to do with what or whom the child is playing with. All these categories could refer to different types of play, such as playing with dolls, running and jumping outside or using sand and water.

PLAY TERMS	DESCRIPTION
Free play	Children playing where adult intervention is absent or minimal.
Structured play	Adult-led tasks (e.g. a modelling activity using clay). The adult demonstrates techniques and how to work with clay and encourages the child to participate and learn how to manipulate the tools and materials. Once mastered, the child knows how to play with clay and this can lead into deeper free flow play.
Free flow play	Children learning through play at the deepest level using their experience of ideas, feelings and relationships and applying these with control, competence and mastery. Free flow play includes symbolic and manipulative play, play with props and rough-and-tumble play. The term 'free flow play' was first used by Tina Bruce, who is a well-known researcher in early years education and play.
Exploration, discovery and investigation of materials	Some early years practitioners and teachers do not categorise these activities as play, but others do.

Children who cannot play freely for whatever reason need adult support to play, such as an adult to hold their hand if they lack confidence or if they are disabled, or special play equipment or environments to assist their play. Children need time to play and if they lead a busy life undertaking activities their parents choose for them, the opportunities for play are fewer. In addition, unhappy children, sick children or those who are dislocated, perhaps as asylum seekers or refugees, need particular help to play. Sometimes practitioners need to show children how to play and then to stand back and let them. If they are emotionally damaged, children may need play therapy to help them to play. Finally children need space to play as cramped and restricted environments do not allow the full scope of play activity.

Theory into practice

Find out the local policy for inclusion of children with special educational needs. Are any special provisions made for play activities? How would you improve provision in your local area to ensure every child has the same chance to play? Why is it important that all children are able to participate in play activities?

As well as the basic necessities of life, children must be allowed to play as a vital part of their healthy growth and development.

The role of the early years practitioner in quality play

Many practitioners who work with young children recognise that there are two levels of play, one where children are just kept occupied and another that contributes to their educational development. Much early years research supports the view that children can spend time in low-level play that has little real benefit for learning and development.

Many practitioners feel that play cannot be left to develop naturally and needs adults to plan, assist and support it to ensure that it aids learning. To ensure children's play brings them the maximum benefits and involvement requires sensitive and knowledgeable adult intervention to ensure that play is of high quality. This means practitioners must not interfere unnecessarily and control play, but must observe children carefully and unobtrusively and extend and support play by introducing new ideas or materials that build on the individual child's interest. They may also need to model playful behaviour to help a child learn to play more effectively.

CASE STUDY

Irena is three years and four months old. Most days she plays with an empty doll's pram and wheels it round and round the outdoor area. She keeps stopping and looking at the children on the climbing frame and other equipment but does not attempt to talk or interact with the other children. Staff have observed Irena for a while and are concerned that she is not making the most of the play opportunities open to her. They have decided to spend time with Irena as she wheels the pram and talk to her as they walk around, suggesting other wheeled toys. They also wheel Irena around the garden laughing and having fun, and other children want to join in. After a week or so Irena seems to have made a friend and they take turns wheeling each other and using the dolls and teddies. They are beginning to use the dressing up clothes.

- Why were staff concerned about Irena? How did they check out their concerns? Why do you think the staff acted in the way they did? Were they successful?

There are other viewpoints regarding play and the basis for some of these can be found earlier in the philosophies of the early educators. Other disciplines, such as playwork, may have very different views of the role of the adult in play and believe that settings should allow for uninterrupted play with minimal adult intervention.

Play and learning

Children will learn well in whatever settings they are in, given the correct conditions. Children's play is one of the most important aspects of their lives. How they play will be the greatest influence on their development and learning but it is not the only influence on learning. Bruce (1996) describes play as co-ordinating a network of developmental and learning strategies. These include the following.

※ **Learning through first-hand experiences:** children cannot learn by proxy. Second-hand experiences, such as watching television or playing computer games, are not likely to bring about quality learning experiences. However, if these build on the child's real experiences, it is more likely to deepen the learning. Listening to stories is not active play, but has other benefits for the child.

※ **Taking part in games with rules:** this allows the child to learn the rules of the game and of their own culture. They learn how rules are negotiated, who has authority and how to belong and be part of a community. For example, in hide and seek the rule is to take turns or to count to 100.

※ **Representation:** children represent their experiences through language, dance and movement, drama and creative expression. They need to represent their own experiences, for example, drawing from close observation of real things.

Moyles (1989) suggests that the learning process is like a spiral. It begins with free play, continues with structured or directed play and then returns to enriched free play as knowledge and abilities are acquired and consolidated. The first session of free play allows exploration, whereas the second brings a degree of mastery and this is followed up by the adult, who provides more structured play opportunities, leading to a new cycle of play and exploration. This spiral goes on and on as children go through these cycles many times.

Example of Moyles' learning spiral

※ **Free play: exploration.** Mina is sitting at the modelling table for the first time. She has been watching other children playing with dough and clay for a couple of days but has never sat down to try it herself. Today she explores the dough by pushing and squeezing it and making holes with her finger.

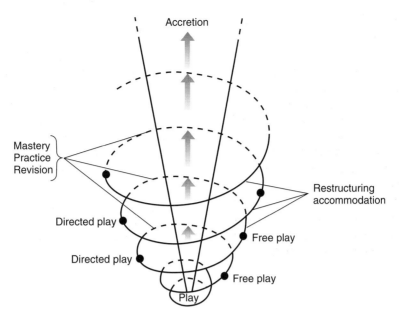

Accretion

Mastery
Practice
Revision

Restructuring
accommodation

Directed play

Free play

Directed play

Free play

Play

Moyles' learning spiral.

* **Mastery.** Mina plays freely several times over the next few days and becomes more and more skilful in the way she handles the dough.

* **Adult provides structured play: baking dough shapes.** When the early years practitioner sets up a dough baking activity to make fruit shapes for the shop, Mina joins in. Over the next few weeks Mina develops real skills in modelling dough.

* **Free play.** Mina starts to investigate clay in exactly the same way.

* **Mastery.** As she is experienced in modelling dough, her skill with clay grows more quickly.

* **Adult provides a structured play activity: making biscuits.** Mina joins in and makes biscuits, she rolls out the paste and cuts out the biscuits with control.

* **Free play.** Mina plays with the cooking utensils in the home corner.

* **Mastery.** She develops her play by entering into a rich sequence of imaginative domestic play centred on cooking.

* **Adult provides structured play activity: cooking bread.** Mina is enthusiastically entering into the cooking activity.

…and so the learning goes on.

Theories of play

Within early years practice there are two main theoretical views of play on which practitioners can base their work with children, which are outlined below. However, it should be noted that playworkers and others working with older children or within different disciplines have different theoretical perspectives that are not covered here.

Psycho-dynamic theories (feelings)

Psycho-dynamic theories were pioneered by Sigmund Freud and built on by workers such as Winnicott (1971) who thought play was the way in which children came to terms with their anxieties and fears. As children develop symbolic play (where one thing stands for another) they begin to act out their deepest feelings and concerns through language and role play. This approach to play is usually used in therapeutic situations. Play therapists often use techniques based on psycho-dynamic theory, such as using drawing and representation and encouraging children to express their feelings on paper. They sometimes use dolls and puppets so that children can express their feelings by pretending it's the doll or the puppet that has those feelings. This is a good way for some children to start to express what are often deep feelings of distress or anger that they simply cannot express openly.

Adults need to observe children carefully so that they recognise if a child needs more specialised help.

Most early years provision will provide opportunities for children to express their deep feelings, such as those of frustration and anger or fear and despair. Vigorous physical activity can often help children to let off steam, as can using a hammer and peg or pummelling clay. Many children will use puppets, masks or pretend play to act out their fears and concerns and this is normal behaviour. Adults have to provide adequate opportunities for children to express feelings and to observe children carefully to ensure that they recognise when a child needs more specialised help.

Social constructivist theory (thinking)

Piaget saw play as the means by which the child's learning comes together and helps the child to make sense of the world. Vygotsky emphasised the importance of other people being involved in play. In particular, he felt that children used play to act out and practise things before they managed them in real life circumstances and that play moved children from the zone of proximal development to the zone of actual development.

Most early years settings base their provision on social constructivist theory and will provide a wide range of activities and equipment for children to use in their learning. Careful observation of children's play and activity will indicate when the child is ready to move on. For example, if a child is drawing circles and dots and recognisable letters, then says 'That's my name', it may be time for the adult to give opportunities for practice and encouragement to write purposefully.

Piaget's stages of play development

Piaget identified the following stages in play development.

* Sensori-motor play (using senses and movement) from birth to eighteen months – e.g. exploring toys or their own hands, looking intently, sucking, banging the object on the ground, throwing objects.

* Symbolic play (where one thing stands for another) from eighteen months to five years – e.g. using language (words stand for something), blocks become cars, dolls become babies, they themselves become someone else, such as a mummy or daddy, when playing in a domestic play area.

* Co-operative play (using games with rules) from five to eight years – e.g. playing chase or hide and seek and making up their own rules or playing a board game and learning to obey the rules or take turns.

Theory into practice

- Investigate how children in your placement can let off steam and express their feelings safely. What activities and equipment are provided to assist in this process? How does this relate to psycho-dynamic theory?

- Look at Piaget's stages of play development. For each stage, think of activities and equipment that could be used with children to promote play development.

Co-operation in play

Early years practitioners work with children during their time at nursery to encourage co-operation, but recognise that children go through different stages before they co-operate in play. Babies and toddlers usually play alone, although they can be said to be aware of others. As they get older, children tend to watch others playing, then play alongside before joining in and co-operating. Co-operative play with rules usually means children make their own rules and play within those rules.

Assessment activity 4.3

Scenario 1: Mark is three years of age and has started at a local nursery school. He has settled well and enjoys the activities. Mark's parents are concerned that he spends a lot of time 'just playing'. They have written a note to the head expressing their concerns.

- Write a note to Mark's parents explaining why the nursery encourages children to join in play activities.

Scenario 2: Shenaz spends a good deal of her time in the construction area playing with large blocks. She is becoming very skilled in building various tall structures but staff have noticed she is becoming frustrated and knocks them down very quickly.

- Prepare a report outlining what the adult could do to support and extend Shenaz's play. Use ideas from Moyles' play spiral on which to base your report.

Scenario 3: Children in pre-school are encouraged to enjoy vigorous outdoor activity, rough and tumble and activities that help them express strong feelings in a safe way, such as pounding clay using a hammer. They are also encouraged to develop 'symbolic' pretend play sequences in a variety of nursery activities, such as domestic play, imaginative play, building and making things.

- Explain to a new student how the psycho-dynamic and the social constructivist theories of play could be used to explain these activities.

Play within the different curriculum frameworks

Birth to Three Matters and the Foundation Stage curriculum emphasise that play is a key tool to assist children's learning and development. When the Foundation Stage was introduced, the emphasis on providing learning through play was welcomed by many early years practitioners who had been concerned by the gradual formalisation of children's learning. The way in which play is provided for does, however, vary according to settings, although the EPPE project (see pages 117–18) notes that children appear to learn best where there is a balance of unstructured and structured play opportunities.

Curriculum provision

The environment that we provide for babies and children can significantly affect how well the early years curriculum is delivered. The first priority is to ensure that it should be physically safe, for example, by providing safe equipment and supervision, including clean and hygienic washrooms and kitchens, safe care routines, home-time routines and clear emergency procedures. The environment also needs to be predictable for the children and encourage their independence, for example, they know where things are, where to put things back and what the normal routine of the day is likely to bring. This does not mean it should be tightly scheduled as flexibility is needed, for example, for spending time when a child comes in with something to show, such as a pet, or when someone has found an interesting insect in the garden. The needs of the child are the guiding principle.

Resources will vary according to the setting but a range of activities should be on offer according to the age and needs of the children.

Activities, resources and equipment

Babies
* Treasure basket play
* Mobiles, rattles and pop-up toys
* Balls
* Stacking beakers
* Fabric and picture books
* Brick trolley

Toddlers
* Heuristic play
* Push-and-pull toys
* Post-it toys
* Sit-and-ride toys, tricycles

Heuristic play provides opportunities for toddlers to explore materials.

* Large connecting bricks, e.g. Duplo®
* Props for role play, e.g. pushchairs, cuddly toys, blankets

Children aged 2–5 years
* Sand
* Water
* Malleable materials, e.g. clay, dough
* Paint, modelling and other creative materials
* Material to explore and investigate, e.g. clocks, circuits
* Props for pretend play, e.g. dressing up, puppets, masks, 'small-world' toys, dolls
* Equipment for large movements, co-ordination and balance, e.g. climbing frames, push-and-pull toys, balls
* Equipment for fine movements, e.g. sewing, threading, puzzles
* Construction toys/equipment
* Graphics and mark-making areas
* Quiet areas
* Book areas

Layout of rooms for babies and toddlers

There is no fixed layout for rooms for babies and toddlers, but the following principles are useful, to include:

* areas where there is plenty of natural light and mirrors

* areas where babies and toddlers can sleep or rest (this can be a separate room)
* areas where nappy changes and bathing can take place safely and hygienically
* space on the floor where babies can move safely
* baskets or low-level storage so that babies and toddler can access equipment freely
* safe areas where babies and toddlers can climb and learn to balance
* division of areas so that non-mobile babies can watch others in safety.

It is also important that rooms for babies and toddlers remain stimulating, especially where they are being cared for over long periods. It is therefore helpful if they can see older children and also that they are given opportunities to change rooms or to spend time outdoors.

Layout of rooms for children aged 2–5 years

The layout of rooms can vary, but the following principles are useful when looking at provision for children of two to five years:

* rooms divided into smaller areas by screen or shelves to give privacy and encourage concentration and talking
* self-service principle, where children help themselves to equipment and return it afterwards
* workshop-style provision of activities according to curriculum plan – children join in as they choose, activities are often facilitated (anchored) by adults, e.g. making things, drawing from close observation
* other areas set up with equipment according to plans and some tables or floor space left empty
* large enough area for children to have circle or story time
* areas for sand and water (indoors and outdoors)
* areas of learning grouped logically, e.g. science next to technology, books next to graphics, creative next to sinks
* layout avoids disruptive through traffic
* easy and constantly available access to outdoors (boots and waterproofs available)

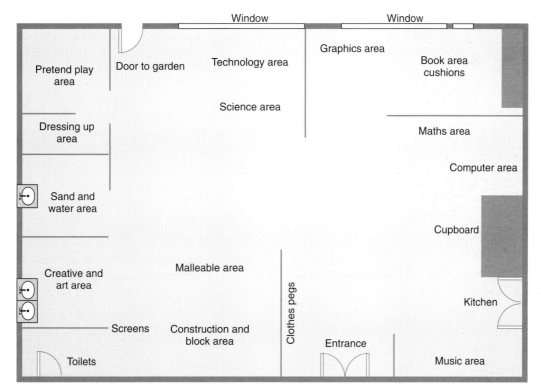

Example of a room layout.

✳ displays at child height, furniture child sized

✳ child has own space to keep things, e.g. in a drawer

✳ comfortable areas for being quiet or using books

✳ opportunities to play outdoors including specific activities such as collecting rain water.

4 Learning opportunities for young children

In order to deliver the curriculum effectively, practitioners have to plan effectively. While children enjoy playing, this alone does not mean that if simply left to it, they would gain a broad range of skills and concepts. This means using the curriculum frameworks and considering the best type of activities, equipment and resources to use with children.

Learning opportunities to promote key concepts

A key part of planning is to identify opportunities that will promote children's learning and development. A skilful practitioner is able to work out when learning opportunities are likely to occur naturally and where learning opportunities need to be planned using resources, equipment and activities.

Using everyday opportunities to promote learning

There are many occasions when learning opportunities will present themselves as part of everyday routines. Identifying and using these opportunities is key to working with all children, but especially with babies and toddlers. Examples of learning opportunities within routines include dressing, when adults might count buttons or poppers, and nappy changing, when adults might draw the child's attention to a hanging mobile.

Learning opportunities from free play

When children are able to access resources and materials for themselves, they are also learning skills and concepts. Free play involves children using a range of materials and resources, such as the sand tray, role play area or construction materials. In terms of planning, most settings

How many buttons are there? One, two, three...

Many everyday routines present learning opportunities.

Learning opportunities from structured activities

This is a key way in which most settings ensure that children cover all areas of the early years curriculum. Structured opportunities are generally recorded in the plans of settings, although it is important to note that activities can be structured at different levels. A highly structured activity would be one where the adult focuses children's attention in particular ways and may instruct them, for example, showing children how to use a salad spinner. An example of a less structured activity would be one where children arrive at the sand tray and find that there are magnetic letters hidden inside.

produce plans showing what materials, resources and equipment will be available for children to use in this way. As it can be hard to predict what individual children will chose to play with and how they will use it, there is always a danger that children will not necessarily gain the breadth of experience necessary to cover the early years curriculum. This means that most settings also plan structured activities that have some input from adults.

Types of planning

While there are no set planning formats, most settings produce three levels of plans ranging from long term through to activity planning. Practitioners working with babies and toddlers are likely to produce medium-term plans along with individual plans. This is because, within a baby or toddler room, the range of development and needs can be extremely wide.

PLAN DURATION	FACTORS TO CONSIDER AND INCLUDE
Long-term plans/strategies (up to a year in advance)	• The ELGs/NC/Literacy and Numeracy strategies • Numbers and ages of children • Patterns of attendance • Available equipment and resources • Significant annual events • Family and community interests and concerns • Organisational factors such as staffing and room availability • Inspection recommendations • Meeting needs of individuals and groups
Medium-term plans (covering period of weeks)	• Planned topics and themes • Needs and interests of the children • Balance of programme • Knowledge and concepts to be gained • Skills to practise • Activities that will be used • Visits • The level of differentiation according to stage of development • Inclusion of anti-discriminatory practice • Health and safety • Existing routines • Arrangements for including children with special needs and English as an additional language

PLAN DURATION	FACTORS TO CONSIDER AND INCLUDE
Short-term plans (usually detailed day to day, week to week or single activity)	• Staff deployment • Preparation of resources • Using visitors or parents who wish to be involved • Timing • Balance across week or day
Individual plans (for individual child's learning and development)	• Plans based on child's identified need, e.g. to encourage eye–hand co-ordination or confidence and self-esteem • Individual plans need to fit carefully with the medium- and short-term plans

Examples of curriculum planning

Fairview Day Nursery has decided to use the theme of 'Festival of Food' with two groups of three-to-four-year-olds. These children either attend the nursery on a sessional basis (each morning) or are part of the full-time groups attending the nursery when their parents are at work. The nursery prepares its own lunchtime meals and snacks. The nursery has decided on this theme as it serves a diverse community who could all contribute and wishes to stress some healthy-eating messages in a non-threatening way. Importantly, the children themselves love cooking activities and have enjoyed visits to local markets. Two of the staff have allotments, as have some grandparents, and children already enjoy visits to the allotment centre.

Remember – there is no right and wrong way of planning and you will find excellent examples in your work placement. The diagram below makes some suggestions.

Knowledge and understanding of the world
- Visit supermarkets, street markets, local allotments
- Help with cooking
- Discuss hot and cold cooking
- Identify healthy lunch boxes
- Understand simple food types and values including junk foods
- Use 'time' words
- Understand rationing and wartime menus
- Develop awareness of world foods and shortages
- Plant quick-growing seeds
- Understand hygiene routines

Personal and social
- Learn about each festival – identify by name
- Provide food for festivals of Hanukkah, Diwali, Christmas
- Become familiar with different customs
- Welcome parents to help prepare and share food associated with different cultures
- Take turns to cook
- Share meals with families
- Dress up in chef's hats and aprons – pretend kitchen and café

Physical
- Develop fine manipulation using cutlery and cooking utensils in context and associate language (peeling, chopping, whipping, mashing)
- Develop large muscles – digging in allotment and preparing ground for planting

Festival of Food

Creative
- Make models of food
- Draw and paint food themes for wall displays
- Design and print menus using IT and vegetable prints

Communication
- Develop co-operative play in pretend shop
- Imaginative play and language in café area
- Make posters for menu of the day
- Write lists and notices
- Recognise print in environment
- Order on-line/phone
- Keep food diaries using cut-out pictures, drawings and papier maché
- Understand social aspect of mealtimes
- Say and make up poems, rhymes and stories about food
- Act and model *The Very Hungry Caterpillar*
- Use food language (portion, helping, tasty, sour, sweet, salty)

Maths
- Buy ingredients
- Understand measuring and weighing vegetables and fruit in market
- Make price comparisons
- Practise selling and buying in pretend shop
- Lay table in café areas counting cutlery 1:1 correspondence
- Use computer and survey children's favourite foods
- Create database of information and then graphs to show findings

Weekly plan based on 'Festival of Food' – learning objectives

✳ Visiting allotment (Monday and Tuesday) and developing understanding of growing things, where some foods come from, how they change when cooked

✳ Talking about war time – developing understanding of time and continuity

✳ Continuing work on personal hygiene

The learning objectives are implemented in the ways shown in the following table.

PERSONAL AND SOCIAL	KNOWLEDGE AND UNDERSTANDING OF THE WORLD
• Sharing and taking turns with tools • Encouraging talk about food likes and dislikes • Cooking in group • Sharing experience of allotment visit • Eating together	• Groups to visit Mrs Ash's allotment with 3 parents • Bringing back potatoes, cooking, mashing with milk and butter and eating • Noting change of appearance of potatoes, texture and taste • Mrs Ash coming to talk about wartime recipes, showing real and dried eggs with pictures of Joel's great granddad digging large field • Washing hands and need for hygiene both after gardening and before eating
MATHEMATICAL DEVELOPMENT	**CREATIVE DEVELOPMENT**
• How many potatoes for each person when they are mashed • Sorting vegetables by colour and size • Setting table ensuring correct numbers of plates and cutlery • Selling vegetables in shop – using calculators and tills • Serving food in café • Maths language	• Printing with potatoes • Vegetable printing • Comparing shapes and patterns • Using prints on menus
LANGUAGE AND LITERACY	**PHYSICAL DEVELOPMENT**
• Wash, wash, wash your hands' song to tune of row your boat • Make posters and menus for café • Develop gardening and food vocabulary • Discuss what it was like in the war • *The Very Hungry Caterpillar*	• Digging potatoes • Using potato masher • Movement activity 'digging', 'raking' and 'stamping' the soil

Activity plan: making mashed potatoes

❋ Ask parents to help. Four children involved at a time.

❋ Prepare kitchen area. Peelers, chopping boards, masher, knives for chopping, wooden spoons, saucepans, salt, butter, milk, potatoes (from allotment), scales, nail brushes, bowls, towels.

❋ Select children in turn so that all can be involved over the week.

❋ Provide aprons.

Areas of learning

❋ *Knowledge and understanding of the world* – life cycle of potato, change of state when cooked, mashing adding butter and milk – butter melting. Watching change of state. Tasting and adding salt and pepper to improve flavour, observing colour, understanding of how root vegetables look when taken out of the ground (children have dug up the potatoes). How to clean and prepare vegetables using brush and bowl of water (fine manipulative skills and hygiene rules for hand washing), cooking.

❋ *Physical development* (control in fine movements and manipulative skills) – peeling user a potato peeler and noting change of appearance under the skin. Chopping using knife.

❋ *Communication* – use of descriptive and mathematical language. Vocabulary – mashed, mashing, peeling, boiling, flavour, dirty, clean, earth, heavier than/bigger than, round, oval, knobbly, smooth, rough.

❋ *Maths development* – language as above, weighing the potatoes.

❋ *Creative* – pattern making on mashed potato.

❋ *Personal and social* – working together, taking turns.

Practitioner's notes on the mashed potatoes activity

All the children participated and enjoyed the activity. Most of the time they were closely involved and talking to adults and each other.

Potatoes were really difficult to peel as the initial wash was not very successful. Using peelers was difficult for Katie as she is left handed (must order left-handed equipment). Children enjoyed chopping but found it hard work as the knives are blunt. Children picked up the language well and were fascinated by the end product as we set the bowl next to a bowl of potatoes from the ground. Jane and Alex could not believe the mashed potatoes were the same thing as the dirty potatoes.

Katie and Anita asked if they could make chips next time.

Most enjoyed eating the mashed potatoes although some needed tomato ketchup and enjoyed making mash pink.

Learning

Discussions with the children as the activity took place showed they all understood how root vegetables look when taken out of ground but only Katie could transfer this knowledge to supermarket situation and that vegetables came from ground – to lorry – to supermarket. Concepts need reinforcement.

Weighing the potatoes – children seemed to understand weighing principles. All understood need and reason to wash.

Use of descriptive and mathematical language – dirty/clean/earth/heavier than/bigger than/shapes/round/oval/knobbly/smooth. Alex could not use appropriate language to cover heavier/lighter, but everyone used terms fluently and accurately.

Children really interested in the life cycle of a potato and asked if they could eat when raw.

Mashing adding butter and milk – butter melting. Watching and describing change of state. Alex, Jane and Anita could describe mashed potato – white, soft, yellow runny butter, but could not grasp change of state, i.e. that this came out of original potatoes from allotments.

Follow-up activities

General

❋ Use potatoes for printing.

❋ Make chips.

❋ Plant in garden to see growth cycle – growing and harvesting.

❋ Continue theme on food.

❋ More opportunities for observing change of state, pictures and books on life cycles.

Individual

Make sure Katie has enough practice with left-handed tools and fine movements are better controlled.

The feedback from activities is recorded against each child's individual record and future plans are based on identified needs.

Common features of plans

Most settings' plans will contain some common features. Some features are specifically used for practical purposes, while other features are used as a way of checking that the curriculum is being covered.

Learning intentions

Many short-term and activity plans will show exactly what children are meant to gain from an activity. A learning intention when providing a toddler a post-it toy might be that the child gains spatial awareness, while a learning intention for making pizzas with three-year-olds might be to learn about how baking changes foods' colour and texture. As most activities actually provide many learning opportunities, writing two or three learning intentions can be helpful in focusing the practitioner when they are working with children. This means that the adult making pizzas might specifically draw children's attention to the colour of the pizza before and after it is cooked.

Curriculum links

Plans need to show how the proposed activities will link to the curriculum. This ensures that the curriculum is fully covered and also provides evidence for Ofsted. This can prevent situations where a practitioner who dislikes paint and creative activities rarely provides it. Curriculum links are also useful because they can help parents to understand why we carry out certain activities.

Vocabulary

Building children's language is a major part of working with young children. Some settings identify specific vocabulary that they feel children's attention should be drawn to. Key words might be shown on activity plans to remind the adult carrying out the activity of the vocabulary that should be introduced.

Assessment opportunities

Some activities lend themselves to observing and assessing children's development, knowledge and skills. Many activity or short-term plans will identify the possibilities for assessing children. This helps the adult to know what they should look out for while working with children. In some cases, opportunities to identify an individual child will be identified.

Differentiation

Many short-term plans will show how an activity can be adapted to meet the needs of specific groups of children or individual children. Differentiation might also indicate how the role of the adult might change. For example, the adult might need to provide extra support or resources for an individual child. Differentiation is essential in order that all children are given equal opportunities to access the curriculum.

Organisation

Short-terms plans are also likely to show some of the practical arrangements about how an activity is to be carried out. Some plans show the resources that are to be used and, where there are several members of staff, plans are likely to show who is responsible for implementing the activity. In baby and toddler rooms, key workers are likely to be responsible for working directly with specific children so that they can get to know and build a relationship with them.

> **Assessment activity 4.4**
>
> - Plan a week's programme to extend creative play development for a small group of children, including one child who is in a wheelchair. Develop at least three activity plans showing how you will ensure that the child in the wheelchair can join in.
> - In discussion with your placement supervisor plan two activities that you could undertake with individuals or small groups of children. Implement and evaluate your plan.

Think it over...

In your work placement, find out what types of assessment are carried out.

Assessment

In order to provide good learning opportunities for children, it is important to assess how children have responded to them. The assessment process should enable us to work out what a child enjoys doing, their strengths and what further activities would be of benefit.

Formative and summative assessment

Most settings use both formative and summative assessment. Formative assessment is where practitioners are constantly monitoring children's responses, strengths and weaknesses either informally or writing about them. Summative assessment is where practitioners draw together information to write a report and literally 'sum' up a child's progress.

Assessment process

Most settings plan for assessment and allocate members of staff who are responsible for assessing particular children. Ideally, the person best placed to assess a child's progress is the key worker, in co-operation with the parents. It is good practice for all young children to have a key worker who spends significant amounts of time with them. In school settings, children are likely to be assessed by their teacher as well as the teaching assistants.

Assessments are usually observation based and staff will watch individual children in order to see what skills or knowledge they have gained. In the early years, it is rare for children to be put in 'test' situations, as this is unnecessary and may cause them stress. It is for this reason that most assessments take place in environments with which the child is familiar.

See units 8 and 11 for further information.

END-OF-UNIT TEST

1 Which major theorist has most influenced current practice and why?

2 Social learning theory says that children learn through copying behaviour they see adults demonstrating. State whether this is true or false and give brief reasons for your answer.

3 Transmission theory encourages children to try new things. State whether this is true or false, and give brief reasons for your answer.

4 Social constructivists believe parents are partners in the education of their children. State whether this is true or false, and give brief reasons for your answer.

5 Why is the adult role less important within laissez-faire theory?

6 Explain the meaning and importance of symbolic play.

7 What equipment in your work placement most resembles that used by Maria Montessori? Describe the equipment and explain how it is used.

8 Describe three key aspects of Froebel's work that influence early years provision today.

9 Explain two theories of play commonly accepted in early years settings.

10 'Adults should leave children to play and not interfere.' Does this statement represent the views of most early years settings? Give reasons for your answer.

11 A parent was overheard to say 'Young children should not just play all day; it's time they got down to the Three Rs'. How would you explain to the parent why the nursery encourages the children to play?

12 'Children can't learn much at home, they need to wait till they go to school.' State whether this is true or false, and give brief reasons for your answer.

13 What are the six areas of learning within the Foundation Stage?

14 From your own experience describe two practical activities you have undertaken with children and state how you identified the key areas of learning.

15 Describe the planning cycle and explain each stage.

References and further reading

Athey, C (1990), *Extending Thought in Young Children*, London: Chapman Publishing

Bandura, A (1993), *Aggression: A social learning analysis*, Prentice Hall: NJ Englewood Cliffs

Bruner, J (1990), *Acts of Meaning*, Cambridge: MA, Harvard University Press

Bruce, T (1991), *Time to Play in Early Childhood Education*, Sevenoaks: Hodder and Stoughton

Bruce, T (1997), *Early Childhood Education*, London: Hodder and Stoughton

Bruner, J (1977), *The Process of Education*, Cambridge, MA: Harvard University Press

Chomsky, N (1968), *Language and Mind*, New York: Harcourt, Brace and World

Donaldson (1986), *Children's Minds*, London: Fortuna

Dowling, M (1995), *Starting School at Four: A joint endeavour*, London: Chapman Publishing

Drake, J (2001), *Planning Children's Play and Learning in the Foundation Stage*, London: David Fulton

Fodor, J (1983), *The Modularity of Mind*, Cambridge, MA: MIT Press

Gopnik, A et al (1999), *How Babies Think: The science of childhood*, London: Weidenfelt and Nicholson

Hutt, J et al (1988), *Play, Exploration and Learning: A natural history of the pre-school*, London: Routledge

Moyles, J (1989), *Just Playing? The Role and Status of Play in Early Childhood Education*, Milton Keynes: Open University Press

National Standards for Under Eights Day Care, (2001), DfEE

Parry, M and Archer, H (1974), *Pre-school Education*, London: Schools Council/ Macmillan Education

Pascal, C and Bertram, T (eds) (1993), *Effective Early Learning*, London: Hodder and Stoughton

Piaget, J (1962), *Play, Dreams and Imitation in Childhood*, London: Routledge & Kegan Paul

Siraj-Blatchford, I (ed) (1998), *A Curriculum Development Handbook for Early Childhood Educators*, Stoke on Trent: Trentham Books

Siraj-Blatchford, I (1994), *The Early Years: Laying the foundations for racial equality*, Stoke on Trent: Trentham Books

Vygotsky, L (1978), *Mind in Society*, Cambridge, MA: Harvard University Press

Manning Morton, J and Thorp, M (2001), *Key Times: A framework for developing high quality provision for children under three years old*, London: Camden Early Years Under Threes Development Group and The University of North London

UNIT 5

Child care practice

What you need to learn

1 The knowledge and understanding required to care for babies and children aged 0–8 years

2 The skills required to care for babies and young children aged 0–8 years

3 Promoting the maintenance of a healthy, safe and secure environment

4 Carrying out safety and emergency procedures

Introduction

The care of babies and young children is central to all aspects of early years work. This unit encourages learners to develop a full understanding of all the routines and care needs of babies and young children from birth to eight years. You will examine the principles of feeding, clothing and communicating with babies and young children. In addition, you will develop the practical skills necessary to implement the full range of care routines effectively.

Safety is an essential basic element for sustaining life and you will discover how to establish and maintain a safe and secure environment for children. You will learn about relevant legislation and how to plan and organise the physical environment, identifying potential hazards and preventing cross infection through effective hygiene procedures. The unit addresses many of the safety and emergency procedures of early years settings and addresses the importance of rehearsing, reviewing and modifying procedures efficiently.

How you will be assessed

This unit is assessed internally.

1 The knowledge and understanding required to care for babies and children aged 0–8 years

In this section you will develop the knowledge and understanding required to care for babies and young children and investigate the reasons why babies and young children need efficient care routines.

The early years services delivered in this country are currently undergoing considerable change. The document *Every Child Matters: Change for children* identifies five key outcomes for children and young people and describes the support needed from parents and carers to ensure these outcomes are achieved. The first three outcomes underpin all work with children and these concepts run through the whole unit.

KEY OUTCOMES	SUPPORT FROM PARENTS AND CARERS
Be healthy	Promote healthy choices
Stay safe	Provide safe homes and stability
Enjoy and achieve	Support learning
Make a positive contribution	Encourage community participation
Achieve economic well-being	Support career aspirations

Routines and care needs of babies and young children

Routines are important for both babies and young children. A good routine will not only meet their care and nutritional needs, but will also stimulate their development. The term 'educare' is now often used in this context, as child-rearing approaches in the past tended to focus more on meeting babies' and young children's physical and care needs, while potentially overlooking the role of the adult in stimulating babies and toddlers. An efficient routine is not only valuable for the children but will ensure efficient working practice for the carer.

Key issues – Birth to Three Matters

When working with babies it is also important to understand the concepts embedded in the Birth to Three Matters framework. Some of the core principles relate directly to the work in this unit.

✳ You should investigate the Birth to Three Matters framework and make a chart identifying the four aspects and associated components. You can then make links with this chart as you work through this unit.

✳ When you are working in a setting with babies and children under three, find out how these concepts within the framework are embedded in the working practice within the setting.

PRINCIPLES WITHIN THE BIRTH TO THREE MATTERS FRAMEWORK	YOUR WORKING PRACTICE
Parents and families are central to the well-being of the child.	You will consult with parents about all matters related to children's routines.
Babies and young children are sociable beings, and they are competent learners from birth.	Your communication with babies and young children is an essential aspect of their care.
Schedules and routines must flow with the child's needs.	While establishing a routine, the needs of the child must be your guiding factor.
Children learn when they are given appropriate responsibility.	As children grow and develop, one of your primary goals will be to encourage their independence.

Routines for children at different ages

The following table identifies core features of the care routines for babies and young children. You will notice how children gain more independence as they grow and develop. A detailed description of the reasons for individual care routines follows.

AGE	CARE ROUTINES
0–1	Babies, who spend considerable time asleep in the first few weeks of life, are totally dependent on the carer for all their needs. Routines will include feeding, sleeping, nappy changing, bathing and time for playful stimulation and interaction.
1–3	Young children begin the process of developing independence in feeding, toilet training, and helping to dress and care for their hair and teeth. While sleeping 10–12 hours a night, they will still need periods of sleep and rest during the day. They still rely on the carer to organise much of their personal care.
3–5	As children start accessing pre-school education, independence skills develop further. They can now feed and dress independently, need quiet periods rather than sleep times throughout the day, and are independent in personal care routines.
5–8	By the time they go to school they are not only able to manage most of their physical needs, but are also socially and emotionally more independent, able to relate to others and take more responsibility for their own behaviour.

Care of skin, hair and teeth

Skin

Skin is the largest organ of the human body and has several key functions which include forming a protective barrier to prevent germs from penetrating into our bodies. As babies are vulnerable to infections, it is vital that babies' skin is kept clean. Their skin is also sensitive and fragile, which means that care must be taken in the selection of skin care products. Advice also changes over time, with products such as barrier cream no longer being used systematically after a nappy change.

It is important to be aware of the different skin types and specific needs of all children. Black skin is often naturally dry and may need regular moisturising with creams and lotions. You should always ask parents for advice about the skin care for their child.

Children's skin needs to be protected from the sun's rays to prevent heat stroke and the occurrence of skin cancer in later life. Current medical opinion suggests that even on a cloudy or cool summer's day the sun's rays can still be harmful to skin. Babies under the age of 12 months should not be exposed to the sun, and particular care needs to be taken between 11 am and 3 pm, when the sun is at its highest. Ensure light-fitting garments, wide-brimmed hats and high factor sun cream are worn. Research into the effects of the sun on the skin is ongoing, so you will need to check for the latest available advice.

Hair

Care of the hair is important and often contributes to the development of children's self-esteem and self-image. Different types of hair require different care and you should ask parents' advice about the most appropriate care. Regular checking for the presence of head lice is essential.

Head lice

Head lice are parasites that live on the human scalp. They have become a common problem in many group-care settings, as children have more head-to-head contact. Children's hair should be checked each week for the following signs of an infestation:

* itchy scalp

* red bite marks

* lice – tiny wingless translucent insects in the hair roots, especially at the nape of the neck

* eggs, known as nits – white or brown specks attached to hair.

Advice as to treatment changes, although thoroughly combing with a nit comb is the traditional method. Other methods include the use of lotions containing pesticides, and electric combs.

Tooth care

As well as chewing food, teeth are important for the ability to speak clearly, so it is important that they are well looked after through good oral hygiene and regular visits to the dentist. The sticky layer of plaque that covers the teeth is home to the bacteria that usually live in the mouth. These bacteria are responsible for producing the acid that softens the enamel and causes tooth decay. Acid in fruit juice and fizzy drinks is also responsible for tooth decay, so should be avoided where possible.

Bathing

The frequency with which babies and children are bathed is often a matter of parental choice. Topping and tailing refers to the process of cleaning the vital parts of a baby, especially their face and hands and nappy area, and is often an alternative to a full bath.

Nappy changing

In Western cultures, babies are put into nappies that require regular changing. There are two categories of nappies: disposables and terry towelling (fabric) nappies. While the majority of parents currently choose disposable nappies, some parents prefer to use towelling nappies as they are re-usable and considered more environmentally friendly.

Adults working with babies should check that stools and urine are normal for the age of the child. At first, all babies produce meconium, which is sticky and greenish-black in colour. After a few days, the stools change according to whether the baby is being breast or bottle fed. Breast-fed babies have stools which are mustard in colour and fairly liquid. They should not smell unpleasant, while the stools of bottle-fed babies are browner, have some smell and are thicker in texture.

Once babies are weaned, their stools become firmer and have a stronger odour. The frequency with which babies pass stools can vary, although medical advice should be sought if no stools have been passed after a week or if the stools are watery, very pale or contain any signs of blood. Medical advice should also be sought if urine is not being frequently passed, as this may indicate dehydration.

Nappy rash

While nappy rash affects many babies under 18 months, it is becoming less common as disposable nappies improve. The rash can cause severe discomfort to babies and therefore preventative steps are essential.

Ammonia dermatitis

Ammonia dermatitis is caused by the production of ammonia as bacteria from the baby's stools breaks down the urine. Ammonia is an irritant that burns the skin and thus causes nappy rash.

The table below describes the most common types of nappy rash. In all situations, seek medical advice if the condition does not improve.

APPEARANCE	CAUSE	TREATMENT
Red rash forming around the genitals. Strong smell.	Ammonia dermatitis	Increase frequency of nappy changes. Wash and gently dry affected area thoroughly. Allow time after changes without a nappy to allow air flow.
Spotty ulcerated rash covering the genitals and bottom.	Ammonia dermatitis	Use steps above, but seek medical advice promptly.
Pink and pimply rash forming around the anus and spreading to the bottom and genitals.	Thrush dermatitis	Seek medical advice – an anti-fungal cream is likely to be prescribed.
Small blisters or pimples around the nappy area.	Heat rash	Avoid using plastic pants if using terry towelling. Leave off nappy for as long as possible.
Brownish-red scaly rash around genitals and anywhere where skin is greasy.	Seborrhoeic dermatitis (similar to cradle cap)	Seek medical advice – an ointment may be prescribed.

Care of skin, hair and teeth for children at different ages

The table below shows the principles of caring for children's skin, hair and teeth at different ages. Note how children need to be given more privacy and independence as they become older.

AGE	PHYSICAL CARE
0–1	All aspects of physical care will be undertaken by the carer.
	Bathing Some babies become very distressed when their clothes are removed, so bathing may not happen every day. As they get older, babies can learn to splash and play and a daily bath becomes more common.
	Nappy changing Nappies should be changed after each feed and immediately following the passing of stools to avoid nappy rash.
	Hair care Babies' hair should be gently washed during the bathing process.
	Teeth It is important to start brushing teeth as soon as they begin to appear. The carer should clean the teeth twice a day with a small amount of baby toothpaste.
1–3	High levels of supervision are required at this age, to prevent possible accidents.
	Bathing **Children should never be left alone in a bathroom or toilet**. Cleaning products must be removed from their reach. Children are likely to need a daily bath or shower. Water must be checked before children enter and bath mats are advised to prevent children from slipping. Adults may need to make washing fun by turning it into a game, as many toddlers intensely dislike having their faces, hands and hair washed. Children's skin needs to be dried carefully to prevent soreness.
	Hair care Hair will need to be combed or brushed regularly. Check with parents about preferred hair products and styles. Many toddlers dislike having their hair washed. Encourage toddlers to wet their hair themselves while they are playing in the shower or bath. Use mild hair products and make sure that a towel is handy to wipe away any water or soap from eyes.
	Teeth Milk teeth should be appearing. It is important that they are brushed twice a day by an adult, as children of this age are likely to just suck the brush. To prevent tooth decay, sugary drinks and foods should be avoided and children should be seen by a dentist.
3–5	Children are taking more responsibility for their personal hygiene. Personal hygiene can be used as a basis for learning topics, such as 'Looking after our teeth'.
	Bathing Most parents will want their children to have a daily shower or bath. Children still need to be supervised at these times and the adult should take responsibility for running and checking the temperature of the water. They should encourage children to wash themselves, but do the 'final check' to ensure that all areas of the body are clean, if necessary.

▶

AGE	PHYSICAL CARE
3–5 (ctd)	**Hair care** Adults should encourage children to brush or comb their hair, but may need to give some assistance. Hair needs to be checked for head lice. Children should be encouraged to wash their own hair, but may need to be given assistance when rinsing.
	Tooth care Children can brush their own teeth, but adults should check and give a final brush. Avoid giving sugary foods and drinks to children. Six-monthly check-ups at a dentist are advised.
5–8	Children should be given increased privacy and the adult should be aiming just to remind and praise children about looking after their hair, skin and teeth. Some children become less enthusiastic and thorough about keeping themselves clean as they get older. Interesting bath products and toys can help if this is the case.

KEY ISSUES

Parents may have differing views on how best to care for their child's skin, hair and teeth. There are cultural and religious variations in the way physical care is provided. For example, Afro-Caribbean children may be massaged after a bath and parents will know which skin care products suit their child best.

- Ask three parents of children at different ages what skin and hair care products they use.
- Use the internet to investigate products for Afro-Caribbean skin and hair.

Think it over...

Watching television

A recent research project from the US suggests that children under the age of two should not watch television. It is suggested that the quick images may cause permanent changes within the brain, and may lead to an increased risk of developing ADHD by the age of seven. However, the National Literacy Trust suggests that, for children aged 2–5, watching some television and talking about it with adults, may aid their language development.

- Using the internet, investigate a range of information about the value of watching television for young children.

Rest and sleep

The exact purpose of sleep is still being researched, but it is already known that the body requires sleep in order to maintain cells and also to process information and for the release of hormones required for growth. Lack of sleep can result in increased susceptibility to infection, a lack of concentration and challenging behaviour. Periods of rest are just as important as sleep, and there should be time each day when children can rest or be involved in some quiet and relaxing activity.

Play routines

Stimulation is essential for healthy development. The early years practitioner will stimulate children's development through effective communication and by providing a range of age-appropriate play activities throughout the day (see unit 11).

Planning, implementing and evaluating routines

Planning a routine

Parents should always be involved in the planning of a routine as they will have particular preferences and knowledge of their own child that should be incorporated into any routine.

Implementing a routine

Implementing a routine requires good planning, patience and good organisation. Most practitioners find that these skills develop with practice, especially as babies and children do not necessarily go along with any planned routine! They are also very aware of changes and react if they sense that their carers are not calm or are

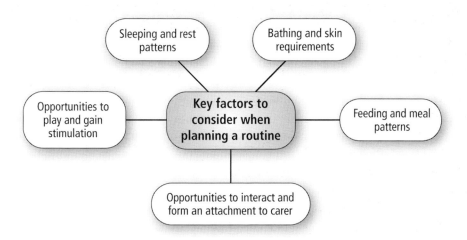

Key factors to consider when planning a routine
- Sleeping and rest patterns
- Bathing and skin requirements
- Opportunities to play and gain stimulation
- Feeding and meal patterns
- Opportunities to interact and form an attachment to carer

hurried. It is essential to be flexible enough to be able to respond to the child's needs and adapt the routine appropriately if required.

✳ Make sure that enough time has been allowed for feeding and various tasks, such as nappy changing, bathing and feeding.

✳ Use any time when the baby is asleep purposefully, such as by making up feeds.

✳ Observe the baby or young child carefully for signs of tiredness or hunger.

Evaluating a routine

Routines are best evaluated by considering how the needs of the baby or young child have been met and how effectively the early years worker has been in implementing the routine. The evaluation process could consider the following questions.

✳ Has the baby or young child:
- showed signs of irritability or tiredness
- eaten a healthy diet and had enough to drink
- had plenty of opportunity for communication and adult attention
- experienced a variety of stimulating activities
- had opportunity for fresh air and exercise
- had appropriate physical care?

✳ Has the early years professional:
- managed his or her time effectively
- kept calm
- shared his or her time with different children

- kept to the schedule as planned
- been flexible enough to meet the needs of individual children?

Toilet training

The term 'toilet training' is in some ways misleading. It suggests that a child can be taught by an adult to use the toilet, but this is no longer the approach taken today. It is now generally accepted that 'toilet training' needs to be a process which is child-led as it relies heavily on the child being physically and emotionally ready. This means that there is a wide variation in ages, with some children moving out of nappies at 15 months, while others are ready at around three years (see also pages 164–5).

Physical activities

Physical activities should be included in all routines, to promote development. Children at different ages have different needs and opportunities can be provided for the following.

0–6 months
- Time without a nappy to kick and play
- Baby gym

6–12 months
- Space to crawl
- Balls
- Objects to explore

1–3 years
- Time outside to run and climb
- Sit-and-rides
- Small slides

3–5 years
- Obstacle courses
- Climbing frames
- Music and dancing

5–8 years
- Races
- Ropes
- Bicycles
- Swimming
- Football

Promotion of self-reliance and confidence

An independent child is a confident child who is able to develop a good self-image and self-esteem, both important aspects of development. The chart below identifies care routines that can promote independence skills.

Feeding

Principles of nutritional requirements

In order to care for babies and children effectively, it is important to have some understanding of how the body uses food. To grow and develop, the body needs a diet that contains food with sufficient nutrients to meet its needs. There are five nutrient groups, with each nutrient having a specific function for growth and the maintenance of health – see table opposite. Many foods contain more than one nutrient and foods that are rich in nutrients are often referred to as 'nutritious' or 'nutrient-rich'. In addition to food, the body also needs water. Water does not contain any nutrients, but has several essential functions in the body, including regulating temperature.

Assessment activity

Jemima is eight months old. She is eating a range of mashed food and has just started finger foods. She wakes at 6 am and has a 45-minute nap soon after 9 am, and a 1¼-hour nap at 1 pm. She goes to bed after her bath at 6.45 pm. Her three-year-old brother Jake goes to nursery from 9 am to 11.30 am and is in bed by 7.30 pm. Six-year-old Julie goes to school.

- Plan a routine which meets the care needs for rest, sleep, stimulation, fresh air and exercise for all three children.
- Explain how the care needs change for all three children.
- Evaluate the effectiveness of your plan in relation to providing care for the children.
- Evaluate your own working practice.

AGE	PROMOTING INDEPENDENCE
0–6 months	Can be encouraged to settle self to sleep.
6–12 months	Begins finger feeding.
12–18 months	Learns to use spoon. Helps with dressing.
18 months–3 years	More confident dressing skills. Toilet training. Learns to use spoon and fork.
3–5 years	Learns to use knife and fork effectively. Washes own hands and face, but may initially need help with drying. Learns to manage simple buttons and fastenings. Can brush own teeth. Learns to dress and undresses alone.
5–8 years	Learns to tie shoelaces. Can dress entirely independently.

NUTRIENT GROUP	FUNCTION	SOURCES	CONSEQUENCES OF DEFICIENCY
Fats	Concentrated source of energy	Oils, butter, cheese, meat, fish, milk	Rarely deficient in the UK, although very low-fat diets can prevent uptake of fat-soluble vitamins, such as vitamin E
Proteins	Growth and repair of cells – excess protein is converted into energy	Animal sources: milk and other dairy products, meat, fish, eggs Vegetables sources – these must be combined: soya, pulses, cereals, nuts, seeds, lentils	Lethargy, failure to thrive and susceptibility to infection
Carbohydrates	Energy Cellulose (commonly known as fibre) assists digestion	Bread, cereals, potatoes, rice, pasta, yams, bananas, fruit juice	Lack of energy – overall tiredness and difficulty in resisting infection
Vitamins Vitamin A – Retinol	Essential for vision in dim light, general health of eyes and skin	Yellow and dark green vegetables, e.g. carrots and spinach; also found in liver, butter and added to margarine	Poor vision, blindness (unusual in the UK)
Vitamin B1 – Thiamin	Responsible for the steady release of energy from carbohydrates	Wholemeal flour and grains, milk, fortified cereal products, potatoes, eggs, vegetables	Beri-beri, where carbohydrate intake is high and vitamin B1 is low
Vitamin B2 – Riboflavin	Using energy from food	Milk, animal products and yeast extract	Sores in corners of mouth (rare in the UK)
Vitamin B6 – Pyridoxine	Metabolism of amino acids; needed for the formation of haemoglobin	Meat, fish, eggs, whole cereals, baked beans, bananas	Deficiency is rare, although excess of this vitamin can cause damage to nerve function
Vitamin B12 – Folic acid	Needed by rapidly dividing cells, such as bone marrow; Folic acid taken before and during the first weeks of pregnancy is known to reduce the risk of spina bifida	Animal products, yeast, eggs, cheese, milk and fortified cereals; Folic acid found in leafy vegetables, yeast extract, breakfast cereals	Anaemia and degeneration of nerve cells – vegans can be at risk if no supplements are taken; deficiency of folic acid can result in anaemia

▶

NUTRIENT GROUP	FUNCTION	SOURCES	CONSEQUENCES OF DEFICIENCY
Vitamin C – Ascorbic acid	Needed for maintenance of connective tissue	Citrus fruits, guavas, blackcurrants, green pepper, as well as other fresh fruit and vegetables; vitamin C is fragile and damaged by heat	Bleeding from small blood vessels and from gums, wounds heal more slowly; disease known as scurvy (rare in UK)
Vitamin D	Helps bone formation	Sunlight, margarine, milk, yoghurt, other dairy products, breakfast cereals	Rickets and deformed bones
Vitamin E	Works as an antioxidant – full role still being researched	Most foods contain vitamin E, especially vegetable oil, nuts, seeds and some cereals	Very rare, but occasionally anaemia in premature babies
Minerals	Many minerals are required by the body. Key minerals include iron and calcium		
Iron	Helps body take in oxygen	Meat, breakfast cereals, bread and vegetables; iron is more easily absorbed into the body when vitamin C is present	Anaemia
Calcium	Strengthens bones, teeth, contraction of muscles including heart muscle, clotting of blood	Milk, cheese, bread, vegetables, yoghurt and other dairy products; vitamin D needs to be present in order for calcium to be absorbed	Rickets, bone deformation

Achieving a healthy diet

It is virtually impossible to see foods just in terms of nutrients, so many dieticians divide foods into groups and suggest that our daily intake of food is composed from each of these groups. It is also important that diets are varied, as relying on only a limited number of foods reduces the likelihood of giving the body the range of minerals and vitamins required.

It is important to consider the age of the child, as nutrient requirements change, with younger children requiring particularly nutrient-rich foods, such as milk, to ensure that their small stomachs are taking in sufficient nutrients. Current advice is that a low-fat, high-fibre diet is unsuitable for young children, especially under two years.

Breakfast
Porridge made with milk, orange juice, toast

Mid-morning snack
Milk and banana

Lunch
Cheese and potato pie, baked beans, and salad, blackcurrant mousse, water

Afternoon snack
Cheese and biscuits and an orange

Tea
Chicken, rice and spinach, fresh fruit salad and ice-cream, milk

A sample menu for a three-year-old.

Snacks as part of the overall diet

Children need to develop a healthy approach towards food, so do not use food as a reward or as a threat! Children's stomachs are small in relation to their bodies, so they need to have a regular intake of nutritious food. Snacks and drinks should be thought of as part of the daily nutritional intake, rather than something additional. Healthy snacks include carrot sticks, tomatoes, apples, bread and rice sticks, while the best drinks to serve are water, milk and, occasionally, fruit juices.

Meeting children's special dietary needs

Some children will have special food requirements because of cultural or religious restrictions or because of a medical condition. When planning meals and snacks for children with special dietary needs, advice and guidance should be sought from parents as the strictness with which families adhere to some religious and cultural restrictions can vary.

The following table is a guide.

	REQUIREMENTS	RESTRICTIONS
Hindus	Mostly vegetarian	No alcohol
Sikhs	Meat must be killed by one blow to the head.	No beef
Muslims	Meat must be 'halal', otherwise considered unclean.	No pork, no shellfish, no alcohol
Jews	Meat must be 'kosher', otherwise considered unclean. Fish has to have scales and fins. Dairy and meat products cannot be consumed together. Dairy products must be prepared using separate utensils.	No pork, no shellfish, no rabbit
Rastafarians	Mainly vegetarian, although take milk products. Foods must be 'I-tal' or alive – no canned or processed foods. Foods must be organic.	No salt, no coffee, no alcohol
Vegans	Vegans do not eat anything that originates from animals. Many vegans will only eat organically-produced plants.	No animal products such as milk or eggs
Vegetarians	Dairy products and eggs can be eaten, providing that the animals are humanely farmed.	No foods that involve the killing of animals
Diabetes	Diabetes is a disorder that reduces the ability of the body to control the amount of glucose in the blood. Fluctuation in glucose level can cause hypoglycaemia or hyperglycaemia. Regular meals and snacks are required to avoid fluctuation in glucose levels.	No foods containing sugar. Follow parents' advice and any diet sheet carefully.
Coeliac's disease	An intolerance to gluten means that it is not digested by the body. The disease can be fatal, causing weight loss and anaemia.	No wheat, rye, barley and oats. Look carefully at processed foods as gluten is often present, e.g. in soups, sauces.
Allergies	Although food allergies are rare you need to be aware of the symptoms, which may include swelling of the lips, face, throat and tongue and tingling and itching in the mouth and lips. Stomach cramps, vomiting and diarrhea and a blotchy skin rash may also occur.	The most frequent allergies are to milk, eggs, fish, nuts, citrus fruits and tomatoes.

Think it over...

Did you know that the following products may contain nuts: breakfast cereals, biscuits and cakes, sweets and chocolate, curries, salad dressings and dips, ice cream, veggie burgers?

- Look in your store cupboard tonight and see how many of your products contain nuts.

Current nutritional practices

There are many concerns about the dietary habits of children and young people today.

The *National Diet and Nutrition Survey: Young people aged 4–18 years* (2000) found that children eat less than half the recommended five portions of fruit and vegetables a day.

The government's Scientific Advisory Committee on Nutrition (SCAN) recommends that children under seven should consume no more than 2 grams of salt a day. Most people do not realise the amount of salt that is hidden in foods such as white bread, baked beans and tinned pasta.

Children who do not drink enough fluids become dehydrated. This can have an effect on behaviour and learning ability.

Research shows that children and young people eat too much sugar. More sugar comes from fizzy drinks than from any other type of food and drink.

Theory into practice

Current issues for healthy diets

Using the internet, prepare a short paper outlining some of the current issues in relation to the diets of children and young people that you could share with parents to support them promote healthy eating within the family. Some websites you can use are:

- www.nutrition.org.uk
- www.food.gov.uk
- www.foodcomm.org.uk

Assessment activity 5.2

Principles of nutritional requirements

You are working as a nanny looking after three children, Dan is eight months old, Matthew is two years old and Rowan is five years old.

- Plan a menu for all three children for breakfast, lunch and dinner and identify any snacks they may have during the day.
- Explain how the menus meet the principles and requirements of a nutritious diet for young children.
- Analyse the challenges that face these children in relation to maintaining a healthy diet.

Infant feeding

In the first four to six months of life, babies rely solely on milk. There are two types of milk: breast milk and formula milk.

CASE STUDY

You are working in a large private nursery where some of the children have specific dietary requirements. Matthew is diabetic and must eat regularly. His carbohydrate and sugar intake must be monitored against his insulin levels. Shabana must have halal meat. Sarfraz has a milk allergy and uses a soya-based product. Lisa is vegetarian. Leon does not like eggs or custard. Rowena has a nut allergy and Imtiaz has coeliac disease and cannot eat wheat, rye or oat products.

- Use this case study to explain why it is important for staff to be aware of the dietary needs of children and explain what might happen to each child if he or she had the wrong food.
- Analyse the advantages and disadvantages of having separate menus for children who have dietary needs.
- Describe a meal that could be eaten by all the children.

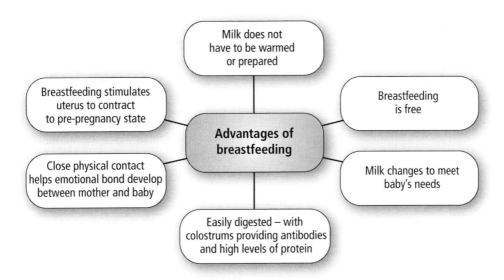

Advantages of breastfeeding

- Milk does not have to be warmed or prepared
- Breastfeeding stimulates uterus to contract to pre-pregnancy state
- Breastfeeding is free
- Close physical contact helps emotional bond develop between mother and baby
- Milk changes to meet baby's needs
- Easily digested – with colostrums providing antibodies and high levels of protein

Breastfeeding

Human breast milk is considered to be the best type of milk for babies to receive, as it changes to meet babies' nutritional needs. In the first two to three days, it is thick and yellowish in colour. This is called colostrum and contains antibodies, to protect the baby from infection, and high levels of protein, to promote growth. Over the following days milk comes in and the quantity of colostrum reduces.

Most babies take the milk directly from their mother's breasts, although milk can be expressed and used in bottles. Expressed milk is often given to premature babies who are not strong enough to suckle, as well as by mothers so that someone else can feed their baby.

Supporting breastfeeding

Breastfeeding is more likely to succeed when mothers have had information about breastfeeding during the pregnancy and have been given help in the first few hours and days after the baby is born. Some mothers need help in getting their baby to 'latch on' to the nipple, as this is a skill for both the mother and baby to learn. Once breastfeeding has been established, most mothers find it pain-free and very rewarding.

Key ways in which breastfeeding mothers can be supported

* Help the mother to rest and relax, such as by changing nappies or helping with household tasks.

* Prepare nutritious meals – breastfeeding mothers need to eat well. Dieting when breastfeeding is not recommended.

* Offer drinks before and during feeds – breastfeeding mothers need sufficient fluid to manufacture milk.

Formula milk – bottle feeding

There are two types of formula milk: cow's milk and soya milk. Soya milk is used for babies who are allergic to cow's milk or whose parents have objections to using animal products. Formula milk is designed to reproduce the composition of breast milk as closely as possible, although it is not as easily digested. Formula feeds are available in powdered form, to which water is added, or in ready-mixed packs which, although costly, can be useful when travelling.

While breastfeeding is strongly recommended, some mothers may bottle feed. Common reasons include the wish to share the feeding with a partner, difficulties in establishing breastfeeding in the first few days or problems in coping with the night feeds. Mothers may also be advised to bottle feed in cases where they have a medical condition which requires that they take medications or where the baby has difficulty feeding or is not putting on enough weight.

Frequency and amounts

You need to follow the parents' advice about the frequency and amount of formula babies eat. A new-born baby may need feeding every two to three hours, progressing to four-hourly as the baby grows. An approximate guide for each feed is as follows:

* New born: 30–60 mls
* 1 month: 90–120 mls
* 2–6 months: 120–180 mls
* 6 months: 180–220 mls

Most of all, it is important to follow the needs of the baby, who will soon let you know if he or she is still hungry.

Weaning babies

Weaning is the process by which babies learn to take foods other than milk. It is an important process because, after six months, babies' natural reserves of iron are running low and milk alone will not be sufficient to meet these or to provide enough calories for the growing baby.

Weaning usually takes place after the age of six months. It is currently recommended that babies should not be weaned earlier than six months because their digestive systems are not mature enough to cope with solid food. Signs that a baby may need to be weaned are:

* wakes in the night for feed after previously sleeping through
* seems hungry after a feed
* lacks energy and sleeps for longer periods.

Stages of weaning

There are three stages of weaning, as shown in the table below. By twelve months, most babies eat a wide range of foods and can feed themselves using their hands. Milk remains an important food in babies' diets during the weaning process but, as milk feeds decrease, the baby needs to be offered drinks of cool boiled water or diluted fruit juice, as more water will be needed to aid digestion.

Foods that should not be given to babies

Advice regarding the safety of foods can vary – always check the current advice. Some foods cannot be given to babies as they pose a health or safety risk.

* **Salt** – salt should not be added to babies' food because the kidneys cannot process it.
* **Sugar** – sugar is not given to babies as it can cause tooth decay.
* **Eggs** – uncooked or partly uncooked eggs, such as boiled eggs, must not be served as they can contain salmonella, which causes food poisoning.
* **Nuts** – nuts can pose a choking hazard and in some children cause a serious allergic reaction.
* **Liver** – liver is no longer recommended for children as it can contain high levels of toxins.

STAGE	FOOD	WEANING PROCESS
Stage 1 4–6 months	Puréed foods	Foods are introduced one by one, with rice, vegetables and fruit being given first. Wheat-based foods should be avoided at first, as they can cause allergies. Foods are mixed with breast milk or formula milk so that they are a runny consistency and easy to swallow.
Stage 2 6–9 months	Mashed or minced foods	Foods are mashed down or minced up so that babies have to chew slightly before swallowing. Meat, fish and well-cooked eggs can be introduced. Foods can be mixed together. Cow's milk can be used for cooking, but formula or breast milk should be given for feeds up until 12 months.
Stage 3 9–12 months	Finger foods	Foods such as slices of bread, fish fingers and pieces of banana are given to babies to encourage them to feed themselves. Babies can be given the same food as the family, providing it is slightly mashed down and does not contain salt or sugar.

Communication with babies and children

As well as providing for care and nutritional needs, babies and young children also need to interact with their carers. Communication with babies helps them to 'bond' or form an attachment with their carer. Research on attachments (see pages 411–13) has shown that children who have formed an attachment with their primary carers will be emotionally secure. Interaction with others stimulates their language and aids overall development.

Communication through touch and eye contact.

Touch and massage

While hearing and vision are still developing in young babies, they are able to process information by touching and being touched. Babies respond to being stroked, rubbed and held, as this makes them feel secure. The use of massage in the everyday care of babies is increasing, although it is traditional in many cultures.

Crying

Babies are born with a range of reflexes (see pages 246–7) including the crying reflex. Young babies rely on crying to signal their needs, although the amount of crying decreases as their communication skills develop. Primary carers are usually able to identify the needs of their baby through the type of crying, with breastfeeding mothers finding that some cries will stimulate the 'let down' milk reflex in their breasts.

Talking to babies and young children

The National Literacy Trust suggests that there is a growing realisation that the language and communication skills of young children are deteriorating. It would appear that there is less emphasis on talking to babies and young children. There are many reasons why this may be the case, some of which include:

* changes in family work patterns
* lack of shared family time, e.g. meal times

* predominance of television in the home
* lack of understanding about the importance of communicating with young children.

It is therefore essential for the professional carer to develop the skills of communication and use them effectively.

Stimulation

Babies and young children learn about their world by taking information in from their senses. This stimulates brain activity and creates pathways in the brain. Babies who have not been stimulated are likely to show signs of developmental delay. As children grow older, they need to be provided with a range of safe stimulating play experiences, supported by a responsive adult who can interact effectively without controlling the play.

Massage

Talking and singing to them

Heuristic play and treasure baskets

Showing them books and pictures

Examples of ways to stimulate babies

Mobiles and displays

Providing safe toys such as baby gyms

Placing baby in front of a mirror

Taking them for 'walks' and pointing out things

Liam is two and a half and lives with his mother in a high-rise block of flats in a deprived area of town. His father is in prison and his mother has had depression since he was born. The health visitor has just arranged a place for him at the local children's centre, as she is worried about his language development.

- Identify why Liam has poor communication skills.

- Explain the importance of communication with babies and young children.
- Analyse the effect of poor communication on Liam's future development.
- Create a list of advice you could give to Liam's mother.

Praise and encouragement

Babies and young children notice and respond to adults' tone of voice, gesture and facial expression as part of the process of learning language. Praise and encouragement helps children to feel secure and promotes self-esteem, confidence and independence.

Theory into practice

Observe three children receiving praise.
- Identify what they were being praised for.
- Describe how they were being praised.
- Analyse how that praise supported or extended the children's development.

Management of a distressed baby

Babies cry as a signal that their needs are not being met. These signals should never be ignored, as they may mean that the baby is in pain or needs feeding. Babies who cry persistently must be referred for medical advice promptly, especially if they are normally easy to settle.

Some causes of crying are as follows.

Colic

* Acute pain in the lower abdomen causing the baby to draw up their knees and scream
* Common in babies under three months
* Often worse towards early evening
* May be linked to the immature digestive system or cow's milk intolerance

Hunger

* Hungry babies may cry
* They may suck their hands
* If over four months they may need to be weaned

KEY ISSUES

- Prepare feeds and meals in advance so that the baby does not have to wait long.
- Offer a sip of cool boiled water if feed is not immediately ready to take the edge of hunger.

Tiredness

* Babies may fight to remain awake, especially as they get older and more alert
* Intermittent crying
* Rubbing the head

Loneliness

* Feels lonely and wants to be picked up
* Can't entertain themselves so rely on adults for stimulation

Pain

* Babies cry when in pain, so a baby should never be left to cry without being checked

Teething

* Common cause of crying in babies as they approach five to six months
* Signs include hot, red cheeks, dribbling and restlessness

* Babies often gain temporary relief by biting on teething rings

Ear infections

* Not uncommon in babies, especially after a cold

* Signs include raised temperature, distressed cries and rubbing of ears

* Medical attention needs to be promptly sought

Nappy rash and **eczema** can also cause babies distress and break their sleep patterns (see page 148).

Separation anxiety

* Babies show separation anxiety from eight to nine months, although it can occur earlier.

* Babies cry as they have formed a secure attachment to their primary carer and react if that person leaves (see pages 410–15).

Recognition of unusual conditions and reporting unusual conditions

There are many sources of support and advice for parents and carers. You might ask the health visitor, call the GP, call NHS Direct or call an ambulance. Your response will depend on the severity of the condition.

> **Think it over...**
>
> For which of the conditions listed in the diagram below would you call an ambulance?

Clothing and footwear

Suitable clothing and footwear is primarily needed for warmth and the protection of skin. It has, however, also become important in our society as a way of projecting a self-image and it is not unusual for quite young children to have clothing preferences.

Although parents are largely responsible for buying and choosing their children's clothes, adults working in home settings may also have an input. Clothes and footwear should be suitable for the time of year and also for the type of play and activity that children are undertaking. Carefully choosing clothes for the activity prevents situations when children are told to 'try to keep clean', which effectively restricts their play.

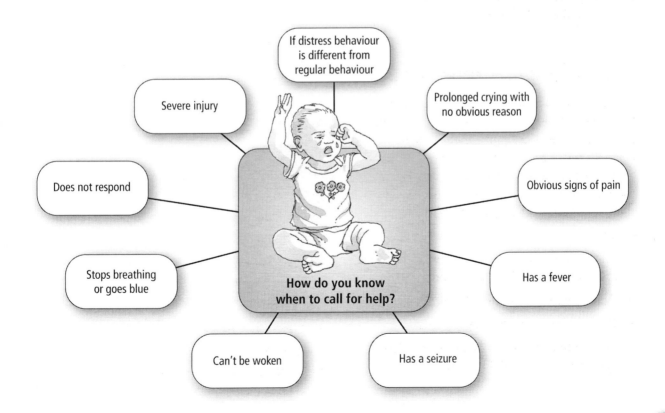

If distress behaviour is different from regular behaviour

Severe injury

Prolonged crying with no obvious reason

Does not respond

Obvious signs of pain

Stops breathing or goes blue

How do you know when to call for help?

Has a fever

Can't be woken

Has a seizure

- Clothes for toddlers and young children need to be easy to put on and take off.
- Garments should be easy to launder.
- Nightwear must conform with safety standards.
- Footwear including socks and tights should be checked for tightness.
- Garments should not restrict children's movements.

Care of clothing and footwear

For reasons of good hygiene and the child's self-image, it is important that babies and children should have clean clothes. It is important that clothes are washed in gentle and non-irritant detergent and you should ask the parents if they have any preferences. Children's feet need to be well supported and shoes should be the correct size and regularly checked for wear. As children grow older, they can be encouraged to care for their own clothes, hang up coats, put clothes away or line up their shoes neatly.

Care of equipment and toys

An important aspect of providing care for babies and young children is the ability to maintain their equipment and toys effectively.

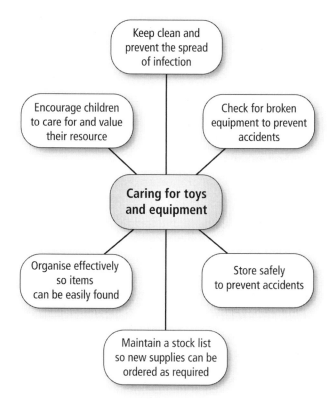

2 The skills required to care for babies and young children aged 0–8 years

This section will support you as you develop the practical skills required to provide care for babies and young children.

Care routines

Nappy changing

The key to a successful nappy change is good organisation and plenty of practice.

Items required for nappy changing

* Disposable gloves (usually provided in settings)
* Clean nappy
* Cotton wool or baby wipes
* Spare change of clothes if necessary
* Changing mat or towel in a safe place where baby is secure
* Nappy sack or access to bin

Method for nappy changing

* Wash hands and put on disposable gloves.
* Remove clothes from lower part of the body.
* Using a wet cloth or cotton wool, remove stools from bottom, taking care to wipe from front to back. Use a new piece of cotton wool for each wipe.
* Wipe girls from the vagina back towards the rectum to prevent the spread of infection.

* Clean nappy area thoroughly, avoiding pulling back the foreskin on a boy.
* Dry nappy area thoroughly.
* Check that clothing is not soiled or damp.
* If possible, allow time for baby to kick without nappy, especially if there is any indication of nappy rash.
* Put on a barrier cream if requested by parents.
* Place clean nappy on baby and dress.
* Place baby in safe place, clean mat and dispose of soiled nappies.
* Wash hands before handling baby.

CASE STUDY

Jodie is in a hurry. She lies eight-month-old Farhan on the nappy-changing shelf. There are no nappy bags left, so she goes to the store cupboard to get a new roll. She comes back and removes his nappy. There are no stools, so she quickly puts on a new nappy and takes him for his dinner.

* Describe any mistakes Jodie has made.
* Evaluate the potential outcomes of her behaviour.

Bathing and care of the skin

The key to a successful bathtime is to be well organised.

Items required
* Baby bath with warm water, 38°C
* Towel
* Non-slip mat (optional)
* Bath thermometer (optional)
* Clean nappy and other items
* Changing mat for nappy change

KEY ISSUES

* Do not leave babies in the bath, or even near water, without close adult supervision.
* Check the temperature of the water carefully.
* Make sure that room temperature is 20°C or slightly above.
* Remove any jewellery, especially watches, which can scratch the baby's skin.
* Be careful to bend from the knees to avoid back strain.

Bathing babies

It is important to be shown how to follow these procedures and to be supervised in doing so.

* Prepare equipment and fill bath. Check the temperature by using a thermometer or dipping in your elbow. It should feel luke-warm.
* Add bath product to water if requested.
* Remove clothes from baby, leaving on the nappy. Wrap in towel immediately.
* Wash face using cotton wool. Wipe gently round the eyes from the inner corner out. Use separate piece of cotton wool for each eye. Using fresh piece of cotton wool, wipe face gently and clean behind the ears and under the chin.
* Keeping the towel around the baby, tuck baby under arm supporting head, neck and shoulders. Baby must be securely held. Practise this position first with a doll if unsure.
* Hold the baby's head over the bath and, using the other hand, wet head to wash hair and scalp.
* Dry baby's head.
* Remove nappy and clean nappy area.
* Hold the baby's arm that is furthest away from you and support the head with your wrist. Lower the baby into the bath.
* Use your spare hand to wash the baby. Allow the baby time to kick and splash.
* Lift the baby back onto towel. Do not allow the baby to become chilled.

* Dry thoroughly, checking that folds of skin around the neck and groin are dry. Rub in moisturiser or massage oil, if requested by parents.

* Put on clean vest and then nappy. Check that baby is warm.

Bathing older babies

As babies become older, they can be bathed in an ordinary bath, although care has to be taken that they do not hurt themselves against taps and that they can't turn on a hot tap. Water should always be kept shallow. Most older babies enjoy bathtime and should be given time to play with the water.

Hair and teeth care

The way in which babies' hair should be cared for depends largely on the type and quantity of hair and also on the family's cultural and religious wishes. Some babies have their hair shampooed and brushed, while others will need their hair oiling and plaiting.

When the milk teeth first come through, some parents use a finger stall to brush the teeth and gums before moving to a soft brush as the babies get older.

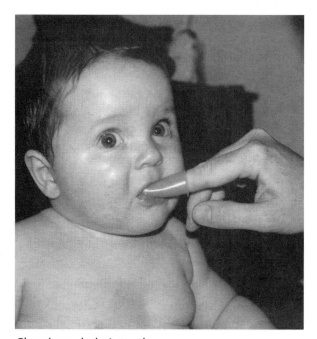

Cleaning a baby's teeth.

Rest and sleep

As with all care routines, being prepared is the key to success. Preparing to put a baby down to sleep involves the following.

* Make sure baby is not hungry.

* Change nappy.

* Have a quiet time, with gentle talking or a short story.

* Place baby quietly in a darkened room.

* Check with parents if the baby likes to have a comforter.

KEY ISSUES

Putting babies to sleep

Cot death, or Sudden Infant Death Syndrome, is thought to be responsible for seven infant deaths a week in the UK (FSID, September 2004). The number of deaths has recently been cut by following these steps with young babies.

* They should be placed on their backs and at the foot of their cots.

* Ensure that babies will not overheat. Room temperatures should be between 16°C and 21°C.

* Cot bumpers, pillows and duvets should not be used in cots.

* They should not be exposed to smoky environments or placed in rooms where adults have previously smoked.

* Mothers and fathers should stop smoking during pregnancy.

* Keep the baby's head uncovered.

* If the baby is unwell, seek medical attention.

Routines

It is essential that you consult with parents or carers to ensure that the home routine can match the setting's routine. Your primary aim is to meet each child's individual needs and adapt that routine as the child develops.

Toilet training

The key to successful toilet training is to make sure that children are relaxed and happy. Toilet

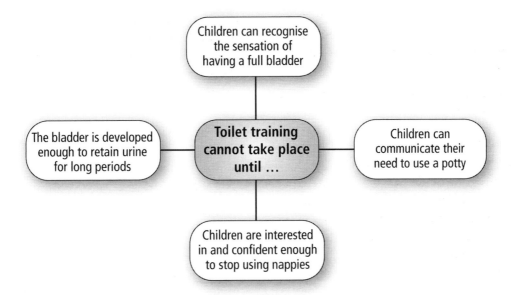

Children can recognise the sensation of having a full bladder

The bladder is developed enough to retain urine for long periods

Toilet training cannot take place until …

Children can communicate their need to use a potty

Children are interested in and confident enough to stop using nappies

training should only take place when children are showing that they are developmentally ready. Forcing children to sit on a potty often results in a child tensing up and so preventing the bladder from emptying. This in turn can lead to the child becoming distressed and associating the potty with the cause of their distress.

Once a child shows signs of being ready to use a potty or toilet adults should:

* make sure that clothes are easy to take off

* make sure that a potty is near the child

* avoid asking children if they need the potty, as this creates potential pressure

Theory into practice

Hand-washing experiment

Ask two children to brush their hands with paint.

- Give one child some hot water, soap and a towel to wash their hands with.
- Give the other child some cold water and a towel to wash their hands with.
- Which method of washing hands is the most effective?
- Decide the age range that this experiment would be suitable for.
- Consider the learning benefits for children.
- Link this activity into the Foundation Stage or other early years curriculum.

* respond quickly when children say that they need the potty

* react calmly to any accidents

* avoid putting undue stress on children by bribing or rewarding them for successfully 'performing' because, if they have an accident, it can make them feel that they have failed

* teach children to wash and dry their hands

* start to teach children about hygiene issues.

Promotion of self reliance and confidence

To help children develop independence, early years professionals will:

* have knowledge of the expected development milestones

* observe the child and talk to parents about the child's developing skills

* encourage the child's independence

* demonstrate and role model new skills

* assist the child in the early stages of learning a new skill

* withdraw support as skills develop

* offer lots of praise and encouragement.

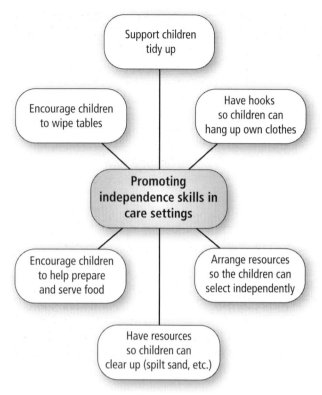

Assessment activity 5.3

To demonstrate your developing skills, create two accounts about three of the following skills. One should be written at the beginning of a placement and the other near the end. Your log accounts should address children at different ages.

- Nappy changing
- Feeding
- Care of hair and skin
- Sleep and rest routines
- Promoting independence and confidence

Describe your practice, evaluate your performance and analyse how your practice meets the care needs of children.

ingesting bacteria and is required until babies are at least six months old although, in group-care settings, this may continue until twelve months to prevent possible cross-infection.

Feeding

Preparation of feeds

Sterilisation

It is important to learn how to sterilise feeding equipment. Sterilisation prevents babies from

Methods of sterilisation

There are several ways of sterilising equipment. Many group-care settings use commercial sterilising units as, although expensive, they are fast and efficient. Whatever method is used, items have to be thoroughly cleaned first.

NAME	METHOD	COMMENTS
Chemical or 'cold water' sterilising	Sterilising fluid or tablets are added to cold water. Items must be completely immersed and remain in solution until required. Check for air bubbles. Items must be rinsed in cool boiled water.	Cheap. Teats and rubber items need replacing frequently. Solution must be made up accurately and needs changing every 24 hours.
Boiling	All washed items are put in a saucepan with a lid. Items have to be completely immersed. Lid is placed on pan and water is boiled for at least 10 minutes, although teats can be removed after 3 minutes. Items are left in the pan until required.	Cheapest method. Teats and rubber items need replacing often. Saucepan kept just for sterilising.
Steam steriliser	Steam circulates in the unit and items reach high temperatures.	Expensive, but fast and efficient. Manufacturer's instructions must be followed. Care must be taken when opening the unit, as steam can scald.
Microwave units	Steam circulates in the unit and items reach high temperatures.	Commercial units must be used for this method. Follow instructions. Allow items to cool. Do not use metal items.

Preparation of a formula feed

Powdered formula feeds are significantly cheaper than the ready-mixed types. Bottles are usually made up in advance and stored in a fridge to save time and prevent babies from becoming distressed when they are hungry. It is important to find out from parents the type of powdered milk that should be used and also the weight of their baby as this, not the age, determines the amount of feed required. Follow the stages described below.

- Check that bottles have already been sterilised.
- Boil kettle – allow to cool to avoid being scalded.

- Read manufacturer's instructions to find out about amounts of water and powder to be used.

- Wash hands.

- Put required amount of water in sterilised bottles.

- Measure the exact amount of milk powder using scoop provided. Level off with a knife. The powder should not be pushed down as this will increase the amount.

- Put powder into bottle.
- Screw on top and shake.

- Allow to cool if bottle is to be given straight away, otherwise store in fridge.

Bottle feeding a baby

As well as feeding providing babies with nutrients, bottle feeding also provides babies with emotional security. This means that whenever possible, babies should be fed by the same people. Follow the stages in the following list.

* Wash hands.
* Warm bottle by standing it in a jug of boiling water.
* Check the flow and temperature of the milk by turning the bottle upside down and allowing it to drip onto your wrist.
* Find a comfortable chair to sit in and have tissues or a towel to hand.
* Gently touch baby's lip with the teat.
* When mouth opens, gently place teat inside.
* Tilt the bottle to make sure that milk is covering the teat end of the bottle.
* Allow baby to take milk at own pace. Some babies can be slow feeders, while others are quick.
* Wind the baby after the feed. Sit baby upright on your lap and gently rub back, or hold baby upright slightly over your shoulder. Use a towel to protect your clothes. Babies sometimes bring up milk when they burp.
* Offer bottle again after winding in case baby is still hungry.
* Throw away remaining milk.
* Change baby's nappy.

KEY ISSUES

* Never leave a baby alone with a bottle.
* Do not heat bottles in microwaves as they can heat the milk unevenly.

Beginning the weaning process

Baby rice mixed with breast or formula milk is usually the first food that is offered to babies when beginning the weaning process, as it is bland and unlikely to provoke an allergic reaction.

Some babies find it hard to take from a spoon and choke or spit out food, so they will need to be introduced to weaning slowly.

* Choose a time when the baby is not tired or very hungry. Most people give the first spoon part-way through a feed.
* Place a bib on the baby and sit the baby on your knee.
* Place a very small amount of food onto a sterilised teaspoon.
* Gently rub the spoon against the baby's lips allowing the baby to suck it in.
* Talk to the baby soothingly.
* Follow the baby's lead – if the food is spat out, try again at the next feed but, if taken, encourage the baby to have another go.
* Do not force the spoon into the mouth.
* Be ready to take action if the baby chokes (see page 192).
* Throw away any unused food.

Assessment activity 5.4

Janine has just returned from shopping with five-month-old baby Chelsea, who is screaming. As she unpacks the shopping, Chelsea's dummy falls on the ground. Janine picks it up, wipes it on her sleeve, gives it a quick suck and pops it into Chelsea's mouth. She collects a bottle from the draining board, boils the kettle and, using a teaspoon, scoops some milk powder into the bottle. When the kettle boils, she adds water to the bottle. Chelsea has started screaming again, so Janine tops the bottle up with cold water and gives it to Chelsea.

* Identify all the mistakes Janine has made.
* Explain the consequences of her actions.
* Critically evaluate two sources of advice about hygiene procedures for feeding babies that have been designed for parents.

Communication

Developing your communication skills is an essential aspect of your work with children.

'Talk to your baby' is a campaign run by the National Literacy Trust to encourage parents to talk to their babies. Investigate current findings about the communication skills of babies and young children. You can use the website www.literacytrust.org.

Holding and supporting

Young babies feel safe and confident when held firmly and securely. For the first few months it is important to support their head whenever you lift them. You may like to practise on a doll until you feel comfortable moving the baby around.

Talking, eye contact and interpersonal skills

Good practice when communicating with babies and young children is as follows.

Do

* Talk to babies while undertaking care routines describing what you are doing.

* Provide lots of eye contact when talking and listening.

* Provide a running commentary when undertaking domestic tasks or out shopping.

* Allow 'turn taking' when babies start making noises.

* Use facial expression to respond to communication and show that you are listening.

* Reinforce communication with touch or gestures.

* As children get older, listen carefully to what they have to say.

* Allow children time to respond.

* Follow children's lead in conversations.

Don't

* Do not ask too many questions.

* Do not use baby talk with toddlers.

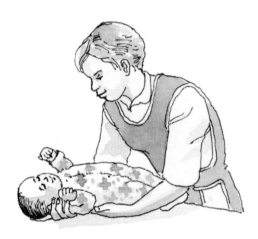

(a) Lift him carefully with your hands under his arms and your fingers supporting the back of his head.

(b) Turn him gently so that he lies cradled in your arms with his head resting in the crook of your elbow and his body resting on your forearm. Your other arm can then go under his bottom.

(c) Babies sometimes like to be held in the upright position with one hand under the bottom and the other supporting the back with the head turned to one side resting on your shoulder.

Picking up a baby.

* Do not correct their pronunciation but simply repeat the word or sentence. For example 'Doddy done' could be repeated as 'Yes, daddy has gone'.

* Do not feel you must fill up every silence, the child may be thinking what to say.

Theory into practice

Imagine you are working in a children's centre and have been asked to prepare a leaflet to share with parents giving advice about the importance of communicating with children.

Stimulation and play

To ensure you provide meaningful stimulation and play you should:

* make time for play

* provide a wide variety of different play experiences

* use good communication techniques

* follow the baby's lead

* notice when the baby is becoming tired or bored.

Praise

To promote good self-esteem, babies and young children need to receive lots of praise.

There are many different ways to praise a child:

* shared praise informal – telling mother in front of the child, 'he has been good today'

* shared praise, formal – showing good work in assembly

* verbal praise – well done, that was excellent

* physical clues – hugs, clapping

* facial reinforcement – eye contact, positive facial expressions

Think it over...

Think about how many times you have been praised in the past week.

* How did it make you feel?
* Can you think of three different types of praise you have received?
* Can you think of three times this week when you have praised someone else?
* What types of praise did you use?

Soothing a distressed baby

In the previous sections you have learnt about some of the many reasons why babies cry. To sooth a distressed baby you should initially try to identify the cause of their distress and alleviate that.

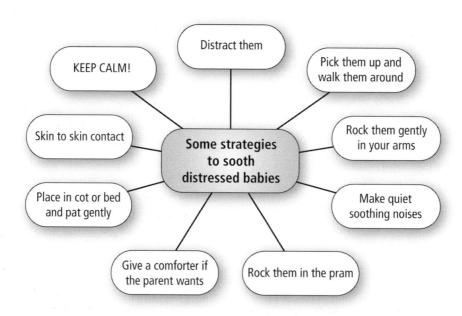

Some strategies to sooth distressed babies

- Distract them
- KEEP CALM!
- Pick them up and walk them around
- Skin to skin contact
- Rock them gently in your arms
- Place in cot or bed and pat gently
- Make quiet soothing noises
- Give a comforter if the parent wants
- Rock them in the pram

Clothing and equipment

Dressing and undressing

One of the key principles in dressing babies is to ensure that clothes are easy to put on and also easy to remove.

* Make sure that buttons on garments are sewn on securely.
* Avoid garments with ribbons, as the baby may choke or be strangled.
* Dress babies in layers of clothes and check that they are not overheating.
* Do not put a baby down to sleep in a hat.
* Check homemade clothes carefully – babies tend to suck and also handle their clothes.
* Make sure that garments are easy to put over a baby's head.
* Avoid garments that are difficult to wash.
* Make sure that any socks or garments with feet allow the baby to move their toes freely.
* When dressing babies make sure that the room is warm before you remove their clothes.

Many babies do not like having clothes pulled over their head, so it is sensible to choose clothes with wide or stretchy necks, clothes with fasteners or clothes that tie at the back. When putting on sleeves or tights it is always easier if you roll up the garment before slipping the foot or hand through.

Care of clothing and shoes

Clothes should be washed regularly. When working in a group setting, clothes that have been soiled should be double-bagged and sent home with the parents. If working as a nanny, soiled clothes should be sluiced clean and washed in a very hot wash using whatever detergent the parents normally use. Shoes should be cleaned regularly and checked for wear. It is particularly important that children wear appropriately fitting shoes, as the feet can be damaged through ill-fitting shoes.

Care of equipment

The care of equipment and toys is extremely important, especially in group-care settings where there is a potential risk of cross-infection and potential for accidents.

* All toys and equipment should be age-/stage-appropriate for children.
* Weight-bearing toys, such as tricycles and climbing frames, should be regularly checked for signs of corrosion, metal fatigue and cracks.
* Equipment and toys that are damaged should be removed and discarded if necessary.

Cleaning feeding equipment

* Rinse as soon as possible following the feed.
* Wash in hot soapy water.
* Clean bottles with appropriate bottle and teat brushes.
* Turn teat inside out and squeeze water through the feeding hole.
* Rinse thoroughly under running water.
* Check for wear and tear.
* Equipment may be cleaned in a dishwasher.
* Sterilise as described on page 167.

Bath and bedding

All equipment must be cleaned carefully on a regular basis. The bath should be cleaned after every use. The bedding does not need to be changed every day unless it becomes wet or soiled. The cot or bed should be wiped down occasionally using a spray cleaner. It is particularly important to keep the high chair clean as there are many corners where food debris can gather and harbour bacteria.

Toys

* Toys that are frequently handled, such as Duplo® bricks, should be wiped down regularly with a mild solution of disinfectant to destroy bacteria.
* Cuddly toys, dressing-up clothes and other fabric items should be regularly machine washed.
* Manufacturers' instructions should be carefully followed when cleaning or using toys and equipment.
* A sand pit should be cleaned out regularly.
* Older children can be encouraged to help wash some toys in soapy water.

Equipment safety check

Cleaning	Date cleaned
Sand tray	------------
Construction toys	------------
Dolls and dolls clothes	------------
Large mobile toys	------------
Baby toys	------------
Painting aprons	------------

Maintenance	Date checked
Climbing frame erected securely	------------
Jigsaws complete	------------
Car box checked	------------
Farm complete	------------
Dolls house	------------
Train set complete	------------
All toys in correctly labelled containers	------------
Containers in correct place on shelves	------------
Home corner equipment	------------

Renewable materials	Date checked
Paint	------------
Glue	------------
Play dough	------------

Signed _____

Sample safety checklist.

Storage

* Resources and equipment must be stored safely.

* Items that children access themselves must be easy to reach.

* The shelves themselves must be securely fixed to the wall.

* Resources such as paint, glue and play dough should be checked regularly for freshness and disposed of appropriately.

* Where large items need to be stored, thought must be given to methods of transportation, as carrying heavy loads may cause injury to a member of staff.

* Staff should be taught safe handling techniques.

CASE STUDY

You work as a nanny in a family with two children, nine-month-old Zoe and three-year-old Robert. On Monday when you arrive at work you notice some dog faeces just outside the gate. The latch on the gate must have broken over the weekend and it is impossible to shut the gate. The father has just finished giving the children their breakfast. 'I'm so sorry, we slept in and I haven't had time to clean up this morning,' he says. The high chair needs cleaning, and Zoe has got cereal all over her stuffed rabbit. Robert, who has only just come out of nappies at night, wet the bed so his bed needs changing. While the father is talking, Robert has been scribbling on one of his books, and Zoe is sucking the ear of her stuffed rabbit.

* Describe the actions you will take as soon as father goes off to work.

* Explain the importance of cleanliness and maintenance to the care of young children.

3 Promoting the maintenance of a healthy, safe and secure environment

Hygiene

Standards of hygiene in the environment

To ensure good standards of hygiene within the environment, settings should:

* address issues of hygiene within the health and safety policy
* include hygiene procedure in staff induction
* develop routines for cleaning the environment, equipment and toys

* provide appropriate hand-washing facilities
* use protective equipment as appropriate
* ensure safe storage of rubbish
* introduce appropriate food-handling procedures
* promote personal hygiene routines
* introduce specific procedures when working with animals
* adopt appropriate measure for dealing with bodily fluids.

Theory into practice

* Using the National Standards relevant in the home country of the UK in which you live identify the hygiene requirements within the standards.
* Examine the health and safety policy within your current work setting to identify hygiene procedures.

Personal hygiene and cleanliness

Babies' immune systems are not fully developed and they are vulnerable to infection. Adults must maintain high levels of personal hygiene to avoid bacteria transferring from their hands and clothing onto babies and children. You should wash your hands:

* after going to the toilet
* before and after changing babies nappies
* following any incident involving bodily waste
* before preparing food or bottles
* after touching animals and pets
* after undertaking domestic cleaning tasks.

Floors and feeding equipment

During any one day a range of cleaning tasks will be completed by an early years professional, making sure the following are clean:

* toilets
* floors
* tables
* cooking utensils
* feeding equipment
* toys and equipment.

You will find that there are separate cloths and brushes, cleaning agents and rubber gloves for different tasks in the different areas.

Assessment activity 5.5

Hygiene and cleaning routines

1 Investigate the cleaning routine in your current work placement. Describe the following and explain the reasons for the procedures that you identify.
   * Where the instructions for each task are kept
   * The time of day when specific tasks are undertaken
   * Appropriate equipment, such as cloths and mops and brushes
   * Appropriate cleaning aids for each task
   * Storage and labelling of cleaning aids
2 Make two posters for the kitchen and toilet wall describing an efficient hygiene routine for each area.
3 Analyse how legislation, policies and procedures support hygiene practices in the setting.

Security

Maintenance of specified adult:child ratios

The National Care Standards for each country identify the adult:child ratios for registered settings to ensure the safety and well-being of the children in the group.

The National Standards in England require that the group size should never exceed 26 children. They also recommend that children should be in key worker groups. This means that each child has a named member of staff who is responsible for his or her well-being and knows all the details of the child and the family. (It does not mean the child spends all the time with that member of staff.)

The minimum appropriate adult:child ratios in sessional care, full day care and out of school care are:

* 1:3 children aged 0–2 years
* 1:4 children aged 2 years
* 1:8 children aged 3–7 years.

UNIT 5: CHILD CARE PRACTICE **173**

Where a childminder is working alone in his or her own home the ratios are:

* six children under the age of 8
* of these six, no more than three children may be under 5 years of age
* of these three, no more than two may be under 2 years.

Control of access, locks to doors, control of visitors and dealing with unwanted visitors

To ensure that the environment is secure, a setting will create procedures for managing access to the premises, with arrival and departure procedures for the children.

This is particularly important if there are situations in individual families where one or other parent may have restricted access to the child. A setting will also want to provide some control over the people who are able to enter the building. All visitors will be expected to sign in when arriving at the setting.

The diagram below identifies some of the security measures taken to ensure:

* the safe arrival and departure of children
* that children are not able to leave the premises unsupervised
* that unwanted visitors are not able to enter the building.

Child collection policy

To ensure safety and security, settings will have a child collection policy, which may include:

* a statement about the importance of collecting the child on time and the distress that not doing so may cause to the child
* a statement to suggest that regular episodes of non-collection might even be seen as neglect
* Social Services may be contacted if no-one comes to collect the child
* procedures for a named emergency contact to be called if the named adult does not arrive
* procedures in place for when a different adult is to collect the child, which may include photographs, passwords and written instructions
* the point at which responsibility for the child transfers from the staff to the parent, which may be when the parent enters the building, or when the parent leaves the building
* a procedure that ensures that some adults can be free to talk to parents and still ensure there are enough staff to attend to the needs of other children.

Locks/buzzers on doors
The locks on doors and gates will be placed so children cannot reach them. Buzzers will alert adults to opening doors.

Named personnel
Settings will ask parents to identify any adults who may collect their child. The child will not be allowed to leave the building with any other adult.

Panic buttons
Many settings now have panic buttons to enable staff to call for help if threatened.

Voice-activated or video access
Some settings may have voice or video identification systems. In large settings staff may have identification badges.

Control of access – security

Care for all children
Settings will have a specific procedure to ensure that all children are cared for whilst other members of staff talk to parents.

Signing in
All settings will record the time children arrive and leave, many settings ask parents to sign their children in and out.

Transfer of responsibility
The policy will identify the point at which responsibility for the child transfers from the staff to the parent. This may be when the parent enters the building, or when the parent leaves the building.

A parent forgets to collect a child
Procedures will be in place to contact the parent or another adult.

Legislation, policies and practice

Health and safety legislation

'Your health, safety and welfare are protected by law. Your employer has a duty to protect and keep you informed about health and safety. You have a responsibility to look after others.' (Health & Safety Executive, 1999)

Everyone working with young children must be aware of their legal obligations in relation to maintaining the safety of the children in their care.

The role of the Health & Safety Executive (HSE)

The Health & Safety Executive is the government agency which is responsible for health and safety. The HSE has responsibility for:

* inspecting some places where people work

* investigating accidents and causes of ill health

* enforcing good standards by advising people how to comply with the law

* publishing guidance and advice

* providing an information service

* carrying out research.

The Health and Safety at Work Act 1974 is the most important piece of legislation relating to health and safety and includes the following.

* Employers must ensure, as far as is reasonably practicable, the health, safety and welfare of employees and those affected by their work. (This includes any person who may enter the premises, such as a caretaker, student or visitor.)

* Settings with five or more employees must have a written safety policy which must include specific procedures to cover emergencies such as accidents and events that require evacuation of the building (see page 194).

* Settings with five or more employees must carry out a risk assessment and show how risks are minimised (see page 187).

* Employers must provide for health and safety in relation to the provision, maintenance and use of premises and equipment.

Additional regulations, addressing specific areas of health and safety, have been added since the introduction of the act.

Health and Safety (Information for Employees) Regulations 1989 require employers to display official posters or provide leaflets for workers giving basic information on health and safety law. This is the reason that health and safety notices or leaflets will be on display in your workplace.

Control of Substances Hazardous to Health Regulations 1994 (COSHH) require that hazardous substances be kept separately in a marked, locked cupboard. It is important that staff are all aware of appropriate methods for using such materials. Instructions about protective clothing and first aid information should also be kept (see page 196).

Reporting Injuries, Diseases and Dangerous Occurrences Regulations 1984 (RIDDOR) require that all settings must provide an accident report book with separate sections for reporting accidents to children and adults (see page 195). All fatal and major injuries, as well as dangerous occurrences not resulting in injury, at work must be reported to the appropriate authority. Any injury that requires a member of staff to take more than three days off work must also be reported. The local Environmental Health or Social Services Department will advise on the reporting procedures.

Health and Safety (First Aid) Regulations 1981 state that there should be at least one person appointed to take charge in an emergency and to be responsible for the first aid equipment. It also requires that someone in each workplace must be trained in first aid (see page 188).

Fire Precautions (Workplace) Regulations 1997 state that it is essential that all settings have plans and procedures for action in the event of a fire and signs showing what to do in the event of a fire should be placed in every room. Regular evacuation practices must be carried out at least every three months and fire extinguishers, smoke detectors and fire alarms should be tested regularly (see page 194).

Electricity at Work Regulations 1989 require that all electrical equipment and systems in non-domestic premises should be safe to use, be properly installed and should be maintained and tested by competent persons. A record of all electrical equipment must be kept, giving details of when each item was tested and the date for re-testing.

Food Handling Regulations 1995 state that settings that prepare or provide food for children must register with the Environmental Health Department in the local authority. They must ensure that people handling food have appropriate training, such as the Basic Food Hygiene certificate.

The National Standards Under Eights Day Care and Childminding: The four home countries each have a set of National Standards which identify a series of 'outcomes' that providers should aim to achieve. Each standard describes a particular quality outcome.

KEY ISSUES

National Standards research

This important piece of legislation affecting early years settings underpins much of the work in this section of the unit, so it is important that you develop a good understanding of the documents.

- Examine a copy of the National Standards from within your home country and prepare a fact file for your reference that details all the specific criteria relating to health and safety within all the individual standards.

Policies and procedures

The implementation of the legislation requires settings to prepare policies and procedures that inform working practices and provide for quality and an agreed framework for action.

The management is responsible for creating the policies and for checking that they are being followed and the staff are responsible for implementing the policies.

As all staff and parents must be aware of these policies you will often find them on a notice board, or in the setting's brochure.

Theory into practice

Using the materials you were given during induction at your current setting, identify the following policies and procedures:

- health and hygiene
- arrival and departures
- child protection
- behaviour management policy
- smoking and drinking policy
- fire procedure
- medication procedure
- illness, accident and emergency procedure.

Food hygiene

All foods may be potentially hazardous if they are not handled correctly. Therefore good hygiene in the kitchen is essential. Anyone who is involved in food preparation should undertake the Basic Food Hygiene certificate. This unit only provides simple basic guidelines as demonstrated in the chart opposite.

Handling and disposing of bodily fluids and waste materials

The legislation which underpins this procedure is to be found in the Control of Substances Hazardous to Health Regulations 1994 (COSHH) (see page 175). The definition of 'substances

Storage
- Correct temperature
  Below 4°C for fridges, −18°C for freezers
- Stock rotation
- Raw food below fresh food in fridge
- All food covered
- Sandwiches should be prepared just prior to eating
- Dry ingredients in air tight containers

Preparation
- Hands washed before and after handling food
- Hands washed between handling raw and cooked food
- Disposable towels used
- Do not reheat food
- Food thoroughly cooked and cooled quickly if going to be stored

Equipment
- Separate areas and equipment for cooked and uncooked food
- Separate chopping boards
- Can openers, slicers, food processors regularly cleaned and sterilised
- Cloths, tea towels, oven gloves boiled frequently
- Disposable towels used for hands and spills

Food hygiene

Cleaning
- Surfaces to be cleaned regularly throughout the day
- Spills cleaned up promptly
- Food containers emptied and cleaned before refilling
- All signs of household pests reported immediately
- Waste disposal into sealed bins which are away from food area
- The bins must be cleaned regularly

Food handler
- No smoking
- Stay off work if any sign of diarrhoea or vomiting
- Complete food hygiene course

---

hazardous to health' is given in Regulation 2 of these regulations and it covers all substances that are capable of causing disease or adverse health effects. It is therefore obvious that bodily fluids, blood, faeces, urine or vomit that may carry infections must be treated as hazardous substances.

While there is general concern about infections such as HIV (and small amounts of HIV have been found in bodily fluids like saliva, faeces and urine) there is no evidence to suggest that HIV can spread through these bodily fluids. However, there is a risk that blood-borne viruses, such as hepatitis B and hepatitis C and HIV, may be spread by blood-to-blood contact.

A child may be HIV positive or have hepatitis without the carers knowing about it, so it is essential that all accidents or incidents that involve bodily fluids are managed by following the appropriate procedures.

Procedures for dealing with bodily fluids will include the following.

* Disposable gloves should be worn at all times.

* Where possible, hands should be washed before carrying out any first aid procedure involving broken skin.

* Hands should be washed after dealing with any spillages, even if gloves have been worn.

* Cover any skin abrasion with a waterproof plaster.

* Blood splashed onto the skin should be washed off with soap and water.

* Splashes of blood in the eyes or mouth should be washed out immediately with plenty of water.

* Spillages should be cleaned up as soon as possible using a solution of bleach, diluted 1 part in 10 parts of water.

* Spillages should be wiped up with paper towels, which are then disposed of as contaminated waste.

* Soiled clothing and linen should be rinsed in a cold wash and then washed in a hot wash, preferably at 90°C.

* Soiled items may be flushed down the toilet, burnt, or double-bagged in plastic bags which have been properly secured, and the waste collected for incineration.

* All gloves or aprons that have been worn must be disposed of with the affected items. Any practitioner concerned about the transfer of blood should seek medical advice from his or her doctor.

Theory into practice

Prepare a log account of a situation where you have had to deal with hazardous waste. Evaluate your actions in relation to the list identified above.

Administration and recording of medication

There are two specific types of medication: those which are prescribed by a doctor and those which can be bought over the counter. In early years settings, only medicines that have been prescribed by a doctor would normally be given.

People tend to think of pills and syrups when talking about medicines, but medications can be administered in many different ways, including:

* pills

* nose, eye, or ear drops

* elixirs or syrups

* inhalers

* creams and ointments

* injections.

The National Standards provide specific guidelines regarding the administration of medications and all settings are expected to create a medications policy. The following aspects will be addressed within the policy.

* The parent must provide written permission.

* The medicine must be prescribed by a doctor.

* Written permission must include the name of the medicine, the dose, the time and instructions for administering the medicine.

* The medicine must be stored in the original container in a locked cupboard. If kept in the fridge, the fridge should ideally be locked.

* When administering medicine, another member of staff should act as a witness.

* The exact time and dose should be recorded and signed by both parties.

* A parent should also sign the record to verify the administration of the medication.

* If children attend different care settings, written information about the days' doses must be shared.

* For inhalers or injections, the practitioner should receive specific training from a health professional on how to administer the medication to that particular child.

Administering the medication

* Two members of staff check the label and the child.

* Shake the bottle.

* Measure the correct dose.

* To keep the label clean, ensure it faces upwards when pouring the dose.

* Sit the young child on the adult's knee.

* Talk to the child calmly.

* Have a drink ready to follow the medicine.

* Praise the child.

Never pour the dose into a drink, as the child may not finish the drink and you will not know how much they have taken. Both members of staff should then complete and sign the medication record.

Happy Days Nursery medication record

Child's name _____

Date of birth _____

Parent/carer's name _____

Emergency contact _____

Name of medication _____

Storage instructions _____

Dose _____

Instructions _____

Time to be given _____

I the parent of _____ give permission for the medication specified above to be administered by the staff at the stated time/s. I confirm that the medication was prescribed by the child's GP.

Signed _____ Date _____

Date _____ Time _____

Medication _____ Dose _____

Administered by _____

Witnessed by   _____

Parent's signature _____

Physical environment

The National Standards address issues related to the physical environment. There should be an area where confidential information can be kept and where staff may talk to parents. Staff should have a room away from the children for their breaks and there should be separate toilet facilities for adults. There should be a kitchen which conforms to environmental health and food safety regulations.

The planning of the layout of the setting will have a direct effect on the children's experiences during the day. Their concentration, behaviour and sense of security will all be affected by the way in which the room has been prepared.

Positioning furniture and fixtures

* Furniture should be of an appropriate size for the children in the setting.

* Special consideration is required when premises are used for two different purposes or age groups, such as a nursery or school which is also used as an out of school club.

* Include some comfortable domestic furniture, such as chairs or sofas, to create a comforting and homely environment.

* Provide a good variety of activities and make them available at all times.

* Provide some core work/play areas to ensure stability and continuity.

* There must be space to move between activities, to ensure no disruptions.

* Provide secure, stable storage at the child's height for self-selection of activities.

* Keep noisy activities away from areas near doors to ensure safety by the doors and a sense of calm for people entering the premises.

* Quiet areas where children can rest or read should be away from the noisy activities.

* Messy activities should be near a source of water for hand washing.

* Provide clear space for energetic play, or move the furniture for part of the session.

* Ensure that fire exits are unobstructed.

* Ensure good visibility throughout the room to aid supervision.

CASE STUDY

Jason has asthma and uses an inhaler. Yesterday his mother brought a bottle of Calpol to nursery and asked you to give him some if he needs it. She said, 'He has a bit of a cold and has had a bad night'. Today she has brought a bottle of antibiotics that the doctor has prescribed.

* What legislation provides guidelines for the administering of medication?

* Explain in detail how you will respond to each of these situations.

* Evaluate the role of legislation, policies and procedures in providing for health and safety.

Adaptations for special needs

When working with children with identified needs you need to consult with parents or any professional who may be working with the child to ensure that you can adapt the environment to meet the child's needs. You may provide:

* ramps or wide doors for wheelchairs

* a quiet environment where background noise is reduced for a child with a hearing difficulty or autistic spectrum condition

* a safe area where a child with a visual difficulty can move around by touching the furniture, or be introduced to tactile materials and resources

* a clear floor for a child with a visual difficulty

* opportunities to take an activity to the child, such as painting on a table rather than an easel.

Supervision

It is important that there are quiet areas in the nursery where children can play in peace – but the staff must also always be able to observe and supervise effectively. The level of supervision will vary depending on the age of the child, the environment they are in and the activity they are

---

Think it over...

Examine the plan of Happy Days Nursery.

• Evaluate the physical layout of the nursery using the information provided above as guidance.

• Identify any potential health, safety or security hazards in the setting.

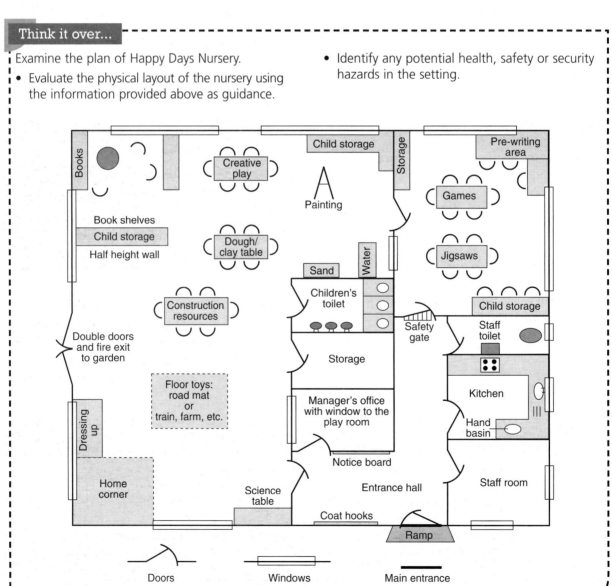

undertaking. There are three distinct levels of supervision.

* **General supervision** – ensuring that you can see the children and are aware of what they are doing, for example, being aware of what the children are doing while playing in the garden.

* **Close supervision** – being on hand while they undertake specific activities to help if required, for example, sitting at the collage table to help with aprons or writing names on the paper.

* **Constant supervision** – interacting with the child during a risky activity, for example, supporting children during a woodwork or baking activity.

Your responsibility is to ensure that children have the appropriate supervision at all times.

Think it over...

After lunch your supervisor is discussing your work for the afternoon. She has asked you to do the following.

* 14.00 – Go into the garden with the toddlers on the physical play equipment.
* 14.30 – Support a cutting activity.
* 15.00 – Support the home corner and dressing up area.
* 15.30 – Support the children in the out of school club making jewellery with beads.

Identify the level of supervision you will use in each situation.

Potential hazards

To ensure a healthy, safe and secure environment you must learn to identify potential hazards and take action to reduce the risk of accident or injury.

Defective equipment

The table below identifies a range of examples of the equipment and resources within an early years setting that will be checked on a regular basis.

EQUIPMENT	WILL BE CHECKED:
Electrical equipment	By qualified electrician
Outdoor play equipment	For rust and breakages
Games and puzzles	For broken or missing pieces
Books	For torn pages or scribbles
High chairs and prams	For cleanliness and safe harnesses
Play houses and climbing frames	For correct assembly and efficient hinges
Fire alarms, smoke detectors and carbon monoxide detectors	For low batteries

Dangerous and non-secure areas

There are certain dangerous or non-secure areas within the setting where accidents are more likely to occur. The following tables identify some dangers and the actions taken to reduce the risks.

POTENTIAL HAZARDS IN THE INDOOR ENVIRONMENT		
AREA	**THE DANGER**	**ACTION TAKEN TO REDUCE RISK**
Toilet	Children locking themselves inside the cubicle Children slipping on wet floors Children falling while climbing on Bacteria flourishing Burns from hot water Cleaning materials	Teach children about toilet safety High locks on cubicle doors Wipe wet floors immediately Child steps for high toilets Appropriate hygiene procedures Ensure thermostat controls temperature Cleaning materials in locked cupboard
Kitchen	Sharp knives and hot equipment	No access to kitchen area

POTENTIAL HAZARDS IN THE INDOOR ENVIRONMENT		
AREA	THE DANGER	ACTION TAKEN TO REDUCE RISK
Floor	Children slipping on wet or polished floor Children tripping on carpet Rubbish left out by another user of the room	Non-slip floor covering Absorbent mat placed under water tray All carpets and mats fixed to floor with nails or tape Sweep and check floor before use each day
Stairs	Children falling	Ensure safety gates always closed Accompany children on stairs, ensuring they hold the hand rail Teach children safe use of stairs
Windows	Children falling out	Safety glass installed Provide window locks and keep key out of reach of children Do not open window further than child safety lock allows
Doors	Children 'escaping' Children trapping fingers	Locks on doors, but keep key in accessible place Check situation in relation to fire doors Supervise home time Provide slow-closing mechanism and internal doors which are open during the session must be fixed open
Plug sockets	Children poking objects into sockets	Socket covers for all sockets not in use

POTENTIAL HAZARDS IN THE OUTDOOR ENVIRONMENT	
Plants	Careful checks must be taken to avoid plants with poisonous leaves and berries.
Safe surfaces	Safe surfaces should be installed under climbing equipment. Areas where bikes are used must be flat and clear. Animal droppings must be cleared and disinfected. Surfaces must be checked for results of vandalism, such as broken glass.
Access and fencing	Gates must be self-closing, at least 1.2m high and locked. Fences must not have horizontal bars that children can climb. Fences and gates must be kept in good repair.
Dustbins and rubbish	Dustbins must be kept out of reach of children. If children are encouraged to pick up litter, they must wash their hands immediately afterwards.
Sun	Areas of shade should be provided. Sun screen and sun hats should be worn. Children should not be outside in the midday sun.

SUBSTANCE	HAZARD	ACTION TO MINIMIZE THE RISK
Cleaning materials Washing-up liquid Toilet cleaners Bleaching agents	Poisoning Bleaching agents Unstable if mixed together Skin irritant	Store in a locked cupboard. Ensure bottles are labelled. Never transfer to another bottle. Never mix different agents, e.g. toilet cleaners. Wear protective gloves.
Bodily waste Faeces Urine Vomit Blood	Transfer of infection	Wear disposable gloves and aprons. Wash hands before and after dealing with incident. Clean area after use. Dispose of bodily waste and soiled nappies in separate container.
Medicines	Poisoning	Keep medicines in a locked cupboard. Follow 'administering medications policy'.

Keep children safe in the sun.

Dangerous substances and spillages

There are many substances in early years settings which may be hazardous. The Control of Substances Hazardous to Health Regulations 1994 (COSHH) require settings to list dangerous materials and show how the risks are minimised. Spillages of any of these substances must be treated seriously and cleared up effectively using disposable gloves and appropriate cleaning cloths, which must in turn then be cleaned effectively or discarded.

Animals in the early years setting

Scrupulous hygiene precautions are necessary in relation to any contact with animals. The following list describes some essential requirements.

* Wash hands before and after handling animals.
* Only introduce animals that are used to children.
* Always supervise children when with animals.
* Dispose of animal waste.
* Keep cages hygienic, with a regular cleaning routine.
* Litter boxes should not be accessible to children.
* Keep all animal feeding utensils separately.
* Do not allow animals near children's food.
* Ensure that animals have regular checks with the vet and follow any vaccination requirements.
* Worm animals regularly.
* Check for fleas and treat appropriately.

KEY ISSUES

Department of Health guidelines recommend precautions for school visits to farms, and this information can be found on the PHLS website – www.phls.co.uk.

Infection

Particular care needs to be taken to limit the spread of infection and efficient hygiene routines are essential (see pages 172–3). Good ventilation can limit the build-up of bacteria and viruses. It should always be possible to open windows to ensure a supply of fresh air to limit the spread of infection.

Lighting

* Lighting can affect mood – a sunny day can make people feel happier.

* Good lighting will avoid eye strain.

* Good use must be made of artificial and natural light.

* Flickering fluorescent light should be avoided – consider the use of daylight bulbs.

Heating

* Hot children are often irritable, cold children lethargic.

* The temperature should be kept at 18–21°C.

* The temperature must be monitored during the day.

* Heating systems must be maintained.

* Radiators must be protected.

* Carbon monoxide monitors should be provided.

Assessment activity 5.6

Undertake a risk assessment of one particular area within your workplace to identify hazards.
* Identify potential hazards.
* Describe procedures for dealing with them.
* Explain how legislation, policies and practice supports the provision of a healthy, safe and secure environment.

Communicable diseases

There are many infectious childhood conditions. Some diseases can be very serious for particular groups of people, such as pregnant women and children with certain medical conditions that make them vulnerable to infections. Immunisation is available for some of the diseases, but not all families participate in immunisation programmes. The Department of Health provides guidance on infection control in schools and nurseries and includes exclusion times. Many settings also provide a policy for the exclusion of children who are ill, to limit the spread of infection.

The following chart identifies the incubation and exclusion time for some common childhood infections and lists some of the specific complications. (Exclusion details are taken from the Department of Health 'Guidance on Infection Control' poster.)

INFECTIONS	INCUBATION	RECOMMENDED PERIOD TO BE KEPT AWAY FROM SCHOOL (ONCE THE CHILD IS WELL)	COMPLICATIONS
Chicken pox	14–21 days	Five days from the onset of rash	Scarring or secondary infection from scratching Can affect pregnancy of a woman who is not immune
Diarrhoea and/or vomiting (with or without a specified diagnosis)		For 24 hours after the diarrhoea and vomiting have stopped	Dehydration

INFECTIONS	INCUBATION	RECOMMENDED PERIOD TO BE KEPT AWAY FROM SCHOOL (ONCE THE CHILD IS WELL)	COMPLICATIONS
Impetigo	1–3 days	Until the lesions are crusted or healed If lesions can be kept covered, exclusion may be shortened	Side effects are uncommon
Measles	7–15 days	Five days from the onset of the rash	Ear and eye infections, pneumonia and encephalitis
Meningitis	2–10 days	The Consultant in Communicable Diseases may be informed and will give advice National Meningitis Trust help line (0845 6000 800) will also advise	Deafness, brain damage or even death
Mumps	14–21 days	Five days after swelling appears	Meningitis (very rare) Infection of testes in young men
Rubella (German Measles)	12–25 days	Five days from the onset of the rash	If contracted by a woman in first three months of pregnancy can cause serious defects in the unborn baby
Scabies	Until treated		
Whooping cough	7–10 days	Five days from commencing antibiotic treatment	Weight loss, dehydration, pneumonia

Children who are not well should not be at school or nursery, even if they are not infectious – neither should children and adults with diarrhoea unless the diarrhoea is known to be of a non-infectious cause (such as coeliac disease).

Methods to minimise/prevent cross-infection

To appreciate the methods used to prevent cross-infection, you need to have an understanding of how infection is spread. The following chart describes the different ways that infection is carried and identifies the precautions that are taken to minimise/prevent cross infection.

Theory into practice

Identify a range of activities you could use with young children to promote issues of hygiene. You should identify activities suitable for both pre-school and school age children. Evaluate your activities making reference to the importance of personal hygiene, food hygiene and maintaining the environment.

MICRO-ORGANISMS ENTER	METHODS OF MINIMISATION AND PREVENTION
Inhalation Breathed in through the nose and mouth	Ensure good ventilation. Encourage hygiene practices, such as covering the mouth when coughing. Use good hygiene procedures in relation to keeping the environment and resources clean. Exclude children with communicable diseases.

MICRO-ORGANISMS ENTER	METHODS OF MINIMIZATION AND PREVENTION
Ingestion Swallowed through the mouth	Use proper hand-washing procedures (see page 173). Practise good food-preparation procedures (see page 177). Use good hygiene procedures in relation to keeping the environment and resources clean (see page 171). Use good hygiene procedures in relation to animals (see page 183). Exclude children with communicable diseases. Safely dispose of waste products (see, page 178).
Inoculation Penetrating the skin through cut or injection	Cover open wounds. Safely dispose of waste products (see page 178). Use separate personal hygiene equipment. Use rubber gloves.

Confidentiality and reporting procedures

Every setting will have a confidentiality policy, and will have been required to register with the Data Protection Commission. The general rule is that information about a child or family should not be shared with any other person unless it is in the direct interests of the child, such as in the case of safeguarding children from harm. While in all general situations confidentiality must be maintained and personal or health details about any child or family must not be disclosed, there are some circumstances where sharing information is essential.

Reporting to the authorities

If there appears to be an outbreak of a particular condition, the setting must report the matter to staff at the Public Health Department. The Consultant on Communicable Disease Control will assess the situation. If the outbreak is food related this must be reported immediately to the Local Authorities Environmental Health Department.

Reporting to parents

Some information must be shared with parents. This can be done through the daily exchange of information, through letters or on an accident form. The following details may be shared with parents:

* any concern about the health of their own child
* specific information might be given to all parents about a particular situation, such as a case of meningitis
* there has been an outbreak of head lice
* a child in the setting is known to have developed rubella
* accidents or incidents.

KEY ISSUES

There is still a considerable degree of public concern in relation to HIV, but personal information about the health status of any child or family member must never be shared with others. The hygiene procedures in place within the setting will ensure that cross-infection cannot take place.

CASE STUDY

You are the manager of an out of school club.
* Jason has nits.
* Five of the children have developed diarrhoea and vomiting last night.
* Farhan has German measles.
* Casey has a nasty weeping sore on her chin.
* Jamilla has eczema.

1 Identify which of these situations you will share with:
   * the parents of the child
   * colleagues
   * all parents
   * the authorities.
2 Explain why you have decided to share this information.

Risk assessment

All settings are required, under health and safety legislation, to undertake risk assessments. While the responsibility for risk assessment ultimately lies with the management of the setting, the most efficient methods will include all members of staff.

Security issues

When assessing the risks involved with security the following issues may be considered:

* responsibility for keys
* responsibility for locking up
* systems for storing money and valuables
* setting alarms
* installation of CCTV
* security for the children (see page 173)
* access to the premises
* arrival and departure procedures
* CRB (Criminal Records Bureau) clearance for all adults.

Five steps for risk assessment

1 Identify the hazard. This may include identifying **who** is at risk (such as a member of staff using a cleaning product) or **what** specifically the risk is (such as bacteria flourishing in the toilet).

2 Identify control measures to ensure the risk is minimised.

3 Identify who is responsible for taking action to minimise the risk.

4 Record the assessment. Ensure that the assessment is dated and signed.

5 Identify a timescale for the review of the risk assessment (this may be an annual inspection of the whole setting, or may be instigated if there is a change of staff or a new piece of equipment is purchased). Monitor and document that the control measures are in fact in place and working effectively.

Settings will undertake risk assessments of:

* areas such as indoor or outdoor environment (see pages 181–2)
* activities such as water play or outings
* times of day such as meal times or arrival and departure time.

Examining the accident book may provide some evidence to identify specific risks and hazards.

Policies and practice

In order to minimise risk, all settings will have policies and procedures in place to inform working practice. They are a legal requirement and ensure quality practice. The management is responsible for creating the policies and for checking that they are being followed and all staff are responsible for implementing the policies.

Theory into practice

* Examine a recent risk assessment undertaken in your current work placement.

Think it over...

Consider the following hazards. Identify what action is taken in your current workplace to reduce the risk.

* Too much sun
* Children locking themselves in the toilet
* Teenagers leaving broken bottle or syringes in the outside play area at weekends

Planning an outing

Outings are a regular feature of all early years settings. They may be a trip to the park, a walk to post a letter or a full-day outing to a wildlife centre or the seaside. Changing environments inevitably means a new set of risks that need to be managed. Schools now follow national guidelines that were produced following a series of fatal accidents on trips, while pre-school settings have to increase staffing levels to comply with regulations.

Prior to any outing, you will be expected to undertake a risk assessment (as described above) to identify hazards such as the venue, traffic, weather or the activity. This list is by no means comprehensive.

In addition to undertaking a risk assessment you may consider the following checklist.

For all outings

* Ensure you have parental consent.

* Ensure children are adequately dressed.

* Take spare clothes, drinks, food, nappies and sun protection.

* Consider how to manage 'stranger danger' or children wandering off.

* Consider first aid/emergency arrangements.

For group-care outings

* Allow sufficient time to plan the outing.

* Find out whether you need insurance.

* Check what staffing ratios you need.

* Cost the trip carefully, allowing for hidden extras, such as a driver's tip or parents who may not be able to contribute.

* Examine transport arrangements carefully. For example, do the coaches have seatbelts? Do volunteer drivers have the necessary experience and insurance?

* Ensure you have children's emergency contact details.

* Ensure that all staff and volunteers understand their role in the trip.

* Prepare and use registers to check that all children are present.

Assessment activity 5.7

You work in a private day nursery. Your manager has asked you to prepare an induction session for new members of staff. The session will include:

* a description of the policies and procedures in the nursery

* an explanation of how these procedures support health and safety

* an evaluation of the role of legislation in the maintenance of health and safety.

---

4 Carrying out safety and emergency procedures

KEY ISSUES

Accidents are the commonest cause of death in children over one year. Those most at risk of a home accident are in the birth to four years group. Most accidents are preventable through increased awareness.

See www.rospa.com for further information.

First aid procedures

First aid is the immediate assistance or treatment given to someone who has been injured or taken ill before the arrival of an ambulance, doctor or other appropriately qualified person. The aims of first aid are:

* to preserve life

* to limit the worsening of the condition

* to promote recovery.

(*First Aid Manual*, 1999)

It is essential that any intervention should not harm the casualty and you should not take action just for the sake of doing something. For this reason it is important that everyone who works with children should attend a relevant paediatric first aid course with a trained instructor which includes:

* dealing with emergencies

* resuscitation

* shock, choking and anaphylactic shocks.

A first aid course will need to be updated every three years.

The following information provides an outline of the procedures to be taken in an emergency, but is no substitute for attending an appropriate course. For further information see www.childcareapprovalscheme.co.uk.

Checking for signs and symptoms

It is important that you have a good procedure for responding to accidents and recognising the signs

```
┌─────────────────────────────┐
│ Assessment                  │
│ Keep calm, don't panic.     │
└─────────────────────────────┘
              │
              ▼
┌──────────────────────────────┐        ┌──────────────────────────────┐
│ Assess the situation         │        │ Assess the casualty          │
│ Ensure the area is safe. If  │        │ An initial assessment to     │
│ a child has put their        │───────▶│ ensure there is no life      │
│ hand through a window and    │        │ threatening condition. Check │
│ there is a lot of sharp      │        │ for consciousness, airway,   │
│ glass, you may do yourself   │        │ breathing, signs of          │
│ an injury. You may need to   │        │ circulation and blood loss.  │
│ consider what to do with     │        │ If necessary start           │
│ other children.              │        │ resuscitation.               │
└──────────────────────────────┘        └──────────────────────────────┘
                                                    │
                                                    ▼
                          ┌──────────────────────────────────┐
                          │ Diagnosis                        │
                          │ You reach a diagnosis by         │
                          │ assessing the signs and symptoms.│
                          └──────────────────────────────────┘
                              │                        │
                              ▼                        ▼
┌──────────────────────────────────┐    ┌──────────────────────────────────┐
│ Signs                            │    │ Symptoms                         │
│ Signs are evidence of a          │    │ Symptoms are sensations that a   │
│ casualty's injuries that you can │    │ casualty can describe. For       │
│ see, hear or feel. For example,  │    │ example, pain, loss of movement, │
│ burns, bleeding from orifices,   │    │ weakness, tingling, dizziness,   │
│ swelling, unnatural shape,       │    │ nausea.                          │
│ abnormal skin colour, noisy      │    │                                  │
│ breathing, groaning, abnormal    │    │                                  │
│ temperature.                     │    │                                  │
└──────────────────────────────────┘    └──────────────────────────────────┘
```

and symptoms of injury. In an accident situation, as a student, your first priority is to summon help from your supervisor, the identified first aider, or the professional services.

Below is a useful procedure for the assessment and diagnosis of injury.

Prioritising treatment

Having completed this process of assessment you need to be able to prioritise your treatment. The following list, taken from the *First Aid Manual* (1999), provides clear guidance.

✳ Follow the ABC of resuscitation.

✳ Maintain a clear airway and breathing: if unconscious and breathing, place in the recovery position.

✳ Control bleeding.

✳ Treat large wounds and burns.

✳ Immobilise bone and joint injuries.

✳ Give appropriate treatment for other injuries and conditions.

✳ Check airway, breathing and pulse regularly and deal with any problems immediately.

Dealing with an unconscious casualty

An important aspect of first aid provision is the ability to deal with an unconscious person. These skills are best practised on a recognised first aid course. The following chart aims only to provide basic guidelines.

THE ABC OF RESUSCITATION

CHECK RESPONSE

Child (1–7)	Baby (under 1)
	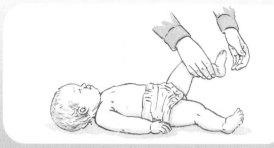
Talk calmly and shake very gently	Gently tap or flick sole of foot. DO NOT SHAKE A BABY

CHECK AIRWAY

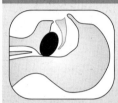 1. When unconscious the muscles relax and the tongue falls back

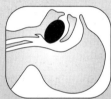 2. When the head is tilted and the chin lifted, the tongue will lift from the back of the throat

Open airway. Tilt head back slightly, one hand on forehead, two fingers under chin	Open airway. Tilt head back very slightly, one hand on baby's head, one finger under chin
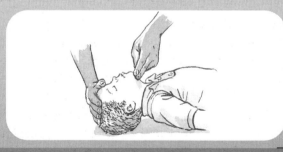	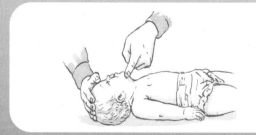

CHECK BREATHING

Place cheek next to child's mouth. Listen for sounds of breathing and watch chest for movement. Listen for up to 10 seconds

If breathing is not present, carefully remove any obvious obstructions from mouth. DO NOT poke down throat. Pinch child's nose, seal lips round mouth and breathe into the lungs till the chest rises. Give five breaths, one every three seconds. Look for signs of recovery	Carefully remove obvious obstruction. Seal lips round mouth and nose and breath into the baby's lungs. Give five breaths, open every three seconds. Look for signs of recovery

Feel the carotid artery by placing two fingers lightly on the side of the neck and observe for other signs of circulation	Lightly press two fingers on inside of upper arm and observe for other signs of circulation
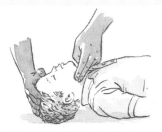	
If there is no sign of circulation, begin cardio-pulmonary resuscitation	If no sign of circulation, or baby's pulse is less than 60 per minute, begin resuscitation
Place heel of one hand one finger's breadth from the base of the breastbone. Press down one-third the depth of the chest five times at a rate of 100 per minute	Place one finger in the middle of the chest between the nipples. Place two fingers below this and use these two fingers to press down one-third of the depth of the chest five times at a rate of 100 per minute
Simple check 5 chest compressions with one hand 1 breath through the mouth	**Simple check** 5 chest compressions with two fingers 1 breath through mouth and nose

The recovery position

You will be able to practise this technique on an approved paediatric first aid course.

* **Step 1** – Place two fingers under the child's chin and place other hand on the forehead, gently tilt the head back.

* **Step 2** – Straighten the limbs and place the arm nearest to you so it lies at right angles to the child's body. Check pockets for any bulky objects.

* **Step 3** – Bring the child's other arm across the chest and place the hand against the child's cheek with palm facing outwards. Holding that hand in position use your other hand to pull up the child's far leg. Hold the leg just above the knee.

* **Step 4** – Gently pull the far leg towards you, rolling the child forward till they are lying on their side. Use your knees to prevent the child rolling too far forwards. Keep your other hand holding the child's hand to their cheek.

* **Step 5** – Bend the upper leg so that it is at right angles to the body.

* **Step 6** – Throughout the procedure, ensure that the child's head remains well back and is supported on their hand to keep their airway open.

Treatment of minor and major injuries

Minor injuries

While it is fairly unlikely that you will have to deal with many major accidents, you will regularly be called upon to deal with minor injuries. Many minor injuries will respond to a cuddle and some adult attention but, however minor the incident, you will always be expected to monitor the child's condition to identify any underlying problem. You may need to call for professional assistance even for what may appear to be a minor injury.

Major injuries

* Assess for danger.

* Give emergency first aid.

* Make it safe.

* Check ABC.

* Protect yourself.
* Keep calm and support others.
* Wear disposable gloves.
* Summon help.

The table below provides some basic information for use in an emergency until expert help arrives and highlights the actions you must not take. Remember, it is essential that any action of yours does not harm the individual or make the injury any worse.

EMERGENCY	ACTION	DO NOT
Bleeding	Lay child down to reduce the possibility of shock. Cover wound with pad or dressing. Apply pressure for up to 15 minutes. If there is a large foreign body in the wound, apply pressure on either side of wound. Raise and support the injured part. Bandage the wound.	**Do not** remove glass or objects from a deep wound. **Do not** apply a tourniquet, as it can worsen the bleeding.
Burns and scalds	Cool with running water for at least 10 minutes. Remove constricting clothing. Cover with a clean cloth.	**Do not** remove anything sticking to the burn. **Do not** apply lotions or plasters.
Choking	If obstruction visible, hook out with your finger. Lean older child forward, or support baby's face down along forearm and give five brisk slaps between shoulder blades. Stand behind child, place fist on lower breastbone, hold with other hand and press in sharply five times. For babies, use two fingers on lower breastbone.	**Do not** risk pushing it further down. **Do not** ever hold a baby or young child upside down and slap their back, as you could break their neck.
Convulsions	Cool the child by sponging with tepid water if they have a high temperature. Clear the area to protect from injury by placing pillows or padding around the child. Sponge with tepid water. Put child in the recovery position once convulsions have ceased.	**Do not** put anything in the child's mouth.
Fractures	Keep the child still.	**Do not** move the child until the injured part is immobilised.
Head injury	Control any bleeding. Monitor for consciousness, headache, drowsiness, vomiting or blood loss from nose, mouth or ears.	If there has been a back or neck injury **do not** attempt to move. **Do not** leave the child alone.
Poisons	Check ABC. Save sample of poison.	**Do not** make the child vomit.
Shock	Lay the child down, raise legs and keep warm. Loosen tight clothing. Treat any injury. Monitor condition.	**Do not** leave the child alone. **Do not** give food or drink.

In any of these incidents you will have called for professional assistance. It may be tempting to put the child in a car to take them to the hospital, but some situations can deteriorate very quickly and you may need professional help and the ability to move through the traffic very quickly.

Assessment activity 5.8

You have taken a group of children to the local park. Suddenly a large dog appears and starts to chase Kerrie. She starts running, looking backwards over her shoulder and crashes into Jack, and they both fall to the ground. The dog jumps on the children and bites Kerrie. Jack hits his head on the ground and is unconscious and breathing, and Kerrie has a deep bite on one leg and a dirty looking graze on her other leg. The other children are all screaming.

Describe what you will do to in relation to:

a) assessing the situation

b) assessing the casualty

c) diagnosing the injuries

d) prioritising treatment

e) providing treatment for both children

f) recording the incident

g) informing the parents.

Remember in most situations you would call your supervisor, or the identified first aider who will make any necessary decisions.

Emergencies

The Health and Safety at Work Act 1974 requires that all settings provide procedures for use in the event of an emergency to ensure that everyone in the setting can respond quickly and effectively during any emergency incident.

EMERGENCIES THAT REQUIRE EVACUATION OF THE BUILDING	OTHER EMERGENCIES
Fire	Accident
Gas leak	Sudden illness
Flood	Intruder
Bomb scare	Missing child

The emergency process

It is not enough simply to plan the response to an emergency situation. The process must involve a cycle of specific procedures as shown in the diagram opposite.

Each setting will prepare procedures that meet the individual needs of its environment. In this section we examine some emergency situations following the process identified opposite.

Fire emergency checklist

All settings will prepare specific procedures that are relevant to their individual situations. However, a fire procedure will include the following guidelines.

* Prominent display of fire procedure notices which inform people of the action to take in the event of a fire.

* Ensure all adults in the building are aware of notices' location and content.

* Provide fire extinguishers and fire blankets in areas where they may be needed, such as the kitchen.

* Provide training in the use of extinguishers.

* Ensure all fire equipment is serviced once a year.

* Fire exits should be clearly signed, unobstructed and checked for ease of opening.

* Evacuation routes should be planned with consideration for the different situations where a fire may occur.

* Fire practices must be carried out regularly at different times of day and using different evacuation routes.

* Fire practices must be recorded and evaluated.

* Registers must be completed as the children enter the building and must include arrival and departure time.

* Registers should include each child's emergency contact number and be held in an accessible place.

* Access must be maintained for emergency vehicles.

Even if you have fire-fighting equipment, the first priority is to evacuate the building. Do not fight a fire unless you know what you are doing.

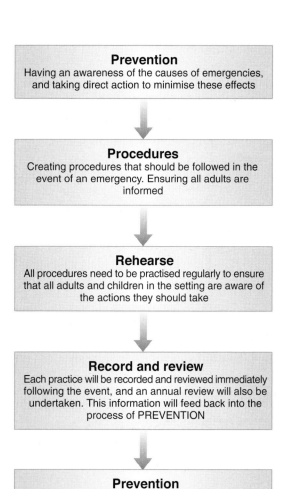

Prevention
Having an awareness of the causes of emergencies, and taking direct action to minimise these effects

Procedures
Creating procedures that should be followed in the event of an emergency. Ensuring all adults are informed

Rehearse
All procedures need to be practised regularly to ensure that all adults and children in the setting are aware of the actions they should take

Record and review
Each practice will be recorded and reviewed immediately following the event, and an annual review will also be undertaken. This information will feed back into the process of PREVENTION

Prevention
And the cycle is complete!

The cycle of specific procedures required to prepare for an emergency.

- Draw a plan of your workplace. Identify the position of the fire procedure notices, fire extinguishers and emergency exits.
- Describe why you think they have been placed where they are.
- Identify three hazardous areas or situations where a fire may occur.
- Describe an evacuation route for each fire situation.
- Explain some measures you could take to limit the chances of a fire starting in these positions.
- Evaluate the role of legislation, policies and procedures in maintaining health and safety in the workplace.

Gas leak emergency checklist

✳ Raise the alarm. (**Do not use an electrical alarm.**)

✳ Turn the gas off at the mains.

✳ Open all doors and windows.

✳ Evacuate the building in a calm and orderly manner.

✳ Phone the Emergency Gas Number (keep the number by the phone).

Flood or bomb scare

For all emergencies that require evacuation of the building, such as bomb scares or floods, it is important to have a list of emergency numbers, and to have identified an alternative safe venue to take the children to.

Accident procedures checklist

Accident procedures are specific to individual settings but will probably include the following points.

✳ A trained first aider must be on duty at all times.

✳ All adults should know who the first aider is.

✳ The person who witnesses the accident should inform a first aider.

✳ The first aider will assess the situation and the injury and summon help if required.

✳ Another member of staff should comfort the other children involved in the incident.

✳ Remaining staff should maintain a normal play environment and move children to another area if necessary.

✳ If necessary, inform the parents or emergency contact if a parent cannot be found.

✳ In an emergency, dial 999 to call an ambulance. A member of staff may accompany the child to hospital if the parent has not arrived (ensure that the adult:child ratio in the setting is still appropriate).

Reporting Injuries, Diseases and Dangerous Occurrences Regulations 1984 (RIDDOR) require settings to provide an accident report book. The member of staff attending to the injury is responsible for completing the accident report and ensuring that the parent signs the report.

Accident report

Name _Farinda Patel_

Day/date _Tuesday 15 February, 2005_

Time _11.45 at home time_

Place _in the pre-school room_

Circumstances of accident _Farinda and another child were running to get their coats. They collided, banged heads and Farina fell to the ground_

Nature of incident _slight bump on the head_

Action taken _Cold water compress_

Person who dealt with injury _Zameera_

Witness _Caroline_

Parent's signature

Injuries must be recorded in the setting's accident report book.

First aid box

The Health and Safety (First Aid) Regulations 1981 require that all settings must provide a first aid box. The box should be green and marked with a white cross and should be waterproof and airtight. It must be kept in an accessible place, so that it can be easily found in the case of an emergency. Examples of what a first aid box may contain include:

* guidance leaflet
* 20 individually wrapped sterile adhesive dressings
* 2 sterile eye pads
* 4 individually wrapped triangular bandages
* 6 safety pins
* 6 medium-sized individually wrapped sterile wound dressings
* 2 large individually wrapped sterile wound dressings
* 1 pair of disposable gloves
* Alcohol free cleansing wipes
* 1 pair of blunt ended scissors
* HSE Standard Kits.

KEY ISSUES

A designated member of staff should be responsible for checking the contents of the first aid box, ensuring that contents are all still 'in date', and replenishing it as necessary.

* Find out who is the designated first aider in your current setting.

Need to rehearse/review and modify procedures

In order to be able to respond effectively in any emergency situation it is essential that everyone knows what to do and has had the opportunity to practise the procedure regularly. All accident procedures must be reviewed regularly and should involve an examination of the accident book. This will enable staff to identify any common features, such as the time of day or specific activities that regularly appear to cause accidents. This information can then be used to improve the accident prevention measures.

Rehearsing the fire procedure

Fire practices should be carried out at least once a term. Staff should ensure that they make provision for any children with special needs who may need additional help to leave the building quickly. It is important that, even in domestic situations, evacuation routes are planned and practised with the children.

If procedures are to be effective, all adults and children in the building need to be familiar with them.

Reviewing and modifying the fire procedure

To ensure that fire practices are meaningful experiences, you will need to prepare criteria for

CASE STUDY

It is the beginning of the new school year. The children joining the reception class are coming into school during the first two weeks. There are some new members of staff, the school secretary, the Year 3 teacher, two teaching assistants, and two midday supervisors. The school runs a Parents as Educators programme where parents volunteer to support work in the classroom. This programme is going to start at the beginning of

Week 3. A small number of these parents have English as an additional language.

* How, and at what time, will you ensure that all adults and children are aware of the fire procedure?
* How can you help parents who are not confident in their use of English?
* What would be the result if some adults were not aware of their responsibilities?

evaluating their effectiveness. Suggestions could include the following.

* How long did it take?
* Was the appropriate exit used?
* Was the 'fire' in a different place from the previous practice?
* Was the alarm at a different time from the previous practice?
* Did all the adults know what to do?
* Did all the children know what to do?
* Did the children remain calm?
* Did someone remember the register?
* Was there a debriefing discussion with the children after the fire practice?

Think it over...

There are three people working in the upstairs baby room with seven babies. During a fire practice last week Shabana and Dan were alone giving the babies their lunch. Natalie had just gone downstairs to collect some clean bibs when the fire alarm went off. It took Shabana and Dan five minutes to get all seven babies out of their high chairs and outside to the collection area. Natalie stayed downstairs to help one of the children who has special needs to get out quickly. Fortunately it was only a fire practice.

• What conclusions would you come to if you were to review this fire practice?
• What difference does the time of day make to the fire practice procedures?
• What difference does the age and ability of the children have to the fire practice procedure?

Theory into practice

• Provide a detailed log account of a fire practice you have participated in.
• Evaluate the effectiveness of your role during the fire practice and identify how you met the requirements of the policy in your setting.
• Identify the legislation which underpins the requirements of the fire procedure in your workplace.

Theory into practice

• Ask if you can look at the accident report book at your current setting.
• Identify a variety of different types of accidents.
• State how they may have been prevented.
• Observe the day, time and place of each accident to identify if there is any pattern.
• List five activities or situations where accidents may occur and describe what you would do to prevent them.

How to recognise and cope with children's emotional reactions to accidents and emergencies

A child who has had an accident will be in pain and frightened and will want to see a parent figure. You should keep the child calm, talk quietly and reassuringly and, if the injury is serious, contact the parent as soon as possible after contacting the emergency services. Other children may also be frightened. You should reassure them, distract their attention, and not apportion blame. They may be feeling guilty already!

How to give information to parents without causing alarm

Parents will obviously be very anxious when they hear that their child has been injured, so the news must be given to them in a calm and gentle manner. While staff may be upset by the incident, they must be careful not to pass on their own sense of anxiety.

In the case of serious accidents, a parent may experience emotional shock and should be treated appropriately. They may demonstrate their distress by being angry and accusative. You should remain calm, and not become defensive or participate in argument. Should the accident have been caused by another child (e.g. biting or hitting), this information should be treated sensitively and public accusations avoided. Following an accident, a parent will be asked to sign the accident book to agree that he or she has been informed about the accident.

CASE STUDY

Sarfraz fell over and bumped his head on the way to nursery. His mother told the supervisor to keep an eye on him in case he showed signs of concussion. The supervisor had to go to a meeting and forgot to tell the nursery staff. However, Sarfraz played happily all morning, and, when he was collected by his childminder, no-one told her what had happened on the way to school.

- Identify what might happen as a result of this.
- Describe the importance of all adults in the setting being aware of their roles.
- Evaluate the role of legislation, policies and practice in supporting the health and safety of children in the setting.

Following a head injury, parents should be provided with information to help them to recognise symptoms of a more serious injury.

Head injury information

Your child has had a minor bump on his/her head today. If you notice any of the following symptoms contact your doctor:

- Intense headache
- Unusually drowsy
- Vomiting
- Unequal or dilated pupils
- Clear fluid or blood from the nose or ears
- Visual disturbance, blurred vision or seeing 'stars'

Recognition of when to call for professional assistance

In any major incident, such as a fire, bomb or gas leak, you should call the emergency services. For

KEY ISSUES

If any of the following occur you must call an ambulance.

- Unconsciousness
- Difficulty breathing
- Severe bleeding
- Serious burns

major accidents, as described on page 192, you should always call for an ambulance.

You may also need to call for professional assistance for what may appear to be a minor injury. The table below provides details of some minor injuries and identifies some specific complications for which you should seek medical attention.

However, the final advice to any early years practitioner is always that if at any time you are concerned about the welfare of the child you should refer the situation for professional assistance.

INJURY	TREATMENT	MONITOR
Bump to head	Apply a cold water compress.	For drowsiness, vomiting, headache, bleeding from ears, nose or mouth
Nose bleed	Tip head forward and pinch nose below the bridge for up to 10 minutes.	If it continues for more than 30 minutes seek medical attention
Grazed skin	Rinse with clean water, do not rub embedded grit. Cover the wound while in the setting to prevent infection and inhibit spread of leaking bodily fluids.	For signs of infection, reddening of skin or discharge
Trapped fingers	Apply a cold water compress.	Check surface of skin for abnormal shape, or possible fracture

END-OF-UNIT TEST

1 Provide a brief description of the care needs of children aged 0–1, 1–3, 3–5 and 5–8.

2 At what age are children ready to be toilet trained? Explain the reason for your answer.

3 Identify three things you can do to prevent nappy rash.

4 Describe a self-reliance skill you could promote for children aged 0–1, 1–2, 2–3, 3–5, 5–8.

5 List three sources of the following: fats, proteins, carbohydrates, vitamin C and vitamin D. Explain why a balanced died is important.

6 Identify three foods that should not be given to babies.

7 Explain the key advantages of breastfeeding.

8 List four methods of sterilisation and describe why it is important to clean and sterilise feeding equipment.

9 Describe the three stages of weaning.

10 List five situations where you would wash your hands, and explain why hand washing is so important.

11 Identify three pieces of legislation that affect the practice in your setting and analyse the role of legislation, policies and practice in the maintenance of health and safely in the environment.

12 Describe four strategies a setting may take to ensure security for all children.

13 List three ways that infection is spread. Analyse the procedures in your setting to limit the spread of infection.

14 Identify five potential hazards in an outdoor environment. Explain the actions you will take to reduce the risks.

15 What will you do in the following situations?

- Fazila has fallen off the climbing frame and is unconscious.

- Daisy is choking on a piece of apple.

- Nathan has put his hand through a window and has some glass stuck in the palm of his hand.

References and further reading

Bruce, T (2004), *Cultivating Creativity in Babies, Toddlers and Young Children*, Hodder Arnold

Bruce, T and Meggitt, C (2002), *Childcare and Education* (3rd edn), Hodder Arnold

Childs, C (2001), *Food and Nutrition in the Early Years*, London: Hodder and Stoughton

Dare, A and O'Donovan, M (2002), *A Practical Guide to Nutrition*, Nelson Thornes

Dare, A and O'Donovan, M (2000), *Good Practice in Child Safety*, Nelson Thornes

Dare, A and O'Donovan, M (2003), *A Practical Guide to Working with Babies*, Nelson Thornes

DfES (2003), *Birth to Three Matters: A framework to support children in their early years*, Sure Start

DfES (2001), *National Standards for under Eights Day Care and Childminding*, Sure Start

First Aid Manual: Authorised manual of the voluntary aid societies (1999), London: Dorling Kindersley

First Aid Manual: St Andrews Association, British Red Cross and St John Ambulance (2002), Dorling Kindersley

Meggitt, C, Stevens, J and Bruce, T (2000), *An Introduction to Child Care and Education*, Hodder and Stoughton

Meggitt, C (2001), *Baby and Child Health*, Heinemann

Meggitt, C (2003), *Food Hygiene and Safety*, Heinemann

Useful websites

British Red Cross – www.redcross.org.uk

Department of Health – www.doh.gov.uk

Food Safety (General Food Hygiene Regulations) – www.doh.gov.uk/busguide/hygrc.htm

Government health – www.wiredforhealth.gov.uk

The Hanen Centre – www.hanen.org

Health and Safety Executive – www.hse.gov.uk

Infection control in schools and nurseries – www.phls.co.uk

National Literacy Trust – www.literacytrust.org.uk

National Standards and Guidance for National Standards – www.ofsted.gov.uk

Nutritional information – www.nutrition.org.uk

Royal Society for the Prevention of Accidents – www.rospa.com

St John Ambulance Association – www.sja.org.uk

Professional practice

Introduction

This unit will help you to look at your own skills in the care of children in the early years and to focus on what skills you need to work effectively as an early years professional. All early years practitioners have to learn to care for children as individuals, promote equality of opportunity to all the children and adults they work with, look at their own development, evaluate their progress and set targets for the future. Understanding the requirements of employers and the demands of working with colleagues is part of professional practice.

Throughout the course of achieving your qualification, you will have the opportunity to work in a range of settings – you will look at both the differences and similarities as you work with children of different ages and with different needs. Using experiences from your placements will help you to complete this unit. You cannot succeed just by writing about caring for children – you must be able to show that you can do the job.

How you will be assessed

This unit is assessed internally.

1 How to observe the individual needs and skills of all children

Observing and identifying the individual ages/stages of the development of children

This section considers how you observe and identify the individual needs and skills of children appropriate to the requirements of the setting. Working with children from birth to eight years of age, you will find out how rapidly children develop and how different they all are. Each child is an individual and this shows from a very young age. Even when babies seem the same – even when they are twins – they can be very different and their parents and carers can tell them apart very quickly, often by their behaviour rather than their appearance. You will need to be able to understand the behaviour and development of children aged 0–1,1–3, 3–5 and 5–8 years.

Observing children is one of the most important skills the early years practitioner develops; observation is a professional skill and an important tool for assessing children. This is different from just watching people, particularly when it is young children, which is always fascinating. Watching children and using the information you notice is also an essential part of becoming a professional; being observant is a key skill of good communication.

> ### Think it over...
>
> Think about two children who you know or have seen; one a baby aged 0–1 years and one a toddler, aged 1–3 years.
>
> - Make some notes on what is the same and what is different about them.
> - Think about how the development of the child has changed between one age and another and note down the kinds of thing children learn to do as they grow up.
> - If you can, compare notes with someone in your group or class.
> - Keep your notes so that you can use them later.

Milestones of development

Understanding how children grow and develop is an essential skill of a professional early years practitioner. The use of observation is one of the keys to identifying the individual needs and skills of children. To understand what you see, you need to know what you are looking for. There are charts for you to check the developmental stage of the observation you are recording in Unit 7.

Children's development is usually divided into four different aspects:

* physical
* social and emotional
* cognitive
* language.

Although children develop at different rates, they all go through the same sequence. The patterns of development always follow the same order, for example, a baby will sit before walking and walk before running. It is usual to refer to a child's stage of development rather than a chronological age although, if you are referring to age, it should be in years and months – a child who is just two years old will be very different from a child who is two years and eleven months.

Observing and recording children and their development

There are certain conventions to be used when you observe children and record what you see. Early years practitioners will be observing all the time and may only need to record these observations in particular circumstances but, as a student, you will need to gather together a collection of observations to contribute to the portfolio of work submitted as evidence for this unit.

You should decide what you are going to observe, such as a particular aspect of the child's development or play, or a particular part of the day like welcomes, farewells, lunch or playtime, and then plan your observation carefully.

You will need to make sure that supervisors know about your observation and get their permission to carry it out. You must also be certain to reassure them that the information you record will be confidential. Children should be referred to by their first initial and age, not their full name, and the information should only be shared with your supervisor and your tutor at college; it should never be discussed elsewhere. This issue of confidentiality is most important.

Your supervisor may ask you to observe a particular child so that your observations can contribute towards planning strategies to help the child's development. The records that you keep and the notes of activities that you make may be a valuable contribution to building up a picture of each child. You will find much more information on observing children in Unit 8. However, here are some basic guidelines.

Firstly, you must give some background information.

* How old is the child (in years and months)?
* Where is the child (place and time of day)?
* Who else is around (adults and children)?
* Is the child a boy or a girl?
* You should also give a description of the child and state any information you have been given about his or her background.

Remember to say 'I have been told that...' rather than making statements that may seem like personal judgements. For example, 'I have been told that the family has many problems at home,' is factual but saying, 'This is a problem family,' is a judgement that is inappropriate and unprofessional.

* Say what you are trying to observe and how you are going to record it. Be sure to add the date, including the year, so that those reading it later will be quite clear about when it took place.
* Write down only what you see and hear; do not make personal comments
* After you have recorded your observation you can then interpret and evaluate it. You should use the developmental charts in this or other textbooks.
* You need to recognise variations between what you see and what you would expect. These should be recorded and reported to your supervisor.

* When you have written your interpretation or evaluation, you can then note any plans you could make to encourage the child's development in the future, such as more complex jigsaws if the child found a jigsaw easy, or a new skill for an older child, such as skipping or knitting.
* Remember to store your observation in an appropriate place and do not leave it lying around – the contents are confidential.

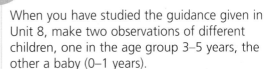

Assessment activity 6.1

When you have studied the guidance given in Unit 8, make two observations of different children, one in the age group 3–5 years, the other a baby (0–1 years).

Observe one child arriving at a setting in the morning. How does the child say goodbye to the carer – quickly and easily or with difficulty? How long does the child take to settle down? Who does the child talk to first? What does the child play with first? Why do you think this is?

Next, see if you can observe a baby playing with something, possibly while eating. What is the baby doing? Which hand does the baby prefer to use? How do the baby and the carer interact? What happens when the baby drops something, does the baby look to see where the item has gone or just go on playing but with something else? Why do you think this is?

As well as noting down what you have seen, try to interpret it so you learn more about how the children are developing.

Observe a child arriving at the setting.

Observing and identifying the development of children with particular requirements

When you have learnt to observe children and interpret your observations using your knowledge of child development, you are then able to identify a child's individual skills and assess his or her individual needs. You will also get to know what to expect for different age groups. However, all children have their own level of skill and their own needs and you can never respond to every child in the same way because each child is different. Some examples follow.

✳ A child who has a hearing difficulty may not be able to sit on your knee and listen to a story told very quietly. This child may need to sit where he or she can see your face in a good light, with you speaking clearly.

✳ A child who comes to nursery and won't do the simple jigsaws may be interested in something more complicated and challenging to stretch his or her skills.

✳ Joining in a noisy outdoor game may overwhelm a child who has never had the opportunity to mix with other children. A gentle introduction to a quiet game with one or two others may be a much better option.

When a child has special needs, you may be the first person to notice. For example, you may recognise that the child can't see the board or is crouching over a book and realise that this child may have visual difficulties. It is important to talk to your supervisor when this happens, so that appropriate referrals can be made if special help or services are required.

Different early years settings

While you are undertaking training for your qualification, you will usually work in three or four different early years settings. You may work in a home with a nanny or a childminder, in a nursery or pre-school group or in a school, hospital, or special needs setting, with both younger and older children. People with different backgrounds, training and skills will run each of them in a different way. Each will have different resources. There may be only one or two adults in a home, but many different professionals, all with particular roles, in a hospital. Some will have rooms only used by them, as in a school but some will share them with other users, such as a pre-school group in a church hall. Even in a primary school, there may be classes in the evenings and equipment may need to be tidied away carefully so that everything is safe and sound.

The table below lists some of the settings you may find.

SETTING	AGE GROUP AND PREMISES	STAFFING	FUNDING AND HOURS	RELEVANT DOCUMENTS AND CURRICULUM GUIDANCE
Child's own home	All ages In a domestic household	Nanny	A salary is paid Hours are by negotiation	Depending on the age group – see notes on page 206
Pre-schools and playgroups	Under fives Often in a shared hall	Qualified staff with volunteers (often parents)	Fees are paid (with grants for education places from LEA) Sessional and some all day	Birth to Three Matters Foundation Stage curriculum National Standards for Under Eights

▶

SETTING	AGE GROUP AND PREMISES	STAFFING	FUNDING AND HOURS	RELEVANT DOCUMENTS AND CURRICULUM GUIDANCE
Childminders	Babies to teenagers In own home	Qualified staff and helpers	Fees are paid (with grants for education places from LEA) All day with some sessional and after-school care	Birth to Three Matters Foundation Stage curriculum National Standards for Under Eights
Private nurseries, workplace nurseries and crèches	Under fives Purpose-built or adapted premises (separate room for each age group)	Qualified staff and helpers	Fees are paid (with grants for education places from LEA) All day with some sessional and after-school care	Birth to Three Matters Foundation Stage curriculum National Standards for Under Eights
LEA nurseries	Threes to fives Purpose-built or adapted premises	Qualified staff and helpers	No fees Mostly sessional – some all-day places	Birth to Three Matters Foundation Stage curriculum National Standards for Under Eights
Integrated children's centres and family centres	Under fives and their families Purpose-built or adapted premises	Qualified staff and helpers	Usually no fees All day and sessional, often before and after school	Birth to Three Matters Foundation Stage curriculum National Standards for Under Eights
Transition groups and nurture groups	Fours as they enter school and fives to sevens Classroom in school	Qualified staff and helpers, usually with special training	No fees Usually sessions away from usual class	Foundation Stage curriculum National Curriculum (depending on age)
Infant schools	Fives to sevens Purpose-built premises	Qualified staff and helpers, sometimes with parent volunteers	No fees Full school day	National Curriculum (UK) National Curriculum Guidelines (Scotland)
Units for children with special needs	Primary and secondary age Purpose-built or adapted premises	Qualified staff and helpers with parent volunteers	No fees Full school day	Foundation Stage and National Curriculum (as above and depending on age)

▶

SETTING	AGE GROUP AND PREMISES	STAFFING	FUNDING AND HOURS	RELEVANT DOCUMENTS AND CURRICULUM GUIDANCE
Hospital paediatric units	Children up to age 14 Purpose-built premises	Nursing staff, key workers and nursery nurses	No fees 24-hour care	Depending on the age of the child – see above
Out of school clubs and before and after school clubs	Usually threes to thirteens Usually shared premises	Qualified staff and helpers with volunteers	Fees are paid Usually an hour or more before or after school	National Care Standards for Under Eights
Holiday clubs and play schemes	Usually threes to thirteens Usually shared premises	Qualified staff and helpers with volunteers	Fees are paid Sessions or full days in holiday times	National Care Standards for Under Eights

All these settings will have to comply with certain standards, such as the space and facilities available, the number of qualified staff and the equipment provided. This information is found in the documents *National Standards for Under Eights Day Care and Childminding*. Settings offering early years education will deliver the Foundation Stage Curriculum. They have to ensure that activities are planned and implemented to allow children to make progress towards the Early Learning Goals. Settings caring for under threes will follow the guidance in the document Birth to Three Matters and those for children of school age will follow the National Curriculum documents. They will be registered with and inspected by Ofsted.

Ofsted reports must be made available to the public, so that those who want to use the service can read them before they decide which is best for their child. All settings will have to take account of the Preventative Strategy, which aims to support and protect vulnerable children and keep them safe from harm. You can find out more about protecting children in Unit 3 of this book.

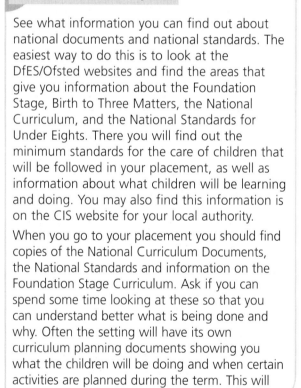

Assessment activity 6.2

See what information you can find out about national documents and national standards. The easiest way to do this is to look at the DfES/Ofsted websites and find the areas that give you information about the Foundation Stage, Birth to Three Matters, the National Curriculum, and the National Standards for Under Eights. There you will find out the minimum standards for the care of children that will be followed in your placement, as well as information about what children will be learning and doing. You may also find this information is on the CIS website for your local authority.

When you go to your placement you should find copies of the National Curriculum Documents, the National Standards and information on the Foundation Stage Curriculum. Ask if you can spend some time looking at these so that you can understand better what is being done and why. Often the setting will have its own curriculum planning documents showing you what the children will be doing and when certain activities are planned during the term. This will help you to plan your work with theirs.

The CIS and EYP

Information about local settings can be obtained from the Children's Information Service (CIS) for your area. It will have a helpline and a website where information about all registered settings can be accessed. Many CIS websites are lively and interesting and you can gain a lot of useful information from them.

The CIS is part of the local Early Years Partnership (EYP) for your area. Representatives of many groups involved in early years come together within the EYP to plan and expand provision for the children in their area. They can provide funding for places, for training, for expanding provision, to help out when there are emergencies and so on. One of their main tasks is to expand provision for all age groups in every type of setting and they work closely with Ofsted to prepare new settings for registration and to support those who are inspected. The EYP will also have a website that you can access. It is part of the education provision made by your local council, so see if you can find it.

Think it over...

Find the address of your local CIS website and explore it to find out about early years settings in your area.

Observational methods

Observations can be recorded in many ways, including: watching the children for a short period of time and then thinking about what you have seen; observing a particular child or group of children at regular intervals throughout the day; using a checklist to see how a child is developing (e.g. physical development) and watching out for and noting a particular event as it occurs during the day (e.g. type of behaviour). Some of the main techniques are listed in the following table.

You will find more information in Unit 8.

NARRATIVE	DESCRIBING OR TELLING THE STORY OF WHAT YOU HAVE SEEN
Event sampling	Focuses on and describes a particular behaviour that you wish to observe or may have concerns about
Time sampling	Notes made at regular intervals, e.g. every half hour, every hour or at the same time of day every week, to compare behaviour
Checklists	A list of areas of development for you to tick off as you see them (good for comparing two children)
Structured	A situation organised to observe something specific, e.g. outdoor play
Longitudinal	A series of observations made over a longer period of time, e.g. every month for a year
Photographic	Photos (with permission), often taken from behind, to show development of a painting or display, with descriptions of what has been observed

CASE STUDY

It is the start of the spring term and you are welcoming children to the reception class. Two children arrive, both of whom are almost five years old. Will comes first and looks around quickly. Spotting the play dough, Will rushes over and immediately joins in, rolling and patting the dough with obvious enjoyment. There are lots of different shaped cutters and he has great fun playing with them and making lots of little dough shapes. He chats away to the other children all the time although this is the first time he has met them and they soon start chatting to him and including him in their play.

Meanwhile, Aaron is standing by the door with his coat on and is holding his teddy. You talk to Aaron gently about his home and his family and things that are important to him. Eventually you get Aaron to come to the book corner and listen to you quietly reading a simple story with lots of bright, clear pictures.

- Why do they behave like this when they are the same age?

Look at the following possible explanations for the differences in the case study and compare them with your own notes.

✳ Will is used to going out and playing with other children and Aaron is not.

✳ Aaron may have been at home a lot and may not have a large family or group of friends nearby.

✳ Will's parents may have many relatives who get together regularly and, for him, large groups of children are not threatening.

✳ Aaron may live away from the rest of the extended family and the nursery may be a very new and strange experience.

These are just a few of the possible reasons – you cannot know from initial impressions why individual children react in the way they do. In order to understand why, you will need to understand much more about the child's background and history. What you can do at this stage is to decide how you will respond to each child, and recognise that each child needs a different response from you to meet different needs.

Aaron and his teddy arrive at school.

2 How to respond to those needs through care routines and procedures

Health and safety

Creating a safe, secure and healthy environment is one of the fundamentally important jobs of an early years practitioner. It is essential that you have an awareness of safety all the time and that you are observing the children's environment for any potential risks and hazards, ensuring that action is taken promptly. When you work with small children, things change quickly and situations arise without warning, however careful you have been. This demands quick responses from everyone, including you as a student.

Assessing the risks

Children have little awareness of the risks in their surroundings and do not realise what the results of their actions will be, so the early years practitioner must watch out for them. Children will be able to play happily in an environment that is safe and secure, and this will help their emotional well-being, especially if the early years practitioner is alert to the sounds and signs of danger. There may be certain safety routines that you have to follow when using particular types of equipment, such as that for indoor active play or, for older children, specific items, such as woodwork tools or sewing machines, whether in school or in an after school or holiday club.

Your role in supervising children is very important. At times, you may feel you need eyes in the back of your head, even if you are looking after one baby in his or her own home and with a parent nearby. When you are helping with a group of children, be careful where you stand and be aware of what is going on around you. It is not good to concentrate so hard on one child working in a corner of the room that you miss all the activity that the other children are involved in everywhere else. You will learn to always sit facing out into the room so as to see as many children as possible, even when the main focus of your attention is one particular child.

When you are working with a baby, you will probably do almost all the physical care of the baby, such as washing hands, bathing, changing nappies – all under the supervision of the baby's carer. It is part of your job to keep the baby clean and tidy so he or she can feel comfortable and you will need to ask about the care routines that the baby is used to and then find out how you can contribute. It is particularly important that you find out how soiled nappies are dealt with, as there are many different methods used. Nappies may be washed down and then taken away for

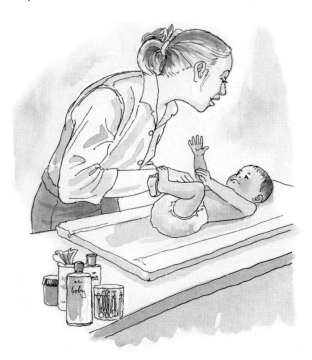

Talking to the baby while keeping her clean and comfortable.

laundering, there may be a disposal bag that is used to take away disposable nappies, which should not be flushed away as they will block the pipes. You must find out the method and use it yourself. It is important that you always wear disposable gloves and aprons for each child you deal with; you must change these for each one and pay very careful attention to your own hygiene, ensuring that you wash your hands carefully and tie your hair back if needed. You should not risk giving a baby any infection that you may have, such as a cold or a stomach upset – if you are unwell then somebody else should be dealing with the baby.

Some older children may still need help and support with going to the toilet and washing their hands, but you should never take a child to the toilet on your own. You will need to be sure that a qualified practitioner is with you at all times so that there can be no allegations made later about how you treated the child. Issues about child protection are uppermost in everyone's minds these days and you must take special care as you are a student and a visitor to the setting.

If you are working in a school or with primary age children, you may be asked to go with other staff when the children have a swimming lesson or take part in sports tournaments or matches and you will have to be alert to the possible hazards and dangers all the time.

It is important that any play area has been checked before the children start to use it and any potential dangers removed or minimised. For example, in an outside area, you can help to check that any glass or sharp stones have been removed, but if you find a broken gate, it may not be able to be repaired quickly and the area may have to be cordoned off, or outside play stopped until it can be made safe. Remember that it is your responsibility, even as a student, to make the situation known to the person who should fix it and take any steps you can to protect others from danger.

The table on page 210 lists ten tips for daily health and safety.

You will find more details about children's health in unit 8.

RISK	ACTION
Check all equipment you use is safe, not cracked or broken.	Report any concerns to your supervisor.
Make sure equipment and areas used by children are clean.	Clean up anything you can do easily and report anything else.
Watch for hazards, such as toys scattered around.	Tidy things up and put them away when not in use.
Check your own hygiene.	Wash your hands before eating and after going to the toilet.
Check your own health.	Don't go near children if you think you have an infection (a bad cold, a stomach upset).
Watch for children that are ill.	Report any concerns to your supervisor.
Watch out for accidents.	Comfort the child, report to your supervisor and keep a note of what happened.
Keep an eye on doors and windows.	If you think a child is missing, report it immediately.
Ensure that hazardous materials that you use are put away safely (even washing-up liquid).	Find out the setting's policies on this.
Be aware of children's medications.	If you are concerned, tell your supervisor.

Assessment activity 6.3

Choose an area of your setting in which to do a hazard check. If possible, choose an outside play area. Use the following system:

1 Look carefully at the area you have chosen

2 Identify any potential hazards you find and note them on the form.

3 Assess the risk from the potential hazard. Is it potentially critical, serious or minor?

4 Prioritise any actions needed.

You should record your findings. The form below is an example of how you might do it.

Risk assessment summary				Assessment area _____						
Form number _____										
Name of assessor _____				Review date _____						

Ref no.	Activity/task	Hazards	Persons in danger	Probability 1 to 3	Severity 1–3	Risk factor	Person responsible	Comments	Results
1	Water play	Wet floor	Children and staff	2	1	Low	Nursery nurse	Wiped up immediately	A

After you have done the hazard check, it is important that something is done with the results. If anything needs doing, give the results to the responsible person so that they can plan the appropriate action. All settings must have a health and safety policy and many, particularly the larger ones, will have a health and safety officer.

You need to read the policy and talk to the officer or other staff to understand what your responsibilities are. Later, when you are employed, you and your employer will work together to ensure that there is a healthy and safe environment for the children in your care. Everyone needs to know that children and staff can play and learn happily and comfortably together.

Care routines and your role

Part of the contribution you can make to the safety of the setting and to the children's feelings of safety and security is to have clear routines that you follow. These are particularly important in the physical care of the child, such as times of day for eating and sleeping, as they ensure that everything that you need to do has been done. They also contribute to giving a structure and framework to the children's day so that they feel happy and secure and know what to expect, such as when you welcome them or say goodbye at the end of the day.

> **Think it over...**
>
> Watch what goes on in your placement and identify the care routines that are in place. How can you contribute to some of these routines according to the age and stage of development of the children with whom you are working?

A care routine

Here is a typical routine for a qualified early years practitioner working on his or her own and preparing a child to go bed.

* Warn the child that bedtime is coming in, say, half an hour. If the child is old enough, tell him or her what time that will be.

* Run the bath before the child gets there so he or she is ready to get straight in.

* Go and help the child finish any activity that he or she is doing and put everything away.

* Make sure that the child is not hungry or thirsty and give a drink if required.

* Take the child to the bathroom, play and talk while the child is in the bath, as well as assisting with washing.

* Dry the child thoroughly and help him or her put on night clothes.

* Help the child to clean his or her teeth.

* Put the child in bed and choose a story together to read before settling down.

* Sing some nursery rhymes and encourage the child to join in.

* Tell the child what you are going to do next (don't make it too interesting!), say good night and leave, turning out the light.

In this routine, the early years practitioner is doing everything with the child. If the child's parents were there too, the routine would need to be adapted so that they had a role too.

In a nursery, where the small child will often fall asleep at the most unexpected times, you may not be able to follow such a routine, but some of it may be needed if you are helping to settle the babies down during the day.

Bedtime – the end of a long day.

3 How to promote a stimulating learning environment for children

Provision for play and activities

Whatever setting you are working in, it will provide a stimulating learning environment. You can see the settings and staffing listed on pages 204–06 and you should find out their main aims and objectives.

Play activities

The key principle of early years care and education is that play and learning are inseparable and are both equally vital to a child's development. Regardless of the setting, there will always be a range of activities and most will include those in the following diagram.

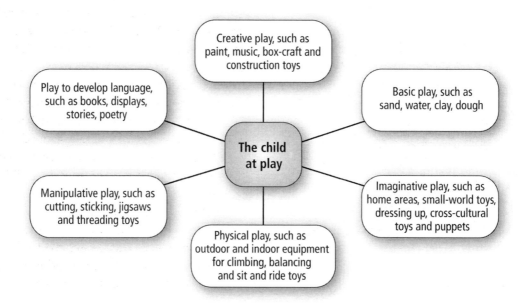

Creative play, such as paint, music, box-craft and construction toys

Play to develop language, such as books, displays, stories, poetry

Basic play, such as sand, water, clay, dough

The child at play

Manipulative play, such as cutting, sticking, jigsaws and threading toys

Imaginative play, such as home areas, small-world toys, dressing up, cross-cultural toys and puppets

Physical play, such as outdoor and indoor equipment for climbing, balancing and sit and ride toys

This is usually the basic provision that all settings will offer, although there may be some differences. For example, a childminder may have a garden so outside play is available all the time, whereas a school may have a playground, which is only available at set times. On the other hand, a school may have an excellent library with plenty of books for children in the early years, whereas a pre-school may have to get all of its equipment out and put it away each session, so may not have as many books available.

Promoting development

Equipment provided needs to promote all aspects of development. This is easy to see in a nursery or school but may not be so obvious in a home setting. However, if you think of playing with a toddler in the garden on a fine day, you will be able to see how this can be achieved. The fact that the child is in the garden will promote physical development. The child will be able to breathe in the fresh air, run about to get exercise for the large muscles and pick up little things to exercise small muscles. You will just need to make sure that little

things that are picked up and examined with great interest do not end up in the mouth – especially if they are small creatures or creepy crawlies!

Intellectual development and communication can be promoted by talking to the child and explaining what things are and, in simple terms, how they work. This could be flowers or trees, the clouds in the sky or the shadows under a tree. Social development will be encouraged by the way you and the toddler interact and work together, perhaps when you are using any outdoor equipment, such as a swing. Finally, emotional development is promoted by the sheer satisfaction and enjoyment gained from playing outdoors in the sunshine.

So you can see that even in this simple way, with the minimum of equipment, every aspect of development can be promoted.

Health and safety

It is important to remember to check health and safety at all times. You have read about this earlier in this unit but, as you have seen above, you will always need to be alert.

Accidents can happen very quickly and, for example, when you are indoors you will need to make sure that any sand that is spilt is swept up and any water on the floor is mopped up as soon as possible. It is easy to slip and fall and this can happen quickly unless swift action is taken. There are always risks outdoors, including making sure the ground is cleared of any debris before playing outside. You will also need to remember that there are hazards for children that do not exist for adults. For example, a small child can drown in very shallow water, so having a pond in a garden where a small child is playing is not a good idea. If one exists, it should be covered or that area cordoned off when the child is outside. No garden tools or chemicals should ever be left where a child can get at them.

You will need to balance common sense with being over-careful, but always err on the side of caution where small children are involved.

More information about play and learning activities is available in Unit 4 of this book.

Flower beds are interesting!

TYPE OF CHILD	SPECIAL NEED OR REQUIREMENT
Children with visual impairments	Textures to feel and enjoy e.g. different papers and fabrics Brightly coloured toys Toys that make noises Good lighting
Children who use wheelchairs	Plenty of space to move about Tables at the right height for the chair Suitable equipment outdoors
Children with auditory problems	Quiet surroundings for stories with a good view of the adult's face Support to join in with others and communicate in a group
Children with learning difficulties	Individual attention Simple toys and equipment to attract and keep attention Patience and understanding from everyone

The needs of children with particular requirements

If children with special needs or particular requirements use the early years setting, it will have special equipment for them so that the environment is as accessible as possible. All settings will ensure that the children are able to communicate with each other and will help you to understand any special methods of communication for children and staff.

Some examples of provision of equipment and support for special needs are given in the table above.

Very often the early years practitioners who work with children with special needs will have had specialist training and plenty of experience of dealing with all types of children. Some schools and nurseries will have a particular unit or base room for the children, but in most settings, children with special needs will be integrated and play alongside everyone else. There will be a SENCO (Special Education Needs Co-ordinator) whose task is to co-ordinate support and services for the child. He or she will work closely with the parents and the child's key worker.

KEY ISSUES

Find out about the work of the SENCO in your setting and ask how you can help with any children with special needs.

Curriculum activities

When you are planning activities, you will usually find that the long-term plans are made by the team you are working with, rather than youself. You will often work under the direction of a teacher or qualified leader and you will be asked to contribute, rather than take responsibility. If you are working in a school, the teacher will usually have topics planned according to the requirements of the National Curriculum. It will be part of your job to use your initiative to enable all children to access the planned learning activity. It is important that you find out about these plans to make sure that you are fitting in with the overall strategy of the setting. Planning is usually in three stages and is likely to follow the pattern set out in the table opposite.

A child who needs your special attention could be encouraged to join in the group, name the colours, talk to the other children, share and take turns, as well as being encouraged to talk to you about what they are doing.

The plan for the whole topic might include collecting special items and information and visits to nearby places. You may be lucky enough to have visitors from the local community. The home area could be turned into a shop, with suitable labels, coins, and things to buy and sell linked to the topic. If you need to do a display or a play

Long-term plans	The team meets to discuss how the aims of each area of learning and each early learning goal can be met, alongside the developmental needs of the children, both as a group and individually. Planning often includes special events such as particular festivals.
Medium-term plans	These will often cover particular topics or subjects which may be the focus of a few weeks' work, a month or even half a term. Examples could include looking at colours and shapes, how things are made or how our bodies work. It is very important that you find out about the plan that will be running when you are in placement, and any work that you do will need to contribute toward it.
Short-term plans	You will have a part to play here, as these will be focused on both individual children and a topic or subject area. For example, you and your team could be implementing a plan around a particular event, you could be working with an individual child to develop language skills and working on a display where you and a group of children work together.

activity for an assessment or to undertake an observation of a particular child, you could include these opportunities within the plan.

Evaluation

When you have carried out the activity or the plan, you should review and evaluate it carefully. This is usually undertaken as a team, with everyone who has been involved getting together to look at what has happened. The team will consider what went well and achieved the aims and what did not go so well and why. Suggestions will be made as to how it could be improved in the future. The evaluation of plans for the activity will need to record what happened, what was used, who was involved, how successful it was and how future plans can be made from the work that was done.

The evaluation of plans for an individual child will record what the child knew before, what has been learned through the activity and what the next activity to help the child to progress needs to be.

Remember that the age of the child or children will affect your planning. Plans could be for a very young child, to encourage a baby crawl or walk or to encourage a toddler to talk. These will be individual and related to that particular child and his or her circumstances. Plans for a group of older children in an out-of-school club will often be negotiated with the children and may be for a specific group activity, such as a visit to the pantomime at the local theatre or an outing to a safari park.

You will find more details on curriculum planning in Unit 4.

Think it over...

What could you provide to help to develop a two-year-old child's language? Think about different kinds of activities and find out about suitable books as well.

Encourage the toddler to talk to you.

```
                  Posters of different              Objects, e.g.
                  places with different        thermometers, windmills,
                    types of weather            sunglasses, umbrellas

      Photographs taken
        by the children                                              Tabletop display
                                          Topic title:
                                          THE WEATHER
      Children's pictures                                            Mobiles, e.g. sun,
     of different weather                                            clouds, raindrops

                  Children's writing              Frieze showing
                  about the weather              all sorts of weather
```

Supporting learning and displays

As you have seen with ideas for activities for special topics, there are many ways to support learning. Displays are important, as are first-hand experiences, and visits. Many teaching assistants will be involved with producing displays, as well as working with groups of children or, sometimes, the whole class. You may be asked to contribute to a learning wall, which will focus on a particular topic and include information to enhance the children's knowledge and excite their interest. You should always consider what the children can contribute and what they can learn from it. However, in all displays, you can use children's own work in many ways, some of which are listed in the diagram above.

Visits and first-hand experiences

To enhance this activity, which is all based on the topic of the weather, your plans could include a walk, perhaps to something that you have arranged with the staff team previously. You might encourage older children to record the rainfall with a rain gauge over a period of time and make comparisons. You could help younger children to make a weather chart and talk about the weather each day to see how it changes. Visits and activities like this, although they are quickly and relatively simply arranged, are enjoyable experiences for the children.

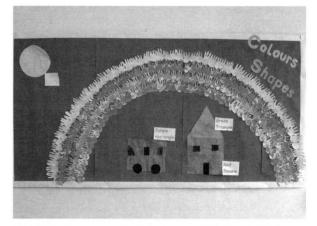

The Weather – a display done with the children.

When children go out, the setting will ensure that the parents have given permission and a qualified member of staff is present. If a child with special needs is in the group, a qualified worker may be asked to visit the area first, to check its suitability. This worker may be asked to be responsible for the child when on the visit.

It can be a good opportunity to teach the children basic road safety, so enough adults are needed for the number of children being taken. You can find out how many from your setting. Everything will be checked before you go to make sure each child is suitably dressed in appropriate clothing and you have everything you need. This could include warm clothes and boots in winter or sun hats and t-shirts with sleeves in summer, when sun protection lotion may also be needed.

Bringing back what you have found and putting it on the display table is an enjoyable task for staff and children together. You may be able to help choose pictures the children have painted or drawn to add to the display, or mobiles they have made. It is important that it is their work, so don't try to help too much and label all work clearly, 'John's pine cones', 'Susan's photograph', 'Sam and Anwara's paintings ', and so on. Labels should be in lower case letters and everything on the table should be safe for children to handle.

Older children will enjoy writing about what they have seen and this is a good opportunity for them to practise their writing skills and then add an illustration.

All children, particularly younger ones, will learn by touching, smelling, listening and tasting, as well as looking, so see if you can find something to display for all five senses. Check your spelling, laminate the labels if necessary, be prepared to maintain the display as it gets used, and plan when it will be taken down and what to replace it with. There should always be more input from the children than from you. You are just the person that makes it all happen.

4 How to work with codes of practice and policies

All early years practitioners will work to a code of practice which they will have learnt through their training and which will have set out the expectations of the setting. These will vary depending on the professional involved, but your primary concern is to comply with the code of practice and underlying values for early years practitioners, such as teachers, playworkers, teaching assistants and childminders. It is interesting to find out about the codes of practice of professional colleagues and to explore the differences and similarities. Codes of practice give guidance on behaviour and good practice in the workplace. They describe a set of standards that all workers are expected to maintain to ensure the quality of the service being delivered. You will find that policies and procedures are often written based on codes of practice.

The values and underlying principles for the early years care and education sector are listed in Unit 1. These principles draw on the UN Convention on the Rights of the Child. They are based on the premise that the earliest years of children's lives are a unique stage of human development, and that quality early years provision benefits the wider society and is an investment for the future.

You should take time to read and understand the values and principles and follow the guidance that codes of practice give you. These are the basis on which all professionals in the sector work, and you must comply with them at all times. The principles underpin all good practice in the sector. If you ever have doubts about the right way to approach a situation, consider how you would apply the underlying principles, and this should inform your actions.

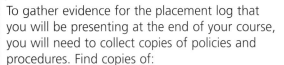

Assessment activity 6.6

To gather evidence for the placement log that you will be presenting at the end of your course, you will need to collect copies of policies and procedures. Find copies of:

• codes of practice
• health and safety policy
• equal opportunities policy
• behaviour policy.

Include a commentary on each and, when you have been in more than one setting, compare them and explain why there are differences and similarities.

Other policies

Each setting will also have a set of policies giving guidance on areas such as health and safety, behaviour and equal opportunities.

Clearly a health and safety policy in the home of a childminder has to be different from the health and safety policy in a large primary school, where there are many children, lots of rooms and plenty of staff available to help in emergencies. However, the basic principles will be the same and key safety concerns such as the administration of medicines and the storage of dangerous substances (such as bleach), as well as the safety and security of outdoor areas, are very similar, although the ways they are put into place are different. It is very important that you read and understand the health and safety policy of your setting so that you will know what to do in emergencies.

The table below lists common policies in early years settings.

TYPE OF POLICY	INFORMATION INCLUDED
Health and safety policy	• checking of equipment, ranging from toys to fire extinguishers • the responsibilities of workers to avoid and report hazards • dealing with emergencies
Equal opportunities policy	• equipment and training of staff • the equal treatment of families and children • the provision of particular play opportunities and equipment
Behaviour policy	• agreements about standards to be expected • how to promote positive behaviour

Look at the equal opportunities policy for your setting. Now consider how equal opportunities are promoted. Copy and complete the following table to make notes on what you find.

ACTIVITY/EQUIPMENT	CHECKLIST	NOTES
Toys and equipment, especially the home corner	Are there different types of dolls or different cooking and eating facilities? Do they promote equal opportunities and cultural awareness?	
Race, religion and culture	What religions and different cultural traditions are celebrated? Find out about each one, including when it is celebrated and how.	
Gender issues – boys and girls	Do the boys and the girls have toys that they prefer to play with in gender groups or are boys and girls encouraged to play with everything? Are there books that avoid stereotypes (e.g. female fire-fighters and male nurses)? Are both boys and girls encouraged to do everything (e.g. carrying things and tidying up)?	
Disability issues	Are there books that include characters with disabilities? Are all children encouraged to join in all activities?	
Different faiths	Are appropriate diets available for children that need them?	

Theory into practice

Talk to your supervisor about the ways that anti-discriminatory practice is promoted in your setting. You may find that there are ways this can be done that may not have been obvious to you, such as specialist training for staff, or policies on the ways relationships with parents are conducted.

Find out how you can contribute to the promotion of equal opportunity in your setting. Your supervisor will be able to help you here and you should make notes about what you find out, checking that you are putting it into practice during the time you are on placement.

5 How to demonstrate workplace expectations of a professional carer and evaluate your own performance

Professional behaviour

Becoming a professional is a process that takes place throughout your training. It is often useful to have a checklist that you consider at regular intervals to make sure that you are behaving in a professional manner. People will judge you by what they see and the way that you behave. If you observe the team that you work with, you will see that they maintain certain standards that are important to them in their work.

Think it over...

Think about the requirements for each setting you are in, as these may change. Use your checklist at regular intervals, so that you think about what is expected of you and how you are working towards achieving the expectations of the profession. You could write it down as a table and note specific examples of things that you did under each heading. You could then make a note of what you felt went well and what did not go so well. Then you could suggest how you could plan to improve your professional performance if you are in similar circumstances at another time.

Assessment activity

Devise a checklist for yourself that you could use to ensure that you are reaching a professional standard. It should include:

- personal presentation, such as standards of dress and cleanliness
- behaviour, such as reliability, punctuality and attendance
- showing enjoyment and pleasure in the children's achievements
- commitment to the job you are doing, which would include attention to the children's needs and skills
- being busy and seeing what needs to be done
- meeting health and safety and other legal requirements and following codes of practice
- speaking and communicating with children and colleagues
- being a good role model
- respecting parents and other professionals with whom you work.

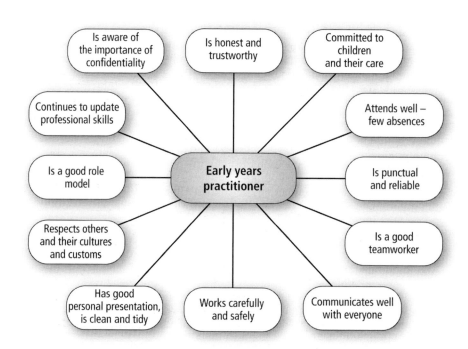

Confidentiality

Below is a diagram of the other professionals you will meet in the settings.

All of them are aware of the need for confidentiality when working with children. You will understand this too. Try to find out what they do and how your work links with theirs. You should understand what their particular specialist knowledge is and how your professional skills and understanding will be able to contribute, so that everyone's roles and responsibilities are clear.

Appropriate interpersonal skills

Communication is an essential part of the job of the early years practitioner. It is important to be able to communicate well with the team in which you are working, as well as the children in your care and their parents and carers. Other professionals may visit your setting and you should be clear about their roles and how they fit with yours.

Verbal and non-verbal skills

There is an interesting debate about how we communicate with each other. We do know that most of the messages we send out to others come, not from the things we say but from the way that we say it. It is thought that between 60 per cent and 70 per cent of communication comes through the non-verbal messages we send out. Much of the remainder depends on our tone of voice, its pitch, the way we speak and the vocabulary we choose, leaving between 10 to 15 per cent for the words themselves.

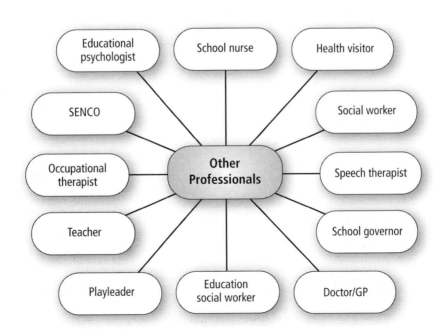

Our body language, such as our face, hands and posture, sends out powerful messages that others pick up, sometimes without us realising that it is happening. This non-verbal communication happens both formally, such as in meetings, and informally, such as when we pass each other during the day. Good communication can contribute to feelings of well-being and self-worth for both adults and children. It is important to listen as well as to talk. We need to hear what the child or other adult says, think about what he or she means and plan what we are going to say in response.

We need to remember that the other person may not think in the same way as we do. Children have very different life experiences to adults and so may see things in a very different way. When a child tries to touch something dangerous and we call out in alarm, the child is exploring in order to find out about it and what it does, whereas we will know what might happen and be alarmed at the possible consequences of their actions.

Assessment activity 6.9

Carry out an activity as you talk to children, either individually or in a group. Make an action plan for yourself to improve your interpersonal skills. Compare your skills in a group with your skills when working with an individual child.

Think it over...

Think about interactions between professionals. Watch yourself and others, as you talk to each other in a professional context either in pairs or in a group. Make notes under the following headings:

- Face and eyes
- Tone and pitch of voice
- Body movements and posture
- Gestures – arms and legs
- Muscle tension – tense or relaxed
- Touch and closeness
- The words and language used (professional jargon, complex vocabulary or another language altogether)
- The respect shown for the other person, particularly when listening

Now think about what you have seen and make notes about how the interactions could have been improved or made clearer.

Communicating with children and families

One of the most important ways to support children in their learning is to communicate with them. In Unit 2 you will have learnt a lot about

Talking to each other – enjoyable for everyone.

communication skills and how to look at your own skills and improve them. You will need to make sure you put what you have learnt into practice in your day-to-day work, especially when dealing with children of different ages, or with children or families who have particular communication needs, such as a need for signing, or for any printed material to be in Braille or in large print.

Look at the case studies below and consider how you could improve communication in each case.

Knowledge of children and parents

Parents will vary in the skills they have and the way they look after their children. It will often depend on how they were brought up themselves and patterns of behaviour and child rearing are often handed down from one generation to another. You may hear a parent say that if something was good enough for them when they were children, it is good enough for their child now. Other parents may be keen to be up to date and well informed

CASE STUDY

A mother arrives at the nursery with her three-and-a-half-year-old daughter, Evie. Both the mother and Evie are beautifully dressed and Evie is very small for her age. The mother seems rather anxious. As Evie comes in the door, she goes straight to a table to sit with the other children and starts playing. Her mother is obviously worried and, as you are nearby, she starts talking to you. She says she thinks that Evie might be bullied, as she is so small. She also says she is not happy about some of the other children who seem rather untidy and not very clean. She says that the children fell out the other day and Evie came home very upset

and told her about it. In your experience, while you have been on placement there, Evie is well settled and able to stand up for herself but you realise that the mother may not see that at home on her own.

- Make some notes about how you should – as a student – communicate with the mother in this situation and how you would refer the matter to a qualified member of staff concerned.

- Discuss your notes with your tutor or supervisor or with others in your student group.

CASE STUDY

A young mother arrives late at the nursery with her two-year-old son. He is in tears and so is she. She wants him to stay at the nursery but she is as upset about him leaving her as about her leaving him. She says that he is very nervy and that you must take special care of him. She says he cannot sit on the floor but must sit on a chair.

The mother tells the child that he must not worry if the other children are rough with him but must tell you when that happens. She adds that he must tell the teachers if the other children upset him and assures him that she really will come back for him later. You know

that unless the child gets away from the mother they will both be upset all morning and the child will never settle. She is going to need some help to be able to leave him and he is going to need help to settle down.

- Write some notes about what you should say to the mother to help her and how you would refer the matter to the appropriate member of staff.

- Write some notes about how you could support the child when his mother leaves him and help him to settle in the nursery.

about all the latest ways of bringing up their child. Parents are central to the life of their children and you need to understand the child and the family together to be able to do your best for the child in your care. Some parents will be happy to leave the care of their child to the staff of the setting, often because they are busy and working. Other parents will be keen to get all the information they can about their child and you will need to make it quite clear that you are a student and not a member of staff. Information about a child should always be given by the staff of the setting.

Think it over...

What could happen if you were chatting to a parent and gave them information about the other children in the group? Would it help them to understand their child better? Would you be breaching confidentiality? How could you make sure that you didn't?

Children and families

Knowing children and their families is very important and you will learn to work in partnership with the children's parents. The diagram below shows some of the ways this can be done.

All methods shown in the diagram should help families and carers to work together with the staff of the setting, so that the best interests of the child can be served.

It is not your role at any time to become involved in arguments or disputes with parents. These do occasionally happen in settings and must be dealt with by a senior staff member.

Using your initiative and procedures for referrals

Another skill of the professional is using initiative appropriately so that you are responsive and adaptable in changing needs and situations. This is a skill that you will need to develop. It is important to decide what you can deal with and what you can't. You may be able to dry a child's tears when he or she is distressed and talk to and comfort him or her but you may not be able to deal with the underlying problem. Consider the following case study situation and make some notes about how you would deal with it. If you can, discuss your ideas with your tutor or supervisor.

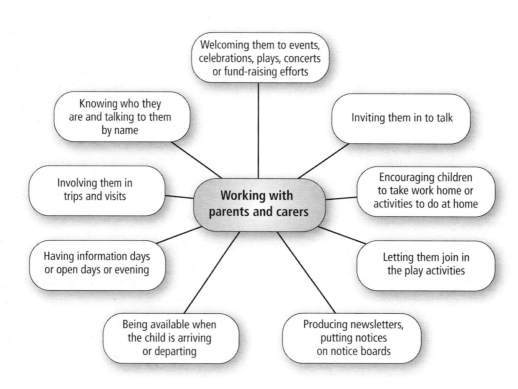

CASE STUDY

You have been working as one of the team in an infant school for some months and have enjoyed working with Emma, a small, quiet, shy girl, who is seven and a half. Emma has always had problems, but as you started at the school as a student on placement when she started, she took a liking to you and always talks to you at some time in the day, often when she is playing in the playground. One morning Emma arrives with her mother and it is clear that both of them are distressed and upset. You go to a quiet place in the book corner and Emma comes to talk to you. She tells you that at breakfast that morning, the police came to her house and now her mother has to go court. It sounds like this is as a result of domestic violence.

Emma's mother has gone but you need to know what to do now. You know that you will need to tell a member of staff as well as looking after Emma and keeping the other children occupied, as you and the teacher have planned. Emma tells you a bit about what has happened at home, but she doesn't want to talk too much. However, you can see that it is serious and Emma seems very unhappy.

- What can you do to help to sort out this unexpected situation?

- Who do you need to refer this incident to?

- Make some notes and try to put them in some order of priority.

Books and stories – a quiet moment to settle down.

Self-appraisal and self-awareness

All professionals, in any field, need to be able to reflect on their own practice. You will be able to undertake some of this with the support of your supervisor by learning to use your annual performance review effectively. Appraisal or review of your working performance will give you the chance to hear about your work from your supervisor and is a useful opportunity to find out about areas of work in which you are performing well and which are your areas of strength. You can also find out about areas of your work where you need some more support and a chance to develop your skills. You will plan targets and tasks with your line manager or a member of the senior management team in your setting.

Reviewing your own performance

In discussion with your supervisor, you should set targets for your own professional development. Your targets must be SMART targets, such as those shown in the table overleaf – these are all linked to improving your planning of activities to show you how it works.

Specific	I will improve my skills in activity planning.
Measurable	I will plan at least one activity for each day for the next two weeks.
Achievable	I will make sure that at least one activity each week is new to the children.
Realistic	I will read *Nursery World* magazine regularly to get new ideas for activities.
Timed	I will review my activity plans and outcomes with my supervisor weekly.

Assessment activity 6.10

Look back at the diagram, which has the early years practitioner in its centre (page 220). Now think about yourself very honestly. Which of the qualities can you say you have? Which are you developing? And which need more work? Now carry out a self-appraisal, as above.

Give yourself realistic dates for each target you wish to achieve, and then make sure you review them on the dates you have set yourself. For some of them, you may want to write down SMART targets, which will help to make things clear for you.

When you set your own personal targets, try to be quite clear about how you are going to develop the skills needed to reach them. Setting yourself challenges is the mark of a professional and a habit you will continue to develop throughout your professional life.

Contributing to the working of the team

Most early years settings will involve you in working as part of a team. Working with colleagues is a skill that you must develop. It is never possible to like everyone you work with but, as a professional, you will work hard at overcoming personal likes and dislikes and recognise the value of the contribution which all staff members make.

In order to become an effective team member you should:

✳ use good communication skills with colleagues just as much as the children

✳ recognise and value the work others do

✳ always ask for help if there is something you are unsure of

✳ never pretend to know more than you do

✳ never allow personal feelings to affect your working relationships

✳ make sure that you are clear about your role in any team projects

✳ never alter team plans or ways of working without getting the agreement of your supervisor

✳ never gossip about colleagues.

Remember – you are there to learn, to enjoy your work and to benefit the children you are working with. Try to become part of the team and do take every opportunity to ask for the help and advice of your colleagues. They were once students just like you!

END-OF-UNIT TEST

1 Give a brief description of the language skills you have observed in children aged 0–1, 1–3, 3–5 and 5–8 years.

2 List the main differences between a child minder, a pre-school playgroup and a nursery school.

3 Identify three hazards that you would look out for when the children are playing inside and three that you would look out for when they are playing outside. Describe briefly how you would avoid them.

4 Explain two reasons why care routines are important.

5 Describe two resources or materials that would encourage:

a) creative development

b) language development

c) physical development.

For each one, state the age of the children for whom it would be most suitable.

6 Briefly describe a curriculum topic you have been involved in with older children. How did it contribute to helping them learn reading, writing and number skills?

7 Describe ways you can play with a young baby to encourage his or her all-round development.

8 How can a good display support learning? List some of the main things you should remember when you are putting up a display.

9 What does a code of practice do? How does it differ from a policy or procedure?

10 Why is it important to read and follow codes of practice? What might happen if you don't?

11 List six qualities that would be expected of an early years practitioner and describe briefly how you have demonstrated them in your work.

12 Explain why it is important to understand confidentiality. Give one example of when keeping information confidential would be appropriate and one when it would not.

13 Describe four ways that people communicate other than by the words that they use.

14 Why do you need to get to know something about the children's families as well as the children themselves? How can this help you become a good early years professional?

15 Explain why you need to review your own performance regularly. When you set yourself targets, they should be SMART – describe what this means.

References and further reading

Birth to Three matters: A framework to support children in their early years (2003), Sure Start Unit

Bruce, T (2004), *Cultivating Creativity in Babies, Toddlers and Young Children*, Hodder Arnold

Bruce, T and Meggitt, C (2002), *Childcare and Education* (3rd edn), Hodder Arnold

Dare, A and O 'Donovan, M (2000), *Good Practice in Child Safety*, Nelson Thornes

Dare, A and O 'Donovan, M (2003), *A Practical Guide to Working with Babies*, Nelson Thornes

DfES (2001), *National Standards for Under Eights, Day Care and Childminding*

DfES (2001), *Guidance to the National Standards*, Ofsted Early Years

DfES (2004), *Removing Barriers to Achievement (Strategy for SEN)*

DfES (2004), *Five Year Strategy for Children and Learners*

Meggitt, C, Stevens, J and Bruce, T (2000) *An Introduction to Child Care and Education*, Hodder and Stoughton

Meggitt, C (2001), *Baby and Child Health*, Heinemann

O'Hagen and Smith (1995), *Special Issues in Child Care*, Balliere Tindall

Useful websites

Children's Information Services websites – look under CIS in your Local Authority's website

Department for Education and Skills – www.dfes.gov.uk

Department of Health – www.doh.gov.uk

Guidance for the National Standards – www.ofsted.gov.uk

Health and Safety Executive – www.hse.gov.uk

National Curriculum documents – www.dfes.gov.uk

National Standards for Under Eights Day Care and Childminding – www.dfes.gov.uk

National Literacy Trust – www.literacytrust.org.uk

Office for Standards in Education – www.ofsted.gov.uk

Royal Society for the Prevention of Accidents www.rospa.com

UNIT 7

Human growth and development

What you need to learn

1 The principles and theories of development in children aged 0–8 years

2 Growth and development from conception to the end of the first year of life

3 The stages of growth and development in children aged 1–8 years

4 The factors involved in promoting children's development

Introduction

To meet the requirements of this unit, you should have a good understanding of the principles and theories underpinning the development of children up to the end of their first year. You will need to be aware of the nature/nurture debate. Knowledge of the biological principles of the process of conception and birth as well as the growth of the foetus will be required. A longitudinal study of a baby in the first year of life will be undertaken which should take place over a minimum period of three months. This will enable you to consider in depth all aspects of growth and development. You will need to have a detailed knowledge and understanding of children's physical, emotional, social, cognitive and language development up to the age of eight years. In addition, you should be able to explain both the positive and the negative factors which influence children's development.

How you will be assessed

This unit is assessed internally.

1 The principles and theories of development in children aged 0–8 years

There are several aspects to a child's development. Development involves both the structure and the function of parts of the body. For instance, a baby during its first few months makes open vowel sounds, often called 'cooing'. The muscles of the mouth and tongue, which are important in producing clear speech, are still very slack. Later, when muscle tone and control improves, consonants can be formed.

As the child grows, body actions become increasingly controlled and complex as physical development takes place. Children's thought processes become more organised and their understanding broadens as cognitive development progresses, sometimes called intellectual development. Babies are born with some skills to enable them to interact with others, mainly parents and carers. However, the social skills and abilities of babies need greater refinement before they are competent in, and adaptive to, the social world around them. This is the process of social development. Feelings or emotions, both negative (such as fear and anger) and positive (such as happiness and pride), have to be both understood and controlled by children. This process is called emotional development. All aspects of development are continually changing as children progress through life.

Holistic development

The development of children is often studied as separate topics. However, each area of development influences the others.

A child is developing physical skills when trying to control the shaped pieces of a jigsaw.

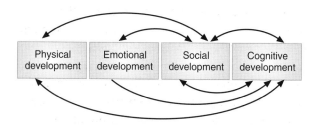

Holistic development.

When successfully completing the jigsaw, the child may express great emotional pleasure by enthusiastically telling the nearby adults about their achievement. To complete the jigsaw, the child has to develop cognitive skills to identify and match the pattern. In addition, the physical skills of fine motor control and co-ordination need to be used successfully.

If unsuccessful the child may show frustration. The resulting social behaviour of throwing the pieces of jigsaw around the room arises due to the child's stage of physical, emotional, cognitive and social development. Hence, development should be seen as a whole or as holistic development.

> **Think it over...**
>
> - Observe a child playing within a group of children.
> - Briefly list the child's development under the headings of physical, cognitive, emotional and social.
> - Comment on how the holistic development of the child has affected the interaction of the child with the other children.

Sequence of development

Children develop at different rates for a variety of reasons. However, development does follow the same sequence. The upper part of the body, especially the brain and head, develops rapidly while the lower part of the body follows more slowly. This is called head-to-toe or cephalo-caudal development. Also, development starts from the centre outwards. This is called inner-to-outer or proximodistal development. Hence, babies can hold their head up before they can stand and wave their arms around before they develop fine control over the use of their hands.

Nature/nurture debate

Every parent hopes for a healthy, beautiful baby who will thrive and reach the expected norms of

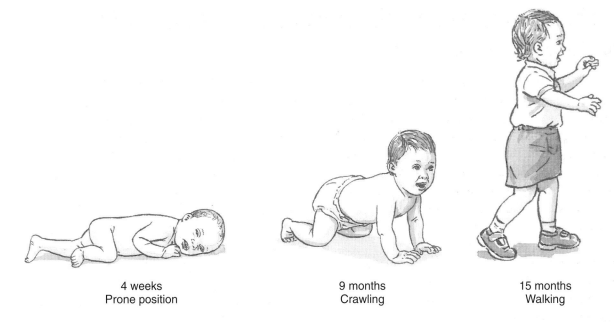

| 4 weeks | 9 months | 15 months |
| Prone position | Crawling | Walking |

Stages of physical development.

development. The potential for growth and development is affected by inherited factors. This is called the interaction with nature. In addition, factors within our environment have a very influential effect on development. This is called the interaction of nurture. There is much debate about how much and in what way either nature or nurture affects the process of development. Supporters of the nature side of the argument believe that intelligence is inborn, or innate, and the child's genes have determined the child's cognitive potential. Supporters of nurture believe that environmental factors, such as the child's stimulating experiences in the early years, have a strong influence on cognitive development. It is generally considered that both nature and nurture interact and influence the developmental process.

Assessment activity 7.1

- Explain an example of your own **head-to-toe** (cephalo-caudal) development.
- Explain an example of your own **inner-to-outer** (proximodistal) development.

Biological principles of conception, embryonic and foetal growth and birth

Conception is based on biological principles but, nevertheless, this does not diminish the aura of miraculous wonder at the creation of another human being.

Most conceptions occur as a result of sexual intercourse but, in a small number of cases, some embryos result from assisted conception techniques such as in-vitro fertilisation (IVF), intra-cytoplasmic sperm injection (ICSI), ovarian stimulation or induction, donor insemination or intra-uterine insemination (IUI). (See the glossary for further information.) All conceptions require the presence of a gamete, or sex-cell, from the male's sperm, and a gamete from the woman's ovum, or egg-cell, in order to form the embryo.

The monthly menstrual cycle allows the release of the ovum. Good health, positive mental well-being and a balanced lifestyle provide favourable conditions for the efficient cyclic process. Factors such as poor diet, ill-health and stress, including both over-excitement and deep unhappiness, can influence the timing of the release of the ovum.

The pituitary gland in the base of the skull controls the menstrual cycle. This cycle usually lasts 28 days and during this time four different hormones are secreted. These are essential if conception is to take place.

Day 1 — Pituitary gland secretes a **follicle-stimulating hormone**. This causes between 10 and 50 follicles to form in the ovary.

The developing follicles secrete **oestrogen.**

Day 5–14 — Oestrogen causes the endometrium (the lining of the uterus) to develop and stimulate the cervix to produce a mucus to help the progress of the sperm into the uterus.

Days 11–17 — Fertile phase when conception is more likely to take place.

Day 14 — One follicle develops fully. When released from the ovary it forms an ovum while the rest of the follicles degenerate. Sometimes, more than one follicle is released. This may result in a multiple pregnancy (twins).

Luteinising hormone is given off by the pituitary gland.

This causes:

- the ovum to be released

- a small gland called the corpus luteum to form in the ovary after the ovum has been released (after ovulation). It secretes **progesterone**. The gland continues to form for the next ten days until the 26th day of the menstrual cycle.

Day 26 — If fertilisation does not occur the corpus luteum degenerates and the hormone progesterone is no longer produced.

If fertilisation does occur the hormone progesterone will continue to be produced during pregnancy. Menstruation will stop and a softening of some of the muscles occurs in the uterus, intestine, bladder and blood vessels.

The ovum is wafted towards the fallopian tubes through the oviduct. The minute hairs in the fallopian tube encourage the ovum to pass along the tube to the uterus. If a sperm cell (a gamete) swims along the fallopian tube and comes into contact with an ovum, it will pierce the jellylike coating around it and the sperm head will then go on to penetrate the ovum's nucleus. The two fuse together to form one cell (a zygote). Normally, the 23 chromosomes from the sperm join with the 23 chromosomes from the ovum to form a set of 46, which form 23 pairs. They are reproduced in every cell of the embryo.

The zygote initially divides into two and continues to divide rapidly, with some cells forming the embryo and some the placenta. These cells, which look like a mulberry, are called the morulla and take four days to travel along the fallopian tube into the uterus. This is now called a blastocyst. It gets attached to the uterus wall by tiny projections called villi. When implanted in the soft wall, it connects into the bloodstream, which allows it to absorb oxygen as well as essential nutrients and so it grows fast. When this stage is complete, usually between ten and fourteen days after conception, the developing baby is now known as an embryo.

Many conceptions do not progress through all the stages of pregnancy. The highest risk of failure to thrive and develop is between fertilisation, the embryo's implantation in the uterus and Week 10. Common problems include:

✳ ectopic pregnancies, when the blastocyst implants in the fallopian tube instead of the uterus

✳ the fertilised ovum, or zygote, failing to implant in the uterus and an early miscarriage resulting.

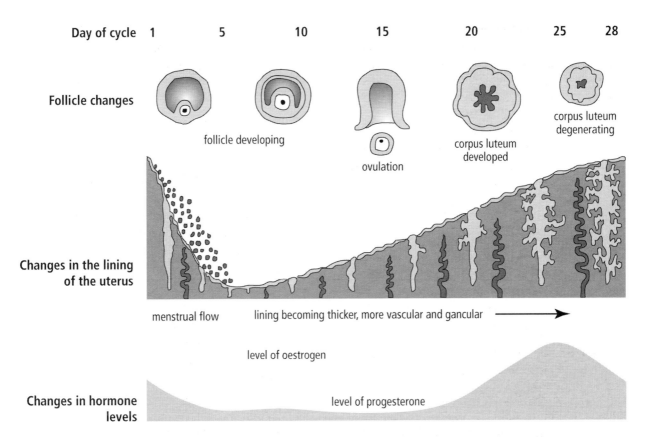

| Day of cycle | 1 | 5 | 10 | 15 | 20 | 25 | 28 |

Follicle changes

follicle developing

ovulation

corpus luteum developed

corpus luteum degenerating

Changes in the lining of the uterus

menstrual flow

lining becoming thicker, more vascular and gancular →

level of oestrogen

Changes in hormone levels

level of progesterone

Changes occurring during menstrual cycle.

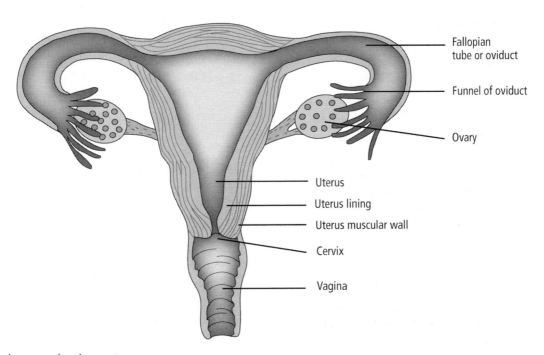

Fallopian tube or oviduct

Funnel of oviduct

Ovary

Uterus

Uterus lining

Uterus muscular wall

Cervix

Vagina

Female reproductive system.

Development of embryo into a full-term foetus

WEEK	STAGE FIRST TRIMESTER (THREE MONTHS) – WEEKS 0–13
3	**Embryonic stage** • First missed period. • Foundation of the brain and nervous system is laid down. • Amnion sac is formed around the embryo, which floats in a liquid (the amniotic fluid). • The placenta is formed, which lies against the uterus wall and acts as the liver, lungs and kidneys for the embryo and the foetus. The placenta is connected to the embryo's circulatory system by the umbilical cord. Nutrients pass through to the embryo and digestive waste products and CO_2 pass from the baby to the mother.
4	• Neural tube closes (otherwise spina bifida occurs). • Length of embryo is about 6.4mm.
5	• Heart beat is detected and embryo is the size of a small seed.
8	• Embryo has 10,000 cells and is about 2.5cm long. • The formation of organs, eyes, ears and limb buds is at a rudimentary stage. • Embryo has developed the startle reflex.
12	**Foetal stage** • All body parts are present, but still need refining. The baby is now called a foetus. • It has developed the sucking reflex, can swallow, roll and somersault. • Organs are functioning. • Downy hair and fingernails are forming. • Foetus measures about 7.5cm.
	SECOND TRIMESTER – WEEKS 14–27
15	• Hears first sounds.
16	• Genitals have formed. A female foetus has around 3,000,000 egg cells in her ovaries. • A greasy substance called vernix, covers the skin of the baby.
20	• Weighs about 460g. • The survival rate of babies born at this stage is very low.
22	• Body grows, bones harden. • Develops reflex to root, and grasp. • Can dream and feel emotions.
24	• Although the lungs are not yet fully developed, with intensive care, the foetus has a reasonable chance of survival. • The eyes open for the first time.
27	• Weighs about 500g and is approximately 33cms long. • Is very active e.g. twisting, somersaulting, kicking.

WEEK	STAGE THIRD TRIMESTER – 28–40 WEEKS
28–32	• Foetus grows rapidly to about 1800g and is approximately 40cm long. • It fills the space in the uterus and so rolls and turns less, but can kick energetically. • The developing brain is able to process more information and respond more effectively, such as recognising the mother's voice. • Starts to develop a rhythm of sleeping and waking.
33–36	• The foetus continues to grow and by Week 35 is about 2800g. It subsequently gains about 280g per week. • The brain develops rapidly and the head grows more than the rest of the body to allow for this. • Myelination of the brain cells starts. • Fine hair covering the body starts to disappear. • The foetus can now swallow, urinate and make breathing movements. • A supply of glycogen forms in the liver, which the foetus draws on, together with its fat reserves, to provide energy during birth and immediately afterwards while feeding patterns are established. • The head will usually 'engage' in the pelvis for first pregnancies but during subsequent pregnancies it may not occur until labour.
37–40	• The amniotic fluid reduces and the foetus grows to fill the space in the amniotic sac. • The foetus at 37 weeks weighs about 3 kilograms and is lying head down. • Birth may take place any time between Week 38 and Week 42.

Genetic information

When a baby is born, friends and relatives are usually very interested in who the baby looks like. We inherit genetic information from both parents. The millions of cells in our bodies arise from the division and subdivision of the single cell formed by the fusion of the ovum from the mother and the sperm from the father. Before a cell divides, its DNA is organised into paired formations, called chromosomes. Human DNA forms 23 pairs of chromosomes. Each part of the pair is very similar, but not identical. Units of DNA form a gene. Chromosomes are made up of hundreds of genes. Differences in details of our make-up are determined by our genes. For example, at a certain point on a chromosome, there is a gene determining the colour of the eyes. The mother may have a gene for brown eyes, while the father has a gene for blue eyes. The 'brown' gene is more dominant than the 'blue' gene, which is recessive and, therefore, not so influential. Consequently,

the child will have the mother's brown eyes. If both parents have blue eyes, the child would have blue eyes.

Genetic information affects other features of physical development, such as height and build. It determines the limits of each child's potential to develop and grow. Currently, much exciting scientific research is unravelling the mystery of our genes and it is hoped that soon scientists will understand much more about how we are formed and function.

Genetic disorders

Many human disorders are due to defective genes, called mutants. Perhaps the most common disease is cystic fibrosis, where the gene is recessive. The gene may have been passed down through many generations without difficulties. However, the medical condition may occur when both the mother and the father are carriers of this recessive gene. Other disorders that are the result of inherited genes

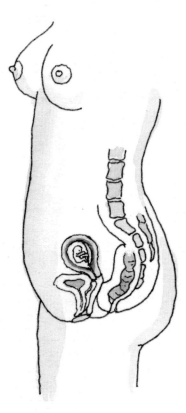

Week 12 – first trimester

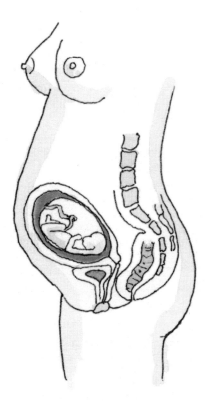

Week 26 – second trimester

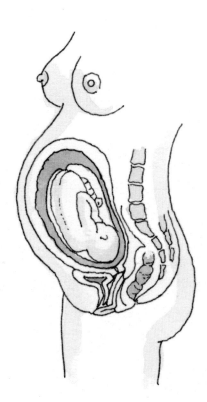

Week 34 – third trimester

Stages of pregnancy.

Age of mother

Under 15 and over 35 – Increased risk of high blood pressure and pre-eclampsia.
Under 15 – risk of under-weight baby.
Over 35 – increased risk of diabetes, miscarriage, stillbirth and a baby with chromosomal abnormalities.

Diet

A well-balanced diet is essential. Nutritional supplements containing folic acid and Vitamin B help prevent neural tube defects and lower the incidence of congenital abnormalities. Excessive amounts of Vitamin A during the first two months of pregnancy can cause birth defects.

Medication

Some medications may cause congenital abnormalities e.g. chemotherapy drugs.

Alcohol

Heavy drinkers or alcoholics usually have smaller babies, with smaller brains and with distinctive physical abnormalities or deformities. Affected babies display foetal alcohol syndrome. This can have long-term consequences including developmental delay, learning difficulties and impaired growth, affecting the functioning of the central nervous system.

Infection

Some diseases:
a) attack the placenta, e.g. viruses such as HIV, and so reduce the nutrients passed to the foetus
b) with small molecules pass through the placenta and attack the foetus, e.g. rubella, syphilis, flu, chicken pox
c) are present in the mucus of the birth canal and infect the baby during birth, e.g. Herpes simplex.

Factors influencing embryonic and foetal growth

Industrial hazards

Exposure to solvents, oils, lead and pesticides can have a radical effect on both embryonic and foetal growth.

Congenital abnormalities

Chromosomal abnormality – a defect in one of 46 chromosomes to be found in every body cell, e.g. Down's Syndrome.
Genetic abnormality – one of the genes found on the 46 chromosomes does not function properly, e.g. cystic fibrosis.
Developmental abnormality during the embryonic stage e.g. cleft lip, spina bifida. The reason for this is not fully understood. Genetic counselling and testing is offered when parents are concerned about congenital abnormalities.

Smoking

Nicotine constricts blood vessels reducing blood flow and nutrition to the placenta. Risk of:

- low birth weight
- miscarriage
- premature birth
- still birth.

Street drugs

Street or recreational drugs may cause congenital abnormalities, low birth weight, or premature birth.

are sickle-cell anaemia and haemophilia, (the latter is transmitted by a sex-linked gene and is only exhibited in males). Some diseases, such as Down's syndrome, arise due to a faulty allocation of whole chromosomes. Early pregnancy tests involving amniocentesis and ultrasound scanning reveal some of these genetic disorders prior to birth.

Factors influencing embryonic and foetal growth

Some factors can enhance or promote growth and the development of the embryo and resulting foetus and baby, while others can inhibit or have a negative effect. (See diagram on page 237.)

Birth

After the long wait during pregnancy, the mother has to work hard during the birth process to reach the moment of wondrous joy as she sees and holds her baby.

The midwife has a lead professional role preparing and managing the birth, and also plays a part in providing a range of other services.

> **Think it over...**
>
> You have been asked to help produce the local health clinic's leaflet on 'Healthy Pregnancy, Healthy Baby'.
>
> - What advice would you suggest should be included in the section Healthy Lifestyles at the Pre-conception Stage?
> - Prepare sections on:
>   - the enhancing factors
>   - the inhibiting factors which can affect the growth and development of the embryo and foetus.

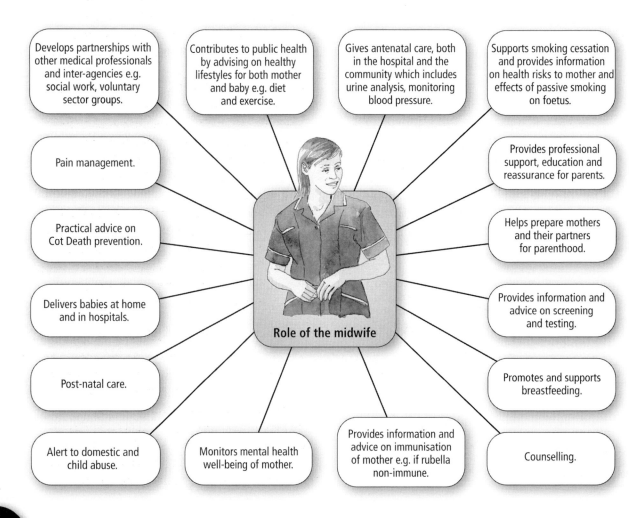

Develops partnerships with other medical professionals and inter-agencies e.g. social work, voluntary sector groups.

Contributes to public health by advising on healthy lifestyles for both mother and baby e.g. diet and exercise.

Gives antenatal care, both in the hospital and the community which includes urine analysis, monitoring blood pressure.

Supports smoking cessation and provides information on health risks to mother and effects of passive smoking on foetus.

Pain management.

Provides professional support, education and reassurance for parents.

Practical advice on Cot Death prevention.

Helps prepare mothers and their partners for parenthood.

Delivers babies at home and in hospitals.

Role of the midwife

Provides information and advice on screening and testing.

Post-natal care.

Promotes and supports breastfeeding.

Alert to domestic and child abuse.

Monitors mental health well-being of mother.

Provides information and advice on immunisation of mother e.g. if rubella non-immune.

Counselling.

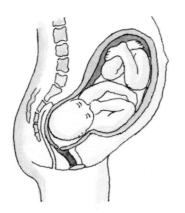

Before labour – head engaged in pelvis, cervix closed.

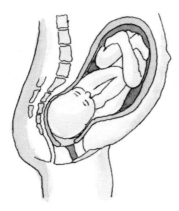

Stage 1 – cervix dilates gradually.

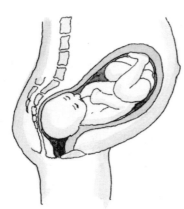

Cervix fully dilated.

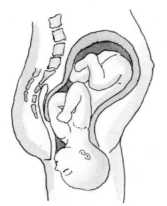

Stage 2 – Baby's head descends through cervix into birth canal, ready to be born.

Birth is a continuous process but is often described as progressing through three stages.

Prior to birth, during pre-labour, the body secretes a number of hormones.

✳ The baby's brain signals via its pituitary gland to the adrenal glands to release cortisol. This stimulates the production of prostaglandins, which are released when the baby has reached full-term. Prostaglandins trigger the uterus to contract. These are known as Braxton-Hicks contractions. These occur over the last weeks of the pregnancy.

✳ Progesterone, relaxin and prostacyclin, as well as nitric oxide, are released, which inhibit the contractions in the uterus.

✳ Relaxin helps to soften the connective tissue in the cervix and so prepare it for opening.

✳ Both baby and mother produce oxytocin.

Stage 1 – This is the longest part of the birth process. It may last up to 12 hours or more. The cervix dilates gradually (opens) from 0cm to approximately 10cm and flattens out. This is called effacement. At first, during the latent stage, the contractions are relatively spaced apart but later, during the active stage, contractions come more frequently and are intense.

At the end of Stage 1, called transition, the baby's head will be on the pelvic floor and contractions maybe very close together, coming every two minutes. It is a very exhausting time.

Stage 2 – This stage is shorter than Stage 1 and may take anything between 20 minutes and 2 hours. The mother has a great urge to bear down and push, resulting in the birth of the baby. The baby's head moves through the cervix, down the birth canal and then out of the mother's body.

Most baby's are born head first, facing the back of the mother. Some babies are positioned before birth feet down on the pelvic floor in the breech position. Nearly all breech births are now delivered by caesarean section.

Stage 3 – The placenta, which is also called the after-birth, and any other material from the uterus, is delivered. The uterus contracts with after-pains. If the contractions are not strong enough the

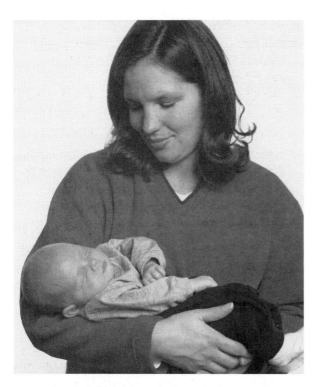

A mother holding her new-born baby.

mother may be advised to put her baby to her breast, as the baby's sucking will release the hormone oxytocin which stimulates the contractions.

Most babies are now able to breathe on their own and have a well-developed sucking reflex, so are able to thrive. About 10 per cent of babies need extra support provided by the special care baby unit (SCBU) or the neonatal intensive care unit (NICU). Babies born before their full term of 40 weeks, or babies who are small or very much below the normal birth weight, may need special or intensive care. A baby which is born before 35 weeks, which has a birth weight of less than 2.5kg, or which has a condition that requires special care may need intensive care.

KEY ISSUES

A healthy mother who has prepared for pregnancy, has regular antenatal care and has a well-balanced life-style is more likely to produce a healthy baby who has the potential to thrive.

Assessment activity 7.2

- Prepare a presentation, as part of a sex education course for Year 6 primary school pupils, to explain the process of birth.

Undertaking a longitudinal study

One way of noting the progressive development of a baby is to carry out a longitudinal study, which involves research over a long period of time.

The research required for Unit 7 will involve following the development of a baby in the first year of life over a period of at least three months. It will enable you to study in depth various factors affecting development.

Before you start your study, you need to give some careful thought to how you will carry it out. Consideration needs to be given to the following.

✳ **Selecting the baby to study**. As you have to undertake the study over a three-month period, you will need to be confident that you will have access to the baby for this period of time. It is advisable to study a baby who has neither a known developmental delay nor an identified disability.

✳ **Liaising closely with the family of the baby**. You will need to explain fully what your study will involve and get the family's written consent for you to undertake the study. Remember, the baby will be the most precious thing a family has and it is, therefore, a privilege to peer into the baby's life.

✳ **The ethical conduct of your study**. Strict confidentiality must be observed. You must be responsible in your attitude to your work. You may be given, or become aware of, sensitive and personal information. This must be treated in confidence and with respect and be used in such a way that it cannot be traced back to its source. When you write up your study do not use the real names of the baby or family nor identify the exact location of where the baby lives. You must respect the culture and beliefs of the family and their circumstances, such as age, any disability, etc. Your attitude must be non-judgemental. Permission must be obtained from the family to take any photographs to include in your study. You cannot force the family to give you any information and you must not hold any data which is not relevant to the study. Any methods used to study the baby must be morally acceptable.

Understanding what is required by the active verbs used in the assessment grid

You need to be aware of what is required when you describe growth and development for pass criteria P4, what is needed to explain growth and development for merit criteria M2 and finally how to analyse enhancing and inhibiting factors affecting the growth and development of the baby for distinction criteria, D1.

The study should include the following.

* *Relevant measurements and observations of all areas of development*
  You will need to study and observe physical, social, emotional and cognitive development. The baby's parents may be willing to report on birth weight and measurements and the results of relevant development screening by the health visitor.

* *Statements of developmental baselines and progress*
  Secondary research will be needed to obtain information on measurements relevant to the age of the child studied, such as centile charts, Apgar Scores or Bayley Scales of Infant Development. To achieve the pass criteria (P4) you will have to **describe** all aspects of growth and development of the baby. However, to meet the requirements of the merit criteria (M2), you will need to **explain** the growth and development.

* *Developmental needs and provision*
  Developmental needs will have to be researched based on the age and stage of development of the baby. You will need to be sensitive to the family's ability to provide for the baby and link your observations to both enhancing and inhibiting factors affecting development – see later in this unit, page 259. It will be necessary to try to obtain some case history of the baby.

* *Routines and procedures*
  You will need not only to describe these, but to explain their relevance and whether they meet the developmental needs of the baby and whether safety and security are considered.

* *Safety and security measures*
  These measures must be of first importance when you are with the baby. You must not put the baby at any risk of harm. The relevance of measures taken by the family or the nursery, if studying the baby in that setting, must be explained. You should discuss with your tutor how to ensure your own safety and security when undertaking your research.

* *Play activities*
  You will need to research suitable play activities for the age and stage of development of the baby. Play to promote all areas of development should be covered. This will link in with other sections, such as developmental needs and provision.

* *Role of significant adults*
  The range of significant adults will vary according to the circumstances of the family. If you are studying a baby in a nursery or with a childminder, you will need to try to find out who are the significant adults in the home environment and the role they play.

* *Role of professionals*
  The range of professionals involved with the baby will vary according to the family circumstances and the health and development of the baby. It will always include a health visitor and GP, but it may also include a social worker, nursery staff or Ofsted inspector.

Planning the methods to be used to gather the required information

Secondary research

This may be useful in order to gather background information and data. It could include literature or book searches, CD-ROMs, documents, reports and information from the internet. Remember to acknowledge your sources and to reference them correctly.

Primary research

You may wish to use questionnaires to gather background information from the family or carer. An interview may enable you to gather more detailed information than through a questionnaire. You can also explore issues raised in more depth.

Observations will be essential during the study. They may take a variety of formats including:

* naturalistic
* written record – narrative
* checklists
* time sampling
* event sampling
* structured.

See Unit 8 and Unit 11 for more detail of these research methods.

KEY ISSUES

- Respect the confidentiality of the baby and its family.
- Ensure the safety and security of the baby during activities undertaken as part of the longitudinal study.
- Undertake your study in a morally correct and responsible manner.

Theory into practice

From your longitudinal study:

- choose one example to illustrate and explain the 'nature' theory of development
- choose one example to illustrate and explain the 'nurture' theory of development
- use these examples to explain whether you think the child's development is due to 'nature', or 'nurture' or is influenced by both nature and nurture.

2 Growth and development from conception to the end of the first year of life

Principles, stages and sequences

We have already considered the debate surrounding the influence of nature and nurture in the development of babies and children, but there are other controversies surrounding the principles of development.

Developmental psychologists have differing views about the nature of the change in development. The issue of quantitative and qualitative change raises interesting questions. Is the development in children just an increase in the amount of the same progress (quantitative), such as increasing the number of the words they can use? Does the development involve different processes at different stages or ages (qualitative), such as when children string words together to form simple sentences?

Quantitative change is seen as a continuum and, therefore, stages are not viewed as being relevant. However, the qualitative approach to change accepts the idea that children at varying stages or ages have new approaches to problems, see the world around them differently and are concerned with different ideas. For instance, Piaget developed his theory of cognitive development based on a qualitative or stage approach.

Recently there has been much criticism of the qualitative or stage approach. For instance, John Flavell argues that children show sequences of development and these are found in a variety of areas, such as in the acquisition of language. They involve both qualitative and quantitative changes, but the sequence for all children follows the same pattern. Progress can vary across different sequences – a child may proceed faster along the language sequence than along sequential change for moral development. Hence, development does not correlate with age, but follows a similar pattern.

Children may reach milestones of development at different ages, for example, when children take their first step or speak their first word can vary greatly. Milestones are often used to measure development, such as when a child can sit without support. These milestones have to be used with care as the whole, or holistic, development of a child should be considered before drawing any conclusions. However, there is a generally accepted range of normal development.

1 month – Held sitting, back a complete curve

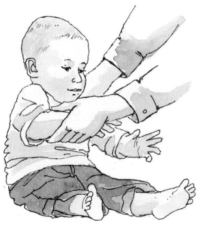

6 months – Held sitting, back straight

9 months – Sitting unsupported

Important milestones – sitting unsupported.

Normal ranges of development

Generally, parents view their child as a unique individual but, nevertheless, are usually eager to compare their child with others. Health professionals use both approaches in assessing and trying to understand children's state of physical and mental health and developmental stages.

In the *nomothetic* approach of assessment, factors have been identified which enable

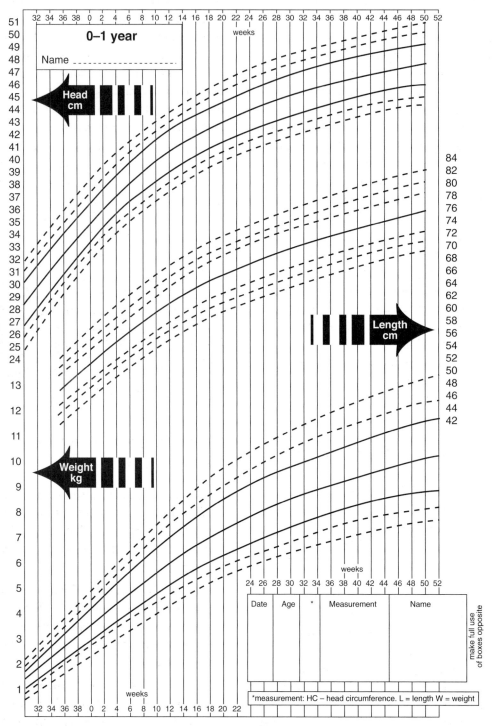

Boys growth chart 0–1 year, from Boys Growth Charts (Birth – 18 years) *– designed and published by Child Growth Foundation 1994.*

children's progress to be compared. These factors are expected to be the normal level of development according to age and other factors, such as racial origin. For instance, children from Thailand are generally smaller than those from Western European countries.

The *idiographic* approach to assessment involves the children's individual progress, with their uniqueness being observed and considered. This approach may be adopted by specialist health professionals, such as child psychiatrists. Children with emotional problems may be referred to a child psychiatrist who will assess the individual child's problems, stage of development and needs. This may lead to the child having an individual therapy or support programme.

When a child is born, parents are given a Personal Child Health Record Book which contains charts on which the child's height, weight and head circumference are plotted.

Information is gained through growth monitoring. For example, at birth the head circumference is measured to help detect any abnormality, such as hydrocephalus. This is due to the accumulation of cerebro-fluid which can cause brain damage and is characterised by a large head.

A small head, such as found in microcephaly, may arise from some abnormality of brain development in pregnancy, or may be a sign of impaired brain growth.

Weight, length and height monitoring is also undertaken. These have to be interpreted with care. For instance, growth hormone deficiency may be linked with normal or even increased weight gain. Temporary slow weight gain or loss may be due to minor illness or family disturbances. Parental build and height also have to be considered. Hence, what is 'normal' for one baby may be of concern for another.

Children's growth is usually plotted on centile charts – nine centile charts were first published in 1993. These resulted from the study of and recording of the progress of thousands of children. They describe current growth very precisely. The horizontal axis, or bottom line, shows the age of the child in weeks up to one year. The vertical axis (down the sides) shows the types of development being measured and are given an age range.

Blocks above the centile line show good development and those which appear below the centile line may indicate some developmental concern.

Centile charts are valuable since they allow a child's progress to be noted and comparisons made. Hence, a child can be compared with him or herself as well as with the average or 'normal' development. The charts can record all areas of development, so a pattern of progress may be evident. Some areas may show advanced development, while others may show slower development. These charts can alert early years practitioners to any progress which may give concern and is deviating from the normal pattern. Hence, this promotes the possibility of early intervention. Centile charts can be used up to the age of twenty, but this rarely happens.

For further details of principles of growth and development see Unit 13.

Theory into practice

If the parents of the baby you are studying are willing to let you see the Personal Child Health Record Book, study this carefully. What evidence does it provide for the development of the baby since birth? Can you give an explanation of the progress recorded so far?

What is meant by physical development?

Physical development is the gradual process by which children develop the use and control of muscles, thus gaining a wider range of movements. Physical development includes the following.

* **Changes in gross motor behaviour** – newborn babies display involuntary 'walking' movements arising from reflex actions. A 15-month-old child can increasingly voluntarily control his or her walking actions.

* **Fine motor development involving the movements of hands and fingers** – the early primitive squeeze grasp shown by some babies as young as four weeks develops into a very

neat and co-ordinated grasp using the forefinger by five years.

* **Changes in some of the sensory organs, such as eyes** – the development of eye muscles enables most babies to see more clearly and over a larger area than at birth.

Why is physical development so important?

As a baby's physical development progresses, new skills are learned. These enable the baby to become involved in more activities and to explore their immediate world. Further complex skills are learned, giving increasing control of activities. With success comes **emotional development**. Babies/children gain self-confidence through the control of their actions, thus promoting their self-esteem. With more mobility, children are able to play with others, thereby promoting their **social development**. The development of both gross and fine motor skills is important. Children become more personally independent, and, for instance, start dressing themselves. Children can then proceed to acquiring more advanced skills which they need, as they grow older, for school, work and leisure.

Children progress at different rates following the same sequence of physical development. The age at which children develop physical skills, such as walking, depends on the maturation of their nervous system, strength of muscles, especially in their legs and back, and achieving balance. For most children physical development is a continuous process until maturity.

Think it over...

Imagine you are confined to bed to lie on your back for three weeks and the muscles in your hands are weak and poorly co-ordinated.

* How would this affect your range of activities?
* How would this affect your awareness of the world around you?

Reflexes

Newborn babies are born with certain reflexes. These are involuntary, automatic, physical responses, triggered by a stimulus and determined by impulses in nerves. Everybody has some reflexes – knees jerk when tapped, which you do not learn to do; this reaction is inborn.

REFLEX	STIMULUS	RESPONSE
Rooting	Stroking baby's cheek	Turns towards the side stroked as if seeking a nipple with the mouth
Sucking	An object put into the mouth, e.g. nipple	Sucks rhythmically
Hand grasp (palmar grasp)	An object, e.g. finger, put into hand	Grasps tightly into the palm of the hand
Startle (Moro) reflex	Baby is startled by bright light/loud noise	Arms and legs splay open, back arches and then arms and legs close as if to hang onto carer to avoid falling

▶

REFLEX	STIMULUS	RESPONSE
Stepping/walking reflex	Baby held upright with soles of feet on a flat surface or edge of table	Makes stepping/walking movements

These reflexes enable babies to survive. They can seek for food and suck without being able to think about their actions. Gradually the reflexes disappear and babies develop voluntary actions – they learn and can choose to do the actions. For instance, the walking reflex disappears after the first few weeks and babies learn to walk at around twelve months.

Development of gross motor control in first year

These are large movements including:

* gross motor actions which involve the use of the whole limb, such as when hopping

* locomotive skills which are movements needed to travel, such as crawling and walking; they develop as shown in the table below.

1 MONTH	3 MONTHS	6 MONTHS	9 MONTHS	12 MONTHS
Head droops if unsupported	Head held erect for a few seconds before falling forwards	Raises head to look at feet	Can lean forward to pick up toy	May stand upright alone for a few minutes
Pulled to sit, head lags	Pulled to sit, little head lag	Sits with support in pram	Can sit alone for 10–15 minutes	Sits confidently on floor for long periods
Lies with head to one side	Lies with head in midline	Lifts head from pillow to look at feet	Can turn body sideways to pick up toy	Can pull up to standing and sit down again
Large jerky movements of limbs	Movements smoother and continuous	Holds arms up to be lifted Can roll over	Moves on floor by rolling Tries to crawl When held, steps purposefully on alternate feet	Crawls Walks around furniture and may walk alone
Arms active	Kicks vigorously Finger play – brings hands together	In cot, lifts legs to 90 degrees and grasps foot	Very active movements	Drops and throws toys purposefully

When these milestones of sitting, crawling and walking are achieved depends upon the development of neuro-muscular co-ordination. Other factors such as the weight of the child and fitness level can also affect progress. For instance, an overweight baby who has little exercise may take longer to be able to walk unaided.

Children's pattern of walking changes as they become more confident. The rate of development is also influenced by the inherited growth pattern from the parents.

Theory into practice

As part of your longitudinal study, study the child's progress towards either:
• being able to sit unsupported or
• walking independently.
Observe the child at the beginning of the study and three months later. Account for the progress made.

Think it over...

Discuss in a group your actions when first learning a physical skill, such as ice-skating or rollerblading.

• How relaxed were you at the different stages of learning? How far apart did you position your feet? How fast were you at first? How far did you attempt to go before choosing to stop? How much practice did you need to improve?

• Did your progress in learning the skill match the progress children make when developing their walking skills?

3 The stages of growth and development in children aged 1–8 years

Further development of gross motor movements

AGE	PATTERN OF DEVELOPMENT
12–15 months	Moves hesitantly and irregularly Poor balance, very unsteady Falls easily, body rigid Legs wide apart, arms outstretched to aid balance Arms and legs used to achieve balance by moving opposite each other
19–24 months	Body less rigid Feet only slightly apart, smooth pattern of walking Arms at side of body and not used for balance Stops and starts safely Runs carefully but cannot go round corners Walks upstairs with support, two feet to a stair Creeps downstairs backwards No attempt to move to catch ball
2–3 years	Can throw ball overhand Kicks balls enthusiastically Tries to catch a large ball by extending arms Can ride a tricycle Walks alone upstairs using alternate feet
4–5 years	Steady stride, arms used in walking action Can walk along a narrow line Runs lightly on toes Skips on alternate feet, can hop a short distance Moves rhythmically to music Skilfully climbs, slides and swings

AGE	PATTERN OF DEVELOPMENT
6–7 years	Can catch ball by holding hands in cup-shape Moves legs, outstretches hands to intercept ball Takes impact of catching by moving body Good balance, both when moving and when static A smooth rhythmical action Arms and legs move in opposition to each other Feet close together When running slightly leans forward, arms swung backwards and forwards Co-ordinated jumping – able to jump a distance
By 8 years	Gross motor movements are precise, e.g. can walk along a thin line with arms outstretched for balance Expert rider of two-wheeled bicycle May develop skills in sports, e.g. swimming, rollerblading

Theory into practice

Observe two children of different ages and stages of motor development. Note their gross motor actions. What locomotion differences between the two children do you notice? Using the information above, identify at what age the toys listed below would be appropriate:

- baby bouncer
- roller-blades
- a toy on a rug for baby to lie on
- tricycle
- a trampette
- two-wheeled bicycle
- push-along wheeled toy.

In order to develop motor control, children need to:

✳ practise, to improve and master the skill

✳ concentrate on small parts of the overall skill – children learn to place two feet to a stair before developing the more complex skill of alternate feet action

✳ pay a lot of attention to the action; later they can do the action almost automatically

✳ have experience of a range of movement activities to develop their memory of motor actions, enabling them to cope with more complex situations.

Development of fine motor skills

At the same time as a child's gross motor movement changes are occurring, so too are their fine motor skills – see the table below. These involve wrist, hand and finger movements. It is important that these skills are fostered so children can develop good manual skills in adult life involving the use of tools and implements.

AGE	PATTERN OF DEVELOPMENT
Birth	Reflexes give automatic tight hand grasp
4 weeks	Hands tightly clenched and will only open when touched Not yet able to control hands
3 months	Watches own hands Begins to clasp and unclasp hands together in finger play Presses palms together
5 months	Primitive squeeze grasp appears but movement of hands uncontrolled Finds it difficult to let go of object Enjoys practising dropping and throwing, e.g. toys, food

AGE	PATTERN OF DEVELOPMENT
6 months	Uses whole hand to grasp objects which are held in palm of hand
9 months	Learns hand-eye co-ordination to pick up small objects – stretches out one hand leading to grasp small objects when catching sight of them Handles objects enthusiastically – passing from one hand to another, turning over, etc. Early pincher grip – picks up small objects with finger and thumb
12 months	Picks up small objects, e.g. crumbs, with confident pincer grip – thumb and tip of index finger Uses both hands freely, but may show preference for one
15 months	Picks up small objects with precise pincer grasp using either hand Releases objects from grip skilfully Manipulates cubes – builds tower of two cubes after being shown Grasps crayon with whole hand in palmar grasp Imitates to and fro scribble after being shown (large, forceful movements)
18 months	Holds pencil in primitive tripod grasp Spontaneous to and fro scribble Builds tower of three cubes after being shown Turns pages of books
2 years	Picks up very small items, e.g. threads, accurately and releases with skill Builds tower of six cubes Holds pencil in preferred hand, well down shaft using thumb and two fingers
2½ years	Holds pencil in tripod position using thumb, middle and index finger Can imitate circle and 'T' and 'V'
3 years	Builds tower of nine bricks Threads large wooden beads on shoe lace Enjoys painting with large brush Cuts with scissors
4 years	Threads small beads Builds towers of ten bricks and makes bridges Holds pencil with good control in adult fashion Draws recognisable house
5 years	Threads large needle alone and sews real stitches Good control in writing and drawing using pencils and paint brushes Colours pictures neatly, staying within the lines
By 8 years	Can build tall straight towers using bricks Drawings and pictures show increased recognisable detail Handwriting is even and may start to be joined Ties and unties laces

A four-year-old child's picture of the Titanic. Jim's picture shows that his fine motor skills are well advanced. He has good pencil control and his drawing is clear. He is starting to form recognisable letters.

Social and emotional development

Children's social and emotional development are closely linked. Social interactions are also linked with language development, which facilitates communication people. Research suggests that newborn babies have an in-built need to form relationships. They watch their carer's face, start to smile and make noises to attract their carers.

Emotional development

John Bowlby thought both babies and mothers had a biological need to stay in close contact with one another. He suggested that an early, close emotional bond by the mother to the baby, which he called an attachment, was important for long-term development.

See page 411 for a discussion of Bowlby's attachment theory and for further information.

Rudolf Schaffer in *Mothering* (1977) puts forward the idea of the three stages of attachment in infancy.

* **First stage** – The baby is attracted to other human beings in preference to other inanimate things in the immediate environment. By six weeks babies smile more at human faces and voices than inanimate objects.

* **Second stage** – At about three months, the baby learns to distinguish between different human beings. The parent or carer is recognised as familiar and other unfamiliar humans as strangers. At this stage, babies do not object to being handled by people other than their parents/carers.

* **Third stage** – At about six to seven months, the baby forms a lasting, emotionally significant attachment to specific individuals and seeks their attention. This is characterised by the ability to miss this significant person/s and fret for them if not present, even for a few minutes. The baby shows fear of strangers and becomes distressed and cry.

Schaffer stressed the importance of the attachment figure (the parent/carer) being responsive to the baby's behaviour and providing stimulation, such as talking and playing with the baby. He held the view that the need for stimulation was inborn.

The baby then selects human stimulation and finally homes in on particular individuals to provide that stimulation. Schaffer and Emerson, as a result of a longitudinal study of babies, concluded that babies may become attached to people who do not carry out the normal caring roles, such as feeding and changing. Thus, the baby is capable of multiple attachments.

For further theories and studies related to attachment see Unit 13.

Think it over...

* At what stage might it be easier for a baby to cope with separation from the mother when being placed in a day nursery?

Developing self-concept

One important aspect of emotional development is developing self-concept, or the way we see ourselves. It is closely linked to self-esteem and revolves around the question, 'How do I feel about myself?'. Self-concept relates to children's view of their own personality and what they can do. It also involves children's perception of how others view them and their abilities.

The theories of self-concept are looked at in Unit 13.

Developing self-concept.

0–3 months	• Babies' first important interactions are with family or carers. • They start to recognise their carer's face and voice and may stop being distressed if they hear, see, smell or feel their parent or carer. • These are the first steps to realising that they and their carer are separate beings.
3–6 months	• Babies start to develop their self-image, so they will gradually, over the next few months and years, discover the kind of person they are as well as what they can do. • Positive interactions between parent/carer and baby are important. They will then learn to value themselves and their abilities and thus promote their self-confidence. A positive self-image enables children to feel they are valued and respected. A negative self-image makes children feel worthless and results in lack of emotional stability during childhood and often into later life. • Babies are able to judge their self-worth by the responses of adults and carers to them.
6–12 months	• The opportunity to play increases, especially if encouraged by an interested adult. Encouragement to play and interact will promote a positive self-image. • Babies are aware of emotions or feelings and are starting to realise that others have emotional responses linked to their interactions. • They are developing their understanding that they exist separate to others. They form a clear image that those around them are important.
1–2 years	• Children are now aware of themselves as people in their own right. They can show this sometimes in negative ways of strong-will reactions to situations, e.g. throwing a tantrum if required to do something which does not interest them such as having to get dressed when absorbed in a play activity. • Children need much obvious praise and encouragement so that their positive self-image is fostered. Their relationships with others will depend on the development of their self-image. • By 18 months, children start to use language that reflects the development of their understanding of self. They use their own name and that of others. They vocally label things as 'mine' and can be very possessive. At times, they show an understanding of 'yours' and 'mine' but often prefer to have possession of both. • Children have not yet developed effective co-operative playing skills, but are starting to play alongside others, with mixed success. • They may start to form friendships with other children, but their peers are not yet significantly influential on their developing self-image. • They are starting to look beyond themselves and understand how others feel – if someone gets hurt they can show sensitivity to their pain.
2–3 years	• Children continue to build up their self-image and self-concept. • Play, especially role-play, is important in developing their understanding of self and others. • They like to imitate others, e.g. when speaking on the telephone. • Feelings of self-worth are enhanced through having special responsibilities and their identity recognised, e.g. acting as a monitor at snack-time or hanging their coat on their named peg at nursery. • Increasing physical skills promote their independence and self-reliance, e.g. being able to dress themselves. This promotes their self-image and enhances their self-concept.

▶

DEVELOPMENT OF SELF-CONCEPT

4–5 years	• Children have usually by now developed a secure self-concept based on their own inner knowledge and understanding. If this is based on the views of others, it is likely to present problems as they will be unable to retain a stable view of themselves. • Acceptance by others, especially other children, is important to them. • They show sensitivity to the feelings of others. • They have internalised the social rules of their environment.
6–8 years	• Children begin to compare themselves with others, e.g. 'I am better than Heather in maths but she can run faster than me in games.' • They are more successful in controlling their emotions and having a private view of a situation, while hiding their feelings. • They are starting to progress from 'Who am I?' to 'What do I want to be?' • Friendship with others is very important to them.

Think it over...

When undertaking a work placement in a nursery or a pre-school, discreetly observe a child absorbed in playing on his or her own with small world characters and talking to him or herself. What role is the child taking? Is this contributing to the development of self-concept?

Personality

What is personality? Helen Bee defines personality as 'a broad range of individual characteristics, mostly having to do with the typical ways each of us interacts with the people and the world around us… and which tend to be persisting aspects of the individual' (Bee, 1989). Much interest is shown by parents in a child's developing personality. Babies of only a few weeks old display distinct personalities.

Personality is thought to be a result of a combination of nature and nurture. In other words, it is influenced not only by what is inherited from parents, but also by our environment. Children's initial temperament affects their developing personality. Environmental factors then come into play.

Our experiences are very important in forming our personality. Some babies are very placid and easily soothed, while others seem to find it difficult to settle. The reaction of parents and carers to difficult children is thought to be crucial in reinforcing this type of temperament or helping not to emphasise it. Some studies, such as Olweus's

(1982), suggest that early aggression in children is a good predictor of later aggressive behaviour. On the other hand, sociability seems to be well established by the age of two years and is a good indicator of it continuing into later stages of development. Environment is very influential in reinforcing and encouraging aggressive and sociable behaviours.

For details of Freud's theories linked to emotional development see Unit 13.

Social development

One important aspect of social development is the development of children's moral or pro-social behaviour. The family's role and that of other adults and children is vitally important in this development. (See the diagram on page 254).

These theories ignore the fact that some people develop part of their moral sense through thinking carefully and logically about their actions. This is looked at in Unit 13.

CASE STUDY

During a work placement in a pre-school, you notice that Ella is very disruptive in the home corner. She handles toys roughly. The toys and other children are often hit and subjected to verbal abuse. She is constantly interrupting the circle time.

• Using the approaches featured in the diagram on page 254, account for this behaviour.

Conditioning
Classical conditioning may influence behaviour, e.g. the visit of a severe-looking great-aunt may cause a response of good behaviour. The child has come to associate the need for good behaviour with the sight of the disapproving old lady.

Role models
They may see members of their family as role models. For instance, an older sibling gets a reputation at school for behaving badly so the younger child feels the need to follow the family tradition by using the other child as a role model. Adults may reinforce this pattern of behaviour by their expectations based on their knowledge of the family.

Some psychologists believe that the rules of what is right and wrong are learnt through...

Social learning
A child may learn behaviour from others who they view as significant to them. This may be parents or other children or perhaps an older brother or sister. For instance, they may develop anti-social behaviour which they have learnt within a dysfunctional family.

Imitation
A younger child imitates the older child's behaviour, e.g. a younger child may copy an older child's use of bad language.

Reinforcement
This good behaviour may be reinforced by a reward of a £5 note if the child's behaviour has been good during the visit.

Aggression

Freud believed that aggression comes from unconscious instinctive drives. He stressed the need to release this energy which would otherwise cause psychological disorders, such as depression. This act of release is called **catharsis** and may take the form of violent behaviour or more acceptable activities, such as sport.

> ### Think it over...
> Discuss in your group your own experiences of dealing with aggressive children. What causes them to become aggressive? How do you deal with their aggression?

There is some evidence to suggest that aggression may have a biological explanation.

Connor's Danish study (1995) showed that if one of a pair of twins is a criminal, then the other twin is much more likely to have a criminal record than the average person. Brown et al (1979) suggested that aggression is probably linked to high levels of certain hormones or chemicals. It is suggested that high levels of testosterone in males, women with pre-menstrual syndrome and increased levels of progesterone are linked to crime and negative behaviour.

Other theories stress that aggression may be reinforced and is, therefore, more likely to be repeated. For instance, parents may encourage boys to be tough and girls to be gentle. However, this is generally considered to be an oversimplified approach.

Patterson et al (1991) studied families, some with aggressive children and some with children who did not have a problem. Families were

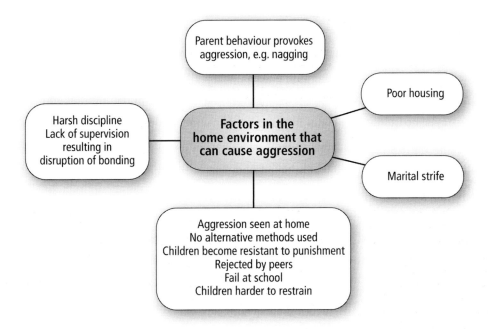

identified where the children were difficult to discipline. These seemed to have certain things in common, such as little affection shown, use of aggression to cope with tensions within family relationships, little use of approval and instead much use of physical punishment. The diagram above shows the kind of home environment which may create aggressiveness.

Ways of managing unwanted behaviour

* Positively reinforce behaviour which is not aggressive, such as by praising a child who helps another child. Aggressive behaviour should be calmly stopped and children given much warm attention when behaving well.

* Provide role models who are not aggressive. It is important that nursery staff always provide an excellent example of non-aggressive, calm, warm behaviour towards the children.

* Remove aggressive cues. For example, playgroups have a policy that there are no toy guns for children to use.

* Use humour and empathy to reduce aggressive behaviour.

* Encourage children to think about and discuss aggression.

* Encourage the aggressor to experience the emotions of the victim, e.g. in role play.

* Give clear guidelines for acceptable behaviour.

* Children should not be put down in any way. This may have a negative effect on their self-image.

* Provide stimulating and challenging activities which are attainable for their level of development. This will prevent children becoming bored or frustrated by unachievable tasks.

* If children misbehave, encourage them to explain why they have misbehaved.

* Carers and parents need to be aware of problems or stress in a child's life which may be triggering unwanted behaviour.

Learning theories

Throughout our lives we develop ideas or concepts and are influenced by what we perceive about the world around us (our perception). Gradually our knowledge develops, together with an ability to reason, solve problems, comprehend abstract ideas and understand why people behave as they do. This is called cognitive development. Various theories explain how children learn and think (see the table on page 256).

MAIN THEORIES	THEORIST/RESEARCH PERIOD	KEY FEATURES
Behaviourism	Watson (early 20th century)	• This is concerned only with observable activities. • Thoughts and feelings have little relevance to learning. • Babies are born with biological reflexes which exist from birth (innate) and all other responses are learned (nurture). • Behaviour changes in response to rewards and punishments. Actions are encouraged by rewards and other actions discouraged by punishments.
Classical	Pavlov (late 19th century)	• A new stimulus causes an existing response conditioning because of an association between two happenings. • Baby's cheek touched gently (*unconditioned stimulus*) → baby turns head (*unconditioned response – reflex*). • Baby's cheek touched + mother talks to baby (*unconditioned stimulus*) → (*conditioned stimuli*) → baby turns head (*unconditioned response*). • Mother's voice (*conditioned stimuli*) → baby's head turns (*conditioned response*).
Social learning (observational learning)	Bandura (1960s/1970s)	• Children learn by observing another (a model) and then imitate, especially if the model is important and loving to them, such as a parent.
Constructivism	Piaget (1920–70)	• Children's understanding of 'reality' is **constructed** through interacting with the world around them and learning through discovery. For more details see Unit 13.

Sensory development

Newborn babies take in, process and use a vast amount of information using their senses of sight, hearing, taste, smell and touch. The process by which each of us gains direct awareness through our senses of the world around us is called perception (Sylva and Lunt, 1998).

Hearing

From birth, babies seem to have an inborn preference for hearing the human voice. Condor and Sanders (1974) carried out some experiments on babies just a few hours old. Tapes of different sounds, including human speech, were played. After two days the babies started to move their arms and bodies in time with the human speech and showed little interest in the other sounds.

Vision

Babies' visual sensory system is not fully mature at birth. Vision is more blurred than in an adult and their eyes focus best at about 25cm. Fantz (1961) carried out research with young babies who were shown different stimuli the approximate size and shape of an adult's head. Babies looked at the face-pattern more than the others so Fantz concluded that babies have an innate preference for facedness. Other studies showed that babies have a preference for increasingly complex patterns and their capacity for differentiating patterns steadily develops.

Assessment activity 7.3

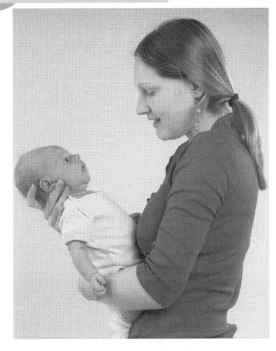

Mother talking to her fifteen-day-old baby.

- Comment on the distance between the mother's face and the baby. How can this influence the baby's perception?
- Comment on the baby's interest in the mother's face and her interaction with the baby. Is this interest to be expected by a baby of this age? Justify your answer with reference to relevant theories.

Perception of depth and 3D objects

Often babies roll and fall off chairs if unattended. They seem to have no sense of depth. Gibson and Walk (1960) tested babies' depth perception. They devised an experiment using a 'visual cliff' which consisted of a glass top covering a drop of several feet. Babies over six months refused to cross the 'cliff' which indicates that they are able to perceive depth.

Development of perceptual judgements

Vurpillot (1976) studied children from the age of 3½ years to 7½ years to discover how they use their perceptual skills. She showed them a series of drawings, all of which were slightly different. She asked them to spot the differences. Vurpillot found that:

* 3½-year-olds perceive anything missing in the picture and differences in form, e.g. round sun changes to crescent
* by 7½-years they perceive changes in sizes but not in detecting changes in location, e.g. the position of the house.

She concluded that younger children's perception is limited by their lack of capacity to gather, record and think about perceptual information, using only a few simple judgements. As children get older, they are able to make more visual comparisons and are more skilled at selecting from a range of information presented to them.

Theories of language development

These are outlined in the table below.

THEORIST/PERIOD OF RESEARCH	TYPE OF THEORY	MAIN FEATURES OF THEORY
Skinner (1930s)	Nurturist Language is taught through imitation.	Parents and carers reinforce and shape children's language.
Chomsky (1960s)	Nativist Language is innate. Children are biologically programmed for language development.	Children are born with all the things needed to produce language (called Language Acquisition Device) and are born with the potential to understand the structure of language (grammar).

THEORIST/PERIOD OF RESEARCH	TYPE OF THEORY	MAIN FEATURES OF THEORY
Piaget (1920s–1970s)	Interactionist input theory	Language results from the children's cognitive development. As the cognitive processes develop so language develops, e.g. during the animism stage of the pre-operational period, children often practise talking to their favourite toys. Language is influenced by the interaction with the environment. Children enrich the input and actively shape their perceptions through making it fit into pre-existing schemas or by generating new ones. They often use an expression which seems logical to them, but does not follow the more complex formal rules of grammar, e.g. a child says 'one mouse' but when another is present a child may speak of 'two mouses'.

Sequence of language development

The table below shows the sequence of development which all children follow regardless of their ethnic origin. There can be considerable variation in the age at which children pass through the stages, depending on the environment and their speed of development.

AGE	PATTERN OF DEVELOPMENT
1–2 months	Cooing – open vowel sounds like oooh, aah and use of gestures. Shows skill of turn-taking in 'conversations'.
6–10 months	Babbling – adds consonants and makes strings of sounds, e.g. dah, dah, dah.
1–2 years	**12–18 months** First words linked to familiar things, e.g. 'Daddy', 'Car'. First one- or two-word sentences with gestures are called holophrases, e.g. child pointing to shoe with male figure, 'Daddy' – meaning Daddy's shoe. First sentences – from 2 years. **Telegraphic speech** (short sentences – two or three words but only essential words, e.g. 'I play ball').
$2\frac{1}{2}$ years	50-word vocabulary. Uses plural, past tenses, prepositions. Generalises speech, e.g. 'I goed' instead of 'I went'; 'three mouses'.
5 years	2500-word vocabulary. Uses complex sentences and questions. Shows an interest in reading and writing. Can listen intently when interested.
By 8 years	Able to pronounce most sounds but may have difficulty with some consonants, e.g. 'v', 's', 'l'. Speaks confidently. Uses most plural and past tenses correctly. Can express abstract ideas, such as emotions, through language. Writes short pieces of writing independently. Can read simple text accurately.

For further details see Unit 13.

Observe three-year-olds in a nursery including both (a) when they play together during role play, and (b) when interacting with adults. Record the language used on both occasions.

- What stage of language development have the children reached? Give examples from your observations to explain your answer.
- How did the adult influence the child's language development?

Language delay and language disabilities

Children mature at different rates. In order to talk, children need to hear spoken language and use their language. In extreme cases where children have little human contact, studies show that they do not learn to speak in isolation. In normal situations children with language delay in the early years can still progress well later.

Fluency – young children often hesitate to search for a word or how to say things. They lose track of what they are trying to say and may start again, taking time to complete what they want to say. If adults get impatient, then fluency can get worse. Most children gradually get more confident and become more skilful in expressing themselves fluently. For a few children, fluency problems may lead to stammering, affecting their confidence and requiring specialist help.

Articulation – most children have difficulties saying some sounds, e.g. 'yellow'. Physical conditions, such as cleft palates, result in difficulties in forming sounds through control of mouth and tongue and need specialist help. Children with mild or severe learning difficulties may have a delay in talking due to difficulty decoding the meaning of sounds.

Deaf children – if the emphasis is on developing oral language, then speech and reading problems may occur. Deaf children can be taught to communicate through lip reading, sign language and oral language at the same time. Most need special schooling.

Difficulty in reading and writing may be due to dyslexia. Children have problems organising themselves, with their memory as well as word recognition. Early identification and support are important.

- Observe or record children at different stages of language development. Identify the children's stage of language development.
- Find out the early learning goals for listening, speaking, reading and writing which children are expected to achieve by the end of the Foundation Stage.

Language and thought

Psychologists have different view on the relationship between language and thought. As adults, we often think using imagery and may struggle to find the right words to express our thoughts. In difficult situations we hear people say, 'There are not words to express what we feel.'

For more information see Unit 13.

4 The factors involved in promoting children's development

Factors affecting development

Factors may have both positive (enhancing) and negative (inhibiting) effects on development.

Social factors

Positive – Families with strong social networks provide opportunities for children to thrive socially and emotionally. Children gain confidence through mixing with others. This enhances language and cognitive experience.

Negative – Little experience of mixing with others in a variety of situations may affect social and emotional development. Restricted social experience and interaction means that there are inadequate opportunities for mental processes, such as those involving imagination and thought, to be fully stimulated. Thus, the potential for cognitive development is not fully realised. Children born into a lower social class are more likely to be disadvantaged, for example having poor health or living conditions, which affects all development.

Economic factors

Positive – Children living in favourable economic circumstances are more likely to have a healthy lifestyle. Their diet may include a wider range of foods, such as five servings of fruits and vegetables per day, thus enhancing their physical development. They may have more social opportunities, such as holidays and joining youth groups. They may have more fashionable, peer-acceptable clothes, thus promoting their self-confidence and feelings of social and emotional well-being. There may be less stress in the home, thus increasing the likelihood of emotional stability. More affluent families may live in an area where schools enjoy a better learning environment. Active parent organisations often generously supplement core school resources. This supports and extends children's cognitive development. In addition, parents may be able to afford more out-of-school learning opportunities, such as music lessons, sports coaching and provide a wider range of toys and equipment including access to computers.

Many factors can affect development.

Negative – Children living in poverty are more likely to have a poorer quality of life. Poor housing, inadequate diet and higher rates of pollution affect physical development. There is more stress and lower educational attainment and aspirations within communities with fewer resources. Potentially, there may be higher rates of crime which may influence children's social and emotional development. However, affluence may also have negative effects. For instance, diets of more expensive convenience and junk food, such as fizzy drinks and chocolate snacks rich in fats and sugar, contribute to childhood obesity. This may have a notable effect on health in adult life. Too easy access to resources and opportunities may present fewer challenges, affecting their drive to develop and progress.

Cultural factors

Positive – Families where books and the expressive arts are valued stimulate children's creativity and widen their cognitive, social and emotional experiences. Some cultural groups value extended families. These enable children to have a good support network which may promote their development.

Negative – Children who live in an unconventional culture may develop moral values which promote anti-social behaviour. Some children in rural areas may have little experience of mixing with people from other cultures, which can affect their social confidence and tolerance within culturally diverse situations later in life.

Racial factors

Positive – Some racial groups are more favoured by society and, therefore, enjoy better opportunities for a healthier and satisfying lifestyle.

Negative – Some racial groups, despite legislation, experience stereotyping and discrimination. This can affect children's physical, social and cognitive development, as well as their emotional stability. They may suffer the psychological effects of not feeling accepted by the dominant race in their community. Different racial groups place different emphasis on the importance of education, which can affect children's educational aspirations and therefore their drive for cognitive development.

Gender factors

Positive – There is an increasing breakdown of traditional discriminatory attitudes to gender differences. All children are expected to have the same opportunities within the caring and educational services. These promote social, emotional and cognitive development for both girls and boys and so widens their future career choices.

Negative – Despite legislation to promote equality of opportunity, discrimination and stereotyping still exist. This can affect children's self-concept and their emotional and cognitive development. Some conditions, such as congenital deficiencies in colour vision, are more prevalent in one gender group. Boys are more prone to colour vision deficiencies.

Motivational factors

Positive – Children who grow up in a stimulating environment, experiencing interested, interactive parental support, are more likely to be well-motivated to learn.

Negative – Children who have few stimulating resources and experience little interest from adults are less likely to be well-motivated to learn and be aware of the world around them. They may start Key Stage 1 with a lower threshold of achievement.

Some children have parents who are over-eager to motivate their children to succeed. This may put undue pressure on them and affect the children's mental and emotional well-being and have major repercussions later in life.

Prior learning and adult expectations

Positive – Parents and carers who have achieved educational success are more likely to stimulate their children, be aware of their holistic developmental needs and actively seek and campaign for the best educational provision for their children. They are likely to have high expectations for their children's achievement.

Negative – Parents with little educational achievement may see educational progress as less of a priority. They may not have the highly developed skills to enable them to access the best educational opportunities for their children.

Provision of health, family and other support services

Positive – Families with favourable economic situations may need less support from such services in order to thrive. The government has a positive strategy of supporting families and children in need through the *Every Child Matters* agenda. This initiative has the vision of all children living happy and healthy lives. It aims to achieve this through five outcomes: being healthy, staying safe, enjoyment and achievement, community participation and economic well-being. Through the Children Act 2004, a raft of measures are being put in place. Local authorities have a statutory duty to merge children's education and social services. Other measures include the appointment of a Children's Commissioner, better integrated planning, commissioning and delivery of children's services, Children's Trusts, the Children and Young People's Plan, as well as extended schools. Other measures include the National Service Framework for Children, Young People and Maternity Services, Ten Year Child Care Strategy, Children's Centres, free nursery education places for all 3- and 4-year-olds, Sure Start and workforce reform involving improving skills and effectiveness of the workforce.

Negative – Neighbourhoods with high levels of deprivation, such as inner cities, often have less effective support services and have more problems attracting health, education and other support workers, such as teachers, doctors and dentists.

Assessment activity 7.4

Analyse how both the enhancing and inhibiting factors listed above may affect the baby's development during his or her first year.

Theory into practice

Identify and describe two recent government strategies which might affect the family and baby you have selected to take part in your longitudinal study.

Developmental delay

Children mature at different rates. However, there is an accepted range of expected ages for different types of development. Some concern may be expressed if a child's development does not come within these ranges, such as if it is below the lower level of the centile chart. This may be due to a variety of reasons.

Premature birth – Development can be seen as a continuous process from conception to maturity with birth just one event along the way. Hence, if a baby is six weeks premature, he or she cannot be expected to reach, during the early assessment checks, the norms for a baby born after 40 weeks of pregnancy.

Physical disability – Resulting from accidents before, during or after birth to vital organs, genetic abnormalities, inherited disease or birth defects may all cause developmental delay. For instance, a club foot may restrict children's mobility and social interaction with others, thus causing both physical and social developmental delay.

Sensory disabilities – A visual or hearing impairment may cause delay in a child's development in other areas. For instance, children with permanent childhood hearing impairment may suffer significant impairment of language acquisition and social isolation.

Functioning of the brain – This may cause developmental delay. Dyslexic children may have delay in reading and writing. If the pre-patterned growth of the nervous system does not occur normally then brain functioning will be affected and normal maturation will be delayed.

The child's environment does not foster maturation – In extreme cases where children have little human contact, studies show that they do not learn to speak in isolation. It is generally thought that we need to hear speech before we can produce it. Severe neglect, privation, abuse, parental depression and family stress can all have a major effect on development.

Poverty – This can radically affect the developmental progress of a child. Poor diets can restrict growth. (It was notable how small some Romanian children were who suffered very restricted diets in the 1980s.) Inadequate housing causing respiratory problems can affect a child's physical development. Exposure to environmental toxins, such as those produced by passive smoking, can also increase the risk of respiratory illness needing hospitalisation and so affecting physical and, possibly, emotional development.

Children's need to explore – Children need to explore and have access to exploratory play in order to learn from experience and to make the necessary cognitive and perceptual connections. Developmental delay can result if the child does not experience the normal rapid change in the nervous system, increasing muscle control and strengthening of bones which permit more exploring.

Lack of strong attachments to a parent or carer – This is linked to developmental delay. John Flavell (1985) argues that cognitive understanding of the existence of a person when absent is needed in order to form an attachment. Children who form strong attachments do appear to concentrate longer on their play (Bates 1982) and develop the understanding of some concepts quicker. Hence, without this attachment the pace of learning is often slower and the progress of understanding important concepts delayed.

Child may have suffered a trauma/shock – If a child has been involved in a terrifying event this may cause emotional developmental delay.

Implications for social and educational development

Early identification of developmental delay is promoted through the well-established series of assessment tests undertaken at birth and regularly through childhood. For instance, universal neonatal screening is undertaken to detect hearing impairment so very early appropriate action can be taken to support the needs of a baby with any hearing loss.

Developmental delay can affect a child's social development. A child with a hearing impairment may have a speech delay and this may add to the difficulties of interacting with other children and adults. Such a child's educational needs may require additional support within the classroom when working alongside other primary school children. The child may have specialist education within a unit attached to a primary school or, where there are severe problems, may attend a special school for children with the same or related needs.

Children with a visual impairment may experience restrictions when socially interacting with sighted children. Autistic children have notable difficulties socialising with others. Both groups of children may need the support of a teaching assistant and specialist resources within mainstream schools or have to attend a specialist unit or school in order for their needs to be met.

Children who have physical developmental delay may not easily be able to interact fully with other children who are making normal progress. For instance, they may not be able to play the rough-and-tumble games popular with primary school children. Hence, the opportunity may be limited to experience and develop the social skills needed to play successfully with their peer group. Children with such delay usually attend primary schools, but may need the support of care assistants, mainly to look after their care needs

The implications of cognitive development delay for a child's social and educational development will vary according to the nature and severity of the delay. Healthy children may readily include children with mild learning difficulties within their play, but may not be so welcoming towards those with more major problems. Hence, children with developmental delay may find themselves socially isolated. Their educational development may be promoted within mainstream schools, special units attached to schools or within specialist schools.

Children with severe emotional problems which are exhibited as behavioural problems, may find it difficult to mix successfully with other children. Such children are usually educated within mainstream schools, but may find their behaviour is such that it creates unacceptable situations which can result in exclusion from school. These children may be referred to special units or special schools catering for such behavioural disabilities. Often the provision to meet such needs is very limited and many children drop out of the educational system and have a high risk of becoming involved in petty and more serious crime.

Often, children may experience more than one type of developmental delay which can compound their problems and increase their social isolation. Frequent medical appointments may reduce the time they spend in the educational system. Hospitalisation can slow children's educational progress unless there is good liaison between the hospital's education service and the child's normal educational provider.

Article 23 of The United Nations Convention on the Rights of the Child provides the basis for the development of legislative rights for a disabled child. It states that the disabled child has the right to special care, education and training. This is to enable the child to live with the 'greatest degree of self-reliance and social integration'.

In this country, the policy has been to include children with developmental delay in normal educational situations wherever possible. This was originally promoted by the Warnock Report (1978). However, the policy is currently being questioned by both Lady Warnock, the committee chair who compiled the report, and other interested agencies. They are questioning the adequacy of mainstream education to provide for the special needs of some children.

A range of Education Acts and disability legislation, as well as the Code of Practice for Special Educational Needs (1994), have strengthened the provision for children with special educational needs. (See Unit 16 for further details.) All settings receiving the nursery education grant have to have a special needs policy and be willing to receive and provide for children with developmental delay. Further education colleges have to provide for the lifelong learning of young people and adults with development disabilities.

The Disability Discrimination Act 1995 aims to challenge barriers causing social isolation for disabled people.

Education, care and voluntary organisations aim to develop independence. A range of aids can help babies and children to interact with others and the world around them. Aids such as walking frames, hearing aids and learning support assistants all play a part in helping to stimulate development and assisting children in living independent and fulfilling lives.

END-OF-UNIT TEST

1 Describe the essential role played by the different hormones in the process of conception.

2 Describe the growth and development of the embryo and foetus from conception through to the end of the second trimester.

3 Explain the factors which can affect the development of the embryo and foetus from conception to birth.

4 Give a brief description of the nature/nurture debate.

5 Describe the monitoring and recording of children's growth.

6 Describe the physical development you might expect of an eight-year-old.

7 Explain Bowlby's attachment theory.

8 Explain how you would ensure confidentiality throughout your longitudinal study.

9 Explain the affects of three inhibiting factors on the development of a two-year-old.

10 Briefly describe the holistic development of a three-year-old.

11 Identify and describe three enhancing factors which might affect the development of a three-year-old.

12 a) Explain what is meant by self-concept.

   b) Why is it important to promote a child's positive self-concept?

13 Describe the expected language development of a four-year-old.

14 Explain three types of developmental delay and their causative factors.

15 Analyse the consequences of two common types of developmental delay for all aspects of a child's development.

16 Describe the language development babies make in their first two years.

References and further reading

Bee, H (2003), *The Developing Child*, Allyn & Bacon

Cheshire, Merseyside and West Lancashire NHS Primary Care Trusts (2005), *Improving Fertility Services*

Gordon, Y (2002), *Birth and Beyond*, Vermillon: London

Hall, D & Elliman, D (2003), *Health for All Children*, Oxford University Press

Hucker, K (2001), *Research Methods in Health, Care and Early Years*, Heinemann

Nolan, Y (2002), *BTEC Early Years*, Heinemann

Sheridan, M *et al* (1997), *From Birth to Five Years: Children's developmental progress*, Routledge

Sheridan, M *et al* (1999), *Play in Early Childhood: From birth to six years*, Routledge

Tassoni, P (2002), *Certificate in Child Care and Education*, Heinemann

Tassoni, P, Beith, K, Eldridge, H and Gough, A (2000), *Diploma in Child Care and Education*, Heinemann

Useful websites

Child development – www.childdevelopmentinfo.com

Every Child Matters documentation – www.dfes.gov.uk/everychildmatters

National Childbirth Trust information on pregnancy and care for babies – www.nctpregnancyandbabycare.com

NHS careers information – www.nhscareers.nhs.uk

NHS giving up smoking advice – www.givingupsmoking.co.uk

Royal College of Midwives – www.rcm.org.uk

Sure Start information – www.surestart.gov.uk

Observation of children

What you need to learn

1 How to be objective

2 Different observation techniques

3 Uses of observation

4 The ethics of observation

Introduction

Observations are a key tool when working with children. They will help you to understand individual children and groups of children. This understanding in turn will help you to meet children's needs more effectively. Observations are not boring. Learning how to observe children is a rewarding skill. It can make the routine parts of working with children become exciting, as you notice details about their progress, interests and interactions.

How you will be assessed

This unit is assessed internally.

Why observe?

Observing children helps us learn more about them and so should, in theory, help us to work more effectively. For example, we might spot a four-year-old who is left-handed and therefore remember to put out some left-handed scissors. Observing another toddler, we might notice she makes a certain movement just before she needs the toilet, meaning we can be prepared for this and therefore avoid accidents. These are examples of small day-to-day needs but, on a larger scale, observing a child might also reveal that he or she is going to require more significant support, such as speech and language therapy. Identifying children who will need this type of support should happen as early as possible in their life, as early intervention in some areas of children's development has been shown to result in positive outcomes. This is one reason why those working with babies and toddlers carry out observations that are then looked at in comparison to milestones or 'expected development'. While a baby who is not crawling at seven months will not give any rise for concern, the same would not be true if the baby was nearing twelve months.

As well as focusing on children, observations should also be used to focus on our practice with children. The term 'reflective practitioner' is often used and means thinking about the impact that we have on children's enjoyment, learning and behaviour. By observing children's responses during sessions and activities, we can reflect upon how effective we are and, from this reflection, consider ways in which we might become more effective.

There are many reasons why professionals might observe children, as the spider diagram below shows.

1 How to be objective

This section looks at objectivity. It is difficult to be scientific about observing children, as there are many factors that might affect their responses, but also our own interpretation of them.

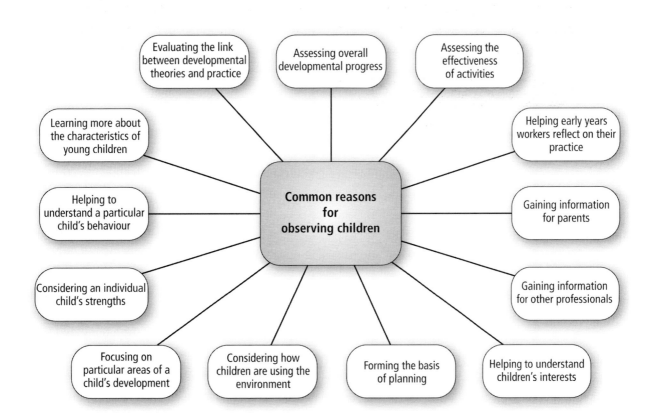

CASE STUDY

Kylie is four years old. She is interested in writing her name and has been spending a lot of time sitting down at the mark making table and having a go. Beth, her keyworker, has noted her interest and has played games with her focusing on her name. She has also been writing Kylie's name in front of her so that Kylie gets a feel of the shapes and how to form them. Beth has been asked to assess whether or not Kylie can write her name. Beth asks Kylie if she would write her name on a piece of paper. Kylie writes her name, but forgets one of the letters and also reverses another letter. Beth is faced with a dilemma as the assessment sheet is a tick box. She must either tick a 'yes' or a 'no'. Beth thinks about the day before when Kylie almost perfectly wrote her name. She ticks the 'yes' box.

- Explain the factors that may have influenced Beth's recording.

- Would an adult who did not know Kylie have reached the same conclusion?

Objectivity versus subjectivity

Objectivity means being able to suspend prior knowledge of the child during the observation and also to suspend any expectations that we might have of the outcome. Observing children in an objective way is surprisingly hard. Being subjective comes much easier – this might mean being influenced by preconceptions and prejudices, or using other information that was not gained during an actual observation.

Observation methods and subjectivity

The way in which we observe children can be linked to subjectivity. Some methods are inherently more subjective than others. That does not mean that they should not be used, merely that we need to understand that this is the case. Observation methods can be grouped into two broad groups: closed and open data.

Closed data methods

Closed data methods focus the observer's attention very narrowly. A good example of a closed data method is a checklist. A checklist usually consists of groups of statements. The observer reads the statements and then considers whether or not this is what he or she is seeing while observing the child – the options in this case would be true or false, yes or no. Closed data methods are considered to be less subjective than open data methods. The major drawback with closed data methods is that they can focus an observer so narrowly that some data might be missed, such as whether children smile as they skip. Closed data methods tend to be good for assessing children's skills and achievements in group situations.

Open data methods

Open data methods allow the observer significantly more freedom as the observation format is not as narrow. The responsibility to decide what to focus on lies more with the observer, even when the situation is prescribed. This increases the potential to be subjective but, on the other hand, can provide more raw data about children. Snapshot observations are examples of open data recording. In this type of observation, the observer jots down what he or she perceives as interesting when watching a child.

Strangers versus familiar faces

Who should carry out observations on children? Adults who work with the children carry out most observations, but this can mean that they already have a view about the child based on their prior knowledge. Strangers on the other hand might be more objective as they see the child with fresh eyes, but this too can be an imperfect solution. Children are likely to react differently when they see an unfamiliar face, especially if they know that they are being observed.

This child knows that an adult is watching. Will it make a difference?

Participative versus non-participative

The way in which observations are actually carried out, whether or not they are open or closed data methods, also needs to be considered. Does the observer join in an activity or ask the child to do a task? If so, the observer becomes a participant in the observation. Participant observations are useful because the observer is likely to collect the information more quickly or to observe a skill that otherwise the child might not show. There are two main disadvantages to participant observations. Firstly, children's responses can change when they know that they are being watched, and secondly, if an open data method is being used, the observer might miss significant pieces of information.

Think it over...

A physiotherapist is visiting a nursery to see how well Josh is managing to cope with the steps. The physiotherapist is only able to spend half an hour in the setting and really needs to watch Josh attempt the stairs to see what type of equipment or support is required if necessary. She has not met Josh before. After saying hello and having a little chat, she asks Josh whether he would show her how he goes up the stairs. Josh does so, but his keyworker, who was also watching, notices that he was much slower than usual.

- Is this an example of a participant or non-participant observation?
- What might have affected Josh's responses?

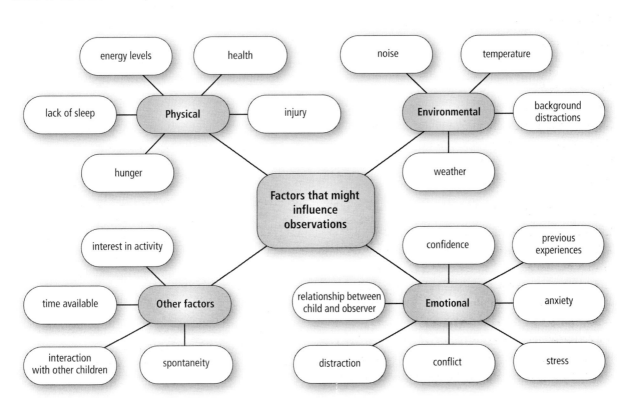

Validity

It is important to realise that there are many factors that will influence the child and also us during an observation. Observations need to be accurate if they are to be valid so it is important to be aware of the influences that might make them less accurate.

Environmental factors

The environment around us and the child can have significant effects. Children's responses might change during a thunder storm or if they hear a doorbell ring. Our ability to observe might also be hampered if we are being interrupted or are distracted by other things around us.

Emotional factors

Children and adults are not machines. This means that our ability to observe can be influenced by what we are feeling and, in the same way, children's responses will be altered by their feelings. A child who has fallen out with a friend at break time might not respond in the same way as a child who is celebrating a birthday. Responses are particularly affected when children feel that they know that they are being watched or when they feel under pressure.

Physical factors

Physical factors are another influence. Children who are tired or hungry may find it hard to concentrate while if, adults are tired, the observation might not be as focused.

Other factors

There are many other factors that influence validity, such as how interested the child is in the activity. The time that we have available to observe is also a key factor, as sometimes we might miss a child doing something because we have left the room! In the same way, some children respond differently according to who they are with. Groups of friends might chat more and be distracted, while a child with unfamiliar children might seem quite quiet.

Naturalistic versus structured

The type of situation in which the child is being observed is important. Naturalistic observations are ones where children are doing something that they normally do, while structured observations are ones where a situation has been created in order to watch the child. An example of a structured observation would be where an early years practitioner has put out stilts in order to see children's balancing skills. The equivalent naturalistic observation would be where a child goes and gets out those stilts for him or herself. Naturalistic observations are likely to help the child relax, although this does depend on whether the observation is participative or not.

Reliability and error

One of the ways in which we can maximise the accuracy of observations is by ensuring that we use a range of methods and also check that the recording methods suit their purpose. The case study on page 268 about Beth's dilemma with Kylie shows how the recording system might prompt the observer to be less than accurate. It is also important when observing children to understand the limitations of different recording methods (see pages 273–80) and to avoid situations where we give the impression that our observations are totally reliable.

Effects of perception

We might imagine that our eyes cannot play tricks on us, but they can, or at least our brain can. What we 'see' is governed partly by what our brain decides to focus on. A good example of this is the way in which some people can see the 'duck' below

What do you see?

while others are able to see the rabbit. If you originally saw the duck, you might find it hard to see the rabbit, until the shape of the rabbit is pointed out to you. What is interesting about these types of perception tests is that it is not possible to see the two at the same time.

The effects of perception mean that two people seeing exactly the same video clip of a child playing may notice different things about the child. One might focus on hand movements and the child's facial expression, while another might notice the way in which the child completes a task and the interaction that is used. This is normal as, when we look at children, there is so much information available, we are unable to take it all in. The brain effectively registers some facets, but loses others.

What influences our perception?

There has been much work looking at the way our perception is influenced. For many years it has been thought that perception is an active process in which we are selecting some features or information over others. Allport (1955) looked at the reasons why we might be pre-disposed to notice some things but not others. He came up with a list which included personality, reward and punishment, individual values and also emotional connotation.

Counteracting the effects of perception

One of the ways that we can make observations more objective is to focus our attention during an observation so that we force ourselves to notice things that otherwise we might miss. Observations that focus on particular aspects of children's responses are called structured observations.

Attitudes, values and beliefs

Our attitudes, values and beliefs can also play a major part in our ability to perceive and select information. What we 'see' is significantly determined by what we expect to see. A good example of this is the way in which we might misread a word in a text such as 'the cat sat on the map and licked its whiskers'. There has been some staggering research that shows that people have 'selective memory' and this is considerably linked to their expectations, stereotypes and beliefs.

Have you worked out that there is an extra word here?

KEY ISSUES

Buckhout (1974) did some interesting research where participants were shown a series of drawings that countered the usual stereotypes. One of these was of two men in a train. The white man was badly dressed and holding a razor in a threatening way towards a black man. The black man was well dressed. Half of the white participants 'remembered' afterwards that it was the black man who was holding the razor. This and similar research is consistent in showing that some people find it very hard to be accurate eye witnesses.

Effects on objectivity

There are many ways in which our own attitudes and thoughts about a child might influence our judgement and affect what we choose to see. If we believe that a child is making good progress, we are more likely to look for information that will support this viewpoint while, in the same way, if we believe a child is not socialising, we may focus on the times when the child is playing alone.

Gender and objectivity

Gender is becoming an issue in children's learning and play. There is conflicting research about whether boys and girls do learn differently. Expectations of how boys or girls might respond in given situations have the capacity to influence our recordings. If you have strong feelings about gender-related play and learning, it is essential to consider whether these will influence you.

Jo is watching Meltem as she plays. She is four years old and has recently arrived from Turkey. Jo thinks that Meltem is not playing with the other children because of the language barrier and has decided to observe her. She observes that when other children try to talk to her, Meltem does not respond. She also notes that when a staff member calls out that it is snack time, Meltem does not move. Again, she thinks that this is caused by Meltem not understanding the word. A few months later it is realised that Meltem has some hearing loss.

- Explain why Jo was unable to realise that Meltem had a hearing loss.

- Consider the consequences of the delay in realising that Meltem was not fully hearing.

- Why is it important to be open minded and as objective as possible when carrying out observations?

Counteracting the effects of attitudes, values and beliefs

A key step in striving for objectivity is to recognise that we hold attitudes, values and beliefs and to recognise what they are. We must also be ready to question how our thoughts might influence what we might see. In practical terms, it is usually a good idea if more than one person observes the same child so that different viewpoints can be considered. It is also worth gaining information from adults who may see the child in a different light, such as parents, relatives or other professionals. As the conclusions drawn from observations can heavily influence the way in which adults work with children, it is also important for us to observe 'positively'. This means looking out for the things that children can do and the times when they respond well. This is especially important if you are observing children because you have concerns about their progress and development.

Bias

Observations can become unreliable if we are not aware of bias, especially when carrying out observations of groups of children. We may, for example, be drawn to a particular child and not recognise what other children are doing. In the same way, we may find that we record children doing similar activities and so might not 'see' the all-round child.

Countering the effects of bias

As with other issues in observing children, it is important that we stand back from time to time and consider how objective our recording systems are. Our records should always show the time and date of any activity. We need to use this information to check we are getting an overall picture of the child that is accurate. This means using a variety of methods, but also ensuring that we see the child in a variety of situations. Some nurseries develop charts to help them see whether or not they are 'covering' a range of observations and situations.

Theory into practice

Aiming for objectivity

- Use a range of different recording methods.
- Consider whether or not there is a bias towards open or closed data collection.
- Observe children in a variety of different situations e.g. naturalistic as well as structured.
- Share observations with others including parents and seek their viewpoints.
- Recognise that a child's responses will be influenced during a participant observation.
- Keep language focused and non-judgemental.

Assessment activity 8.1

Prepare an information sheet that considers the issues around objectivity when observing children. The information sheet should:

- explain how different ways of observing children might affect objectivity
- consider how the observer's perception, values and beliefs might affect objectivity
- describe the steps an observer might take to become more objective.

2 Different observation techniques

There are many different methods by which we can observe children. We have seen that, in order to build an overall picture of a child, it can be helpful to use more than one technique. This section looks at the different methods and also considers their advantages and disadvantages.

Observational techniques

As well as actually recording information, most practitioners almost instinctively get used to looking at children and their responses. The way that a child walks into a room can often tell us quite a lot about feelings. Observing children informally can also help us to decide what further areas we need to look at in more depth. Sometimes practitioners might have a 'hunch' that the child is not happy or that there is a deeper underlying issue. This hunch is our observational skills in action.

What strikes you about this child?

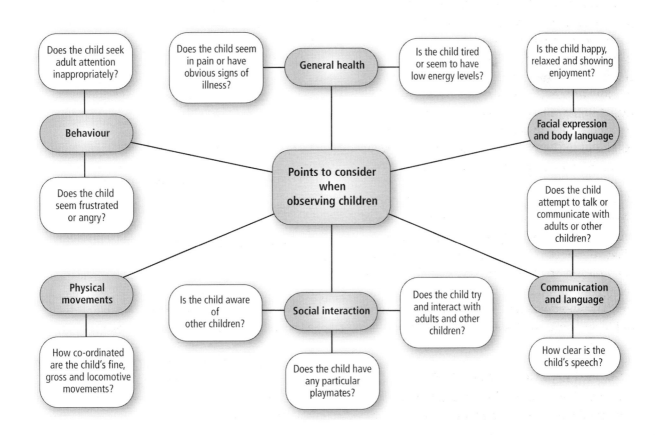

Date: 18/12/05	Child's name: Ayse	Age: 5 months
Time: 14.30		
Presentation of new toy		

Ayse sees the rabbit and frowns. She smiles. She smiles again and gurgles. Both hands reach for rabbit. Rabbit is hidden. Ayse stops smiling. Frowns. Rabbit reappears. Ayse smiles. Laughs. More smiles. Hands reach again towards rabbit. Rabbit is pulled towards her. Ayse brings rabbit towards mouth. Holds rabbit whilst mouthing. Rabbit is made to disappear again. Ayse takes hand to mouth. Rabbit reappears. Ayse squeals and smiles. Laughs and looks at mother. Rabbit is bounced slowly up and down. Ayse moves head and continues to focus on rabbit. Rabbit is held still. Ayse reaches for rabbit with both hands. Rabbit bounced again.

An example of a written record.

Cross-sectional observations

Cross-sectional observations look at several children's responses. We might, for example, look at how a baby reacts when a toy that he or she is playing with is hidden and then see how another toddler in the same situation reacts. Cross-sectional observations can also look at groups of children of the same age and see whether their responses are similar.

Longitudinal observations

Longitudinal observations track one child over a period of time. They are interesting because we can see how a child's responses change and how he or she develops skills.

Written narrative/running record

This method is probably one of the most straightforward. It requires the observer to put into writing what is being seen. There is a surprising amount of skill required though, as it can be hard to find descriptive language quickly and to be able to write it down. This is a very subjective method of recording. The speed at which the observer must write and act means that only a small amount of information can be recorded and its selection is likely to be subjective. The language that is used to record can also be subjective. Observers will not have the time to consider carefully the vocabulary that is being used and will probably put down the first word that comes to mind, for example, 'snatches' as opposed to 'takes quickly'. Most observers using this method find it helpful to take a pause from time to time so that they can finish off a sentence. Afterwards, notes need to be written out so that they are legible.

When to use this method

This is a versatile method and is often used as a starting point for future observations. You can choose to record any area of development or look at the child more holistically and note down things of interest as they occur. This method is often used to provide a 'snapshot' for parents.

How to use this method

You will need a reliable pen and notepad. You will also need to consider whether to be a participant or non-participant observer.

Begin by noting the start time of the observation as well as the context. Then, as you watch the child, write down what you are seeing. This method is sometimes referred to as 'running commentary' because the observer is providing a commentary. Most observers find that they need to stop after a few minutes, as they are unable to write quickly enough to record everything that a child is doing or

---

Assessment activity 8.2

- Ask your placement supervisor if you can observe a child engaged in imaginative play. Use written record as a technique. Your observation should include the start and end times. You should also make a note of the context and the age of the child in years and months.
- Write a report that evaluates:
  - your effectiveness in using this technique
  - factors that might affect the objectivity of the observation
  - your personal learning from using this technique.

saying. It is good practice to note the time of each 'stop' and 'start' so that anyone reading it later does not assume that it is continuous.

Key advantages

* No preparation required

* Very versatile

* Provides a 'portrait' of a child and so is popular with parents

Structured recording systems

Some observation methods focus the observer's attention onto specific elements of a child's responses or skills. These methods are useful because they provide some degree of objectivity.

Target child observations

Target child observations note the actions and responses of a particular child over a continuous period of time. Target child observations require the observer to be very focused and to work intensively. Observers use codes to ensure that they can record what the child is doing minute by minute.

When to use this method
This method is often used to learn about individual children and, while they can be used to provide a holistic observation, are generally used to focus on children's social and language interaction.

How to use this method
This is an observation that does need to be planned ahead. It requires the observer to only focus on one child and so means that the observer is not able to work with other children at the time.

* Begin by deciding which child is to be observed.

* Consider whether this will be a participant or non-participant observation.

* Prepare a recording sheet (see example below).

Child's name: Rajeet				
Age: 3 years 4 months			Date: 22/10/05	
Minute	Activity	Language	Task	Social Group
1	TC pouring with teapot.	→ TC ←	Water	Sol
2	Uses teapot to pour water onto boat.		Water	Sol
3	Fills teapot. Repeats pouring onto boat.		Water	Sol
4	Fills teapot with spoon. Pours onto boat.	A → C 'I wouldn't want to be in that boat.'	Water	A
5	Pours onto duck. Duck bobs up.	A → C 'Is that fun? Is the duck finding it hard to swim?'	Water	A
6	Shakes duck. Drops duck back into water. Fills teapot.	C → A 'Look duck comes back. Look. The duck bounces.'	Water	A
7	Shakes water out of boat. Uses beaker to fill teapot.		Water	1C
8	Passes boat to C.	TC → C 'You have boat. Silly old boat.'	Water	1C

Social grouping code

TC	Target Child
Sol	Solitary
C	Child
A	Adult

Language code

→ TC ←	Target child talking to self
C → C	Child talking to target child
TC → C	Target child talking to child
TC → A	Target child talking to adult
A → TC	Adult talking to target child

An example of a target child observation.

* Read through and check that you can remember the codes that are to be used.

* Write the start time on the sheet and use a stopwatch or clock thereafter.

* For each minute, record what the child is doing. Use codes to ensure that you can keep up to date with the recording.

Key advantages

* Provides detailed information about a child's activity over a continuous period

* Codes can be used to enable the recorder to write more effectively

Checklists

Checklists are usually straightforward and easy to use. The observer reads a statement and considers whether the child's actions or responses correspond with it. They can be used in a variety of contexts. While they are an example of a structured assessment, they can be completed in a non-participant situation. For example, you might sit and watch a group of children playing and from this note down particular skills that a child has. Many nurseries and schools use standardised checklists as a way of checking that children are reaching developmental milestones or targets for learning. When checklists have been designed well, they can help the observer to be objective. Some types of checklist ask that the observer should also 'evidence' their conclusions, such as the Foundation Stage profile.

When to use this method

Checklists work well when the wording is accurate and focused. This tends to mean they are suited to considering aspects of children's development, such as 'can count three buttons without touching them' or 'turns head in response to sound'. This method can establish a baseline which means that you can carry out a follow-up at a later date and look out for progress.

How to use this method

This method needs a little preparation. It is important to have the checklist sheet in front of you and to read it first. This way you will be able to focus on observing the child rather than on the sheet. It is also important to decide whether you will need to ask the child to complete tasks or whether the context in which you observe the child will provide evidence of the skills.

Assessment activity 3.3

* Ask your placement supervisor if you can complete a checklist observation on four children of a similar age.
* Write a report that evaluates:
  ○ your effectiveness in using this technique
  ○ factors that might affect the objectivity of the observation
  ○ your personal learning from using this technique
  ○ learning that can be gained by carrying out the same observation technique on a group of children.

Behaviour	With support	Without support	Comments/evidence
Matches 3 colours			
Puts together 4 piece puzzle			
Names big and little objects			
Counts to 3 in imitation			
Points to a picture of a boy or girl			
Points to long and short objects			
Copies building a bridge using 3 blocks			
Names times of day: morning, afternoon, evening			

An example of a checklist.

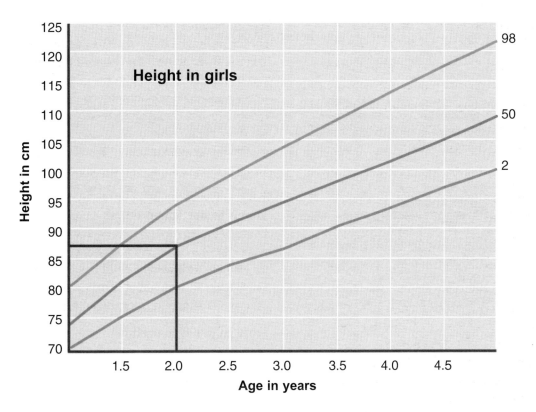

An example of a centile chart.

It is important also to remain as objective as possible, especially if the checklist statements are open ended.

Key advantages

* Simple to use
* Can provide an ongoing assessment
* Useful for assessing development and concepts

Graphs and charts

Strictly speaking graphs and charts are not really 'observations' as they are used to record information rather than to observe children. There are many situations in which graphs and charts might be used. They include tracking children's growth and also providing information about a child's performance, such as the number of times per night that a baby wakes up over a week. Graphs and charts can allow us to see quickly any trends that are developing, such as a baby's weight gain slowing down.

Time sample

Time samples are interesting and versatile. They provide information about a child's activity at regular intervals, for example, what a child is doing during a session at ten-minute intervals. Time samples can be structured and can be used with codes, but equally they can be freer with observers simply using a running commentary style when the sample is taken.

When to use this method

This is a useful method to use to look at a child's activity over all or part of a session. It is less intensive than the target child or the written narrative and leaves the observer free to look at other children in between the samples. It is a good method for looking at children's all-round development in a range of contexts, such as social interaction while the child is playing indoors with the sand, but also twenty minutes afterwards when the child might be outdoors on tricycles.

How to use the method

The starting point for this method is to decide how structured the time sample needs to be. A structured recording will mean that a sheet will need to be drawn in advance and you will need to be familiar with codes. You will also need to decide how often you will 'sample' the child's activity. This

Date:	4/1/06		
Name:	Connor	Age: 3 years 4 months	
Time	Observation		
9.35	Connor is sucking his left thumb. Looks around the room. Stands close to mother. Mother is stroking his hair. Connor takes thumb out of mouth.		
9.40	Connor is at the sand tray. Both hands smoothing the sand. Standing next to James. Talking.		
9.45	Connor is at the sand tray. Scooping a hole using both hands. Buries James' hands. Laughing and eye contact between them.		
9.50	Connor is at the sand tray. Digging hole. Puts in a car. James puts in another car.		
9.55	Connor hiding behind book shelf. Squatting down. James runs over.		

This is an unstructured time sample. Recordings have been made at five-minute intervals.

may partly depend on the length of time you intend to observe. For example, five-minute intervals for observations that last for less than an hour, and fifteen-minute intervals for all-day observations. It is unlikely that sample times greater than fifteen minutes will be very informative.

Once you have determined the range of the time sample, the next step is simply to record what you see when it is time to observe. It is a sample and so you should look to see what the child is doing and then record. While it can be helpful to observe the child in the interim, it is important only to record at the sample times.

Key advantages

* Provides information about a child's activity over a longer period

* Can be used to provide information about children' overall development

Event samples

Event samples are sometimes referred to as 'frequency counts'. The aim of these observations is to find out how often a specific type of behaviour or response takes place and also the context in which it occurs. They are often used when a child is showing unwanted behaviour, but can be used more broadly. They can help a practitioner to work out reasons behind certain responses, but also provide evidence to show whether the number of responses or incidents are increasing or decreasing. Event samples are not strictly observations, as recording takes place after the 'event' or incident has occurred.

When to use this method

Event samples focus narrowly on a particular response of a child. We might decide to investigate how often a child has a tantrum and the context in which this occurs or we might look at how often a child interacts with other children.

How to use this method

A sheet that directs the user to the type of information to be collected has to be drawn up. There are no 'standard' formats, as the recording columns should reflect the observer's requirements for information. Commonly

Event	Time	Situation	Social group	Dialogue
1	9.16 am	Curren is hovering near the painting table	Susan + 2 children	A–C 'Do you want to come and paint a picture too?' C–A nods head
2	9.27 am	Curren is finishing painting	Susan + 2 children	A–C 'Have you finished?' C smiles 'It's a lovely picture. Tell me a little bit about it.' C–A 'It's my mum. Can't take my apron off.' A–C 'Wait still, I'll do it.' Curren hands apron to Susan and runs over to sand area
3	10.12 am	Curren is waiting for his drink at snack time	Curren is sitting next to Ahmed. Jo is handing out drinks	A–C 'Milk or squash, Curren?' C–A 'Milk.' A–C 'Can you remember the magic word?' C–A 'Thank you.' A–C 'Good boy.'
4	10.19 am	Curren is putting on his coat in the cloakroom area	Jo + 5 children	C–A 'Can't put coat on.' A–C 'Keep still. There you are. You can go out now.'
5	10.36 am	Curren is waiting for his turn by the slide	Jo + 2 children	A–C 'Good boy. It's your go now.' C smiles C–A 'I go fast down now.'

An example of an event sample.

collected information includes date and time, as well as background context. The example on page 278 shows an event sample that is focusing on the number of times a child interacts with adults in a setting. In this situation, it will be important to see who exactly the child does talk to and for how long. It will also be useful to find out whether the child initiates the contact or whether it is the adult.

Once the recording sheet is drawn up, it is only filled in when the specific behaviour or response is noted. In settings where several adults might work with a child, the person who was working with the child at the time might fill in the recording sheet.

Observing groups

It can be useful to observe groups of children together. This is not always easy to do, but can provide interesting information about how children interact with each other and also use the environment.

Sociograms

Sociograms are a way of finding out about children's friendship preferences. They are not a perfect tool, especially with children under four years old, as many children choose their playmates according to the play activity, rather than a friendship loyalty.

Sociograms are not strictly an observation method as we are relying on what children tell or show us, rather than observing directly.

When to use this method

This method suits children in the reception class upwards or slightly young children who are in full-time group care. The danger of asking children in sessional care situations is that they are likely to base their responses on who they have most recently played with. This means that a child who has been absent due to illness or a holiday might be 'forgotten'.

How to use this method

The simplest way of using this method is to ask individual children, when they are alone, who they most enjoy playing with. You then need to write down their responses. You might also be interested in finding out what they like doing with this child, such as playing outdoors, as this can help you build up a picture of whether children are choosing playmates on the basis of shared play interests.

Once you have talked to each of the children in the group, a simple chart is drawn up such as the one shown above. Note that while you might find that some children are named more frequently than others, you cannot assume that children who are rarely or not named do not have friends. In schools, some children make friends with children who are in different classes. The next step from a sociogram is to observe individual children and see the quality of their social interactions.

Key advantages

✳ Can identify children who may need support with social skills

Mapping

Mapping is used to see how children move around the setting and how long individual children stay with particular activities.

Name of child	Child 1	Child 2	Child 3
Kerri	Grace	Niamh	Matthew F
Robert	Matthew F	No other name given	No other name given
Zainab	Samantha	Kerri	Grace
Samantha	Kerri	Zainab	Grace
Matthew F	Anthony	Naseer	Jo
Jo	Naseer	Anthony	Matthew F
Helen	Grace	Kerri	No other name given
Naseer	Anthony	Matthew F	Jo
Anthony	Naseer	Matthew F	Jo

An example of a sociogram, showing children's friendship preferences.

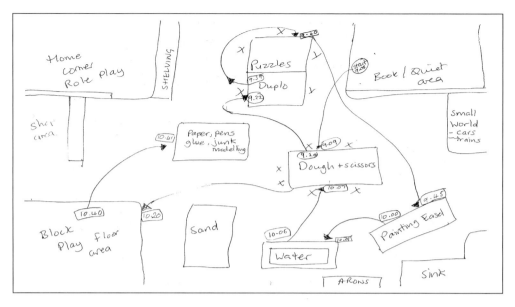

An example of mapping.

When to use this method

This can be useful to see how effective the provision is or when you have many children who do not appear to settle down to activities. Mapping can give us insights into which materials and activities are the most attractive to children.

Using this method

Begin by drawing a floor plan which shows the main activities and equipment that is available. The plan needs to be fairly accurate, although it does not have to be to scale. You will also need an accurate watch, preferably digital and a coloured crayon for each of the children whose movements you are mapping.

When you are ready to start the observation note children's movements and times as they move around during the session. Use a different coloured crayon for each child that you are observing.

Participant observations

At the beginning of the unit, we saw that children's responses might be affected according to whether or not they knew they were being observed. One of the key things when planning an observation is to consider whether or not the observer needs to be 'part of the action'. The advantages of participating are that we might gain a greater understanding of a child's play if we are part of it and also we may influence what children do in order that we can assess more quickly their skill level.

Tips for participant observations

✳ Try to record discreetly

✳ Look relaxed and be aware of children's responses to you

✳ Consider what effects you might have on the children's play

Non-participant observations

Where you are not directly involved in the observation, you will need to be as unobtrusive as possible. Children who see someone standing nearby with a camera or clipboard can change their responses completely. Older children are often curious as to what you are doing and you will need to find a way of dispersing their interest!

Tips for non-participant observations

✳ Look for somewhere out of sight to observe from.

✳ Have everything to hand to avoid distracting children.

✳ Try to sit, rather than stand.

✳ Avoid direct eye contact with children.

✳ Be ready to abandon the observation if children become acutely aware of your presence.

Planning to observe

While we informally observe children all the time, carrying out formal observations and assessments requires some preparation. If you are a student,

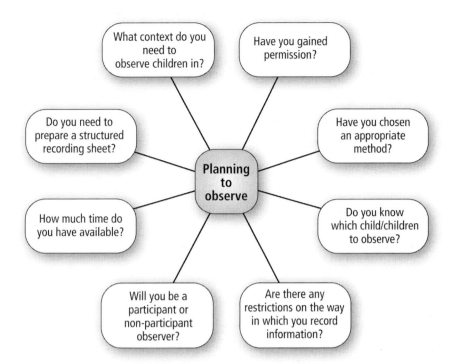

Planning to observe

- What context do you need to observe children in?
- Have you gained permission?
- Do you need to prepare a structured recording sheet?
- Have you chosen an appropriate method?
- How much time do you have available?
- Do you know which child/children to observe?
- Will you be a participant or non-participant observer?
- Are there any restrictions on the way in which you record information?

you need to talk carefully to your placement supervisor about the types of observation that you wish to carry out. This is not only courteous but also essential in terms of planning and permission, as we will see. Placement supervisors can also help students to think about the best context to observe particular activities.

Gaining permission

It is essential to begin by checking that you have permission to observe. As a student this means checking with the placement supervisor or, if your placement is in a home situation, directly with the parents. You should never begin an observation without checking and, even if on a previous occasion permission has been granted, do not make any assumptions that it will still be granted. It is also important to talk to a placement supervisor about the scope of your observation and to find out if there are any restrictions about how the observation is to be recorded. Permission is an important area in its own right and is covered later on in the unit (see page 288).

Timing

It is important to think about how much time you will need to set aside to observe a child or group of children. If you are working as part of a staff team,

this needs to be planned so that the adult-ratio can be maintained. As a student, you will also need to consider whether the timing is convenient for the nursery or school. Some structured observations, such as checklists, might also require that individuals or groups of children be diverted from the usual routine of the setting. This can cause great upheaval if not planned ahead.

Choosing technique and situation

We have seen that different techniques have advantages and limitations. It is important to think about what you need to observe and to check that you are using the best technique. You will also need to consider whether or not you intend to be a participant or non-participant observer, as well as the context that you wish to observe.

Preparing to observe children

While some techniques need little in the way of preparation, others require preparation. You should, for example, make sure that you have read the statements carefully on checklists or tickcharts, while a time sample will need drawing out.

It is also helpful to work out where best to 'hide' if you are hoping to observe children unobtrusively.

Comparison of methods

METHOD	USES	INDIVIDUAL	GROUP	ADVANTAGES	DISADVANTAGES
Written/ narrative record	All areas of children's development	Yes	No	No prepared sheet required Flexible method	Difficult to maintain recording May miss information Potentially subjective
Time sample	All areas of children's development Understanding children's interests	Yes	Yes	Useful for observing an individual or small group of children over an extended time	Interesting responses or behaviour may fall outside of the time slot
Checklist	Skills and concepts	Yes	Yes	Simple to use	Can be inflexible
Target child	Social and language interaction	Yes	No	Provides detailed information on an individual child	Method needs practice
Event sample	Specific behaviours and responses	Yes	No	Useful for monitoring specific aspects of a child's behaviour or responses	Recording sheet has to be well designed. Other staff may not notice and fill in sheet
Sociogram	Development of friendships	No	Yes	Useful to identify children who are not settled within the group	Is not reliable with children under four years Many factors may affect the outcome, e.g. if a particular child has been absent for a while
Mapping	Concentration/ children's interests	Yes	Yes	Useful to find out which areas of an environment hold children's interests	Intensive, but little information about the quality of children's activity or skills is recorded
Audio recording	Language	Yes	No	Can be replayed, which makes analysing language easier	Sound quality can be poor Other children may also be recorded at the same time

▶

METHOD	USES	INDIVIDUAL	GROUP	ADVANTAGES	DISADVANTAGES
Video recording	All areas of development	Yes	Yes	Helps bring observations to life Parents enjoy having a record of their children	Other children whose parents have refused permission may stray into shot Can be an intrusive method for children and other staff
Photographic		Yes	Yes	Helps bring observations to life Parents enjoy seeing photos	Other children whose parents have refused permission may stray into shot Does not show what has happened before or afterwards

Limitations with methods and recording

Most people find that they develop a favourite method of recording that they enjoy using and that they become skilled at. Having said that, it is important to use a variety of methods and also to be aware of their limitations.

Pre-coded method limitations

Where a coded method such as a target child observation is used, it is essential for the observer to be familiar with the coding system. Most practitioners find that at first they are very slow, but with practice can record quickly. It is also possible to develop your own codes but, if you do so, you must explain what these are in the form of a key on the bottom of the recording.

Checklist limitations

Where checklists are being used, it is essential that you read the statements through and check that you understand what the child needs to do. It is also important to consider whether the checklist is age appropriate. Checklists can be drawn up by practitioners or students. If you choose to design your own checklist it is important to make sure that the statements are not too vague, as this can lead to confusion.

Written method limitations

Methods where you write down notes or sentences have inherent difficulties. Firstly, you need to be fast enough to get the information down. You also need to be aware that while you are writing, you may 'miss' some important action. There is also a real danger that you might not understand what you have written or be able to decipher it. It can therefore be useful, when planning an observation, to make sure that you have time afterwards to read and copy out what you have written. It is also another reason why methods that use codes can be helpful.

3 Uses of observation

At the start of the unit, we looked at some of the common reasons why adults observe children. Observations, while interesting for their own sake, are usually carried out in order to benefit the child or group of children in some way. We may, for example, decide to look at the way in which the room is laid out to see if it fosters independence, or we may observe an individual child to see if he or she is able to recognise his or her name. This section looks at the use of observation in supporting children.

Interpretations

Once we have finished observing children, we need to draw some conclusions from our findings. This is always best done after the observation is finished, rather than during it. If we draw conclusions during the recording process, there is always the danger that this will influence the actual observation. A child who is finding it hard to recognise his or her name may notice that the adult seems a little disappointed. This might then affect how the child approaches the next task.

Assessment activity 8.4

Prepare a presentation for other students about observation techniques and their limitations. Your presentation should focus on at least three different techniques that you have tried, which may include those carried out for assessment activities 8.2 and 8.3.

Your presentation should:

- describe the techniques that you have tried
- explain what you have learnt by using them
- evaluate their effectiveness.

Interpreting an observation

Interpretations are rarely objective. Our own knowledge about child development, the child and the setting is likely to shape our conclusions about what we have seen. The type of method will also influence the scope of the interpretations.

Interpreting written records, time samples and target child

With these types of observation, the starting point is the record. It is worth reading through the record and imagining that you do not know the child. The crucial skill when interpreting is often to be able to think afresh. Consider the reasons behind children's responses, including the environment, other children and the responses of the adults present. Think also about the skills and interests that the observation is revealing about the child. Where previous observations of the same type have been used, it will also be important to look at the correlation.

Interpreting checklists, event samples, mapping and sociograms

These types of observation may provide us with closed data. They are also observations that often build on previous ones. If this is the case, the starting point may be to look at a previous observation in order to gain some type of base line. Could the child cut on a straight line with scissors last month? How many times did a child have a tantrum last week? From considering previous observations, the next step is to piece together what is different or new about this observation. Where there are significant changes, we need next to consider what may have caused these. There are many reasons why children's skills and responses change. Adult intervention, maturation or practice are common denominators.

Note that with sociograms, some children are likely not to have been named by their peers. Do not assume that this is because they are unpopular or do not have anyone to play with. The only way to determine this is to carry out another observation, such as an event sample or target child, that looks particularly at the child's social interactions. In the same way, you cannot assume from mapping that a child who stays for a long period of time at an activity enjoys it. It is possible that the child was distracted, or was simply happy to stay there because a friend was there.

Assessment

When interpreting, you may also need to assess a child's progress in relation to other children of the same age, curriculum objectives or theories of child development. Assessing children is not about judging them, but it can help us to consider whether their needs have been identified and whether we are meeting them. It is important that assessment is not seen as labelling children.

Comparison to milestones

As part of the interpretation process, you need also to consider how the child's responses, skills and concepts match the milestones or 'expected development' for the age group. This is quite an important step in many observations. If you have not researched the milestones for the age range

CASE STUDY

Jo has observed Lizzie who is two years old. Lizzie was playing with other toddlers in the room. She walked over to another girl and pulled a cuddly toy out of her hand. The other child tried hard to hang on. The tussle resulted in Lizzie falling on top of the other child. Both children cried. In her interpretation, Jo wrote about Lizzie's unsociable behaviour and concluded that she needs to be told off more often when she is aggressive.

- At what age are most children able to show co-operative behaviour?
- Why is this knowledge important in interpreting this observation?
- Consider how Jo's conclusion might influence her future work with Lizzie.

you are working with, there is a danger that you will draw inaccurate conclusions. This is particularly important when observing children's behaviour, as the case study above shows.

Relation to child development theorists

It can be useful to read up on the aspects of child development that you have observed. Child development theorists can often help us to understand the child's responses and therefore develop our professional knowledge. As a student, you will be expected to be able to make the links between what you have observed and the theories of child development (see Unit 13). The danger of not reading or refreshing our knowledge about child development theory is that we may come to unreliable conclusions about what we have seen.

Achievement of curricular objectives

Observations are sometimes carried out in order for us to see how children are progressing in relation to a curriculum. This can be helpful as it allows us to determine whether we are providing the best opportunities for groups of children, as well as considering whether individual children need more support. While many settings are required to carry out some assessment in relation to curricular targets, it is important not to lose sight of children's ages. Many targets are not age-related, but stage-related, such as the end of Key Stage 1 or the end of the Foundation Stage. This means that curricular targets that might be relevant for a child who is born in October are

hard to meet for a child who was born nine months later in July.

Using observations for future play/learning activities

It is essential that observations are used to meet children's needs. This means that as part of the interpretation process, we need to consider what actions we need to take.

Children's interests

We may need to consider what the observations revealed in terms of children's interests. Were children genuinely enjoying the activity that they were engaged in? If this is the case, future plans for play and activities should build on it. We may, for example, think about additional toys that have a 'pop-up' function for the toddler who is fascinated by a pop-up toy. Noting children's interests and dislikes is essential as, if we plan as much as we can around children's preferences, they are more likely to show wanted behaviour and also to concentrate.

Extending children's play

Sometimes as a result of the observations, we will realise that children's play needs to be extended. We may realise that a child who has been playing on a simple sit-and-ride toy now needs one that has steering. In the same way, we may notice that a child has mastered a skill or concept and that we might need to introduce a further challenge or idea.

Extending children's play.

Reinforcement activities

There are often times when children have nearly mastered a skill or concept, but are not completely confident. A child, for example, may sometimes recognise the number 6, but only in some situations. Observations might help us to plan further activities that will reinforce in different ways the skill or concept that the child needs to master.

Considering approaches to behaviour

Event samples and other observation methods may help us to consider whether current approaches to managing children's behaviour are effective. We may also use observations to understand more of the context of what children are doing. As part of the interpretation, we may be able to think of how to change the context or approach.

Adult support

As well as looking at children's interests, we may also need to consider what further adult support is needed. This might mean thinking about the help that we offer children or the way in which activities are presented. The case study below shows an example of this.

Effectiveness of provision

Observations that consider groups or focus on how children use the environment can help us to reflect on the effectiveness of our provision. If we note that many children of a similar age are not reaching the expected milestones for language, we may need to consider whether the way in which we work with children needs to change. In the same way, if we note that many children's behaviour deteriorates in the outdoor area, we may need to plan more effective play opportunities.

Reporting to parents

It is now understood that children gain when we work in partnership with parents. In terms of observations, this means sharing what we have observed and our thoughts with parents. This is an essential part of working effectively. As parents should have given staff permission to carry out observations in the first place and should wherever possible have developed a day-to-day relationship, sharing observations should not be difficult. It is also good practice to find out information about children's responses at home. This is because children do show different skills and reactions when they are in the home setting. Where there are concerns about a child's development, it is important to pool information with parents.

CASE STUDY

Polly was looking at the observation that she had written about Harry. She noted that he seemed hesitant about using the climbing frame, but had been interested in it. This made her think about whether next time the climbing frame was available she should actively work with Harry to boost his confidence. A few days later, Harry was standing by the climbing frame. She decided to stand next to him and ask him if he wanted to try to climb. She reassured him that she would stand next to him and watch him. He slowly began to climb. Polly encouraged him and Harry beamed because he was pleased with himself.

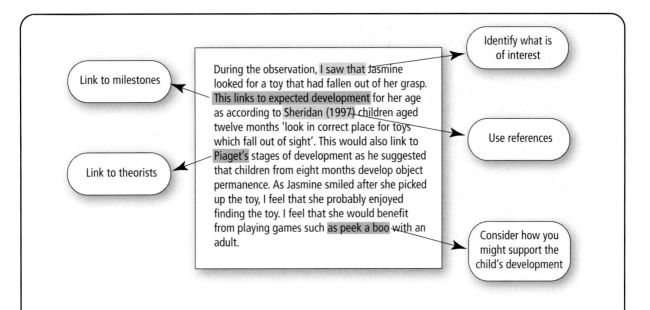

During the observation, I saw that Jasmine looked for a toy that had fallen out of her grasp. This links to expected development for her age as according to Sheridan (1997) children aged twelve months 'look in correct place for toys which fall out of sight'. This would also link to Piaget's stages of development as he suggested that children from eight months develop object permanence. As Jasmine smiled after she picked up the toy, I feel that she probably enjoyed finding the toy. I feel that she would benefit from playing games such as peek a boo with an adult.

- Link to milestones
- Identify what is of interest
- Use references
- Link to theorists
- Consider how you might support the child's development

Carrying out and interpreting observations forms part of the assessment process on childcare courses. Your ability to interpret an observation can provide evidence of your knowledge of child development, theorists and also practice. If you are writing an interpretation as part of an assessment you will need to bear this in mind. Student interpretations tend to be longer and more detailed than ones that are carried out in the workplace. When writing an interpretation you should:

* go through the observation
* highlight what is of interest
* for each point of interest you should:
   * write about what you think it demonstrates about the child
   * think about how it links to milestones or curriculum objectives or child development theories
* use references to support your ideas
* consider future support and/or play activities to promote the child's development.

Point to remember when talking to parents

* Explain the limitations of the observation method.

* Focus on children's strengths as well as weaknesses.

* Be honest and straightforward about what you have seen.

* Ask for parents' views.

* Talk through ways in which the child might be helped.

Particular difficulties

Early identification and support of children whose progress is not similar to expected development can make a significant difference. This means that if an observation seems to suggest that a child has a particular difficulty, it is important to take this further. As children's performance and behaviour can change according to what they are doing, who they are with and also from day to day, it is often useful to collect further information. An observation might be repeated later on in the day or a different method might be used. It is also important to double-check from a reliable source, such as a book, the expected development for the age of child that you are assessing. If you have concerns about what you have seen as a student, your first port of call should be your supervisor. If you are a member of staff, you may need to talk to the child's keyworker and/or the parents.

Suspected neglect or abuse

Occasionally, observations might reveal that a child is the subject of abuse or is being neglected. This is why it is essential that you understand what the child protection policy and reporting procedures are in the early years setting in which you are a student or are working. It is usual to reassure the child, but to avoid making comments or even asking further questions. Any notes that you take should be factual, dated and signed. You should also avoid the temptation to change, re-write or make legible your original notes.

Psychological or legal advice

Observations are sometimes used to provide information for other professionals and occasionally are used in courts of law. It is important where you are asked to provide observations in such cases to ask for detailed advice about what you should be recording and the format. The need for accuracy and avoiding assumption is paramount.

4 The ethics of observation

There are some key issues relating to the ethics of observing children that we need to be aware of. These include permission as well as the dangers of not ensuring that observations are accurate.

Protocols to observe

Every setting will have its own system of observing and keeping children's records. It is important that either as a student or staff member that you understand and follow these rules.

Permission

Observations on children cannot be carried out without the permission of parents. This is not only good practice, but is also necessary to comply with the Data Protection Act. Children's records contain personal information. Parents need to know for what purpose their child is to be observed and how this information is to be kept. It is also good practice to show them the types of observation methods that are used. Most settings have consent forms and it is good practice for these to be regularly reviewed. It is also good practice for parents to give separate permission for student observations to take place, as these may be read by others outside of the setting (see also pages 32–3 for more on confidentiality).

When asking parents for permission, it is important that they can give informed consent. This means that they should know exactly what the observation will mean for their child and how it will take place.

CASE STUDY

Katherine has a four year old child. She has signed a consent form so that the nursery can carry out observations. She did not realise that this might include photographs and that sometimes the photographs might also be used in other ways. She is horrified to see that a photograph of children playing which includes her child is in the local paper. She is worried because she is staying with her daughter in a woman's refuge as her ex-partner has physically attacked them both. She is worried that he will now be able to find them as the nursery has been named.

- Why is it important that informed consent is obtained from parents?

- How might parents feel if they do not feel that they have given informed consent?

Consultations, involvement and reporting

It is often useful to talk through with parents what might be recorded during an observation. They may have particular interests or concerns that they wish us to consider. It is important afterwards to share the information that we have collected with parents and to talk through our conclusions. Involving parents in the observation process is thought to have many benefits. It can help us to learn more about the child, but also can help parents to feel involved with the work that we are doing. It is important that parents do not feel that the observation process is one where children are compared and that it is a competitive process. This means that we have to be extremely careful in the use of our language. Terms such as 'he's one of our best' or 'she's about average' are misleading and not helpful in this respect.

Explicit authorisation

While parents need to give permission before observations can take place, there may be occasions where explicit authorisation is required. A physiotherapist may wish to see how the child is managing in the setting. This type of observation is likely to fall outside of the usual perimeters of what parents have granted permission for. In such cases, it is essential that explicit authorisation is given from parents. It is also important to be aware that settings should not ask other professionals in to observe a child without having gained this type of permission.

Confidentiality

There are many issues about the confidentiality of observations. Observations have the potential to provide information about children that could put them at risk. For example, an estranged and abusive parent might find out about the setting that a child attends.

Storing observations

Children's records in early years settings have to be kept in a secure place. This is usually a locked filing cabinet. Access to records is usually limited to the child's keyworker and the manager. Children's records are covered by the Data Protection Act (see also page 33). With student observations, it is usually suggested that names are changed and details about the setting are not so specific that it would be easy to recognise its location. In the same way, it is important not to put the child's date of birth and to instead put the age in years and months. As a student, you should be careful about your observations and you should avoid photographs as, if you were to lose your work, someone else might identify a child.

Disclosure of information

Observations about children are confidential. This means that they should not be shared with people other than those directly working with the child and who have a need to know and their parents. Where parents are separated, it is important to know whether both parents have access to records. Occasionally, children's records might be disclosed to other professionals if there is a child protection issue.

Rights

Children and their families have rights and these need to be considered during the observation process. It is important, for example, that any language that is used about the child is accurate and factual. A good test is always to consider whether you would be happy for the same to be said or written about you!

Rights of refusal and non-participation

As part of their rights, parents can decide that they would prefer for their child not to be observed or that they would like to 'opt out' from some situations. This might mean parents say they would not like photographs to be taken of their children or videos, while they might be happy for other types of methods to be used.

Responsibility

It is not always apparent that we have significant responsibility when we carry out observations, but we have. Conclusions that we reach about children can affect their longer-term development both positively and negatively. This is partly

In 1968 two researchers, Rosenthal and Jacobson, carried out an experiment in which they told classroom teachers that some of the children they were due to teach were likely to make significant progress in the school year. They named these children (who had actually been chosen on a random basis) and then monitored their progress later. The researchers were then staggered to find that the named children had made the 'predicted' progress! They associated the children's progress with the teachers having high expectations of these children and the children in turn living up to these expectations. The link between expectations of others and actual behaviour is known as the self-fulfilling prophecy.

Accuracy

We have seen that observations must not be used to 'label' children. Accuracy is therefore essential when carrying out and interpreting observations. A good tip is always to check that you have evidence for your conclusions and also that you have researched carefully in terms of milestones and theories of child development.

Purpose

It is important to focus on the purpose of observing children. At the start of the unit, we saw that the key purpose is to ensure that we can meet children's needs. It is important that this focus is kept and that observations are not used in ways that may be harmful for children.

linked to the expectations that we and other adults might develop as a result of assessments. An adult who believes that he or she is working with a child who is not good at mathematics might not provide activities that are stimulating and challenging. The term 'self-fulfilling prophecy' is used to explain the phenomenon whereby children's performance can be determined by adults' expectations of them.

The importance of understanding the self-fulfilling prophecy

The above experiment, although based in a school setting, shows clearly that the way adults think about children will influence their behaviour and achievement – if we show children we believe in them and have high expectations of them, they will demonstrate this behaviour to us.

In pairs, using the self-fulfilling prophecy theory can you explain why:

- labelling children as difficult or naughty can be unhelpful
- conclusions drawn from observations have to be accurate
- observations need to be on-going?

1 Ask your supervisor if you can observe a child using any of the observation techniques described in this unit. You should discuss with your supervisor the scope of the observation and how it might be used. Your observation should contain:
- the date and context of the observation
- the child's age in years and months.

2 Produce an interpretation for the observation. Your interpretation should include:
- information about how the child's responses linked to their expected development
- how the child's responses linked to child development theory
- suggestions as to how the child's future development might be promoted.

3 Produce an evaluation of your observation. The evaluation should consider:
- the ethics of your observation
- the effectiveness of your chosen method
- factors that might affect the objectivity of your observation and interpretation.

END-OF-UNIT TEST

1 Describe the main purposes of observations in early years settings.

2 Explain the difference between closed and open data.

3 Give three reasons why observers might find it hard to be objective.

4 Describe three factors that might influence a child during an observation.

5 Explain the advantages and disadvantages of participant observations.

6 Describe three different observation techniques.

7 Give one advantage and one disadvantage of using written records.

8 Explain why it is important to consider expected development when interpreting observations.

9 Describe what an observer should do if a child's responses gave them cause to believe that a child was being abused.

10 Why is it important that permission is sought before observations are undertaken?

References and further reading

Bentzen (2004), *Seeing Young Children: A guide to observing and recording behaviour*, Delmar

Hobart, C and Frankel, G (2004), *A Practical Guide to Child Observation and Assessment*, Nelson Thornes

Meggitt, C and Sunderland, G (2000), *Child Development: An illustrated guide*, Heinemann

Sharman, C (2004), *Observing Children*, Continuum International Publishing Group

Research methodology for early years

What you need to learn

1 The purpose and role of research in early years

2 Research methods relevant to early years

3 How to gather, present and examine research information

4 Implications and ethical issues in using research

Introduction

This unit provides an understanding of research, the research process and its application in the early years setting. Through increasing your understanding of research and by providing the opportunity to develop your research skills, you will be better placed to complete many of the activities required for other units, in particular Unit 8 Observation of Children and the optional Unit 20 Early Years Project. As the project unit is about putting research methods into practice, this chapter includes information to help you conduct a research project. Where this information is not part of this unit, it has been placed in separate sections entitled 'Working towards your Early Years Project (Unit 20)'.

How you will be assessed

This unit is assessed internally.

1 The purpose and role of research in early years

Have you ever been shopping in your local high street and been pounced upon by someone holding a clipboard who just wants a few minutes of your time, only to ask a seemingly endless stream of questions? If so, then you will probably have been involved in market research to determine, for example, different people's shopping preferences. You will almost certainly have completed a registration card after purchasing a new mobile phone or mp3 player that will have involved ticking a number of boxes answering a variety of questions, and if you have a store reward card then data on all your purchases will have been collected and analysed to determine your shopping habits and preferences.

You may have taken part in the National Census or even been interviewed about your views on some topic in the news. These are examples of social research.

In science classes at school you will have carried out experimental investigations that are the basis of scientific research. You may have been involved with scientific medical research as a result of being asked by your doctor to be involved in the trial of a new type of drug.

Research is used in all sorts of different ways and can be regarded broadly as a tool to develop a better understanding of the world we live in. Organisations and professionals concerned with young children are continually undertaking research for many different reasons. These can be for:

* extending knowledge and understanding of issues relating to early years

* identifying needs

* evaluating services to highlight gaps in provision

* monitoring progress

* informing and improving policy and practice.

The range of research is vast. It often reflects issues of political importance simply because a large amount of research is commissioned or funded by central government. Organisations such as universities, private research companies, public services or voluntary groups conduct the research on behalf of the commissioning body or they may have their own source of funding that will enable them to carry out research independently.

Types of research

There are many different ways of undertaking research and all involve the use of what is termed **primary** and **secondary** research. Primary research is the gathering of information by the person or persons carrying out the research. Primary research provides up-to-date and hopefully relevant information about the topic being studied. You will use primary research to carry out your own studies, such as observing children in a nursery or classroom or carrying out a survey of parents.

Secondary research is the use of information that others have collected. You will undertake secondary research to gather information for the completion of much of your coursework. The information you obtain may come from a variety of sources and will be based upon the published work of the original researcher or an interpretation of this work by someone else.

Secondary research is an essential part of primary research, as the researcher needs to be fully aware of what other people have studied in relation to their own work. It may be that one piece of research is based upon the work of someone else or that the same research is being carried out in a different context, in a different place or with different people.

The type of information obtained by primary or secondary research can be identified as either **quantitative** or **qualitative**. Quantitative information describes information or data that is in the form of numbers, such as the number of children attending different forms of day care provision. Qualitative information is descriptive and in the form of the written or spoken word, such as mothers' experiences of childbirth.

Further distinctions can occur as a consequence of research in the early years field involving the study of people. These include **cross-sectional** and **longitudinal** studies. A cross-sectional study is based upon the investigation of people at a particular moment in time. Such research may form part of investigations into the differences or relationships that can occur between individuals or groups, such as finding out about the difference in ability of children to conserve. Alternatively, longitudinal research studies individuals or groups over a period of time, in some cases many years, for example, studying the development of a baby for the first six months of life.

The problem with longitudinal studies is the time required to complete them. While the example given might be feasible for you to carry out, others may not – it is unlikely that you could complete a lifetime study of the social and emotional development of twins during your course.

Secondary research

You will have seen from the previous section that secondary research is something you do as part of your studies, whether or not you are doing any primary research and you will also do secondary research both prior to as well as during any research project. As such, background information on undertaking secondary research is presented here rather than after the primary research section.

Secondary sources

As already stated, secondary research involves finding out facts and figures on topics you may be

Research can be a communal and wide-ranging activity.

studying that have been produced by others. Some thought needs to be given to potential sources of such information.

Books, newspapers, magazines, specialist publications

Books obtained from your school or college will probably be your main source of information initially, particularly if you have not had experience of using other sources. While your tutors may direct you to some books and provide a booklist, you will have to search out others for yourself. This can be quite a task if a library is well stocked. However, most libraries now possess computerised search facilities and these can be a great source of help in finding resources that cover the area of work you are studying. As well as the school or college library, your local library may have useful material and, depending on where you live, it may be possible for you to access more specialist libraries, such as universities or local authority education centres, which usually have libraries for teachers (access to such facilities may be restricted or involve paying a subscription).

Libraries often subscribe to, and keep back copies of, one or more daily newspapers, magazines and more specialist publications produced for people working in specific industries/organisations. The types of publication you might find helpful include:

* *Nursery World* – a weekly publication for early years curriculum professionals

* *Nursing Times* – a weekly publication produced for nurses and other professionals in the health and caring services; often contains specialist articles relating to children

* *Times Educational Supplement* – published weekly, covering newsworthy topics and developments in education

* *Social Trends* – published annually, this is an invaluable source of official statistics covering, amongst others, information on families, housing, health, education and work

* *Regional Trends* – similar to *Social Trends* but contains information on a regional basis; useful if you want data relevant to the area you live in.

People

By talking to people who work in early years settings, your tutors, family and friends, you can get different views and ideas on subjects. Such views may reflect changing attitudes towards parenting and education and, as such, support or refute information obtained from books.

Organisations

There are voluntary and statutory organisations that you will have found out about by reading other parts of this book and through input from your tutors. They can be an invaluable source of help and information on specific topics.

While the statutory services are available throughout the country, voluntary organisations may be concentrated in larger towns or cities. However, a good starting point to look for such organisations is your local newspaper or the library. While many organisations offer support to sufferers and carers, they are usually more than happy to talk to students, or provide students with information that helps to further their cause.

Computers and the internet

Computers can be used to obtain information from CD-ROMs, the internet or intranets. CD-ROMs are digitally recorded stores of information. Some are like electronic encyclopaedias, containing textual and visual information on a wide range of topics. Others are digital copies of the publications mentioned above that are updated annually. CD-ROMs are now the usual source of computer programs, many of which have an educational content.

The internet, as a worldwide information base, allows access to an enormous range of research information either as full publications, reports, summaries or abstracts. Search engines such as Google, Yahoo, Ask Jeeves or MSN can be used to find information on subjects of interest or to look for current areas of research. However, you can waste an awful lot of time searching the web and getting nowhere. You need to be quite specific in your search, but not so specific that the search engine comes up with nothing. Most search engines have help facilities to assist you in your quest. Note that to gain access to some research reports and papers of many research journals sites you must register or pay a subscription fee.

To get you started, here are some sites that contain abstracts, summaries or complete reports of research for which you do not have to register or subscribe:

* www.dfes.gov.uk/research – research page of the Department for Education and Skills website

* www.surestart.gov.uk – website for Sure Start

* www.ecrp.uiuc.edu – a bilingual journal on the development, care, and education of young children

* www.ltscotland.org.uk/earlyyears/publications.asp – the early years page of the Learning and Teaching Scotland website that has easy-to-follow links through its publications page to summaries and full reports of early years research undertaken in the UK

* www.rand.org/research_areas/children – RAND is a non-profit research organisation providing access to research from around the world in a wide range of subjects via a range of links; it is not easy to navigate round, but it allows you to look at research undertaken in other parts of the world.

Intranet sites are local versions of the internet used by organisations for exchange of information within that establishment. It is more than likely that the place where you are studying has its own intranet that may have pages devoted to your course and contain links to websites considered useful for your course. Other organisations that have intranets may choose to allow you access via an internet website, but may limit use to specific parts of that site.

Other media

TV, national and local radio as sources of up-to-date information are often used to reflect current attitudes and opinions about different issues. However, like newspapers, they may reflect the biased views of the publishers and in order to attract a maximum audience will latch onto subjects that are topical, such as the Louise Woodward case in America, or the supposed link between the MMR (measles, mumps and rubella) vaccine and autism.

Museums

These are often disregarded but are potentially useful in terms of local history and the subsequent social changes in local communities. Such changes may reflect on a wide range of issues relating to parenting and the development, education and experience of children in a community. Many museums, such as the Beamish Museum in Country Durham, operate interactive displays or operate as living museums to reflect social history.

Using secondary research

Remember that information obtained from secondary sources is second-hand. As such it may be biased towards the views of the person or organisation that has produced it. In addition, the information may be out of date as the book or article may have been written some time after the original research was undertaken and you may be reading the material some years after publication. You should always treat such information with

---

KEY ISSUES

The purpose and role of research in the early years can be illustrated by the range of research on literacy and numeracy in the UK relating to the introduction of the literacy and numeracy hours in primary schools. Research in this field initially highlighted the fact that the literacy and numeracy standards in the UK lagged behind those of other countries (*identified need*). Other research, not just in the UK, investigated different methods that could contribute to improving standards (*extended knowledge and understanding of issues relating to early years*). Research since the introduction of the literacy and numeracy hours has focused on the effectiveness of the programme leading to modifications, but also to questions as to whether it is the best way of addressing standards (*monitor progress, inform and improve policy and practice*).

The bracketed and italicised notes identify the purpose of the research using the headings as shown in the following assessment activity.

Assessment activity

To develop your research skills you should know how to conduct an information search or literary review and be able to identify examples of research that will help you understand the research process.

Go to your local or college library and look for texts on the subject or chapters or articles in books or publications. Note down the titles, the authors, date and place of publication (see Producing a bibliography on page 323).

Now carry out a search on the internet. Try using different search engines to identify online information on the literacy and numeracy hours. Check out some of the website addresses and, if they seem to contain relevant information, note down or copy the titles of the research together with their author and website address. If you have not used the internet before, ask your tutor, school, college or local library to help.

For each piece of research you identify determine its purpose in terms of whether it:

- extends knowledge and understanding of issues relating to early years
- identifies needs
- evaluates services to highlight gaps in provision
- monitors progress
- informs and improves policy and practice.

---

caution and have evidence from different sources to support your work and provide a balanced picture.

Primary research

While secondary research can provide the background and basis for many of your studies, you will also need to be familiar with the process of primary research and the different primary research methods used. Whatever the nature of the research being undertaken, researchers make use of different methods to help them answer the questions they have posed. These include:

* surveys/questionnaires

* observations

* interviews

Working towards your Early Years Project (Unit 20)

For any project you undertake, the first three statements in the cycle are all about planning. The more effort put into planning and organising your activities, particularly where the research is a project for which you have been allocated a term or longer to complete, the better the end result. Once you have planned the research, you are then ready to collect the data, after which you need to sort it out ready for presentation and analysis.

At the end of this unit a checklist is provided to help you with the organisation and planning of any research or project you undertake (see page 324–5).

Identifying a topic to research

As far as any research you undertake is concerned, any ideas may arise as a result of:

- reading or hearing about something that you think would be interesting and enjoyable to find out more about
- your own thoughts or experiences
- the ideas of others.

Your tutor may be able to get you started by suggesting topics that previous students have investigated or you may be able to use observations or other activities expected of you in placement.

The research question or hypothesis

Having selected the topic or list of topics that you would like to, or are thinking about, studying, you must now begin to refine your ideas focusing on what you would specifically like to find out. This will lead to producing a **research question** or **hypothesis**.

A research question simply states the question or questions you want your research to answer. A hypothesis is a special type of research question that tends to be used in surveys or experiments. It proposes the existence of a relationship between variables or factors and tends to suggest how the relationship will be tested (see Experimental method, pages 303–5). Students often find identifying a research question one of the more difficult parts of the whole process and consequently try to opt out of making a decision about this until later. This is an error that results in students being unclear about the focus of their study. Time needs to be given to what you hope to find out. This part of the research process will involve you in doing some secondary research, reading around the topic, looking at recent research and talking to others. In this way you will begin to find out more about the area you are going to study that can then lead to the selection of a specific topic.

* case studies

* experiments

* action research.

You might find by reading specialist books on research that these methods are presented in different ways and that there are others. Each method has its own advantages and disadvantages and will consequently be used by researchers in different circumstances.

Before considering each method in turn, together with an explanation of the method and examples of its application, you need to be aware of the processes that must be gone through to plan research effectively.

Research is regarded as a cyclical process that involves the following general approach.

1 Identify a topic to research (research commissioned by a government body or other organisation generally dictates the subject matter being researched).

2 Produce a research question or hypothesis (this may again be dictated by the commissioning body and can be based upon the research programme's aims).

3 Select research and sampling methods (designing) and consider any ethical issues involved in conducting the research.

4 Collect the information.

5 Present the information.

6 Analyse the information.

7 Evaluate and discuss the research and its implications.

Discussion and evaluation of the research can lead to further or continuing investigations to complete the cycle.

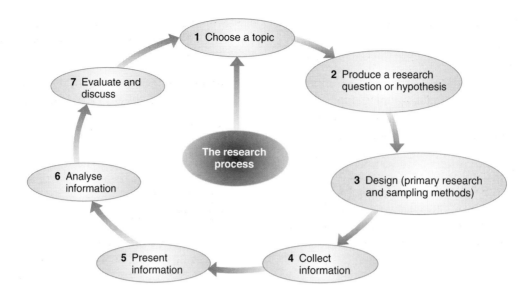

The research process

1 Choose a topic

2 Produce a research question or hypothesis

3 Design (primary research and sampling methods)

4 Collect information

5 Present information

6 Analyse information

7 Evaluate and discuss

2 Research methods relevant to early years

This section concentrates on giving you information about the different methods you were introduced to earlier and how to use them.

Surveys

Survey research is based upon asking questions. This can be in the form of a questionnaire or an intensive one-on-one, in-depth interview.

Questionnaires

Questionnaires are usually a pen-and-paper exercise that people complete through a mail drop or group activity, or as a one-on-one structured interview.

Advantages of postal questionnaires

* They are relatively inexpensive to administer, apart from the cost of photocopying and postage stamps.

* They can be sent to a large number of people.

* Respondents may fill them out at their own convenience.

Disadvantages of postal questionnaires

* Response rates from mail surveys are often very low.

* They are not the best way of asking for detailed information.

The disadvantage of response rate can be overcome by carrying out the survey face to face. This also allows for questioning the respondent to clarify any questions or to gain a more insightful response. If you decide to use this method it is important for personal safety that you conduct the activity in a small group and that you have some form of identification.

Alternatively, a group-administered questionnaire is an effective way of getting people to respond to a questionnaire. It guarantees a high response rate and can draw on people who are readily available, such as in college, a school or workplace, though it may limit the total number of people surveyed and can create a biased sample (see Sampling methodology, pages 307–8). Respondents are handed the questionnaire and can be asked to complete it immediately or you can offer to collect it the following week or whenever is convenient.

How you administer the questionnaire is relatively easy compared to producing it. You might think it is easy to run off a few questions about, for example, the views of parents on raising children and keeping pets. You will find that it takes time, thought and practice to ensure that the questions give you the answers you are seeking. You will also find that you need to undertake a trial to find out if it works (see

Checklist for carrying out a research project on pages 324–5).

The types of question you can ask vary and include the following.

Closed and open questions – closed questions lead to a yes/no answer whereas open questions prompt the respondent to say something more. 'Are you married?' is a closed question, 'What are your views on marriage?' is an open question. Closed questions give information that can be easily quantified while open questions allow the respondent to express their own views. The difficulty with open questions is that respondents may have slightly different views, making the presentation and analysis of such information more difficult.

Information gathering questions usually ask for some numerical data.

* How many children do you have?
* What is your age?
* In what year were you born?

(The last question is regarded as a more sensitive way of asking someone their age than the second.)

Category questions offer a number of possibilities, only one of which the respondent can fit into.

* Are you: Male ☐ Female ☐
  Married ☐ Single ☐

* Tick which age group you fit into:
  15–25 ☐
  26–35 ☐
  36–45 ☐
  46–55 ☐
  56+ ☐

The use of categories such as age groups is another way of obtaining information that may be regarded as sensitive. It can, however, be useful to allocate people to age ranges if you want to see if there is any difference in response to your questionnaire between age groups, such as attitudes or changes to parenting between younger and older age groups.

Ranking questions are used to place answers in order and are useful for obtaining information on views or attitudes.

* Number the following emotional and social needs of children in order of importance.
  Security ☐
  Discipline ☐
  Love ☐
  Encouragement ☐
  Responsible behaviour ☐

* In order of importance number your preferred method of pain relief during childbirth.
  Gas ☐
  Pethidine ☐
  Epidural ☐
  Breathing and relaxation techniques ☐

Scale questions can also be used to obtain information about attitudes and beliefs, but must be used with care.

* Tick the box that best describes how you feel about the following statements:

Children should be smacked if they:

	Strongly agree	Agree	Disagree	Strongly disagree
hit or bite another child	☐	☐	☐	☐
wet themselves when being toilet trained	☐	☐	☐	☐
have a temper tantrum	☐	☐	☐	☐
play with their genitals	☐	☐	☐	☐

The above scale question is quite controversial and may not be appropriate within a college-based project. However, it helps to illustrate how controversial topics may be investigated without having to ask someone directly about the subject, such as whether they smack their children.

A less controversial subject for using a scale question might be as follows.

✻ Tick the box that best describes your views on:

	Strongly agree	Agree	Neither agree nor disagree	Disagree	Strongly disagree
Breastfeeding	☐	☐	☐	☐	☐
Fluoridation of water	☐	☐	☐	☐	☐
Homework for infant school children	☐	☐	☐	☐	☐

In this example note how an extra column has been added to include the neutral response of neither agree nor disagree. While this allows people to express a neutral view, it can result in people avoiding the subject.

Creating the questionnaire

In addition to the style of questions used you also need to consider the construction and presentation of your questionnaire. The following pointers should be taken into account.

✻ Keep your questions as simple as possible. Two or three simple questions may be easier to answer than one difficult one.

✻ Do not ask too many questions. If there are too many, people will get fed up.

✻ Make sure your questions are unambiguous, for example, 'Should a child be disciplined for being naughty?' begs the response, 'What form of discipline are you referring to and how do you define naughty?'

✻ Do not ask leading questions that imply a particular response, for example, 'Do you think that it is better to breastfeed rather than bottle feed a new baby?' – the response may well be, 'Yes, but I'd rather bottle feed.'

✻ Avoid grouping together questions that have a negative or sensitive context or, if you are seeking a more personal view, place them towards the end of the questionnaire, for example, asking people's views on abortion, child abuse or drugs.

✻ Do not ask too many open questions as they can take time to answer and are difficult to analyse. Again these are best placed towards the end of the questionnaire and can be a useful way of getting a response to more contentious subjects.

✻ Type or print your questionnaire in a format that is clear and legible.

✻ Set the questionnaire out so that simple closed questions that only require yes/no or one-word answers come first, followed by ranking and scale-type questions and finishing with open questions to allow subjects to express their opinions more fully.

✻ Ensure that you include an explanation of who you are, where you are from and the purpose of the questionnaire. Also provide clear instructions and a statement to assure respondents that the questionnaire is confidential (see page 320).

Interviews

As you read through this section you will see that interviews, particularly at their simplest level, are no more than extended survey questionnaires. However, interviews are a far more personal form of research and can provide more detailed information, particularly on sensitive subjects. They are usually carried out on a one-to-one basis. While interviews are generally easier for

Conducting an interview.

The following questions were put together by a group of childcare students to find out about mothers' views on breastfeeding and bottle feeding. Read through the survey then see if you can answer the questions that follow.

1 Please indicate which age group you fit into
  a Under 20
  b 20–30
  c 30–40
  d 40+
2 How many children do you have and what are their age and gender?
3 Did you breastfeed or bottle feed?
4 If you breastfed please state how long you breastfed each child for.
5 If you did not breastfeed any of your children please identify which type of infant formula milk you used
  SMA ☐   Cow & Gate ☐   Milupa ☐   Farley's ☐   Other ☐
6 Number each statement in order of importance
  a Breast milk contains all the nutrients a baby needs.   ☐
  b Bottle feeding is more convenient.   ☐
  c Breastfeeding is time consuming.   ☐
  d Breastfed babies are less prone to infections.   ☐
  e You know how much your baby has had when bottle feeding.   ☐
7 Tick the box that best describes how you feel about each statement

	Strongly Agree	Agree	Disagree	Strongly Disagree
You should follow the advice of health professionals in deciding whether to breastfeed or bottle feed.	☐	☐	☐	☐
You should make up you own mind on whether to breastfeed or bottle feed based on the experiences of friends and family.	☐	☐	☐	☐

Questions
- Identify which questions are of the category, rank or scale type.
- How could you improve the presentation of questions 2, 3 and 4 and make it easier for you to summarise the results?
- Suggest what is wrong with questions 3, 4 and 6?
- Why is question 5 unnecessary?

the respondent, especially if what is sought is opinions or impressions, they are not necessarily easier for you. Interviews can be very time consuming and they require good communication skills to complete effectively. Interviews can be of different types.

✳ **Structured** interviews are based on a set of questions requiring specific answers and are not very different from a questionnaire.

✳ **Open-ended** interviews may have little, if any, format and may take the form of a discussion.

✳ **Semi-structured** interviews are a bit of both. If you use this form of research, semi-structured interviews are probably the most appropriate procedure to follow.

You are most likely to use interviews to find out about people's feelings, attitudes and experiences of, for example, childbirth, raising children, caring for a sick child, managing children's behaviour or the education of children. As a result, you will tend to choose one or more people to interview from those you know, have had contact with or have been put in touch with by your tutor or workplace supervisor.

As a consequence of knowing or having been introduced to the person to be interviewed use the following guide to help you complete the process.

1 Give a brief explanation of the purpose of your interview and make arrangements as to the date, time and place of the interview. This will help prepare both the interviewee and yourself for the event.

2 Make preparations for recording the interview. You can choose to use a tape recorder or take notes, both of which have their advantages and disadvantages as shown in the table below.

TAPE RECORDING	NOTE TAKING
Able to concentrate on interviewee, what he or she has to say and the questions to be asked	Need to give attention to both interviewee and note taking
Can make respondents anxious and not able to talk about sensitive issues	Can be distracting
Provides a complete account of what has been said, but can take a long time to transcribe and analyse	Allows a summary of what has been said to be noted, and the main features identified, so analysis is easier, important facts or remarks may be missed

Whichever method is used, ensure you have the agreement of the interviewee and, if note taking, have a spare pen or pencil and devise a system for abbreviating certain responses such as 'Q:' for your question, 'A:' for the respondent's answer, 'DK' for don't know, and so on.

3 In conducting the interview, you need to take into account the beginning, middle and end. The beginning includes making appropriate opening remarks that puts interviewees at ease and does not ask too much of them. This can be achieved by explaining who you are, where you are from and re-emphasising what the research is for. The main thing here is not to be long-winded. Also, provide reassurance that the interview will remain confidential. This can also include asking simple questions that only require one-word or short answers, such as 'How many children do you have?', 'What age and gender are they?' These simple questions can be memorised, enabling you to give attention to the interviewee so helping to establish a trusting, honest, and non-threatening relationship that can lead into a more open-ended discussion about the main issues.

4 If you are interviewing more than one person for your research, you must ensure that the questions asked are exactly the same, as altering them in any way can change their whole meaning and, as a result, the response you get.

5 Ask all the questions in the order arranged prior to the interview so that nothing is missed out either by you or the interviewee. Do not finish people's sentences for them because it might not have been what they were going to say.

6 If the beginning of the interview has gone well, it should lead naturally into the middle part of the interview, where you hope to elicit a more open or detailed response for which you may find the following techniques helpful.

- **Silence**: One of the most effective ways to encourage someone to say more is to do nothing at all – just pause and wait. It works because people are generally uncomfortable with pauses or silence and it suggests that you are waiting, listening for what they will say next.

- **Encouraging remarks**: Something as simple as 'Uh-huh' or 'OK' after the respondent completes a thought can encourage the respondent directly.

- **Elaboration**: Asking a question such as 'Is there anything else you would like to add?' can result in the respondent providing more information.

- **Ask for clarification**: Asking the interviewee to talk in more detail about something said earlier can allow the discussion to explore new areas. This type of question also shows that you have been listening, which can encourage the interviewee.

- **Reflecting**: By repeating back part of what the respondent has said, you say something without really saying anything new. For instance, the respondent just described a traumatic experience from childhood. You might say 'What I'm hearing you say is that you found that experience very traumatic.' Then you should pause. The respondent is likely to say something like 'Well, yes, and it affected the rest of my family as well. In fact, my younger sister...' and so on.

7 When the interview ends, conclude by thanking the respondent and offering him or her the opportunity to read your completed work or at least a summary of it.

8 Do give the respondent time to ask any further questions about you, your course or your research before you leave.

9 You may have observations about the interview that you weren't able to write down while you were with the respondent. You should therefore immediately go over your notes and include any other comments and observations, making sure you distinguish these from the notes made during the interview.

The experimental method

The experimental method is a standard scientific procedure whereby the researcher, possibly after some preliminary work:

✳ proposes a research hypothesis by which they hope to explain the initial findings

✳ designs an experiment or series of experiments to test the hypothesis.

The hypothesis can be in the form of a very precise question, statement or prediction that suggests a relationship or difference between two or more factors or variables where a **variable** is something that changes or can be changed. For example, asthma has been on the increase for a number of years and various reasons have been proposed, including the increase in use of diesel engine cars or an increase in the number of dust mites. Asthma, cars, and dust mites are all variables.

A **relationship**, often referred to as a **correlation** or **association** between variables, results from changes in one variable being *related* to changes in another. For example, the number of children suffering from asthma may be correlated to the increase in house dust mite infestations through increased use of central heating.

A **difference** between variables can be regarded as changes in one variable causing an *effect* in another variable. For example, 'girls learn quicker than boys' is often referred to as a cause and effect relationship.

The hypothesis can also be written in one of two formats: the **experimental** and the **null** hypothesis.

Theory into practice

Interviews require good communication skills and take practice. If you are unsure about conducting an interview, try this activity to practise.

In groups of three, take turns in being an observer, interviewer or interviewee. Choose a topic which each of you feels able to talk about. Jot down some questions that will require closed and open answers. Start by the interviewer asking a simple question with the observer making notes on the responses. Move on to more open questions and note the responses, to see if the interviewee says more.

If you found this easy, try repeating the exercise with a controversial or sensitive topic such as abortion, embryo research or cancer.

CASE STUDY

What not to do in an interview

Suzanne chose to do a project on childbirth and decided to interview her friend, Danielle about her experience of childbirth as she was due to have her first baby.

The project was scheduled for submission four weeks after the birth of the baby which Suzanne thought would give her plenty of time to complete the assignment. However, Suzanne hadn't bargained for Danielle's baby not being born until two weeks after her due date and Danielle didn't come home from the hospital for five days as the baby was slightly jaundiced. Suzanne visited Danielle in the hospital and planned to arrange the interview for when she got home, but in the excitement of seeing the new baby and Danielle wanting to know about what was going on Suzanne forgot. Fortunately, Suzanne managed to see Danielle in hospital again before she went home and this time organised the interview so that it gave her a few days to write up the assignment.

When Suzanne went round to Danielle's she was about to feed the baby. Suzanne hadn't prepared any questions as she thought that as she knew Danielle so well it wouldn't matter, so they just chatted about her experiences. Suzanne realised it might have been a good idea to bring a notepad and pen. Suzanne asked Danielle if she had a pen and paper, but at that moment the midwife arrived. The midwife asked Danielle about the birth and how she was getting on while Suzanne held the baby. When the midwife left the baby was ready for a feed. No sooner had she finished feeding the baby when the door bell rang and another of Danielle's friends had come round to see her and the baby. Suzanne realised she had to go as she'd arranged to go into college to see her tutor about her progress with the project.

In a bit of a panic Suzanne didn't know whether to go into college, but in the end took the plunge and found that by talking through what she had discussed with Danielle and what she had overheard said to the midwife it was obvious that she had gathered an awful lot of information. Suzanne's tutor suggested she spent the rest of the day getting her thoughts down on paper, checking any facts with Danielle the next day and she would still have time to complete her report in time for the deadline.

Suzanne didn't mention to her tutor that she had previously arranged to go to the cinema with her boyfriend so was left having to decide what to do. As you can guess Suzanne went to the cinema and ended up writing up the assignment the night before the hand-in date, by which time she had forgotten a lot of what she knew and consequently failed the assignment.

- What should Suzanne have done differently to ensure the project was successful?

---

* The **experimental hypothesis** predicts the outcome of an experiment, for example, 'the number of children suffering from asthma increases with increased numbers of house dust mites'.

* The **null hypothesis** does not predict an outcome. In other words, it states that there is no effect or relationship between variables, for example, 'there is no relationship or correlation between the number of children suffering from asthma and the increased numbers of house dust mites'.

The next step is to design a suitable experiment that will prove or disprove the hypothesis. The idea is to look at how one variable alters in response to changes in the other. With the cause-effect type of experiment the researcher deliberately alters the variable known as the **Independent Variable** (IV) that is thought to be causing the effect and measures changes in the other **Dependent Variable** (DV). The problem with this approach, particularly when applied to research on humans, is that there may be many other factors that could influence the results.

These are called **confounding** or **extraneous variables**. In the case of asthma and dust mites, diesel engine cars are extraneous variables and in the differences in learning between girls and boys, age, levels of intelligence, social class and income of parents are just a few of the confounding variables to be taken into account. Consequently, the effect of such variables has to be eradicated or minimalised. This can be achieved by attempting to control as many of the factors as possible by ensuring the subjects are of the same or similar age, the same gender, and so on. Alternatively, the experiment can be designed in such a way as to minimise the effects of such variables. This can be achieved by using one of two approaches.

✳ **Repeated measures design**: This type of study is carried out by working with one group of subjects so that each subject experiences both experimental conditions. For example, in an experiment looking at the effect of providing water during classes on children's attention span, each child experiences both conditions: having no water or water at different times.

✳ **Independent subjects design**: In this case, each experimental condition is experienced by two different groups of subjects. For example, in the effects of water on attention span, two groups of children would be chosen, one of which has water available and the other of which does not.

Theory into practice

The following experiment, presented as a step-by-step guide, will provide you with an example of how you could use the experimental method to investigate a subject of your choice. It shows how the experimental and null hypotheses are presented and the need to design a suitable test based on Piaget's theories of cognitive development and conservation.

Step 1 Initial research into problem

• Secondary research based on background reading shows you that up to the age of about six or seven years children are unable to conserve amounts or quantities, so you decide to look into the conservation of mass.

Step 2 The hypothesis

• You produce an experimental hypothesis stating that children under six years cannot conserve mass, compared to children over the age of seven. A comparable null hypothesis would state that there will be no difference in the ability of children under the age of six, compared to children over seven, to conserve mass.

Step 3 Designing the experiment

• You now need to design an experiment to test your hypothesis. This involves selecting the children to take part in your study and designing a way of testing the hypothesis.

• Selecting the children involves taking a sample (see Sampling methodology, pages 307–8) of under sixes and another group of over sevens. In selecting the children you also hope to manage or control some of the extraneous variables that could affect the outcome.

• The design of the experiment is quite easy since you could use playdough moulded into two balls of the same size with each child asked if there is the same amount of playdough in each ball. Those children who answer correctly can proceed to the next part of the test which involves rolling one of the balls into a different shape so that the child can see, and the child is again asked if each ball contains the same amount of dough. This would be repeated for every child and the results noted.

This experiment could be extended or redesigned to study the conservation of capacity (volume), length or number and could form part of a project in your placement having gained the appropriate permission (see pages 318–21).

Observations

This section provides an overview of observation as a research method and is dealt with in more detail in Unit 8.

Observation can be defined as the recording of facts or data through close examination of situations or events.

There are two principal types of observation: **participant** and **non-participant**. In the former, you, as the observer, become involved in the activities you intend to observe. In non-participant or passive observation you observe as an outsider and do not become involved. In all likelihood you will probably find yourself undertaking observations through placement activities that incorporate aspects of both types of observation. A good example would be during play activities where you might be assisting younger children while observing the interaction between individuals.

Observations can also be regarded as either structured (formal) or unstructured (informal). Structured observations are based upon pre-determined criteria that will measure the duration, frequency, type or consequences of events.

Observing a music class.

The opposite of a structured observation is the open-ended, unstructured approach. At the extreme, this method involves the researcher having some vague notion of what they wish to study but, through the observation process, gathering information that provides a focus for developing a research question or hypothesis (the opposite of what has been suggested so far). The advantage of this approach is there are no pre-conceived notions or expectations about what the outcome of the research will be. As such, a large amount of information is gathered which, over time, can begin to show patterns that can then lead to broad generalisations. Herein lies the problem with this type of research – you need time both to carry out the research and to analyse the information.

The advantages of the observation method is that it is adaptable to many situations, can reveal unexpected relationships, draws on data not available using other methods, and can be used in conjunction with the experimental method, for example, the observation of behaviour before and after the introduction of a behaviour modification programme to assess its success or otherwise.

Case studies

The case study is not a method in itself, but an approach to research that is based upon the observation of an individual, organisation or culture. Case studies take into account historical evidence and are used to study the consequences of past and present events on the subject being studied. They can provide a unique insight into an individual or organisation, but can be intrusive; therefore care must be exercised in carrying them out to ensure you have informed consent and to maintain confidentiality (see pages 318–21).

The gathering of information for a case study should initially be focused upon the collection of historical information to prepare what is called a case history. This will usually be based upon interviews with the parents, teachers or other people associated with the child being studied, followed by observations of the child in different settings depending upon their age, such as at home, playgroup or school, outdoors or in social groups. Case studies also form part of a social worker's kit in relation to child abuse and, while it would be inappropriate for you to be taking such an approach, you will find case studies very useful for finding out about the effects of disabling conditions, such as Down's syndrome, cystic fibrosis or autism, on a child's physical, emotional and social development. More in-depth studies may also consider the effects on the family or carers and the implications for health, education and social services.

Case studies are particularly useful for early years research being undertaken by students, as they allow the opportunity to study something in depth over a relatively short space of time. They are also valuable for studying individual children as they enable a picture of the child to be revealed, from which conclusions about things like their patterns of behaviour, their learning or their socialisation skills can be drawn and used to assist their development.

Sampling methodology

As well as choosing the primary research methods, some thought has to be given to the subjects who will be involved with the research. It is necessary to consider some form of subject selection process since it won't be possible to include everyone. This selection process is known as sampling. A sample is regarded as being representative of the group or population of people from which it is taken. Researchers hope to be able to draw conclusions about the population as a result of their work on the sample.

Taking the example of Piaget's experiment on conservation discussed in the experimental method (see page 305), the purpose of the experiment is to see if there is any difference in the ability to conserve between children under six and children over seven years old. Obviously, it would be impossible to carry out the study on all children, so the way forward is to observe a small number of children who can be regarded as representative of children under six and children over seven years old. This group (or groups) of children will become your **sample** and the group from which they are selected is the **population**. For your work to be truly representative of the whole population, the sample selected must be **random**. This means that everyone in the population has an equal chance of being chosen to take part in your study.

Not all forms of sampling are random and the method chosen to select your sample will for the most part be dependent on the nature of the study, how easy it is to gain access to the people you hope to do research on and how much time you have. The table on pages 308–9 lists the types of sampling methodology.

While quota and opportunity sampling are the most likely methods you will use, whichever method you employ there may be people chosen who either do not start/join in or do not finish/give up. Never pressurise people into taking part.

Assessment activity 9.2

You have been commissioned to carry out a research programme into the extent and value of childcare provision in your area. Using the research process model on page 297 and the information presented on research methods, produce a plan and design for the project, explaining your choice of methods.

CASE STUDY

Andrea and Mahesh are undertaking a survey into parental preferences and purchasing habits in choosing and buying babies' nappies. They decide that the best way to get a suitable sample of people would be to take an opportunity sample based on people buying nappies from a local supermarket. As part of their questionnaire is about whether there are any differences between the purchasing habits of males and females, their tutor suggests they try to obtain a sample size of at least 15 males and 15 females. At the supermarket they very quickly reach their target sample size for females, but find that males who are buying nappies are few and far between. By lunchtime they have only got two questionnaires completed by males so in the supermarket café they decide to cheat and complete another 13 questionnaires based on the results of the two they had already done. Having completed the survey and feeling rather pleased with themselves at having finished the work so quickly they spend the rest of the day shopping.

On submitting the assignment for marking they realise their mistake when the tutor calls them in to ask why they appear to have a varied set of results for female shoppers, but those for the males seem to be identical!

TYPE OF SAMPLE	WHAT IT IS	HOW TO DO IT
Random sampling	Subjects are selected at random from a list created by yourself or someone else, e.g. class register, telephone directory or electoral register.	Everyone in a list is allocated a number and then a random number generator is used to select a sample of appropriate size. A random number generator is like the machine that spews out the Lotto numbers every week. Most calculators have a random number generator button that will perform this task for you.
Systematic sampling	From a list, every *n*th case is selected, e.g. every fifth or tenth person.	If you wanted to choose five children from a class of 25, everyone is allocated a number from 1 to 25, then the 5th, 10th, 15th, 20th and 25th child is selected.
Stratified sampling	Stratified sampling involves taking a random or systematic sample from groups within a population.	Say you want to find out if there is any difference in educational attainment or learning ability between girls and boys. You take a random or systematic sample from within the two groups.
Quota sampling	Quota sampling is more or less the same as stratified sampling, but relies on the groups coming from a conveniently available population.	In the stratified sampling example above, the school in which you are on placement would be a convenient population from which to take your sample of boys and girls.

▶

TYPE OF SAMPLE	WHAT IT IS	HOW TO DO IT
Opportunity sampling	This is simply based on taking a sample of subjects from those readily available.	This is the most common form of sampling. The sample is selected from people you are associated with, e.g. students at your college.
Voluntary and snowball sampling	This involves people volunteering to be part of the research sample and may lead to others becoming involved through word of mouth.	You simply ask people if they wish to take part.
Purposive sampling	This is the selection of typical or interesting cases and is particularly suited to case study research or the investigation of a specific problem, e.g. a congenital disease.	The difficult part of this is finding people who wish to take part in your research. Usually the people come from those you know, but can be identified through your placement.

3 How to gather, present and examine research information

Data collection and presentation

Having determined what method or methods you will use and the sampling strategy you will employ, you need to start collecting your data/information.

It is important here to plan your activities. It would not be wise to organise a survey questionnaire in your local high street when the weather forecast is for gales or heavy showers, or to find you had forgotten your recording materials when carrying out an observation or interview.

Whichever method you use it will be necessary to carry out the following to ensure the research is undertaken in an effective and efficient manner.

1 Check your tutor is happy with what you are going to research and how you are going to do it. Make sure your tutor has vetted your questions for a questionnaire, interview or case study or the way you intend to conduct an experiment or observation.

2 Obtain written permission from anyone who may have some responsibility for your research. Verbal permission is adequate for a simple survey.

3 Organise when and where the research will be undertaken.

a Is it at college, in a school, nursery or playgroup, your local high street or shopping centre, at your own house or that of a relation or friend?

b Timing can be important. For instance, Mondays tend to be quieter in town centres, young children may be more tired in an afternoon if you are conducting an observation or experiment, parents may be in too much of a rush to get involved when they are dropping off or picking up children from playgroup, school or nursery.

4 Organise and prepare any materials or resources required.

a Photocopy adequate numbers of questionnaires, having a few for spares should any get spoilt.

b Have you got/do you need paper, pens or flip charts for you or the participants to write on?

5 If you are conducting the research in a group make sure:

a everyone knows what they are doing

b everyone follows the same procedures

c everyone uses the same style of questioning; the way a question is asked can alter its whole meaning.

Having got yourself organised you can now begin to collect the information/data. Once completed, the information collected will need to be prepared for presentation. This will be dependent upon whether it is qualitative or quantitative.

As explained on page 293, qualitative data is descriptive information and can therefore be regarded as information collected in the format of words, while quantitative data is based upon numerical information. You may find that your study produces both types of information.

Dealing with qualitative information

Qualitative information may be in the form of directly written words, such as that transcribed from an interview or written notes that summarise what occurred. Both forms may reflect some selectivity on the part of the person who provided the information or by the researcher in summarising the information. In effect, this shows that some analysis has already taken place and further analysis involves additional selection and refinement of the data.

Initially you should take time to organise or manage the data so that the analysis and refining process becomes easier. While you can do this in many different ways, here are some suggestions to assist you with the process.

* Use different coloured highlighter pens to highlight words or passages that say the same thing, that support or refute your research question and support or refute theoretical arguments.

* Add notes or comments alongside highlighted words or phrases that can help you relate the information to the research question or theory. This can include adding references to articles or books on the subject.

* Use a coding system to process information that repeats itself or could be grouped, for example, males and females, different ages.

* Use tables to categorise words or phrases in particular groups. Open questions from an interview or questionnaire may elicit a wide range of responses. However, it may be

possible to identify words or phrases that mean the same thing, allowing them to be grouped together. You need to be clear about how you have done this in presenting the data to show that you have avoided being biased.

* Cross out information that is irrelevant.

Once you have processed the information in the above fashion you can begin to select and summarise those bits of data that support or refute your research. While this might seem like doing the whole thing again it allows you to present a coherent argument in favour of or against your research question. It also enables you to tie your research into the information you will have gained by means of secondary research.

Where the information can be categorised into groups, as with words or phrases that occur frequently, then the information may be summarised as numerical values – for example, five respondents to an open-ended question on experiences of childbirth referred to the desire for giving birth naturally rather than with medical intervention, while four preferred to have medical assistance. In such cases the information can then be regarded as quantitative.

Dealing with quantitative data

Quantitative data will be based upon direct measurements – categories that have been assigned a value (such as the number of males and females or the number in specified age groups), percentages or averages. Percentages and averages can form part of the next step to summarise and refine your data in order to make it clearer. You may also have obtained data as a result of secondary research that you need to prepare for presentation. Numerical information can be termed **discrete** or **continuous**. Discrete data is usually based on whole numbers that fit into categories, such as the number of boys and girls in a class. Continuous data is any numerical value within a range and can be a fraction of a whole number, such as heights and weights.

The purpose of data presentation, be it discrete or continuous, is to make it easier to digest. This is achieved by taking the following steps.

* Organise the data into tables. Tables allow information to be set out in a structured way

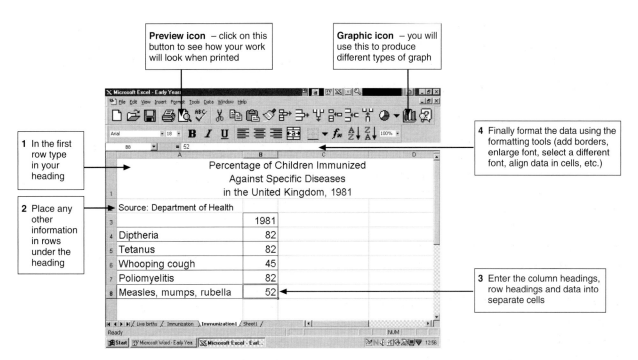

Preview icon – click on this button to see how your work will look when printed

Graphic icon – you will use this to produce different types of graph

1 In the first row type in your heading

2 Place any other information in rows under the heading

4 Finally format the data using the formatting tools (add borders, enlarge font, select a different font, align data in cells, etc.)

Percentage of Children Immunized
Against Specific Diseases
in the United Kingdom, 1981

Source: Department of Health

	1981
Diptheria	82
Tetanus	82
Whooping cough	45
Poliomyelitis	82
Measles, mumps, rubella	52

3 Enter the column headings, row headings and data into separate cells

Entering data into a spreadsheet (created in Microsoft Excel).

and can show simple trends and differences between numbers where there is not too much information.

* Use graphs to summarise more complex information that is difficult to digest from a table.

* Prepare statistics to analyse data in order to establish the proof or otherwise of the research question or hypothesis.

Modern computer programs enable you to complete all the above by entering the data into a spreadsheet program. Such programs include Microsoft Excel, Lotus 1-2-3 and more specialised statistical packages such as MINITAB, SPSS (Statistical Package for Social Science) and STATVIEW.

The figure above shows some data entered into a spreadsheet that is easily formatted into a table. Graphs can then be produced and formatted to show off your results to best effect. The difficulty is in deciding which graph is the most appropriate. The whole purpose of a graph is to make large amounts of data, or more complex data, more easily interpreted than might be possible from a table. This does not mean all data should be displayed graphically. The following information on the different types of graph is designed to help you choose which type to use given the data you have collected.

Pie charts

Pie charts are used when you have a single value for each category or set of data collected. They show each set as a percentage of the whole. The table below shows the number of three- and four-year-olds in education in England, Scotland, Wales and Northern Ireland in 2000, together with the total.

It can be seen that each bit of data is a proportion of the total. To produce the pie chart each value in the table has to be converted into a percentage of the total. Each percentage has then

REGION OF UK	ENGLAND	WALES	SCOTLAND	NORTHERN IRELAND	TOTAL
Number of 3- and 4-year-olds in early years education (thousands)	1190.6	55.6	100.7	32.9	1379.8

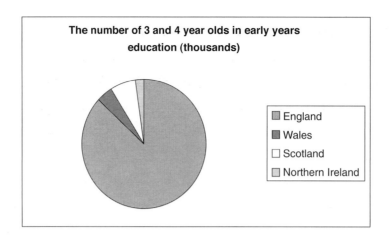

The number of 3 and 4 year olds in early years education (thousands)

- England
- Wales
- Scotland
- Northern Ireland

Pie chart.

to be converted to the number of degrees as part of the 360° that make up a circle prior to constructing the chart. The figure on page 312 shows the pie chart for this data produced using a spreadsheet program that does away with the need for changing to percentages and degrees required for producing the chart by hand.

It is important to note that if we did not know the total number of children we could not work out the proportion of each and a pie chart could not be produced. For example, it would be impossible to produce a pie chart of different types of behavioural difficulty existing in a school because we are unlikely to know the total amount of behavioural problems exhibited. You should also avoid a pie chart where there are more than six sets of data, as the information begins to look confused.

Bar charts

These can be used as an alternative to pie charts for displaying data as either percentages or whole numbers and can be used where there are too many categories to display in a pie chart. The table below gives the availability of day care places for children in England and Wales in 2001.

TYPE OF DAY CARE	THOUSANDS
Day nurseries	285
Childminders	305
Playgroups	330
Out of school clubs	152.8

The types of day care are distinct from one another, so the resulting bar chart displays each group as a separate bar or line. It does not matter how wide the bars or gaps between the bars are.

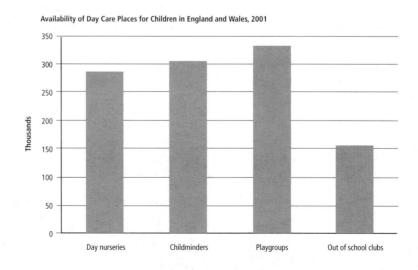

Availability of Day Care Places for Children in England and Wales, 2001

Bar chart.

Percentage of children receiving MMR vaccine in the UK from 1980–2003

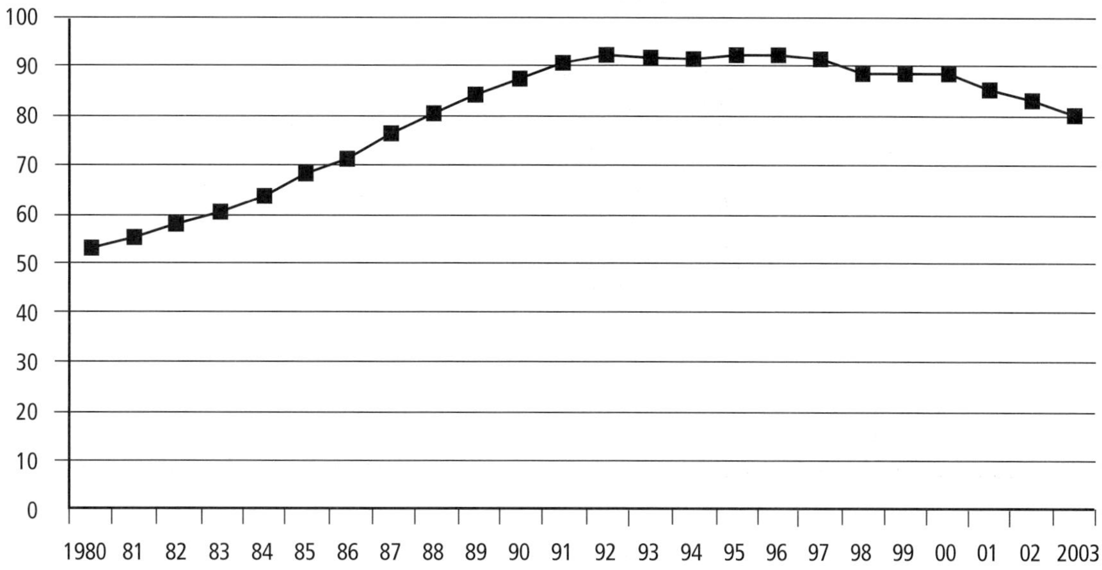

Line graph.

Line graphs

When you have a considerable amount of data, especially when it is based on measurements taken over a period of time, the line graph is the best choice. The figure above shows the change in the percentage of children receiving the MMR vaccination from 1980 to 2003. This type of chart allows several lines displaying changes to several groups of data over a period of time to be displayed. This should only be done if it is necessary to compare different groups of data. As with the pie charts, avoid having too much data, because there will be too many lines.

Sometimes students aren't sure whether to join the data points with a line or a curve. A simple rule of thumb is that if the points for the graph when joined together look like a curve, then draw a curve. If the points form a line, connect the points to form a line. If points are scattered you can draw a line of best fit (see Scattergrams, page 314).

Frequency distributions (frequency histograms and frequency polygons)

These are rather more sophisticated graphs that are often confused with bar charts. They are used exclusively with continuous data. The data is grouped into what are termed class intervals, where the number or frequency of values falling into each class is found. In order to produce a frequency distribution the raw data requires some manipulation prior to entering into a spreadsheet. This involves producing a tally chart (see below) and then entering the class intervals and frequency into a spreadsheet.

Creating the chart is easier with some programs than others, but an IT tutor should be able to help you through any difficulties.

If you wish to compare frequency distributions of two or more sets of data it is preferable to present the frequency distribution as a frequency polygon rather than a frequency histogram. A frequency polygon is simply a line joining the tops of each bar at their mid-points, though it is not necessary to do

Live birth weights of babies born to a random sample of 128 women

Weights (g)	Tally	Frequency
1000–1499		0
1500–1999		0
2000–2499	||	2
2500–2999	卌 卌 ||||	14
3000–3499	卌 卌 卌 卌 卌 卌 卌 卌 卌 ||	47
3500–3999	卌 卌 卌 卌 卌 卌 卌 卌 卌	45
4000+	卌 卌 卌 卌	20

Tally chart.

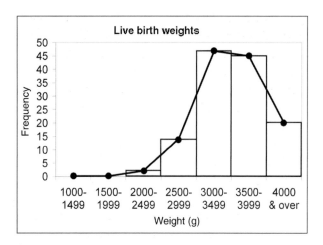

Live birth weights

Frequency distribution.

this when using a spreadsheet as you can simply follow the same instructions as for a line graph.

Scattergrams

Scattergrams are used specifically for displaying the results of correlational studies – data collected to compare one variable with another. It simply involves plotting the results of one variable against the other as a series of markers. The pattern created by the marks once the scattergram has been completed can indicate whether or not there is a relationship between the two variables. If it appears possible to draw a straight line through the markers then a relationship exists. In a spreadsheet the computer can draw in the line.

This trend line describes either a positive or negative correlation. If positive it shows that as one variable increases so does the other, for example, as the social class increases, so the instances of breastfeeding increase. If negative, as one variable increases the other decreases, for example, the increase in media attention given to supposed problems associated with vaccination correlates with a decrease in the number of children being vaccinated.

However, just because a correlation exists does not mean that a change in one variable results in a change in the other. For example, did you know that the amount of bananas imported into the UK after World War II correlated with an increase in the number of pregnant women? It is possible that the change in both variables is due to some other unrelated factor. Another example is the rise in asthma among children during the 1980s and 1990s. It has been found that this increase correlates well with the increasing use of diesel engine motor vehicles. Researchers proposed that this was due to the size of soot particles in vehicle exhausts polluting the air and irritating the lungs. However, there is also a correlation between the increase in rates of asthma and the use of double glazing, central heating and fitted carpets in homes, which encourage the increase in numbers of dust mites that also irritate the lungs. Consequently, don't be tempted to draw a

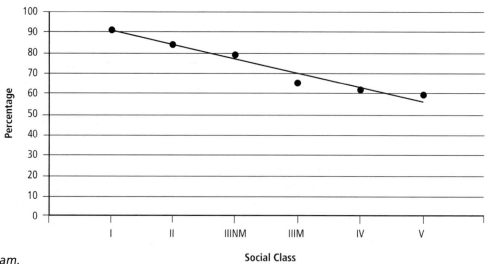

Scattergram to show the relationship between the percentage of mothers who breastfeed and the social class of the partner

Scattergram.

conclusion about a correlation unless it is at least backed up by the research of others – your secondary sources.

Mean, median, mode and standard deviation

Apart from graphs, numerical data can also be simplified and made more meaningful by determining the **mode**, **median** or **mean**. These terms describe different forms of averages known as measures of **central tendency**. The mode is the most frequently occurring number in a set. The median is simply the middle value in a set of results that have been arranged in ascending or descending order. The mean, as you are probably already aware, is calculated from adding up all the values and dividing by the number of values to give the 'average'.

The median is used where the data is discrete and is often used in conjunction with the **range** (the difference between the lowest and highest values in a set of data) to summarise the data. The range gives a measure of the spread of the data. While this is satisfactory for many circumstances, the range will include extreme values and, as a consequence, may not be representative of the majority of the data. For example, school SATS results may include one or two very high or very low scores, with the majority clustered around the median. As a result, it may be more appropriate to use the **interquartile range** covering the middle 50 per cent of the data.

Think it over...

The following questions based on the graphs and charts above ask you to extract relevant information from your tables and charts and draw relevant conclusions, skills required for the discussion and analysis section of research.

1 With reference to the pie chart, what is the percentage of three- to four-year-olds in Scotland as a proportion of children in the UK?

2 With reference to the bar chart:

   a which is the most widely available type of day care provision in England and Wales?

   b why do you think there are fewer day care places for under-five-year-olds in out of school clubs?

3 With reference to the line graph, suggest why there was a decrease in MMR vaccination rates between 1997 and 2003.

4 With reference to the frequency distribution chart, why aren't there any gaps between the bars of the graph?

5 With reference to the scattergram, a line of best fit has been added to show that there is a negative correlation between the proportion of mothers who breastfeed and partners' social class. How would the scattergram appear if:

   a the correlation was positive?

   b there was no correlation?

Assessment activity 9.3

The following are examples of activities you could complete to demonstrate that you can:

- carry out a basic research task using one method of data collection and present the results
- draw conclusions based on the results.

These are just ideas and you or your tutors may come up with something more appropriate.

- Investigate any changes in the numbers of children attending local playgroups, nurseries and out of school clubs.
- Carry out a survey on parents to find out what time children of different ages go to bed.
- Carry out a survey of parents to find out how much, when and what they read to their children.
- Research the cost of using disposable nappies compared to non-disposable ones.
- Carry out case studies of experiences of childbirth.
- Carry out Piaget's study into conservation on groups of children of different ages.

To be considered for a higher grade you will also need to:

- evaluate the research task and make recommendations for improvements
- use the information in section 4 to help you with this part of the activity.

The median and range, or interquartile range, are useful when working with discrete data but where the data is continuous the mean and another statistic, the **standard deviation**, tend to be of more value. This is because the standard deviation, while giving an idea of how much the data is spread either side of the mean also excludes extreme values and, as a result, is more representative of the majority of subjects in the sample. While it is difficult to generalise, the larger the standard deviation, the greater the spread of the data about the mean.

The standard deviation is rather more difficult to calculate than the mean. However, scientific calculators that have statistical functions can determine the standard deviation at the same time as the mean. Alternatively, the standard deviation can be obtained from data entered into a spreadsheet.

The standard deviation and mean can be used to determine whether two sets of data, such as reading test results before and after an intensive reading programme, are **significantly different** from one another. The early years syllabus does not expect you to take your data analysis this far. However, if you would like to extend your knowledge of statistical analysis, the statistics books in the references and further reading section will show you how this can be done, though it might be preferable to seek the help of a tutor who would be able to offer you more structured guidance.

Working towards your Early Years Project (Unit 20)
Discussing and evaluating your results

This is perhaps the most skilled part of the research process and as far as any research project you complete is concerned, tutors use what is produced in this part of a report to confirm decisions regarding the award of higher grades.

It is best to start the discussion with a review of the problem you chose to investigate together with the research question or hypothesis. This sets the scene and also helps to focus your mind on the purpose of the data collection and presentation.

You should then look at your results and summarise what they show. The idea is to highlight those features of your results that are important to your research question or hypothesis – in other words, whether the information supports or refutes the research question or hypothesis. Preparing your report for a presentation is a good way of summarising and picking out the most important features.

In the same way, you need to compare your findings with the information obtained through secondary research. Does this information support your study or contradict it? Differences between your work and those of others may reflect real differences due to the local nature of your research or it may highlight weaknesses in your study. Alternatively, the results may reflect something you hadn't thought of that could lead to the need for further research. In this case, you should attempt to suggest what that research could be.

If your results fail to support your research question or hypothesis, do not be tempted to manipulate them; instead draw on the information provided in the next two sections (Use and misuse of statistics and Validity and reliability) to evaluate the presentation of your data and the research and sampling methods used.

A further way of preparing your discussion is to talk to people who have had some involvement with your research and see if they agree with your conclusions, including your tutor. You could also sit down with someone else on the course and tell them what you have found out. If it makes sense to them then it should make sense on paper. You can do the same for them.

If your research was part of a group project, even better. While you will probably be expected to submit individual reports you can discuss your findings and help each other to draw relevant conclusions, and evaluate and justify your approach to the topic.

If your research was based on interviews with just a few people or a case study, then it can be appropriate to discuss your findings with them. Not only can they make suggestions or identify things you have missed, but it also keeps them fully informed in line with the ethical requirements for informed consent.

4 Implications and ethical issues in using research

Use and misuse of statistics

Statistics provide a valuable tool for presenting and interpreting information so that the results of research are more readily understood. The misuse of statistics can arise as a result of problems with different aspects of the research process and not just the presentation and interpretation of the results. Such difficulties include the following.

* **Lack of clarity in the research question or hypothesis**. If you are unclear about the focus of your study it can lead to selecting the wrong methods and consequently the production of data or information that is difficult to explain. It may also lead to a misreading of the results in trying to make them fit the hypothesis or research question. For example, you may have chosen to observe the behaviour of young children in a playgroup, but not clarified what sort of behaviour it is you are interested in. In all likelihood you will observe a wide range of behaviours and frequency of such behaviours that may produce too much information to organise and simplify with ease.

* **Use of inappropriate methods**. The methods used must allow you to gather information that will support the research question or hypothesis. This means choosing methods that enable you to find out what you want to and that it is reproducible (see Validity and reliability on page 318).

* **Unrepresentative sampling**. Remember that the purpose of sampling is to use people in your research who are representative of the whole population, which relies on obtaining a random sample of subjects. As discussed earlier, this is no easy task and there is often bias within a sample, whatever the sampling method chosen. In particular, the most common sampling method used by students is the opportunity sample. As the people chosen are probably following some further education course like you then the sample is biased towards students and misses out on all other people.

* **Inaccurate recording of information (sloppy techniques)**. Failure to construct a questionnaire with care or to undertake a trial can result in questions being misunderstood and answers being ambiguous. If you are administering a questionnaire as a group, failure for everyone to follow the same procedure can give misleading results. The results of an interview that you haven't prepared for in terms of questioning or recording may bear little resemblance to the actual interview itself and is more open to being biased towards your own views. A poorly prepared observation sheet or failure to conduct an experiment with care and precision will give inaccurate results.

* **Inappropriate presentation or misinterpretation of data**. The following example serves to show how results can be presented in such a way as to change their meaning or to give misleading information. The figure below compares the attainment of children at Key Stage 1 in two schools, A and B. You can see that school A appears to be far more effective at enabling the children to reach Level 2 of Key Stage 1 than school B. However, what you don't know is that school A is an independent school and school B has three times as many pupils as school A, and the children entering the schools come from different social backgrounds.

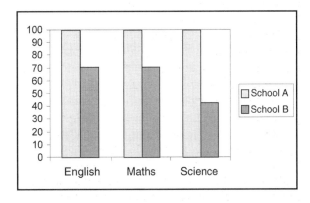

Percentage of children at National Curriculum Level 2 (Key Stage 1) in two schools.

How to avoid misusing information

- Be clear about what you are trying to find out: ensure your research is focused.
- Be sure to use the most appropriate method or methods for your study.
- Try to ensure your sample is representative of the population in which you are interested.
- Don't try to use statistical methods in presenting your data to make it fit your research question when it doesn't – be honest. In using graphs, make sure they are accurate.
- Don't misinterpret the data – don't say something is true when it blatantly isn't or say the results don't show anything when they do. Look carefully at the data and use all the results.
- Don't try to draw conclusions that don't exist. These can become discussion points for further research.

Validity and reliability

These terms have already been mentioned with respect to one or two of the different primary research methods and they need to be taken into account when selecting the most appropriate method to use.

* **Validity** is about whether the results you obtain using a particular method tell you what you want to find out.

* **Reliability** is to do with the method being reproducible – if someone else repeated your work would they get the same answers?

A method may be reliable but not necessarily valid. While some methods are more reliable and others more valid, it is probably true that the level of reliability and validity is dependent upon how carefully the research has been undertaken. This surprisingly comes down to the conscientiousness of the researcher! One way of improving reliability and validity is to use more than one method in your study and you will find in reading many research reports that the researchers draw on a range of methods.

Ethical issues

Before undertaking any primary research that involves questioning, experimenting or observing people, the ethics of conducting the research and any issues of confidentiality that may be raised must be considered.

Ethics has been an issue in research ever since World War II when the Nazis were found to have submitted individuals to horrific experiments that resulted in death, disfigurement or psychological trauma. The Nuremberg trials that followed the war made researchers aware of the dangers of carrying out experiments on non-consenting subjects and it led to the development of a code of ethics for working with human subjects. Even so, there have been many cases of research carried out since the war that have subjected people to physical and/or psychological pain.

One famous experiment on obedience carried out during the 1960s by Stanley Millgram involved allowing participants to administer electric shocks to other people they could see. Unknown to the participants, the subjects being electrocuted were actors faking increasing discomfort as shocks were applied. Participants were told that they had to continue applying shocks of increasing voltage even though the person being 'electrocuted' appeared to be in obvious pain. While the experiment proved that people would follow 'orders' irrespective of the suffering they may cause, the justification for such deception of participants was regarded as immoral. Not only had Millgram deceived the participants, but had attempted to alter their behaviour and used secret recordings to observe them.

While such dishonesty may be unethical, many drug trials rely on deception to determine the effects of new drugs. Such trials, known as blind trials, involve two groups of volunteers, one of which receives the drug and the other a placebo (normally a simple sugar pill). This experimental type of research works on the basis that any effect of the drug will only be seen in the group taking the drug as neither group knows whether they are taking the placebo or the drug under test. It has been found that some drugs have had as much effect on the placebo group as the test group!

Anyone participating in research is now covered by the United Nations Declaration of Human Rights, which is supported by European legislation enshrined in the EU Directive on Data Protection (1995) and nationally by the Data Protection Act (1998). Organisations conducting research implement a code of ethics to ensure these rights are protected. Such codes include the need for participants to give their informed consent. This is particularly important where research involves vulnerable groups such as children and should also take into account parental/guardian consent. This means that all involved are fully informed as to the nature and purpose of the research, what will happen and how and where it will take place. It also gives participants or their guardians the right to refuse or to withdraw at any time and to anonymity. Many researchers also include the requirement to debrief those involved about the nature of the research and why any deception may have been necessary.

As far as any research you undertake is concerned, you would be unwise to set about a project if it could cause distress to the people involved either as a result of the methods chosen, the sampling process or the reporting of the work. As such, you should follow any policies and procedures that the organisation where you are studying has in place for students undertaking research. Such information should be available from your tutor. Alternatively, or in addition, the following code of practice can be followed to ensure your research meets basic ethical codes.

* Gain permission from appropriate authorities (employers, teachers, tutors) to conduct the research. This is important, as you may need the support of such people if any problems occur. It is generally recognised that research undertaken at this level will be underwritten by your tutors and/or workplace supervisors, due to your inexperience.

* Ask the subjects or, where children are concerned, their parents or guardians, if they wish to take part.

KEY ISSUES

The publication of research and role of the media

The vast majority of published research is only read by those with an interest in the work – the commissioners of the research, other researchers and those who may be affected or influenced by the research findings. The media will report research findings if they regard it as being in the public interest. The effect of media interest can be profound as, for example, in the case of the MMR vaccine and autism.

Referring back to the chart showing the change in vaccination rates against measles between 1980 and 2003 (page 313) you will see that there was a steady increase in the percentage of children being vaccinated between 1980 and 1996 from 53 per cent to 92 per cent.

In 1998, research was published that suggested a link between the MMR (measles, mumps and rubella) vaccine and increasing rates of autism in the population. This was widely reported in the media, despite it being the only research at the time suggesting such a link. As a consequence, vaccination rates fell from a peak of 92 per cent and continued to fall to around 80 per cent in 2003, despite evidence showing there was no risk to children's health and also other researchers questioning the validity and reliability of the original work.

Research has continued to be published confirming that there is no link between MMR and autism. The media has reported the results of this research and the government, National Health Service and other public and voluntary groups have sought to persuade the public of the safety and benefits of vaccination. However, the subject continues to be shrouded in controversy, as there are many organisations that still support the findings of the original research and seek to influence the public in spite of research that suggests other factors may be involved in autism and its increase among children.

* As a consequence of the first two points, be in a position to explain your research.

* Be able to reassure participants, or again their guardians, about the measures taken to maintain confidentiality.

From 1946 to 1956, 19 boys with learning difficulties at the State Residential School, Fernald, Massachusetts (USA) were fed radioactive iron and calcium in their breakfast cereal. The goal of the study was to gather information about nutrition and metabolism. The parents, who consented to the study, were not told about the radioactive substances.

This research provides an interesting topic for group discussion as it raises a number of issues that should be taken into account when planning any research project that involves vulnerable groups. Alternatively, ask yourself the following questions about this research.

- Is research dating back some 50 years relevant in modern society?

- Would it have been more ethical for the research to be carried out on children without learning difficulties?

- Should the research have been conducted if the parents had been fully informed?

- If it were known that the radioactive iron and calcium were harmless would this have made any difference to whether the research was carried out?

Confidentiality

With regard to confidentiality, you must ensure the anonymity of all participants. This involves the following.

✳ Change the names of subjects, particularly when using interview, observation, experimental and case study methods where the sample size might be small. False names, letters or numbers can be used instead, e.g. Fred, Miss X, subject 9.

✳ Avoid descriptive language that could give away a person's identity as can occur in case studies – 'Mrs Y, the leader of the local Labour party', would lead to immediate identification. You need to think whether such information is important to your study and if so, how else it can be worded, e.g. subject 8, a local politician.

✳ In conducting taped interviews, take care when transcribing the taped interview into a written format so as to avoid identifying the interviewee. It is important to recognise that the interviewee has the right to request that all or part of the tape is erased or destroyed at any time, and in any case the tapes should be erased once you have completed your work.

Another issue concerns what you may find out as part of your research. When gaining permission to conduct the research you need to be clear about what you must do in the event of being told or finding out something of a confidential nature. If you find out or suspect that abuse has taken place, you need to know what your responsibilities are and to whom you should refer. These responsibilities should also form part of the information given to potential participants before the research is carried out.

Authenticity (plagiarism and summarising information)

When a piece of research is made available to the commissioners and/or public it is expected that the person or persons undertaking such research have been honest and open about the research undertaken, information and data gathered and its presentation. The misuse of any secondary information is generally a result of plagiarism – the direct copying of someone else's work, which is against copyright law. However, copyright does allow for other work to be used for research purposes, as long as the original author is acknowledged. The use of secondary information means that the researcher, and this includes anything you produce for assessment that uses other peoples work, must produce a summary of the original. A direct quote can be made where the information contains specific facts or data relating to the study, but the information should be enclosed within quotation marks. Whether the information has been summarised or a direct quote used, a reference or acknowledgement to the author or producer of the information and its source must be included (see Producing a bibliography on page 323).

With the advent of computers and the internet, plagiarism has become a problem where students cut and paste large chunks of material for inclusion in their work. It has been known for students to copy information from publications and not even take the trouble to remove the original author's name! Teachers and lecturers are becoming more adept at spotting such transgressions and students may be asked to do the whole assignment again.

Assessment activity 9.4

Conduct your own literature search to identify a current piece of research from which you can identify the purpose, methods used, any ethical issues and its effects on policy and practice in the early years sector. To be considered for higher grades you will need to analyse the purpose and role of the research, consider how the results of the research could be misused and evaluate its impact on current practice.

CASE STUDY

Exemplar research

The assessment for this unit includes the ability to identify an exemplar piece of research and to look at its purpose, the methodology used, any ethical issues involved and its effects on policy and practice.

To give you an idea of how this might be approached, an early years tutor asked her students to investigate a current piece of major research called EPPE (the Effective Provision of Pre-School Education) using the Sure Start website (www.surestart.gov.uk). In the research page of the Sure Start website they found a reference to EPPE and were able to access the full report. In addition they were also able to access other websites relating to the research via the Department for Education and Skills (www.dfes.gov.uk/research) and University of London Institute of Education (www.ioe.ac.uk). The information was very detailed and they did not understand all the terminology used but, by going back to their tutor, they were able to

get such terms explained. As a result, they identified the purpose of the research, the methods used and its effects on policy and practice, though it took a little more determination to gather information on ethical issues, as these followed expected practice and were therefore not mentioned in any detail within the research papers.

In many respects you have the freedom to put forward different points of view when carrying out the analysis, but in doing so you should back up your arguments with evidence from other research. For example, Sweden does not start formal education until the age of seven.

As the students in the case study found, the ethical implications were more difficult to explain so you may need to draw on information within the Implications and ethical issues section on pages 317–21 to discuss what the researchers would have been expected to do to ensure the research was conducted ethically.

The following is an extract of summary information about EPPE to introduce you to the research programme.

The EPPE project is a longitudinal study of a national sample of young children's development (intellectual and social/behavioural) between the ages of 3 and 7 years. The project was set up to investigate the effects of the child's home background and pre-school education from the age of 1 to 7 years, and the researchers collected a wide range of information on over 3000 children, their parents, their home environments and the pre-school settings they attended, using a range of methods (child assessments, interviews, case studies and observations). 141 pre-school settings drawn from local authority day nurseries, integrated centres, playgroups, private day nurseries, maintained nursery schools and maintained nursery classes were investigated. Centres were selected from five regions that were chosen to cover a range of socio-economic and geographical areas including rural, metropolitan, shire county and inner-city. The regions were selected to include ethnically diverse and socio-economically disadvantaged communities. A sample of children who had no or minimal pre-school experience was recruited to the study at entry to school for comparison with the pre-school group.

EPPE demonstrated the positive effects of high quality provision on children's intellectual and social/behavioural development.

Use the website links in the case study to find research papers on EPPE. Use these to gather more detailed information on the purpose, methods used and effects on practice than given in the case study. From the information gathered you should be able to explain or analyse why the research was carried out and its impact on current practice. Here are just a few things that could be considered in conducting this analysis.

- Who commissioned the research?
- Do the commissioners of the research want confirmation that more formal pre-school education works? Is this because more formal pre-school education would result in:
  - better educational attainment throughout school
  - better behaviour in school
  - better behaviour in the home
  - improved social skills
  - a standardised programme of pre-school education, whatever the setting
  - children better able to integrate when they enter primary school?
- Would the above always be regarded as a positive outcome? Some people, organisations and governments believe that young children develop intellectually, socially and emotionally more effectively in a less formal environment.
- What would be the effect of the research concluding that more formal pre-school education was ineffective? For example:
  - a return to less formal under-five provision
  - closing down of pre-school centres in schools
  - the reverse of the outcomes above.

Working towards your Early Years Project (Unit 20)
Producing a bibliography

In producing your work you will hopefully have used a range of books, articles and other sources. Since you have summarised or extracted sections from such material for inclusion in your work, it is essential that you acknowledge the producers or providers of this information. Consequently, you need to produce a reference section, bibliography and/or acknowledgements section. While these words can be used to mean the same thing they are used here as follows.

- A reference section is generally used for acknowledging information taken from the original author(s) work.

- A bibliography, or further reading list, is used for information extracted from more general textbooks where the author has drawn a wide range of material together from different sources.

- An acknowledgements section is to identify and thank those people who have given help or support or have contributed directly to your work by being a subject (remember not to identify anyone for whom confidentiality was promised).

You do not have to use this system and your tutors may prefer everything to be acknowledged within a bibliography only. However, whatever form you use, adopt a style or format for identifying information and material used.

One of the most commonly accepted formats for referencing is known as the Harvard system. Within the body of your report any book, periodical, newspaper report and so on used must identify the author, the year of publication and the page number(s) referred to. For example:

> Observation is particularly suited to the study of phenomena such as non-verbal communication and tactile skills (Lynes, 1999, p. 315).

If the author's surname is part of the sentence, then the date and page number(s) are sufficient.

> Lynes (1999, p. 315) suggested that observation is useful for studying non-verbal communication and tactile skills.

If reference to a table or diagram is made, then the following is appropriate.

> Analysis of the results (White, 1995, p. 13, table 2)...

> White (1995, p. 13, table 2) in his results showed that many single mothers...

If you have copied or used part of a table or diagram from another source this must also be acknowledged. This is normally done by identifying the author of the work and year of publication after the title of the table or diagram.

At the end of the assignment the information sources referred to are listed alphabetically by surname. The format depends on the type of resource referred to and is best shown by example as follows. For textbooks use the following.

> Gibb, C and Randall, P (1989), *Professionals and Parents, Managing Children's Behaviour*, Basingstoke, Macmillan Education.

For articles from newspapers, periodicals or magazines use this method, with the article title in quotes and the periodical name in italics.

> Lynes, D (1999), 'Using observation for data collection', *Professional Nurse*, Vol. 14, No. 5, pp. 315–17.

Websites should be referenced in the same way as above, with the author, year of publication, title and the website address, rather than the publisher (unless this is known). You should also include the date on which you assessed the site. Sometimes it may not be clear who the author is, in which case use the name of the organisation. For example:

> BBC News (2005), 'No link' between MMR and autism,
> http://news.bbc.co.uk/l/hi/health/4311613.stm.

Seek advice from tutors with regards to other types of resource you may have referenced.

Some of this may appear rather confusing, but once you have got used to the idea you will find that it helps in organising and presenting your work in a logical manner.

Working towards your Early Years Project (Unit 20)

Checklist for carrying out a research project

1 Find out how much time you have got. You may have been given a deadline that only allows you a few weeks or even days to complete the work. Alternatively, you may be looking at a whole year. Whichever it is, you will need to plan your time effectively to ensure the work is completed on time and is of the standard that you feel justifies the grade you are aiming for. Don't leave things to the last minute, particularly with a longer-term project.

2 Select a topic. If you only have a short period of time you need to select a topic that does not involve more complex secondary or primary research. For instance, it would be no good choosing a topic that involves obtaining information from obscure sources or is reliant on postal questionnaires. You may not get the information back in time, if at all. The following may assist in generating ideas for topics.

Your tutor may be able to get you started on suggesting topics that previous students have investigated, but you and your fellow students could try a brainstorming session. This is a popular technique used by businesses and organisations to generate ideas. It is sometimes referred to as 'thought showering', felt by some to be more politically correct that brainstorming.

You need a flipchart and marker pens. Your tutor may have given you a broad idea to think about or left things very open. As a class, or in smaller groups of four to seven, agree who will write down the ideas (they need to be written large so everyone can see). The group should then start to think about what they could research and any idea that is suggested should be written down, no matter how silly it may seem. Sometimes it can be difficult to get started, but ideas will soon flow easily. From the list, choose two or three topics that sound interesting. Either as a whole class or in groups, discuss the ideas to see if they are realistic (in the time allocated, with the resources available, considering relevant ethical or confidentiality issues, etc.) and what research methods could be used. Your tutor will help you with this process. This should result in a research idea that you can begin to consider in more detail.

Another starting point is the course syllabus, which should be available through your tutor. The syllabus identifies the outcomes and assessment evidence requirements for the units you will be studying. By reading through these it should be possible to identify a topic that could be based upon a research project. Indeed, your tutor may give some direction or set specific assignments to ensure you meet such outcomes and assessment criteria. A number of units, both core and optional, refer to research projects as possible means of assessment.

Talking to other people can be invaluable for helping to generate ideas and may include any of the following.

Family – by virtue of being your parents/guardians, your mother and father will have a wealth of knowledge about bringing up children and, apart from seeing how difficult a job it is, you may be able to gain information from them that will enable you to focus in on your study. Other relations may also be of assistance, not only as potential parents themselves, but possibly as someone who works with or on behalf of children.

Employers and workplace supervisors – if you work in a 'caring' organisation, either voluntarily, through an organised placement or as an employee, you could ask for advice and may find that they would like you to carry out some research for them. As you will be expected to carry out observations on children through placements, these may become part of your research project.

3 Start reading around your chosen topic to help in focusing on your study in order to produce a research question or hypothesis. A research question simply states the question or questions you want your research to answer.

A hypothesis is a special type of research question that tends to be used in surveys or experiments. It proposes the existence of a relationship between variables or factors and tends to suggest how the relationship will be tested (see The experimental method, pages 303–5). Students often find identifying a research question one of the more difficult parts of the whole process and consequently try to opt out of making a decision about this until later. This is an error that results in students being unclear about the focus of their study. Time needs to be given to what you hope to find out. This part of the research process will involve you in doing some secondary research, reading around the topic, looking at recent research and talking to others. In this way you will begin to find out more about the area you are going to study that can then lead to the selection of a specific topic.

One way to focus on a subject for the purpose of identifying a suitable research question or hypothesis is to produce a spider diagram to explore the different issues relating to a chosen subject.

4 Select the primary research and sampling methods appropriate to your study. With a short-term project, choose just one or two research methods that will provide information quickly, whereas a longer-term study should involve a variety of methods and allow a more in-depth investigation to be carried out.

5 Identify what resources you will require to complete your study. Do you need specialist equipment? Where will you get such equipment? Will there be a charge and how long can you have it for?

6 Produce an action plan that identifies your research topic, research question or hypothesis, resources required for the primary research and secondary resources, as well as an approximate time allocation for each section. Submit this to your tutor for approval.

7 Conduct a pilot study of any survey you have planned. You may be quite happy with a questionnaire you have produced, but when it comes to people answering the questions, problems can arise over the meaning of words or misinterpreting of questions. Consequently, it is advisable to practise using your questionnaire on a small number of people to see whether questions need modifying to make them clearer. This is called a pilot or trial study, the results of which may still be used if you have not had to make any changes.

8 Continue reading around the subject, making notes that provide background information and that support or refute your research question or hypothesis.

9 Draft an introduction and have it checked by your tutor.

10 Carry out the primary research. Be prepared to answer questions people may have about your research and, if they were actively involved, remember to thank them at the end.

11 Collate and present the results.

12 Analyse, discuss and evaluate your research.

13 Make recommendations for practitioners/users/policy makers.

14 Relax!

Your research as a presentation

You may be asked to present the findings of your research to your peer group or others as part of the assessment process. You will not be alone in dreading this part of the project and being unsure about what you should put into the presentation and what to leave out. A good way of tackling this is to produce an abstract or summary of your work. This is a paragraph or two of 100–200 words that states:

- the purpose of your research, the research question or hypothesis
- the methods chosen
- the most significant results that either support or refute your research

- the conclusions drawn, together with any implications and suggestions for further work.

The abstract can then be the basis for your presentation, which can be expanded on with reference to:

- aspects of secondary research
- interesting parts of the data collection process (for example, the interview that went wrong)
- tables, diagrams and charts that display quantitative findings to good effect
- acknowledgement of the people who took part.

END-OF-UNIT TEST

1 Explain what is meant by the terms primary, secondary, qualitative, quantitative, cross-sectional and longitudinal research.

2 Identify three forms of secondary information.

3 Identify the main primary research methods.

4 In surveys, how would you differentiate between a questionnaire and an interview?

5 What are the differences between a structured, semi-structured and unstructured interview?

6 In preparing a questionnaire, in what order would you place the following types of questions (i) open ended; (ii) closed; (iii) scale; (iv) category?

7 Produce an experimental and null hypothesis for the observation that girls appear to achieve academically more than boys.

8 Read the following extract of a case study on an autistic child and undertake secondary research to see how the child's symptoms match up with what would be expected.

The child was developing like a 'normal' child until she reached the age of two and a half. Soon after she reached this age she began to isolate herself from others, stopped talking and feeding herself, and started to hit her head and bite her hand. She would also avoid eye contact and have 'crying' episodes for long periods of time, then she would stop and laugh for no reason. She began to spend a lot of time sitting looking out of the window at clouds and trees as they moved.

9 Select the most appropriate graph/chart to present the following category of data.

   a The number of children being immunised against measles, mumps and rubella (MMR) between 1985 and 2000.

   b The number of children achieving different attainment Levels for Key Stage 1 in English, Mathematics and Science in a school for the year 2000.

   c The weight of babies at birth.

10 Select the most appropriate measure of central tendency for the following:

   a The number of parent helpers attending a school on each day of the week over a year.

   b The amount of time children spend watching television.

11 Decide whether the mean, median or mode would best summarise the following data.

Twenty-four children in a class were asked how many books they had read in the past month. The raw results were as follows.

Child	1	2	3	4	5	6	7	8	9	10	11	12	13	14	15	16	17	18	19	20	21	22	23	24
Number of books	3	5	2	6	4	4	5	1	1	3	4	7	6	6	4	3	1	2	6	8	5	6	2	4

What do the results suggest?

References and further reading

Bell, J (1993), *Doing Your Research Project* (2nd edition), Buckingham: Open University Press

Blaxter, L, Hughes, C and Tight, M (1996), *How to Research*, Buckingham: Open University Press

Corston, R (1992), *Research Methods and Statistics in the Social Sciences*, Durham: Casder

Davenport, G (1988), *An Introduction to Child Development*, London: Unwin

Hucker, K (2001), *Research Methods in Health, Care and Early Years*, Oxford: Heinemann

Hyman Marshall, P (1997), *Research Methods: How to design and conduct a successful project*, Plymouth: How to Books

MacNaughton, G et al (2001), *Doing Early Childhood Research: Theory and practice*, Maidenhead: Open University Press

Owen, D and Davis, M (1991), *Help With Your Project: A guide for students of health care*, London: Edward Arnold

Peterson, R (2000), *Constructing Effective Questionnaires*, London: Sage

Robert-Holmes, G (2005), *Doing Your Early Years Research Project: A step by step guide*, London: Paul Chapman

Answers

Answers for Think it over, page 301

* Category = question 1, rank = question 6 and scale = question 7.

* Combine all the questions together as a small table so respondents can tick a box or put relevant information into it.

* Question 3 does not allow respondents to say if they breast and bottle fed babies. Question 4 does not include bottle-fed babies. Question 6 contains a negative statement about breast feeding and there is an imbalance between the number of statements for breast and bottle feeding.

* Why would you need to know about different types of infant formula when the survey is about breast versus bottle-feeding?

Answers for Think it over, page 315

1 7.3%

2 **a** Playgroups.

   b Out-of-school provision is not offered by all schools.

3 Parents were concerned about a suggested link between the MMR vaccine and autism (see Key Issues – The publication of research and role of the media, page 319).

4 Unlike the bar chart, which is used when you have a single value for each category or set of data collected, this type of chart is used exclusively with continuous data. There are no gaps between the bars because the class intervals flow on from each other.

5 **a** The data points would result in a line of best fit that showed that one set of data increased as the other increased.

   b The data points would be randomly scattered and not suggest the existence of a line of best fit.

Child health

Introduction

This unit ensures that all early years practitioners gain a knowledge and understanding of the ways to promote, maintain and preserve children's health. Promoting health and preventing ill health are key aspects of an early years practitioner's role, and an understanding of the government's key themes and targets is essential to these aspects. It is important to be able to recognise signs and symptoms of ill health in a child, and know to whom these changes should be reported. It is also necessary to develop the skills required to work with children and their families, and to understand the pressures that ill health can bring to the whole family.

How you will be assessed

This unit is assessed internally.

1 The need for, and approaches to, health promotion

What is health?

To be healthy means very different things to different people, but it is generally associated with physical health rather than aspects of health such as mental or social health. The World Health Organisation (WHO) describes health as 'a state of complete physical, mental and social well-being and not merely the absence of disease or infirmity'. While some people think that being healthy relates to the ability to resist infection and to cope with life's stresses and strains, others might feel that good health is a person's ability to cope physically, emotionally and mentally with day-to-day life. To some people, however, good health might mean the absence of any illness and simply 'feeling well'.

Types of health

Although the World Health Organisation's definition only includes physical, mental and social health, health is generally considered to also include emotional, spiritual and environmental/community/societal health – in other words, a more holistic approach to health.

Health education and health promotion

Health education focuses on the prevention of illness in an individual, whereas health promotion, according to the World Health Organisation, is 'the process of enabling people to increase their control over, and improve, their health'. It emphasises being healthy and improving health rather than focusing on illness. It also incorporates wider community issues, such as anti-smoking campaigns and employee health.

Approaches to health education

There are many approaches to the health education issue which can be categorised in the following ways: primary, secondary and tertiary health education, and individual, community (or group), and organisational (including within education settings) health education.

Primary prevention

This aims to improve the quality of health by giving people information and advice on staying healthy. Most health education aimed at children falls within this category and includes care of the teeth, personal safety, road safety and healthy eating. It also aims to prevent ill health through, for example, the immunisation programme.

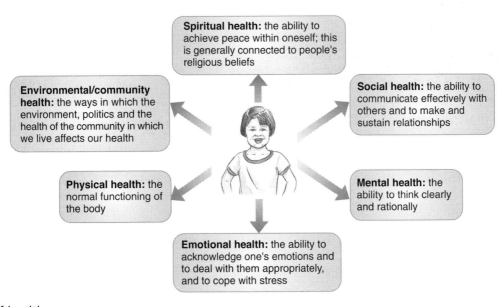

Types of health.

Secondary prevention

This aims at early detection and treatment of conditions in order to prevent further complications or worsening of the condition. It can also involve educating people to change their behaviour in order to restore good health. This could include teaching obese children about their diet and encouraging exercise through sports schemes.

Tertiary prevention

This aims to reduce the impact of a chronic illness or disability by teaching children how to reach their maximum potential. This could involve the use of hearing aids in a child with hearing difficulties, or specially adapted wheelchairs.

Individual health education

Most health education will be aimed at individuals and their particular health needs and can include leaflets and posters on smoking, healthy eating and safety in the home.

Community or group health education

This can involve local campaigns to improve health or the formation of self-help or pressure groups. Local groups for twins, or those with asthma or epilepsy are sometimes formed to give advice about how to cope with situations or conditions. These groups also come under the category of secondary health education.

Organisational health education

In early years settings, this can be about developing policies on promoting the health of staff and children. Settings might, for example, develop a policy on dealing with head lice, infectious diseases or asthma.

Approaches to health education and promotion by health educators

Health educators approach health promotion in different ways, as illustrated in the table below.

Health educators and health promoters

Health education and promotion can be provided both formally and informally to parents and their children.

* **Formal** health education targets a specific group at a specific time. For example, antenatal and postnatal classes run by community midwives and health visitors or sex education in schools as part of the National Curriculum.

APPROACH	AIMS	EXAMPLES
Medical	To prevent ill health by a series of public measures. This is used most by doctors, health visitors and school nurses.	The immunisation programme and health screening of children.
Educational	To provide information and/or the necessary skills to enable the child or parent to make an informed choice.	Teaching of personal safety to children.
Behavioural	To encourage people to change their behaviour or habits.	Campaigns to stop smoking or to improve diets.
Empowerment	To help people identify their own lifestyle changes and to facilitate them in developing the skills, confidence and self-esteem to change. This can be used on an individual basis or within the community.	Parenting classes for young teenage mothers. Building up children's self-esteem through personal safety role plays (e.g. the Kidscape programme).

* **Informal** health education is done on a one-to-one basis or through television, the media or magazines, and provides information to those who are seeking it. Peer groups and the family also have a strong influence in promoting health at all ages.

Everyone can be involved in promoting health, and early years practitioners and parents will be constantly doing this through activities and day-to-day routines, and by being good role models.

The role of health educators and promoters

There are a number of organisations and professionals who promote health and provide health education.

The World Health Organisation (WHO)

The objectives of the WHO are 'the attainment by all peoples of the highest possible health'. Its main functions are to set worldwide standards for health, to give guidance and co-operate with governments in strengthening health programmes. Its role encompasses:

* promoting improved standards of teaching and training in the health professions
* researching ways of preventing infectious diseases
* co-ordinating health work internationally
* promoting improvements of nutrition, housing, sanitation, economic or working conditions.

National Institute For Health And Clinical Excellence (NICE)

In April 2005, NICE combined with the Health Development Agency to form a new organisation, also called NICE. Its role is to provide guidance on the promotion of health, and the prevention and treatment of ill health, to healthcare workers, the local authorities, the voluntary sector and general public. It also has a role to provide guidance on new technologies and appropriate treatment and care for specific conditions. The centre is focusing on three key areas important to government policy:

* promotion of the health of children and young people
* accidental injury prevention
* drug misuse.

NICE is also producing guidance on the following areas which were identified in the 2004 'Choosing Health' White Paper:

* obesity, diet and nutrition
* exercise and physical activity
* alcohol
* sexual health
* mental health
* smoking and tobacco control.

See www.nice.org.uk for more information.

National voluntary organisations and pressure groups

Voluntary organisations strive to educate the public and promote particular health issues. They may also put pressure on the government to change policies (such as the Society for the Protection of Unborn Children). The National Childbirth Trust, for example, provides antenatal classes and promotes breastfeeding, and part of the National Asthma Campaign's role is to educate the public and schools about asthma.

The media

The media have a very important role to play in informing the public about health issues and most organisations concerned with health will issue press releases in order to keep the press updated with accurate information. Magazines also promote health and are often the most popular source of health information for young people.

The primary health care team

The primary health care team's role within the community is to provide health education and to promote health, to detect and treat illnesses and conditions and to provide a caring service. Health education is an increasing and essential part of the team's role. The health visitor, for example, works closely with parents, giving advice and support on all parenting skills.

The school nurse

The school nurse's role is mainly concerned with screening, but the role is extending into other areas, such as promoting health education within the classroom.

The dentist

Teaching on dental hygiene and the prevention of tooth decay is one of the dentist's roles. The school dentist service also visits children in schools.

The health promotion unit

This unit provides training, courses, exhibitions and advice and support on any health initiative. It also offers a free loan service of health education videos, displays, books, project packs and CD-ROMs, and provides leaflets and posters.

Education services

Teaching on health issues is part of the PSE programme within schools and this area is being targeted in the National Healthy Schools Scheme (see page 333).

Others

There are many others who have a role in health education including the police (teaching children to protect themselves, road safety and crime prevention) and the fire brigade (fire awareness).

The early years practitioner

Early years practitioners need to know and understand how to maintain their own personal

Promoting dental health is important.

health, as well as that of the children in their care, and to be a positive role model. It is also their role to help teach children about their bodies and how to care for them as part of the Foundation Stage Curriculum and the National Curriculum. Healthy eating, for example, can be used as a focus in activities within 'Knowledge and understanding of the world' in the Foundation Curriculum, and can be incorporated into the science curriculum in Key Stage 1 and 2. Examples of topics could include:

* healthy eating
* exercise
* care of the teeth
* sun awareness.

These topics could be covered by:

* incorporating activities into the curriculum
* having 'health days', when outside professionals come in and do health activities with the children
* having talks with parents
* holding assemblies to include health issues
* creating displays and interest tables.

Theory into practice

Devise a detailed plan for an activity about one of the following topics:
• healthy eating
• hygiene
• caring for your teeth.
In what ways would the activity help the children to gain a better understanding of the topic?

Health promotion programmes

Health promotion programmes can vary in their extent. Some may target one particular class in a school and some will target the world population. The World Health Organisation (WHO) has managed to achieve the eradication of smallpox, while other diseases, such as polio and leprosy, are rapidly decreasing. The WHO believes that an effective school health programme can be one of the most cost-effective investments a country can make to improve health and education. They have numerous programmes running including HIV, smoking, immunisation, 'walking to school' and breastfeeding (see www.who.int for current programmes).

Current health promotion campaigns in the UK

In February 1998, the government produced a document called 'Our Healthier Nation', which aimed to reduce deaths from cancer, heart disease, accidents and suicides by 2010. This paper identified that 'many of our attitudes to health and the influences on our lives are set in childhood… education is one of the most important ways of giving children and young people a healthy start in life.' In October 1999, the Department of Health and the Department for Education and Employment (now the Department for Education and Skills) launched the 'National Healthy Schools Scheme' to support teachers in their role as health educators and to promote healthy schools.

The strands contained within the Healthy Schools Programme are shown in the table below.

PROGRAMMES	AIMS
Safer Routes to School	To encourage walking and safer travel.
The National Healthy Schools Network	To provide information via a National Healthy Schools Network newsletter.
Wired for Health	To inform teachers and children about health issues in schools through the www.wiredforhealth.gov.uk website.
Cooking for Kids	To teach children about healthy eating, basic cookery skills and food hygiene.
Healthy Teachers	To promote health in teachers.

There are numerous other health promotion programmes which benefit children, including the following.

CAMPAIGN	AIMS	MAIN MESSAGE	METHOD
National School Fruit Scheme and the 5-a-day campaign	To increase the consumption of fruit and vegetables and reduce the risks of cancer and coronary heart disease and many other chronic diseases. To develop a positive attitude to fruit.	Everyone should eat at least 5 portions of a variety of fruit and vegetables each day. Eating patterns developed in childhood will continue into aulthood.	Children of 4–6 years should have a piece of fruit or vegetable every day in school. Booklets for schools, leaflets for parents, and curriculum materials are provided.
Sun safety	To reduce the risk of skin cancer by reducing sunburn and exposure to sun in children under 15 years.	Wear protective clothing. Teach children to apply sunscreen regularly. Use water resistant sunscreen with SPF factor of at least 15. Keep babies in the shade.	Leaflets. Website which offers worksheets and guidance.

Evaluating the success of a programme

In order to ensure that programmes are successful and cost effective, evaluations will be completed. For example, evaluation of the pilot for the National School Fruit Scheme (which can be found on the Department of Health website) found that:

* 25 per cent of children and their families ate more fruit at home after the scheme

* half of all parents think the scheme has increased their awareness of the importance of fruit for a healthy diet

* 95 per cent of parents say their child usually ate the fruit provided at school.

Theory into practice

In your work placements, investigate the success of the '5-a-day' and 'Sun Safety' programmes. Interview teachers and children to discover the impact of these programmes on the children.

Government targets

There are numerous government targets for health, including those set by the Department of Health. With the Department for Education and Skills (DfES), they have produced the National Service Framework for Children, Young People and Maternity Services, which establishes a 10-year plan. This includes the improvement of children's health by reducing child poverty and inequalities in health. The framework sets standards for children's health and social care which they aim to meet by 2014.

* **Standard 1** – Promoting Health and Well-being, Identifying needs and Intervening Early. This includes a new Child Health Promotion Programme to reduce health inequalities and promote a healthy lifestyle.

* **Standard 2** – Supporting Parents. This includes providing appropriate information and education, as well as support.

* **Standard 3** – Child, Young Person and Family-Centred Services. This aims to provide services to meet individual needs.

* **Standard 6** – Children and Young People who are Ill. This plans to give advice and appropriate services to children who are ill or injured and high-quality care to those with long-term conditions so that they may participate in everyday life.

* **Standard 7** – Children and Young People in Hospital. Children should be provided with high-quality care in an appropriate setting and be treated with respect

* **Standard 8** – Disabled Children and Those with Complex Health Needs. Children are to receive well-coordinated services which meet their needs and which promote social inclusion.

* **Standard 9** – The Mental Health and Psychological Well-being of Children and Young People. This standard promotes effective assessment, treatment and support of children with mental health problems.

* **Standard 10** – Medicines for Children and Young People. Children should have safe and effective medicines prescribed and given by professionals who have adequate support, advice and training.

The framework plans to raise standards of children's health in all settings, including schools and nurseries.

Assessment activity 10.2

* Choose three different health promoters (one international or national organisation, and two professionals) and describe their role and approaches in a health promotion programme. Describe how they convey information to children, and explain how these programmes might affect the health of children.

* Evaluate the four programmes, including justified conclusions on their effectiveness.

In order to complete this activity you should do the following.

1 Choose three different health promotion programmes which you have seen used in your placement, such as 5-a-day, dental hygiene, sun safety, or personal hygiene.

2 Research the role and approaches of one of the health educators in each of these programmes. Your local Health Promotion Unit will have information on this.

3 Show how the health promoters pass the information to the children, for example, through activities, worksheets, role play or visits.

4 Explain how the programmes will affect the health of the children – what difference, if any, are these programmes going to make to the health of the children?

5 Evaluate the programmes to decide on their effectiveness with the children in your placement. You can do this by using questionnaires or by interviewing the staff, children and parents; quizzes may also assess a child's understanding of the activity. You can then use these to evaluate the success of the programme. The conclusion should use the information gathered in order to ascertain the effectiveness of all of the programmes.

2 The causes of ill health

Factors which affect children's health

In order that you can understand how to help maintain and improve children's health, it is important to know what factors can influence a child's health. The table that follows summarises some of these factors.

IMPACT OF SOCIO-ECONOMIC FACTORS ON HEALTH

FACTOR	EFFECT
Social class	Research has shown that children who are born to parents who are unemployed or who are manual workers are more often ill than children whose parents are professionals. These children are far more likely to be hospitalised, be ill or die than children of professional parents. In 1998, Sir Donald Acheson produced a report which highlighted the fact that the gap was widening between the health of professional people and those who are unemployed or are untrained manual workers, and the government has since being trying to address this issue. Further reading: 'Acheson Report, Independent Inquiry into Inequalities in Health', (1998) – www.archive.official-documents.co.uk/document/doh/ih/part2c.htm
Income/expenditure	There is an inverse proportion between wealth and health – the poorer the family, the greater the health risks. Children from socially deprived families are less likely to attend screening and developmental checks or to have their immunisations. Children who are born into poverty are more likely to: • eat a poor diet • live in poor housing conditions • die younger from accidents or illness • be ill and hospitalised • have decayed teeth • be born premature or have reduced birth weight • be bottle fed. Further reading: Social Exclusion Unit – www.socialexclusion.gov.uk
Housing	Living in crowded, damp conditions increases the risk of accidents and respiratory infections. 11 per cent of childhood accidents are a result of badly designed housing and dangerous fittings. Infections such as tuberculosis, bronchitis and gastroenteritis are more common where there is poor housing, and asthmatics are twice as likely to live in damp homes. Poor housing can also cause children to have sleep problems. Further reading: Shelter – www.england.shelter.org.uk/home/index.cfm
Employment/ unemployment	Some occupations are more at risk of accidents or from catching infectious diseases. Unemployment can cause mental health problems and stress-related diseases. Due to a poor income, families who are unemployed are more likely to have a poor diet and housing conditions. For parents in low-income groups there can also be a shortage of affordable and appropriate child-care.
Age	The younger children are, the more vulnerable they are to infection and illness. At the other extreme, the elderly are also very susceptible to ill-health
Gender	Boys are more likely to die in childhood than girls, mostly because they are more likely to have accidents. Boys are also more likely to have a chronic condition in childhood, although this trend changes in mid-adolescence. Girls, however, are less likely to participate in sport than boys.

▶

IMPACT OF SOCIO-ECONOMIC FACTORS ON HEALTH	
FACTOR	**EFFECT**
Culture	There is evidence of a north-south divide in health, with children in the south generally having better health than those living in the north. Unemployment is higher in some ethnic groups, particularly in Afro-Caribbean groups, and overcrowding is also more common, especially in Pakistani and Bangladeshi households. Some conditions are more common in different ethnic minorities, for example the infant mortality rate is higher in babies of Pakistani origin.

Assessment activity 10.3

A new nursery has been established in a large housing estate where unemployment is high and many of the flats are overcrowded. There is a diverse mix of cultures, including some refugees who have apparently lived in great poverty.

- Produce a report describing the potential impact of socio-economic factors on the health of the children in the nursery.

Causes of illness

There are three main causes of illness – microbiological causes (when a micro-organism or germ enters the body), genetic causes and environmental causes.

Microbiological causes

Germs which enter the body and cause illness are called micro-organisms, and these are divided into four main groups: bacteria, viruses, fungi and parasites (which include protozoa). Some germs are non-pathogenic and aren't harmful to humans, such as the lactic acid bacillus which turns milk into yoghurt, and the organisms that live in the bowel and manufacture Vitamin K, which is essential in the blood-clotting process.

- **Bacteria** need warmth, moisture and food to multiply, but can be treated by antibiotics. Examples include: impetigo, ear infections and whooping cough.

- **Viruses** invade a living cell, multiply and then are released when the cell dies. There is no effective treatment of viruses and they are usually controlled by vaccinations. Examples of viruses include HIV, colds and mumps.

- **Fungi**: there are very few fungi which cause harm to humans, but those that do include thrush and athlete's foot.

- **Parasites** are large enough to be seen and include head lice, scabies and threadworm.

- **Protozoa** are one-celled organisms, such as toxoplasmosis which can be caught from cat litter trays.

Genetic causes

We cannot change our genetic make-up, and everyone will inherit factors from both parents that will affect their health. Some conditions, such as sickle cell disorder (see page 349) and cystic fibrosis (see page 345), are passed on from one or both parent to the child. Sometimes there can be a chromosomal abnormality such as Down's syndrome, where there is an extra chromosome (genetic factor). Other disorders are familial – this means that there is a tendency within the family to have certain conditions, such as asthma, eczema or hay fever.

Environmental causes

We generally have less control of these factors, because they are often organised at national level.

Theory into practice

Using the leaflet on air pollution at www.defra.gov.uk/environment/airquality/airpoll/pdf/airpollution_leaflet.pdf and the information on www.airquality.co.uk, as well as any other information you can find, research the air quality in your local area and compare it to two different areas.

- What differences do you notice and why might there be a difference in the different areas?

* **Air**. High levels of air pollution can cause eye irritation, coughs and breathing difficulties in those who are sensitive. This may include some asthmatic children or children with chronic lung conditions, such as cystic fibrosis.

  Air quality is monitored by DEFRA – the Department for Environment, Food and Rural Affairs. It provides a free air pollution information service, where anyone can find out the levels of pollution in their local area. This can be found at www.airquality.co.uk.

* **Water supply**. In the UK the water supply is well regulated by DEFRA and there are few problems with water-borne diseases such as cholera. However, there have been some well-publicised incidents where the water supply has become contaminated and caused ill health.

* **Sewage and waste control**. This is essential for community health. A poor water supply can spread infections such as polio and typhoid.

How infection can be spread

Infection can be spread very quickly from one child to another through a variety of ways, as shown in the table below.

Methods of preventing illness

There are a variety of ways to prevent illness and the early years practitioner needs to ensure that he or she is vigilant within the setting in order to prevent the spread of infections.

Environment

The immediate environment within an early years setting needs to be kept clean in order to prevent illness. Adequate ventilation will decrease germs but the setting also needs to be warm; school classrooms should be kept at 18°C. Proper disposal of waste and good personal hygiene of staff and children will also prevent illness. In the child's wider environment, adequate housing and play areas, clean air and water and good sanitation are also necessary to prevent illness. A good cheap transport system will also provide easy access to health care.

For information on providing a safe environment see Unit 5, pages 172–8.

Nutrition

An adequate diet is essential in order for children to remain healthy. See Unit 5 for details on a healthy diet and care routine.

WAYS THAT INFECTION CAN SPREAD	EXAMPLES OF INFECTIONS
Droplet infection: speaking, sneezing, coughing and kissing	Colds, coughs and tuberculosis, rubella
Hands: contamination from air-borne droplets, urine and faeces	Gastroenteritis, colds, tapeworm
Bodily fluids	Hepatitis, sexually transmitted diseases and HIV
Contaminated water	Polio
Contaminated food	Food poisoning
Animals	Rabies (from dogs), toxoplasmosis (from cats)
Insects, e.g. flies	Food poisoning
Dust	Diphtheria

Public health

Public health is the promotion of health to the whole population and includes many factors, such as good transport, housing, the environment and governmental legislation. Public health measures relevant to childcare include training on food hygiene and health and safety for staff. Environmental Health Officers enforce legislation relevant to housing conditions, manage pest control and deal with general public health related matters. The Centre for Disease Surveillance and Control (CDSC) monitors and responds to national outbreaks of notifiable infectious diseases; the law requires notification of some infectious diseases. The child's GP or doctor will inform the local authority in the case of an infectious illness, such as meningitis, food poisoning, measles and mumps. This will ensure that any outbreaks of infectious diseases are quickly picked up.

Education

Many infections can be avoided if children are taught how to wash their hands correctly and are regularly encouraged to do so. You also need to act as a positive role model by washing your own hands frequently and correctly. Regular health education on all subjects will help children to understand how to prevent illness and why it is important.

Immunisation

Immunisation is the use of vaccines to give immunity from a specific disease. They consist of a minute portion of the weakened bacteria, virus or of the toxins which they produce. These stimulate the immune system to produce antibodies against the disease. It is recommended that children have immunisations for the following reasons.

* They prevent a child from getting diseases and the associated side effects.

* They protect children who haven't been immunised (this is known as herd immunity – these children are less likely to be exposed to the disease itself).

* It is cheaper to immunise than to care for the children who suffer from side effects of the illness. Moreover, some diseases can lead to long-term problems and even death.

The table below outlines the immunisation schedule.

From September 2005, the BCG vaccination programme delivered through schools has been replaced with a programme which targets individuals (including babies) who are at the greatest risk. This will include those living in areas with a high tuberculosis (TB) rate, or whose parents or grandparents were born in a country with a high TB rate.

Care of a child following immunisation

Serious side effects to immunisations are rare, but some babies may have a mild reaction, often within the first 48 hours. These include irritability, a mild fever or soreness, redness or a small lump around the injection site. It is often advised that infant paracetamol is given afterwards (with

AGE	IMMUNISATION	HOW GIVEN
2, 3 and 4 months	Diphtheria, whooping cough (pertussis), tetanus. Polio and Hib (one type of meningitis)	One injection
	Meningitis C	One injection
12–15 months	Measles, mumps and rubella (MMR)	One injection
$3\frac{1}{2}$–5 years (before school starts)	Diphtheria, whooping cough, tetanus and polio	One injection
	MMR	One injection
13–18 years	Tetanus, diphtheria and polio	One injection

parental consent) if any of these symptoms appear. Serious symptoms, such as a high fever or convulsions, need to be seen immediately by a doctor.

The polio virus will be excreted in the baby's faeces for up to six weeks so hand-washing is particularly important when changing nappies, and babies shouldn't be taken swimming during this time.

Child health screening

Every child is checked regularly to ensure normal growth and development and to detect any health problems or conditions. This is known as child health screening and is important because:

* conditions are treated as early as possible

* appropriate care can be provided for the child and the family

* the child can be referred to specialist help if required

* parents know how their child is developing

* genetic counselling can be offered to parents if applicable – this shows the likelihood of having a child with a particular genetic condition.

Developmental charts

Every health area will have their own chart on which development is recorded. The personal child health records contain graphs on which the weight, height and head circumference are plotted; these are called centile charts (see Unit 7, page 244).

Health screening and developmental checks

The main ways of checking on a child's development and health are by:

* measuring height, weight and head circumference (the latter in the first year only)

* a physical examination

* observing the child during structured or unstructured activities

* asking questions of, and listening to, the parents and/or carers about the child's development and health.

The midwife and paediatrician do neonatal checks, but the health visitor and occasionally the GP do all the subsequent checks. Each developmental area is checked to ensure that the child is developing at the expected rate, as well as examining specific areas, such as hearing.

Each health authority will do checks at slightly different times, but most will follow a similar format. The way these checks are recorded will also differ from area to area. Health education and advice are also given during these checks.

The checks are normally done at the following times:

* a neonatal check

* 6 to 8 weeks

* 6 to 9 months

* 18 to 24 months

* 3 to 3½ years

* checks at school entry.

If any problems are picked up from checks, the child will be seen more regularly by the doctor or health visitor, or will be referred to a specialist if necessary.

Development is recorded.

The role of the early years practitioner in child health screening

Although health professionals do the health screening, early years practitioners will be in daily contact with the children, so are in a very good position to identify any possible problems. Hearing problems, particularly glue ear, where there is intermittent hearing loss, is a common condition which can be detected by this means. If there are concerns about a child's health or development, the child's parents should be informed.

Lifestyle

Prenatal factors

There are many factors that can affect a child's health before he or she is even born. The health and lifestyle of the parents, but particularly of the mother, has an important impact on the future health of the child.

Diet

A healthy diet is necessary for normal growth, development and health. A malnourished child is likely to be unwell more often and to develop vitamin deficiencies. Children who are breastfed are less likely to have gastroenteritis, sudden infant death syndrome, respiratory and ear infections and allergies than bottle-fed babies. It is therefore important to encourage children to eat a healthy diet, including five portions of fruit and vegetables a day (See Unit 5).

Exercise

Regular exercise reduces the incidence of coronary heart disease in adults. It has been shown that children (particularly girls) take much less exercise than is recommended, and therefore it is important for the early years practitioner to encourage children to exercise every day. Regular exercise and a healthy diet can prevent obesity. Emotionally, exercise can help cope with stress and is also important socially.

Smoking

Children who grow up in a smoky atmosphere, and therefore passively smoke, have a higher incidence of respiratory and ear infections and asthma. These children are also more likely to smoke themselves. The long-term risks of smoking include a higher risk of heart disease, chronic respiratory infections and of developing cancers, especially of the lungs.

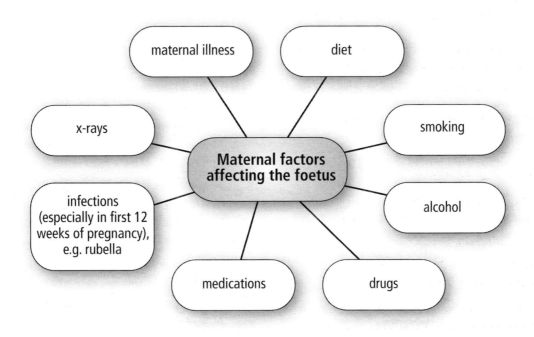

Exercise is good for physical and emotional health.

Assessment activity 10.4

The children in Noah's Ark Nursery are continually getting colds; two children have had scabies and two others have had gastroenteritis.

- Describe the causes and types of illness in the children and produce a poster to show how the setting can prevent illness in children.

Common childhood illnesses

When working with children, it is important for you to be able to recognise some of the common illnesses, and to know when it may be necessary to contact the child's parents or to call a doctor. Children sometimes do not have the experience to know that they are unwell, or the vocabulary to tell someone how they are feeling.

It is therefore important to observe children for changes to their behaviour or physical or emotional well-being in order to detect signs of illness. It is also important to be able to report information about a child's health to the parent.

Types of illness

* An **acute** illness has a rapid onset of signs and symptoms but is short term; however, it can be severe. Examples include meningitis and a cold.

* A **chronic** illness is prolonged, with little difference in symptoms from day to day. Chronic illnesses often have acute episodes. Examples include asthma and sickle cell disorder.

Signs that a child is unwell

Children's behaviour sometimes changes when they are becoming unwell before any specific signs and symptoms develop.

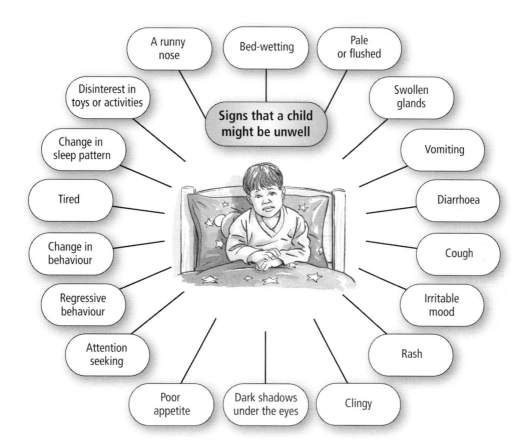

Signs that a child might be unwell:
- A runny nose
- Bed-wetting
- Pale or flushed
- Disinterest in toys or activities
- Swollen glands
- Change in sleep pattern
- Vomiting
- Tired
- Diarrhoea
- Change in behaviour
- Cough
- Regressive behaviour
- Irritable mood
- Attention seeking
- Rash
- Poor appetite
- Dark shadows under the eyes
- Clingy

Illnesses of the upper respiratory tract and ears

Respiratory infections are the most common of the childhood illnesses. There are over 200 viruses that cause cold symptoms – which is why children seem to get one cold after another! Children are particularly prone to infections when they first start nursery or school because they are suddenly exposed to more germs.

Colds

Colds are caused by viruses and are spread by coughing, sneezing or by contact with secretions on toys and other surfaces. Cold-like symptoms are often the first sign of more infectious illnesses, such as chicken pox. Colds often last for five to nine days, but children may have a runny nose for one to two weeks after this. Colds can spread to the lungs and to the middle ear and can also trigger an asthma attack. Signs and symptoms include a runny nose, a sore throat, sneezing, watery eyes, and a slight temperature.

Sore throat and tonsillitis

The tonsils are fairly enlarged in a child because they are active in preventing infections. If there is a large invasion of germs, the tissues swell and become inflamed which usually causes pain. With tonsillitis, the throat initially becomes sore; the infection then spreads to the tonsils which become enlarged.

Coughs and chest infections

Coughing in children is usually associated with an upper respiratory infection and can sometimes follow a cold. It is one of the body's defence mechanisms to rid itself of irritants, chemicals or germs. Coughs can be caused by viruses or bacteria, dust, smoke, tuberculosis and asthma (a dry cough at night can sometimes be an early sign of asthma).

Earaches and middle ear infection (otitis media)

Middle ear infections are very common in children under eight years and often follow respiratory infections. They are caused by a virus or bacteria and some children have frequent attacks, especially children who are bottle fed, live in a smoky house or have frequent colds. Some of the signs and symptoms include painful ears, difficulty in hearing, vomiting and raised temperature. In severe cases the eardrum can perforate (a burst ear drum) which causes the ear to discharge pus and the pain to fade. To help relieve the feeling of tightness in the ear, get the child to yawn or swallow, and give them plenty to drink. Do not pack the ear with cotton wool if the ear discharges or allow the child to sleep with a hot water bottle. Contact the doctor immediately if the child:

* has a stiff neck

* is unsteady on the feet

* had a head injury before the earache

* has a high fever and appears very unwell

* has clear fluid draining from the ears.

Asthma

Asthma is fairly common and affects more than 1.1 million children in the UK, which is one in ten children. It can occur at any age, and half of all children will grow out of it. There is often a family history of asthma, hay fever or eczema.

Causes of asthma

The airways in an asthmatic become oversensitive to certain conditions or triggers. These triggers cause the muscles around the airways to tighten, the lining of the airway to become inflamed and the airways themselves to fill with mucus. These cause the airways to narrow, which causes the symptoms of asthma.

The 'triggers' which can cause the airways to become more sensitive are:

* an allergy to one or more irritants, such as pollen, house mite dust, cats, dogs or horses (the allergen – substance which causes an allergy – is in the fur, saliva and urine)

* chemical irritants such as tobacco smoke, exhaust fumes, perfumes and household cleaners

* exercise

* cold air

* chest infections

* emotional stress, such as anxiety or excitement

* food, especially peanuts, seafood, eggs and some additives and food colourings

* mould (especially in damp living conditions)

* air pollution – although there is no evidence that this can cause asthma, it can be a trigger if the child has asthma.

There is also a higher incidence of asthma in children whose mothers smoked in pregnancy and in those who were bottle fed.

Signs and symptoms

The symptoms vary in each child, and can range from mild to very severe or life threatening. Attacks may be very occasional or frequent and are a major cause of absence from school. The first signs might be:

* a persistent cough, especially in cold air, after exercise or at night

* colds which go 'straight to the chest'

* breathlessness and wheezing when the child exhales (breathes out)

* tightness in the chest.

During an attack there may also be:

* difficulty in speaking

* grey-blue colour, especially around the lips

* a dry tickly cough.

The child may be frightened and anxious.

Management of asthma

This consists of medication and controlling the triggers. Medication consists of two types.

✳ The **relievers** are used to treat the acute symptoms. They open up the air passages in the lungs and are given in syrup form, tablets or in an inhaler, which will always be blue.

✳ The **preventers** reduce inflammation in the airways and prevent attacks or reduce their severity. These are usually brown but sometimes in a maroon or orange inhaler, and they need to be taken regularly.

Children under five years of age or who have difficulty using an inhaler might use a spacer device, such as a Volumatic or Nebuhaler, where the child inhales the drug as a mist. For under-twos, there is a Babyhaler, which has a soft mask.

Care and treatment of a child with an asthma attack

✳ Keep calm and reassure the child.

✳ Help the child find a comfortable position.

✳ Give the child the relief inhaler.

✳ If the inhaler has no effect after five to ten minutes, call 999.

✳ Check and record the child's breathing and pulse every ten minutes.

KEY ISSUES

Supporting children with asthma
- Know the local education authority's and the setting's policy on asthma.
- Know the signs, triggers, care and first aid for an asthma attack – the school nurse can give a talk if necessary.
- Be aware of children's triggers when planning activities and trips.
- Ensure that children have immediate access to their inhaler.
- Always take an asthmatic attack seriously.
- Keep the setting well ventilated.

Cystic fibrosis

Cystic fibrosis (CF) is an inherited condition which affects the respiratory and digestive systems. The mucus produced by the lungs is thick and sticky causing the airways to become infected or blocked, which therefore causes difficulty in breathing. The ducts in the pancreas also become clogged with mucus which prevents the digestive enzymes produced here from digesting fats in the digestive tract. This results in poor weight gain. For further information on cystic fibrosis, see Unit 16.

CASE STUDY

Dominique is a five-year-old in a class at your placement. There are several children in the class with asthma, but Dominique's frequent asthma attacks mean that she has frequent absences from school. Triggers to her asthma include: the house dust mite, cats and other animals with fur, cold weather and exercise. To prevent her attacks, Dominique has a preventer inhaler which she takes at home; she brings her reliever inhaler to school, and she always has to use it before exercise. Dominique wasn't able to go on the school trip to the farm last term due to her condition.

- Obtain research from the Asthma Campaign website, www.asthma.org.uk, and produce a fact sheet for staff on asthma to include:
  - definition of asthma, the causes and common triggers
  - the management of asthma
  - the latest research on asthma.
- What are the signs and symptoms of an asthma attack and the first aid treatment?
- Find out about your placement's policy on asthma.

Disorders and infections of the digestive system

Vomiting

Vomiting is a symptom that is very common in children and can be associated with an infection anywhere. Some children will be sick every time they have a slight fever, if they are excited or frightened. However, there are many causes and it is important to note the time of sickness, the colour, any pain or diarrhoea and whether the child appears unwell.

Causes of vomiting
* Travel sickness
* Meningitis (see page 352)
* Food poisoning
* Gastroenteritis (see page 347)
* Hepatitis
* Appendicitis
* Pyloric stenosis (causing projectile vomiting in newborn babies)
* Food intolerance
* Possetting (babies less than one year old are slightly sick after feeds – this is normal)
* Urinary tract infection
* Whooping cough
* Respiratory infections and tonsillitis (see pages 343–345)
* Ear infections
* Concussion (following a head injury)
* Excitement
* Stress
* Over eating (often associated with children's parties)
* Sunstroke or heat exhaustion

Diarrhoea

Diarrhoea (frequent runny stools) is fairly common in children and is often due to an infection. It can be distressing for a child and it may cause accidents in younger children, when unable to get to the toilet in time. Diarrhoea is not an illness in itself, but, like vomiting, is a symptom of many different conditions.

Causes of diarrhoea
* Toddler diarrhoea (see page 347)
* A side effect of some medicine (especially antibiotics)
* Food poisoning
* Gastroenteritis (see page 347)
* Food intolerance

KEY ISSUES

Care of a child who is vomiting
* Reassure and stay with the child.
* Ensure there is a bowl nearby and disinfect after use.
* Support the child's head when vomiting.
* Wash the child's hands and face after vomiting and encourage rinsing of the mouth with water.
* Allow the child to rest/lay head on soft towels in case of accidents.
* Change clothes when necessary.
* Encourage sips of water to prevent dehydration.
* Once the sickness has stopped, provide small portions of dry food, such as toast – this should be started gradually.

KEY ISSUES

Care of a child with diarrhoea
* Reassure the child – it can be very distressing.
* Give regular drinks of clear fluid to prevent dehydration.
* Keep a potty nearby, if possible, for a younger child.
* Keep spare pants handy!
* Avoid going out (except if toddler diarrhoea).
* If gastroenteritis is suspected, isolate the child from others and send home.
* Good hygiene is important – ensure that the child washes hands after using the toilet.
* Soak soiled pants in Napisan solution before washing.

* Excitement, nervousness or stress
* Chronic constipation, which can cause an overflow of diarrhoea

Toddler diarrhoea

Toddler diarrhoea can affect healthy children of one to three years, and is characterised by watery diarrhoea containing undigested food. The child should be seen by the doctor to exclude other disorders, but there is no treatment other than chopping food up smaller. The child should grow out of it by the age of three years.

Gastroenteritis

Gastroenteritis is an irritation or inflammation of the stomach and intestines and is contagious. Because the infection is in the bowel, proper hand washing is essential. It is much more common in bottle-fed than in breastfed infants. This can spread very quickly from one child to another in a nursery.

Skin conditions and infection

One of the main functions of the skin is as a protection against the environment – if the skin becomes broken, then infection can easily enter the body. Skin conditions and infections are fairly common in children and often cause great discomfort and itchiness. It is important that children are kept away from the early years setting if their condition is infectious, because these infections spread very quickly among children.

Some of the most common skin conditions and infections are shown in the table below.

CONDITION AND CAUSE	SPREAD	RECOGNITION OF CONDITION	TREATMENT AND CARE	POSSIBLE COMPLICATIONS
Scabies *Insect*	Direct contact (the insect burrows under the skin and lays eggs), clothing and towels.	Tiny grey swellings appear, particularly between the fingers or on the wrist, armpits or sides of feet. Intense itching especially at night. Waking frequently at night.	See a doctor. All the family will need treatment with an insecticide lotion. Isolate the child.	Scratching can also cause impetigo.

CONDITION AND CAUSE	SPREAD	RECOGNITION OF CONDITION	TREATMENT AND CARE	POSSIBLE COMPLICATIONS
Cold sore *Herpes simplex virus*	Direct contact. Triggers can be: cold weather, the wind, sunlight, or having a cold.	Starts as tingling around the mouth. Small blisters which form a crust after 1–2 days (these are smaller and more regular than impetigo). Itching.	Often disappears on its own. Anti-viral cream may be used early on. After infection, the virus lays dormant until a 'trigger' restarts the infection. Use lip salve in the winter and sunscreen in summer.	
Impetigo *Bacteria – usually Streptococcus or Staphylococcus*	Contact with other children. Break in the skin caused by a cut, insect bite or eczema. Chapped lips.	Small blisters (often around the mouth and nose) which crust and ooze. The area spreads rapidly.	Antibiotic cream which needs to be applied using gloves, or medicine. Child should be isolated. Discourage the child from touching the area. Separate towels and flannels should be used. Personal hygiene is very important.	If untreated it spreads rapidly. Can cause generalised infection and septicaemia (blood poisoning).

Eczema

Eczema affects about one fifth of all school-age children. It can start as early as two months and 60–70 per cent of children grow out of it by adulthood.

Characteristics

* A dry, itchy rash which becomes red and starts to weep. In very young children it can affect the face, scalp, trunk and the outside of the arms and legs. In older children it can affect the bends of the elbows and knees, the feet and the hands.

* The skin can become broken and be raw and bleed.

* Itchiness, especially at night.

Caring for a child with eczema

Each child's eczema is very different and therefore it is important to discuss the child's treatment and care with the parents before coming to the setting. It is also important to keep updated on the child's condition. Some children are unable to touch paint, playdough, sand, clay or even water without causing the eczema to flare up, so it is important to find out from the parents what the child is unable to touch or use. This can potentially restrict the opportunities available for the child and, to ensure equality of opportunity, the early years practitioner needs to be aware of the child's needs and ways of coping with these in the classroom. The table on page 349 includes some suggested strategies.

POTENTIAL DIFFICULTY	POTENTIAL STRATEGY
Contact with soap	Special emollients brought from home.
Contact with paint, salt, dough, clay, sand or water.	Cotton gloves can be worn or plenty of cream applied first.
Swimming	Emollient cream can be applied beforehand. Remind the child to dry properly and then to reapply cream afterwards.
Pets	Some children will need to avoid pets altogether.
Becoming hot which will worsen the itching.	Seating away from the radiator and windows. Plastic seats may be covered if necessary.
Uniform	Children are better having cotton next to their skin and should avoid getting overheated.
Scratching Lack of concentration due to itching	Distract the child as much as possible. Try to avoid saying not to scratch because it can make it worse or build up resentment. Further applications of cream may help
Cooking: children should avoid contact with any food they are allergic to.	Use different ingredients for all of the children. It is important to know if any of the children has a severe reaction to a food such as anaphylactic shock.
Worry over schoolwork, friends or appearance can affect some children's eczema.	Encourage the child to talk over any worries with the staff.

Think it over...

- How could you help to build confidence and self-esteem of a child with eczema within the setting?

Sickle cell disorder

Sickle cell anaemia is an inherited red blood cell disorder. Some children will be born with the disorder which will be inherited from both parents, while others may be born with a 'sickle cell trait' which means that they are carriers. Sickle cell trait cannot turn into the disorder and these children will usually be perfectly healthy.

In the UK, sickle cell anaemia is most common in people of African and Caribbean descent. Normal red blood cells are doughnut shaped but sickle red blood cells become hard, sticky and shaped like sickles, which can clog the flow of blood to an area of the body. This can cause pain and anaemia.

Role of the early years practitioner

* Children with sickle cell anaemia may be absent more frequently because of crises or infections, which may require treatment in a hospital setting.

* Allow children to drink plenty of water – they may need to keep a water bottle with them. This will necessitate frequent visits to the toilet as their kidneys cannot retain water as well.

* Try to prevent children from becoming over heated or exposed to cold temperatures.

* Because of their anaemia, children with sickle cell may get tired before others and a rest period may be appropriate.

* Encourage gym and sports participation but allow children to stop without undue attention.

* Some young children will be on permanent antibiotics to prevent infection.

CASE STUDY

Jacob and his brother have sickle cell anaemia. Jacob has frequent periods of absence from school, whereas his younger brother has fewer health problems. When Jacob is at school he has to be careful about getting overtired during exercise, and he needs to drink water regularly to prevent dehydration. Last week, he had to be collected from school by his mother due to a crisis, when he had pain in the arms, legs, back and stomach. His hands were also beginning to swell and he felt extremely tired.

- Obtain research from the Sickle Cell Society website: www.sicklecellsociety.org and write a fact sheet for other students on Sickle Cell Disorder. Include a description of the disorder and signs of a crisis, as well as ways in which a child can be supported.

Infectious diseases

ILLNESS, INCUBATION TIME, IMMUNISATION, METHOD OF SPREAD	SIGNS AND SYMPTOMS	CALL DOCTOR IMMEDIATELY IF	SPECIFIC TREATMENT/ COMPLICATIONS
Chicken pox (varicella) (common in children under 10 years) Can be uncomfortable, and serious in very young babies, children who are HIV positive or taking medications for childhood cancer (and adults, especially pregnant women) *Incubation time:* 11–21 days *Method of spread:* droplet infection	• Rash starts on head and behind the ears • Pink spots turn to blisters which dry and form scabs • Spots often come in crops – new batches appear over a few days • Slight fever and headache • Child may *feel* well • Intense itching	• Coughing • Seizures • Abnormal drowsiness • Unsteady when walking	• Sodium bicarbonate in a cool bath and calamine lotion to relieve itchiness • Keep child cool as warmth makes the spots and itching worse • Dress in loose cotton clothing • Soft food if the mouth is affected • Scarring • Secondary infection from scratching, especially impetigo • Pneumonia • Chest infection • Encephalitis (inflammation of the brain)
Measles Caused by a virus, is highly infectious and can be serious	• Generally unwell initially • Koplick's spots (blueish white spots) appear on the cheeks	• Severe headache • Earache • Vomiting • Rapid breathing • Drowsiness • Seizures	• Conjunctivitis • Otitis media • Bronchitis • Pneumonia • Encephalitis

ILLNESS, INCUBATION TIME, IMMUNISATION, METHOD OF SPREAD	SIGNS AND SYMPTOMS	CALL DOCTOR IMMEDIATELY IF	SPECIFIC TREATMENT/ COMPLICATIONS
Measles (continued) *Incubation time:* 10–14 days *Immunisation* is available for children at 12–15 months *Method of spread:* droplet infection	• Temperature, runny • nose, red eyes and cough • A flat, blotchy red rash starts behind the ears and on the face, and spreads to the rest of the body • Photophobia (dislike of bright light) – nurse in a slightly darkened room		
Mumps Viral infection of salivary glands – not usually serious except in adolescent boys *Incubation time:* 14–24 days *Immunisation:* children can be immunised against mumps at 12–15 months as part of MMR *Method of spread:* droplet infection	• Generally unwell initially • Fever *After 1–2 days:* • Swelling and pain on one or both sides of the face under the jaw line – lasts for five days • Dry mouth • Loss of appetite • Confirm diagnosis with doctor – it is a notifiable disease	• Severe headaches and signs of meningitis • Abdominal pain	• Orchitis (inflammation of the testes) in adolescent boys which very rarely can cause infertility Rarely: • Meningitis • Encephalitis • Deafness in one or both ears
Rubella (German measles) A viral infection which causes a mild illness which is not serious (except to pregnant women: it has serious effects on the unborn child) *Incubation time:* 14–21 days *Immunisation* is available for children at 12–15 months *Method of spread:* droplet infection	• Slight fever and generally slightly unwell • Swollen glands behind the ears and at the back of the neck • Rash of tiny flat pink spots which are not itchy and start on the face and spread to the body and limbs. These only last for a few days	• Joint pain • Any sign of meningitis	• Encephalitis • Can cause serious defects to the foetus if a woman contracts rubella in the first 12–16 weeks of pregnancy • Because the child can be infectious for 5–7 days before the rash develops, inform pregnant women who have had contact with the child

▶

ILLNESS, INCUBATION TIME, IMMUNISATION, METHOD OF SPREAD	SIGNS AND SYMPTOMS	CALL DOCTOR IMMEDIATELY IF	SPECIFIC TREATMENT/ COMPLICATIONS
Meningitis Infection of the lining of the brain and spinal cord – always very serious *Incubation time:* 2–14 days *Immunisation*: Hib vaccination can prevent one type of viral meningitis in children under four years (see page 339) and there is also a meningitis C vaccine available	Children can develop these signs and become seriously ill very quickly: • Signs of cold/flu initially • Drowsiness • Loss of appetite • Restlessness • Temperature • Nausea or vomiting • Severe headache • Photophobia (dislike of bright light) • Stiff neck • Joint pains *In the late stages there may also be:* • a rash: flat purple or pink spots which **do not** fade if pressed* *Babies may also:* • arch their backs • have a shrill cry • have a bulging fontanelle **The rash in meningitis is very distinctive, and can be recognised by doing the glass test. Press a glass over the spots. If the rash is due to meningitis, the rash will not fade when pressed, whereas other rashes will.*	• As soon as meningitis is suspected	• Antibiotics in bacterial meningitis • Will be nursed in hospital • Darkened room • Brain damage • Deafness • Epilepsy • Death

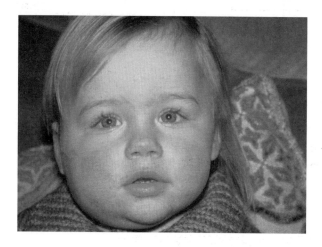

A child suffering from mumps.

General care of a child with an infectious illness

✳ Isolate the child.

✳ Give paracetamol to reduce the temperature (with parental consent).

✳ Ensure child drinks plenty of fluids.

✳ Foods should be soft.

✳ Allow child to rest as much as they wish.

✳ If the child has an itchy rash:

- keep the nails short – cotton mittens could be used for young children

- discourage the child from scratching, especially on the face – scratching can lead to permanent scarring.

3 The impact of ill health on children and families

Ill health can cause stress within the family, especially if it is chronic or life threatening. But even short-term illnesses can cause problems in the family. The effect of the illness on the child and family will depend on:

✳ whether the child is at school or early years setting

✳ the child's age and stage of development

✳ the parents' work, and whether they would need to take time off to care for the child

✳ the illness itself, whether it is acute, chronic or life threatening

✳ the type of treatment

✳ previous experiences of illness

✳ how the family copes with the illness and the support they receive

✳ how often the child is away from school or the early years setting – this may affect their development

✳ whether the child needs hospitalisation.

Potential effects of illness on a child's development

Chronic and life-limiting conditions can have a dramatic impact on a child's development, especially if this involves frequent nursery or

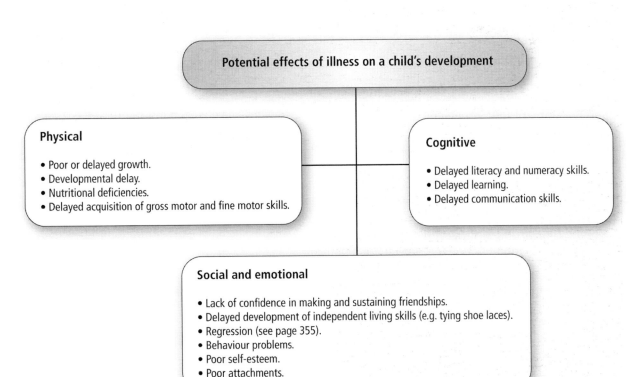

Potential effects of illness on a child's development

Physical

- Poor or delayed growth.
- Developmental delay.
- Nutritional deficiencies.
- Delayed acquisition of gross motor and fine motor skills.

Cognitive

- Delayed literacy and numeracy skills.
- Delayed learning.
- Delayed communication skills.

Social and emotional

- Lack of confidence in making and sustaining friendships.
- Delayed development of independent living skills (e.g. tying shoe laces).
- Regression (see page 355).
- Behaviour problems.
- Poor self-esteem.
- Poor attachments.

school absences. These effects can be due to lack of independence, stimulation or play opportunities or from bullying. Medications can affect the concentration of children and have other side effects which affect the child's learning. Even a condition such as 'glue ear' can affect children's development; when a child has fluctuating hearing loss they will miss important information in class and among their friends, and behaviour problems are also common, due to high levels of frustration.

The impact of illness on children's physical development

Physical development may be affected by chronic or life-limiting conditions; an acute illness rarely has long-term effects except when complications may occur, such as a perforated ear drum causing some ongoing hearing difficulties following an ear infection. The impact could include the following.

* **Poor or delayed growth**. Children who are unable to eat sufficiently may have poor growth or a 'failure to thrive', which may be a result of congenital abnormalities or from conditions where food is not absorbed properly.

* **Developmental delay**. Where children are not able to move sufficiently, they will not be developing their muscles. For example, babies who have to have their feet in plaster for some time will be unable to start walking.

* **Nutritional deficiencies**. Some children don't absorb some types of food properly, and this could lead to deficiencies if not treated early.

* **Delayed acquisition of gross motor and fine motor skills**. Children who are unwell for periods of time will be tired and will lack the energy to develop physical skills. It will therefore often take them longer to reach their developmental milestones.

Children's physical needs

Children's physical needs will change, often considerably, during illness.

* Their appetite will often decrease and therefore nutritional needs will change.

* They will often need more fluids to drink, especially in acute illnesses.

* Their need for sleep and rest will usually increase.

* Clothing will need to be appropriate to their illness.

* They may need more help with personal hygiene and have more washes instead of baths.

* The need for warmth and fresh air may change, especially if they have a temperature.

These physical needs, and the ways in which you can minimise the effects of illness on physical development, are discussed in further depth on pages 359–61.

The impact of illness on children's social and emotional development

Social and emotional development can be affected in the following ways.

* Friendships can suffer if a child has frequent or prolonged absences from nursery or school. This can cause a lack of confidence in keeping friendships and it is very important that friends should be encouraged to visit the child, if possible; letter writing, emailing or sending pictures to each other can also help to maintain friendships.

* Delayed development of independent living skills may occur. Some children are more dependent on their parents and carers to help in their day-to-day care; for example, when children are confined to a wheelchair they may need help going to the toilet. It is important for children to gain as much independence as possible by allowing them to do what they are able, even if it takes longer for them to do it for themselves.

* Behaviour problems may occur as a result of frustration, especially when children cannot do what their friends are able to do. This can cause tantrums, aggressiveness or attention-seeking behaviour. Behaviour problems can be due to regression (see page 355).

* Poor self-esteem can develop because children with health problems often miss school and are not always able to keep up with their peers or do everything that their friends are able to do. This can also lead to depression in some children.

* Poor attachments can develop when young babies are unwell and need frequent hospital visits, as parents are not always able to stay with the baby all the time, especially if there are other young children in the family. This can occasionally lead to poor attachments with the parents and rest of the family.

Regression

If emotional needs are not being met, then the child may regress. Regression means that the child reverts back to the behaviour of a younger child. This can happen with any illness and is normal for a short period of time, but over longer periods can affect development. It is important to recognise this and provide reassurance, routine and extra attention.

Signs of regressive behaviour

* Behaviour typical of an earlier age group and refusal to do things that they previously did, e.g. talk, feed or dress themselves

* Playing with toys from an earlier age group

* Excessive crying

* Lack of concentration

* Inability to learn

* Clinginess

* Aggressiveness

* Unusual behaviour, such as head banging

Children's social and emotional needs

In order to minimise the effects of illness on a child's social and emotional development, it is important for the early years practitioner to support the child and family. Children who are unwell need more support than usual, and will need to be cared for by someone they know and trust. Children in hospital cope far better if they have a parent or carer with them, and hospitals cater for this by providing beds and facilities for parents.

In the home environment, sick children need the security of their normal routine as much as possible. Mealtimes and bedtimes should, where possible, continue as normal. It can be very worrying for a child to be ill and young children may not have the right vocabulary to express how they are feeling. Allow children to express their fears and validate their feelings. There is nothing worse than feeling scared and confused and not being able to talk about it. Some children will become clingier when unwell and behaviour changes might be noticed in others. They need to be reassured that they are going to get better and that they are still loved. It is often better to make up a bed on a sofa in the sitting room so that the child knows that the carer isn't far away.

In a nursery and school setting, all staff should have an understanding of chronic conditions and ensure that they provide activities that are achievable and help raise the child's self-esteem. However, it is also important that a child with a chronic condition is not overprotected.

If a child is seriously ill, it is usually better to be honest with the child about their condition and explain what is to happen in a clear and simple way. Part of growing up is learning how to deal with frustration, pain and loss. As carers, we can teach children effective ways of handling tough times with honesty and love.

Play is still very important for a child, even when ill. When children are first unwell, they often need to sleep more, but in between periods of sleep and rest they can quickly become bored and frustrated. In hospitals, play workers help children to work through their fears and worries using play. They can also explain what may be involved in their treatment through play.

The impact of illness on children's cognitive development

Children who have to be absent from a learning environment for a period of time will lack the stimulation offered by that environment and will also be restricted from learning through observation and imitation of others. If this pattern of absence continues, they can get further and further behind in all aspects of their learning, including the following.

* **Delayed literacy and numeracy skills**. Children require regular repetition to develop reading skills, so frequent absences from school can delay the development of reading and numeracy skills. When children are unwell, they may not have the energy to concentrate for any length of time, which can also affect their learning.

* **Delayed communication skills**. Language development can be affected by chronic illness due to lack of friendships. Some children, however, develop very good language skills from being in regular contact with a variety of adults.

Children's cognitive needs

Children often sleep for longer periods when unwell and they aren't interested in much, except perhaps being read to. During recovery, however, they may become bored and frustrated, and require activities that are short and simple, and need little concentration. Children often play with toys and read books which are suitable for a younger age group when unwell, and the carer needs to plan appropriate activities throughout the day.

Children who are unwell for some time can miss out on work from school and their learning can then be affected. In order to minimise the effect of ill health on a child's cognitive development, therefore, the early years practitioner should try to provide activities that can stimulate the child at the right level, but that don't cause the child to become frustrated. It is important that children be given the opportunity to have work from school, if appropriate, in order to minimise any disruption to their education. In hospital, the play worker may provide activities to help stimulate the child's mind. A home tutor is sometimes provided if the child is going to have a prolonged absence from school.

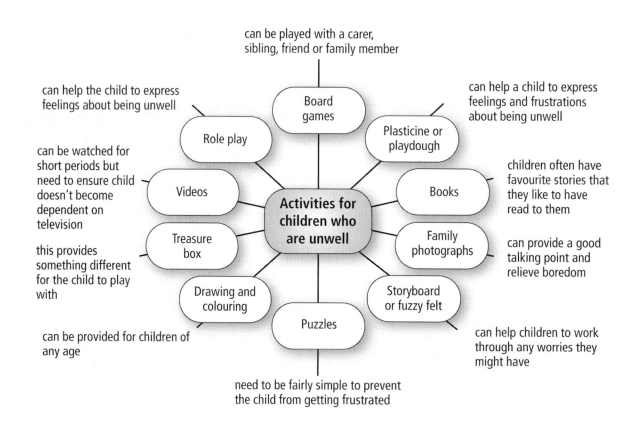

Needs of parents and other family members during a child's illness

The effect on the family of the child's illness

Even a short illness can cause disruption to family life and routine. If the parents work, alternative childcare may need to be arranged. Chronic, long-term and life-threatening illnesses may cause the family to make adaptations to many aspects of their lives to meet the needs of the child and other family members. A child's illness may therefore affect the family in a number of ways as described in the table below.

Even a short illness can cause disruption to family life and routine.

The needs of siblings

When a child is unwell this can upset the routine of other children and can also cause a variety of different emotions to surface, especially if the child is seriously unwell. Siblings often have ambivalent feelings towards each other – they are the best of friends one minute and mortal enemies the next. Illness can cause them to feel guilty if they think unkind thoughts about their sibling, and they might also feel that they have caused the illness in some way. Other children might feel jealous of the attention the ill child is getting or feel confused. Siblings may become attention seeking or develop behaviour problems and they therefore need time spent with them by themselves.

Older siblings may be expected to help more in the house and behave more responsibly; as

EFFECT ON FAMILY	NEEDS OF FAMILY
Physically: It can be physically demanding to care for an unwell child, especially if any lifting is required. Lack of sleep can also lead to exhaustion.	Help with childcare or respite care for the child can give the family a break from their caring role.
Emotionally: There is always a multitude of emotions, such as fear, uncertainty, anxiety, insecurity, guilt and depression, which arise when a child is ill, especially when there is a long-term illness, or if hospitalisation is required.	Support and information can help parents feel that they're not on their own.
Financially: If a parent has to give up work either temporarily or permanently, it can have huge financial implications on the family. If a child is in hospital, this can also cause more expense.	A social worker could advise on financial help.
Isolation: It is often not possible for the parent to have the same contact with friends or work colleagues when a child is ill, and this can cause the parent to feel isolated, especially if the care is very demanding.	Families can be encouraged to share experiences and gain help through support groups.

one child explained: 'Just for once, I wish I wasn't the one that my parents say that they can always rely on'. If the child is seriously ill, siblings can worry that their brother or sister may die or that they may also catch the illness. Siblings therefore need time with parents and carers in order to express these feelings and have the details about their sibling's illness explained in a simple way. They should be included in family discussions and know in advance whether there will be any change to their routine, such as who might pick them up from school. It is important that the early years setting knows what is happening at home and about any change to the routine, in order that staff can support the child appropriately.

4 Treatment and care routines for children with health problems

Different care settings for children who are unwell

Home

Most children who are unwell will be cared for at home because this is the place that can provide them with the security, comforts and attention that they require. At home, a bed can be made up in the sitting room if necessary, so that the child is not far away from the parent or carer. Children can have their own toys and comfort objects and have their favourite foods cooked.

Hospital

Occasionally children need to be admitted to hospital but a parent or carer can always stay with them throughout the stay – it is very frightening for children to be admitted, especially in an emergency, when there is little time to prepare them. Many children will have the experience of attending an accident and emergency department. It is useful if children have played 'hospitals' and have read books on hospitals in an early years setting.

If the child is having a planned admission to hospital, the early years practitioner may be able to help prepare the child. Generally, the child should start preparations two weeks before admission. The child can visit the hospital and look at booklets or videos that the hospital may produce. The early years practitioner could play hospitals with the child and read books about hospitals. Children get very worried about being in hospital; these worries include being separated from their parents or carers and being left alone. Children have a poor concept of time and even a trip to the toilet will seem a long time. Some children believe that they are being punished and others become acutely anxious. Children who are well-prepared for hospital are more likely to co-operate with hospital procedures and have a better recovery rate. The hospital will advise the child on what should be brought in, but the child's comforter and some favourite toys or books are also important.

Hospice

Children with a life-limiting condition may be admitted to a hospice, especially if they have a lot of pain that needs to be controlled.

Hospices offer respite, emergency and terminal care and 24-hour support at home through a community team. The team also runs support groups for family members. Hospices enable children to have their physical care done by an experienced team, allowing time for the family to spend quality time with them. Activities are also organised by specialist playworkers.

Early years settings

If a child becomes unwell in the early years setting, it is important that he or she is removed from the other children and given a place to rest with an adult nearby. If children are feeling sick they need a bucket and easy access to a toilet. The parent(s) should be called straight away because it is unfair for the child to be kept at the setting, and there is also a greater chance of other children catching an infectious illness.

If a child has a chronic condition such as asthma, epilepsy or diabetes, then all staff need to know about the condition and any particular support that is required. The parent(s) should provide all this information and the school nurse can provide training if necessary.

Caring for the child's physical needs

Warmth

Children will need to be kept in a warm but well-ventilated room; if infectious, the child will need to be isolated from other children, but children will often prefer to be cared for in the sitting room on the sofa, rather than in their own bedroom.

Food and drink

Children are often not very hungry when unwell, but this is not generally a problem as long as they are drinking plenty of fluids. Food doesn't always

Make sure the child is warm and comfortable – whether in bed or on the sofa.

taste the same as usual, so it is important that the food is nutritious and presented in small appetising portions.

However, it is far better to allow the child to have a favourite food than eat nothing at all! Food such as ice cream, fromage frais, toast and marmite, puréed fruit, eggs, ice lollies (made with fruit juice) will all provide the child with some energy and also with vital nutrients. It is often better to offer regular snacks when a child is unwell.

It is very important that the child drinks frequently while unwell to prevent dehydration. It is better to offer children their favourite drink, but drinks which are high in vitamin C, such a diluted orange juice or squashes, are ideal and will help them fight infection. To encourage a child to drink, use a special cup with a straw, or make ice lollies or flavoured ice cubes from fruit juice and water; these should be offered at least every hour.

Personal hygiene

It is important that the child's normal hygiene routine continues, although washes may be more acceptable than a bath. Hair brushing and teeth brushing should continue as normal, although this may also be done after a child has been sick. The child will need to wash their hands frequently, especially if they have an infectious illness.

Carers must also ensure that they provide a good role model and take the following precautions.

* Wash hands after contact with the child's bedding, tissues, clothing and bodily fluids.
* Wear gloves if in contact with bodily fluids.
* If the child has an accident, use gloves and cover the area with a bleach solution (consult the setting's policies), wipe over the area with disposable towels, which should be disposed of according to the setting's policy, and then wash the area with soapy water.
* Use tissues instead of hankies and dispose of them into a bag.
* Ensure that the room is warm but well ventilated in order to disperse germs.
* Wash the child's bedding on a high heat to destroy germs.
* The child may need their own towel, especially if they have an infectious skin condition.

- Toys should be washed thoroughly.
- If a child has sickness or diarrhoea, cover their bed sheet/sofa with soft towels, because these are easy to wash on a high heat.
- Children are more likely to wet the bed when unwell, so you may need to use a mattress protector.

Rest and sleep

Most children require more sleep when they are unwell, giving the body time to recover. Children should therefore be encouraged to rest wherever they feel comfortable and be given quiet and simple activities to do.

Control of the child's temperature

When a child has an infection the body temperature is raised in order to fight the infection. The normal body temperature of a child is 36.5–37°C, and will vary throughout the day, often being higher in the evening, after exercise and bathing, and in hot weather. Babies, who have a very immature temperature-regulating mechanism, can show large fluctuations in temperature and can develop high temperatures very quickly. The temperature is usually taken under the armpit or by using a fever strip on the forehead in young children and babies. The temperature will be 0.5°C lower than if taken by mouth.

Thermometers

There are four different types of thermometer which can be used.

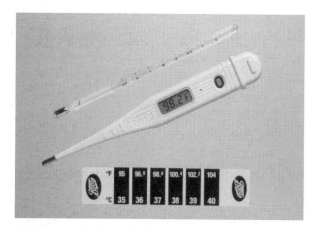

Different types of thermometer.

- A digital thermometer is unbreakable, easy to read, accurate and fairly quick to use.
- A mercury thermometer can be hazardous if made of glass because it contains mercury, which emits fumes if the glass is broken. It is accurate and cheap but is difficult to read and should never be placed in a child's mouth. There are plastic ones available.
- A fever strip is not as accurate as other methods but is cheap and very easy to use by placing the strip onto the child's forehead. The strip changes colour and shows the temperature of the child.
- An infrared thermal scanning thermometer is very accurate and it only takes a few seconds when it is placed in the ear to take a reading. It is expensive but very easy to use on children.

KEY ISSUES

Taking a child's temperature using a digital thermometer

It is important that you note down the child's temperature so that you can inform the parent (or GP, if necessary).

- Ensure that the thermometer is cleaned and collect a book or toy to distract the child.
- Explain to the child what you are going to do. Try it on a teddy first if the child is anxious.
- Sit the child down. Turn the thermometer on.
- Place the thermometer under the child's arm, ensuring that the bulb is directly in the armpit. Hold it in place.
- When the digital thermometer bleeps, record the temperature.
- Clean the thermometer and put it out of reach.
- Inform the parents if there has been a big change in the reading.

Care of a child with a temperature

A high temperature can cause febrile convulsions (see page 361); therefore the child should be cooled if the temperature exceeds 37.5°C.

- Maintain room temperature at 15°C (60°F) and remove clothing down to the underwear.
- Offer sips of cool drink regularly.

* With parents' permission, paracetamol syrup (e.g. Calpol) can be given to children over three months.
* Fan the child.
* If the temperature is over 38.5°C, tepid sponging can be done – dip a sponge into lukewarm water, and sponge over the child's skin but do not dry. Repeat until the temperature falls below 38.5°C. The temperature should not fall too quickly because it can cause shock. *Never* use cold water.

Febrile convulsions

These can occur in children of six months to five years due to a rise in temperature. Children who have had a convulsion have an increased risk of further convulsions. It is frightening dealing with this and it is important to know whether the child has a history of convulsions.

> **Theory into practice**
>
> You are caring for Michael and Sophie in the home setting. Sophie is an active and inquisitive two-year-old and Michael, who is four, is feeling very unwell with tonsillitis.
>
> * Plan a routine for one day for both children, including your role in caring for Michael.
> * Michael is to be admitted to hospital in two weeks to have his tonsils out. What might the early years practitioner's role be over the next two weeks and on admission to hospital?

Who to contact when a child is unwell

Generally, it is not advisable to have children who are unwell at an early years setting. The following may be contacted when a child is unwell.

The parent/guardian

The parent should be informed if the child becomes unwell, has an accident or if their condition changes while in your care. If the parent is unavailable, the emergency contact should be phoned.

The general practitioner (GP)

Occasionally it may be necessary to contact the child's GP if the carer is unable to contact the

parent and is concerned about the child's condition.

The emergency services

In an emergency call 999 (or 112) for an ambulance and be ready to answer some questions about the child and about the signs and symptoms. The parent would need to be informed and the child's key worker, first aider or head teacher may accompany the child from an early years setting.

It will depend on the setting as to who will contact the above.

* **Home setting** – if caring for a child at home, the early years practitioner will generally contact the parents initially when concerned about a child. It may occasionally be necessary to contact other services in an emergency situation.
* **Nursery setting** – the child's key worker will initially be informed if a child is unwell, but it will generally be the manager's responsibility to call parents and other services if necessary.
* **School setting** – the first aider will generally care for a child initially, but it will usually be the head teacher who calls parents in a primary school.

> **KEY ISSUES**
>
> ### When to call for help
>
> An early years practitioner should always call for help when concerned about a child. This could include:
> * breathing difficulties
> * unconsciousness
> * signs of meningitis: severe headache, photophobia (dislike of bright light), high temperature, nausea, stiff neck and/or a rash, flat purple spots which do not fade if pressed
> * severe pain
> * convulsions
> * unconsciousness
> * jaundice
> * unusual symptoms or behaviour
> * first aid emergencies
> * signs of dehydration
> * severe or persistent vomiting/ diarrhoea
> * no urine produced for 6–8 hours.

Records of a child's health

If you are caring for children in their own home, it is good practice to ensure that you record any change in their health and any medication which you have been requested to give. In all other settings, it is important to keep accurate records of:

* the name, age and address of the child
* parents' or guardian's contact numbers – at home and at work
* two further contact names and their telephone numbers
* the GP's name, address and telephone number
* long-term illnesses, allergies, conditions or operations
* medication
* special diet
* difficulties with hearing, speech or vision and whether glasses are worn
* immunisations.

These records of a child's health are confidential, and should only be seen by those who really need to know. Parents might not want some information to be disclosed in case the child is treated differently. It is also very important not to discuss the contents of the record sheet with anyone else. Records should be kept in a locked cupboard and be updated regularly, usually manually.

When caring for a child at home, the practitioner needs to make records of the child's illness in order to show the parents, or doctor, if necessary. These need to contain:

* the child's temperature
* date and time of any medication given
* any changes in the child's condition, e.g. if the child develops an earache or a rash. If the carer becomes concerned about a child's condition they should always contact the child's parents and/or seek medical assistance.

Procedures and regulations for administering medicines

Standard 10 of The National Service Framework for Children, Young People and Maternity Services, 2004, is 'Medicines for Children and Young People'; this gives guidance on the administration of medicines in all childcare settings.

- **Early Years and Childcare Settings** – These settings are required to stick to 'The National Standards for Day Care and Childminding of Children under Eight Years Old'. Medicine is included in Section 7 and requires that the setting has a policy which should include:
  - medicines being stored in their original containers, which are clearly labelled, and are locked away
  - medicines are usually only given if prescribed by a doctor for that child
  - written parental permission is given
  - records are kept of all medication and these are signed by the parent
  - training is given by a health professional for any medicines which require medical or technical knowledge.

- **Schools** – Guidance for schools is provided by 'Supporting Schools with Medical Needs', which aims to help schools to draw up their own policies.

  The National Service Framework for Children, Young People and Maternity Services states that staff should be adequately trained to give medicines by local health care professionals (such as school nurses). Schools need to have a policy on medicines and procedures for staff for administering, recording and storage of medicines. Staff also need to follow the prescriber's instructions.

- **Home** – The National Service Framework also gives some guidance for administering medications in a home setting. This includes support and advice on side effects and storage of medicines, being provided by healthcare professionals to parents/carers. Childminders follow 'The National Standards for Day Care and Childminding of Children under Eight Years Old' which includes having written records of medicines and ensuring that they have a thorough understanding of any medical condition and medication.

The practice of administering, recording and storing medicines

Giving medicine

Children often need medicine when unwell, but medicines are potentially dangerous and therefore great care should be taken in giving and storing them. It is best to avoid giving medicines if at all possible but if this is part of your role, ensure that you have been adequately trained.

Children under the age of 12 years are usually supplied with medicines in syrup form which are flavoured and often sugar free. They are supplied with a 5ml spoon or a syringe (for babies and young children). Most children are happy to take their medicine, but some are not so eager! Try offering their favourite drink afterwards, making it into a game or, if the taste is a problem, the child's parent could talk to the doctor about changing the flavour.

Record of medicines

Each early years setting will have a policy on this, and will require the parent to complete a form before any medicine can be given in the setting. If you are caring for a child at home, the parent should record all instructions for medicines. In most settings the first aider gives medicine. If you are caring for a child at home you must get permission from the parent before giving medicine.

KEY ISSUES

Giving medicines to children

- Before giving medicine ensure you know the reason for the medicine, the dosage, storage (some medication needs to be stored in the fridge), side effects and whether it should be given before or after food.
- Read the label on the medicine to ensure that it is the correct one.
- Check the dose and the time that the medicine should be given.
- If you are giving a medicine from the pharmacist, such as paracetamol, check that the dose you have been asked to give matches the instructions provided.
- Check the expiry date.
- Wash hands.
- Shake the bottle if necessary.
- Always use the measure that is provided with the medicine (teaspoons are not equivalent to 5ml measure).
- Explain to the child about the medicine and sit the child down, preferably on your knee.
- Pour medicines from the bottle with the label facing upwards, to prevent drips ruining the label.
- If using syringe, point this towards the inside of the cheek and give slowly to prevent choking.
- Ensure the child takes the full dose – medicine should never be added to drinks because the full dose might not be drunk.
- Give the child a drink after taking the medicine.
- Store the medicine correctly according to instructions.
- Record the date and time that you gave the medicine.
- For a baby, sterilise the syringe.
- If a child develops a side effect, such as a rash or diarrhoea, inform the GP before the next dose is given.
- It is important, when taking antibiotics, that the course is finished even if the child appears to get better, otherwise infection might reappear.
- A pharmacist should dispose of any unused medicines.

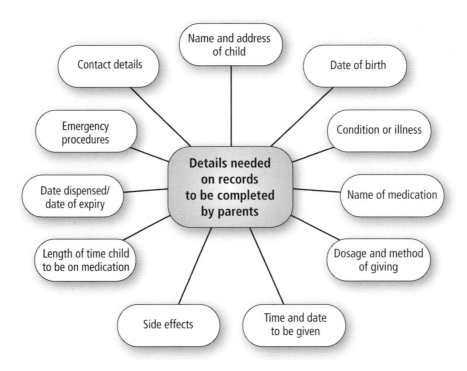

A mind map with central node "Details needed on records to be completed by parents" connected to: Name and address of child, Contact details, Date of birth, Emergency procedures, Condition or illness, Date dispensed/date of expiry, Name of medication, Length of time child to be on medication, Dosage and method of giving, Side effects, Time and date to be given.

DATE	NAME	TIME	NAME OF MEDICATION	DOSE GIVEN	ANY REACTIONS	SIGNED	PRINT NAME
20/10/05	Jessica Butler	12.15	Epilim	5mls	None	HED	H. Eldridge
20/10/05	Sophie Eldridge	13.00	Amoxycillin	5mls	None	MJ	M. Jackson

An example form to record details of mediation given to a child.

Storage of medicines

Medicines may be dangerous to anyone for whom they are not prescribed. The Control of Substances Hazardous to Health Regulations 1994 (COSHH) requires that the setting protects others from this risk. Medicines are therefore kept in a locked cupboard out of the reach of children in an early years setting. Inhalers (which need to be easily accessible), and medicines, which need to be in a locked fridge, are the exception to this. It is important in a home setting that medicines are kept out of reach of children. Children can very quickly find an open medication, including those with a childproof lid – these only delay a child for a few seconds. Care must be taken never to keep any medicines in a handbag because children find these very quickly.

Assessment activity 10.6

- Describe the treatment, care and medication routines for two children (one with an acute illness and one with a chronic condition) in different settings, and describe the role and responsibilities of the early years practitioner.
- Using an example from one of your work placements, explain the role and responsibilities of the early years practitioner when a child is unwell.
- Justify ways in which two different settings could alter and improve their treatment, care and medication procedures and routines to benefit children and their families. You may wish to use examples from placements, although these shouldn't be identified.

END-OF-UNIT TEST

1 What different types of health are there?

2 What is the early years practitioner's role in promoting health to children?

3 What environmental factors can affect health?

4 Name three different types of micro-organism and give three characteristics of each.

5 Name five different ways in which infections can be spread.

6 Which immunisations are given at two, three and four months and when is MMR given?

7 Why is it important to screen children's health and development? Give two ways this can be done.

8 What six signs indicate that a child is unwell?

9 What are the signs and symptoms of meningitis?

10 What could trigger an asthma attack and how should you deal with this?

11 What preventative measures can be taken in the setting to avoid gastroenteritis?

12 What signs indicate dehydration in a baby and how would you deal with this?

13 What is the normal temperature of a child and how would you reduce it if it were high?

14 What would you do if a child had a febrile convulsion?

15 What information needs to be included in a child's health records?

16 Where should medicines be stored?

References and further reading

Acheson, D (1998), *The Acheson Report: Independent inquiry into inequalities in health*, HMSO

Department of Health (1999), *Saving Lives: Our healthier nation*, HMSO

Department of Health (2003), *Every Child Matters*, HMSO

Department of Health (2003), *Keeping Children Safe*, HMSO

DfES (2001), *National Standards for Under 8s Day Care and Childminding*, Sure Start

Hall, D and Elliman, D (2003), *Health for All Children*, Oxford University Press

Keene, A (1999), *Child Health: Care of the child in health and illness*, Stanley Thornes

Meggitt, C (2001), *Baby and Child Health*, Heinemann

Naidoo, J and Wills, J (1998), *Practising Health Promotion: dilemmas and challenges*, Balliere Tindall

Stretch, B (2002), *BTEC National Health Studies*, Heinemann

World Health Organisation (2003), *Solid Facts*

Useful websites

Department of Health – www.dh.gov.uk

BBC Health Online – www.bbc.co.uk/health

Chartered Institute of Environmental Health – www.cieh.org

Department for Education and Skills (DfES) – www.dfes.gov.uk

Wired for Health – www.wiredforhealth.gov.uk

World Health Organisation – www.who.int

UNIT 11

Play and learning activities

Introduction

Play is essential to all children's development and acts as a natural learning medium. Through play children develop skills and language and learn about their immediate environment and those in it. This unit will help you to develop an understanding of the benefits of play and your role in maximising those potential benefits.

How you will be assessed

This unit is assessed internally.

1 The nature and value of play

It is increasingly being recognised that play should be central in children's lives, both in and out of early years settings. This section looks at the stages and types of play as well as the benefits from different types of play.

Definitions of play

Play is not as easy to define as one might at first think, although the following characteristics, as provided by Catherine Garvey, are often agreed upon.

* Play is pleasurable and enjoyable. Even when not actually accompanied by signs of mirth, it is still positively valued by the player.

* Play has no extrinsic goals. Its motivations are intrinsic and serve no other objectives.

* Play is spontaneous and voluntary. It is not obligatory but is freely chosen by the player.

* Play involves some active engagement on the part of the player.

* Play has certain systematic relations to what is not play.

Motivational value of play

One of the difficulties, when providing play, centres around the role of the adults and the way in which adults might structure play opportunities for children. How can play be 'real play' if adults have chosen and planned it, bearing in mind that one of the key characteristics of play seems to be that it should be spontaneous and voluntary? This is a fair question and, in reality, what tends to happen is that adults are using play as a vehicle for learning. We know that children respond to playful experiences and that they are likely to be motivated to learn if it is used as a tool. Play is so fascinating and pleasurable that children are often able to persevere at a self-chosen activity, concentrate and repeat skills.

Play activities and learning experiences
Stages of play

The way in which children engage in play changes as they develop new skills and learn how to relate to others. Play begins early on in life. A young baby enjoys being played with and quickly learns how to smile and gain the attention of adults. By eight months, most babies are starting to enjoy peek-a-boo and will even initiate this type of play by pulling something over their faces. The way in which children are gradually able to play together with children of their own age suggests that there are social stages to play. These were recorded by Mildred Parten in 1932 and are still referred to today. Note that the age guide in the table below has to be considered as very approximate and that, although most older children are capable of social activity, there will be times when they wish to play alone.

AGE	ACTIVITY	DESCRIPTION
0–2 years	Solitary activity (or play)	Babies and toddlers spend time playing 'in their own world'. Babies, for example, may spend time touching, feeling and talking to their toes.
2–4 years	Parallel activity (or play)	Children are beginning to notice other children and may play alongside each other. They may also imitate each other's play. Gradually children then become more and more involved in each other's play.
4–7 years	Collaborative (also known as co-operative) play	Children are able to play co-operatively together. They can decide how they want to play and make up rules for their play. They can also play complex games that require turn taking.

AGE	ACTIVITY	DESCRIPTION
7+ years	Competitive	Some children, from around six or seven years onwards, enjoy play that is collaborative and often structured, but also has a competitive dimension. Good examples of this are children playing board games, e.g. chess as well as sports, e.g. football, tennis.

The links between stages of development and play

The speed at which children's play becomes more social and sophisticated depends on their overall development, so adults need to be able to observe children playing in order to assess their play needs.

The following table shows the stages of play and development that most children show, although it should only be used as a broad guide.

AGE	STAGE OF DEVELOPMENT	SOCIAL STAGES OF PLAY	FEATURES OF PLAY	EXAMPLES OF RESOURCES/ EQUIPMENT
0–6 months	During this period, babies gain some control over their limbs. They learn about communication by cooing and babbling.	**Solitary play** Babies enjoy playing with adults and older children, but also play and 'talk' by themselves.	Senses are used to gain pleasure and explore. Repetitive actions are used.	Baby gyms, rattles
6–12 months	Most babies become mobile in this time. Babies are learning to gain adult attention by smiling, babbling and, towards 12 months, pointing.	**Solitary play** Additionally, babies often show things to adults and initiate movements which will gain adult responses, e.g. dropping a toy on the floor.	Senses are still being used. Play is repetitive and exploratory.	Activity quilts, balls, books, pop-up toys
1–2 years	Toddlers are mobile and gaining gross and fine manipulative skills. They can feed themselves and can stack bricks and manage very simple puzzles. Language is just developing, with first words emerging at 12–14 months. By 2 years, many children are beginning to put two words together. Children are very reliant on adults and want to be close to adults.	**Solitary play** Most activity is still likely to be solitary.	Trial and error learning. Repetitive movements and play. Toddlers 'talk' to toys. Imaginative play is developing.	Push-and-pull toys, dolls, trolleys

AGE	STAGE OF DEVELOPMENT	SOCIAL STAGES OF PLAY	FEATURES OF PLAY	EXAMPLES OF RESOURCES/ EQUIPMENT
2–3 years	Children's overall co-ordination is becoming developed, although strength is often lacking. Many new words are learnt. Sentences are short, e.g. three words, and not always understood by others. Children often need adults to support their play and to help organise games.	**Parallel play** Children begin to notice other children playing and will happily play alongside.	Children enjoy imaginative play and imitate adult gestures, words and movements. Children may take each other's toys and equipment. Sensory play is also enjoyed, e.g. water, sand. Play can be repetitive with children gaining mastery of their movements.	Dressing-up clothes Props used in the home, e.g. tea sets, telephones Water, sand, paint and dough
3–4 years	Children are usually confident at this age. Most children are well co-ordinated and are able to snip/cut with scissors, run and partly dress themselves. They feel grown up as they are usually out of nappies. Language is usually understood by others and by 4 years, speech has become fairly fluent. Children require significant adult support.	**Parallel/ co-operative play** The way in which children play is usually determined by their level of confidence and language skills.	Play is often imaginative play with children playing alongside or with others. Children also enjoy physical activities such as riding tricycles and climbing. Some play is beginning to be more planned, e.g. a child may tell an adult that they are making a house out of bricks.	Small world play, e.g. farm animals, train sets Dressing-up clothes and home props Water, sand, paint and dough
4–6 years	Friendships are beginning to be formed. Single-sex groups are not unusual. Language is usually fluent with only minor errors. Physically, children are well co-ordinated. Children often require adult support and help.	**Co-operative play** Children are able to play together, share equipment and respond to each others' play.	Imaginative play remains important for some children, although other children are more interested in games involving physical skills, e.g. football, riding bicycles, or making things, e.g. construction toys.	Climbing frames, bicycles Drawing and painting Construction toys Creative materials

AGE	STAGE OF DEVELOPMENT	SOCIAL STAGES OF PLAY	FEATURES OF PLAY	EXAMPLES OF RESOURCES/ EQUIPMENT
6+ years	Friendships are important to children. Children are starting to see others' points of view and can negotiate. Children are becoming increasingly independent.	Co-operative play	Children begin to have strong play preferences, e.g. some children enjoy making things while others may enjoy physical games.	Very dependent on children's preferences – creative materials, board games, complex construction toys, footballs, climbing frames, hoops, dressing-up clothes

Assessment activity 11.1

Carry out the following structured observation using free description (see page 273).

* Observe two children of different ages playing with the same piece of equipment, for example, give a football to a child of twelve months and then later to a child of four years.

* Analyse the differences in the way in which the children have played.

* Evaluate the extent to which their play links to their stages of development.

* Consider ways in which their play links to theories of child development.

Types of play activity and learning experience

Play can be grouped into types, although remember that for children play is simply play! Categorising play into types helps practitioners to plan effectively, as each play type has particular developmental benefits. Categories of play can vary from setting to setting, but in this unit play has been grouped into:

* imaginative play

* creative and sensory play

* exploratory, technological/investigative play

* vigorous physical play.

Imaginative play

This type of play is also referred to as 'pretend play' or 'role play'. It particularly stimulates children's language as at first they talk to themselves and later talk to each other. The language used often reflects the language that they have heard, with children sometimes using imaginative play to make sense of situations that they have encountered.

Physical development

* Develops fine manipulative movements and hand-eye co-ordination, e.g. pretending to pour drinks.

* Develops gross motor skills during play, e.g. pretending to go shopping by getting on a tricycle.

Communication, language and literacy

* Develops an awareness of social language, e.g. children 'practise' intonation, vocabulary that they have heard and expressions.

* Develops an awareness of non-verbal communication, e.g. children use facial expressions and hand gestures.

* Develops interest in 'writing' as some children begin to write as part of their play, e.g. writing out a shopping list, calling the register.

Cognitive development

* Imaginative play is often used by children as a way of interpreting the 'adult world', e.g. children often practise using 'numbers' in their play.

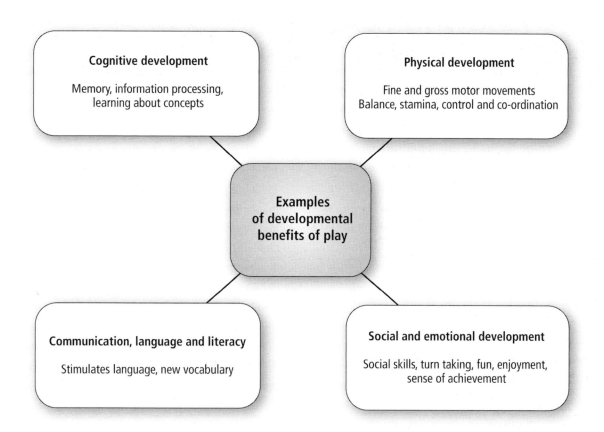

Cognitive development

Memory, information processing, learning about concepts

Physical development

Fine and gross motor movements
Balance, stamina, control and co-ordination

Examples of developmental benefits of play

Communication, language and literacy

Stimulates language, new vocabulary

Social and emotional development

Social skills, turn taking, fun, enjoyment, sense of achievement

---

* Develops problem-solving skills, e.g. children may turn a table into a bed to suit their play needs or look for ways of making a blanket from a coat.

Social and emotional development

* Develops and rehearses social conventions, e.g. children practise 'how to behave' and often act out the consequences of not behaving.

* Develops understanding of gender and social roles. Children, as part of trying to make sense of their world and their role in it, try to explore gender and adult roles through their role play.

* Develops and explores friendships.

* Provides enjoyment and freedom, e.g. by creating their own world, children can feel 'released' from the world of adult expectations.

Resources for imaginative play

Imaginative play is seen as important for children's development. Many settings provide a range of materials to support this type of play – see the table below. In home settings, children often use 'real' props rather than ones specifically made. A feature of this type of play is the way in which children are adept at making one object stand for another, for example, a box becomes a car or a piece of dough becomes a cake. They also adapt environments to suit their play purposes, for example, a bench outdoors becomes the garage while the tricycle becomes a car.

ROLE PLAY	SMALL WORLD PLAY
Materials for home corner, e.g. tea set, cooking utensils, bed, cooker, pushchairs, dolls and teddies, etc. Dressing-up clothes Materials for a shop or office, e.g. cash till, shopping bags, typewriter, note pad	Duplo people, animals Fisher Price people Playmobil people Farm animals

TYPE OF CREATIVE PLAY	FEATURES	RESOURCES
Collage	Children from as young as 2 years enjoy selecting and feeling different textures and finally sticking them.	Glue, selection of paper, fabrics, laces, ribbons, buttons, feathers, newspaper, magazines
Painting	Most children enjoy painting and printing with brushes, rollers, sponges and also with their hands.	Selection of paints, large brushes, rollers, fine brushes
Musical instruments	Children love to use musical instruments and can quickly learn to identify a beat or rhythm. Exploring the sounds of instruments helps children's auditory discrimination.	Homemade shakers and rattles, a selection of un-tuned percussion instruments such as tambours, drums and rattles; tuned percussion instruments, such as xylophone, chime bars
Junk modelling	From a selection of paper, boxes and other materials, children enjoy creating 3D models.	Wide selection of interesting textures and materials which might include boxes, bubble wrap, corks, plastic lids, matchsticks, straws, tubing
Drawing and mark making	Early drawing and mark making forms part of the process of learning to write and communicate through symbols.	Selection of paper, typewriter, crayons, charcoals, pastels, felt tips, board markers, rubbers, etc.

Creative and expressive play

Creative play is a broad heading to encompass materials and play that encourage children to express themselves. It is important to differentiate between creative play and activities which are adult-led and result in children making things to a set formula. Creative play should allow children to be expressive and to bring to their play an interpretation of their own ideas. For example, they may choose to paint but will not necessarily use the 'proper' colours. Another key feature of creative play is that it does not have to have a definite purpose or end product – only the purpose that the child ascribes it. For example, a three-year-old may enjoy the texture of ribbons and laces and may choose to stick different pieces onto a piece of paper.

Opportunities for creative play

Many settings provide varied opportunities for creative play. To maximise learning opportunities for creative play, it is important that, wherever possible, children are provided with a varied range of resources, as shown in the table above, and are encouraged to explore the materials freely.

Sensory play

Sensory play is sometimes referred to as 'play with natural materials'. It includes traditional nursery activities such as sand, water and malleable materials like dough. Sensory play has the capacity to hold some children's attention for long periods of time as the sensory nature of the materials seems to help them to focus. It is not unusual for quite sociable children to prefer to play in parallel with sensory activities. For example. two four-year-olds may stand side by side at a sand tray and, while looking occasionally across at each other, may not actually play together.

Opportunities for sensory play

Most early years settings aim to provide for at least one type of sensory play. The equipment that is put out often shapes how children will use the materials, such as dough with scissors as opposed to dough with moulds and rollers. Some examples are given in the following table.

TYPES OF SENSORY PLAY	FEATURES	EXAMPLES OF RESOURCES – THESE ARE USUALLY ROTATED TO ENCOURAGE CHILDREN TO PLAY IN A VARIETY OF WAYS
Sand	Sand can be provided in walk-in large pits, free-standing trays or also in small trays on tables. Children tend to spend time scooping, digging and shaping sand, although the dampness of sand will affect the way that they play.	Equipment for scooping and pouring, e.g. spoons, spades, bottles, egg cups. Toys with wheels, e.g. trucks. Animals, e.g. dinosaurs, farm animals. Objects for hiding, e.g. shells, beads, 'treasure'. Equipment for printing and making sand castles
Water	Water is usually provided in large trays. Children tend to enjoy changes in the water tray, e.g. inclusion of ice cubes, bubbles or coloured water.	Items for floating, e.g. boats, corks, ducks. Toys for 'washing' dolls' clothes, dolls, plastic animals. Equipment for pouring and scooping, e.g. beakers, bottles, tubes, funnels.
Dough, plasticine and clay	Dough is used for children to model with as well as to pound and cut. Dough is versatile, as there are many recipes which provide different textures.	Tools, e.g. cutters, rollers, scissors. Moulds. Plates and cake tins to encourage children to make items for their role play.
Gloop	Gloop is cornflour combined with water. It forms a runny paste.	Trays and spoons, although many children simply use their hands.

Exploratory and technological/investigative play

Most children enjoy looking at things work, investigating and seeing what things can do. This area of play is about children acting almost as early scientists and mathematicians. They may go outdoors and look closely at things, want to dig and pour water into a hole or create a shelter. Indoors they might be interested in programmable toys, computers and technology. This is not a 'traditional' area of play, but one that reflects the growing interest in technology and also the realisation that children should also be spending time outdoors playing.

Combining play types

As children do not see play in terms of 'types', they tend to combine play materials to support their ongoing play. The climbing frame may become the house, dough may be used to make cakes for the home corner or farm animals may need to go for a swim in the water tray! Insisting

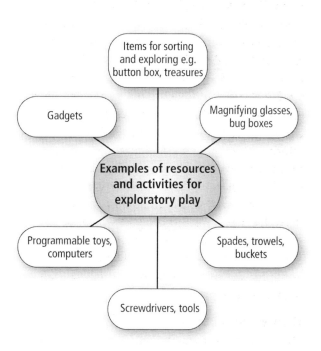

that play materials can only be used in a certain way or have to remain in certain places generally inhibits children's learning experiences and creativity. It is good practice therefore for settings to be as flexible as possible and, unless materials or equipment are likely to be damaged, to try to allow children to combine materials.

Play experiences

Planned and spontaneous play

In order to implement the early years curriculum, children will need a variety of play experiences, both planned and spontaneous. Spontaneous play experiences are often those that the children find the most rewarding because they are often child initiated and thus of interest to them. Sometimes spontaneous play arises out of planned activities – for example, a practitioner may decide to encourage children to sort buttons, but a child may discover how to play tiddlywinks with the buttons. This spontaneous play could then be used by the practitioner to further other learning by asking the child about the buttons which are the easiest to use.

Spontaneous play can arise from a planned opportunity.

Structured and free play

Structured play is sometimes the term used when adult involvement is an essential part of an activity, such as planting bulbs. In recent early years curricular documents, the terms 'adult-directed activity' or 'adult-initiated activity' are often used instead of 'structured play'. These terms reflect the growing view that if play is highly structured, it is unlikely to be in essence 'play', as play by its nature should emanate from the child.

There are many advantages of structured play or adult-directed activities. If sensitively led, they can support specific areas of a child's development or enable coverage of a particular area of the curriculum. An adult, for example, may put ice cubes in the water tray and ask a group of children to observe and play with the cubes to see if they float or sink. This activity would help children to notice the properties of ice

and through the activity they may learn specific vocabulary.

In contrast, free play is play that is completely chosen by the child and relies on children's interests, hence the growing trend to call this type of play 'child initiated' or 'child led'. There are many advantages to this type of play as children are able to spend time following their own interests and set their own challenges.

Most settings aim to provide a mix of play opportunities, some of which would be considered as structured play and others as free play. The table opposite shows the advantages and disadvantages of structured and free play.

Combining free and structured play

As both child-initiated play and activities involving adults have advantages, there is a growing trend towards combining both ways of working with children. The Foundation Stage curriculum advocates play as a vehicle for learning, but gives practitioners a vital role. To achieve this way of working, many settings now look for a combined approach as illustrated by the case study opposite.

FREE PLAY OR CHILD-INITIATED ACTIVITIES		STRUCTURED PLAY OR ADULT-DIRECTED ACTIVITIES	
ADVANTAGES	**DISADVANTAGES**	**ADVANTAGES**	**DISADVANTAGES**
+ Children can set their own goals. + Children concentrate for longer periods when play is self chosen. + Children are more likely to be creative. + Child-initiated activities are less pressurised as the child is responsible. + Children learn how to choose. + Children can gain in confidence by being self-reliant. + Children can repeat activities until they feel they have mastered them.	– Children may not gain specific language or may choose not to engage in co-operative play. – Sometimes child-initiated play can be repetitive and not challenge the child. – Child-initiated play can be stereotypical. – Some children find it hard to cope with choice. – Children may not get a range of skills. – Children with learning difficulties may not receive sufficient adult input.	+ Coverage of the curriculum is ensured. + Children can gain specific vocabulary and skills. + Areas of the curriculum, such as mathematics, need to be delivered sequentially in schools.	– Children's attention span is shorter during adult-directed activities. – Children may feel that they have failed if the adult's expectations are too high. – Activities may not be sufficiently challenging or creative.

CASE STUDY

Anna, an early years practitioner, wants to encourage several children who are four years old to practise their sorting skills as part of delivering the mathematical development area of learning within the Foundation Stage. She puts out a large tray of buttons on a table. Two children come and start playing and touching the buttons. Anna asks them to show her their favourite buttons. She gives each child a small box to put their favourite buttons in. As the children show her their favourite buttons, she comments on them, saying 'This one is shiny. This one has four holes'. She then asks the children if they could find her some black buttons with four holes. After three or four minutes, Anna leaves them to carry on playing.

The children make up their own sorting game using the small boxes that Anna has left.

Evaluate the effectiveness of this approach to learning by considering the following questions.

- How has the early years curriculum been implemented?
- How are the children learning through play?
- How is the practitioner able to meet individual children's needs and interests?
- How did the practitioner's intervention extend the children's skills and language development?

Extension of play opportunities

Practitioners need to look at ways of extending children's learning while they are playing. This can take many forms and requires a flexible and thoughtful approach.

✳ **Providing further equipment**. A practitioner may feel that a child could benefit from a more challenging jigsaw puzzle or could be given further choice of materials in order to make the play more enjoyable.

* **Asking questions**. Sometimes practitioners may ask questions to stimulate children's thinking and thus learning about a situation, e.g. 'What would happen if you mixed the colours?' It is important that questioning is not carried out in the form of an interrogation and that the question is worth asking!

* **Playing alongside or with children**. Practitioners can play alongside children as this may help children to gain ideas, e.g. a practitioner may start to make a model and children might then take some of the ideas and incorporate them into their own models.

Language and communication activities

Children are more likely to remember and gain new vocabulary if it is introduced to them in an enjoyable way. Many settings working with young children play games such as picture lotto or guess what is in the feely bag.

Role of adult

These types of games often need an adult to direct and support the children. Adults need to be careful not to 'take over' so that they are speaking more than the children! It is also important to allow young children enough time to reflect and find 'the words' that they need. You must remember that most children are not able to internalise speech and thought until they are six or seven years old. This means that young children are likely to call out the answers or speak even when in theory it is not their turn. To avoid disruption, games tend to work better when played in very small groups.

Drama and role play

Imaginative play encourages children's speech and language development. To develop children's overall language, many early years settings 'theme' the role play area so that children begin to use new expressions and vocabulary (see the diagram below). Themes tend to work well when children have had some actual experience so that they draw from it into their play.

Role of adult

Children learn new vocabulary and expressions by hearing. This means that when introducing a new theme into the role play area, adults will need to introduce the target language. This can be done by having a visitor into the setting, such as a vet to talk about how animals are cared for, if the role play area is an animal hospital. Language can also be introduced by reading a book or story to children and also by the adult at first taking a role in the area.

Music and rhymes

Songs, nursery rhymes and counting rhymes all stimulate children's language. Research carried

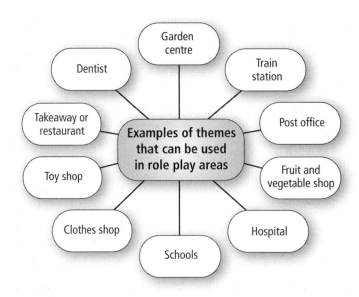

out in the 1980s suggested a correlation between children's achievement in reading and their knowledge of traditional nursery rhymes. This is likely to exist because children learn to focus on patterns, rhymes and phonetic sounds in words as they speak or sing them. There are many songs that have actions or dances and these are particularly enjoyed by children.

The use of traditional nursery rhymes is controversial in some settings as many nursery rhymes promote stereotypes and violence. There is also a school of thought which suggests that they should be learnt by children in order to keep a strong historical tradition alive. Many settings choose a compromise and combine traditional rhymes with modern songs and, where necessary, alter words.

Role of adult

Adults need to be familiar with a range of songs and games and also, where necessary, to learn new ones. Traditional nursery rhymes often have several verses and these should be used so that children gain the pattern and sounds. It is also important for songs to be carefully planned and not just rely on children choosing them as

otherwise their 'repertoire' will not develop. It is also a good idea to use props, especially with counting rhymes, as they help give meaning to the 'numbers' that the children are hearing. Nursery rhymes and songs have a huge advantage in that they can be done at any time and so it is good practice to 'burst' into song at odd times especially if children are waiting or are bored, such as at home time while waiting for their parents.

Poetry and literature

From as early as four months old, children can be introduced to books. In early years settings, a range of stories and poems will help children develop an interest in reading. Children who enjoy handling books and listening to stories and poems are more likely to be motivated to learn to read. Children's vocabulary and expressions are extended by hearing stories and poems and they also learn to associate print with reading. Poems and books can be used as starting points for a themed play during a session as the example below shows.

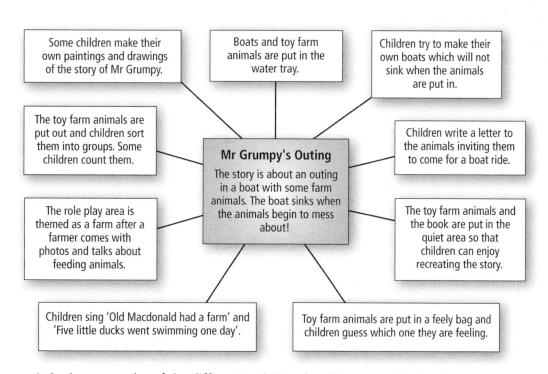

Mr Grumpy's Outing: examples of the different activities that this story might lead to.

Using the early years curriculum:

- discuss how the activities in Mr Grumpy's outing would link to the curriculum
- explain the developmental benefits of these activities
- produce a short-term plan with identified aims and objectives for one of these activities.

Role of adult

It is essential that the experience of listening to stories and rhymes is a pleasurable one for children, otherwise they will not become motivated to learn to read for themselves. To achieve this, stories and rhymes are best shared with a very small group or even individual children. This allows for children to make comments about the story or ask questions and 'dwell on' pages that they find particularly interesting. Young children also rely heavily on pictures and will need to spend time looking at and enjoying the pictures. To help children learn to identify print with the words being spoken, it is good practice for adults to run their fingers under the words as they are reading. This also helps children to learn that in English, print runs from left to right.

Whole-group story time is very difficult to manage with young children as they are unable to 'hold in' their thoughts and tend to call out. The Foundation Stage curriculum in England, for example, does not give this as a model for working with three- and four-year-olds, suggesting instead individual and small-group sharing of books. In settings where whole-group story time is being used, it is essential to use props and look for ways of making the story time interactive. This might mean choosing books with a repeated refrain which mean that children can join in.

Communication of information and reconstruction of events

Children need to be able to use language in a variety of ways, including being able to describe events, give information and ask questions. Young children need plenty of support and practice at gaining these skills. Activities to help children

gain these skills need to be carried out in small groups or with individual children. Children often benefit from the use of puppets, props, photos and objects which help them to visualise and sequence their thoughts. Adults often have to model language with young children as the case study below shows.

CASE STUDY

Mike, an early years practitioner, has brought in a teddy bear. He tells a small group of children that teddy wants to see what happens in a nursery class. The children take turns at 'showing' teddy around and during the session he joins in. Towards the end of the session, Mike asks pairs of children to use a telephone to tell 'teddy's mum' what he has been doing. To model the language to some of the younger children, Mike often talks to 'teddy's mum' first. The children listen to Mike and then often repeat the same expressions and phrases when it is their turn. Mike planned this activity to encourage children to use description and also to recount events.

Role of adults

Adults need to model new language to children. They may need to help children by asking them questions which help to sequence events – for example, 'Do you remember what happened after story time?' Large group situations should be avoided as they can create unnecessary stress as younger children may not be able to 'get out' what they want to say quickly and before older children call out. This can in turn cause some children to stammer or stutter.

Expression of emotion

Language development is linked to behaviour. Children who are articulate are often more able to control their behaviour and also to express their needs without being aggressive or attention seeking. Learning to express one's feelings requires specific language. Activities that can help children to do this include using puppets who 'say' what they are feeling, choosing stories where central characters express their emotions and also looking for ways of helping children talk about things that make them happy, sad, angry or jealous.

Role of adult
Adults need to model language that children will need. They also need to look for opportunities to talk about emotions, especially when children are experiencing potentially stressful events in their lives, such as the arrival of a sibling, moving house, changes in family structure or a visit to hospital. There are many resources, including books and puppets, that can be used to trigger discussions.

CASE STUDY

Jaswinder, an early years practitioner, uses a teddy and some other cuddly toys to talk about feelings. Teddy tells Jaswinder that he is feeling sad. None of his friends want to play with him. Jaswinder asks another cuddly toy why. The cuddly toy says that teddy never wants to share any of his toys and that last time they played, teddy hurt him. He says that teddy makes him feel unhappy. Jaswinder asks a child or a small group of children what they think the problem is. Jaswinder asks the children if they can tell teddy what he should do. This activity can be used to introduce specific vocabulary and also to help children think about sharing and friendships.

Speaking and listening activities
A good starting point when considering speaking and listening activities is to revisit children's stages of language development including their ability to internalise thought and process information (see Unit 13). Child development theories suggest that children will find it hard to process information gained by the spoken word alone (i.e. listening) as they rely heavily on images to process information. In the same way, they find it hard to wait for their turn to speak because they cannot internalise their thoughts which results in them needing to talk in order to think. It is therefore good practice for speaking and listening activities to be interactive and carried out with small groups of children. Some examples are given in the table below.

Role of adult
Adults have to remember that children's ability to absorb the spoken word in the absence of pictures or gestures is limited. This is why many young children appear to find it hard to sit and listen. Listening activities need therefore to be kept focused and interactive, for example, 'put your hand up when you hear a bell'. It is also very hard for young children to listen to each other – as young children do not have 'entertainment' skills. This means that activities relying on large groups are unlikely to meet the needs of all the children.

SPEAKING ACTIVITIES	LISTENING ACTIVITIES
Feely bags – children have to describe what they are feeling to the others. Guess what is in the box – children have to ask questions. I went to the shops and I bought… (for young children put out real objects).	Simon says... Sound lotto. Guess the sound (one child hides behind a screen and the other children guess or point to the instrument that is being played). Stop and go type games – children run around and make certain movements according to the instructions.

Self-expression

Activities that encourage self-expression help children gain confidence, build imagination and develop language and fine manipulative skills.

Role play, dance and drama

Although the role play area can be used to stimulate children's language, it should also be a place where children can go, dress up and take on any role that they wish. As children get older, they may wish to plan their play with others and this then becomes 'drama'.

Children can also show self-expression when moving to music. Children enjoy having space and music to move to. Props such as ribbons and scarves can be put out as some children enjoy moving and creating shapes with them.

While concerts and plays organised by adults may be enjoyed by children, it is important to understand that generally they are not good vehicles for self-expression as they originate with the adult rather than with the child.

Creative art

Drawing, painting and making models are all ways of encouraging self-expression in children. The key to helping children show their creativity is to provide them with a good choice of materials rather than to show them what to make. Most settings provide a drawing and writing table as well as malleable materials and paint.

Role of adult

In order for children to be able to express themselves, adults have to give them choices and a feeling of 'freedom'. Children will need to feel that there is no 'right way' or 'wrong way' and that whatever they do will be free of judgement. Adults have therefore to learn to take a 'step back' and support rather than direct children. It is also important that adults praise children for what they are doing, rather than for what they are producing – 'You look like you are enjoying painting' rather than 'Well done, that's a lovely painting'.

Physical development

There is increasing research to suggest that children's physical development is important in order to help their literacy. Physical skills also give children confidence and independence as, for example, they can put on their coats or complete a jigsaw. Physical skills can be divided into gross and locomotive motor skills and fine motor skills, although some activities encompass both types of skill (see table below).

ACTIVITY	SKILLS PROMOTED	COMMENTS
Obstacle courses – indoor and outdoors	Promotes gross and locomotive skills and develops general co-ordination and balance.	Obstacle courses are enjoyed by children and can be varied according to children's stage of development. Hoops and play tunnels, as well as beams, can be used to encourage children to use a range of movements.
Parachute games	Promotes listening skills, co-ordination and gross motor and locomotive skills.	Parachute games can be used indoors as well as outdoors. Tablecloths or sheets can be used to improvise as parachutes.
Tricycles, scooters, roller skates and bicycles.	Promotes hand-eye co-ordination and gross locomotive skills and also helps children to learn about speed and distance.	Children need to gain in confidence to use these pieces of equipment. Protective headgear should be offered where possible in case of falls. Children enjoy the feeling of speed and independence.

ACTIVITY	SKILLS PROMOTED	COMMENTS
Climbing frames, seesaws, swings	Balance, co-ordination and gross motor skills, spatial awareness.	This type of equipment helps children to gain in confidence as they enjoy the sensations of climbing and swinging.
Throwing and catching	Gross motor skills, hand-eye and foot-eye co-ordination.	Young children will need significant input before they can throw and catch.
Kicking	Co-ordination, perceptual skills.	There are a range of balls, bean bags and coils available. Children will also enjoy simply throwing and then collecting objects. Children enjoy kicking from an early age although children find it hard to play co-operatively with a football until they are older.
Running games	Gross motor and locomotive skills, co-ordination, spatial awareness.	There are a range of 'running games' that can be enjoyed by children, e.g. chase or what's the time Mr Wolf?. Young children also appreciate catching bubbles that have been blown into the wind or running with ribbons.

Fine motor skills

Children need to develop the muscles in their hands to allow them later to use tools such as scissors with accuracy and also in order to be able to write.

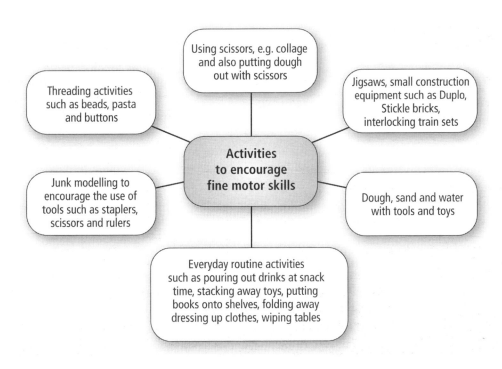

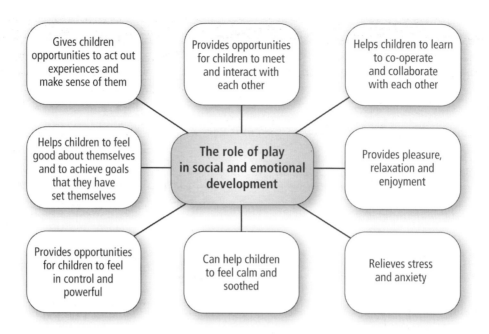

The role of play in social and emotional development

- Gives children opportunities to act out experiences and make sense of them
- Provides opportunities for children to meet and interact with each other
- Helps children to learn to co-operate and collaborate with each other
- Helps children to feel good about themselves and to achieve goals that they have set themselves
- Provides pleasure, relaxation and enjoyment
- Provides opportunities for children to feel in control and powerful
- Can help children to feel calm and soothed
- Relieves stress and anxiety

Role of adult

Many physical skills involve practice and early failure can discourage children from continuing. This means that activities need to be planned to ensure that, while presenting some level of challenge, the child is likely to succeed. Children also need to gain in confidence before attempting some activities, such as climbing or attempting to ride a bicycle. Adults therefore need to adopt a sensitive approach to encouraging children to attempt such activities and avoid pressuring children.

Therapeutic nature of play

Social and emotional development

While play was once viewed as a waste of time, now we know that it benefits children's social and emotional development. Sensory activities such as sand, water and dough, as well as role play, are particularly seen as helpful. Being encouraged to play often helps children who have witnessed or been the subject of distressing events in their lives, including bereavement and abuse.

2 How to plan, prepare, evaluate and further develop play and learning activities

Adults working with children need to be able to plan and implement activities. This section looks at ways in which planning might take place and also at the role of evaluating activities ready for further planning.

Planning and preparation

Providing for children's play requires good organisation to ensure that there are sufficient materials, equipment and support to meet the needs of all children. This means that nearly all settings have some form of formal planning system in place, although the extent and type of plans can vary enormously.

Planning for the early years curriculum

In the UK, at the time of writing, there are several early years frameworks. Frameworks reflect the needs of the home countries and also the ages of the children. Each country within the UK has, or is developing, a framework for the under threes as well as one for pre-school and school-age

ADVANTAGES	POTENTIAL DISADVANTAGES
Provides cohesiveness in play and learning. Enthuses children to learn about particular topics. Helps staff remain focused and motivated. Can provide a way of involving parents and even the community as a whole.	Can be difficult to tie in all areas of the curriculum into the theme – this can result in 'false' or contrived links. The play needs and interests of all children may not be met. The theme may act as a restriction and staff may not put out certain activities because 'they do not link to the theme'. May lead to an adult-led rather than a child-led curriculum.

children. Settings in receipt of government funding need to show that they are implementing the curriculum for their country.

School settings working with children aged six years and above in the UK have to plan using the country's National Curriculum.

Thematic and non-thematic frameworks

Many settings choose to deliver part or all of the curriculum using themes. The idea behind themes is that play and learning activities are interlinked and children benefit from a cohesiveness. There are hundreds of popular themes including 'myself', 'growing' and 'colours'. It is generally accepted that 'themes' are not really appropriate with babies and very young children, although many settings working with children over three years tend to have some type of theme. There are criticisms as well as advantages of using themes in planning. These are outlined in the table above.

Types of planning

There are several types of planning and, as this changes from setting to setting, it will be important to find out the type of planning that your setting uses. Good plans are based on correct assessment of children's stages of development and interests.

Long-term planning

The length of long-term plans varies incredibly. Some settings view a long-term plan as anything over six weeks, while in school settings it usually refers to a full academic year's work.

Common features of long-term plans

* Outlines how curriculum is to be delivered.

* Considers the themes that are to be used over the period.

Medium-term plans

Medium-term plans are in some settings called curriculum plans. The length of a medium-term plan depends on the long-term plan. In some schools a medium-term plan shows coverage for half a term, while in some pre-school settings it shows coverage for a fortnight or a month.

Common features of medium-term plans

* Details types of activities to be offered.

* Shows how the activities link to the Early Years or National Curriculum.

* Indicates the order in which the activities are to be carried out.

* Shows learning outcomes.

Short-term plans

Settings that plan for a month may also have short-term plans which show what is to happen each week or each session. Settings may refer to these type of plan as 'session planners' or 'weekly planners'.

Common features of short-term plans

* Contains details of staffing and resources.

* Includes order of activities to be carried out.

* Details of how individual activities may be adapted or extended to suit particular children.

* Shows learning outcomes for activities.

Role of adults
- Will there be sufficient adults to ensure effectiveness of activity?
- What level of supervision is required?
- What type of support will children need?
- How should children be supported during the activity?

Preparation of setting
- How much preparation time is required for the activity?
- Where will the activity be located?
- How will the activity be made appealing to children?

Meeting the needs of children
- How do the activities meet the needs of individual children?
- How do the activities link with the curriculum that is being followed?

Factors that will influence the effectiveness of play and learning activities

Resources
- Are there sufficient resources available?
- How attractive are the resources?
- Are they suitable for the purpose of the activity?

Health and safety constraints
- Are the materials/toys suitable for the age/stage of the children?
- Has the area been checked for hazards?
- Are the toys/materials clean and safe?
- Is the location of the activity suitable and hazard free?

---

* May show which activities are to be assessed.

* Details the role of the adult in supporting specific children.

Activity plans

These can be referred to as detailed activity plans or even in schools lesson plans. Activity plans are not used in every setting, but tend to be used by students to help them show that they can plan a single activity effectively.

Common features of an activity plan

* Shows resources.

* Shows staffing.

* Has specific learning outcomes.

* Demonstrates how needs of individual children will be met.

* Details the role of the adult.

Curriculum planning

A curriculum can be thought of as a programme of activities or learning outcomes. Some settings plan an overall curriculum, which may be based on areas of development or on areas of learning from the curriculum they are following. Other settings may produce a separate curriculum plan for each area of learning or subject. For example, some schools have a curriculum plan for literacy, another one for mathematics, and so on.

Ensuring plans meet children's individual needs

It is now good practice to ensure that activities and equipment meet children's individual needs and interests. This means observing children and also talking with parents. Parents can help us find out about their children's strengths, needs and also play interests.

Structured play and free play

As well as thinking about the activities, practitioners also have to think about the balance between structured and adult-directed play, and play that is child-led or 'free'. It is essential that children do have sufficient time to explore and set their own challenges in the way they want and there has been some concern that time and opportunities for 'free play' have been crowded out.

Differentiating the curriculum to meet children's needs

Within the planning process, play and learning experiences need to match children's needs. Experienced practitioners choose activities and resources that will allow the curriculum to be differentiated – one child may simply observe and play with ice cubes in the water, while another may be asked to find a way of keeping the ice cube from floating.

Factors for consideration

There are a range of factors that will influence the effectiveness of play and learning activities – see the diagram opposite. By planning ahead, settings avoid confusion, duplication of activities and are able to check that sufficient resources are available.

Assessment activity 11.2

In order to carry out this assessment activity fully, you should gain the advice and permission of your placement supervisor.

- Produce an overall curriculum plan for at least six weeks showing a range of play activities that would be suitable for your placement setting.
- Choose five activities from the curriculum plan and produce activity plans for each of them.
- Implement the activity plans, keeping notes for later evaluation (see Assessment activity 11.4).

Your curriculum plan should contain:

- a detailed rationale for the play activities chosen which considers the potential learning benefits from the plan

- detailed links between the early years or National Curriculum and the curriculum plan.

Each activity plan should contain:

- an explanation of how the activity is to be implemented
- an examination of the role of the adult in extending children's learning during the activity
- an exploration of the factors that might affect the success of the activity
- detailed links between the activities chosen and the stages of development of the children
- analysis of the potential developmental benefits of each activity.

Role in formal learning

Many activities that help children to learn skills and concepts are now being planned using play as a tool. We have seen that children are responsive to play and so combining play with learning intentions can be extremely effective. The key to doing this successfully is to consider what children naturally enjoy doing and finding ways of building learning into them. The table below shows how activities can be planned to promote children's learning while they are playing.

AREA OF LEARNING	EXAMPLE OF PLAY ACTIVITY
Literacy	*Reading* Children can learn to recognise their names by playing a treasure hunt game. Adults hide names outdoors and children see if they can find their own name. Children can then develop this into their own game – they may write notes to each other and hide them or want to hide each other's names.
Mathematics	*Subtraction* The sand tray has 10 sand castles on it. Children roll a dice and take it in turns to squash down the sand castles. Children can develop this game by making their own sandcastles and choosing to knock them down.

AREA OF LEARNING	EXAMPLE OF PLAY ACTIVITY
Science	*Blowing bubbles* Children are given a range of bubble mixtures and shapes through which they blow bubbles. Adults might help them to notice that bubbles are always spherical. Children can develop this game by trying to blow the largest bubble.
ICT	*Using programmable toys* Adults show the children how a toy robot works and together they make a maze for the toy robot to travel along. Children can develop this by building their own maze and seeing if they can programme the robot to move through it.
Knowledge and understanding of the world	*Learning about immediate environment* Adults give children magnifying sheets. Children explore how to use them and make their own discoveries about what is outside.

Encompassing diversity

In the planning process, thought has to be given to what has been dubbed the 'hidden curriculum', or underlying messages that children will be learning besides the ones intended. Are the activities in any way discriminatory? Will the activities help children to take a positive view of the differences in others and around them? Are the activities reinforcing undesirable stereotypes? These key questions should be at the forefront of practitioners' minds when planning and evaluating programmes.

Note that the Foundation Stage curriculum reflects the growing sentiment that, before children can learn about the cultures and beliefs of others, they should feel secure about their own background and values and that by covering major festivals that are not part of a child's life you actually devalue and trivialise them, as a young children cannot conceive of things beyond their own world. This represents a major change in thinking as early years settings have previously been encouraged to celebrate a variety of religious festivals outside of their immediate experience.

Implementation

The way we actually work with children is important to their enjoyment and learning.

Interpersonal skills

Adults working with children need to be friendly, approachable and send out through their body language these messages. Children often reflect how comfortable they are feeling through their behaviour and concentration. A good play activity can therefore be ruined if children do not feel at ease and are worried about being told off.

Observations and monitoring of children's activities

We can learn enormously by simply watching children as they approach activities and while they are engaged in play. These observations should help us to decide whether we need to intervene or interact with children. Observations should also help us to reflect upon whether an activity is working well and is meeting children's developmental needs and interests. It is good practice to observe children and then use the information gained towards future planning. A child, for example, who is fascinated by mixing red and yellow paint together, should have future opportunities to explore further the effect of mixing. Observations skills form the basis of how to plan for children under three years and this is reflected in the Birth To Three framework in England and the equivalent framework in Scotland.

Communication skills

Good communication is essential when working with children. A good style to adopt is a 'chatting' style in which children are equal partners in the interaction. This allows them to talk freely rather than feel that they have to give a 'correct answer'. Questions need to be asked sensitively and ideally we should only ask a 'real' question rather than one that tests children's knowledge. With younger children we need to provide a running commentary style of speech. This helps them learn new vocabulary in context and encourages them to tune in to speech patterns. Pointing out things and remarking on them is, for example, a way in which a young child can work out what the topic of conversation is, while also learning vocabulary that is linked to it. This style is also useful with children whose home language may be different to that of the setting and who are not yet fluent (see also Unit 5).

Awareness of when to intervene

One of the great skills of working with children is to know when and how to intervene. It is useful to think about what children will gain from any intervention and whether the intervention will disrupt children's play. Sometimes children can solve their own disputes and squabbles while at other times they may need an adult. It can be useful to stand by and move closer rather than always directly intervening so that the situation can be monitored. When intervening with older children, it is worth seeing if they can suggest a solution to their difficulty. With babies and toddlers, distraction usually serves as a wonderful tool.

Involvement of children

It is now good practice for children to be involved not just in the play and learning, but in other aspects such as tidying away and setting out. This is important as children gain many skills and it also helps their feelings of self-reliance and confidence. It is also important during an adult-directed activity to think about ways of encouraging children to take ownership even though the adult is central. This might mean asking children for their thoughts, giving them plenty of choices and looking for ways of making sure that they are active rather than passive. Plenty of props might be used at a small-group story time or children could go and collect all the

things that they think that they would like to use to make a card.

Awareness of safety

Adults have to keep safety in mind, although it is important that this is not used as a reason to become controlling. During sessions, it is worth thinking about the noise level and the quality of the noise. Children should be talking, chatting, laughing and even singing, but shouts and shrieks might mean a little further investigation. It is also essential that adults should discreetly think about the way equipment is being used to prevent accidents. It is good practice for to keep a general overview of what is happening around you even when you are involved with a group of children. (See also Unit 5.)

Evaluation

While play and learning activities are ongoing, we need to assess and evaluate their effectiveness. The focus should be on the children and considering how well the activities reflect children's needs.

Children need a good range of resources and activities in order for them to enjoy playing and learning. Reflecting on how well an activity has worked for individual and groups of children can help us to plan for the future. It is important to focus on the role of the adult during the activity, as well as the responses of the children. This can help us to think about the contribution that we are making to children's enjoyment and learning.

* Did most children appear to be engaged and interested in the activity?

* Can you identify the ingredients that helped children to be interested – e.g. the activity was sensory and children were active?

* Were children encouraged to take control and be active during the activity?

* How much input from you was needed?

* Why was this input needed?

* How did you encourage children to be active in their play and learning?

* What did the children learn from the activity?

* Was this learning planned or spontaneous?

* How could this learning be reinforced or built upon?
* What did individual children gain from the activity?
* What was your role in helping children to learn?
* What types of resources were used?
* Were there sufficient resources?
* Which resources attracted children's attention?
* What further resources could have been used?
* What were the limitations of this activity?
* How could these limitations be addressed?

3 Individual learning plans

This section looks at the role of individual learning plans. Individual learning plans are particularly suited to the needs of babies and young children, but are also used with older children.

What is an individual learning plan?

During the planning process, practitioners need to consider the individual needs of children and ensure that play opportunities will encourage their overall development. Many settings, particularly those working with babies and toddlers, produce outline plans that identify the needs of children and give strategies for meeting these needs. These types of plans can be known as individual learning plans or play plans.

Development of assessment and plans

The starting point for individual learning plans is the child. This means that practitioners begin the process of drawing up an individual learning plan or play plan by assessing the child's development, interests and needs.

Ways of assessing children

There are several methods that can be used to assess children's development. Ideally, a range of methods should be used to gain a full picture of the child, although in practice this rarely happens, as most settings find it hard to release one member of staff to carry out observations. It is also important to look at children in a range of situations and in group situations as well as when they are playing alone or with one other child.

Some settings also use commercially devised programmes or, since the advent of the Foundation Stage and Birth To Three Matters in England, use a scheme devised by the early years team in their area.

The table below briefly describes various observation methods, but see Unit 8 for a fuller description.

METHOD	KEY FEATURES	COMMENTS
Free description – also known as Specimen record Narrative record	The observer records whatever they see. Simple, flexible method.	This method allows the observer to be spontaneous as no special equipment or planning is required. This method is particularly prone to observer bias as the observer has to choose, while working, what to focus on.
Time sample	Observer notes down what child is doing at regular intervals. More than one child can be observed at a time.	This method allows the observer to record a child over a period of time and build up a picture of what the child does.

METHOD	KEY FEATURES	COMMENTS
Event sample	Observer looks out for and records particular behaviours or responses, e.g. every time a child interacts with an adult.	This method 'catches' specific features of a child's development or behaviour.
Checklist/Tick chart	Observer has a series of statements or questions relating to specific skills or behaviours.	This is a common method used in settings as checklists and tick charts are quick and simple to use. These methods often do not allow the observer to note how easily or confidently the child manages tasks.
Pre-coded observations with a target child	Observer 'tracks' one child for a period of time using codes and symbols to save time.	This type of observation can be very informative if the observer is able to provide a full and detailed picture of the child's movements.

Factors affecting viability and reliability of assessments

It is very hard for practitioners who are closely involved with children to be completely objective when observing and assessing them. This is known as observer bias. The danger of observer bias is that the observer tends to home in on behaviours or skills that confirm their current view of the child. One way of limiting observer bias is by setting clear aims for observations. For example, noting down every time a child interacts with an adult to gain a picture of a child's interactions with adults.

It is also important, when completing checklists or tick charts which require adults to ask children to do certain tasks, to remember that children may not always 'perform' well if they think that they are being watched or tested. Many skilled practitioners therefore try to incorporate these type of assessments into planned play opportunities, for example, by putting out some buttons for children to play with and then asking them if they would like to count how many there are.

With babies and young children, it is also important to remember that the focus of their play and interests can change in a few days. A baby may suddenly 'discover' their feet or a toddler may spot a car that previously was not of interest to them.

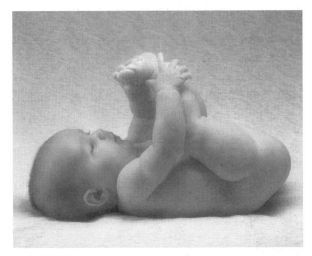

A child discovers a new toy – feet.

Use of assessment

Once a practitioner has completed some observations, it is important to develop an overall picture of the child's development. What strengths and interests has the child shown? Are there any areas where the child has specific developmental needs? It is also good practice for early years settings to involve parents in the process. Parents see their children in a different context and will be able to provide additional information. It is also important to find out what parents feel are the priorities for their child. For example, a parent of a toddler may want to concentrate on feeding skills.

Implementation

The actual layout and content of an individual learning plan can vary, with some settings choosing to keep them quite brief. Most plans contain a résumé of the child's developmental progress and some aims for the future. It is important that these aims are achievable, otherwise the child may be put under pressure. Plans also have to be looked at when drawing up curriculum plans and overall plans for groups of children. Activities can then be added that reflect children's play interests, but also link to any developmental needs that they have. Babies and toddlers particularly benefit from this individual approach.

Reviewing and modifying plans

Once an individual learning plan has been drawn up, it is important for it to be reviewed regularly. Most settings review their children's progress each term or every three or four months. With babies and toddlers, individual learning plans may be reviewed and modified each week. In settings where the child has a key worker, the key worker may be responsible for implementing the plan. The key worker may plan particular activities for the child or make sure that activities designed for a whole group are adapted to meet the child's needs.

Think it over...

Matthew is three years old. His individual learning plan aims to promote his interaction with other children as, although he plays alongside other children, he rarely talks to them. A small group of children, which includes Matthew, is to play sound lotto. Matthew's key worker puts Matthew with a slightly older child to play the game together as this will encourage Matthew to work with another child. She encourages them both and Matthew begins to make eye contact with the other child.

- Suggest two other activities that might encourage Matthew to interact with other children.

Assessment activity 11.3

In order to carry out this assessment activity, you will need to gain the advice and consent of your placement supervisor. Choose one child in your placement setting.

- Assess the overall development of the chosen child by carrying out five observations. You should use at least three different methods of observation and observe the child in a range of situations.

- Using your observations as a basis, produce an individual learning programme for the child.

- Produce and implement three activity plans based on the individual learning programme you have devised (keep notes during the activities for later evaluation; see Assessment activity 11.4).

The individual learning programme must contain:

- analysis of the observations linked to the child's stage of development and child development theory

- an evaluation of the child's overall development and subsequent needs

- a rationale of the aims and learning outcomes you have suggested for the child

- an explanation of how the proposed learning outcomes are to be evaluated and measured.

Each activity plan should contain:

- an explanation of how the activity is to be implemented

- an examination of the role of the adult in extending the child's learning during the activity

- an exploration of the factors that might affect the success of the activity

- detailed links between the activities chosen and the stages of development of the child

- analysis of the potential developmental benefits of each activity

- detailed links between the play activities chosen and the individual learning programme.

4 The role of the adult

The role of the adult is central to how well children are able to play and learn when activities are delivered using play as a medium.

Planning and preparation

The key to working well with children is often in the planning and preparation. This means that good organisational skills are required.

Environment

Children play and learn well when the environment meets their needs, but also interests their curiosity. A good layout helps children to move around safely, but also allows them to get on with their play. Enough space needs to be provided for each type of play activity so that children do not become frustrated because other children 'walk' across their game or the table is not large enough for them to put out all the farm animals that they want. The environment also has to be safe for children. Good planning means allowing time before and during sessions to check that areas are clean, especially outdoor areas where vandals or animals may have created hazards. It is also important that time is spent thinking about storage and accessibility. Messy cupboards and drawers where nothing can be found means that neither children nor staff can find things. It also makes it harder for children to be given and take responsibility for tidying up and looking after their environment.

Materials and equipment

Planning and preparation are needed so that sufficient resources are put out and ones that will actually grab children's attention and interest. The way that they are put out can also make a difference. Where children are spending several hours in a session, it will also be important to think about how the materials and equipment might be varied throughout the day so that if children's interest wanes, there will be something else for them to do that they will enjoy. In settings that share resources, planning is essential to avoid situations where two members of staff are both hoping to use the same resource with children.

Discussion with children

Children always play better and enjoy their learning more when they are involved and when their interests are reflected. Adults can make a difference to play and learning by observing children as they play and also talking to them about what they would like to do. It is good practice to also make materials and equipment accessible for children to pick up and use when they want to.

Discussion with other adults

It is important for everyone working with children during a session to know what is going on. This means that volunteers, parents and staff should all have an idea of what is planned and the type of learning and play opportunities that are being created. Everyone also needs to know what their role is and also how best to work with individual children in the setting, some of whom may have an IEP (see Unit 16).

Safety

Planning play opportunities should be done with safety in mind. This does not mean that safety becomes an excuse to prevent children from having fun or from doing things that will challenge them. Thought needs to be given as to the level of supervision that will be required during a session and during particular activities. Ideally a balance should be struck so that there might be some activities that children can do and enjoy without too much adult support, while others might need adults to supervise closely.

With babies and young children, safety is paramount, especially when choosing equipment and materials (see also Unit 5).

Extension of play activities

During activities, sensitive practitioners will also be looking for scope to extend children's language, skills or thinking. This requires an amount of skill and knowledge of child development as the practitioner has to consider the children's stage of development, their interest in the activity and ways of developing the children further. Opportunities to extend children's learning are sometimes built into the activity, or they can be spontaneous.

CASE STUDY

Jo has planned a series of activities to improve cutting skills for four-year-olds. She put out some scissors on the dough table and three children are happily snipping and cutting away. Jo sits with them and flattens a piece of dough. She draws a line on the dough and then cuts it along the line. One of the children looks at what she is doing. She then flattens another piece of dough and draws a line on it. She passes it to the child who smiles and then has a go. Jo notices how the child handles the scissors and how easily he is managing the scissor action. Jo also notes that the child is almost able to cut on the line.

- Discuss the advantages of this type of assessment.

- Consider ways in which this assessment will help further planning of activities.

Methods of evaluation

It is important for practitioners to evaluate the effectiveness of their plans and ways of working with children. Ongoing evaluation helps us to consider whether we are meeting the needs of children and also helps us to consider what further activities they may need.

Setting and using criteria for evaluation

To assist the evaluation process, it will be important to set criteria for success during the planning process so that the success of strategies or activities can be measured. Criteria for evaluation is often seen on individual learning plans, school curriculum plans and individual education plans for use with children with special needs (see Unit 16). Setting some criteria for evaluation is essential in situations where a child needs to have mastered a concept or skill before being presented with a further task. Judging whether the child has met the criteria will therefore help the practitioner to decide whether further reinforcement and practice is needed or whether a child is ready to move on. An example of a curriculum area where this is particularly useful as an approach is maths. A child who cannot count accurately to five will not be ready to carry out an activity which involves counting to ten.

Building assessment tasks into activities

Most evaluation criteria involve checking whether children have gained the intended learning outcomes. This is difficult to measure unless some type of assessment is carried out either during or after the activity. A child may appear to have understood a concept or may have happily played with materials, but not necessarily have learnt anything new! By building in some assessment into the activity itself, practitioners can see what the child has understood and learnt. It is important that the assessment is not seen in any way as a test, as this would undermine the child's confidence. Good assessment happens as part of the activity.

Student evaluation

As a student, you will need to show that you can evaluate the effectiveness of your work as well as the activities. Student evaluations can also be used to provide evidence of:

* knowledge of child development

* ability to assess accurately a child's stage of development

* understanding of the early years curriculum

* awareness of your strengths and weaknesses

* ability to review and plan effectively.

Producing a student evaluation

There is no set format for producing student evaluations, although most contain:

* an overall introduction to the nature of the plan and the intended learning outcomes

* a brief review of how the plans were implemented

* an analysis of how the children responded and an evaluation of the effectiveness of the activity or activities

* an analysis of the effectiveness of your role and your planning

* detailed recommendations of how to extend the child's learning

* detailed recommendations of how to improve and consolidate your practice.

Gaining information for evaluations

One of the key ways of gaining information for use in later evaluations is through careful observation of children during the activity. Most students find it helpful to keep a pad of paper near them to make notes.

* How engaged are children in the activity?

* Do children appear to be interested and enthusiastic?

* How easily are children distracted?

* Do children appear settled?

* How confident do the children seem?

* Are their bodies relaxed or tensed?

* How easily are children managing the activity?

* Are there any children who appear frustrated or bored?

* How much support is being given in order for children to manage the activity?

* Is support being given because the activity is too challenging?

* Are the children active or passive?

* Are the children using language during the activity?

* What has interested the children during the activity – can this be used as a starting point for further activities?

Self-evaluation

In order to analyse the effectiveness of your practice, it can be useful to ask yourself the following questions.

* How well have I prepared for this activity?

* Is this activity meeting the needs of all the children?

* Are the learning outcomes planned being gained by the children?

* What other learning is taking place?

* How much control have the children over their learning?

* Am I encouraging children to be spontaneous and to develop their own thinking?

An activity in progress. How successful do you think it is?

- Produce an evaluation of your curriculum plan and associated activity plans (see Assessment activity 11.2).
- Produce an evaluation of your individual learning programme and associated activity plans (see Assessment activity 11.3).
- In each evaluation you should:
  - explain how the plans were implemented
  - analyse the responses of the children in relation to child developmental theory
  - consider the effectiveness of your planning based upon self-evaluation, responses from children and feedback from others
  - evaluate your role in implementing the plans and extending children's learning and play
  - examine your effectiveness in meeting children's play and developmental needs
  - consider ways of improving your professional practice.

END-OF-UNIT TEST

1 What is meant by the term 'parallel' activity?

2 List the developmental benefits of imaginative play.

3 Suggest three toys that might be given to a child aged three years.

4 Describe the advantages of free play.

5 What factors might an adult take into consideration when choosing activities and equipment for children?

6 List three activities that will promote children's spoken language skills.

7 Why is it important that young children work in small groups or individually with adults?

8 Why are observations important when working with children?

9 List four pieces of equipment that would promote children's physical development.

10 What is an individual learning plan?

References and further reading

Bruce, T (2001), *Learning Through Play: Babies, toddlers and the foundation years*, Hodder Arnold

Drake, J (2005), *Planning Children's Play in the Foundation Stage*, David Fulton

Hucker, K and Tassoni, P (2005), *Planning Play and the Early Years*, Heinemann

Lindon, J (2001), *Understanding Children's Play*, Nelson Thornes

Tassoni, P (2002), *Planning for the Foundation Stage: Ideas for themes and activities*, Heinemann

UNIT 13

Developmental psychology

What you need to learn

1 How children's behaviour develops

2 How early relationships are formed

3 How children process and use information

Introduction

Most early years practitioners find it useful to have a basic knowledge of child psychology as it helps them to work more effectively with children. Using psychology can help them to manage children's behaviour, help children to settle in, and also consider how best to present activities.

How you will be assessed

This unit is assessed internally.

1 How children's behaviour develops

The term 'behaviour' is used widely within psychology and it is worth noting that its use is not limited to appropriate or inappropriate actions that children might show. The term behaviour takes in all responses and actions that children might make. This section begins by considering some of the main issues in psychology before considering the ways in which children's behaviour develops.

Issues in developmental psychology

Why study children?

There are many different branches of psychology, but developmental psychology looks at the skills and thoughts that we have and considers how we might have acquired them. It studies how we grow and develop and includes areas such as how we learn, and language and personality development. Having an understanding of how children learn will help us when planning activities, while knowing about the way children learn language will enable us to provide the best conditions for this.

The nature versus nurture debate

Many of the early theories of psychology were influenced by the idea that we inherited skills, abilities and behaviour. Work by behaviourists such as Skinner has since shown that our behaviour can also be shaped. The issue for many psychologists is to define how much of our skills, personalities, and so on, are inherited and how much is influenced by our environment, as most psychologists accept that both influences are probably at work.

A practitioner who fundamentally believes that children's abilities and personalities are with them when they are born may take a non-interventionist approach, saying for example 'boys will be boys' or 'she's very shy'. A practitioner who believes that nurture has a bigger impact may take a different stance, believing that the children's progress and behaviour will be a reflection on their own abilities as an educator.

Continuity versus discontinuity

Is development continuous or does it occur in stages? Some theories discussed in this unit are 'stage' theories, such as Freud's psychosexual stages of personality and Piaget's stages of cognitive development. Such theories are based on the idea that development passes through defined and separate stages and that each stage will have recognisable features. For example, in language development children babble before they speak words so babbling is seen as a stage in itself. Others feel that development is more gradual or a continuous process.

> **Think it over...**
>
> Many early years practitioners may feel that children don't jump from stage to stage, but that development is often so gradual that it is hard to see, although over a few weeks they can see that children's development has progressed.
>
> - In your work setting, ask staff what they think. Do they think that children's progress fits into stages or that development is continual? Ask if there are any areas of development which seem particularly stage-like.

Nomothetic versus idiographic

This debate looks at whether we are all unique (the idiographic approach) or whether we share essential characteristics and have some differences (the nomothetic approach). This debate is particularly relevant when we consider our personalities.

Main theoretical perspectives

There are four main theoretical perspectives that keep occurring in developmental psychology. While originally these were often seen as competing perspectives, increasingly today psychologists find that there are often overlaps between the different perspectives.

The perspectives are:

* biological
* social
* psychoanalytical
* cognitive.

The table below shows some of the key theorists that have influenced developmental psychology.

Biological perspectives

Biology has a major influence on psychology. This is partly historic as the study of psychology grew out of the disciplines of philosophy and biology. Biological perspectives reflect the 'nature' element of the nature versus nurture debate. Areas such as aggression and the way in which we react instinctively in certain situations are sometimes linked to biological processes.

Social perspectives

Theories that have a social perspective look particularly at the influence of others on children's development. These perspectives link particularly to the 'nurture' element of the debate within psychology. Examples of social perspectives within psychology include the influence of parents on children's behaviour and the way in which social relationships affect us.

Psychoanalytical perspectives

Psychoanalytical perspectives consider the role of the subconscious on our actions. This area of psychology remains one that is quite controversial and it is particularly associated with Freud.

Cognitive perspectives

Cognitive perspectives look at how children's actions are influenced by their thoughts and ability to process information. These perspectives also focus on the way in which thinking changes as children develop language and also mature.

NAME	PERSPECTIVE	KEY THEORY	COMMENTS
Freud, Sigmund	Psychoanalytical	Psychosexual stages of development	Freud made a distinction between our conscious and unconscious minds.
Erikson, Erik	Psychoanalytical	Psychosocial stages of development	Erikson produced his theory based on Freud's work. He considered that our personalities carry on developing into adulthood.
Bowlby, John	Biological	Maternal deprivation	Bowlby showed in his work that for healthy development, babies and young children need to form a bond with their parents or key carers.
Bandura, Albert	Social	Social learning theory	Bandura showed that children can learn through imitating others.
Skinner, Burrhus Frank	Biological	Operant conditioning	Skinner suggested that behaviour can be manipulated through the use of reinforcements.
Pavlov, Ivan	Biological	Classical conditioning	Pavlov, through his work with dogs, showed that humans can learn through association.
Piaget, Jean	Cognitive	Stages of cognitive development	Piaget suggested that children's thinking passed through stages.
Vygotsky, Lev	Social	Zone of proximal development	Vygotsky placed emphasis on the importance of adults to help children understand concepts.

Acquisition of behaviour

When the term behaviour is used in ordinary conversation, we may think of actions of some kind – good or bad. Psychologists use the term in a different and broader way. For them, the study of behaviour encompasses the way we learn and form attitudes, as well as how we behave towards others.

Acquiring behaviour through learning

Behaviour and learning are linked. It is through behaviour that psychologists can see that learning has taken place. If we can understand how we learn, we can be more effective in our teaching and improve society. Psychologists in this area are interested in the process of how we learn rather than what we learn.

There are several theories that explain the learning process, broadly dividing into two strands: the behaviourist approach and social learning. There is also a third strand which centres around how children learn to think and develop thought processes.

The importance of learning theories in psychology

Learning theories are extremely important as they can be applied to many situations. This means that when studying other aspects of child development, such as language or behaviour management, the same terms and theories will keep reappearing.

Behaviourist approach to learning – conditioning

This approach suggests that learning is influenced by rewards, punishments and environmental factors. The term **conditioning** is often used by behaviourists – it means that we learn to act in a certain way because past experiences have taught us to do or not do something. We may know this as 'learning by association' – for example, not touching a flame because we were once burnt. There are two types of conditioning which are well documented: classical conditioning and operant conditioning.

Classical conditioning

Ivan Pavlov was a physiologist who, while studying dogs, noticed that they always started to salivate before food was put down for them. He concluded that the dogs were anticipating the food and were salivating because they had learnt to associate the arrival of food with other things such as footsteps, buckets, and so on. He devised an experiment where he fed dogs while a bell was sounded. Normally dogs do not salivate when hearing bells, but the dogs began to associate the bell with food and would salivate simply on hearing the bell.

Applying classical conditioning to humans
Pavlov's work was built on by Watson, who showed that it was possible to use classical conditioning on humans. In a famous experiment he was able to make a baby of eleven months afraid of a white rat. The child had previously shown no fear of rats, but by pairing the rat with something that did frighten the child, the child was conditioned to be afraid of the rat.

Theory into practice

Mary was five years old and had gone to bed without being afraid of the dark. One night she was violently sick and her room was in darkness. Afterwards Mary cried if no light was left on at night.

Classical conditioning can help us to understand how some children might develop seemingly irrational fears – for example suddenly being afraid of the dark, particular foods or animals.

Operant conditioning

The basis of the operant conditioning theory is that our learning is based on the type of consequence or reinforcement that follows our initial behaviour. BF Skinner (1904–1990) is recognised as being a key figure in developing the behaviourist approach to learning theory and in particular for developing the theory of operant conditioning. His work was at first based on EJ Thorndike's Law of Effect.

Operant conditioning – Thorndike's law of effect

The original concept of operant conditioning was first pioneered by EJ Thorndike, although he did not use the term operant conditioning. Thorndike (1898) showed, through experiments with cats, that the results of behaviour would affect subsequent behaviour. He called this the 'law of effect'.

In his experiments, hungry cats were put into a 'puzzle box' which had a lever that allowed the cats to escape. The cats could see, from inside the box, a piece of fish which they were able to eat every time they escaped. At first the cats took about five minutes to escape and did so the first time purely through trial and error. Subsequently they were able to reduce the time that it took them to escape until they were able to escape in less than five seconds.

Thorndike suggested that the cats learnt to operate the lever because their behaviour had been rewarded or 'stamped in' by being able to escape, and in particular by eating the fish.

Skinner

Skinner adopted and furthered the work of EJ Thorndike into the now accepted model of 'operant conditioning'. While Skinner accepted the work of Pavlov and Watson, he suggested that most humans and animals learn through exploring the environment and then drawing conclusions based on the consequences of their behaviour. This means that we tend to be active in the learning process, which is an important difference from classical conditioning.

Skinner divided the consequences of actions into three groups:

* positive reinforcers
* negative reinforcers
* punishments.

Positive reinforcers are likely to make us repeat behaviour where we get something we desire. For example, we may buy a new food product after having tried and liked a free sample! Skinner suggested that using positive reinforcement was the most effective way of encouraging new learning. Positive reinforcers for children include gaining adults' attention, praise, stickers, sweets and treats.

Negative reinforcers are likely to make us repeat behaviour as well, but this is in order to stop something from happening to us – for example, we may continue to wear oven gloves to stop us from being burnt.

Punishers are likely to stop us from repeating behaviour. For example, we may learn to stay away from an electric fence after receiving a shock.

Theory into practice

Operant conditioning is often used to encourage children to show wanted behaviour, although many parents and early years practitioners will think of it as offering a bribe! A child may be given a sticker if they have helped to tidy away. In this way, the child will be more likely to help in future as their behaviour has been positively reinforced.

Unexpected positive reinforcers. Skinner found during his experiments that it was often hard to predict what would act as a primary reinforcer and that it was sometimes only after the event that this became clear. An example of this is when children sometimes deliberately behave badly in order to attract their carer's attention. If they manage to attract the attention, they are more likely to show the behaviour again, even though they might be told off. Gaining the carer's attention in this case is the positive reinforcer.

Primary and secondary reinforcers. There are some reinforcers that give us instant pleasure or satisfaction or meet a need. These are referred to as primary reinforcers. Chocolate is a primary reinforcer, because most people find that once they put it into their mouths, they enjoy the taste.

Secondary reinforcers are different because they in themselves do not give us satisfaction, but we learn that they symbolise getting primary reinforcement. A good example of secondary reinforcement in our daily lives is money. Coins and notes in themselves do not give us reward, but we learn that they can be used to buy something that will give us primary reinforcement. The learning that is used when making the association with money and being able to get something is classical conditioning.

Frequency of reinforcement. Skinner looked at the effect that giving positive reinforcements at different intervals would have on behaviour. How long would behaviour be shown without a positive reward before extinction takes place? Interestingly, he found that unpredictable reinforcement works better than continual reinforcement. This would seem to work because it teaches the learner not to expect a reward or reinforcement every time – hence they keep on showing the behaviour just in case a reinforcement is given.

In everyday life, this is one of the reasons why gamblers find it so hard to stop playing. They know that they will not win every time, but carry on just in case they get lucky.

Delaying reinforcement. Delaying positive reinforcement, for example saying to a child that they can have a sticker at the end of the week, makes the effect of the reinforcement weaker. Immediate positive reinforcements are the most effective, partly because the behaviour is then more strongly linked to the reinforcement.

Social learning theory

This is another widely accepted learning theory. The key figure among social learning theorists is Albert Bandura (1925–). Social learning theorists accept the principles of conditioning, but suggest that learning by classical and operant conditioning alone would not explain other behaviours. Social learning theorists are particularly interested in looking at moral and social behaviour (see also Unit 4 and Unit 7).

Bandura's Bobo doll experiment

Bandura's famous experiment, often referred to as the Bobo doll experiment (1965), showed that children can learn behaviour by watching adults. Bandura showed a film to three groups of children. The film showed an adult in a room with a Bobo doll (a large inflatable doll). The three groups saw different versions.

* Group A saw the adult acting aggressively to the doll.

* Group B saw the adult being aggressive to the doll, but at the end of the film, the adult was rewarded with sweets and lemonade by another adult.

* Group C saw the adult being aggressive to the doll, but at the end a second adult appeared and told the adult off.

After the film, each group of children was shown in turn into a playroom that had a variety of toys, including the Bobo doll. The reactions of the children were recorded.

Group C were the least aggressive to the doll, but there was little difference between groups A and B. This suggested that they were less influenced by the reward that had been offered to the adult.

A follow-up to the experiment asked the children if they could demonstrate how the doll had been attacked and were rewarded for doing so. There was little difference between the three groups, showing that they could all imitate the behaviour they had seen.

Early years practitioners may agree that children learn through observational learning. A toddler may try to cross their legs in adult fashion after seeing an adult. If children do learn through observational learning, this has powerful implications for early years practitioners. We must act as good role models for children and be responsible when children are with us.

Reference group

It is thought that children's behaviour is also shaped by their reference group. In young children this is their families, but with older children, this extends to their peers. Reference groups provide children with models for behaviour and so can influence their behaviour. This can be particularly observed in adolescents who may develop their own fashion styles within a group.

Effects of parenting styles

As part of the social perspective on children's behaviour, some work has looked at the effects on parenting styles on children's behaviour. Parenting styles are usually grouped into four categories, as shown in the table below. It is important to realise that few parents consciously choose a style.

The development of self

Who are we? What are we like? These are fundamental questions for children, almost like being able to place oneself on a map. The development of self-concept is the process by which we gather information about ourselves. Self-concept is important because it is closely linked with self-esteem. It is useful to understand the difference between the terms used when talking about self-concept.

* **Self-concept** is our vision of our whole selves, which includes our self-esteem, our self-image and our ideal self.

* **Self-image or self-identity** is the way in which we define ourselves – who we are, where we live, our gender, etc.

* **Ideal self** is our view of what we would like to be.

* **Self-esteem** is also referred to as self-confidence. Once we have developed a self-image and an ideal self, we then judge ourselves: how close are we to being the person we want to be? This judgment either gives us high or low self-esteem.

PARENTING STYLE	FEATURES	OUTCOME FOR CHILD
Authoritarian	High levels of control and demands on child. Low levels of warmth, negotiation and communication.	Low self-esteem. Lower achievement in school. Subdued/aggressive tendencies.
Permissive	Low level of control. High levels of warmth and communication. Indulgent.	Slightly lower levels of achievement in school. Less independent and mature. May be aggressive, if aggressive behaviour is allowed at home.
Authoritative	High level of control, but balanced by high levels of warmth and response to child.	High levels of achievement. Independent. High levels of self-esteem.
Uninvolved	Low levels of control. Low levels of warmth and responsiveness.	Low levels of achievement in school. Low levels of self-esteem.

Developing self-image

Children gradually develop a self-image. The first step for children is to be able to recognise themselves. A well-known test to see if children can recognise themselves is to put a touch of red lipstick on a baby's nose and then put the baby in front of the mirror. A child who is beginning to recognise themselves will touch their nose, rather than the nose in the reflection. Most babies are doing this by eighteen months old.

How do we learn about who we are?

Robert Selman's levels of social role-taking

Role play or role-taking is also seen as important by Selman, who concludes that children develop in their abilities to understand themselves and others – see the table below.

How self-esteem and self-image are linked

Once we have established what we think we are like (our perceptions of ourselves), we then consider whether we are happy with the result. People with a high self-esteem will be reasonably happy about their self-image, whereas people with a low self-esteem feel that they are not 'measuring up'. This means that self-esteem and self-image are linked. The process of how we come to make our judgments has been researched. There seem to be three main factors that affect this process which carries on through our lives:

* reaction of others to us

* comparison to others

* ideal self-image.

Why does self-esteem matter?

Low self-esteem is linked to low achievement. Children who have low self-esteem will be less likely to put themselves in challenging and new situations. They have low expectations of what

ROLE-TAKING STAGE	AGE	DESCRIPTION
Stage 0 Egocentric role-taking	3–6 years	Children assume that everyone will be the same and feel the same as they do.
Stage 1 Social-informational role-taking	6–8 years	Children see that others do not act the same or appear to have the same feelings, but do not understand the reasons behind this.
Stage 2 Self-reflective role-taking	8–10 years	Children accept that others have different points of views to theirs, but find it hard to bring together the different perspectives.
Stage 3 Mutual role-taking	10–12 years	Children can understand two points of view at the same time, and realise that other people can do the same.
Stage 4 Social and conventional system role-taking	12–15 years	Adolescents are beginning to have a more detached view on how other people may be feeling and are able to understand behaviour in the light of this.

they can do and so do not meet their full potential. This means that early years practitioners must raise children's self-esteem through praise, showing genuine warmth and affection.

Coppersmith's study of self-esteem

Coppersmith (1967) carried out a large study in which hundreds of boys aged between nine and ten years underwent a series of tests to discover whether there was a link between achievement and self-esteem. Although the boys came from similar social backgrounds, he found that where the boys had high scores of self-esteem they were also achieving more highly. He found that boys with lower self-esteem consistently underestimated themselves.

Coppersmith then looked to see if there was a link between self-esteem and parenting. Using questionnaires and interviews, he found that children with high self-esteem had parents who had set firm boundaries but who had allowed them some freedom and security. Later, Coppersmith looked at the same children as adults. He found that men who had high self-esteem as children in the study had fared better in their education and careers.

Interpersonal theories

One of the ways in which we might develop a self-image is by considering the reactions of others to us. This is sometimes referred to as the 'Looking Glass' effect. This established theory was put forward by Cooley who suggested that, in order to for us to know what we are like, we need to see how others react to us. This theory is particularly important for adults to consider, as it means that we must be positive towards children so they are able to see themselves positively.

Symbolic interactionalism

A slightly different approach was taken by Mead (1934) who suggested that we develop self-image as a result of interacting with others and that role play is an important part of this process for children. Mead suggested that children's role play allows them to understand different points of view. This would suggest that home corner play is particularly valuable for young children.

Personality development

One of the greatest influences in psychology is Sigmund Freud. He is particularly famous for his psychosexual theory of development, often used to explain our unconscious thoughts and actions.

Freud's structure of personality

Freud suggested that there are three parts that make up our personality: the id, the ego and the superego. Not all of these parts are present at birth and they develop with the child.

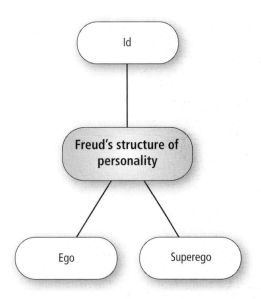

The id

This is the instinctive part of our personality, governed by the drives and needs of the body, such as hunger and pleasure. The id does not consider how meeting our desires and wants will affect others and so is often thought of as the selfish and passionate component. Freud suggested that babies only have the id when they are born – hence a baby will cry and cry until it is fed, regardless of how tired the carer is or whether there are other children who also need feeding. Getting the desire or need met is known as **gratification**.

The ego

The ego has a planning role. It works out how to meet the id's needs and desires in the best way. The ego develops from the id in the first few months – as babies might learn that by smiling in some situations, they are more likely to get their needs met, while in others it is better to cry. In some situations the ego may sometimes make the id wait for its demands to be met – a child may learn that if they snatch a cake from a tray, they may have it taken away from them, but by waiting to be offered it, they will eventually get it. The term **deferred gratification** is used when this happens.

The superego

The superego develops later in childhood and is that part of our personality that gives us our 'conscience'. It tries to control the ego. It comprises of two elements: the conscience and the ego-ideal.

* **The conscience** will punish the ego if it misbehaves, i.e. does something that the superego considers wrong. This is the source of our guilt.

* **The ego-ideal** will reward the ego if it shows good behaviour, with pride or high self-esteem. This is the source of our pride and confidence.

Freud's psychosexual stages

Freud believed that our personalities are based mainly on biological needs or drives – the id factor! He felt that the main drives were sexual and aggressive ones and he shocked Victorian and Edwardian society by suggesting that the sexual drive was present in babies and children. The energy behind these drives, Freud called **libido**. He suggested that there were five stages through which we pass in childhood and on which our libido concentrated. The stages linked to physical development of the body. Freud felt that if we did not pass through these stages satisfactorily, part of our energy or libido would be stuck – or fixated. This would affect our behaviour and personality.

Oedipus complex

One of the theories that made Freud famous is the Oedipus complex. In the Greek tragedy, Oedipus falls in love with his mother and kills his father. Freud suggests that in the phallic stage, children fall in love with the opposite sex parent – hence the title of the theory. They then see the other parent as a rival. This is also a stage where children have become aware of the physical differences between men and women. Freud argued that the absence of a penis is thought by children to be as a result of castration. This leads boys to fear being castrated: 'castration anxiety'. Boys therefore have a decision to make – should they continue to love their mothers and risk being castrated by their fathers? Freud suggests that the conflict is resolved because boys decide to try and make a friend of their fathers by copying and admiring them.

For girls the situation is slightly different. Freud called this the female Oedipus (or Electra) complex. Girls will believe that they have already been castrated and develop 'penis envy'. Eventually realising that they cannot have a penis, they develop a desire for a baby and turn to their fathers. Freud is not so clear why girls then begin to develop closer ties with their mothers. He suggested that the ties are not as profound and that a girl tries to identify with the mother, fearing that her mother will stop loving her.

Theory into practice

It is interesting that many children do have strong links with the opposite sex parent. We may hear the expression 'he's a mother's boy' for example or hear a girl saying that one day she is going to marry her father. The phallic stage does correspond with children often showing very sex-stereotypical play. Freud would argue that this play helps the child to identify and copy the actions of the parent they fear.

It is also interesting to note that boys do sometimes hold their penises at this age, particularly when they are anxious.

Erikson's theory of personality development

Erikson was influenced by Freud's work, but considered that the social environment, such as parenting and friendships, also affects personality. He accepted Freud's theory of the structure of personality being divided into three, but did not feel that Freud's work went far enough. He considered that our personalities were not fixed, and that we kept on changing during the course of our lives. His stages of personality development are life stages and are linked to social stages. He considered that at each stage, we face a dilemma or conflict and that, like Freud, the outcome of each stage would determine our personality.

Personality – a behaviourist approach

Do children learn some aspects of their personality from their parents through imitation and reinforcement? This would be the behaviourist and social learning approach to personality development. Many children share some characteristics of their parents. They can also develop similar attitudes to them. The difficulty with this approach is that it does not explain why children brought up in the same families can be so different.

Acquiring gender role

Gender concept and sex role concept is an important part of self-concept and image. Our gender and the expectations of our gender become part of our self-image. It is important not to confuse gender concept with sex role concept. Sex role concept is learnt alongside gender concept and means that children come to understand how, as a boy or girl, they are expected to act.

Gender identity

Children need to understand if they are a boy or a girl. By nine or ten months, babies are already starting to respond differently to male and female faces. By the age of two years, most children can correctly pick out a same sex picture (Thompson, 1975). Children seem to be using clues such as hair length and dress. Understanding gender identity is the first step in the gender concept process.

Gender constancy

Children also need to understand that regardless of the way people dress, act or cut their hair, they remain either male or female. This is called gender constancy. Understanding that some things remain the same, even if their appearances change links to Piaget's theory of conservation (see also page 408) which suggests that this understanding marks a significant stage in children's cognitive development.

Sex concept

This is always an interesting area, in the light of equal opportunities practice and policies. How do children learn the sex roles that are associated with gender and how are these learnt? The table below outlines some of the stages of the development of gender concept and sex concept.

AGE	STAGE OF DEVELOPMENT
9–12 months	Babies react differently to male and female faces.
18–24 months	Toddlers start to show preferences for gender stereotyped toys.
By 2 years	Children can point to a picture of a same sex child.
$2\frac{1}{2}$–3 years	Children identify differences between genders by using clues such as hair length and style and dress.
3–4 years	Children begin to associate tasks and objects with gender. Some roles are determined through gender.
5–6 years	Children have acquired the concept of gender stability. They know that gender is not dependent on type of clothes or hair cut.

Sex role behaviour

Researchers have found that sex role behaviour is often shown earlier than we imagine. By 18–24 months children start to show some preference for play things, with boys choosing building blocks and cars, and girls choosing dolls and 'caring' toys (O'Brien, 1992). Even so, many children of this age are still not showing understanding of their own gender. Children as young as three years start to show a preference for playmates of their own sex.

Children also seem to be quickly aware of stereotypical roles – tasks and occupations that are seen as men's or women's work are identified by children as young as three years.

How do children learn these stereotypes and sex role behaviours?

There are three strands of thinking that relate to learning theories and theories of personality.

Social learning theory – Bandura

This theory suggests that children learn sex role behaviour by the way in which they are played with and with what they see. Children will imitate their parents' and carers' roles and actions. There is some research to support this approach as parents seem to respond in different ways to boys and girls (see page 400).

Cognitive development theories of gender

The idea behind one widely supported theory by Lawrence Kohlberg (1966) is that children develop an understanding of what it is to be a boy or a girl – a schema – and behaves in such a way as to fit in with their understanding once they have understood that gender is permanent and they will always be a boy or girl. This would explain why some girls at around three years old refuse to wear trousers, because they know that they are a girl and believe that wearing trousers is what makes a boy a boy!

Gender schema theory

Another cognitive development theory put forward by Martin (1991) builds upon Kohlberg's

Do girls learn about their gender by imitating their mothers?

theory. It suggests that children begin to develop an idea of what it is to be a boy or girl at around two or three years and show behaviour to match this. As they grow up they learn more about gender roles and sex roles and adapt and develop their ideas or schemas. It differs from Kohlberg's theory because the original schema is developed even though children have not shown an understanding that gender is permanent.

Aggression

In many early years settings guns are banned, but children may still go around waving a stick and pretending to be shooting each other. This begs the question whether aggression is instinctive or whether it is learnt – the nature versus nurture debate again.

The biological perspective – nature

This considers whether aggression is an inborn instinct that has its roots in the survival of the species. This is an appealing theory – animals fight each other to protect their territory and their mates. One of the most famous ethologists is Konrad Lorenz, who believed that the fighting instinct in animals has parallels with aggression in humans. He notes that fighting is often ritualised in animals – the triumphant male shows enough aggression just to make his point. Shows of aggression without actual violence lead to the other party backing off and appeasing the aggressor. Through ritual aggression, animals avoid killing each other. According to Lorenz, humans have inherited the 'warrior' instinct, but no longer ritualise aggression because they have developed weapons. Weapons where the aggressor no longer needs to make face-to-face contact with the other party have meant appeasement rituals, such as cowering or begging for mercy, are no longer so effective. Lorenz also suggested that aggression in animals and humans is spontaneous, as though the aggression has built up inside and needs to show itself.

Criticisms of Lorenz's theory of aggression

* Where does the 'warrior' instinct come from? Evidence about early man suggests he was a

hunter-gatherer rather than a warrior fighting other tribes, so he would not have the basic instinct to attack.

✳ Animals do frequently kill each other. Lorenz talks about ritualised aggression where animals do not actually destroy each other. Although this can be seen, there are also many documented cases where groups of chimps have attacked and killed each other. It is also not uncommon to find animals eating their young offspring.

✳ Aggression is inevitable. Lorenz's idea that aggression builds up inside and needs an outlet has been criticised by other ethologists and biologists who suggest that aggression in animals is shown as a result of environmental factors – if food is plentiful, territorial fights might not be needed.

✳ Aggression is learnt behaviour. Lorenz did not consider that learning played a part in aggressive behaviour. Studies have, however, shown a correlation between learning and aggression (see below).

Think it over...

Many early years practitioners plan time for physical play or activities that allow children to be 'legitimately aggressive', believing that children need to 'vent their aggression'.

• Is this the case in your setting?
• What happens if the children are not able to go outside for vigorous play activity?

Frustration–aggression hypothesis

A theory known as the frustration–aggression hypothesis combines the instinctive nature of aggression with learning theory. It was put forward by Dollard *et al* in 1939, although was later revised. The basis is that, although there is an inborn aggressive instinct, it tends to be triggered when people are feeling frustrated. This linking of frustration with aggression may explain why some children have dolls or objects onto which they heap their anger. The later theory proposed by Miller (1941) suggested that, although aggression can be triggered through frustration,

other factors may prevent the aggression from being shown, such as realising that any aggression might be punished afterwards.

Aggressive-cue theory – nurture

This theory builds on the frustration–aggression hypothesis, but looks carefully at why aggression is not automatically shown when people become frustrated. This theory suggests that although frustration causes anger, it might not necessarily cause aggression. Experiments carried out by Berkowitz (1966, 1967 and 1993) suggested that, in order for aggression to be shown, there need to be some other triggers. Triggers used in experiments included weapons being available and participants seeing violent films. The aggressive-cue theory would therefore explain why sometimes we can cope in some situations when we are angry, whereas in similar situations we might show some types of aggressive behaviour.

Aggression and biological factors

There is some support for believing that aggressive behaviour might be linked to biological factors such as hormones, drugs or alcohol. Chemicals produced by the brain may lead us to be more highly aroused and therefore more prone to show aggressive behaviour. A study in 1979 by Brown *et al* looked at levels of serotonin. Low levels of serotonin are likely to produce high levels of arousal and therefore possibly aggressive behaviour. There have also been cases where women suffering from pre-menstrual tension have committed acts of aggression. These acts have been linked to the higher levels of progesterone produced prior to menstruation.

Social learning theory and aggression

The social learning theory approach suggests that our behaviour is shaped by what we have seen. Bandura's Bobo doll experiment (see page 400) seems to support this view. Children who had seen violent behaviour seemed more likely to show aggressive behaviour, whereas children who had seen how adults and other children control their anger were more likely to cope when they were angry. Although this theory is valuable, Bandura warns that not all children will be aggressive if they have seen an aggressive act.

Development of social behaviour

Pro-social behaviour is the type that we tend to encourage in young children, such as comforting another child or sharing equipment. Psychologists have studied this behaviour to consider whether pro-social behaviour is instinctive or learnt.

Moral development

At what age are children able to judge right from wrong? In the UK the age of legal responsibility is one of the lowest in Europe. The boys involved in the murder of Jamie Bulger faced criminal prosecution as our legal system felt that, although they were 10 years old, they were at an age to know right from wrong. The Early Learning Goals for England suggest that by the end of the reception year 'most children will understand what is right and wrong, and why'.

Psychoanalytical – Freud and moral development

Freud suggested that moral development was also part of personality development. He suggested that moral behaviour is controlled by the superego (see page 404). He also suggested that children would be influenced by their parents through the process of identification during the phallic stage. Freud believed that children identify; that is to say they try to be the same as their same-sex parents. This would mean that a boy who had an authoritarian father would be likely to show the same characteristics.

Piaget's theory of moral development – a cognitive approach

One of the most famous approaches to understanding moral development is a cognitive stage model. This cognitive approach was put forward by Jean Piaget. Piaget used a clinical interview approach, asking children to explain how they were playing games and telling them stories. He suggested that children's moral development was a three-stage process (see the diagram below).

Children often worry about how an adult will react. Do they learn about right and wrong from these reactions?

Pre-moral (0–4 years)

Children learn about right and wrong through their own actions and consider the results of adults around them.

Moral realism (4–7 years)

Children's moral development is greatly influenced by the adults in their lives. Their judgments very much depend on what they think the adult's expectations would be.

Moral relativism (8–11 years)

Children are preoccupied with justice and following rules. This means that children have developed a concept of fairness. By 11+ years, children understand the concept of equity – that treating people in exactly the same way may not result in fairness. Children who do not understand their homework may need more of a teacher's time than those who do. The motives for people's actions are also considered by children.

If moral development follows a stage process, with children learning more as they develop, it would mean that an 'age' approach to children knowing right from wrong is not a helpful one. It also means that it is difficult to 'teach' children right from wrong.

• What do you think?

Kohlberg's theory of moral development – a cognitive approach

Lawrence Kohlberg's work on moral development is well known. He built on Piaget's description of moral development and suggested that, as with other cognitive areas, moral reasoning is linked to stages of development. He suggests that there are three levels of moral development that are subdivided into stages. The table below outlines the three levels and stages.

Pre-conventional

This is divided into two stages. At this level, children are not being guided by their own moral reasoning, but following their parents or carers. They are doing this to either seek reward or to avoid punishment.

✴ **Stage 1: Punishment and obedience.** The child finds out about what is wrong and right through seeing the consequences of their actions.

✴ **Stage 2: Individualism, instrumental purpose and exchange.** The child is learning that some actions and behaviours are rewarded. The child is also learning to avoid behaviours that might mean punishment. By the end of this stage the child is also beginning to enjoy helping people and has learnt the 'if I help you, you might be able to help me' approach.

Conventional

The next level of moral development consists of an awareness of group behaviour and the idea of what is and is not acceptable in society.

✴ **Stage 3: Mutual interpersonal expectations, relationships and interpersonal conformity (often known as the 'good boy/nice girl' stage).** In this stage children come to believe that good behaviour pleases other people, such as friends, teachers and parents. Children are also becoming aware of the motive factor – 'he meant to help really'.

✴ **Stage 4: Social system and conscience (also referred to as law and order orientation).** This is a widening-out stage – before, children were wanting to show good and correct behaviour to please people they knew. In this stage, we become more aware of society's needs and interests and what is deemed by society to be right or wrong. People in this stage are keen to obey regulations and laws.

Post-conventional or principled morality

This level is very different to the others. At this level, people are not accepting the morality of the group or society unquestioningly. Demonstrators who break laws, such as animal right's campaigners who illegally set animals free, would be demonstrating this level of morality.

✴ **Stage 5: Social contract.** At this stage rules and regulations are seen as useful tools to

AGE	LEVEL	STAGES
6–13	Pre-conventional	1 Punishment and obedience 2 Individualism, instrumental purpose and exchange
13–16	Conventional	3 'Good boy/nice girl' 4 Law and order
16–20+	Post-conventional/ principled	5 Social contract 6 Universal ethical principles

make sure that there is some protection and fairness in society. People working at this level are prepared to tolerate rules being broken, if they do not see that they are fair or just rules.

* **Stage 6: Universal ethical principles.** This last stage was in some ways an unclear one for Kohlberg and a difficult one to test. People working at this stage would be extremely principled people who are not swayed by society and have inner principles which they have developed. People in history who may have reached this level were often killed or persecuted because they were often seen as troublemakers as they would be unwilling to compromise their position.

Testing moral reasoning

Kohlberg used hypothetical stories to test his theory (see Think it over below). His ideas have also been tested in many countries by John

Snarey (1985) to see if his stage theory was relevant to other cultures. The result of his studies showed that the development of moral reasoning did fit the stage and level model, although in some societies, a norm of Stage 2 reasoning was shown.

Behaviourist approaches

Behaviourist approaches to moral development would consider that children learn right from wrong through being reinforced. A child who is given praise because they helped another child would have this pro-social behaviour reinforced. Behaviourist approaches to moral development focus on rewards and also punishments, but the criticism of this approach towards moral development, is that it will only give children a 'black and white' view of morality. This approach does not explain why adults sometimes act altruistically.

Think it over...

A man was trying to save his wife's life. He could not afford to pay for the special medicine she needed. He asked the only chemist who sold it, but the chemist would not give it to him. Later the man broke into the chemist's shop and stole the medicine. Should he have stolen the medicine?

Try out this example of one of Kohlberg's stories to look at the reaction of children you work with. (The story has been simplified and adapted so that you can use it with children aged four plus.)

Assessment activity 13.2

Using at least three observations of one child in a setting, prepare a report about how the child is learning behaviour. The report should:
- analyse how the child's behaviour is being managed or reinforced in the setting
- evaluate ways in which the child is learning behaviour
- consider how the theories of how children learn behaviour link to practice.

---

2 How early relationships are formed

The study of children's early relationships and their importance in a child's overall development did not really start until the 1950s when John Bowlby published *Maternal Care and Mental Health*. The result of this and subsequent research has had noticeable and continuing

effects on early years practice. This means that adults working with babies and children need to have a good understanding of the stages in attachment, attachment theory and the effects of separation.

Key terms

There are many key terms that are used in relation to the study of early relationships.

* **Attachment**. An attachment can be thought of as a unique emotional tie between a child and another person, usually an adult. Research has repeatedly shown that the quality of these ties or attachments will shape a child's ability to form other relationships later in life. Attachment is often seen as a process.

* **Critical period**. Some theorists have speculated that an attachment must occur within a set period of time.

* **Innate sociability**. This is the theory that humans are designed to make attachments and form relationships.

* **Reciprocal behaviour**. Attachments and relationships are often mutual. A mother has strong feelings for her baby, while the baby has strong feelings for her.

* **Monotropy**. In early theories of attachment, it was proposed that babies made only one key attachment.

* **Multiple attachments**. Later theories of attachment proposed that babies were able to simultaneously make several strong attachments.

* **Socialisation**. This is the process by which babies and young children gradually form a variety of relationships.

* **Separation**. This is the term used when a parent or main attachment leaves the baby or toddler.

* **Separation anxiety**. This is the effect on babies and toddlers when they leave their main carers.

* **Deprivation**. This is the term used when babies and toddlers are separated on a long-term basis from their main attachment.

* **Privation**. This is the term used when no attachment is made.

Bowlby's theory of attachment

The work of John Bowlby has greatly influenced social care policy, early years practice and research into early relationships. Immediately after World War Two, he was asked to investigate the effects on children's development of being brought up in orphanages or other institutions. In 1951 his findings showed that meeting children's physical needs alone was not sufficient – children were being psychologically damaged because of the

AGE	STAGE	FEATURES
6 weeks–3 months		Babies begin to be attracted to human faces and voices. First smiles begin at around 6 weeks.
3 months–7/8 months	Indiscriminate attachments	Babies are learning to distinguish between faces, showing obvious pleasure when they recognise familiar faces. They are happy to be handled by strangers, preferring to be in human company rather than left alone – hence the term indiscriminate attachments.
7/8 months	Specific attachments	At around 7 or 8 months, babies begin to miss key people in their lives and show signs of distress – e.g. crying when they leave the room. Most babies also seem to have developed one particularly strong attachment – often to the mother. Babies also show a wariness of strangers, even when in the presence of their 'key people'. This wariness may quickly develop into fear if the stranger makes some form of direct contact with the baby, e.g. by touching them.
From 8 months	Multiple attachments	After making specific attachments, babies then go on to form multiple attachments. This is an important part of their socialisation process.

absence of their mothers. The term 'maternal deprivation' was used to describe this effect. He reached this conclusion by looking at the life histories of children who had been referred to his clinic. He noticed an overwhelming trend – most of these children had suffered early separations from their mothers and families.

Main features of Bowlby's theory

* **Monotropy.** Bowlby believed that babies need to form one main attachment and that this relationship would be special and of more importance to the child than any other. Bowlby suggested that in most cases this relationship would be formed with the mother, but that it could be formed with the father or another person.

* **Critical period.** Bowlby was greatly influenced by ethologists such as Lorenz and he believed that, in the same way, humans too would have a 'critical period'. He felt that babies needed to have developed their main attachment by the age of one year and that during a child's first four years, prolonged separation from this person would cause long-term psychological damage.

* **Children need 'parenting'.** Bowlby showed through his findings that simply meeting a child's physical and care needs is not enough for healthy growth and development. Children need to have a main attachment in their early lives who gives them consistent support. His early papers suggested that the mother should play this role, although his position changed in later years.

* **Children show distress when separated from main attachment.** Bowlby outlined a pattern of distress that babies and children show when separated from their carers. This is often referred to as **separation anxiety** (see page 415) He also made links to show that when adults had been separated from their mothers in infancy, they would not form deep and lasting relationships. He called this effect **maternal deprivation**.

Criticism of Bowlby's work

There are many criticisms of Bowlby's work and his work has been superseded by other pieces of research. When looking at the criticisms of his work, it is, however, important to remember the political, economic and social climate of the time.

The role of the mother was overemphasised

This has been a major criticism of Bowlby's early work. At the time of writing, women were the traditional care-givers and, economically after the war, the government was keen for women to return to their traditional roles within the home. Bowlby's later work did emphasise that babies could form an attachment with someone other than the mother.

Attachments to more than one person were not explored

Bowlby placed a lot of emphasis on the importance of one single attachment. Subsequent research (Schaffer and Emerson, 1964) has shown that as children get older, they can develop equally strong attachments to other figures, such as their fathers and siblings (see table, page 411).

Quality of the substitute care was not taken into consideration

Bowlby did not take into consideration the effect of being in poor-quality care. This means that it is hard to be absolutely sure that the psychological damage done to the children was only the result of 'maternal deprivation'. Later studies have suggested that good-quality care can help children to adjust to separation as they are able to substitute the main attachment to another person (Hodges and Tizard, 1989).

Maternal deprivation as a concept was too general

Michael Rutter criticises Bowlby's 'maternal deprivation' as being too general. Factors such as discord in the family, the nature of separation and the quality of attachments made would all affect outcome. This explains why some children are more adversely affected by their earlier experiences than others (see also Key issues box about Koluchova, page 416).

Schaffer and Emerson's work on attachment

Until the 1950s, it was generally thought that babies and children automatically formed the strongest relationships with the people who fed them and met their physical needs. This is sometimes referred to as 'cupboard love'! Several pieces of research have shown that this is not necessarily true. One strong piece of research by Schaffer and Emerson (1964) showed that babies and children can form equally strong attachments to their fathers, even when the father is not the main giver. Over a period of 18 months they visited babies at 4-weekly intervals and found that most children, by 18 months, protested equally when they were separated from either the mother or the father. This piece of research showed that care-giving alone did not automatically mean that a child would form a main attachment.

Theory into practice

One of the major concerns most parents have when leaving babies with nannies or childminders is that children will attach themselves to the care-giver and not know who their parent is. Although in theory this is possible, it is unlikely, providing the parents spend time responding to and interacting with the baby. This is the idea behind 'quality time', where the quality of the interaction and responsiveness of the parents is more important than the actual time spent with children.

The role of fathers

Recent research has highlighted the importance of a father's role in children's social and emotional development. Fathers seem to offer a different type of contribution, which is nonetheless valued by babies and children. Research also shows the following.

* Most children aged 7–30 months chose their father to be playmates in preference to their mother (Clarke-Stewart, 1978).

* Fathers hold their children in order to play with them, whereas most holding by mothers is linked to care-giving or restricting (Lamb, 1977).

* Fathers play in different ways with their children, giving children more vigorous physical play (Parke, 1981).

* Strong attachments to both parents, rather than just one, also seems to help children in unfamiliar situations (Main and Weston, 1981).

Theory into practice

Interestingly these pieces of research also coincide with a greater public awareness of the importance of fathers, although ironically, due to an increase in divorce and separation, a large proportion of children grow up in families without fathers. The understanding that men relate in different ways to children is also a reason why many early years settings are trying to employ male members of staff.

Development of attachment

It is important for early years practitioners to be able to identify when babies and children have made attachments. This can generally be observed through looking at their behaviour. There are four broad indicators that babies and children might show:

* actively seeking to be near the other person

* crying or showing visible distress when that person leaves or, for babies, is no longer visible

* showing joy or relief when that person appears

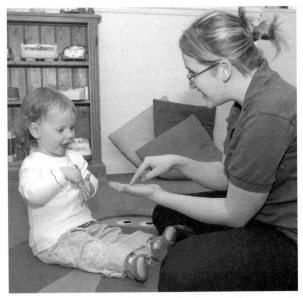

Spending time with children helps develop attachment.

* acute awareness of that person's presence, e.g. looking up at them from time to time, responding to their voices, following their movements.

Helping attachments to form

There are some practical ways in which attachments can be helped to form. Practitioners working with babies and toddlers need to focus on these particularly.

Feeding

The moment when babies feed is special, as the baby is relaxed, secure and nestled into the adult. It is important that, during this time, the adult focuses on the baby. It is good practice in settings to ensure that the same person feeds the baby. This helps an attachment to be made. It is interesting to watch parents as they feed their babies. They may talk softly, stroke their babies' cheeks or head and make eye contact. These attachment behaviours need to be duplicated in early years settings.

Physical contact

Attachments are also reinforced through the handling of the baby. Cuddling, comforting and rocking are obvious ways in which parents and keyworkers respond to babies. Lack of physical contact can be damaging for babies, so it is now considered good practice for those working in early years to spend time holding, rocking and responding physically to young children.

Time and care-giving

While babies seem to recognise who their parents are, they still do need to spend sufficient time with them to build up an attachment. In the same way, babies and young children will feel more secure if they are regularly spending time in an early years setting, rather than sporadically.

Research shows that simply responding to children's physical needs does not necessarily guarantee attachment, and most strong relationships also have an element of care-giving. This might be passing a toy to a baby who is pointing towards it, as well as other tasks such as bathing and washing.

Sensitivity and responsiveness

The way in which a parent or key worker responds and is sensitive to a child seems to be one of the strongest indicators of a strong attachment. Where there are strong attachments between babies and parents or key workers, the adults seem to be tuned in to what the babies want. This means that they can recognise the different types of cries easily and can interpret what the baby wants and needs.

Looking at the quality of attachments

There has been some research that has looked at the quality of babies' early attachments. It would seem that where babies and children are 'securely' attached they are able to explore and develop their independence. Babies and children whose attachment is less secure seem to show either indifference or clingy types of behaviour.

The 'strange situation'

The quality of attachments was looked at by Ainsworth, who is considered, alongside Bowlby, to a be key figure in this area of pyschology. Ainsworth and her colleagues (1978) created a scenario by which babies' reactions to being left with a stranger and then reunited with their mothers (and/or fathers) was measured. This scenario is now widely used to study attachment behaviour. The scenario is known as the 'strange situation' and is divided into eight parts, with each part lasting about three minutes. During the experiment, the baby (a one-year-old) has some time alone well as with a stranger.

1 Parent and baby enter room.

2 Parent remains inactive, baby is free to explore room.

3 Stranger joins parent and infant.

4 Parent leaves room.

5 Parent returns, settles baby and stranger leaves.

6 Baby is alone in the room.

7 Stranger returns and interacts with baby.

8 Parent returns again and stranger leaves.

Ainsworth and her colleagues were particularly interested in the reactions of the baby to the parent when they left or returned and the way in which the parent interacted with the baby. They categorised the behaviour into three types.

* **Type A: Anxious-avoidant.** Baby largely ignores parent and shows little signs of distress when parent leaves, continuing to play. Baby ignores or avoids parent on their return. Baby dislikes being alone, but can be comforted by stranger.

* **Type B: Securely attached.** Baby plays while parent is present, but shows visible distress when parent leaves and play is reduced. Baby is easily comforted on return of parent and carries on playing. Baby cries when alone because parent is not there, but can be partly comforted by stranger. Reactions towards stranger and parents are markedly different.

* **Type C: Anxious-resistant.** Baby is wary and explores less than other types. Baby is very distressed when parent leaves and actively resists stranger's attempts to comfort. Baby wants immediate contact with parent on return but is ambivalent, showing frustration and anger alongside clinginess, e.g. wanting to be held but then immediately struggling to get down.

Why are some children more securely attached than others?

Ainsworth came to the conclusion that the quality of attachment depended on the parenting that the baby received. Where parents were able to sense and predict their babies' needs and frustrations, the babies showed type B behaviour. This meant that they were able to explore and play, knowing that their parent was a safe base.

What happens when babies and children are separated from their main attachments?

Most early years practitioners will notice that, as children become older, they find it easier to separate from their parents. This is because they have formed other attachments to staff and, as they get older, to other children. They have also learnt that, although their parent is absent, he or she will return. Babies and toddlers, however, find it difficult to cope with the absence of their main attachments and will show distress.

Separation anxiety

Bowlby noted that there seemed to be a pattern to the way children reacted if they were separated from their main attachments. This pattern is often referred to as separation anxiety. Separation anxiety is clearly seen in babies from around seven months and seems to reach a peak at around twelve to fifteen months. Older children will show separation anxiety if they are separated for long periods, such as if a parent dies or goes away for a period of time.

There seem to be three distinct stages of separation anxiety, as shown in the table below.

STAGE	FEATURES
Protest	Children may cry, struggle to escape, kick and show anger.
Despair	Children show calmer behaviour, almost as though they have accepted the separation. They may be withdrawn and sad. Comfort behaviour, e.g. thumb sucking or rocking, may be shown.
Detachment	Children may appear to be 'over' the separation and start to join in activities. The child is actually coping by trying to 'forget' the relationship – hence the title 'detachment'. The effects of detachment may be longer lasting, as children may have learnt not to trust people they care for.

What are the effects of parents leaving their children to go to work?

A number of studies in the US have compared groups of children – those with working parents and those with a parent who has stayed at home. One of the largest studies (Kagan *et al*, 1980) would suggest that children receiving high-quality day care fare no differently from children whose parents stay at home. However, the importance of good standards of care and attention cannot be emphasised enough!

Privation

There is a difference between the terms 'deprivation' and 'privation'. Deprivation means that a child has made a main attachment and then has been separated from the person. Privation means that the baby or child has never formed a main attachment. Fortunately, an increased awareness of child abuse and child protection has meant that cases of extreme privation in the UK are rare. There are, however, some famous case studies that have helped psychologists look at privation in children. Below is the case study of the Czech twins reported by Koluchova in 1972.

KEY ISSUES

The Czech twins reported by Koluchova (1972)

In 1967, twin boys aged seven years were found to be in a neglected state in Czechoslovakia. They had been cruelly treated and beaten by their stepmother and had often been locked in a cupboard together. They had little speech when they were rescued and after spending two years in a children's home were fostered. Follow-up reports in 1976 suggested that they had made significant progress in their speech and cognitive development and by 1984 they had completed an apprenticeship. They also seem to be psychologically stable and had developed a good relationship with the foster parents.

This case study seems to show that children can form main attachments to each other – almost as a survival mechanism. This and similar case studies cast doubt on beliefs that poor early experiences will automatically create irreversible damage on children's social and cognitive development.

Assessment activity 13.3

Produce a report about attachment and settling-in procedures. Your report should:

- be based on information that you have collected about settling-in procedures at two different settings that care for children aged four years and under
- analyse the settling-in procedures studied, in relation to attachment theories
- examine the influence of attachment theories on early years practice
- evaluate factors that might affect the settling-in process.

Historical theories of child rearing

Since the beginning of the last century, there have been texts widely available on child rearing. They are interesting to look at in terms of social history as they provide insights as to the prevailing attitudes towards children at the time of their writing.

Truby King

One of the earliest influential experts was Truby King. Today, his method is much maligned. He is known for suggesting that babies should spend many hours outdoors, be toilet trained early on and that they should be fed on a schedule. From today's viewpoint this seems harsh, but his focus was to prevent infant mortality. By cutting down contact and also putting the baby outdoors, the baby was less likely to pick up infections such as diphtheria. It is worth remembering that at this time there were no antibiotics or bottled milk if breastfeeding failed. Nappies were often not changed regularly as washing was not easy. Interestingly, Truby King was considered to be a hero of his time as his practices were credited with reducing the overall number of infant deaths.

Benjamin Spock

Benjamin Spock was influential in the UK in the 1950s and 60s, although he began writing in the US in the 1940s. His books were child-centred as he was influenced by the work of paediatricians, but more particularly psychoanalysts. He urged parents to move towards more flexible approaches to their children and stressed the importance of building relationships. He is known as being 'permissive', but in his later texts he revised his position and aimed to give a more balanced view.

Penelope Leach

Penelope Leach has written many books, but one of the most influential was *Baby and Child* which appeared in 1977. Penelope Leach's approach is child-centred, arguing that by responding to babies' needs, parents will themselves feel happier.

Sheila Kitzinger

Sheila Kitzinger looks at child rearing from both a child's and a woman's point of view. Interestingly, her books are mostly about pregnancy, childbirth and breastfeeding. She draws upon other countries' and cultures' traditions to draw out what she believes is instinctive and natural in terms of childbirth and rearing.

Gina Ford

Gina Ford's *Contented Little Baby* book caused much debate. She advocated that mothers have a definite routine and structure for their newborns. The book was and still is a bestseller, but some experts have suggested that it is not child centred and is a backward step in parenting terms.

Birth To Three Matters

The increase in the number of babies and toddlers being cared for in settings has prompted the arrival of frameworks of practice for professionals. Scotland and England have developed frameworks that help practitioners to identify key aspects that will promote emotional as well as other areas of development. Good practice today centres on meeting the individual needs of babies and toddlers, observing them closely and thinking carefully about their attachment needs.

Assessment activity 13.4

Using either Birth To Three Matters or another current framework for the under-threes, carry out the following tasks.

- Identify practical ways in which practitioners are supposed to work with babies and toddlers.
- Explain the role of observations in the framework.
- Consider how the framework reinforces the importance of the emotional development of babies.

---

3 How children process and use information

From birth onwards, we are constantly being bombarded with information – light, sounds, tastes and language. The way we process this information, sometimes filtering it out, has been a focus of research in recent years. This section looks at the following aspects of processing and using information:

* Piaget's approach to cognitive development
* Vygotsky's and Bruner's theories of cognitive development
* the information-processing approach to learning.

Piaget's theory of cognitive development

Jean Piaget was a zoologist who became interested in children's cognitive development as a result of working on intelligence tests. He noticed that children consistently gave similar 'wrong' answers to some questions and began to consider why this was. Piaget used his own children to make detailed observations and gradually developed a theory of learning. This theory is sometimes referred to as a **constructivist approach** as he suggested that children constructed or built up their thoughts according to their experiences of the world around them. Piaget used the term **schema** to mean a child's conclusions or thoughts. Piaget felt that this was an ongoing process, with children needing to adapt (hence Piaget's term **adaption**) their original ideas if a new piece of information seemed to contradict their conclusions.

Understanding why children think differently to adults

Piaget's belief that children develop schemas based on their direct experiences can help us to understand why sometimes young children's thinking is so different to ours. Piaget also suggested that, as children develop, so does their thinking. He grouped children's cognitive development into four broad stages. (See also Unit 4.)

Sensori-motor stage (0–2 years)

This is the first stage of children's lives. It begins at birth with babies using their reflexes to survive. Babies are also very reliant on using their senses in the first two years, especially taste and touch. Babies' first schemas are physical ones, with babies learning to repeat and then control their movements.

Pre-operational stage (2–7 years)

During this stage, children develop their skills at using symbols (language). Many early years practitioners will find that children in this stage are using a lot of imaginative play: where children use objects to stand in a representational way – sticks become guns, cardboard boxes become cars. Piaget did divide this stage into two further substages – pre-conceptual and intuitive – although there are four main features which run through both of these substages.

* **Egocentrism**. Children can only see things from their own perspective.

* **Conservation**. Children find it difficult to understand that things can remain the same, even though their appearance might change.

* **Centration**. Children are beginning to classify objects and make associations, but are often only looking at one attribute at a time, e.g. sorting objects according to size, but not size and colour.

* **Animism**. Children believe that objects must have feelings, e.g. 'That wall is bad, it hurt me'. Children's drawings can also be animistic.

An example of an animistic drawing – this cat is smiling.

Concrete operations stage (7–11 years)

This stage marks a great leap in children's logical abilities. They begin to use rules and strategies to help their thinking. Piaget called this the concrete stage because children are helped in their thinking when they can do it in practical ways, for example, using counters to find the answer to the sum 15 – 9.

Theory into practice

Children in the concrete operations stage will need plenty of practical support to help them. For example, they may use their fingers to help them count or need to see something actually laid out or acted out for them to understand it.

* Find out about the national Numeracy Strategy in schools. What is the balance between practical and mental mathematics?

* Ask one teacher in Key Stage 1 and another in Key Stage 2 how easily children find it to carry out mental calculations.

Formal operations stage (11–15 years)

The main difference between this stage and the concrete operations stage is that children are now able to manipulate thoughts and ideas to solve problems, without needing practical props. This means that, in theory, tasks such as map reading can be done without having to turn the map around to work out whether a turning is on the right or left.

Criticism of Piaget's work

Piaget's work has been very influential and widely accepted, but there have been many criticisms of his work as further research has been carried out.

Piaget's research methods may have been biased

Piaget did use clinical interviews as the major research method with children. This method is open to bias, but Piaget did carry out hundreds of interviews and the type of data that was collected is qualitative, but very informative. Piaget also used experiments, but the tests he constructed have also been criticised (see page 419).

Does cognitive development really happen in stages?

This is one of the criticisms of Piaget's early work, although from the 1970s Piaget suggested a spiralling process and considered that at times children will show features of more than one stage at once. This he referred to as *d'ecalage*, but maintained that children would not be able to skip whole elements of the stages and progress to another stage.

Piaget may have underestimated children

One of the most widely accepted criticisms of Piaget's work is that the ages that he gave for children's thinking are inaccurate. He underestimated children's level of thinking. One of the reasons given for his inaccuracies is the types of task that he used with children.

Research by McGarrigle and Donaldson (1974) showed that by making the tests of conservation more child-friendly – they used a naughty teddy to mess up the counters – children as young as four were able to conserve.

Piaget's tests of object permanence have also been evaluated and some researchers, such as Bower (1977), suggest that babies do remember that there are objects, but either lack the necessary physical skills to find the object or are fooled by the way the object has been disappeared. Bower showed this in one experiment when a screen is put between the baby and a toy that they have been handling. The toy is then removed and when the screen is lifted the babies are surprised to see that the toy is no longer there.

Think it over...

In your work setting, consider the following questions in relation to Piaget's theory of how children learn.

- Is there an assumption that children need to work at their own pace – are children grouped according to their stages of development or according to their ages?
- What types of activity are chosen that encourage learning through discovery (e.g. children using beakers and water to find out about properties of water)?

Piaget may have underestimated how training and practice can help children

Piaget suggested that the cognitive development of children was heavily linked to maturation and therefore children could not be 'fast-tracked' through the stages. There has, however, been some research which suggests that children can achieve tasks if they are given experiences to help them. For example, Bruner felt that five- and six-year-olds can be taught to conserve, although training is only partially effective.

Other constructivist approaches to cognitive development

Although Piaget's work is well known, there are two other approaches which are in some ways similar to Piaget's and have also influenced early years practice: Vygotsky's theory of cognitive development and Bruner's developmental theory.

Vygotsky's theory of cognitive development

Vygotksy's work was not published in English until the early 1960s, even though his work was known in Russia in the 1920s and 1930s. He believed that children's social environment and experiences are very important. He considered that children were born to be sociable and that by being with their parents and then with their friends they acquired skills and concepts. Vygotsky saw children as 'apprentices', learning and gaining understanding through being with others. The term 'scaffolding' is often used alongside Vygotsky's ideas, as the idea of the child being helped by adults around them to learn concepts is a strong feature of his work.

Vygotsky also suggested that maturation was an important element in children's development and that we needed to extend children's learning so that they could use their emerging skills and concepts. He used the term **zone of proximal development** to define this idea, although we might think of this as potential.

Bruner's developmental theory

Jerome Bruner's work was influenced by Piaget, but particularly by Vygotsky's work. Bruner's is not a stage theory as such, but he suggests that children

MODE	AGE (APPROX.)	DESCRIPTION AND USE
Enactive	0–1 years	Learning and thought take place because of physical movements.
Iconic	1–7 years	Thoughts are developed as mental images.
Symbolic	7+ years	Symbols, including language, are used in thinking.

gradually acquire cognitive skills which Bruner refers to as modes of thinking – see the table above.

Information processing theory of cognitive development

Information processing (IP) theories of cognitive development consider the actual processes used when information is presented to us. Information is constantly being gathered in the brain through our five senses – we may hear a sound in the street while also having the television on. Some information we store and use, while others we filter out and disregard. Information processing theories often use similar language to the terms used in computing, as they suggest that the brain acts in similar ways. In much the same way as computers, IP theorists suggest that tasks are broken down as part of the process involved in handling information. This breaking down into stages is often referred to as 'task analysis'.

Memory

Memory is an important component in our ability to process information. It was not until the 1950s that memory was really studied by psychologists and at present the most influential work carried out on memory has been by Atkinson and Shiffrin. They have proposed a 'multi-store' model which looks at the way information is coded and retrieved.

Theories about the way we store and retrieve information vary, but most psychologists agree that there is a process system to our memory – a simplified version of this process is shown below.

Primary and secondary memory (short- and long-term memory)

Most psychologists also agree and have worked on the concept which William James (1890) suggested, that memory storage is divided into two parts – commonly called short- and long-term memory. Our short-term or (primary) memory is the one we use when we are holding a new telephone number for a few seconds before dialling it. An hour later we might not remember the order of the digits. By contrast, the long-term memory can hold information for a few minutes or for a lifetime. The long-term memory is seen as having unlimited capacity – this may come as a surprise if you are someone who has difficulty remembering things, but storage capacity is completely different to the process of retrieving information.

Storing information

In order to be able to retrieve information from either our long- or short-term memories, we have to encode it. If information is not encoded properly, it will be lost to us. Researchers are still looking at the way we encode information, but it would seem that our long-term memory uses three main methods: visual, semantic (signs, written and spoken language) and acoustic. In addition, we may also learn some of the following strategies that help us hold onto information that we do not want to forget.

* **Rehearsal.** Repeating to ourselves what we want to remember. For example, repeating a telephone number or practising actions to a song.

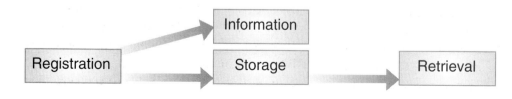

* **Clustering or chunking.** This involves grouping pieces of information – rather than remembering a telephone number as 0-0-3-3-5-6-0-6-7-9-9-7, you would remember it in clusters or chunks 00-33-56-06-79-97. Children as young as two years can begin to chunk information.

* **Elaboration.** Elaboration means finding connections between things that need to be remembered. If you find a person's name difficult to remember, you might think about one feature about that person to help you. Mnemonics, such as Never Eat Shredded Wheat to remember the points around a compass, are forms of elaboration.

Assessment activity 13.5

Produce an information sheet for other students on the theories of cognitive development. Include the following.

* Outline each of the following theories: Piaget, Bruner and Vygotsky.

* Analyse the differences and similarities between these theories.

* Evaluate each theory's contribution to current early years practice, using examples based on your placement experience.

Language development

Language, either spoken or written, plays an important part in most people's lives. Some psychologists, theologians and philosophers would suggest that our ability to use language to communicate and think separates us from the animal kingdom.

Understanding the structure of language

It is important to have some understanding of the structure of language. All languages have rules which are understood and used by both the speaker and listener. These rules are often usually referred to as grammar. By following the rules of grammar, speakers and listeners can understand each other. Linguists who study the structure of language use the term grammar to describe the 'package' of a language. This package is formed of three key elements.

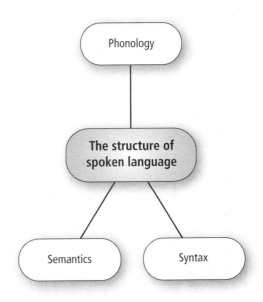

Phonology

Languages have a sound system – phonology. When we hear someone speaking, we may recognise the language that they are using, even if we cannot speak it. This recognition may be based on listening to the sounds that are being used. The individual sounds that are used in a language are called phones. Some languages use fewer phones than others – there are 40 phones used in English. Individual sounds that are combined together are called phonemes.

Semantics

Languages are composed of words or units of meaning. When we learn a language we also have to learn what these units are and how they can be changed. For example, if we add 'less' onto the end of some words, it changes their meaning.

Syntax

Finally, we have to learn the rules for using the words and how their place in a sentence can change their meaning. 'The cat ate the mouse' has a different meaning to 'The mouse ate the cat', even though the same words have been used.

The sequence of language development

A good starting point when considering language development is to look at the pattern by which children learn to speak. It is interesting to note that babies and children, in whichever country they are born, all follow a similar pattern. The first year of a baby's life is spent trying to 'tune in' on the language that they are hearing and learning the skills of communication, such as making eye contact or responding to others' facial expressions and words. This first year is often known as the pre-linguistic phase and is now considered to be vital in children's overall language development.

The major stages in language development are shown in the following table.

STAGE PRE-LINGUISTIC STAGE	AGE	FEATURES	COMMENTS
Cooing	6 weeks	Cooing	Babies make cooing sounds to show pleasure. These early sounds are different to sounds made later on, mainly because the mouth is still developing.
Babbling (phonemic expansion)	6–9 months	Babies blend vowels and consonants together to make tuneful sounds, e.g. ba, ma, da.	Babbling has been described as learning the tune before the words. The baby seems to be practising its sounds. Babies increase the number of sounds or phonemes. This is sometimes called phonemic expansion. All babies, even deaf babies, produce a wide range of sounds during this period.
Babbling (phonemic contraction) Echolalia	9–10 months	Babies babble but the range of sounds is limited.	The range of sounds or phonemes that babies produce are used in the language that they are hearing. At this stage it would, in theory, be possible to distinguish between babies who are in different language environments. At 10 months babies are also understanding 17 or more words.
LINGUISTIC STAGE			
First words	Around 12 months	Babies repeatedly use one or more sounds which have meaning for them.	The first words are often unclear and so gradually emerge. They are often one sound, but are used regularly in similar situations, e.g. 'ba' to mean drink and cuddle. Babbling still continues.
Holophrases	12–18 months	Toddlers start to use one word in a variety of ways.	Toddlers use holophrases to make their limited vocabulary more useful for them. One word is used in several situations, but the tone of voice and the context helps the adult understand what the toddler means. Most toddlers have 10–15 words by 18 months.

STAGE LINGUISTIC STAGE (CTD)	AGE	FEATURES	COMMENTS
Two-word utterances – telegraphic speech	18–24 months	Two words are put together to make a mini sentence.	Toddlers begin to combine words to make sentences. They seem to have grasped which are the key words in a sentence – 'dada gone' or 'dada come'.
Language explosion	24–36 months	A large increase in children's vocabulary combined with increasing use of sentences.	This is a period in which children's language seems to evolve rapidly. Children learn words so rapidly that it becomes hard for parents to count them! At the same time the child uses more complicated structures in their speech. Plurals and negatives begin to be used, e.g. 'No dogs here!'
	3–4 years	Sentences become longer and vocabulary continues to increase.	Children are using language in a more complete way. Mistakes in grammar show that they are still absorbing the rules and sometimes misapplying them. Mistakes such as 'I wented' show that they have learnt that '-ed' makes a past tense. These type of mistakes are known as 'virtuous errors'.
Fluency	4–5 years	The basic skills of the language are mastered.	Children have mastered the basic rules of English grammar and are fluent, although will still be making some virtuous errors.

Theories of how children use language

The nature versus nurture debate appears once more when we look at the theories of how children learn language.

Skinner's operant conditioning theory – behaviourist perspective

This is a 'nurture' theory as Skinner suggests that we learn language mainly because when babies try to communicate, their efforts are rewarded or reinforced in some way – babies may get a smile from a parent if they gurgle. Skinner used this idea of reinforcement to explain why babies stop making some sounds – he reasoned that when babies made sounds that parents did not recognise, they would not receive any attention, while sounds which were recognisable were noticed and reinforced. He called this process selective reinforcement. This approach would explain why children speak in similar ways to their parents, using the familiar phrases and intonation.

However, there have been criticisms of Skinner's theory. For example, the theory does not explain why all babies and children follow the same pattern of gaining language. If Skinner's theory were correct, you would expect to see that children's language would develop very differently depending on the amount and type of reinforcement that adults and others were giving. This is not the case, however, as most children seem to pass through the same stages. Also, the theory does not explain why children speak in different ways to adults around them, for example, 'dada gone'. If children are learning by imitating what they are hearing and not having incorrect sounds or sentences reinforced, why do they say things such as 'wented' or 'swimmed'?

Noam Chomsky – nativist perspective

Chomsky's work on language is based on the idea that our ability to learn language is instinctive. This is a 'nature' or nativist theory. His theory has been widely accepted as it is comprehensive and, unlike Skinner's ideas, explains why all babies' language development follows a pattern. He is famous for suggesting that humans have a Language Acquisition Device (LAD). This is not an actual physical part of the brain, but a structure within our brains that allows babies to absorb and understand the rules of the language they are being exposed to. The brain is able to analyse the language and work out the system that the language uses. This is a complex process, but explains why children can quickly understand and then use their language creatively and correctly without ever being formally taught or 'knowing' the rules.

Relationship between language and thought

There seems to be a strong link to language and thought, although there are different views of the relationship between them. Piaget differed in his views from Vygotsky and Bruner, because he suggested that language was a tool that was used by us, whereas Vygotsky and Bruner suggest that language organises and drives the thought process.

Vygotsky

Vygotsky suggested that thought and language begin as two different activities – when babies babble they are not using babbling as a way of thinking. At around the age of two years, they merge and at this point children use language to help them think. Vygotsky also differentiated between two types of speech – inner speech, which helps us to think, and external speech, which we use to communicate with others. An example of inner speech would be when we say either aloud or inwardly 'Then, I am going to...' as a way of directing ourselves. Between the ages of two and seven years, Vygotsky felt that children were not able to use them in distinct ways and therefore their speech was often a blend of the two, with young children often providing a running commentary of what they are doing. Vygtotsky referred to this early speech and thought as egocentric.

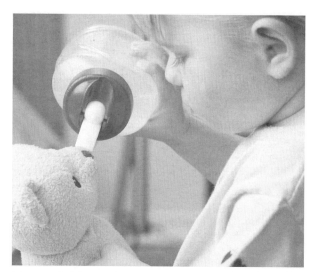
Young children often talk aloud.

Bruner

Bruner suggested that language is also linked to thought and that this was why children were able to develop a symbolic mode of thought. Previously children were using visual imagery to hold and use information in their learning, but language allowed them to use abstract, symbolic thoughts.

Application of theories to professional practice

Piaget

Although Piaget had no particular recommendations about how his theory should be used to teach children, his work did have an effect on educational practice. There are two main strands: **readiness** and **learning by discovery**. Both of these strands were used to suggest that an individual approach to children's learning should be taken.

Readiness

If children's thought processes cannot be 'fast-tracked' this means that we can only work at the child's pace. If a child does not have the concept of conservation of number, this would mean that there is no point in teaching children addition or multiplication.

Learning by discovery

The way that children develop their thinking is by reviewing their schemas and adapting their ideas (accommodation) to new information. In order to do this children will need a wide range of experiences.

Vygotsky

Vygotsky's work has been influential – he suggests that people working with children need to extend and challenge their thoughts so that their zone of proximal development can emerge. He also stressed the importance of social interaction and the need for adults to work alongside children. He also felt that children could guide and develop each other's potential and peer group teaching was a feature of Marxist education. It is also interesting to note that although Vygotsky saw that direct teaching was important, children also needed to be active in their learning.

Bruner

As Bruner felt that language and thought were interlinked, he also felt that it would be possible to support children's cognitive development by teaching them to use symbols. He also looked at the role of the adult in asking questions that would guide children's thinking and draw their attention to particular aspects of any activity.

END-OF-UNIT TEST

1　What is meant by the nature versus nurture debate?

2　Briefly explain the theory of operant conditioning.

3　What is the difference between operant and classical conditioning?

4　Why has Lorenz's theory of aggression been criticised?

5　Explain how the social learning theory may be used to explain differences in personality.

6　Explain the role of the id, ego and superego according to Freud.

7　What were the key effects of Bowlby's work on early years practice?

8　What are the major criticisms of Bowlby's early work?

9　List Piaget's stages of cognitive development.

10　Why were Piaget's research methods criticised?

11　What are the differences between the nativist and the behaviourist perspectives of language development?

12　Give two practical examples of the way in which a major theoretical perspective has influenced early years practice.

References and further reading

Bee, H (1999), *The Developing Child*, London: Longman

Bukatko, D and Daehler, M (1997), *Child Development: A thematic approach* (3rd edition), London: Houghton and Mifflin

Gross, R (2001), *Psychology: The science of mind and behaviour* (4th edition), London: Hodder and Stoughton

Gross, R, McIlveen, R, Coolican, H, Russell, J and Clamp, A (2000), *Psychology: A new introduction for A Level* (2nd edition), London: Hodder and Stoughton

UNIT 16

Children with special needs

Introduction

It is estimated that one in five children will at one time or another in their school career need some additional support in order to access learning. The term 'special needs' is an extremely broad one and takes in children who may have short-term educational needs, alongside those who are gifted and those who have inherited a severe learning difficulty. The number of children who are considered to have a special need means that a good understanding and awareness of special needs is important for early years practitioners and adults working with children. This is an interesting and changing area within education. There is plenty of debate currently as to how best to help children who need specific help.

How you will be assessed

This unit is assessed internally.

1 Special needs and its causative factors

Models of disability

A good starting point when looking at this area is to consider the way in which society views disability. This has affected the care and education of people with disabilities. Two models of disability (or attitudes towards disability) are usually contrasted – the medical model and the social model.

Medical model of disability

The medical model of disability is in many ways the traditional way of thinking about disability. It reflects society's faith in doctors and perhaps has come about because of the advances in medical knowledge. The medical model views disability as something that must, whenever possible, be cured and, where that is not possible, a feeling of failure results unless the person can be made to 'look' or 'act' normally. The medical model of disability therefore treats people with impairments as victims and patients – words such as handicapped, incurable, suffering and wheelchair-bound are associated with this attitude. The medical model of disability tends to put the emphasis more on the condition rather than on the person. The tendency to label people according to their impairments stems from this attitude – 'the one who's wheelchair-bound' rather than 'James, who uses a wheelchair'.

Social model of disability

The social model of disability reflects a new attitude towards people with impairments. It considers that first and foremost they are people with rights and feelings. The social model of disability has been a very empowering one for many disabled people, as it emphasises their

The social model of disability means that children are not seen as helpless and passive.

CASE STUDY

Emma was born with one arm foreshortened above the elbow. Her mother was determined that this should not affect Emma's life and she refused anyone to feel sorry for Emma or consider her a victim. Emma was given a prosthesis (false limb) which, although uncomfortable and restricting, made her look like other children. At home Emma never wore her prosthesis as her family completely accepted the way she looked without it. Emma learnt to ride a horse, manage everyday tasks and was to all intents and purposes a very happy and confident child. She left school and started to work in a restaurant. As she became older she gradually started to question society's attitude towards disability and began to feel unhappy that she was in effect disguising her disability. One day she decided that she would no longer wear her false arm. Her employer was unhappy about this decision. He said that seeing a person with only one arm would make customers feel uneasy and it could affect his business. Emma turned the argument around and said that if she had spent her life learning to cope without an arm, perhaps his customers could spend five minutes learning to see her without one, especially as they had already learnt to cope with seeing his bald head!

rights to make choices, question values and asks whether it is society with the real problem. The social model of disability has meant that terms such as 'mentally handicapped' and 'wheelchair-bound' are now considered unhelpful. The case study below shows clearly how attitudes have changed and the social model of disability is now being increasingly accepted as the way forward.

Definitions of special educational needs

The term 'special educational needs' is widely used, but is also a matter for debate as it is often argued that all children have special needs. It is worth noting that there is a growing trend to use the term 'additional needs' or 'particular needs' as an alternative. The reason behind the growing reluctance to use the term 'special needs' is that many parents and professionals feel that this term labels children in a negative way. This is interesting as the term was considered to be quite revolutionary and was designed to avoid potential discrimination.

At the time of writing, however, the term is still used in legislation and other documents, although it is essential to remain aware of any changes. There are several definitions of special needs. Definitions often reflect the attitudes of society and they gradually change over time. The following definitions are used in current legislation.

Education Act 1996

Children have special educational needs if they have a learning difficulty which calls for special educational provision to be made for them. Children have a learning difficulty if they:

✳ have a significantly greater difficulty in learning than the majority of children of the same age

✳ have a disability which prevents or hinders them from making use of educational facilities of a kind generally provided for children of the same age in schools within the area of the local education authority

✳ are under compulsory school age and fall within the two definitions above or would do so if special educational provision was not made for them.

Disability Discrimination Act 1995, Section 1 (1)

People have a disability for the purposes of this Act if they have a physical or mental impairment which has substantial and long-term adverse effect on their ability to carry out normal day-to-day activities.

Children Act 1989, Section 17 (11)

Children are disabled if they are blind, deaf or dumb or suffer from a mental disorder of any kind or are substantially and permanently handicapped by illness, injury or congenital deformity or such other disability as they may be prescribed.

Labelling and stereotyping

One of the dangers of using any classification system is that people can be stereotyped. This means that instead of seeing the person, we hear the label – this is one of the things that disabled people find most frustrating. The danger of labelling and stereotyping is that people working with children with special needs can concentrate more on the condition and the disability than on what the child can actually do. This means that the child's potential is not fulfilled and is one of the reasons why integration into mainstream classes is considered a preferred option wherever possible.

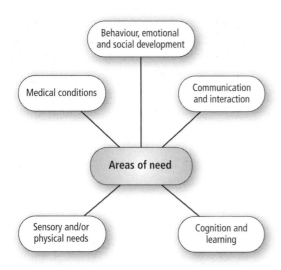

Behaviour, emotional and social development

Medical conditions

Communication and interaction

Areas of need

Sensory and/or physical needs

Cognition and learning

Classifications of special need

There has been an increasing reluctance to 'categorise' children for the reasons given above, but five areas are given in the SEN Code of Practice that is used in England and Wales. The code is clear that some children will need support in more than one area.

Causative factors

Identification

There are several ways in which children with special needs are identified. Wherever possible, early identification is sought which has meant that many routine tests are carried out before babies are born. Early identification is not always possible because some needs and difficulties only become noticeable as a child develops. The table below outlines the main ways in which a child with special needs might be recognised.

WHEN?	TEST	IDENTIFICATION
Pre-natal tests	Ultrasound scan Blood tests Amniocentesis Chorionic villus sampling	Tests are carried out during pregnancy. Where a family has a medical history that might indicate a possible difficulty, specific tests will be carried out. Modern technology has meant some life-saving operations can be carried out in the womb. These include heart surgery and repairing the lesion in the spine of babies who have spina bifida.
At birth	Apgar tests Blood tests Physical examination	At birth babies are carefully checked. In some cases immediate operations might be carried out.
During health surveillance checks	Physical examinations including height, weight and head circumference Speech and language	The need for early identification means that parents are offered regular health surveillance checks for their babies and children. Health visitors and family doctors normally carry out these health checks.
Recognition by parents or other family members		Parents might have a concern about their child (especially if they have had more than one child). They may report their concern to their health visitor or to the family doctor.
Recognition by early years practitioners		Early years practitioners may carry out observations or notice that a child has specific difficulties compared to a child of a similar age.
Recognition in school settings	Diagnostic language and numeracy tests	Some children will have their needs identified in schools because teachers may carry out routine educational tests or they may notice discrepancies in areas of a child's performance, e.g. a child may be orally very fluent, but have difficulty in remembering and recognising letters.

WHEN?	TEST	IDENTIFICATION
During an illness or following an accident		Sometimes identification will be made during a routine visit to the family doctor, e.g. a cough that is persisting or while other medical conditions are being investigated. In addition, there are some illnesses that can cause an impairment, e.g. measles can occasionally cause hearing impairments.

Causes of special needs

Many parents of children with special needs find it very helpful to understand the cause of their child's condition. It can affect whether they go on to have another child, inform them of support organisations and also help them deal with their own feelings of guilt. Many parents, especially mothers, are afraid that they might have taken something or done something to cause the condition. Unfortunately, although scientific knowledge has developed enormously, not every condition has a clear cause.

Hereditary factors

Many conditions are thought to be caused by hereditary factors, which means they were passed down to the child via one or both parents. In some cases, such as Down's syndrome, the condition can even be traced to the presence or absence of specific chromosomes, whereas in others the condition is caused by a damaged chromosome. Substantial medical research is now being done to identify the genes within our chromosomes and to define their effects on our bodies. Some conditions are only seen in particular races. For example, sickle cell anaemia affects Afro-Caribbean children, while others affect only one gender, such as haemophilia in boys.

Prenatal factors

Some conditions are thought to be caused during pregnancy. The foetus is particularly vulnerable in the first few weeks of life and often before a woman knows that she is pregnant. This means that drugs taken for medical reasons as well as for recreational use, excess alcohol and smoking can sometimes have an effect on the developing baby. Recently, scientists are becoming more aware of the need for women planning on becoming pregnant to take extra supplements before conception. Conditions such as spina bifida seem to be linked to a lack of folic acid in the woman's body. Diet during pregnancy can also be a factor, for example it is known that eating un-pasteurised foods can lead to women contracting listeria. Illnesses contracted during pregnancy can also cause damage to the embryo – for example, rubella can cause sensory impairments. Towards the end of the pregnancy, some women also develop high blood pressure (hypertension). In some cases this develops further into pre-eclampsia which is a serious condition and can affect the health of both mother and unborn child.

CASE STUDY

Wendy is Sophie's mother. She realised that Sophie was not making the same developmental progress as other children during Sophie's first year. She was keen for Sophie to be checked out and was at first disappointed when the doctors could not find out what exactly was wrong, although they could recognise that she had some learning difficulties. It was several years before the exact cause of Sophie's learning difficulties was recognised – a chromosomal disorder. Wendy was relieved as she had been worried that she might have unknowingly taken something during the pregnancy to cause the condition. It also meant that she could conceive another child knowing that it was unlikely for a subsequent child to have the same disorder. Once Sophie's disability had been recognised, it was also easier for Wendy to get support as there was a voluntary organisation for children with the same disorder.

In many cases, doctors will intervene and induce the birth which may mean that the baby is born prematurely.

During the process of birth

The process of birth itself can be the cause of some conditions. Damage to the brain can be caused by lack of oxygen during the first moments of life (asphyxia). Similarly, some babies suffer physical damage during the actual delivery. Some babies are also born too soon (prematurely) and this can lead to several difficulties as the lungs are often not mature enough to allow the baby to breathe independently (bronchopulmonary dysplasia).

Postnatal factors

Postnatal factors cover illnesses, accidents and diseases that the child might be subject to during childhood. For example, a child might fall off a bike and have a brain injury, or contract meningitis and develop a hearing impairment. It is now known that shaking a baby or toddler can cause severe brain injuries. The environment where the child lives can also have an effect on general health and some conditions such a asthma can be triggered by pollution, damp and chemicals. Sometimes the way that children are receiving care in the home can contribute towards learning or behavioural difficulties. Children might be exposed to a tense and aggressive atmosphere or their carer might not be coping with the demands of parenthood. Children in these situations might develop emotional and behavioural difficulties. Finally, child abuse of any kind can also mean that children develop special needs.

Conditions present at birth

Down's syndrome

Children with Down's syndrome have one extra chromosome in their genetic make-up. The diagnosis of Down's syndrome is often made at birth as the baby's facial features have certain characteristics, although women who have had an amniocentesis test will be aware that they are carrying a Down's syndrome baby.

Impact on child

Children with Down's syndrome develop and learn in the same way as other children, although their progress will be slower and their eventual ability to reason in the abstract is often limited. The extent of their learning difficulties varies enormously from individual to individual, although many children are able to remain, with support, in mainstream settings. Some children go on to be able to lead relatively independent lives in sheltered accommodation.

Cystic fibrosis

Cystic fibrosis is a disease that is present at birth and is caused by a recessive gene. A child with cystic fibrosis will have both parents who are carriers of the gene. Diagnosis is usually made early on in a baby's life as the baby may be failing to put on weight and also have recurrent lung infections.

Impact on child

Children with cystic fibrosis have difficulty in digesting food properly and are unable to take in all the nutrients required for a balanced diet. They are also prone to chronic lung infections, diabetes and pancreatic disorders. Children with cystic fibrosis often require daily physiotherapy to clear their lungs of mucus which builds up. Tablets are also required at meal and snack times to help children digest their food.

While children with cystic fibrosis do not have learning difficulties as such, they may need extra support due to absences caused by the disease, which is physically tiring and can shorten the lifespan of a child due to the damage caused to the lungs. Children with cystic fibrosis may not be able to join in physically demanding activities and may quickly feel tired. The nature of the disease can affect children's ability to concentrate.

Cerebal palsy

This is a general term to describe disorders which prevent the brain from controlling muscles in the body. There are a multitude of causes of cerebal palsy, including birth injuries, maternal infection in the first few weeks of a pregnancy, head trauma and genetic disorders.

There are three main types of cerebal palsy with some people having a combination of two or more.

* **Spastic cerebal palsy.** One or more limbs are stiff and the muscles are contracted.

* **Ataxic cerebral palsy**. Difficulty in balancing, controlling whole limb movements and focusing.

* **Athetoid cerebral palsy**. Involuntary movements caused by muscles contracting and then stiffening.

Impact on child

The extent to which a child may be affected can vary enormously, with some children having only slight indications of cerebral palsy. While children with cerebral palsy may have difficulties with co-ordination and use of their limbs, they will not necessarily have learning difficulties.

Muscular dystrophy

There are 20 known types of muscular dystrophy. The commonest type is Duchenne, which affects boys only. Muscular dystrophies are genetic conditions. They cause the cells in the muscles to break down and gradually be lost. This causes increasing loss of movement and can eventually lead to reduced life expectancy

Impact on child

The gradual deterioration and loss of movement is distressing for parents and children. The aim is to maintain as much independence for the child as possible.

Spina bifida and hydrocephalus

Spina bifida is a congenital disorder which occurs early in pregnancy. The vertebrae in the spine do not properly form, leaving part of the spinal cord exposed. The spinal cord serves as the passageway for messages to be passed to and from the brain from the limbs. Any blockages can result in loss of sensation and use of the limbs. Hydrocephalus often accompanies spina bifida at birth. Hydrocephalus is sometimes referred to as water on the brain and is the result of a build-up of spinal fluid in the brain. In order to prevent brain damage, the excess fluid is drained.

Impact on child

The extent of damage to the body depends on how exposed the spinal cord is, with the severest type of spina bifida (myelomeningocele) often resulting in partial or complete paralysis from the waist down. Children with severe spina bifida will often require a wheelchair for mobility and will remain incontinent. Many children with spina bifida do not have any learning difficulties, although they may need extra support in terms of coping with their disability.

Physical disabilities

Epilepsy

Epilepsy is the term used when the brain shows abnormal electric activity. This can result in 'absences' where a child or person simply seems to have 'shut down' or makes involuntary twitches and movements or, at its most extreme, dramatic convulsions or seizures.

In the past, children with epilepsy were discriminated against as it was thought that they were 'mentally deranged' or even that the devil had taken control of their minds. It is now known that epilepsy in itself is not linked to a person's mental state and that children with epilepsy do not have learning difficulties. There are three types of epilepsy.

* **Partial**. Where a person may be conscious of feeling 'strange'.

* **Generalised absence** (previously called *petit mal*). Where a person 'switches off' and afterwards has no recollection of what they were doing or thinking about.

* **Generalised tonic clonic** (previously called *grand mal*). Where a person falls unconscious and has a seizure. Seizures are often dramatic with a person arching their back and then going on to make large involuntary movements before the body relaxes. A person may then regain consciousness and feel dazed or fall into a deep sleep.

Most children with epilepsy take medication which suppresses extraneous brain activity. Medication can cause drowsiness, especially at first when the dosage is being fixed. If children have a seizure, it is important to clear the area of anything that may cause them to injure themselves and stay on hand until the seizure has finished. They should then be put in the recovery position until they feel better. Children may then need to rest.

HIV

HIV stands for human immunodeficiency virus. Once a person has the HIV virus, they may later develop AIDS (acquired immune deficiency syndrome), although some people with the HIV virus are at present showing no signs of developing AIDS. It is AIDS that people fear as the virus attacks the immune system, preventing the body from fighting off bacteria, viruses and cancers and thus it inevitably shortens the lifespan.

Children with HIV are likely to have gained this virus from their infected mothers, either in the womb or through breast milk. In the past, a relatively small number of children may have contracted the virus through having received contaminated blood products, although careful screening now makes this unlikely.

Children with HIV pose no risk to other children or staff, providing that the usual procedures of wearing gloves when dealing with bodily fluids, including blood, are followed. Children with HIV have often been discriminated against because of a widespread and unfounded fear of HIV. Children with HIV have no particular learning difficulties, although they may show emotional and behavioural difficulties caused by the awareness of the disease and in some cases bereavement of their parents.

Asthma

Children with asthma have difficulty in breathing. Asthma affects one in ten children, and can occasionally be fatal, which is why when a child has an attack, the correct medication should be available. Children with asthma do not have learning difficulties as a result of this condition, although they may get behind academically due to prolonged absences from school. If it is properly controlled by medications, there should be no restriction on active play for children with asthma.

Eczema

Eczema is a skin condition which is caused by an allergic reaction. Eczema can cause severe itchiness, dryness of skin and discomfort. Children with eczema do not have learning difficulties, but may find it hard to concentrate and in severe cases may not be able to touch certain play materials, such as sand or dough.

Sickle cell anaemia

Sickle cell anaemia is an inherited blood disorder which causes the red cells to be 'sickle' shaped. This in turn prevents the normal flow of blood and causes anaemia. Sickle cell anaemia is prevalent among people of African or Caribbean descent. The symptoms of anaemia include tiredness and lethargy, and poor blood flow can create pains in the arms, legs and back.

The disease also causes children to have difficulty in fighting off infections and adults caring for children need to be vigilant for signs that the child is having a crisis that will require immediate medical attention. Children with sickle cell anaemia do not have learning difficulties, but may fall behind with their work due to prolonged absences and constant fatigue which may affect concentration.

Diabetes

Diabetes is a disease where the pancreas is unable to produce sufficient insulin to maintain blood sugar levels in the body. Untreated, the disease

---

CASE STUDY

Holly has diabetes and was diagnosed when she was a baby. She is six years old and has several injections a day. She has been taught how to test her blood sugar level and understands how important it is to have her snacks. Holly's friends know that she has extra food and that she can't have chocolate without checking first. She is doing well at school.

- Why is it important not to assume that all children with a medical condition will have learning difficulties?

- Explain why it is important for Holly to take some responsibility for managing her diabetes.

can be fatal, although this is extremely rare. Children who have diabetes are likely to require daily injections of insulin and will have a diet to follow which will exclude sugar. They are also likely to need regular meals and snacks to prevent low blood sugar.

Impact on child
Children with diabetes have no particular learning difficulties and generally the disease goes unnoticed by the other children.

Coeliac disease
Children with this disease have an intolerance to gluten. Gluten is found in wheat and many other cereals, such as rye and oats.

Impact on child
Children have no learning difficulties and, as with diabetes, the disease usually goes unnoticed by others. Adults caring for children with this condition must be careful not to offer any products containing gluten and adhere to the dietary arrangements agreed with the parents.

Dyslexia
Dyslexia is a global term used to describe specific learning difficulties in reading and writing. It is sometimes referred to as 'word blindness'. It is usually recognised when children reach seven or eight years and have made limited progress in reading and writing, although they may be performing well in other areas of the curriculum.

Impact on child
The needs of children with dyslexia are often very different and the type of support required can vary among individuals. Most children, however, develop low self-esteem as literacy skills are often valued in schools by teachers and the children's peers. The causes of dyslexia are not completely understood, although there appears to be an inherited tendency and a difference in the way the brain processes information. Dyslexia appears to affect boys more than girls and there is a correlation with children who have not crawled as babies.

Dyspraxia
This is a developmental disorder that affects children's control and co-ordination. The term is relatively new, as before many children were seen as just being clumsy. The cause of dyspraxia is not fully understood, but it appears to be linked to the brain's ability to process information effectively.

Impact on child
The impact on the child is likely to relate to the extent of the dyspraxia. Children can become frustrated by their difficulties in co-ordinating movements. They may also be isolated as they may not be able to join in games, such as football, or other activities unless support is given. Dyspraxia can also affect children's learning, as they may have difficulty in organising thoughts as well as actually writing them.

Gifted children
While gifted children are not usually defined as special educational needs children, there is an increasing recognition that they do have particular needs. The Special Educational Needs Code of Practice 2001 does not cover gifted children but, at the time of writing, the government is developing initiatives to identify and support gifted children.

Parents of gifted children often report that their children have behavioural or emotional and social difficulties. These can be the result of frustration, boredom or low self-esteem, as children feel that they are 'different'. Traditionally, many parents have found that the education system cannot cater for their child's needs and some parents have decided to educate their children at home.

Communication difficulties
There are a range of disorders which cause children to have difficulty in responding and communicating with others. Autistic spectrum disorders are the most common.

Autism and Asperger's syndrome
The causes of autistic spectrum disorders are currently unknown although there is some speculation that there may be some genetic factors at work. Children who have autistic spectrum disorders find it hard to understand and communicate with other people, including their own families. Some people liken autism to being 'trapped in a bubble'; seeing others, but not being able to share their world.

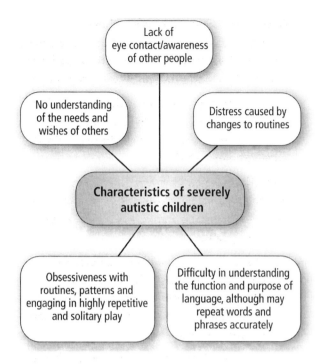

Impact on child

The extent of autism can vary enormously, with children who have slight tendencies towards autistic behaviours usually being diagnosed with Asperger's syndrome. Children with Asperger's syndrome are usually able to use language effectively, but find it hard to guess what others want or are thinking and so find it hard to socialise effectively. Their play is often highly structured and individual.

Parents of children with autistic spectrum disorders can feel isolated as their child's behaviour is not conducive to shopping or social occasions, especially as members of the public cannot see the 'disability' and assume that the behaviour is a result of poor parenting.

Assessment activity 16.1

Produce an information sheet for other students about two different groups of children who have 'special needs'. This should be based on at least three different sources of information and should provide information about:

- the causative factors
- the impact on children and their families
- further sources of information for parents.

Terminology

This section looks at the definitions that are used in relation to special needs. It also looks at some of the factors that may create disabilities as well as some types of disability. The section ends by looking at the current terminology that is used by professionals in the sector.

Getting the terminology right

A good starting point is the language and terms that are used in relation to special needs. Language is a powerful tool; words and phrases can reveal our deep-seated attitudes and so getting the language right when talking about special needs is important. There has been quite a shift in thinking about disability in the past 20 years and this has been reflected in the language we use and it is quite possible that it will change again to reflect further changes in society's thinking. An example of this is the current debate within some organisations such as SCOPE as to whether the term 'disabled people' should be used.

The key to working successfully with anyone who has special needs is to think about the person, not about the condition. At the time of writing the following words are often used.

* **Impairment**. The loss or abnormality of development of growth – a hearing impairment means that a person has a loss of hearing.

* **Disability**. The restrictions that the impairment causes – a person with a hearing disability has a disability in hearing.

* **Handicap**. The disadvantage that the person has in relation to others in certain situations. Note that the person is not themselves 'handicapped' – they are being handicapped by the situation. A person with a hearing impairment is being handicapped when announcements are being broadcast in an airport because they have a hearing disability. Their disability does not prevent them from reading the signs and getting onto the aircraft and so they are not being handicapped.

Terms to avoid

* Handicapped person
* Wheelchair-bound
* Sufferer, victim, crippled with
* Spastic
* Mental
* Idiot, imbecile
* Mongol, mongoloid
* Congenital

Keys to good practice

* Remember that children should not be labelled or only known for their disability or need.
* Avoid drawing attention to the child's disability, difference or condition unless it is relevant.
* Ask children or their parents about their preferences in terms of language.
* Listen carefully to the language that they use.
* Check out with support organisations the terms that are currently being used.

Other terminology

There are some words that are used specifically within this area of education. Understanding what they mean is useful.

* **Inclusion**. This is the concept that children should not be segregated from other children because of their disability.

* **Individual Education Plans**. These are programmes designed to focus on the needs of an individual child. In Scotland they are being referred to as Individualised Education Plans.

* **Equal opportunities**. This is the concept that all children should be able to achieve their potential and barriers that might prevent them have to be removed.

* **Anti-discriminatory practice**. This is the practice of thinking about potential barriers to children's learning and inclusion and actively removing them

* **Labelling**. This occurs when adults have categorised a child, e.g. 'she's very bright'. Labelling is dangerous as it prevents people from seeing the individual child and noticing individual changes.

* **Stereotyping**. This occurs when people have made blanket assumptions about a child based on what they think they know about a disability. These assumptions might not be relevant to the individual child.

* **Statements**. Known as Record of Needs in Scotland and soon to be changed to Co-ordinated Support Plans. These are legally binding documents that record the provision and support that children who have been formally assessed require. These are usually provided only where a child's needs are particularly complex.

2 Key legislation

This section looks at key and current legislation that affects children's rights. It also goes on to consider how children are identified and assessed and also considers the role of the multi-disciplinary team.

Key reports and legislation

Legislation often reflects the attitudes of society. There has been both an increasing awareness of the rights of children and also the rights of disabled people and this is reflected in some legislation. This is a changing area and so it is essential to keep up to date, especially if you work in Northern Ireland or Scotland. Many of the principles embedded in English legislation apply to legislation specific to Scotland, Wales and Northern Ireland, but there are also differences.

Legislation affecting children's rights

United Nations Convention on the Rights of the Child (UNCRC)

The UNCRC was drawn up in 1989 and gives children and young people under the age of 18 their own special rights. The UK is a signatory and it was ratified in 1991 (see also Unit 1).

The following articles are relevant in an early years setting.

* **Article 2**. The right to be protected from all forms of discrimination.
* **Article 3**. The best interest of the child to be the primary consideration in all actions concerning children.
* **Article 12**. A child's rights to express his or her views freely. A child's view to be given due weight in keeping with the child's age or maturity.
* **Article 13**. A child's right to freedom of expression and exchange of information regardless of frontiers.
* **Article 28**. A child's right to education with a view to achieving this right progressively on the basis of equal opportunities.

Children Act 1989

The Children Act was the first Act that brought together many pieces of legislation related to children, and was based on the idea that children have rights following the adopting in the UK of the United Nations Convention on the Rights of the Child (UNCRC). It sought to protect all children, but also looked at the needs and rights of vulnerable children. In respect of children with special needs the following points are important.

* Children's welfare must be given priority.
* Parents are important.
* Children need to be listened to.
* Local education authorities have legal duties towards all children, but especially vulnerably children.

'Every Child Matters' and Children Act 2004

Following the tragic death of Victoria Climbie, a report was commissioned into her death and the failure of the authorities to protect her. The Laming report provided many recommendations that in turn prompted the government to produce a Green Paper called 'Every Child Matters' (ECM). This was widely received and is at the basis of today's policies concerning children's services in a programme known as Every Child Matters Programme for Change.

The programme places better outcomes for children firmly at the centre of all policies and approaches involving children's services. These outcomes are:

* be healthy
* stay safe
* enjoy and achieve through learning
* make a positive contribution to society
* achieve economic well-being.

The Children Act 2004 is the legislative spine that helps to implement the Every Child Matters programme.

Legislation relating to children with special needs

In addition to legislation that relates to all children, it is also useful to see how reports and legislation relating to children with special needs has developed.

Education (Handicapped Children) Act 1970

This piece of legislation made all children the responsibility of the local education authority (they had previously been the responsibility of the health service) and, as a result, full-time education had to be provided for them. This meant that many special schools were built in the 1970s to provide an education. Towards the end of the 1970s, the consensus changed towards trying to integrate children into society. This was a backdrop to the now famous Warnock Report.

Warnock Report 1978

In 1978 a report was published by a committee chaired by Mary Warnock. This report was to prove one of the most influential pieces of legislation to affect disabled children in the 20th century. In 1981, many of the recommendations suggested by the committee became law. The committee had undertaken a comprehensive study of the whole area of disabled children, their education and their needs. The committee took evidence from parents, the voluntary sector, educationalists and the medical profession.

Introduction of the term 'special educational need'
For years, people had talked about handicapped children, or labelled children according to their disability. The report suggested a title of 'special

education need' (SEN), which would include any child who needed some form of extra support. The report suggested three types of support:

* special means of access to the curriculum

* changes to the curriculum

* changes to the environment – including emotional or social support.

The term 'special educational need' was an all-encompassing one and went from children who had slight difficulties with their reading and writing to children who had major care needs. It also included children who had short-term needs that were causing them difficulties in fulfilling their potential alongside children who had long-term needs. In this way it focused professionals on the idea of how to meet the needs that the children might have, rather than on the condition or cause of them. This was a major breakthrough and one that the Warnock Report will be noted for.

Education Act 1981

This Act was heavily based on the recommendations of the Warnock Report and gave local education authorities legal duties to fulfil. The act placed a clear responsibility on local education authorities to provide support for children who have special educational needs. It also introduced the process now known as 'statementing'. This is the process by which children are assessed by a team of professionals alongside the parents and a statement is drawn up of how the child's needs are to be supported. The statement of special educational needs is a legally binding one and commits the local authority to providing for the child.

The Act is also important because it gave parents power for the first time. Parents were to be involved in the process of producing a statement and deciding on the best course of education for their children but, more importantly, the parents were given the legal power to challenge local education authorities.

Statementing and funding

The idea behind producing a statement was to ensure that children with special educational needs were given support. By recording their needs and the action required to meet these needs,

children were supposed to be more likely to have these needs met. See pages 443–4 for more on statementing.

Education Act 1993

This Act was built upon the Education Act 1981 legislation and is currently legislation in England and Wales. Its key points are summarised below and are important because they still form the basis of the Education Act 2001.

KEY ISSUES

- **Code of Practice.** The Act required that the Secretary of State for Education publish a code of practice which was to give local education authorities and others practical guidance in following the legislation. The Code of Practice was in effect between September 1994 and December 2001.

- **Parents.** The 1993 Act made it clear that local education authorities needed to work alongside parents. It also established special educational needs tribunals that would hear cases where parents and local authorities were able to agree. Parents' rights of appeal were extended and information was published to help parents understand their rights.

- **Definition of special educational needs.** The Act stated that where health services identified that a child under five years old might have special educational needs, they had a duty to both the local education authority and the parents. It also stated that they should pass on information about voluntary organisations that might be able to help parents. This meant that health services, the voluntary sector (including charities such as Scope and Mind) and the local education authority have to work together.

- **Assessment of children under two years.** The Act gave parents the right to ask for the child under two years to be assessed and if appropriate be given a statement of special educational needs.

Special Education Needs and Disability Act 2001

This Act has been fairly well received by major disability charities and is divided into two sections. Part 1 of the Act reforms the framework of special educational needs to strengthen the rights of parents and children to access mainstream education. Part 2 extends the Disability Discrimination Act 1995 to education, extending the civil rights of disabled children and adults in schools, colleges and universities. Key features of the Act include:

* the right of children with special educational needs to be educated in mainstream schools (where this is what parents want and where it is appropriate for the child)

* the requirement of local education authorities to arrange to provide parents of children with special educational needs with advice and information, and a means of resolving disputes with schools and local education authorities

* the requirement for local educational authorities to comply with orders of the special educational needs tribunal

* the requirement of education settings to tell parents where they are making special educational provision for their child and allow schools to request a statutory assessment of a pupil's special educational needs

The Disability Discrimination Act has meant that early years settings must make reasonable adjustments to accommodate children with special needs.

* the introduction of disability discrimination rights in the provision of education in schools, further education, higher education, adult education and the youth service

* the requirement not to treat disabled students less favourably, without justification, than non-disabled students.

Carers and Disabled Children Act 2000

This legislation came into force in April 2001. It is designed to help the people who care for children to get their needs met alongside those of their children. The idea behind this law is to help carers manage more effectively. They may be given respite vouchers as well as being offered services directly from social services.

Disability Discrimination Act 1995

The aim of this Act is to ensure that services and employment opportunities are not denied to disabled people on the grounds of their impairment. An example of this would be if a disabled person using a wheelchair wanted to go into a restaurant. The owners of the restaurant must now make sure that they provide the same level of service to the disabled person as for any other member of the public. They can no longer say that they cannot serve wheelchair users.

The Act was divided into seven parts, with parts being gradually phased in to allow time for businesses and employers to make necessary adjustments. It created a National Disability Council to advise and work with the government on matters relating to disability and ways to introduce all parts of the Act. A further Act was later passed to create a commission in response to disappointed campaigners. The commission now has statutory powers to enforce the Disability Discrimination Act.

Additional Support for Learning Act (Scotland)

This Act will form the basis of special education provision in Scotland. It was presented in the Scottish Parliament in the autumn of 2005. A Code of Practice will then be produced to give further guidance. If you work in Scotland, it will be essential to have a copy of the Code of Practice.

The main features of this Act are:

❋ **The Co-ordinated Support Plan (CSP).** Instead of having a Record of Need (the equivalent of a Statement), children will have a Co-ordinated Support Plan. The CSP is intended to ensure better co-ordination of services from education, health and social work.

❋ **The right of extra help to more pupils.** The new Act introduces the wider concept of additional support needs (ASN) and extends the right of extra help to more pupils. Education authorities have a new duty to identify and support all children who would benefit from extra help with their learning. This is interesting as it takes on the concept that many children need support from time to time.

❋ **Parental involvement is vital.** In the same way that the English Code of Practice recognises the role of parents, the new legislation stresses the need for parental involvement. It ensures that parents:

- will have the right to request that their child's needs be assessed
- will have the right to be accompanied by a supporter at any meetings with the education authority
- will have the right to independent mediation
- will have the right to use local dispute resolution services
- will have the right to take Co-ordinated Support Plan disputes to the new Additional Support Needs tribunal
- will have the right to be accompanied by a supporter at tribunal
- will have the right to use advocacy services
- will be able to request a place at an independent special school (rare in England).

SEN Code of Practice 2001 (England and Wales)

This Code of Practice was implemented in January 2002 and acts as the key guidance for local education authorities, schools, early years education settings and parents.

Fundamental principles

The Code of Practice outlines the following principles.

- ❋ A child with special educational needs should have these needs met.
- ❋ The special educational needs of children will be met in mainstream schools or settings.
- ❋ The views of the child should be sought and taken into account.
- ❋ Parents have a vital role to play in supporting their child's education.
- ❋ Children with special educational needs should be offered full access to a broad, balanced and relevant education, including an appropriate curriculum for the Foundation Stage and the National Curriculum.

The philosophy behind the Code of Practice

Behind the Code of Practice there are several themes which represent trends in society.

Inclusion
The Code of Practice forms part of the government's drive towards establishing an 'inclusive' society. This trend is generally welcomed by voluntary organisations representing groups who are traditionally discriminated against. Therefore the aim of the code is to look for ways of keeping children who have special educational needs within mainstream school and early years settings by supporting them.

Involvement of children
The Code of Practice emphasises that children have rights and that they should be involved in making decisions and exercising choices. The importance of recognising the views of children was one of the main themes of the Children Act 1989 and also forms two of the articles of the United Nations Convention on the Rights of the Child. The Code of Practice clearly states that, from an early age, children should be involved in making decisions where possible, including the drawing up of individual education plans, as well

as during the statementing process and subsequent reviews.

Acknowledgement of the role of parents
The importance of parents in supporting their children and also in educating them is recognised within the Code of Practice. There is emphasis on making sure that parents are informed when settings have concerns about their children and also emphasis on gaining the expertise of parents when discussing arrangements to meet the needs of children. The Code of Practice also reminds local education authorities of their duty under the Education Act 1996 to provide parents of children with special educational needs with advice and information.

Assessment procedures

It is increasingly being recognised that early identification of special educational needs is essential in order to support children and their families and also, in some cases, to minimise the impact of the special needs.

Identification of special needs in early years settings

The Code of Practice 2001 requires all early years settings that receive government funding to have a special educational needs policy and appoint a member of staff to be the special educational needs co-ordinator (SENCO) (see page 452 for the role of SENCOs).

Theory into practice

Find out about the special educational needs policy in your setting. How is the policy implemented?

Graduated response

The Code of Practice uses the term 'graduated response' within the context of identifying, assessing and providing for young children (see diagram).

At this level, the setting will be providing most or all of the support for the child, although advice and help from local education authorities and other external agencies may be sought. In some cases, children will be provided with extra adult support, but in other cases, the staff in the setting may differentiate the curriculum or concentrate on particular activities with the child.

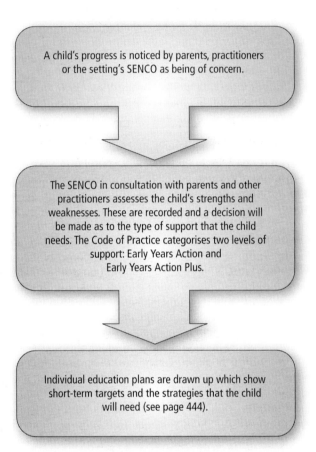

A child's progress is noticed by parents, practitioners or the setting's SENCO as being of concern.

The SENCO in consultation with parents and other practitioners assesses the child's strengths and weaknesses. These are recorded and a decision will be made as to the type of support that the child needs. The Code of Practice categorises two levels of support: Early Years Action and Early Years Action Plus.

Individual education plans are drawn up which show short-term targets and the strategies that the child will need (see page 444).

Early Years Action Plus level

At this level, the setting has identified that it will need additional support in order to meet the child's needs. It may approach the local education authority or other external agencies with records of the child's progress and previous individual education plans.

Requests for statutory statements

Where additional support is required beyond the scope of Early Years Action Plus, education settings, external agencies or the parents may request a statutory statement from the local education authority (see Statutory assessments, page 443).

Identification, assessment and provision in the primary phase

In theory, many children with special educational needs may have already had their needs identified by the time that they begin their primary education. The Foundation Stage in England now spans the pre-school and primary sectors. Individual education plans from the child's pre-school settings are likely to be passed to the primary school. The assessment process suggested by the Code of Practice is similar to that of the early education settings, with primary schools using a graduated response.

School Action level

At this level, the school will make plans to meet the child's needs and the SENCO will draw up individual education plans in association with class teachers, parents and other professionals. The implementation of the individual education plan is the responsibility of the class teacher, although advice can be gained from the SENCO.

School Action Plus level

At this level, schools will seek the assistance of external support and involvement. An educational psychologist may assist in drawing up individual education plans, although any involvement of external support will require the consent of parents.

Statutory assessment

Where a school is still concerned that the child is not making adequate progress, they may seek a statutory assessment from the local education authority.

Statementing

A statement is a legal document that outlines a child's special educational needs and the local authority's duties towards the child. The process by which a statement is drawn up is often referred to as 'statementing' (see the diagram below).

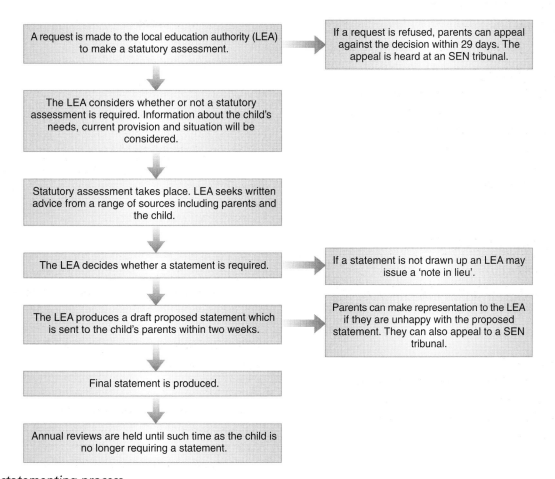

The statementing process.

The trend towards reducing the number of statements

Since statementing began there have been concerns that too many children were gaining statements which were not required, as they were already receiving sufficient support. It was often felt by local education authorities and others involved in the statementing process that too much time and money was spent on preparing reports and reviewing previous statements when the money would be better allocated in actually making provisions.

One of the reasons given for parents and schools asking for a statement for a child was budgetary. By having a statement, schools could often ask for additional funds while parents could in theory take a local education authority to court if the support indicated in a statement was not given. Changes in school funding to include a budget to support children with special educational needs has meant that fewer statements should be required.

Individual education plans – short-term plans

These are considered to be essential in helping a child to make progress and are used in all of the home countries. Individual education plans are normally drawn up by the SENCO together with staff members who work with the child and also the parents. They contain:

* short-term targets for the child (usually three or four at a time)

* details of the teaching strategies

* the provision to be put in place (this includes resources)

* when the plan is to be reviewed

* criteria for success, e.g. that a child may be able to put on a coat alone

* outcomes, e.g. a brief evaluation once the plan has been implemented.

Role of the multi-disciplinary team

Most families and children with special needs will gain support from the many different agencies and professionals. Before 1994, many parents became very frustrated as there seemed to be little communication between many of the different professionals and agencies. This meant that time was wasted in giving the children the support that they needed. The Code of Practice 1994 improved this aspect of supporting families as it stressed the importance of inter-team collaboration. The Every Child Matters programme continues to stress the importance of collaborative approaches. Increasingly, teams of professionals involved in delivering services to children and their family are working out of the same centres. This might mean that a child will go to a nursery where, on site, there is also a speech and language therapist, physiotherapists and an education psychologist. An outline of the roles of different professionals and agencies is given below.

SENCO

The role of the SENCO is now well established within settings. This is the person who is responsible for co-ordinating the polices and liaising with other professionals.

Key worker

It is increasingly understood that one person needs to develop a strong and individual relationship with a child and the parents. The key worker will spend time with the child and will be the person who in practice works alongside the child and gets to know his or her strengths and interests. Individual education plans will be implemented by the child's key worker. In many schools, the child's key worker will also be the teacher or classroom assistant.

Educational psychologist

Educational psychologists consider how children learn and so are used to help identify learning difficulties in children. They visit schools and settings regularly and work alongside parents and professionals in the setting. They draw up individual educational programmes and give guidance to staff as to how they can be implemented. Where a child needs a statement or has a statement, they will be involved in the assessments and drawing up of the statements.

Physiotherapist

A physiotherapist helps to identify a child's main physical problems, working alongside other professionals and parents. They often devise a programme of exercises or treatments which they either administer themselves or help parents and others to learn how to administer.

CASE STUDY

Oliver is three years old. His mother and the portage worker (see page 449) have decided to work on Oliver's feeding skills. The aim for this week is to get Oliver to put his fingers around a spoon. Three times a day, his mother will enclose his fingers around a spoon at meal times. She will praise him during this process.

Speech and language therapist

Speech and language therapists work with children who have some difficulties with their language. They identify the causes of the problems and devise speech and language programmes. These may include exercises, advice for parents, early years practitioners and other professionals. The range of children that they work with can be quite wide and includes children with cleft palate and lisps, as well as children who are autistic.

Community paediatrician

Paediatricians are mainly based in hospitals and clinics. They have specialised training in children's medicine and children are referred to them via their family doctor for diagnosis. They make regular assessments of children's progress and medical needs. They are able to refer children to other health services, such as speech and language therapy and dieticians.

Community nurse

In some areas, community nurses visit schools and settings to help provide advice and support. They may undertake general health promotion work with parents or they may work with particular children and their families. Integrating health and education is a major focus of the Every Child Matters programme and so some early years centres will have a community nurse based at the centre.

Family doctor (general practitioner)

The family doctor has general training in medicine. The doctor forms part of the community health team and act as a base for a child's ongoing medical treatment and notes. The family doctor will often have been the person who referred the child to the paediatrician when impairment was suspected.

Child psychologist and psychotherapist

These professionals are often used when children show emotional and behaviour difficulties. They work with other professionals to determine the root cause of the unwanted or disturbed behaviour. Play therapy or family counselling is often used as a way of helping children and their families. Child psychiatrists may sometimes be called upon to give guidance to other professionals in some cases.

Educational welfare officer/education social worker

The main function of these professionals is to liaise between home and families in cases where school attendance is infrequent. (It is an offence for children not to be in some sort of full-time educational provision.) Their role is particularly helpful in cases where children are refusing to attend school (school refusal). They are often able to work alongside parents, the child and other professionals to make sure that children's needs are being met.

Special needs support teacher

These teachers travel between schools or visit children in their homes or in pre-school settings. They are able to help a wide range of children and are often seen as useful sources of support and guidance. Special needs support teachers tend to build up a good relationship with the child and may even work with children when they are admitted to hospitals.

Classroom assistant/learning support assistant

There are many variations on the title used for classroom assistants. Their main purpose is to support an individual child or group of children within a classroom under the direction of the classroom teacher. They may also be responsible for carrying out the activities listed in the individual education plan, as well as recording the child's progress. Most classroom teachers, SENCOs and special needs assistants work closely together and draw up the individual education plan.

Social worker

The majority of social workers are employed by the local authority, although some are employed by voluntary organisations. They are generally deployed in teams according to specialist areas – some social workers are involved in caring for older clients, others for adoption and fostering work. Children with special needs often have an assigned social worker as they are seen as potentially vulnerable. Social workers are often able to provide guidance, advice and practical support for families and as such are often welcome visitors.

Respite carer

Respite carers care for children for short periods of time so that their parents can have some time out. Respite care may be for a few hours, a weekend or for a week. Respite carers may look after the child in their own homes or may work in a residential centre.

> **Assessment activity 16.2**
>
> Sam is four years old. He attends a local pre-school in England three mornings a week. The staff have become concerned about his language development. He has made some progress over the past six months, but the staff feel that he will need further support.
>
> - Produce a flow chart which shows how this child may have his needs met in relation to the latest legislation. The flow chart should also show the roles of a range of people in the assessment process.
> - Explain which professionals may become involved with Sam if his language development is considered to be seriously delayed.
> - Produce a sample individual education plan for Sam.

3 Equal opportunities and anti-discriminatory practice

Early years practitioners have a key role in promoting equal opportunities and anti-discriminatory practice. This section considers some of the ways in which this might be done in settings. For more information on equal opportunities and anti-discriminatory practice see Unit 1.

Promoting equal opportunities and anti-discriminatory practice in early years settings

Building self-esteem

Positive self-esteem is important in all children. Having good feelings about yourself can give you security and confidence. It enables you to cope with setbacks and helps you take on challenges. Low self-esteem is often associated with depression and with lowered levels of achievement and friendships. Sadly, children with special needs can often have low self-esteem. This is partly because they may compare themselves unfavourably with other children and also because they may not be given opportunities to become independent. Self-esteem can also be lowered by people around them doing too much for them and thus taking control away from them.

In some cases, this means that children become very passive, because adults around them reward

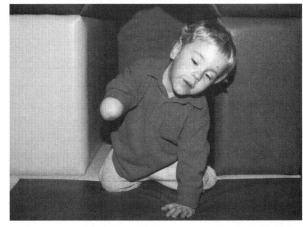

Happiness is crawling through a tunnel without help!

them for 'being so good' – which actually means that they have kept still and allowed the adult to take control. This is sometimes referred to as 'learned helplessness'. In the long term it can mean that children's potential is not being developed, as the focus becomes their condition or disability.

Adults working with children with special needs must therefore encourage children to be active rather than passive and build in them self-reliance and self-confidence. This is achieved through praise, positive expectations and giving children unconditional love.

Empowerment

The word 'empowerment' is often used in connection with the idea of people taking responsibility for decisions that will affect them. Previously, disabled people tended to have things either done for them or done to them. They were often protected and treated as helpless victims to be nurtured. Currently this attitude is being revised and people working with children with special needs have to make sure that whenever possible they are empowering children. This means giving children choices and looking for ways in which we can develop their independence.

In an everyday routine, this might mean asking children to choose what they wear, the colour of the pen they use or which activity they want to do first. Empowerment has become a key feature of many disability campaigning groups. This campaigning has resulted in changes to legislation, voluntary organisations and education policy.

Advocacy

Today great care is taken to involve parents and children with special needs in the decision-making process. Generally, parents act as advocates for their children or the children are able to speak for themselves if the issues are explained to them. Where, for some reason, there is no one available to represent the child, an advocate will speak for the child. The advocate will be thinking about the needs and wishes of the child and putting these forward. Advocates are particularly used in cases where children are being 'looked after' by the local authority.

Promoting children's rights

As part of their role, early years practitioners need to be aware of children's rights and actively aim to promote them. This means checking that their setting is working actively to involve children and empowering them. Organisations that actively promote children's rights include Save the Children and Unicef. Both organisations have information about how best to listen to children and involve them.

Cultural and religious norms

Promoting equal opportunities and anti-discriminatory practice also means thinking about how best to understand and meet the needs of children whose families have cultural and religious preferences. Most settings find that talking to parents directly and learning about their needs and wishes is the best way. This is an area where making assumptions can lead to discrimination – for example, a vegetarian family not being asked if they would like to help at a barbecue because it is assumed that they will not be pleased if there is any meat available.

Stereotyping and labelling

Stereotypes are assumptions that are made about groups of people. Stereotypes and labels can be both positive and negative. The difficulty is that they ignore the individual. An example of a positive assumption that is commonly made is that everyone who speaks English can read it. While this is the case with many people, there might be some individuals who do not read. Letters that are sent home might therefore present a difficulty. Settings that promote equal opportunities and anti-discriminatory practice try hard to reflect on their practice and consider whether they are making any assumptions.

Challenging discrimination

Children with special needs and their families can sometimes be discriminated against. Assumptions are sometimes made about them which affects the way others react. Children might not be given the opportunity to look at books because a practitioner thinks they are not capable. All practitioners have a duty towards children and so need to challenge discrimination. As part of their anti-discriminatory policy, settings should have a procedure to follow where a practitioner has concerns (see also Unit 1).

Developing an inclusive environment

The recognition of promoting equal opportunities has meant that settings are becoming more inclusive. Inclusive settings think about all aspects of their practice and check that they meet the needs of all children and their families. Thought is given to every aspect, from how welcoming the setting is down to whether or not the session hours really meet the needs of the local community. Information might be sent out in a range of formats to ensure that no one is left out and the views of parents are actively sought.

Communication strategies

Being able to communicate is one way in which children can feel part of an environment. Finding ways to communicate with children is a priority as it means that their needs, interests and feelings can be sought. There are many different systems available to help children communicate.

Picture exchange communication system

This is a visual system which is used with children. Pictures on cards mean that children can choose a picture that represents what they want to do or show and then give it to the adult. The exchange of cards is central to the system as it teaches children about the nature of communication.

Braille

Braille is a well-known and widely used system of written language for the visually impaired who are unable to read large print. It uses sequences of raised dots that can be felt and therefore read. A machine called a Perkins brailler can be used to transcribe text into Braille and vice versa.

Makaton

Makaton has become increasingly used to support speech and language development with children who have communication difficulties. It is based on signs that resemble actions or objects. Makaton is often chosen as the major sign language in many schools because it is easy to learn. In terms

of creating an inclusive environment, this means that other children can pick it up easily as well.

British sign language (BSL)

British sign language is a different language to Makaton. Users of BSL have a complete language and can make complex and abstract statements.

Policies within the early years settings

Policies are documents that explain how settings intend to work. They are important as they provide the framework that staff should follow. The need to ensure that children are treated fairly should be reflected in the range of policies within a setting.

Special needs policy

All early years settings are required to have a special needs policy. They need to show how they will ensure that children who have a disability or learning need will be supported. The SENCO in a setting is usually responsible for ensuring that the policy is followed and is also updated to reflect the latest thinking and legislation.

Equal opportunities and anti-discrimination

These policies are brought together in most settings. They should explain how a setting works to ensure that children are not discriminated against on account of their gender, race, culture or disability. This policy should be closely tied to the special needs policy.

Ofsted requirements

All settings caring for children are inspected. In England the inspection process is carried out by Ofsted. All inspectorates, however, check that there are policies relating to anti-discriminatory practice and special needs and they look closely to ensure that the policies are regularly reviewed and that they are reflected in everyday working.

✱ **Standard 9: Equal Opportunities**. The registered person and staff actively promote equality of opportunity and anti-discriminatory practice for all children.

CASE STUDY

Mark's hand-eye co-ordination is a focus of his IEP. He enjoys playing with the construction materials. When it is time to complete the weekly planning sheet, his key worker thinks about his needs and how these might be linked into the overall planning. Many other children also enjoy playing with construction materials and so it is decided to link a mathematics activity with it. In this way, Mark's IEP can be implemented without taking Mark away from the other children.

Meltem finds it hard to concentrate and sit still at story time. Her key worker changes her approach to story time by introducing small hand puppets and props. All the children are given one, but this makes it easier for Meltem to cope.

- Why are these approaches examples of inclusive education?
- Why is it important for staff to consider the needs of individual children when planning?

✳ **Standard 10: Special Needs (including Special Educational Nerds and Disabilities)**. The registered person is aware that some children may have special needs and is proactive in ensuring that appropriate action can be taken when such a child is identified or admitted to the provision. Steps are taken to promote the welfare of the child within the setting in partnership with parents and other relevant parties.

Differentiation of the curriculum and activities

One of the ways in which an inclusive environment is put into practice is by checking that activities and the curriculum are suitable for all children. This means that plans should reflect individual children needs and be structured in a way to accommodate them.

Portage

Portage is a system that was developed in the US and has been adopted, although often modified, in the UK. It concentrates on helping children under five by working with parents in their home. It is based on the idea that early stimulation can help children with special needs. A portage worker will visit the home (in some areas this is a volunteer, whereas in others it is a trained teacher) and will carry out some assessments on the child. The parents and the portage worker together decide which skill or area of learning should be worked on. A step-by-step approach is decided upon with the parents being largely responsible for carrying out the programme. To support the

programme, families are visited at least once a week by the portage worker where the child's progress is discussed. Portage workers take on the role of being a 'support' rather than a professional and parents are very much seen as equal partners.

Individual Education Plans (IEPs)

We have seen earlier that IEPs are a central part of working with children with special needs. IEPs help adults working with children to focus directly on specific aspects. It is good practice that wherever possible the activities suggested in the IEPs are linked to the main curriculum.

Access and safety within the physical environment

As well as looking at the curriculum and activities, early years settings also need to look for physical ways of allowing children to access the curriculum. Adjustments such as ramps and widened doors are becoming more common as the SENDA legislation ensures that settings must make reasonable steps to ensure access. Where buildings cannot accommodate physical changes, staff have to consider ways of ensuring that children are not discriminated against because of mobility needs. Sometimes this means relocating activities so that they can become more accessible.

As well as meeting physical needs, some children will also require areas where their personal care needs can be met with some degree of privacy. Children might need to take medication or be changed. Staff have to be sensitive to how this is done and it is usually the responsibility of the key worker.

4 Effective parent–professional partnerships

It is now recognised that parents form an important role in children's lives. Their role has been increasingly strengthened through legislation. This means that professionals are now likely to be working effectively with them. This section looks at issues for families, ways in which partnerships should be developed and the role of the statutory and voluntary sector. The section ends by considering effective communication.

Issues for families

There are significant effects on families who have children with special needs. The following highlights some of the common issues. Interestingly, few parents want pity or to be cast in the role of the hero. Most parents find that, even when they are under stress, they still can find time to enjoy and cherish their child.

Stress on family

The families of children with special needs often have their own special needs. Couples can find that their own relationship is put under enormous stress at times. It is not uncommon for couples to split up soon or shortly after a child is found to have special needs, especially if they are complex or severe. Many parents of children with special needs find that so much of their time and energy is used in caring for the child, that it is hard to find the extra time for each other or for themselves, especially where there are other children in the family.

Social need

Some parents find that having a child with special needs, particularly learning difficulties or emotional and behavioural difficulties, is isolating. Public places can be nightmares to negotiate and finding friends who can cope with the behaviour of the child can be difficult. Most parents find that local support groups give them opportunities to make friends.

Information

Parents can also find it difficult to get information, although this situation is now improving.

Legislation means that professionals have to involve parents in decision making. The internet has opened up more opportunities as parents can 'talk' to other parents and also search the web for information that is available in this country and also internationally

Financial issues

Money is another source of worry for most families as in many cases one parent has to give up work in order to care for the child. Places with childminders or in day nurseries for children with special needs are rare, especially if the child has complex needs that require experience or specialised training. This means that the family income is often hit and many families, especially lone parents, find themselves reliant on state benefits.

Effects on siblings

Siblings in some families can also be affected. While there are sometimes some negative effects, such as not being able to have as much attention from their parents or not having as many opportunities to socialise or play, there are also some positive effects too. Some siblings are given responsibility which helps their self-confidence. They may also develop positive and caring relationships.

Thinking about the future

Finally, the future of their children is often a major concern for parents – most parents expect their offspring to lead independent lives at some point,

---

Assessment activity `16.3`

Interview a parent of a child who has been identified as having special needs.

Write a report based on the interview which:

- considers what type of support the child and family are receiving
- explains the difficulties, including discrimination, that the child and parents have encountered
- evaluates the effectiveness of key reports and legislation in supporting the child and the family.

but for some parents of children with special needs this will not be the case. Most parents cope with the future, simply by blocking it out and living one day at a time, especially where a child has a life-threatening condition.

Working partnerships

Parents and families are often forgotten when we think about children with special needs. Previously, parents had to fight to gain information from the medical profession about their child's needs and condition, and then fight local authorities to get the support they needed. Most parents of children with special needs became seasoned campaigners and often helped each other by forming support groups. The need for campaigning and fighting has not completely gone away as many parents believe that there are insufficient resources within the system.

Over the past few years, the relationships between professionals and parents has begun to change. Parents' expertise about their child is seen as valuable and decisions are taken jointly.

The Code of Practice 2001, which is used in England, outlines seven key principles for practitioners working with parents. It could be argued that these principles would apply to working with parents in any situation.

1   **Acknowledge and draw on parental knowledge and expertise in relation to their child**
    This principle reminds us that parents will usually be able to share some valuable advice, thoughts and strategies with us.

2   **Focus on the children's strengths as well as areas of additional need**
    This principle is about remembering that children are 'whole people' and are not problems that need curing or sorting out. Think about the language you are using and also about how it might sound if it was said to you.

3   **Recognise the personal and emotional investment of parents and be aware of their feelings**
    Parents love their children unconditionally and see them as valuable. If we focus only on the child's areas of needs, parents will feel that we do not really know their child.

4   **Ensure that parents understand procedures, are aware of how to access support in preparing their contribution and are given documents to be discussed well before the meeting**
    As meeting with parents and working through individual learning plans is an essential part of supporting children, this principle is about making parents feel at ease. It is also about ensuring that parents can properly contribute.

5   **Respect the validity of differing perspectives and seek constructive ways of reconciling different viewpoints**
    This principle is about understanding that parents will have, and are entitled to, their own opinions about what is best for their child.

6   **Respect the differing needs that parents themselves may have, such as a disability or communication and linguistic barriers**
    Some parents may have particular needs that prevent them from contributing. Inclusion means thinking about parents' needs and looking for ways of meeting them. This might mean translating documents, encouraging parents to bring along a friend or putting up a travel cot so that a baby can be brought along.

7   **Recognise the need for flexibility in the timing and structure of meetings**
    This principle reminds us that parents may have jobs, difficulty in transport or other commitments. Partnership with parents means that we look for times which everyone finds convenient, not just us.

Cultures, beliefs and expectations

As well as the principles above, good partnerships also need to respect that parents may have different ideas from us about what is best for their child. There are many reasons why this may be the case, but sometimes culture can play a part. Parents' own experiences may also be an influence. Deaf parents may have strong feelings about whether their child, who is also deaf, should learn sign language. Parents' expectations can also be different to professionals. Their main goal for their child might be toilet training, while a teacher may focus on the child being able to enjoy a book.

The role of SENCOs

In all education settings that receive government funding a member of staff will be appointed to take on responsibility for co-ordinating the special educational needs policy and also the needs of children with special educational needs. SENCOs have a key role in developing and maintaining partnerships, as they have frequent contact with parents, other professionals and the children. SENCOs do not necessarily work directly with individual children, although many settings will include this as part of their role. In some schools, SENCOs are part of the senior management team. SENCOs play a vital part in liaising with parents and social and health services to make sure that children are having their needs met. The Code of Practice 2001 sets out the role of SENCOs in early years settings as well as in primary settings.

The role of the SENCO in early education settings

* Liaises with parents and other professionals.
* Advises and supports other members of the team.
* Ensures that individual education plans are in place.
* Collects, records and updates information about individual children with special educational needs.

The role of the SENCO in primary schools

* Oversees the day-to-day operation of the school's special educational needs policy.
* Co-ordinates provision for children with special educational needs.
* Liaises with and advises fellow teachers.
* Manages learning support assistants.
* Oversees the records of all children with special educational needs.
* Liaises with the parents of children with special educational needs.

* Contributes to the in-service training of staff.
* Liaises with external agencies including the local education authority's support and educational psychology services, health and social services, and voluntary bodies.

Involvement of children

The empowerment of children as a model of working has affected the way in which decision making and services are provided. Wherever possible, children are involved in decision making and their interests are put first. This is a legal requirement. Involving children in their own education and care means that children's needs are met more easily. It also means that the outcomes are better. Children who are interested and enjoy what they are doing usually gain more from an activity. In the same way, children who feel that they have some control over where they go and who they stay with are more likely to settle more easily.

Involvement of parents

The need for parents to be involved in decisions about their children was first recommended in the Warnock Report and was then enshrined in several Acts including the Children Act 1989. The

Involving children means providing choice and listening to them.

move to working in partnership with parents can be seen in the following ways.

* Information is transferred from home to school using 'home books'.

* Parents are encouraged to take part in exercises and programmes at home, such as carrying out physiotherapy, administering drugs or following a portage programme.

* Parents can express choices about schooling arrangements for their children.

* Parents can challenge the local education authority's decisions at special educational needs tribunals.

* Parents are involved in decisions about children's medical treatment.

Meeting the needs of parents

Traditionally, the needs of parents were not always thought about. Now it is recognised that to work well with the child means thinking about the parents too. A more holistic approach is starting to be taken, although the quality is variable across the UK. Social workers, for example, are often attached to families where a child has complex needs and are meant to find ways of supporting families both financially and in terms of care that falls outside the scope of educational services, such as holiday play schemes or respite care.

The key worker role

One way in which parents' needs are met is by using key workers. Over the years, it has been recognised that parents and children benefit when one person in particular works closely with them. This role is often referred to as key worker or 'named person'. The key worker is often able to get to know and understand the needs of the children and the parents, as trust often builds up. The key worker usually works on a day-to-day basis with the child and will act as a major point of contact for all other professionals, as well as the family.

Respite centres

Respite centres provide either sessional or, quite often, short-term residential care for children. They are hugely popular with families as they enable parents and other siblings to have 'free' time. This is used in a variety of ways by parents. Where they have other children, they may use this time to focus on them. Parents often also need this time to mentally and physically rest. Caring for a child with complex needs is often demanding in many ways. Children also like going to respite care. Activities are planned which may include parties and children often build new friendships there. Respite carers work closely with parents to ensure a smooth transition between home and centre.

Assessment activity 16.4

Produce a report that looks at the services and support that a family with a child with special needs receives. The report should be based on interviews with the family, but should not compromise the child or the family's right to privacy and confidentiality. The report should include:

• details about the child's special needs and the impact on the child and family

• an evaluation of the support that parents receive from statutory and voluntary organisations

• an analysis of the effectiveness of the approach to parent partnership working.

Statutory and voluntary support

The trend over the past few years has resulted in closer collaboration between the statutory and voluntary sector. Professionals from different groups work in multi-disciplinary teams (see pages 444–6).

The role of the voluntary sector

Charities were originally founded either because the state did not provide facilities or the standards of care were very poor for disabled people. Once welfare reforms were introduced in the 1940s it was expected that charities would no longer be needed as social benefits and assistance became statutory provision. This was not the case as it quickly emerged that there was not enough provision or funds to provide the quality of care required, thus the voluntary sector has carried on

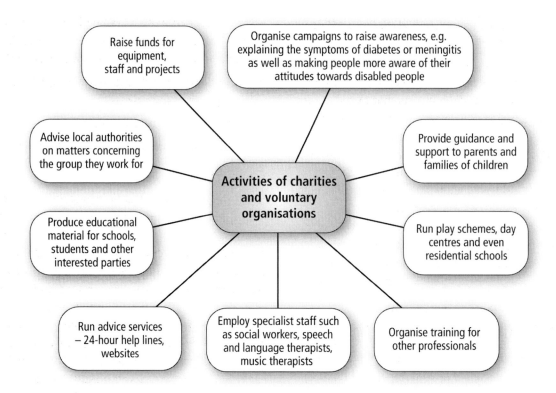

Raise funds for equipment, staff and projects

Organise campaigns to raise awareness, e.g. explaining the symptoms of diabetes or meningitis as well as making people more aware of their attitudes towards disabled people

Advise local authorities on matters concerning the group they work for

Provide guidance and support to parents and families of children

Activities of charities and voluntary organisations

Produce educational material for schools, students and other interested parties

Run play schemes, day centres and even residential schools

Run advice services – 24-hour help lines, websites

Employ specialist staff such as social workers, speech and language therapists, music therapists

Organise training for other professionals

its traditional role in raising funds for specific groups of people and children. In the past few years, the role of the voluntary sector has become not only broad but also very professional. Many positions in voluntary organisations are paid ones, recognising the transition from perhaps amateurish attempts at helping to being thought of as specialists in their field. The diagram above shows the type of activities that many charities and voluntary organisations carry out.

There is a variety of statutory provision, as well as voluntary and private organisations. There is an increasing trend for provision to be holistically organised rather than splitting it into health and education. This helps with interdisciplinary working. It also means that children and their parents are not constantly travelling or making separate appointments. This means that a speech therapist might be based in the same centre where a child attends nursery or a social worker might make an appointment to talk to parents at a Sure Start centre.

Provision is variable

At the time of writing, the type of provision available for children is hugely variable. Even within the same region or city, children may receive different types of services. The trend, however, remains towards multi-disciplinary working and integration of services between health, education and social services.

Residential care and education

Despite the move towards inclusive and integrated education, there is still a need for some children to be cared for in residential centres, although only a very small minority of children need this type of help. Many of these specialised centres are run by voluntary and private organisations but are funded by local authorities, although some of them are privately run. These centres tend to help children with complex needs where the family would have difficulty in caring for them at home, or where children need short-term respite care, although there are also private schools that specialise in educating children with specific learning disabilities such as dyslexia. School services are responsible for inspecting and checking that these centres are providing good care, education and protection for the children.

Provision within mainstream classes and settings

This is the favoured option wherever possible for children. The advantages of receiving education alongside other children means that expectations tend to be higher and that children with special needs are not 'ghettoised'. Support can vary according to the needs of the child. Some children have permanent one-to-one help; often a special needs assistant who only works alongside them and changes classes or group in early years settings with them at the end of the year. Other children might have a support teacher who works regularly with them, while other children might be given extra attention by the classroom teacher.

Units within mainstream schools

In some areas where special schools have been closed, local education authorities have provided units within mainstream schools. The units allow children to have access to specialised equipment and low staff ratios. Children may visit the unit for certain periods during the day or they may spend most of the day there.

Special schools

There are still many special schools to help children whose needs cannot be met within mainstream provision. These include children with complex needs. Special schools have many advantages for these children including:

* specialist equipment such as multi-sensory rooms, hydrotherapy pools
* specialist staff trained and experienced in working with children with special needs
* special schools often take children from 2 to 19 years of age which means that children do not have to move site and readjust to new staff
* on-site speech and language therapists and occupational therapists
* active parent support groups
* small, homely atmosphere with 40 to 60 pupils.

Support groups

Many voluntary organisations support parents directly. They provide advice and guidance but also contact with other parents who are travelling a similar road. Support groups are usually run by parents themselves and are often specific to an illness or disability. They can often provide up-to-date information and, more importantly, a friendly contact. This is often invaluable support for parents. Some support groups also have a campaigning or awareness-raising function. They may raise funds for further research or towards the employment of a professional.

The importance of effective communication

Professionals working with children need to communicate well with parents. This is essential as otherwise children's needs cannot be met. In the past there have been difficulties with professionals communicating with parents and even with each other. Parents have rightly found this frustrating, but the Children Act 2004 puts an obligation on professionals working with children to share information.

CASE STUDY

Kylie is four years old. She loves music and has several favourite songs. At the moment Kylie is reluctant to play in the sand. She also has a favourite towel that she likes drying her hands on and likes the light on at night. She attends a mainstream nursery attached to a school. She has a key worker, speech and language therapist and also a physiotherapist. The family also has a social worker because Kylie is classified as a 'child in need' and social services provide respite care one night a week. Kylie has limited communication and adults working with her use signs and gestures, although this is not always reliable.

* Explain why good communication between professionals is required.
* Evaluate the importance of a good parent–professional relationship.

Good systems of information are particularly needed where children and families are being supported by several different professionals who work in different areas, as the case study on page 455 shows.

Modes of communication

There are different ways in which communication might take between parents and professionals.

Letters

Letters can keep everyone up to date and are particularly useful for sending factual information. They can also be stored and referred to if needed later on. It is important though to ensure that letters are carefully written and that their tone is sensitive. It is also worth remembering that not all parents might have English as their first language or find it easy to understand the written word.

Home-setting books

Where children cannot talk about what they have been doing or where information needs to be shared on daily basis, home-setting books are

Home-setting sheet.

used. They are usually informal diaries and help key workers and parents to understand, on a daily basis, the needs of the child.

Meetings

Meetings are often the most useful way of passing information between different parties. Meetings work well when everyone feels that they can contribute. They also have an advantage in that people at the time can comment straight away or can clarify something if they have not understood. Meetings need to be documented in some way so that afterwards everyone can agree and remember what has been decided. Anyone who has been unable to attend a meeting needs to be updated afterwards and so is it is usual for minutes or 'notes' to be taken.

Reviews

Reviews are meetings, but they have a particular purpose. A review meeting considers children's progress and looks at ways of further supporting the child if this is still needed. It is now expected that parents will attend and be actively involved in the review meeting, as well as children where this is appropriate. Where a child already has an IEP, this will be looked at to see how effective it has been. A new IEP might be drawn up during the review meeting or the existing one might be amended.

As well as reviews being used to consider IEPs, they are also used to look at other aspects of a child's care and education, such as what further support a family needs or how well a programme of physiotherapy is working.

Telephone

Phone calls can be useful for sharing information informally with others. Parents might phone into a setting to say that their child has not slept well

KEY ISSUES

Communicating

There is an ongoing debate between groups and individuals about whether hearing-impaired children and other children with language difficulties should as a priority be taught to speak or whether they should learn to sign. In some ways this debate has echoes of the medical versus social model of disability.

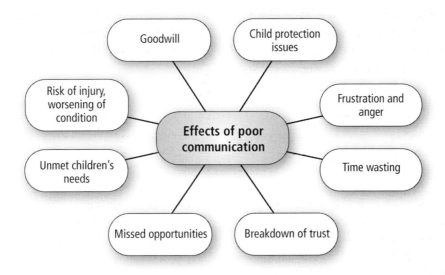

or has had some difficulties, while a setting might call a parent to ask whether some replacement medication can be sent in. Phone calls have the advantage of being fairly instant in terms of communication, without people needing to be present. For parents who are unable to come in person to a setting this can be helpful. It is always a good idea for settings to keep a log of phone calls and messages as, otherwise, information might not get passed along or at a later time might be disputed.

Impact on parents and professionals

It is hard to underestimate the possible effects when communication breaks down or systems are not put in place. The spider diagram above shows the potential impact that poor communication can have on children, parents and professionals.

Child protection issues

Poor communication can lead to children being put at risk. A child might be collected by an unauthorised person or information that might protect a child from further abuse might not be communicated between professionals.

Frustration and anger

This can particularly affect parents where they are not kept informed of the processes that are taking place or feel that they are not being involved in decision making.

Time wasting

Poor or lack of communication often results in time being wasted. Decisions, action or treatment might be delayed because critical information is not in place or funding authorisation has not been gained. For parents, poor communication systems might mean hours wasted in waiting rooms or travelling to and from centres.

Breakdown of trust

Poor communication can also lead to a lack of trust. There is a real danger that parents can lose confidence in the people that work with their child.

Missed opportunities

Poor communication can mean that parents and other professionals might not know what other services, equipment or opportunities are available to support the child. Parents might find that they struggle at home over the summer holiday only to find out that there was a play scheme on offer which was run by a different service.

Unmet children's needs

As well as missed opportunities, poor communication can mean that children's needs are not properly met. Parents might find that information that they have given a professional has not been passed on and so no one working in the setting knows how best to work with a child. In the same way a speech and language programme might not be reinforced because information has not been passed on to the child's key worker.

Risk of injury, worsening of condition

In extreme cases, lack of information can be the root cause of harm to the child. A child with an allergy might be given a substance that causes a severe reaction, while failure to administer medication may lead to a worsening of a medical condition.

Goodwill

Where communication becomes strained or is ineffective, people can lose their motivation. The feeling of 'why bother' can take over. Goodwill is something that is central to working with children.

Assessment activity `16.5`

Produce an information sheet about working in partnership with parents. The information sheet should also contain a case study that acts as an example of how an effective relationship has helped a child with a long-term special need.

The information sheet should:

- identify the benefits of working in partnership with parents
- explain the key features in building effective parent–professional partnerships.

END-OF-UNIT TEST

1 How is disability represented in the medical model of disability?

2 Explain ways in which disability can affect a child.

3 List three features of the Disability Discrimination Act.

4 Explain the purpose of an Individual Education Plan.

5 Give two reasons why it is important to empower children who have a disability or special need.

6 Why is the Disability Discrimination Act 1995 seen as being important?

7 Explain why effective communication between parents and professionals is essential.

8 List three professionals who may be involved in the care and education of a child who has multiple disabilities.

9 What are the arguments in favour of inclusive education?

10 Explain three features of the role of the SENCO in an early years setting.

References and further reading

Useful addresses and support groups

Children's Rights Office, 235 Shaftesbury Avenue, London, WC2H 8EL

Contact a Family, 170 Tottenham Court Road, London, W1P 0HA

Council for Disabled Children, 8 Wakely Street, London, EC1V 7QE

Cystic Fibrosis Trust, 11 London Road, Bromley, Kent, BR1 1BY

Diabetes UK, 10 Parkway, London, NW1 17AA

Disabled Living Foundation, 380–384 Harrow Road, London, W9 2HU

Down's Syndrome Association, 155 Mitcham Road, London, SW17 9PG

Epilepsy Action, New Anstey House, Gateway Drive, Yeadon, Leeds, LS19 7XY

The Equality Learning Centre, 356 Holloway Road, London, N7 6PA

HAPA Play for Disabled Children, Fulham Place, Bishops's Avenue, London, SW6 6EA

Hyperactive Children's Support Group, 71 Whyke Lane, Chichester, West Sussex, PO19 7PD

Integration Alliance, Unit 2, South Lambeth Road, London, SW8 1RL

In Touch, 10 Norman Road, Sale, Cheshire, N33 3DF (links families with children who have rare specific disorders and syndromes)

MENCAP, 123 Golden Lane, London, EC1Y 0RT

National Association for Special Educational Needs (NASEN), House 4–5, Amber Business Village, Amber Close, Amington, Tamworth, B77 4RP

National Association of Toy and Leisure Libraries, 68 Churchway, London, NW1 1LT

National Asthma Campaign, Providence House, Providence Place, London, NW1 0NT

National Autistic Association, 393 City Road, London, EC1V 1NG

National Childrens' Bureau, 8 Wakely Street, London, EC1V 7QE

National Playbus Association, Unit G, Amos Castel Estate, Junction Road, Brislington, Bristol, BS4 5AG

One in Eight, Disability in Action, 78 Mildmay Grove, N1 4PJ (pressure group that challenges media stereotyping)

Scope, 6 Market Road, London, N7 9PW

Sickle Cell Society, 54 Station Road, Harlesden, London, NW10 4UA

Glossary

Abstract Brief summary of a study and its results. States what the study was about, how it was done and what the results showed.

Acute illness Sudden illness that is usually short-lived (e.g. tonsillitis, ear infection). Symptoms might change from one day to next. Some cases may be severe.

Advocacy When a person communicates on behalf of someone else.

Areas of deprivation Areas of the country identified by the government in which an above-average number of deprived families live and for which special help and support is provided. Sometimes these are the areas where **Sure Start** is based.

After-school club A club that meets after school, on school premises or nearby, providing activities for children until the end of the working day. If it takes children under eight and meets for more than two hours, it will be registered and inspected by Ofsted.

Ageism Discrimination on the grounds of age.

Animism When a child attributes feeling and intentions to non-living things (e.g. toys).

Antibiotics Medication which kills bacteria.

Anti-discrimination Actively opposing discrimination.

Assisted conception techniques Treatments that allow people to conceive by means other than sexual intercourse, including **in-vitro fertilisation (IVF)**, **intra-cytoplasmic sperm injection (ICSI)**, **intra-uterine insemination (IUI)**, **ovarian stimulation or induction** and **donor insemination**.

Attachment Close emotional bond between baby and carer.

Bacteria Pathogenic organism that can cause infections.

Bayley Scales of infant development Infant IQ test, which tests sensory and motor skills (e.g. motor response to a dangling ring) and cognitive tests (e.g. testing uncovering a toy hidden by a cloth to test for object permanence at eight months).

Bias Something that could alter, or interfere with, the results of a study.

Breakfast club A club that meets before school, on school premises or nearby, and provides breakfast and activities until school starts. If it takes children under eight and meets for more than two hours, it will be registered and inspected by Ofsted.

Carotid artery The main artery carrying blood to the head.

Case conference Meeting of professionals representing different agencies (e.g. health, police, education) to keep each other informed and make decisions about a particular case.

Chastise To punish by physical harm or beating.

Checklist Pre-set list for observing and recording specific activities or aspects of development.

Child Protection Register A list of names of children who are deemed to be 'at risk', held by Social Services departments.

Chromosome Collection of a large number of genes. Each gene is a unique segment of DNA, which determines one element of the hereditary make-up of the body (e.g. eye colour).

Chronic illness Prolonged illness (e.g. asthma, glue ear), where the signs and symptoms change very little from day to day. Some chronic illnesses have acute episodes.

Colostrum Fluid rich in antibodies, produced from the breasts following the birth of a baby.

Congenital Condition that a baby is born with. Can be hereditary (e.g. cystic fibrosis) or the result of conditions during pregnancy (e.g. disease resulting from medicine taken by mother during pregnancy).

Correlation A statistical term describing the presence of a relationship between variables. A *positive* correlation or association is one where an increase in one variable results in an increase in the other variable being considered. A *negative* association occurs when an increase in one variable results in a decrease in the other variable.

Cross-sectional study Snapshot of a group of people at one point in time.

COSHH Control of Substances Hazardous to Health Regulations (1994): legislation that requires medicines and chemicals to be stored correctly.

Culture The total range of activities, beliefs, values, knowledge and ideas shared by a group of people from the same tradition or background.

Curriculum An outline of knowledge, skills or concepts to be presented to children.

Curriculum plan A programme of activities.

Deficiency A lack of a particular substance (e.g. vitamins).

Deprivation Term used when babies and children have formed an attachment, but are subsequently separated.

Development The increase in the complexity of body actions, thinking processes and also feelings and social interactions. It is partly influenced by the genetically determined programme of maturation and partly by interaction with the prevailing environment.

Disability The consequence of an impairment, or other individual difference. The disability a person experiences is determined by the way in which other people respond to that difference.

Discrimination Unfavourable treatment of individuals or groups of the population based on prejudice.

Distraction hearing test A hearing test done at approximately eight months.

Diversity Having variety; being different; accepting that we are not all the same.

Donor insemination Conception technique which involves placing sperm into a woman's womb.

Droplet infection An infection spread by coughing, sneezing or spitting.

Early years curriculum Everything children do, see, hear or feel in the early years setting, whether planned or unplanned.

Eclampsia Type of epilepsy that can occur during pregnancy (at late stages) and which can be fatal to both baby and mother.

Ectopic pregnancy Occurs when the fertilised ovum (blastocyst), instead of passing down the fallopian tube and then implanting itself in the lining of the uterus (endometrium), settles in the fallopian tube. Ectopic pregnancies rarely last more than two or three months.

Egocentrism The inability to imagine things from another's perspective.

Equality Having the same rights as other people.

Ethnicity Identification with a group (ethnic group) which shares some or all of the following features: lifestyle, culture, religion, nationality, language, history, geographical area.

Ethnocentrism Viewing the world from the perspective of one particular ethnic group.

Event sampling Observing and recording certain events as they occur (e.g. aggressive behaviour).

Febrile convulsion Fit caused by a raised temperature in children under five years.

Extended school provision Provision, usually based at or near a school site, that goes beyond the normal school day and the activities usually found in a school. Can include **after-school clubs**, parent-and-toddler clubs, health checks, social work support, relationship counselling, basic literacy classes and parenting skills classes. Provision is based on what is needed in the community which the provider serves.

Folic acid B-vitamin that can be found in some enriched foods and vitamin pills and which is very important in the development of the embryo and foetus during the early stages of pregnancy.

Free-flow play When a child learns through play at the deepest level, using experience of ideas, feelings and relationships and applying these with control, competence and mastery. Adult intervention is absent or minimal.

Frequency Number of times an event occurs.

Frequency histogram Chart of numerical values ranging from the lowest to the highest (class intervals), showing the number of times each value occurs (frequency).

Full day care Facilities that provide day care for children under eight for a period of four hours or more and which are not domestic premises.

Gamete Sex cell, which is either a sperm or an ovum.

Gender discrimination Practices that discriminate on the grounds of gender difference (sometimes known as sexism).

Genetics The study of inherited conditions.

Genetic counselling Tests and screening done on a man and woman who have a history of an inherited condition. Gives the couple the potential risks of having a child with the condition.

Head circumference Measurement of baby's head to ensure correct growth.

Health education Focuses on the prevention of illness in an individual.

Health promotion Encourages people to increase their control over, and improve, their own health.

Hepatitis Inflammation of the liver caused by a virus.

HIV Human immuno-deficiency virus; the virus that causes AIDS.

Holophrases Word and gesture combinations.

Homework club Club that meets after school, especially to support children as they do their homework.

Homophobia Hatred or fear of homosexuals.

Hypoglycaemia attack Sudden drop in the level of blood sugar in the body, often associated with diabetes.

Hypothesis Statement that predicts the relationship between variables, i.e. the relationship between the independent and dependent variables. A hypothesis can be written as an *experimental hypothesis* that predicts the outcome of the study or as a *null hypothesis* that does not predict the outcome of the study.

Immunisation The use of vaccinations to prevent specific illnesses.

Immunity Body's ability to resist infection.

Incubation period Time between infection with a micro-organism and development of any symptoms.

Insulin Hormone necessary in enabling the body to use and store sugar in the form of glucose.

Interpersonal interaction Ways in which people communicate with each other.

Interpreter Someone who translates speech from one language to another.

Intra-cytoplasmic sperm injection (ICSI) A variation of **in-vitro fertilisation** in which a single sperm is injected into the ovum

Intra-uterine insemination (IUI) Conception technique in which sperm is placed in a woman's womb, through the cervix.

In-vitro fertilisation (IVF) Conception technique in which ova are collected from a woman and fertilised, by a man's sperm, outside the body. Usually, one or two resulting embryos are then transferred to the womb. If one of them attaches successfully, a pregnancy results.

Learning wall A display in a setting that is created by staff, without the help of the children, to enhance and illustrate a topic or subject being studied as part of the curriculum

Longitudinal study Study of an individual or group of people over a period of time.

Malnourished Lacking in essential nutrients.

Marginalised groups The socially excluded: groups of people on the fringe of mainstream society and who feel unimportant and uninvolved (e.g. travellers, asylum seekers, those in poverty, the elderly, those who lack basic skills, e.g. the ability to read or write).

Maturation Genetically determined programme of progressive changes leading to full development.

Micro-organism Organism such as bacteria or a virus that cannot be seen (also known as microbe).

Minority ethnic group People who belong to ethnic groups that are not in the majority.

Moral realism Action that is judged by the intention of the person doing the act and not by the outcome.

Multiculturalism Recognition and sharing of different cultures in our society.

Myelination A greasy substance, myelin, forms an insulating sheath around nerve fibres.

Naturalistic observation Study that observes behaviour as it occurs naturally.

Nurture group Small class of children within a primary school, to which children with particular problems at home or at school can be withdrawn from their normal classes and given extra help and support until they are ready to return.

Observation Report of a study or examination on what is happening, without deliberately intervening in the course of events. Observation can be *participant*, where the researcher is part of what is happening, or *non-participant*, where the researcher observes from a distance.

Ofsted Office for Standards in Education: responsible for registering and inspecting all early years settings and schools.

Out-of-school care Facilities that provide day care for children and operate during one or more of the following periods: before school, after school, during school holidays. If the facility takes children under eight and meets for more than two hours, it will be registered and inspected by Ofsted.

Ovarian stimulation or induction Conception technique involving a course of fertility drugs, which are used to control or stimulate a woman's ovulation.

Paediatric nurse Nurse who specialises in the care of sick children.

Paediatrician Doctor who specialises in the care of sick children.

Phonemic awareness Understanding of the sounds that individual letters (phonemes) make.

Placebo Fake treatment given to people in a control group so they don't know whether they are in an experimental or control group. A placebo should not have any effect; however, occasionally, if someone in the control group believes they are getting a real or active treatment, they can experience effects, good or bad.

Population Group of people or objects with particular characteristics.

Portage System of structured teaching of skills to children in their homes by parents under the guidance of a specially trained professional.

Pre-eclampsia Condition that can occur from week 34 of pregnancy and disappears after birth. Symptoms include accumulation of water in the tissues (e.g. swollen ankles) leading to extra weight gain, high blood pressure and protein in the urine. May lead to **eclampsia**.

Prejudice Having preconceived opinions about a group or individual that results in negative effects.

Premature Baby born before 37 weeks of completed pregnancy.

Privation Term used when babies and children have not formed a main attachment.

Qualitative Information gathered in narrative (non-numeric) form (e.g. a transcript of an interview).

Quantitative Information gathered in the form of numbers.

Race The categorisation of people based on common descent (e.g. nation or tribe), who may have common attributes (e.g. skin colour, general physical appearance).

Racism Practices that discriminate because of colour, culture, race or ethnicity.

Range Measure of the variability of quantitative data. The difference between the highest and lowest values in a set of data.

Referral Passing on information to a person or agency more suited to deal with the issue.

Regression Reverting to behaviour of an earlier age.

Reflective practitioner Someone who is able to review the way in which they work and identify and plan for necessary changes, developments and improvements.

Reinforcers Consequences that might encourage or discourage repeated actions.

Reliability Concerned with the consistency and dependability of a research method. It is an indication of the extent to which the method used gives the same answers at different times, with similar yet different groups of people and irrespective of who administers it.

Research question Clear statement in the form of a question of what a researcher wishes to find out.

Sample Subgroup of a population selected to represent the entire population. Ideally, all people or objects in the population have an equal chance of being chosen. This will give a random sample. Some samples may not be truly random and as such may be subject to bias.

Screening Programme that examines all children to detect certain conditions, illnesses or disabilities.

SENCO Special Education Needs Co-ordinator. Person with responsibility for providing support for children with special needs.

Separation anxiety Unhappy response by a child when the attached carer leaves. The response is usually in three stages: (1) protest, e.g. crying, (2) despair, child becomes calmer but apathetic, and (3) detachment (if situation continues for weeks or longer), gives up hope and ignores attachment figure on return.

Sessional care Facilities that provide day care for children under eight for a period of less than four continuous hours and which are not domestic premises.

SIDS Sudden infant death syndrome. Sudden and unexplained death in an infant. Also known as cot death.

Social learning theory Theory of learning that suggests we learn by imitating others.

Standard deviation Statistical measure of how far things vary from the average result (the mean).

Statistic Characteristic of a sample.

Stranger fear Distress shown by a child if a stranger appears and moves nearer. Babies tend to move away and cling to their attachment figure.

Structured play Activities that are planned and usually led by adults.

Sure Start Programme of activities and support in **areas of deprivation**, funded by the government, to support parents to be, families and children to become less disadvantaged and succeed better in life. They may focus on such issues as reducing teenage pregnancies, stopping smoking in mothers-to-be, encouraging breast feeding and teaching better parenting skills. They work particularly with fathers to involve them in the care of their children.

Time sampling Observing and recording what a child is doing at regular intervals for a short period.

Transition group Small class of children in a school, set up to help children's transition from one setting to another (usually nursery to infant school).

Trial study Initial use of research method, usually a questionnaire, to test its effectiveness (sometimes known as pilot study).

Validity Extent to which a particular research method produces results that are likely to be accurate and free of **bias**.

Variable Factor or characteristic of a person or object that varies, i.e. can have different values. Variables include things like age, height, gender, how much someone smokes, number of children, etc. In experimental research the variable that is assumed to cause or influence the outcome of the experiment is called the *independent variable*. The independent variable is altered in some way to observe its effect on a factor or characteristic of the person or object. This factor is called the *dependent variable* and is the variable that can be measured. Other factors may affect the results of the experiment and these are called *confounding variables*.

Virus A very small micro-organism which can cause disease. It cannot be treated with antibiotics.

Zygote Fertilised ovum.

Index